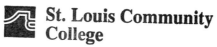

Encyclopedia of
Fable

ABC-CLIO LITERARY COMPANION

Encyclopedia of
Fable

Mary Ellen Snodgrass

ABC-CLIO
Santa Barbara, California
Denver, Colorado
Oxford, England

Library of Congress Cataloging-in-Publication Data

Snodgrass, Mary Ellen
    Encyclopedia of fable / Mary Ellen Snodgrass.
       p. cm. — (ABC-CLIO literary companion)
    Includes bibliographical references and index.
    1. Fables—Encyclopedias. I. Title. II. Series.
PN980.S66 1998 398.2'03—dc21   98-46845

ISBN 1-57607-026-3 (alk. paper)

04 03 02 01 00 99 98   10 9 8 7 6 5 4 3 2 1 (cloth)

ABC-CLIO, Inc.
130 Cremona Drive, P.O. Box 1911
Santa Barbara, California 93116-1911

This book is printed on acid-free paper ∞ .
Manufactured in the United States of America.

Man, in his simpler states, always felt that he himself was something too mysterious to be drawn. But the legend he carved under these cruder symbols was everywhere the same; and whether fables began with Aesop or began with Adam, whether they were German and Medieval as Reynard the Fox, or as French and Renaissance as La Fontaine, the upshot is everywhere essentially the same: that superiority is always insolent, because it is always accidental; that pride goes before a fall; and that there is such a thing as being too clever by half. You will not find any other legend but this written upon the rocks by any hand of man. There is every type and time of fable: but there is only one moral to the fable; because there is only one moral to everything.

G. K. Chesterton
1916

CONTENTS

PREFACE

The plan of *Encyclopedia of Fable* is to present the genre of fable and its major subgenres—cruelty joke, exemplary tale, *pourquoi* story, and storytelling—along with major bodies of fable, characters, situations, creators, collectors, translators, illustrators, and performers as a method of defining and exemplifying the wealth of world literature that belongs in the domain of illustrative wisdom lore. For ease of use, I have put extensive textural commentary under author and title where fables are identifiable, for example, Zora Neale Hurston, Ivan Andreyevich Krylov, *Androcles and the Lion*, and *Panchatantra*, and under the focal characters of Anansi, Brer Rabbit, Chauntecleer, Reynard the Fox, the trickster, and Uncle Remus. Period entries discuss the types of fable that colored the Middle Ages, Renaissance, and eighteenth and nineteenth centuries. Subgroupings of fable appear under specific categories: African, African-American, American, Babylonian, British, Celtic, Christian, French, Greek, Hispanic, Jewish, Latin, Native American, and Oriental.

The sixty-eight entries in this work appear alphabetically. Ample citations appear in original languages with translation for application to the study of fable in French, Middle English, Uncle Remus dialect, Gullah, and Latin. To assist readers, I have also translated less common literary terms, titles, and allusions. Significant to the canon of fable are extensive biographies of major contributors—Richard Adams, Aesop, Hans Christian Andersen, Valerius Babrius, Ambrose Bierce, Geoffrey Chaucer, John Dryden, John Gay, Johann Wolfgang von Goethe, Jacob and Wilhelm Grimm, Virginia Hamilton, Joel Chandler Harris, Zora Neale Hurston, Tomás de Iriarte, Ivan Andreyevich Krylov, Jean de La Fontaine, Gotthold Ephraim Lessing, Sir Roger L'Estrange, Bernard de Mandeville, William March, Marie de France, George Orwell, Phaedrus, Beatrix Potter, Jalal ad-Din ar Rumi, Antoine de Saint-Exupéry, William Shakespeare, George Bernard Shaw, Robert Louis Stevenson, James Thurber, and Oscar Wilde. To assist the student, writer, scholar, and classroom teacher, I have included several appendixes. The first of these is a general time line of fable, followed by a list of the major authors of fables and their works. Next comes a time line of cinema versions of major works, such as *The Lion King*, *Aladdin*, and *Song of the South*. This is followed by an alphabetical list of sources of fables with dates of original publication, then lists of primary and secondary sources. Finally, readers can turn to the general index to look up authors (Charles Dickens and Isak Dinesen), illustrators (Gustave Doré and A. B. Frost), titles ("The Ransom of Red Chief" and "Babette's Feast"), story types and subgenres (Mormonia, jataka tales, Talmudic lore, Jack tales, and cumulative stories), storytellers (Diane Wolkstein, Louise Bennett, and Frankie and Doug Quimby), translators (Richard Burton), adaptors (Richard Strauss), ethnic types (Songhay, Cherokee, and Hmong fable), terms (kamishibai, Zen fable, griot, *Volksmund*, and *satori*), languages (Gullah and Bantu), tribes and nations (Kootenai and Abenaki), and characters (Gluscabi and Daddy Mention). Overall, *The Encyclopedia of Fable* opens the world of fable to the scholar, researcher, linguist, philosopher, storyteller, teacher, librarian, and general reader. Enjoy!

ACKNOWLEDGMENTS

Reference Department
Oxford Public Library
Oxford, England

Peter Dargin
Author and storyteller
New South Wales, Australia

Barbara Haywood
Mark Schumacher
Walter Clinton Jackson Library
University of North Carolina
Greensboro, North Carolina

Avis Gachet
Wonderland Books
Granite Falls, North Carolina

Frances Hilton
Chapter One Books
Hickory, North Carolina

Reference Department
Houghton Reading Room
Harvard University
Cambridge, Massachusetts

Des Kenny
Book consultant
Galway, Ireland

Burl McCuiston
Reference Librarian
Lenoir-Rhyne College
Hickory, North Carolina

Reference Department
Renfro Library
Mars Hill College
Mars Hill, North Carolina

Betty Santos
Book merchant and critic
Native Books
Honolulu, Hawaii

Dr. Werner Schulz
Professor of German
Lenoir-Rhyne College
Hickory, North Carolina

INTRODUCTION

From early times, the comparison of humans to animals has been the life's blood of witty, comic, and disturbingly accurate morality tales known as fables, which presented in digestible form the bad news that people behave and misbehave in predictable fashion. These brief illustrative stories of human foible, national embarrassment, and cultural downfall, which have served as moral and ethical instruction, made an early appearance at world centers of literary ferment. In Babylon they appeared as early as 2300 B.C.E., in Greece in the sixth and fifth centuries B.C.E., in India in the fifth century B.C.E., and in Rome in the fourth, third, and first centuries B.C.E. More recent periods of productivity have added to the world canon a delightfully rich variety of stories:

- The twelfth century produced the *Carmina Burana*, Nivard's *Ysengrimus*, the fables of Marie de France, *The Owl and the Nightingale*, and recensions of Aesop.

- The thirteenth century carried Reynard the Fox across Europe to France, Italy, Germany, Holland, Belgium, and England.

- In the fourteenth century, the pre-Renaissance blaze of innovation and imagination created *Gesta Romanorum*, Giovanni Boccaccio's *The Decameron*, and Geoffrey Chaucer's *The Parliament of Fowls* and *The Canterbury Tales*, the enduring best-seller from Middle English.

- Seventeenth-century fabulists and fable users included William Shakespeare, Ben Jonson, Nicholas Nevelet, Giambattista Basile, Francis Bacon, Aphra Behn, John Dryden, Sir Roger L'Estrange, Rabbi Moses Wallich, and the charming Frenchman Jean de La Fontaine.

- The eighteenth century was a remarkable era of fable translation and illustration and produced the original works of Bernard de Mandeville, John Gay, Gotthold Ephraim Lessing, Voltaire, Tomás de Iriarte, and Germany's major contributor to world fable, Johann Wolfgang von Goethe.

- The nineteenth century equaled previous eras in productivity, adding technological advancement and artistry to fable illustration and the talents of Ivan Krylov, Jacob and Wilhelm Grimm, Washington Irving, Hans Christian Andersen, Charles Dickens, Lewis Carroll, Mark Twain, Robert Louis Stevenson, Beatrix Potter, Oscar Wilde, Henry Van Dyke, Ambrose Bierce, Hilaire Belloc, and two star fabulists: Rudyard Kipling, spokesman for the English Empire, and Joel Chandler Harris, creator of Uncle Remus and collator and transmitter of the West African tales of the trickster Brer Rabbit.

- Spilling over into the twentieth century were additional creations by Potter, Kipling, and Harris plus the works of George Orwell, Kenneth Grahame, Mark Twain, O. Henry, George Bernard Shaw, Zora Neale Hurston, T. S. Eliot, Antoine de Saint-Exupéry, Isak Dinesen, James Thurber, Henry Van Dyke, Elie Wiesel, Richard Bach, Isabel Allende, Virginia Hamilton, Gabriel García Marquez, Joe Hayes, Grace Hallworth, Dan Yashinsky, Jim Weiss, J. J. Reneaux, Gayle Ross, Dayton Edmonds, Joseph Bruchac, and three lesser known figures whose work has received too little acclaim—Jacquetta Hawkes, Anne Bodart, and William March.

Like cataloging the sands of the desert or the stars in the firmament, the study of fable is, despite its rewards, tedious and difficult. The great works of the genre alone are an armload.

- *A Thousand and One Nights*

- Aesop's fables

- *The Panchatantra*

- *Noctes Atticae* by Aulus Gellius

- the fables of Marie de France

- the anonymous *The Owl and the Nightingale*

- *The Parliament of Fowls* and *The Canterbury Tales* by Geoffrey Chaucer

- *The Hind and the Panther* and *Fables Ancient and Modern* by John Dryden

- Gotthold Ephraim Lessing's fables

- "The Sorceror's Apprentice" and *Reineke Fuchs* by Johann Wolfgang von Goethe

- a lifetime of fable writing by Jean de La Fontaine

- "The Wonderful Tar-Baby Story" by Joel Chandler Harris

- *A Christmas Carol* by Charles Dickens

- *Fables* and *Dr. Jekyll and Mr. Hyde* by Robert Louis Stevenson

- *The Story of the Other Wise Man* and *The Christmas Tree* by Henry Van Dyke

- "The Gift of the Magi" by O. Henry

- *Animal Farm* by George Orwell

- *Mules and Men* and *Tell My Horse* by Zora Neale Hurston

- *The Little Prince* by Antoine de Saint-Exupéry

- *Fables for Our Time* and *Further Fables for Our Time* by James Thurber

- *The People Could Fly* and *Her Stories* by Virginia Hamilton

- *Watership Down* and *Tales from Watership Down* by Richard Adams

In addition to these works are the incidental fables that enliven segments of other titles:

- the Torah and the Koran

- the writings of Plato and Aeschylus

- Livy's Roman history

- Horace's *Satires*

- Aristophanes's *The Birds* and *The Wasps*

- Rumi's Sufist sermons

- William Shakespeare's *Coriolanus*

- Elie Wiesel's *Les Portes de la forêt*

- Isabel Allende's *House of the Spirits*

- Rachel Carson's *Silent Spring*

Beyond the grasp of the literary historian, however, lie the myriad land-marks of the anonymous griots, tellers of stories that have no title, no date, and no specific piece of ground on which to pitch their tent. Among these are the Old Man Coyote stories told by the Indians of the American Southwest, the fool tales and wisdom lore of Yiddish savants, jataka tales of the Buddha during his earthly incarnations, Zen "aha" stories, Gypsy tales, and shark lore of the Pacific rim.

The originality and verisimilitude of world fable is a tribute to the genre itself, which includes stories of foolish error, social blunder, and personal over-reaching, often to the humiliation of such classic dolts as Anansi, Till Eulenspiegel, Mr. Bear, Ysengrim, Simple, El-ahrairah, and Chaunticleer, the rooster who grows so enamored of his own voice that he fears the loss of it will stop the sunrise. Along with folly literature are the subsets of trickster lore, cruelty jokes, exempla or admonitory tales, *fabliaux*, and *pourquoi* stories, the fables that conclude with a change in nature itself. The tellers of each model may withdraw into the anonymity of the mesmerizing griot, scop, Kamishibai, storyteller, or kahuna or may sparkle in personalities as memorable as Scheherazade, Rumi, Uncle Remus, the Brothers Grimm, Dr. Jekyll, the Little Prince, Jonathan Livingston Seagull, or the Ghost of Christmas Past.

Taken as a whole, fable is a rich, varied, and satisfying branch of literature that shares much with its near kin—allegory, anecdote, parable, and folktale. Unique in the reverence it has earned, fable bears within lively fictional scenarios the gift of advice, admonition, and right thinking. As a character builder, it has given the parent, preacher, teacher, and political exhorter just the right story to lighten a spiritual load or ease a ticklish situation. Because of its simple parameters and unassuming style, fable has made a home among the Sufi, Christian, Buddhist, and Zen seekers of truth and continues to appear in the words of the storyteller, ecologist, feminist, pulpit minister, and classroom teacher. As technology pushes the imagination toward a complex landscape in the virtual world beyond the chaos of the here and now, readers still turn to the soul-based wisdom of the fabulist.

Encyclopedia of
Fable

ADAMS, RICHARD

A fresh addition to world fabulists, Richard George Adams produced *Watership Down* (1974), a suspenseful, best-selling beast epic that earned the Carnegie Medal and a Guardian Award for children's literature. An Englishman and native of Newbury, Berkshire, he was born May 9, 1920, to Lilian Rosa Button and George Beadon Adams, a surgeon. Young Adams was a soldier in the British army during World War II and returned to complete an M.A. in history at Worcester College, Oxford, in 1948. For 26 years he worked at the Ministry of Housing and Local Government, then retired in 1974 to write his world-wise epic rabbit tale and an extensive canon of fantasy novels: *Shardik* (1974), *The Plague Dogs* (1977), *Tyger Voyage* (1976), *The Iron Wolf* (1980), *The Girl in a Swing* (1980), and *Maia* (1984). Among Americans, his fables and fantasies have brought him a devout readership, the California Young Readers' Association Medal, and honorary residencies at Hollins College and the University of Florida. Currently living on the Isle of Man with his family, he is a fellow of the Royal Society of Literature and former president of the Royal Society for the Prevention of Cruelty to Animals, a clue to his interest in animal lore.

Adams wrote *Watership Down,* his mythic beast fable, from 1972 to 1974, composing aloud during motoring trips to Stratford to entertain his daughters, Juliet and Rosamond. This oral technique parallels the child-centered storytelling tradition of the nineteenth century, which spawned Joel Chandler Harris's Uncle Remus tales, Robert Louis Stevenson's *Treasure Island*, Lewis Carroll's *Alice in Wonderland*, Beatrix Potter's *The Tale of Peter Rabbit*, Oscar Wilde's *The Happy Prince*, and Rudyard Kipling's *The Jungle Book*. As did fable-makers before him, Adams used knowledge of the natural world and indigenous creatures to flesh out the milieu of his hero, Hazel the rabbit, who successfully defends a band of survivors on an exodus like that of Moses and the Hebrew children fleeing the seven plagues of Egypt and Pharaoh's army. The title suggests the hang-tough determination of Noah, whose ark, the prototypical "watership," survives world cataclysm and makes possible a second chance for life on earth. Each episode of the mythic flight reflects the structure and purpose of fable by demonstrating a human *hamartia*, the concept from Greek tragedy of "missing of the mark," the archery term that typifies human flaw.

Rich in themes of survival, synergy, martyrdom, and mythic pilgrimage, *Watership Down* opens on Sandleford Warren, a real stretch of lush, grassy hill country bordering greater London and only minutes southwest of Heathrow Airport. A pell-mell, every-man-for-himself nightmare of terror and annihilation, the opening scene depicts the undersized Fiver warning his brother Hazel of a free-floating, doom-laden aura. After unsuccessfully reporting Fiver's prophecy to the Chief Rabbit, Hazel persuades Fiver, Pipkin, Blackberry, and Bigwig to cross the Enborne River and leave their native warren. This eventful segment is so true to the classic paradigm that it could precede an Aesopic moral warning of complacency, or, as Joel Chandler Harris's Uncle Remus worded it, "Watch out w'en youer gittin' all you want. Fattenin' hogs ain't in luck." (Bartlett 1992, 536)

The episodic trek breaks into stages that progress toward an idyllic home far from human tampering. Newly arrived on Cowslip Warren, the ingenuous travelers assume they have outraced an evil destiny and located a utopia. Before them lies a verdant, promising environment where sleek-haired domesticated rabbits are protected by humans and plumped on carrots, clover, and apples. But Hazel's band learns a harsh lesson about the dangers of pseudo-paradise when a twisted copper snare nearly beheads Bigwig. Fearing the worst, Hazel intones a wistful rabbit proverb, "My heart has joined the Thousand, for my friend stopped running today." (Adams 1972, 120) Adams dramatizes the brush with death as a reminder that no earthly retreat is far enough away from human treachery. Following a hasty getaway, in Chapter 18, the animals pause to regroup and plan their next move. An intrinsic moral rounds out the episode: Wiser and glad to be alive, they recognize each individual's contribution to their safety as they savor hard-won success.

Like Virgil narrating the false starts of Aeneas in the *Aeneid* (19 B.C.E.) or John Bunyan relating Christian's missteps in *Pilgrim's Progress* (1678), Adams sees his column through multiple deceptive havens. The second stop on the rabbit migration is Watership Down, an Edenic grassland and unpopulated warren just waiting for occupants. In the tradition of their legendary hero, El-ahrairah, Hazel assumes leadership yet maintains his congenial, humble nature. Like Moses led to the top of the mountain, Hazel flies over Nuthanger Farm aboard Kehaar, a friendly kestrel. Hazel catches sight of caged rabbits and returns to set them free, but the heroic raid levies a hard price. Hazel is shot in the leg and nearly bleeds to death before he is rescued. Again, the elements of fable encase the episode in a word of caution: No hero undertakes a project of these proportions without encountering pain and loss.

For the next segment of his beast epic, Adams returns to pragmatism by having the all-male coterie plot their future, which will require a suitable proportion of male to female rabbits. Like the Romans capturing the Sabine women to serve as producers of the next generation, Hazel's band adds the does Clover, Haystack, and Boxwood to the growing commune. But Hazel's confidence in his pioneering expedition is soon dashed by Holly and Bluebell, who report that Sandleford Warren is no more. Sutch and Martin, Ltd., of Newbury, the embodiment of human destruction of nature, has poisoned underground chambers and shot those animals that fled suffocation. A yellow bulldozer, symbol of deadly technology, finished the job. Just as Fiver dreamed, the old warren's doom was swift and far-reaching. In Chapter 21 Holly prophesies that humankind will never rest until the earth is rid of animals.

The major confrontation of *Watership Down* reflects heroic style rather than fable. After Hazel's band challenges General Woundwort, dictator of the Efrafa warren, the rabbits enlist other animal troops to defeat tyranny. Chapter 50 returns to utopian description as the victors embrace their rewards—fragrant wild clematis, patches of long grass, and a fall sky foretelling the first frosts of October. Wind rustles beech limbs as the rabbits, increased in number by renegades from Woundwort's compound, prepare subterranean chambers for winter. Thinking over the price the rabbits' epic struggle has cost in suffering, terror, and loss, Silver concludes that the struggle went beyond nature. In a hollow near Ladle Hill, mother Vilthuril tells her young how El-ahrairah guided the rabbits to a promised land carpeted with green, sweet grass. In blessing, the night sky glitters with Perseus, the Pleiades, Cassiopeia, Pisces, and Pegasus. The rabbits depart from the chill and continue their storytelling underground. In the epilogue, Adams extols Hazel for political acumen and persistence in seeking a viable life amid nature's bounty. The next spring, the aged, weary leader greets death by slipping out of his earthly body and frisking across Watership Down as though he were young.

The novel received mixed reviews—some sneering, cynical, and picky; others profoundly impressed by Adams's anthropomorphized cast of rabbits, their reverence for rabbit lore, and the instinctive flight from extermination that links all nature in a struggle for survival. Adams was alternately lauded for the grandeur of his undertaking and reviled as a would-be J. R. R. Tolkien, T. H. White, L. Frank Baum, or Lewis Carroll. As did Robert O'Brien in *Mrs. Frisbee and the Rats of NIMH* (1971), Adams reminds readers that the rhythms of animal behavior are inborn but can be thrown out of sync by human greed and urban sprawl. The fragile, isolated corners of unadulterated nature depend on vision and sacrifice if they are to survive. Six years after Adams published his animal dystopia, Nepenthe Films released a color animated version, a realistic plunge into mayhem, group loyalty, martyrdom, and reward. Voices for the animals are the facile yet mature sounds of John Hurt, Ralph Richardson, Zero Mostel, and Denholm Elliott.

A quarter century after publishing *Watership Down*, Adams reprised the setting and characters in *Tales from Watership Down* (1997), a collection of 19 interrelated tall tales, fairy and ghost stories, *pourquoi* stories, and journey lore. He draws on the milieu of *Watership Down* for the rhapsodic descriptions of England's green spaces, envisioning:

> A low saddle between two hills of the grassy country they were crossing on their journey home. Clumps of oxeye daisies were already in bloom here and there, and there were patches of mauve sainfoin. As they stopped to nibble the fresh grass, a light breeze began to blow, bringing from below scents of sheep and river plants. (Adams 1996, 107)

On the life-freshening grassland, Adams sets a series of adventures told from the point of view of individual rabbits. In the Aesopic tradition is "The Sense of Smell," a story of the godlike trickster El-ahrairah's protection and assistance to rabbits who lack the olfactory sense that judges food from offal and friend from enemy. At the close of the episode, El-ahrairah petitions the King of Yesterday for a brighter future for small animals and raises a prophetic battle cry: "My people shall become to the human race the greatest scourge and tribulation in the world. We will be to them, everywhere, a relentless bane and affliction. We will destroy their greenstuff, burrow under their fences, spoil their crops, harass them by night and day." (Adams 1996, 29) As the beneficent tale draws to a close, the king enfolds the rabbit prince and declares, "Be it so. . . . Take my blessing to your people, and with it the Sense of Smell, to be theirs forever."

Adams emulates the style of the *Panchatantra* with his illustrative stories-within-stories. He begins "The Fox in the Water" with a contemporary interest in foxes, then segues directly into an episode of the ongoing rabbit epic—El-ahrairah's battle against a pair of foxes who destroyed the peace of his warren. On the way to an encounter, the trickster narrates a conservation story to Yona the hedgehog. Because he encourages Yona to coexist with human gardeners by devouring snails, the speaker turns his tale into a *pourquoi* story, which ends in the traditional prophetic mode: "And from that day to this, hedgehogs have frequented human gardens and been welcome." (Adams 1996, 59) The episode then develops into a trickster tale, after El-ahrairah learns from the snake how to hypnotize the fox and banish him and his troublesome brood forever.

The didactic element in Adams's animal lore is a blend of exigency and grace. In each episode, rabbit society rallies against fearfully indistinct threats, as with Blackberry's warning, "There's no place so lonely that men won't get to know about it if there are too many rabbits there." (Adams 1996, 204) The rabbits perceive danger in time to apply to their lord protector for assistance, advice, and leadership. Like a wandering Dionysus, he patrols an earthly path. Like Moses at the Red Sea, he studies the quandaries that stymie ordinary rabbits before confronting the jagged, flesh-rimmed hole in the sky or before leading his wards to safety across the marsh. El-ahrairah's intervention, which seems both heroic and divine, is a bulwark against animal treachery, human cunning, and the unknown. He demonstrates the importance of patience, observation, wise counsel, and compassion for the weak and needy. Banking on keen senses and otherworldly intuition, he saves lesser animals from invaders, brigands, and tyrants and restores their luxuriant greensward to an idyllic place of safety and contentment. Amid abundant foliage on moonlit evenings, the rabbits, like human listeners the world over, retell their cache of stories to restore belief in the good and true.

In addition to novels, Adams has also published story anthologies that are more faithful to the traditional confines of fable than *Tales from Watership Down*. In his introduction to *The Unbroken Web: Stories and Fables* (1980), a collection of 19 multinational tales, he lists two qualities of fable: "First, they are full of surprises and marvels. The essence of fiction is that the hearer is dying to learn what happens next, or if he already knows, he is eager to hear it again and to take fresh delight in his wonder. Second, they are most admirably witty, neat, and adroit." (Adams 1980, flap) To assure reader delight, Adams varies his tone from somber and frightening to mysterious, fascinating, colorful, and intriguing. Transcending the barriers of language, custom, and time, the fables follow the time-honored convention of the unidentified but intimate narrator. Adams selects first Constance Cripps, the fictional nanny of naughty Master Richard, to relate in English dialect a *pourquoi* story, "The Cat in the Sea." Adams's second speaker chooses *franglais* in the Polynesian story "The Giant Eel." Under the storytelling power of this anonymous go-between, who initiates the listener with a new stock of wisdom lore, the reader enjoys the immediacy of front-row involvement.

Adams comments that story emulates the universality of dreams, the individual's nightscapes based on emotion and experience. Thus, story shares with dreams a need to be retold and becomes a part of the collective folklore of all human experience. By way of clarification, Adams quotes Marcel Proust's statement, "One cannot properly describe human life unless one shows it soaked in the sleep in which it plunges, which night after night sweeps round it as a promontory is encircled by the sea." (Adams 1980, 10) Like dreams, the fable can serve a one-person audience and need not make the quotidian kind of sense that real life demands. Disregarding the physical laws of probability, the fable draws on talking animals and plants. This imaginary framework the rapt listener accepts in what Aristotle termed the willing suspension of disbelief.

Adams stresses that the fable is not nonsense. It expresses an intrinsic reality, a meaning that listeners both enjoy and need. In an image that is the source of his title, he envisions outside the earth "a second, incorporeal, gossamer-like sphere—the unbroken web—rotating freely and independently of the rotation of the earth. It is something like a soap-bubble, for although it is in rotation, real things are reflected on its surface, which imparts to them glowing, lambent colours." (Adams 1980, 10) Adams declares that humanity lives within the outer web, an impenetrable surface that soaks up human experience like an inhaled vapor. The storyteller is the connection between earthly experience and the diaphanous oversphere, which retains the essence of life's complexity and meaning. Because the rotating web continually moves above the earth, it passes over all points on the globe, spreading above all people the stories that belong to and unify the human family.

In composing his collection of fables and stories, Adams retains folklore's lack of sophistication and dependence on stereotypical characters, but he rejects the convention of anonymous beings by supplying a more definite setting and cast. "A Hundred Times," a riddle story, reexamines the long-lived relationship between king and peasant. An Eskimo *pourquoi* story, "The Crow and the Daylight," pits beast against the light. With a similar motif, "The Nightingale" explains how birds were created and colored from God's paintbox except for the drab nightingale, whose tongue God tipped with gold. The Polynesian tale "The Giant Eel" reflects Adams's gift for exotic allure through the union of Hina and her island mate, "Maui Tiki-Tiki a Taranga, fisher-up of islands." (Adams 1980, 87) A grim vengeance tale, "Mice in the Corn," describes a ruined Welsh lord who tries to hang a mouse on a tiny gallows. More in the Aesopic mode are "Back of the Moon," an updated version of Horace's "The City Mouse and the Country Mouse," and "The Woodpecker," a charming dialect story of a nosy old woman whose neighbors tire of her intrusions. After she opens a parcel addressed to someone else, she releases a cloud of insects, "fahsands of 'em, hoppin' and flyin' an' scuttlin' all arahnd everywhere, some aht the winder and some under the bloomin' door an' some in 'er 'air an' all sorts." (Adams 1980, 44) A magician changes her into the long-beaked bird and condemns her to "pokin' into trees and posts and old fences, and anywhere where she reckons she's got a chance to catch some more of them insects what she let aht the box." (Adams 1980, 46) Adams's reprise of the sin of Pandora demonstrates his affection for hero and miscreant alike and extols the theme of redemption, which condemns the snooper to an unending job of gathering up nuisances.

See also Christian fable.

Sources Adams 1972, 1980; Bartlett 1992; *Contemporary Authors* 1994; Gilman 1974; Maddock 1975; Mano 1974; Prescott 1974; "Rabbit's Tale" 1997; "The Real *Watership Down* Homepage," http://members.aol.com; Samuels 1974; Smith 1974.

AESOP

The most accessible of moral fabulists from the ancient Mediterranean, Aesop (ca. 620–560 B.C.E.), is a semilegendary character described as slave, shrewd teller of explanatory and representational stories, and the Greek father of the Western fable. According to a preface written by the fourth century C.E. fabulist Avianus, a Roman imitator, Aesop was divinely commissioned to found the genre. In Avianus's words, "My pioneer in this subject, you must know, is Aesop, who on the advice of the Delphic Apollo started droll stories in order to establish moral maxims." (Duff and Duff 1982, 681) Because metaphoric lore such as fable, allegory, and parable was invented after the time of Homer two centuries earlier, Aesop may have achieved popularity less for origination than for the novelty of his witty beast stories, whose brevity is a welcome break from ponderous epics. His classic miscellany of 350 satiric beast satires lampoons the standard human failings of pride, arrogance, greed, and folly. G. K. Chesterton accords the fabulist a left-handed acknowledgement in his declaration that, within human history, "whatever is authentic is universal: and whatever is universal is anonymous. In such cases there is always some central man who had first the trouble of collecting [fables], and afterwards the fame of creating them." (*Aesop's Fables* 1968, v)

The facts of Aesop's biography are sketchy. Legend contends that Aesop was not a continental Greek but a Semitic enslaved in Thrace—or possibly an islander from Samos, a Phrygian from Cotiaeum, or a Lydian, although these suppositions are tenuous. Chesterton notes the peculiar coincidence that both

Aesop and Uncle Remus, a pair of fabulists oppressed by masters, were fascinated by the comparatively free choice enjoyed by the animal kingdom. Although of obscure origin, Aesop caught the attention of Eugeon (or Euagon) of Samos, author of *Horoi Samión* (sixth century B.C.E.), who named Aesop's hometown as Mesembria in Thrace. Aesop also merited mention as "maker of stories" in Book II of Herodotus's *Histories* (ca. 425 B.C.E.). Less than a century later, Aesop earned secondhand praise in Plato's *Phaedo* (ca. 345 B.C.E.), in which the doomed philosopher Socrates whiles away his final days in prison by translating Aesop into verse, and by Aristotle, who, in *Constitution of the Samians* and Book II of *Rhetorica* (ca. 330 B.C.E.), refers to an instance when the storyteller impressed the Samians during the trial of an embezzler by reciting "The Fox and the Hedgehog." Although it is probable that Aesop never issued collections of his iambic beast fables, which, in his milieu, were not serious enough to rate publication, he received at least two notable tributes. Around that same time period, the sculptor Lysippus created a likeness of him in Athens; some two millennia later, the seventeenth-century Spanish painter Diego Velázquez painted Aesop's portrait.

According to legend, Aesop was no stranger to labor. He worked first for Xanthus and then for Iadmon (or Jadmon). His second master freed him as reward for his brilliance. Five centuries after Herodotus's description, the biographer Plutarch named Aesop as the court counselor of King Croesus in Sardis, Lydia. Other nebulous traditions move Aesop about the eastern Mediterranean, placing him on the Black Sea, in modern Bulgaria or Romania, and as far south as Phrygia, a landmass south of the Black Sea in what is now eastern Turkey. Unfortunately, no literary historian can reconstruct Aesop's life, although it appears certain that he was a contemporary of Sappho of Lesbos, who flourished late in the sixth century B.C.E., and that a tablet on the Troad dated to that same century B.C.E. records the Greek name *Aisopos*. Details are hopelessly marred by surmise and outright fiction. The comic playwright Alexis of Thurii repeats some of the innuendo about Aesop the trickster in a play, *Aesop* (ca. 350 B.C.E.), which was lost in antiquity. In the early third century, the poet Poseidippis eulogizes the fabulist in *Aesopia*, an elegy that allies Aesop with a fellow slave, Doricha, who became the famed courtesan Rhodopis.

In the fourteenth century, the translator Maximus Planudes, a monk and envoy from Constantinople, wrote a spurious introduction to Aesop's life and fables. A lengthy work in the Christian tradition, the biography is hopelessly anachronistic and steeped in the stylistic detail and virtues of the Middle Ages. Planudes perpetuates legends and isolated anecdotes claiming that Aesop was born hideously deformed with an oversized head, drooping jaw, and wry neck. Large, bumbling, and hunchbacked, he stammered when he spoke. As is common in victim lore, the boy Aesop compensated for unsightly physical appearance with a piercing intelligence. Legend has it that he was sold into slavery and transported to Aristes of Athens, who placed him under the management of Zenas, a cruel and devious superintendent of field workers. Falsely accused of eating his master's figs, Aesop was unable to defend himself verbally. Instead, he vomited up the contents of his empty stomach and asked his accuser

Nineteenth-century print of Aesop relating his fables.

to force the real culprits to do the same. Because the results were obvious, Aesop was exonerated.

According to Planudes, the next day Aesop elevated himself through genuine piety. He helped Ysidis, a lost priest, by leading him out of the sun to a shady fig tree, offering him bread, olives, and a dessert of figs and dates, then setting him on the right road to Athens. For his kindness, Ysidis prayed that the gods would reward the wretched slave with divine beneficence. While Aesop slept at the noon hour, the goddess Isis blessed him with a clear, sweet voice and an understanding of all birds and beasts. At the goddess's command, he achieved an instantaneous mastery of fable. When the slave boy awoke, he was a different person.

Upon Zenas's return to the fields, he discovered that Aesop was able to relate plainly the overseer's former cruelties and could inform Aristes of the other slaves' sufferings. Zenas ran to meet his master in town and to accuse Aesop of blasphemy and of slander against Aristes. The master was outraged and gave Zenas full control of Aesop. By chance, a slave buyer came through the area seeking animal and slave stock for the fair at Ephesus. Zenas pointed out Aesop, whose ugliness repulsed the slave dealer. Aesop pursued the merchant, promising to serve him as manager of shy, inexperienced slave boys. For three gold coins, Zenas gladly parted with him.

Though small and weak, Aesop quickly proved himself useful and astute. On his master's journey to Ephesus, Aesop volunteered to shoulder the heaviest burden—the slaves' supply of bread for the journey. His fellow slaves admired his spirit until they realized that the loaves dwindled at each meal, leaving

Aesop to carry an empty basket over the final leg of the journey. At the market, the merchant sold all his stock except the fabulist, a musician, and a grammarian. To rid himself of the three, the merchant sailed with them to the island of Samos off modern Izmir, Turkey, and sold them to Xanthus, a philosopher and teacher, who paid only 60 coins for Aesop and 3,000 coins for the other two.

In lengthy episodes in which Aesop deflates his masters by making them look foolish, he proved himself so wise and cautious that the villagers of Samun sought his advice. When Croesus sent formal demands for tribute, the villagers chose Aesop as their emissary. Moved by his fables about the locust, an insect that does no harm and makes sweet harmony, Croesus exempted the Samnians from taxation. Aesop, now an honored savant, dedicated his life to teaching useful fables and spreading worthy counsel. He journeyed to the court of Lycurgus, king of Babylon, where Aesop's adopted son Enus plotted against his father and turned Lycurgus against him. While Aesop hid in a tomb, Enus usurped his possessions. After the king repented of his murderous urge, the servant charged with executing Aesop returned him to court to assist Lycurgus in answering a difficult riddle posed by Nectanabo, king of Egypt. The frail old fabulist then renewed his parental custody of Enus, who was so shamed by his greed and treachery that he leaped to his death from a tower.

As emissary to Egypt, Aesop quickly established a reputation for wisdom and cunning by answering King Nectanabo's riddles. On return from collecting an outstanding debt that Egypt owed Babylon, Aesop delighted Lycurgus, who commissioned a gold statue of Aesop, which the Roman imitator Phaedrus noted in the epilogue of Book II of his fables. Lycurgus also dispatched the old storyteller on a tour of central Greece, which allowed him to see much of the area, including Sardis, Corinth, and Athens.

According to Eusebius, a fourth-century bishop, and to Plutarch's *Banquet of the Seven Sages* (second century C.E.), Aesop died at Delphi in 564 B.C.E. He had arrived at the sacred center of Apollo worship in central Greece as a courier from Croesus of Sardis to distribute gold among the citizens. Instead, he insulted them by accusing them of milking truth-seekers who came to the oracle for advice. Local plotters then hid Apollo's treasured wine bowl in Aesop's luggage, pretended to search for it, and found him guilty of sacrilege. In punishment, they hurled him to his death from the Delphian crags. Plutarch's *Vita Aesopi* [Life of Aesop] (ca. 100 C.E.) corroborates the story as a plausible requital for slighting Apollo by naming Mnemosyne as the head of the Muses. In the episode, Aesop chooses unwisely by taking refuge at the Muses's shrine. Before his execution as a common thief, he predicted that Greece and Babylon would join forces to avenge his death. As he had foreseen, Delphians suffered reprisals as well as internal discontent, disease, and famine. Zeus's oracle advised them to propitiate the angry gods by raising a temple to Aesop.

No clear motivation exists for Delphi's savagery beyond envy of a former slave; however, Plutarch's version gains credence by including Iadmon's grandson, who purportedly demanded payoffs in recompense for the senseless killing of a harmless elder. Another telling claims that a Delphian carried bags of gold to Samos to offer Iadmon's household because their city had suffered a plague and their collective guilty conscience forced them to atone for the old man's murder. Whatever the cause of Aesop's cruel death, there rose from his life story the forbidding warning of "the blood of Aesop."

Traditionally, Aesop's comic prose tales are described in the same mode as the clever dialect adaptations of African lore written by Joel Chandler Harris—a blend of original beast fables and collected moral stories that Aesop may have derived from earlier sources. To free them of weighty human baggage, he tended to strip them of human characters and recast them with anthropomorphic animals, both domestic and wild. Often, the animals appear in pairs—bull with calf, dog with fox, hen with swallow, and wolf with lamb. In some tales, such as "The Old Woman and the Wine-Jar," "The Countryman and the Snake," "The Boy and the Scorpion," and "The Ass and His Purchaser," simple-minded folk interact with animals and often come up short in comparison by displaying poor judgment, venality, or questionable character. A pragmatic ethicist, Aesop salted these brief stories with sensory detail—the plop of frogs into a pond, the shriek of the porker nabbed by the shepherd, and the hum of flies about the honeypot. He concluded each with a clearly stated universal moral, usually lauding caution, moderation, planning, and judgment.

The oldest written compendium of Aesop's stories, which contains 231 fables, is the Augustana codex, named for its location in Augsburg, Germany. The manuscript, which was unknown to Phaedrus and only faintly influenced by Babrius, appears to derive from the second century C.E. Subsequent generations have embraced Aesop and recast him according to the styles and tastes of the times. About two and a half centuries after he flourished in the eastern Mediterranean, Demetrius of Phalerum (or Phalereus) systematized the oral canon of folklore, myths, aphorisms, trickster motifs, and animal yarns into a single written manuscript. The text survived for 500 years. Augmented and refined, Aesop's canon took on new meanings and settings in the four volumes produced by Roman freedman Gaius Julius Phaedrus (ca. 15–50 C.E.) during Tiberius's reign. Further adaptation appears in the versions of Roman fabulists Valerius Babrius (second century C.E.) and Avianus (fifth century C.E.). These romanized stories deviate from the eastern Mediterrean influence but maintain two key qualities: an admirable wit and a didactic intent suited to molding the character of young children, who studied both the ethics and rhetoric of fable as models for their own writing. As did the mentor in the Indian *Panchatantra* and Zen disseminators of jataka tales, teachers of royal youth chose fables as sound expressions of statecraft and discretion, both essentials to princelings.

Throughout the Mediterranean, the fables flourished into modern times. The clergy read them from the pulpit, calligraphers added them to illuminations, tapestry makers copied their graphic images, and other artists and artisans depicted them in fresco, wood, ivory, and stone. Educated people retained and profited from Aesop's images—the cat's paw, the goose that laid the golden egg, sour grapes, and dog in the manger—and his simple, aphoristic homilies:

- Some men will never accept servitude.

- Don't complain—there is always someone worse off than you.

THE · HARE AND THE · TORTOISE·

THEY STARTED TOGETHER, AND THE TORTOISE KEPT JOGGING
ON STILL, TILL HE CAME TO THE END OF THE COURSE. THE
HARE LAID HIMSELF DOWN MIDWAY AND TOOK A NAP; "FOR,"
SAYS HE, "I CAN CATCH UP WITH THE TORTOISE WHEN I PLEASE"

"The Hare and the Tortoise," an illustration from *Aesop's Fables,* ca. 1890s

- Changing place does not change your nature.
- Don't consort with evil companions.
- Don't tempt trouble.
- Don't undervalue the ordinary.
- Fine feathers don't make fine birds.
- Expect times when the small triumph over the weak.
- Familiarity breeds contempt.
- Ignore tiresome yappers who hate being ignored.
- There is strength in numbers.
- Danger lies where you least expect it.
- Look before you leap.
- Necessity is the mother of invention.
- Pride goes before a fall.
- Slow and steady wins the race.
- Speak up—the squeaking wheel gets the grease.

Aristophanes claims that the verses were favorite dinner recitations as well as sources of the Greek comedic allusions—the fox and the grapes, the ostentatious peacock, the foolish pup, the one-eyed doe, the proud lion—that permeate Greek comedy.

Throughout history, the Western canon has paid homage to Aesop. He is mentioned in Christopher Marlowe's *The Jew of Malta* (ll. 2139–2143) and in William Shakespeare's *King Henry VI, Pt. 2* (V, v, 25–26). In the seventeenth and eighteenth centuries, additional citations appear in John Dryden's *The Hind and the Panther*, John Donne's *Epigram—Mercurius* and *Satire V*, and Oliver Goldsmith's *Epilogue Spoken by Mr. Lee Lewes*. In the Romantic and Victorian eras, John Clare speaks of Aesop in "Written in Prison"; Rudyard Kipling opens *The Fabulists* with a four-line tribute to the master fable-maker. In the twentieth century, literary historians and scholars—notably Ben Edwin Perry, compiler and editor of *Aesopica* (1951)—scramble to preserve the earliest reliable sources of oral lore.

Still faithful to Aesop's tradition of oral delivery, performers and updaters of Aesop's fables thrive in library, concert hall, children's literature, and family circle. A modern proponent of Aesopic lore, Jim Weiss, founder of Greathall Productions, Benicia, California, aims to make fables more widely accessible and enjoyable. In 1990, he produced *Animal Tales*, a tape suitable for young children featuring Aesop's "The Crow and the Pitcher," "The Lion and the Mouse," and "The Tortoise and the Hare," plus Geoffrey Chaucer's "Chanticleer and the Rooster" and Horace's "The City Mouse and the Country Mouse." Harper Caedmon features an audiocassette of Aesop's fables performed by film star Boris Karloff. Philadelphia's storytelling maven Mary Carter Smith maintains a career in platform performance, audiocassette, and print publication of updated Aesop's fables. A traditional griot in African robes and headdress, she arms herself with a cowtail switch and takes the stance of the mighty mythopoet to enhance her authority. In 1993, she taped *Mary Carter Smith—Nearing Seventy-Five,* a program featuring "Tales of Aesop from Jamal Koram."

See also fable.

Sources Aesop: Five Centuries of Illustrated Fables 1964; *Aesop's Fables* 1968, 1993, n. d.; Blackham 1985; Cooper 1921; Duff and Duff 1982; Feder 1986; Flaceliere 1962; Green 1965; Hammond and Scullard 1992; Herodotus 1961; Howatson 1989; Komroff 1935; Lang and Dudley 1969; Lesky 1966; Mantinband 1956; Newbigging 1895; Perry 1962; Smith, Mary Carter 1993.

 # AFRICAN FABLE

The sheer size and variance of climate, topography, and cultures stymies a thorough, unified study of African literature, which draws on the interrelation of animal with land and human inhabitants with a habitat that refuses to be tamed. Much African animal lore, after its adulteration by European intrusion, lost its characteristic tie with plateaus, rain forests, grasslands, deserts, and deltas. Yet Africa's fables retain the complexity of human societies and their ambivalence toward nature, especially during chaotic times wrought by flood, fire, drought, disease, infestation, and famine. According to Harold Courlander's overview of Africa's early past, the vitality of its lore derives from change. Owing to crisscrossing migrations, traders passing over camel caravan routes and river highways, and village-to-village swapping of oral traditions, African animal lore has been hybridized and blended from preliterate times to the present. Indigenous African oral tradition, though moderated by Islam and Christianity, perpetually integrates borrowed and enhanced ideas and truths, modulating the common strands of creation lore, song-chants, *pourquoi* stories, fool tales, and nature-based and human-based proverbs. The result is the familiar interlacing of details, beliefs, and themes that colors the Zairian and Thangian trickster hare with attributes of the Yoruban tortoise, Dahomey's rascally Jack, and Ghana's clever Gizo, the trickster spider who superimposes heroism over villainy.

The rise of the sub-Saharan or black African city-states and empires accounts for the collection and systematizing of native cycles of myth and legends. Liberally dotted with exotica attained from Arab, Mediterranean, Indian, and Oriental contacts, these bodies of literature demonstrate a willingness to receive world lore into local culture.

The first African literature to take shape was that of the Soninke of Ghana, who came to power in the fourth century C.E. and remained until the mid-thirteenth century, when their gold trade with Berber Muslims ceased and rebellion of satellite states weakened their authority. A jocular Soninkan fool tale, "The Messenger to Maftam," illustrates the theme of character in the test of

Mamadi, a virtuous man who tells no lies. In the traditional overturning of the plans of schemers, Mamadi retains his reputation by foiling Bahene, a Soninkan chief who tries to force Mamadi to lie. Unlike more pious versions of the test story, folk origins emphasize the insubstantial explanations of Mamadi, whose reputation derives more from witless confusion rather than devotion to truth.

To the east, the Kanem-Bornu dominance of Lake Chad created a weak but persistent empire that slowly took shape in the ninth century and lasted until the European empire builders arrived. From its lore comes "The Two Traders," a Solomonic story that unmasks a trickster and spendthrift who steals his fellow trader's goods. When brought before the king, the thief pretends to be deaf and dumb, but a clever ruse forces him to speak.

At the demise of Ghana, the Mandingo (or Mandinka) superstate of Kangaba took shape in Mali and spread its influence north into the African Sudan, east to the Niger River, and west to the Atlantic Ocean. A briefer segment of African empires, the Malian hegemony lasted 300 years until its demise in the sixteenth century. A witty Malian repetition story, "The Song of Gimmile," illustrates in the recurrence of a humorous refrain the comeuppance of the haughty King Konondjong, who refuses to reward a bard for his song-tales. To retaliate, the singer's friend spreads a catchy ditty:

> Konondjong, king of the Gindo,
> He is fat, his neck is flabby.
> Konondjong, king of the Gindo,
> His teeth are few, his legs are swelled.
> Konondjong, king of the Gindo,
> His knees are bony, his head is bald.
> Konondjong, king of the Gindo.
> (Courlander 1996, 81)

After the king pays the bard to stop Gimmile's song from spreading, the bard retorts a truth that immortalizes his trade: "A song that is not composed does not exist; but once it is made, it is a real thing."

The Songhay city-state of Gao functioned as a subject nation until Mali's decline, at which time the Songhay briefly held sway on Africa's west coast before falling to Moroccan insurgents around 1600. A valued part of the Songhay literary tradition is the multigeneric epic of Askia Mohammed, a Malian ruler from 1493 to 1528. Within the rhythmic, repetitive lines, the griot interposes additional elements—historical side notes, genealogy, proverb, praise poems, and etiological fables that account for natural phenomena.

Wedged between the Kanem-Bornu and the Songhay was the Hausa civilization east of the Niger, creator of the mother lode of surviving indigenous fables. A small power composed of seven states, the Hausa produced a lively literary tradition that collector Robert Sutherland Rattray revealed to English readers. Among the Hausan fool tales and hero stories is a simplistic logic tale, "Leopard, Goat, and Yam," which pictures in words the concern of a traveler ferrying his yam, goat, and leopard across the river. In short order, the story concludes, "He took the goat over first and then the yam. He then recrossed the goat and ferried over the leopard, returning a fourth time for the goat." Within the sight gag lies the wisdom of a traveler who must guard yam from goat and goat from leopard. Less sanguine is "Life and Death," the stark allegorical rivalry tale of yin and yang. The fable concludes amicably with the combatants sharing a calabash of water as they journey the earth. A similar morality tale, "The Friend and the Lion," is an open-ended ethical debate over human behaviors that asks hearers to settle which friend is the better man. The device of audience involvement survives in the Caribbean and African-American dilemma tale, a form of group participation story that sparks discussion of right choices.

Significant to the settlement of the Western Hemisphere were the Yoruba, a flourishing, iron-working, bronze-casting, and trading people south of the Niger who spawned the cities of Benin, Oyo, and Ife. A subset of the Yoruba, the Edo of Benin grew steadily influential through cultivation of markets along the rich Niger delta. Yoruba trickster lore features Ijapa, a shifty tortoise whose character flaws mimic the worst of human behaviors. Humorous and abysmal exploits comprise the cycle of battles against Ijapa's evils. In one of the more positive settings, "How Ijapa, Who Was Short, Became Long," the tortoise outwits the boa by plaiting a long tail. He uses it to encircle a feast to mimic the boa's inhospitality to guests. As Brer Terrapin in African-American lore, Ijapa survives in a new environment and language, but maintains his position as chief exploiter and rascal.

Liberia, the modern state raised to prominence by former slaves, enjoyed the cosmopolitan atmosphere of a trader nation versed in the ways of the outside world. One Liberian story that demonstrates a form of Eastern exotica is "Fembar's Curiosity," a morality tale about a man who knows a serpent's secret and who divulges it to his insistent wife, even though he pays for the indiscretion with his life. The crisp *epimythium,* or concluding moral, reminds hearers that the curious often pay for their probing when they "insist upon knowing something that it is better for one not to know." (Abrahams 1993, 138)

Along the Zaire River, the Congo and Loango empires thrived in the fifteenth century, as did their fables. An enigmatic story, "The Bird Messengers," suggests the difficulties of living among peoples of differing cultures who might assist each other if they possessed a common language. From pagan times, the story of the god Nzambi and the crab told in "Who Beats Nzambi's Drum?" results in severe rebuke for the presumptuous crab and a curse that makes him headless and the prey of humans. In both examples, the people of the Congo and Loango stress survival as a controlling theme and purpose of storytelling.

Active to the northeast of black Africa, the Semitic Kush empire grew from tentative beginnings in 350 B.C.E. to considerable power by the second century C.E. The Mensa lore that distinguishes Kushite literature is true beast fable. Rich in *epimythia,* the stories survive as sources of everyday wisdom. From "The Two Donkey Owners" comes the philosophy that creatures instinctively long for freedom. From "The Prophet and the Hyena" the Mensa derive the saying that a false vow is like the hyena's promise to stop eating carrion. Richer in the knowledge of power is the proverb from "The Leopard in His Old Age," which asserts that goats will mock a toothless old stalker. Overall, Kushite morals reflect a simplistic world view.

Ethiopia's kingdom of Axum was the next northeastern power to evolve, beginning in the late third century C.E. A thematic strand unites some of Axum's stories around the search for justice. "The Donkey Who Sinned" perpetuates cynical beliefs that courts prey only on the weak while allowing the strong to continue their dissolute ways. A similar narrative, "The Goats Who Killed the Leopard," depicts the grief-stricken leopard exacting vengeance on the blameless goats because the real villain, the elephant, is too large for the leopard to attack. More propitious for the victim is "The Judgment of the Wind," a paean to creation that leads to an elemental conclusion that all things act according to nature and are therefore blameless. In celebration of the natural scheme of things, the wind sings, "Therefore, let us dance and sing in thanks because all things are as they are." (Courlander 1996, 545) The story concludes with a wry turn: the farmer, caught in the snake's coils, hands him a drum, then flees to safety when the snake releases him to grasp the drum. The fabulist balances homage to esthetic appreciation of the animal kingdom with praise for the quick-witted who must dash from danger when there is an opportunity.

During the stabilization of land-based cultures, the widespread Bantu people moved across the girth of the continent from the Niger to the Indian Ocean. At home in their final destinations in modern Kenya, Tanzania, Zimbabwe, Botswana, and South Africa, this highly adaptive group absorbed and internalized many traditions while spreading their numerous dialects across the heart of the African landmass. Among the Mbindu of Angola, short instructive animal fables are common commentary on shrewdness and gullibility and preachments against immorality, as in "Frog and His Two Wives," a disparagement of polygamy. Brief, direct fables such as "Squirrel and the Kingship" and "Dog and the Kingship" illustrate the universal belief that inborn failings prevent lowly beasts from rising too high in the animal kingdom. Explanatory tales such as "Dog and Jackal" and "The House-Hog and the Wild Boar" account for the difference in domestic and wild animals, often by reflecting on the fate of animals that grow too fond of the easy barnyard life.

See also African-American fable; trickster.

Sources Abrahams 1993; Alston 1994; Arnott 1963; Courlander 1996; Hale 1996; Lang and Dudley 1969; Mbitu and Prime 1997.

AFRICAN-AMERICAN FABLE

A long-lived amalgam of African, Caribbean, and North and South American lore, African-American folk literature vibrates with life, hope, wisdom, dialect grace, and a wry cynicism indigenous to slavery. According to Henry Louis Gates's "Narration and Cultural Memory in the African-American Tradition," the preservation of the homeland's encoded messages came at a price: "The strictest, most brutal forms of punishment were meted out to those Africans insistent upon retaining their own languages, calling themselves by their true names, or those intent upon continuing those cultural practices, such as religious ceremonies, that they had brought with them through the barbarous

Middle Passage." (Goss and Barnes 1989, 15) By the time black Americans gained their freedom, they celebrated cultural and spiritual emancipation by recovering their own stories, the common coin shared by Langston Hughes, Harriet Jacobs, Zora Neale Hurston, and Alice Walker. The multitude of lore serves as a filter through which hearers process real events and build a foundation for evolving values and judging behaviors.

Today, African-American literature teems with the wealth of Africa. From Senegal, black tellers derive the humor of set-tos between the dog and hedgehog; from Gambia come fool tales of the lion king's subjects, which pit the wily ape against the foolish wolf. Good humored foolery fuels "The Frog's Saddle Horse," a situational comedy from Angola that depicts an audacious frog astride the mighty elephant. Madagascar widens the disparity between living things with "The Boar and the Chameleon," "The Cat and the Rat," and "The Guinea Hen and the Crocodile," a *pourquoi* story that forever separates the two in nature by alloting water to the crocodile and dust baths to the peafowl. Like their African forebears, Caribbean griots exploit the resilience of the small survivor with dramas, dances, mumming, and fables of Anansi the spider, the region's perennial trickster and forerunner of Jack, hero of the American Jack tales. In folklorist Zora Neale Hurston's opinion, as expressed in *The Negro, an Anthology* (1934), the rabbit remains "far in the lead of all the other [tricksters] and is blood brother to Jack. In short, the trickster-hero of West Africa has been transplanted to America." (Hurston 1995, 837)

In assessing New World wisdom narrative, Richard M. Dorson surmises that, overall, American folklore is too new, too diverse, too educated, and too inhibited by modernity to have produced a national folk ethos. Only the slave culture, he declares, possesses a unified storytelling tradition. In Roger D. Abrahams's *Afro-American Folktales*, the author explains why African folktale survived: for a people coerced into slave ships and auctioned into bondage in unknown lands, wisdom lore, fables, songs, epic genealogies, dances, and prayers were the only baggage that survived the mass kidnapping. Stripped of the cultural arts and institutions developed by proud African kingdoms and denied membership among America's elite "buckra" (whites), resourceful black drays and mammies maintained links to a distant homeland with stories and fables.

An outgrowth of the unnatural slave-master paradigm, fables improvised by black griots were shared in good company. As illustrated by Gary Paulsen's young adult novel *Nightjohn* (1993), lore and learning were usually related in nighttime blacks-only privacy, far from the plantation's big house. As examples of self-preservation, these sessions shared the rich legacy of creation myth, *pourquoi* stories, episodes involving meddlers and simpletons, revenge tales, vignettes of trickery and mischief, *agon* or competition stories, ghostly visitations, shrill jokes, and rambunctious foolery that comprised free entertainment and instruction for residents of the quarters. But beneath the surface bonhomie lay timely lessons: "The Rat in the Whiskey" warns that alcohol mocks truth; "The Bear Meets Trouble" reprises the terrors of post-Emancipation nightriders; "Playing Dead in the Road" anticipates the passive resistance of Gandhi and

Martin Luther King. These relics of ancient civilizations are favorites of a coterie of African-American storytellers, particularly Caribbean poets and raconteurs Paul Keens-Douglas, a Barbadian entertainer, the Trinidadian teller Grace Hallworth, and folkteller Ken Corsbie, a native of Georgetown, Guyana, who grew up in a community that valued "ol' talking," a Guyanan term for traditional fables and proverbs.

The African-American reverence for story pervades the arts. Captured by artist Eric Green in a symbolic painting entitled "Tales," a rural setting colors the background with neat vegetable patches flanking a sharecropper's cabin. Listeners, rapt to the fabulist's art, stretch out on the bare ground beneath an aged and battered oak. The Crayola-bright hues of clothing contrast with the blackness of faces and hands and the monochromatic gray bark of the oak. The scarred bole, a symbol of the indomitable black race, reaches truncated limbs to the sky in parallel to the tellers' arms, which ply the air in the ecstasy of narrative. Green's composition delineates the immediacy of black folk stories, the life-affirmation of mimicry, and the endurance of folkways that sustain and uplift at the same time that they entertain.

The patois of humble stories reflects the blending of cultures throughout the New World—Guadaloupe, Martinique, and Dominica among the French islands; the British possessions of Haiti, Jamaica, and Antigua; Guyana on the South American coast; the bayou Creole of Louisiana; the Gullah culture of Charleston and the offshore islands of Georgia and the Carolinas; and the cane fields, docks, and chain gangs of the Uncle Remus South. Original stories dot travelogues, daybooks, and plantation epistles from the early nineteenth century. Nameless characters of fable coexist with Anansi, the self-incriminating scamp of the West Indies, and Ti Malice, the rascal of Haiti's oral tradition. They reach their height in Brer Rabbit, the star of the editorials, features, journals, and anthologies that Joel Chandler Harris published in the four decades following the Civil War. Later compendia of lore—particularly Zora Neale Hurston's two volumes of southern and Caribbean games, hoodoo, and folklore, *Mules and Men* (1935) and *Tell My Horse* (1938), and Virginia Hamilton's award-winning *The People Could Fly: American Black Folktales* (1985)—establish the place of the female folk collector/griot in world literature.

Much of the luminous grace and outrageous joy of Afro-American lore forms a necessary oral barrier between despair, deprivation, and demoralization and the will to thrive. Competitive lore, in the words of Richard Dorson, yokes inequalities: "The slow inchworm outdoes the speedy 'hoppergrass,' the elephant turns the tables on the jackal, the crane finally pins the slippery eel, dirtdauber refuses to learn from the bee, the ox posthumously punishes the traitorous mule, who is whipped with rawhide whenever he balks." (Dorson 1959, 67) Brer Rabbit's witty rejoinders and Anansi's exhibitionism relieve the dangerous urge of a captive people to strike back at oppression. To enhance his superb essay on Afro-American folk wisdom, Roger Abrahams cites the fable of Sis Goose, who sues the fox for ejecting her from swimming in the pond. It is too late for Sis when she notices that the sheriff, judge, attorneys, and jury are all foxes. Not only do they find her guilty, they kill and devour her in the courtroom to which she had fled for justice. The moral comes as no surprise to a minority: If all the folks in power are foxes, the goose can expect no justice.

Crucial to oral delivery of beast fable are the ideophonic sounds of the characters. A blend of gobble-gobble, caw-caw, and baa-baa provide the comedy that veils hard lessons from nature. The voicing of each creature provides individuality and color, for example, to this barnyard conversation:

> Fowl cock say, "Marster, t'ief come."
> Sheep say, "Nevah!"
> Guinea Fowl say, "You did it, you did it."
> Duck say, "A-wa, a-wa, a-wa."
> Turkey say, "It's your habitual practice, it's your habitual practice."
> Hog say, "Good, good."
> (Abrahams 1985, 25)

Richard Baughman, in *Story, Performance and Event: Contextual Studies of Oral Narrative* (1986), includes a fable about a thief fleeing across a swamp that requires skillful voicing to establish the source of accusation. Bayou tellers report that the robber fled a tobacco barn with his pockets jammed with golden leaves. As he made his way through canebrakes and into a spooky fen, he heard a disembodied frog cry of "Thief, thief!" As he jerked around in search of his accuser, he muttered defensively, "What did I steal?" A high-pitched shriek in the top of a live oak echoes, "Tobacky! Tobacky!" Without a teller accurately duplicating the sounds of frogs and birds, the story fails to establish that the thief's guilty conscience turns innocent swamp sounds into oral indictment.

One of the outstanding black storytellers in the United States, Charlotte Blake Alston, of Silver Spring, Maryland, has mastered beast fable in varied styles, including participation story, rhyme, call and response, and morality tale. Performing with the John Blake Jazz Quartet and the Carolyn Dorfman Dance Company, Alston regales general audiences in the griot tradition. For maximum appeal, she dresses in striking African robes and toques and sets her cadence to the drum and *shakere*. Her stories stress humor through gesture and kinetics, facial expression, and accents. As president of the Philadelphia-based "Keepers of the Culture," an Afrocentric teller's guild, she supports inclusion across the arts of genuine African lore, such as the Ashanti fable, "Who's in Rabbit's House," "How Raccoon Got His Dinner," and "The Ant and the Crumb." At annual appearances with the Philadelphia Orchestra, Alston dramatizes classic fables: "The Lion's Whiskers," "The Tall, Tall Tale," "The Yam Story," "Did You Feed My Cow?," "Hambone," and "Shoo Turkey," a favorite of young listeners.

A unique figure in African-American lore is Brother Blue, the performance persona of Dr. Hugh Morgan Hill, a familiar barefoot street teller in the Boston area who blends personal experience with fable from the *Panchatantra*, Buddhist jataka tales, Aesop's fables, and European and Bible classics. Painted with butterflies and armed with tambourine, harmonica, saxophone, umbrella, and fool's bells, the self-proclaimed "Storytellin' Fool of New England" strolls through prisons, homeless shelters, and community centers, gesturing and clowning with painted hands, balloons, ribbons, and puppets. His grasp of traditional lore has won him the Zora Neale Hurston Award and, in 1996, a place in the prestigious National Storytelling Association Circle of Excellence.

Other folksayers have evolved idiosyncratic methods of spreading black culture. California actress-teller Ellaraino focuses on African and African-American tales, participation stories, ring games, and story circles. A winner of a National Education Association commendation for imaginative re-creation of trickster lore, she carries the teller's staff, dresses in Afrocentric style, and plays traditional African musical instruments while performing animal fables and conducting workshops such as *Africa!* and *Critters and Creatures . . . Famous and Lesser Known.* Billed as a "griartist," her contemporary, New Jersey–based teller Adisa Bankole preserves in oral tradition the motifs of the African diaspora. A dynamic performer in traditional African dress, he was a featured teller at the 1997 National Black Storytellers Festival and shared the stage with veterans Daddy Junebug, Baba Jamal Koram, and Sister Caroleees Reed. He seeks the cultural liberation of audiences by re-creating fables and wisdom lore of the ancient African folksayer, which he learned from his great-grandmother, the family history keeper. For the Hamilton Art Center, he created "Ebo: How the Lion Got His Roar," a lesson in listening. His original fables include "Binsee Bee" and "Elika the Elikoo Bird," both lessons from the African past.

Another contemporary preserver of Caribbean and Ghanian Anansi stories is Linda McNear Goss, a Philadelphia storyteller born in Alcoa, Tennessee. A fancier of world beast fables and myths, she tells how-and-why tales and trickster stories from the Anansi-the-spider tradition and Uncle Remus's lore. After leaving a teaching post at Center City's Philadelphia School, she became a "gatekeeper of history" for workshops, church meetings, and school gatherings. The thrust of her career is an ongoing battle against the dehumanization of technology. For performances of her children's book *The Frog Who Wanted to Be a Singer,* she becomes the frog, fingering an imaginery bass fiddle and burbling, "Dooba! Dooba! Doop-Dee-Doop! . . . Blurrrrrrp!" (Goss 1989) The story, which is featured in Holt, Rinehart and Winston's eighth-grade reader, *Elements of Literature,* and in *Treasures of Literature* from Harcourt Brace, expresses her signature use of fable as empowerment lore.

See also Brer Rabbit; Hamilton, Virginia; Harris, Joel Chandler; Hurston, Zora Neale; Uncle Remus.

Sources Abrahams 1985; Alston 1994; Burrison 1989; Cooper 1921; *DISCovering Multicultural America,* http://www.galenet.gale.com; Dorson 1959, 1967; Faison 1989; Goss 1996, 1981; Goss and Barnes 1989; Goss and Goss 1995; Hurston 1995; Jones 1969; Lang and Dudley 1969; Miller and Snodgrass 1998.

 # AMERICAN FABLE

The lore of Europe, Africa, and Asia accompanied settlers on their trek to the New World, where it thrived in schoolrooms and pulpits, by campfires and hearthsides. English colonists who valued books tended to shelve Aesop's works alongside the King James Bible and John Bunyan's *Pilgrim's Progress*, a triad that illuminates the didactic mindset of newcomers to North America, particularly Puritans and Calvinists. Crucial to their emigration was the intent to begin anew in a pristine land and to leave behind old faults and failings. Ironically, they left behind oppression but served as the conduit of Old World lore to the new land. The humorless, repressive townships that sprang up along the New England shore reveal a determination to stamp out in children and adults all evidence of frivolity and sin by replacing Europe's literary romances and nonsectarian textbooks with wisdom literature.

Along with fool tales and riddles, the fable retained its vigor among settlers, who intentionally passed them to the young. From Pennsylvania Dutch lore come anecdotes about Till Eulenspiegel, foolish farmers, shrewd Quakers and Amish, and Yankee peddlers. A beast fable that overturns sanctimony is the story of the cruel farmer who visits his animals on Christmas Eve. According to a pious legend, the coming of the Christ Child is a magical moment in the stable, where animals suddenly acquire the power of speech. Hiding in a corner haymow, the farmer discovers that his animals are indeed able to talk among themselves. But to his dismay, they confer about how to waylay him and stomp him to death. Before he can flee, the animals carry out their plot. The story says much about agrarian values, which disdain farmers whose style of husbandry calls for animal abuse.

Also taking shape in American colonies and outlying islands were stories from West Africa, the homeland of most New World slaves. A favorite theme among the enslaved was the timeless tradition that early Africans had wings and could fly. One plantation fable tells of a wicked overseer who systematically works field hands to death. Unaware that he has acquired a winged woman in his last batch of row tenders, the overseer continually lashes and berates her for nursing her baby when she is supposed to chop weeds. With the encouragement of an aged fellow slave, she leaps into the sky and bears her child to safety. Subsequent acts of cruelty cause the old slave to send others forth from bondage. When the master realizes that one disrupter is responsible for the flight of his property, he orders the old man beaten to death. The story ends with a mass flight from the plantation and over the edge of the horizon toward the slaves' African motherland. A psychological narrative that supplants hazardous escape plans with wish fulfillment, the story lightens the slaves' hearts with a magical solution to plantation torment—sprout wings and fly away.

From the *coureurs de bois* [woods runners] of French settlements along the St. Lawrence Seaway, Great Lakes, and Mississippi Valley came a vigorous corpus of folksay—the silly doings of Foolish John flourished alongside shoutsong, macabre voodoo and devil tales, monsters, and sea serpents. Paralleling sea stories of the Flying Dutchman are the land-based episodes of the *chassegalerie*, the flying canoe, which carries its paddlers far from home, and the mystic fiddler, who charms the constellations with his lively tunes. Prominent in this body of fantasy tales is the tradition of *loup-garou*, the werewolf, who dwells among mortals in human form until the powers of nature evoke its bestial form, usually late at night. In "Joe Hamelin and the *Loup-Garou*," the animal speaks with the voice of a dead man. More in keeping with fable are the animal stories, as demonstrated by the Cajun favorite "M'su Lion Makes a Big Mistake," in which the lion learns the hard way about the pitfalls of bragging, and "M'su Carencro and Mangeur de Poulet" [Mr. Buzzard and the Chicken Hawk], a survival tale that describes how the buzzard tricks the chicken hawk and eats him for dinner.

The United States made its contributions to fable by summoning these multiple strands of imported folk wisdom for New World applications.

- Against the backdrop of the American Revolution, Boston-based author, diplomat, and inventor Benjamin Franklin wrote new fables and adaptations of older works, including a reprise of the lion king motif, tales from the Arabian classic *A Thousand and One Nights*, and an original work, "The Ephemera: An Emblem of Human Life," a reflection on the long history of the common fly.

- During the heated debate over abolitionism, Underground Railroad conductor and lecturer Harriet Tubman drew on illustrative fable for her public defiance of slavery.

- Nineteenth-century transcendentalist and essayist Ralph Waldo Emerson composed "The Mountain and the Squirrel," a standard lopsided *agon* or competition motif that pits the mountain against the squirrel. Most of the retort comes from the squirrel, who "[thinks] it not disgrace/To occupy my place" and concludes, "If I cannot carry forests on my back,/ Neither can you crack a nut." (Komroff 1935, 427)

- Noted humorist and author Mark Twain produced "A Fable," a borrowing from Rudyard Kipling's *The Jungle Book* (1894). Published in *Harper's Magazine* in December 1909, the story, a satire of critical assumptions about art, ends with a wryly bestial moral: "You can find in a text whatever you bring, if you will stand between it and the mirror of your imagination. You may not see your ears, but they will be there." (Twain 1958, 602) A posthumous collection, *Fables of Man* (1972), displays Twain's mounting depression, which shadowed the unpublished works of his later years.

- Late nineteenth-century poet Alice Cary, a native of Cincinnati, Ohio, wrote verse ballads and fables and kept a sparkling literary salon in New York. Along with occasional verse, religious poems and hymns, narratives, and nature and home poems, she produced a smattering of fables, including "The Grateful Swan," a predictable tale of virtue rewarded, and "Barbara Blue," a harsh warning about avarice, which concludes with the tumble of an apple thief over a wall and into a river. Cary composed for children "Three Bugs," a lilting competition for sustenance that ends with the losing bug trouncing and devouring his tormentors. Gleeful for her survivor, the fabulist exults:

  And so there was *war* in the basket,
  Ah, pity, 'tis, 'tis true!
  But he that was frozen and starved at last,

A strength from his weakness drew,
And pulled the rugs from *both* of the bugs,
And killed and *ate* them, too!
(Cary and Cary 1884, 169)

A less violent competitive motif, "A Fable of Cloud-Land," contrasts two clouds, one large and boisterous, the other modest, but helpful. The 14-quatrain poem leads to three verse morals, an appropriate proportion for Victorian-era didacticism. The theme of utility stresses the value of the small cloud to agricultural productivity.

- To illustrate the importance of accepting one's place, Alice's sister, humorist Phoebe Cary, created a fool tale, "The Chicken's Mistake," about a chick that wants to swim like a duck. After the disobedient babe drowns without a peep, Cary extends the moral over four laborious quatrains that remind the young reader:

  For all we have our proper sphere below,
      And this is a truth worth knowing.
  You will come to grief if you try to go
      Where you were never made for going.
  (Cary and Cary 1884, 320)

  Phoebe Cary also wrote a number of lengthy didactic narratives that restate classic fable in verse dramatizations. "The Crow's Children" sets up the crow for loss after she lies to the hunter about the color of birds that eat his garden. "Dappledun," another warning fable, describes a horse who founders from gluttony. A lesson in covetousness, "The Envious Wren" ends the complainer's litany when the farmer's wife snatches up the hen to stew for dinner. The burden of didacticism spirals to the detriment of "They Didn't Think," a narrative of a disobedient mouse, turkey, and robin, all of whom suffer death for refusing to listen to their elders. In the ponderous style of the times, Cary belabors the issue with a loaded question, "Can't you take a warning from their dreadful fate?" (Cooper 1921, 318)

- Nearly a century later, choreographer Pearl Primus, a Trinidadian by birth, collaborated with her husband, Percival Borde, to produce "Earth Theater," a stagy dance form rich in costume, gesture, and drama. Her original folk choreography reached its height in *Impinyuza* (1990), a folkloric dance that Alvin Ailey's troupe performed at the City Center in New York. The pulsing core of the steps reflects Primus's immersion in Rwandan lore of the Watusi, whom she had visited on a study tour of West Africa.

New World apologue, or moral tag, of the twentieth century also adorns and elucidates serious literary works. Perhaps the most compelling statement of modern fable form comes from novelist and activist Alice Walker, whose essays shed light on feminism, child advocacy, equal rights, and humanism. She credits her homeland with inspiring her with this claim:

No one could wish for a more advantageous heritage than that bequeathed to the black writer in the South: a compassion for the earth, a trust in humanity beyond our knowledge of evil, and abiding love of justice. We inherit a great responsibility . . . for we must give voice to centuries not only of silent bitterness and hate but also of neighborly kindness and sustaining love. ("Alice Walker" 1996, 2)

In a reflective treatise, *In Search of Our Mother's Gardens: Womanist Prose* (1983), she summarizes the sufferings of black women in terms of fable: "Black Women are called in the folklore that so aptly identifies one's status in society 'the *mules* of the world,' because we have been handed the burdens that everyone else— *everyone* else—refused to carry."

See also African-American fable; Hispanic fable; Native American fable.

Sources "Alice Walker Web Page" 1996; Blackham, 1985; Blain et al. 1990; "Brewer: Dictionary," http://www.bibliomania.com; Brunvand 1996; Burrison 1989; Cary and Cary 1884; Connelly 1929; Cooper 1921; Creeden 1994; Dailey 1994; *DISCovering Multicultural America,* http://www.galenet.gale.com; Feinberg 1967; Green 1965; Harris 1955; Hobbs 1986; Komroff 1935; Krappe 1964; Leach 1967; Newbigging 1895; Perry 1959; Polley 1978; Reneaux 1992, 1995, 1997; Rosenberg 1997; Ross 1961; Sherr and Kazickas 1994; Twain 1958; Walker 1983, 1994–1995.

ANANSI

Known by a lengthy list of names—Uncle Anansi, Buh Nansi, Compé [Pal] Anansi, Compé Czien [Brother Spider], Kwaku [Uncle] Anansi, Anancy, Aunt Nancy, Sister Nancy, or just plain Nancy—the trickster spider is indigenous to folktales from Africa, the Caribbean, and the American South. The duality of his heroism and villainy replicates similar traits in tricksters the world over— the rascally coyote of North American Plains Indian lore, the Yoruba tortoise Ijapa, the monkey of the Indian *Panchatantra*, and Brer Rabbit, the unifying character of Joel Chandler Harris's Uncle Remus tales and of folksay collected by Zora Neale Hurston and Langston Hughes.

Among the Ashanti of Ghana, the clowning and connivance of Kwaku Anansi suggests the myriad devices by which one human outwits or humiliates another. In "Anansi Owns All the Stories That Are Told," the spider cleverly outmaneuvers the hornet, python, and leopard to prove to the sky god Nyame that he deserves to possess all oral narrative, the true landscape in which he flaunts his mother wit. In "The King's Drum," Anansi displays the flip side of his duality by helping to organize the animals to build a drum as a communication device for the kingdom. When they search for the laziest animal to carry the drum, the monkey refuses to help, thereby confessing his shirking to the rest of the animal kingdom. Without recourse to sleuthing or deception, Anansi unmasks the shiftless monkey, whom the king names official drum carrier. From this perpetual tug of war between rivals and adversaries, the highly energized, inventive lessons fuel the cycle of spider stories that allot to the schemer/planner his due of ridicule and scorn as well as respect and thanks for creating natural phenomena or initiating customs and institutions among native people.

Significant to Anansi's exploits are puzzles, rituals, and dilemmas common to human interaction. In "The Hat-Shaking Dance," the spider performs the expected show of grief for his dead mother-in-law. Of his excesses, the storyteller says:

> Anansi was the kind of person that when he ate, he ate twice as much as others, and when he danced, he danced more vigorously than others, and when he mourned, he had to mourn more loudly than anybody else. Whatever he did, he didn't want to be outdone by anyone else. And although he was very hungry, he couldn't bear to have people think he wasn't the greatest mourner at his own mother-in-law's funeral." (Courlander, 1996, 148)

In a ludicrous attempt to hide a plate of beans from the mourners, Anansi stows them in his hat and jigs about from the scalp-searing pain. Caught in yet another deception, he begs the tall grass to hide his shame. The story ends in a *pourquoi* explanation of the furtive behavior of spiders, still hiding their bald heads from jeering villagers. In a more dastardly show of chutzpah, the Jamaican "Anansi Drinks Boiling Water" describes the spider's nerve in the face of trial by ordeal and his clever stall to give the calabash time to cool. Although the character is a liar and cheat, he earns respect for survival instincts and courage under fire, the inborn traits and learned behaviors that served slaves and the resultant black underclass for centuries.

As demonstrated in parallel episodes of Brer Rabbit and Brer Fox or of the medieval Ysengrimus and Reynard, the delight of trickster stories lies in the proportioning of wins to losses—of Anansi the victor and of Anansi the fool. A resilient motif in Anansi lore prefigures "Brer Rabbit and the Tarbaby," the most loved fable of the Uncle Remus canon. By pretending to be dead, Anansi schemes to lie idle in his grave, sneak out at night to raid the yam patch, and grow fat while doing no work. Concerned over the missing vegetables, Anansi's wife and sons shape a gum-man to catch the thief. Just as Brer Rabbit mires up in the tarbaby centuries later, the original Anansi sticks fast from kicking, punching, squeezing, and butting with his head. By morning, he flees rescuers to hide his humiliation in the dark of the rafters, the preferred home of spiders to this day. Thus, the story strips away the terrors of the dark and, by extension, of death, by reminding children that the spider crawls away from the light to conceal a caper gone wrong.

Anansesem (Anansi lore) is a favorite of storytellers for its intriguing twists, familiar repetitions, and dependable guile. According to the Ashanti story, "Anansi Proves He Is the Oldest," the redoubtable spiderman displays unlimited pluck. On the spur of the moment, he polls the animals one by one, then settles the matter by claiming that there was no earth created in which to bury his father, so Anansi buried him in his head. In Jamaican teller Louise Bennett's dialect tribute in "Anancy an Him Story," the old spider reveals himself to grandmas as they put little ones to bed:

Sometimes wen de ole oman dem sleepy Anancy tie up dem face wid him rope an wake dem up, meck dem talk bout him. So dem tell dem pickney Anancy story, de pickney dem tell smaddy else, dat smaddy else tell an tell, so till me an all dah tell Anancy story.

[Sometimes when the old woman gets sleepy, Anancy ties up her face with his rope and wakes her up, makes her talk about him. So she tells the pickaninnies Anancy stories, the pickaninnies tell somebody else, that somebody else tells and tells, and so tells me and all who tell the Anancy story.] (Goss & Barnes 1989, 40–41.)

Thus, millennia after its inception, the creative genius of Anansi's rescue from the river, his creation of debt or of dance, his riding horse, or his naming of children remains strong among Western audiences. In Bennett's estimation, it isn't the teller who perpetuates the spider, rather, "is Anancy meck it."

In the late twentieth-century American storytelling renaissance, Anansi thrives in oral performance. Rhode Islander Len Cabral, grandson of a Cape Verdean immigrant and a founder of the Spellbinders Storytelling Guild, features "Ananzi's Narrow Waist" and "Ananzi and Common Sense." A master of kinetic, mimetic characterizations, Cabral travels the United States and Canada with his lore. His art appears in textbooks by Houghton-Mifflin and Silver Burdett & Ginn. In collections and periodicals, he has published such animal fables as "The Lion's Whisker" and "Nho Lobo." Cabral's contemporary, three-time Emmy winner Bobby Norfolk of St. Louis, Missouri, enhances his storytelling with African drums, kalimba, and period costume. His original tellings of Anansi lore include two audiocassettes: *Why Mosquitoes Buzz in People's Ears* (1987) and *Norfolk Tales* (1988). Closer to the black African source is the career of teller Grace Hallworth of Trinidad, West Indies, a collector and performer of Anansi trickster lore, beast fables, and audience participation dilemma stories. A former librarian and winner of the Kate Greenaway Award, she helped to revive oral performance in Hempstead, England, and on tours of the United Kingdom. As a patron of the 250-member Society for Storytelling in Birmingham, England, she has carried Anansi lore throughout Britain and the Carribean and has published his stories in an audiocassette, *Anansi's Secret* (1985), and in her children's books, *Mouth Open Story Jump Out* (1984), *Cric Crac* (1990), and *Anansi at the Pool* (1994).

See also African fable; African-American fable; trickster.

Sources Abrahams 1985; Burrison 1989; Courlander 1996; Creeden 1994; Goss and Barnes 1989; Hallworth 1984, 1990, 1994; Miller and Snodgrass 1998; Rosenberg 1997.

 # ANDERSEN, HANS CHRISTIAN

The beloved storyteller and travelogue writer of Odense, Denmark, Hans Christian Andersen survives in fables and children's stories translated into most world languages. He is best known for "The Emperor's New Clothes," "The Little Match Girl," "The Ugly Duckling," "The Princess and the Pea," "The Little

Mermaid," "The Snow Queen," "The Red Shoes," "The Little Fir Tree," "The Tin Soldier," and "The Nightingale." Born in a tenement on April 2, 1805, to an educated shoemaker and his superstitious wife, Andersen was forced to attend a school for slum children after his father died in 1816, leaving the family destitute. Like his friend, novelist Charles Dickens, Andersen worked in a factory. He journeyed to Copenhagen in 1819, where he hoped to become an actor. For three years he endeavored to sing, dance, act, and write for the Royal Theater. But after his voice changed, he lost his job and all hope of a theatrical career.

At age seventeen, Andersen published a book that failed miserably and was sold for scrap. Jonas Collin, a theater director and patron of the arts, acquired royal patronage for him from King Frederick VI, who paid the boy's tuition to a grammar school at Slagelse. Andersen educated himself enough to pass exams admitting him to the University of Copenhagen in 1827. He chose writing over a scholarly life and supported himself by translating, composing opera lyrics, and writing his first play, *Love in St. Nicolai Church Tower* (1829). A financial success, *Fodrejse fra Holmens Kanal til Østpynten af Amager i aarene 1828 og 1829* [A Walk from Holmen's Canal to the East Point of the Island of Amager in the Years 1828 and 1829] brought critical comparison to German fantasist Ernst Theodor Hoffmann. After two sound attempts at novels—*O. T.* (1836) and *Kun en spillemand* [Only a Fiddler] (1837)—Andersen found the courage to return to drama and produced a slave play, *Mulatten* [The Mulatto] (1840).

Throughout Andersen's life, emotions and pride dominated his choices. A failed love match sent him roaming over Europe. From his travels, he derived a profitable autobiographical novel, *The Improvisatore, or, Life in Italy* (1835), which prefaced a series of travel books, including *En digters bazar* [A Poet's Bazaar] (1842), *I Sverrig* [In Sweden] (1851), and *I Spanien* [In Spain] (1863), along with a more detailed autobiography, *The Fairy Tale of My Life* (1855). As his confidence grew, he broached a new genre: fable and fairytale. He composed pamphlets containing 168 of these famous tales, each an original story about outcasts and outsiders told in simple but appealing vernacular. The first book of fairytales and fables, *Eventyr, fortalte for børn* [Tales, Told for Children] (1835), was followed by two sequels: *Eventyr* (Tales) (1837) and *Billedbog uden Billeder* [A Picturebook without Pictures] (1840). The Andersen collection, spanning 37 years and six volumes, was published in 1872, three years before his death, as *Fairy Tales and Stories*, one of the world's favorite storybooks for children. Its popularity brought him fame and the friendship of poet Heinrich Heine, composer Franz Liszt, and novelist Victor Hugo.

Actor Danny Kaye immortalized Andersen's hard life in the 1952 film *Hans Christian Andersen*, which depicts the storyteller as a cobbler making shoes for Copenhagen's prima ballerina. Scripted by Moss Hart, the movie features Frank Loesser's original fable-songs "The Inch Worm" and "The Ugly Duckling" plus "Anywhere I Wander," "The King's New Clothes," "I'm Hans Christian Andersen," "Wonderful Copenhagen," "No Two People," and the Oscar-nominated "Thumbelina."

Among the Danish storyteller's fables and stories are philosophical, satiric, autobiographical, and Swedish tales. A standard *agon* or competition story, "The

Hans Christian Andersen, Danish poet, storyteller, and novelist

Jumper," follows the paradigm of contest lore with a beautiful bride as the prize. Both the grasshopper and flea complain that they jumped the highest, but the king chooses the goose to wed the lovely princess. Andersen's light-hearted matching of human with fowl concludes with offbeat black humor: the flea joins the foreign legion and is killed in action. Bemused at the caprices of fate, the grasshopper, like the fabulist in his early years, sits at the castle moat to ponder injustice. A whimsical retelling of Aesop's tortoise and hare contest, Andersen's "The Races" ridicules panels of judges. By expanding on the witless comments of the fence-rail, mule, fly, and wild rose, the fabulist illustrates a committee's lack of objectivity. The plot winds down to absurdity with the mule's declaration that the judges chose as a prize free admission to the cabbage patch in anticipation of the hare's tastes. The snail's experience precipitates appointment as "one of the first judges of swiftness in racing," which the mule considers a good beginning for future judgings. ("Hans Christian Andersen's Fables" n.d.) Neither fable is particularly appealing because of the overload of private vendetta that quells Andersen's creativity.

Other of Andersen's fables are more promising. "The Flax," a recycling story, follows the plant through its life as a garment and its rebirth as the rag content in paper. The flax's existence ends in a blaze of glory when children burn the paper as tinder, setting the plant's spirit free. The scene of children poking at embers has the ring of realism, as though the fabulist were describing a scene he had observed or perhaps lived in his childhood. A similar verisimilitude marks "The Storks," a *pourquoi* story that pictures children chanting a fly-away rhyme to the elegant bird that typically nests on the Danish housetop. Also sparked by jolly dialogue and intriguing story line is "The Toad," which strays from light illustration to heavier philosophy by contrasting the outlook of poet and scientist. Devoid of the magic and illusion that became Andersen's trademark, his fables combine stark Aesopic truths with realistic glimpses of the teller's homeland.

The autobiographical element in Andersen's fables dominates "The Daisy," a morality tale that pictures a mundane daisy among the gaudier finery of roses and tulips. A parallel to the fabulist's lifelong struggle against Copenhagen's elite, the story dwindles to bathos, or anticlimax, as the daisy dies of thirst along with her friend the lark. In the end, her faithfulness and sacrifice count for nothing. Also venting Andersen's frustration as a social outcast is "The Bell," a pursuit tale that draws a king's son beyond other seekers of a golden bell tone. After arriving at a sea view on the far side of a dense forest, the prince exults in coastal splendor:

> The whole of nature was one large holy church, in which the trees and hovering clouds formed the pillars, the flowers and grass the woven velvet carpet, and heaven itself was the great cupola; up there the flame colour vanished as soon as the sun disappeared, but millions of stars were lighted; diamond lamps were shining, and the king's son stretched his arms out toward heaven. ("Hans Christian Andersen's Fables," n. d.)

The story founders as illustrative apothegm, or moral, because of the final two sentences, which picture a poor boy shod in wooden clogs who reaches the sunset simultaneously with the prince. Andersen dramatizes deep subjective longings in his vision of the privileged and the underprivileged clasping hands while beneficent spirits rejoice with hallelujahs.

Sources Andersen, "Fairy Tales," http://www.math.technion.ac.il; Green 1965; "Hans Christian Andersen Museum," http://www.odkomm.dk; Rosenberg 1997.

ANDROCLES AND THE LION

Derived from a story in Aulus Gellius's *Noctes Atticae* (Attic Nights) (ca. 180 C.E.), later anthologized by Romulus, the tenth-century Roman fabulist, *Androcles and the Lion* is the anomaly of fable grown into Christian satire of martyrdom, cruelty, religious hypocrisy, and fanaticism. Playwright George Bernard Shaw overlays comedy with derision in his whimsical two-act beast drama, subtitled "A Fable Play." The light repartee ostensibly amuses, but underneath, Shaw soaks with vitriol his improbable match of man with lion. In a prefatory essay, appended December 1915, he justifies a preference for Christian principles and distaste for orthodoxy and describes how church tyrants have contorted a hopeful message into church fascism. To the would-be Christian, Shaw predicts the hierarchy's overthrow of simplistic faith:

> It is not disbelief that is dangerous in our society: it is belief. The moment it strikes you (as it may any day) that Christ is not the lifeless harmless image he has hitherto been to you, but a rallying centre for revolutionary influences which all established States and Churches fight, you must look to yourselves; for you have brought the image to life. (Shaw 1951, 56)

A final warning predicts a backlash of the unchurched: "The mob may not be able to bear that horror." Shaw's well-honed prose targets religious sects that carry their private agendas to un-Christian extremes. He cites as an extreme example of distortion the divine right of kings, an earth-bound model of a despot's power over the masses.

The play's prologue presents the familiar caricature of the hypersensitive male mated to the harsh Amazon in a hackneyed sight gag: the hero Androcles, a spindly-limbed, watery-eyed, overburdened tailor, and his buxom, slatternly wife Megaera, whom he calls "my precious, my pet." (Shaw 1951, 114) It focuses on the puny, *frau*-tyrannized husband. Out of deference to social custom, he caters to a pampered shrew, who carries nothing while her stringy husband strains under a double load of packs on their trek from Rome. Her carping and self-pity set the stereotypical scene of downtrodden mate condemned to a life of placating a hard-case malcontent. At the first sign of the lion, Androcles, a Christian in faith and actions, offers himself as decoy to save his "Meggy" from a terrible death. The silly infantilism of "Andy" fleshes out the spare lines of fable with tender solace for the lion:

> Did um get an awful thorn into um's tootsums wootsums? Has it made um too sick to eat a nice little Christian man for um's breakfast? Oh, a nice little Chris-

tian man will get um's thorn out for um; and then um shall eat the nice Christian man and the nice Christian man's nice big tender wifey pifey. (Shaw 1951, 115)

The extended mushy pantomime between tailor and beast ends with a rapturous waltz, to which Meggy grouses, "you havnt danced with me for years." (Shaw 1951, 116)

Having created an incongruous *menage à trois* in the prologue, Shaw opens Act I with a seriocomic test of faith. Set on the outskirts of Rome, the play proper presents a military column marching a coffle of Christ worshipers to the emperor. Shaw takes a quick poke at Christian hymns, which the Romans forbid, except for "Onward Christian Soldiers." Suitably martial by centurions' estimation, the song was popularized during the Crusades, Christianity's attempt to force-feed orthodoxy to Muslims. A second butt of satire is rejection of the term "persecution" to describe acts of the emperor. Rationalizing gladiatorial brutalities, the captain clarifies that throwing Christians to lions is an appropriate ritual, whereas throwing the emperor to the lion would be persecution. In further proof of opportunism, the captain romances Lavinia, a comely political prisoner, and urges her to offer incense on the altar as a gesture of courtesy to Rome. Shaw's epilogue clarifies his attitude toward manipulation of Androcles, Lavinia, and the other innocents. He contends that people crowded to witness carnage in the Roman arena, "not because they really cared twopence about Diana or Christ . . . but simply because they wanted to see a curious and exciting spectacle." (Shaw 1951, 158)

Shaw broadens fable into dark comedy with death jokes that overlay colosseum spectacle with fearful jest. Overseeing the Christians-to-the-lions exhibition is the emperor, who frees all but one prisoner, the one reserved as food for the lion. Ironically, the menagerie keeper chooses the lone Greek, Androcles, a weakling non-Roman, because of his reputation as a sorcerer and animal tamer. As Shaw later observes, "My martyrs are the martyrs of all time, and my persecutors the persecutors of all time . . . Androcles is a humanitarian naturalist, whose views surprise everybody." (Shaw 1951, 155) Unhampered by the playwright's noble intentions, the farce ends in low comic pantomime of the one-to-one events of the original fable: "Androcles, supporting himself on his wrists, looks affrightedly at the lion. The lion limps on three paws, holding up the other as if it was wounded. A flash of recognition lights up the face of Androcles." (Shaw 1951, 150) The emperor cowers while Androcles waltzes with Tommy the lion. The play concludes with a challenge: the emperor makes Androcles the slave of anyone brave enough to lay hands on him. Androcles exults to the lion, "Whilst we stand together, no cave for you: no slavery for me." (Shaw 1951, 154)

Shaw's satiric fable ridicules a variety of character types: cultists who enjoy flouting custom and rule, elitists who elevate themselves through rank or power, and perfectionists who set themselves up for failure by overreaching. A deeper layer of satire comes from the play's study of a period of history when Rome valued might over virtue, when the imperial hierarchy appeased a bloodthirsty mob with barbarism. Beyond this second level of satire, Shaw develops

Androcles as a character who derives strength and power from an unusual source. As fable, the play far exceeds the usual confines and themes of moralistic animal lore. Composed before the term "black comedy" existed, Shaw's stage fable toys with a terrorizing scenario in the antechamber of the Roman arena, where human martyrs tremble at the roar of animals that their remains will soon feed. Anticipating the twentieth century's preference for a blend of horror and sardonic gags, the playwright surprises the audience with its ability to laugh at human sacrifice.

See also Shaw, George Bernard.

Sources Bermel 1982; Brockett 1968; Gassner and Quinn 1969; Hill 1978; Hornstein et al. 1973; Magill 1958; Shaw 1951; Snodgrass, *The Encyclopedia of Satirical Literature*, 1997.

 # *ANIMAL FARM*

The modern age pressed the simple Aesopic fable into heavier allegorical motif in the least humorous of twentieth-century beast stories, George Orwell's grimly dystopian *Animal Farm* (1945). Using bestiality as a mirror for the post–World War II political scene, he exposed the soullessness of Marxism and its tyranny of the laborers it purported to liberate from the exploitive overclass. Central to the fable's mordant humor is an Aesopic caricature that depicts human foibles in the words and actions of common farm animals. With humanity and compassion for the lowest social order, Orwell re-creates the poignant paralysis and vulnerability that gradually return a rebellious underclass to its former servitude.

Orwell's elaborate fable parodies the takeover of propagandists, tyrants, and authoritarian governments that deceive unsuspecting victims. Setting his sheep, horses, cows, pigs, dogs, ducklings, goat, raven, and donkey amid the idyllic agrarianism of Manor Farm, he builds an allegory that characterizes Adolf Hitler, Benito Mussolini, and Josef Stalin and their cynical plot to uplift then enslave the unwary farmyard. Overlaid with irony and satire, the story depicts beasts whose glorious overthrow unseats Farmer Jones, a decadent, undependable human despot. Innocent of the dangers of revolt, the rebels find themselves entrenched in a dismaying animal police state supervised by a porcine pretorian guard. Under a barnyard version of nazism, fascism, and hard-line communism, the animals struggle to survive a terrifying opportunism that threatens them with starvation and overwork.

Early in March, the animal uprising in Orwell's beast fable begins with a classic touch of superstition: the prophetic dream of Old Major—originally named Willingdon Beauty—a venerable 12-year-old Middle White boar. He convenes a general session of animal residents, and, with altruistic fervor and polished oratory, typifies the hopelessness of slavery:

> Man is the only creature that consumes without producing. He does not give milk, he does not lay eggs, he is too weak to pull the plough, he cannot run fast enough to catch rabbits. Yet he is the lord of all the animals. He sets them to

work, he gives back to them the bare minimum that will prevent them from starving, and the rest he keeps for himself. (Orwell 1946, 19)

The prophet exhorts his listeners to "get rid of Man" and rectify millennia of wrong by establishing and governing their own uniquely bestial society. Like Karl Marx's sweeping generalizations about the utopian communist state, Old Major's damning conclusion—"All men are enemies. All animals are comrades"—proves faulty. (Orwell 1946, 21) The farmstead rally ends in an overwhelming majority support for a coup. With a blast of number six shot, Jones disrupts their disorder and quells the fervent strains of "Beasts of England," a stirring "Internationale" comprising seven noble verses set to a heartening tune, "something between *Clementine* and *La Cucaracha*." (Orwell 1945, 22) Three days later, Old Major dies of natural causes and is interred in the orchard. The downturn of chaos suggests that, temporarily, human technology can stamp out with a single blow the hopes of the downtrodden.

In the vacuum of a leaderless state, Orwell predicts the type of demagogues who typically arise from the frightened citizenry. Old Major's protégés—three opportunistic pigs named Snowball, Napoleon, and Squealer—list simplistic principles of animalism to guide their dream state. With biblical majesty, they title their manifesto the Seven Commandments:

1. Whatever goes upon two legs is an enemy.

2. Whatever goes upon four legs, or has wings, is a friend.

3. No animal shall wear clothes.

4. No animal shall sleep in a bed.

5. No animal shall drink alcohol.

6. No animal shall kill any other animal.

7. All animals are equal.

(Orwell 1946, 33)

On Midsummer's Eve, Farmer Jones, like the recalcitrant Romanov tsar Nicholas II, angers the animals by drinking to excess and forgetting to tend the stock. In retaliation, a miniature Russian proletariat arises to oust Jones, his family, and workers. Self-governing for the first time in animal history, the pigs, eager to create the perfect farm, make a public display of burning whips, blinkers, nosebags, reins, and halters, all evidence of human oppression. In a public show of piety and state ceremony, they reconfirm their unity by conducting a ritual burial for Jones's hams.

Orwell's fast-paced fable illustrates how quickly good intentions can go awry. Having taught themselves to read and write, the pigs seize the initiative. In place of Jones, now a porcine troika supervises labor, challenges other animals to surpass productivity under human management, and retains for the supervisory elite the fruits of Animal Farm's first harvest. Eventually, Snowball condenses the Seven Commandments to a single precept: "Four legs good, two legs bad." (Orwell 1946, 41) Moreover, by keeping the other animals overworked and in a perpetual state of tension and anticipation, the pigs conceal their duplicity while plotting the next stage of the power play. The episode suggests that gullibility is often a prologue to victimization.

To manage the willy-nilly barnyard disorder, Orwell creates one of fable's enduring humanesque animals: Napoleon, a fierce, secretive, taciturn Berkshire boar of 24 stone who sets ambition over principle. Cunningly self-serving, he deceives his rival, the ingenuous Snowball, and, as a control over minor defections, trains nine puppies into a parody of a jackbooted hit squad. To the question of Sunday morning meetings he responds by barring future such incidents of wasted time and empanels a puppet committee of pigs, headed by himself. Lacking concrete plans for Animal Farm, Napoleon achieves political aims by subverting Snowball's authority and by seizing psychological control through militant posturing, intimidation, and brainwashing. A fable in itself, this sequence mirrors the ominous motifs of classic Aesopic lore, which characteristically anticipates torture, maiming, exile, and death as appropriate punishments of the unwary.

Orwell swells his fable into beast epic by pitting animals against villagers. In mid-October, the experimental farm suffers an unforeseen setback after Jones coalesces a party of neighbors at his pseudo war room, the taproom of the Red Lion pub in Willingdon. Among his henchmen is Mr. Pilkington, a gentleman farmer who prefers sporting events to farm labor. The mob fuels a countermove to rout the animal rebels. Orwell heightens the absurdity of the melodramatic *coup d'etat* mentality by floating rumors of animal torture, cannibalism, and free love. At the glorious Battle of the Cowshed, Napoleon, a Stalinesque despot, and Snowball, a student of Julius Caesar's battlefield strategies, lead a squadron of pigs to victory. At the high point of the engagement, Boxer the cart-horse unintentionally fells a stable boy with a lethal blow of his iron-edged hooves to the skull. Snowball ripostes with a demagogue's inflammatory sloganeering: "War is war. The only good human being is a dead one." (Orwell 1946, 49) To honor bravery, the animals create a decoration, "Animal Hero, First Class," which they confer on Boxer; they exalt themselves with the evolving legends of the Rebellion and the Battle of the Cowshed. Thus, the self-sustaining mystique of military might cloaks mayhem in ribbons and warmongering frippery.

Orwell stresses the role of revolution in creating a snowballing chain of violence and treachery. Peace at Animal Farm is shortlived; Snowball and Napoleon, who vie for supreme command, fight over the erection of a labor-saving windmill, a highly visible goal destined to ennoble the builder. When the matter comes to a vote, Napoleon unseats his rival by a surprise tactic: he vanquishes Snowball and summons nine savage, brass-adorned dogs, the equivalent of Germany's SS and Italy's Brownshirts. Snowball scampers away to Napoleon's boast of "Tactics, comrades, tactics!" (Orwell 1946, 62) No longer threatened, Napoleon oppresses the other animals by enforced compliance, overwork, and reduced rations. To heighten fanatic nationalism, he exhumes Major's skull to serve as a graphic totem to unity.

Like Russia's stream of ill-fated five-year and ten-year plans, the scheduled accomplishments of Animal Farm fail to materialize. Boxer, a dimwitted dupe,

A still from the movie version of *Animal Farm*, 1955

pushes himself to serve the overlord even more slavishly than before by vowing "I will work harder" and reconvincing himself that "Napoleon is always right." (Orwell 1946, 65) After the animals labor 60-hour workweeks plus Sundays to complete the projected windmill, it collapses in a gale. Orwell satirizes political scapegoating in Napoleon's projection of failure on Snowball, who allegedly lurks nearby, sabotages the mill, and disrupts farm progress. The pigs, more firmly in power, hire Mr. Whymper as intermediary. They negotiate with humans in Willingdon and move into the farmhouse, rephrasing the Seven Commandments to accommodate luxuries for the ruling party. To the threat of a pullet uprising, Napoleon applies an embargo on hen feed, which results in nine dead chickens. To hush up the brief internal defection, he issues an official lie, "that they had died of coccidiosis." (Orwell 1946, 77)

To account for the rapid decline of Animal Farm, Orwell derides the false goals that undermine Napoleon's grandiose plans. Following a dismal winter, a second foray, led by Farmer Frederick the next fall, results in a setback after Animal Farm loses ground to human invaders. The farmer's forces blow up the windmill, but the animals prevail. All residents of Animal Farm rededicate themselves to completing the mill, but something is lacking from their initiative. At a spiritual low, Clover weeps for shattered ideals:

> If she herself had had any picture of the future, it had been of a society of animals set free from hunger and the whip, all equal, each working according to his capacity, the strong protecting the weak. . . . Instead, —she did not know

why—they had come to a time when no one dared speak his mind, when fierce, growling dogs roamed everywhere, and when you had to watch your comrades torn to pieces after confessing to shocking crimes. (Orwell 1946, 85)

Dredging up the dismaying circumstances of his assignment to Spain during Franco's rise to power, Orwell re-creates a terrifyingly real political scenario, a nightmare of false dreams trounced by hobnailed boots.

A cameo within the text, the fable of Boxer, the overachieving drayhorse, creates an autobiographical picture of Orwell's youthful idealism and its eventual cessation during Hitler's rise to power. After wearing himself out with physical labor and misguided devotion to Napoleon, 12-year-old Boxer longs to retire, but the pigs deceive him and dispatch him to the local knacker. Against the counterpoint of Squealer reading a readjustment of harvest figures and work goals, the faithful horse drums a feeble tattoo on the walls of the van to summon his compatriots to action. In Orwell's fable, timing is all. The cabal grasps firmly its control of the barnyard. Squealer, the head propagandist, substitutes rhetoric for truth by falsely reporting that Boxer died in the hospital and that his last words confirmed Napoleon as leader. The poet Minimus (Latin for *smallest*) composes a sycophantic paean to the acknowledged leader.

Creating simple animal parallels, Orwell demonstrates the spiky rhythms of revolution. His farmyard regression stresses how the day-to-day fight for subsistence subverts the immediacy and thrill of rebellion. Years pass in scandal, chicanery, and graft; the original rebel heroes die off, leaving a younger generation who know Manor Farm, Old Major, and idealism only through the memories of their elders. Because of the youngsters' sketchy knowledge of history, Napoleon deceives his followers with a craftily reworded credo: "All animals are equal but some animals are more equal than others." (Orwell 1946, 123) The divisive motto is the beginning of the end. With the assistance of his human cohort, Mr. Pilkington, Napoleon strengthens control over the land, which he renames Manor Farm. The pigs, in imitation of Jones, walk on their hind legs. The other animals, still in Napoleon's power, perceive that the tyrannical police force has developed human habits. As *epimythium,* or moral, Orwell concludes, "The creatures outside looked from pig to man, and from man to pig, and from pig to man again; but already it was impossible to say which was which." (Orwell 1946, 128)

Orwell's achievement hinges on the success of his main character, the crafty Napoleon. The animals, cowed by Napoleon's audacity, ask no questions. Their leader's presumption impels him toward greater atrocities. In Chapter 7, he executes the disobedient, even those whose offenses are slight. In despotic style, "they were all slain on the spot. And so the tale of confessions and executions went on, until there was a pile of corpses lying before Napoleon's feet and the air was heavy with the smell of blood, which had been unknown there since the expulsion of Jones." (Orwell 1946, 83) The silent majority enhances Napoleon's bold power grab and heinous public purge. As the old generation dies off, the generation born under animal tyranny views Napoleon's excesses as normal and necessary.

Orwell's satire of human power-mongering suggests that Europe's mid-twentieth-century takeovers succeeded because of their direct and brutal cowing of a fearful majority. In the end, Napoleon prevails by blitzkrieg, the lightning foray that undercuts Snowball. By blaming setbacks on his former rival, the barnyard amalgam of Hitler and Stalin turns rivalry to advantage with specious arguments and grandiose proclamations. Lolling in the Joneses' house and enjoying whisky, human beds and clothing, and the best farm produce, Napoleon remolds political principle to his own ends. He appears in full strutting glory in Chapter 10, "majestically upright, casting haughty glances from side to side, and with his dogs gambolling round him. He carried a whip in his trotter." (Orwell 1946, 122) A formidable warlord, he manipulates farmstead hirelings who lack his brash savvy.

A wry literary tour de force, Orwell's engaging animal fable combines powerful episodes—a litany of intolerable farm conditions, a revered elder's vision of an animal utopia, waves of revolt and counterrevolt, undermining of the master plan to make Manor Farm into an animal-run haven, regressive internal strife, and the coercion of lesser animals by an imperious superstructure. A brilliant and cohesive satire composed for the enlightenment and edification of the postwar generation, *Animal Farm* symbolizes the ease with which conniving and traitorous usurpers terrorize and crush the working class. By altering truth to shift blame, the pig faction subjugates a gullible, poorly educated nation with dreams turned to nightmare. Just as animal babies born after the initial overthrow have no direct knowledge of farm history, Orwell implies that the human generations born after World War II lack an understanding of the insidious nature of the totalitarianism and fascism that ignited world leaders into global war.

See also Orwell, George.

Sources Alok 1989; Calder 1987; Connelly 1986; Oldsey and Browne, eds 1986; Orwell 1946; Snodgrass, *The Encyclopedia of Satirical Literature* 1997.

 # BABRIUS, VALERIUS

Greek fabulist Valerius Babrius (also Babrias, Barbius, or Babirius) produced the oldest extant compendium of Greek fables. The author, a Greek from the Ionic colonies, is difficult to peg in time and place and is usually classified as a hellenized Roman living early in the second century C.E. in Syria. He cites his homeland since the time of Ninus and Belus as the fount of fable, from which evolved *The Book of Achiqar* (ca. 2000 B.C.E.), an Assyrian collection of wisdom lore. He readily names Aesop as his major source, and, in the prologue to Book II, cites an unknown storyteller named Cybisses as the father of Libyan fable. Textual evidence, such as mention of holy monks and verses from the writings of St. James, establishes that Babrius lived in the Christian era and at least peripherally under Christian influence.

Babrius's works spawned imitators some time after the completion of his second book. To add to the mystery of his role in the history of fable, his ten anthologies of fables have not survived except for scraps containing 200 models. Added material comes from later sources; for example, two fables appear in the *Hermeneumata* [Principles of Interpretation] of Pseudo-Dositheus (207 C.E.). Babrius's name surfaces in the fourth-century encyclopedic citations of the poet Avianus, the writings of the grammarian John Tzetzes, and the commentary of Suidas, an eleventh-century critic. Also, a hazy reference to Babrius's fables occurs in Quintilian's *Institutio Oratoria* [Oratorical Instruction] (ca. 96 C.E.).

Written in scazon or choliambic meter, a Roman style of spondaic stress in iambic meter that concludes with an accent on the last two syllables [∧ ′ | ∧ ′ | ∧ ′ | ′ ′], Babrius's verse collection of simple didactic stories, published about the second century C.E., imitates Aesop and adds no innovations to the canon of world fable. Babrius's urbane satire places his beast tales in cosmopolitan settings and among the court figures surrounding the Olympian gods, far from the bucolic barnyard and forest milieu of Aesop. However, according to Swiss editor Isaac Nicholas Nèvelet, who produced the *Mythologia Aesopica* (1610), Babrius deserves credit as more than a mere imitator of prototypical fables. He appears to have adapted Aesopic lore into the parlance of his own time and to have been schooled in neo-Babylonian lore as well. Other idiosyncratic clues from his texts include mention of friendship with Arabs and the incidence of modern terms, such as Piraeus, Athens's harbor, which did not exist in Aesop's time.

The prologue to Babrius's orderly collection introduces the boy Branchus to the Golden and Silver ages, a lyric myth found in Herodotus's *Works and Days* (eighth century B.C.E.). The speaker contends that animals at one time had the power of speech and shared human vocabulary, as demonstrated by the mule's musings on his family tree in "Only a Half-Breed" and the peaceful alliance of all beasts in "Once in Utopia." Babrius contends that in these prehuman times, pines and laurels as well as creatures talked, a phenomenon he demonstrates with "The Fir Tree and the Bramble." The insightful exchange between the proud and the lowly results in a remonstrance on the order of "the bigger they are, the harder they fall." In later settings, beasts converse freely with humans—the fish with the sailor and the sparrow with the farmer. With a brief tribute to Aesop, the originator of beast lore, the speaker concludes, "I shall set before you a poetical honeycomb, as it were, dripping with sweetness." (Perry 1965, 5) He proves his promise by imparting the wisdom of classic lore, such as "The Farmer and the Cranes," which draws on Homer's belief that the cranes overcame the pygmies in annual battle. Also from early Greek tradition is "Too Many Friends," which relies on Hesiod's belief that a stag lives four times the life span of a crow. The fables intermingle stories of human, divine, and animal interaction—"Heracles and the Ox-Driver," "Hermes on Sale," "The Lion and the Bowman," "The Goat and the Goatherd," and "The Farmer Who Lost His Mattock"—with pure beast fables, such as "The Horse and the Ass" and "The Fighting Cocks," a tale of hubris in which the wounded loser survives and the winner exults but finds himself carried away by an eagle. For divine characters, Babrius favors Zeus in six stories and mentions Hermes in seven instances. Other stories focus on abstract concepts, as with "Truth and Falsehood." One centers on a talking object, "The Boasting Lamp."

Much of Babrius's drama wilts from heavy verbiage, as is the case in "Fleece Me, but Don't Flay Me," in which a sheep tongue-lashes his mistress at length for nipping his bare hide. Another, "Three True Statements," is a glib exchange of retorts between adversaries rather than a true vignette or clever escape. Other fables lack development, such as "Yes and No," the insulting reply of a seer to a eunuch, "An Unwelcome Partner," displaying the antipathy between ox and ass, and "One Toils and Another Complains," the vehicle for a snarling complaint from a wagoneer who wearies of a squeaky wheel. In such narratives, the lack of dramatic tension reduces the effect from fable to flaccid exemplum, or sermon, and strips the genre of its charm and universality.

Demonstrably less facile than the great writers of aphorism, Babrius composes moral tags in Aesopic style, as with the familiar ant and grasshopper story, which concludes, "Dance in the winter, since you piped during the summer." A minority of Babrius's aphorisms are accurate and satisfying:

- Nothing whatever is entirely pleasing to the fault-finder.

- Everyone believes his own child to be handsome.

- You'll not escape what is bound to be.

- Many have been saved by not succeeding.

- A fool fails to keep small but certain profits in the hope of acquiring uncertain ones.

- No one escapes the penalty for perjury.

The elements of comparison are usually clear in Babrius's *epimythia,* or morals, but his composition lacks music, wit, and agility, the strengths of such memorable Frankliniana as "A stitch in time saves nine" or "Neither a borrower nor a lender be." Consequently, his moral reminders go down like sour medicine and occasionally leave an aftertaste.

As with his morals, Babrius's fables vary in length, complexity, and development. His eighth story, "Rough Fare," and "The Arab and His Camel" each have only four lines. "Bonded Brotherhood" is five lines long; Babrius's version of "The Goose that Laid the Golden Egg" is a compact seven lines. The seventeenth fable, "The Cat as Fowler," has only six lines compared to the 24-line story of "The Mice and Their Generals" and "The Nightingale and the Swallow," a 28-line poem derived from the complex misogynistic myth of Procnis and Philomela. The longest model, "The Stag without a Heart," requires 102 lines to tell the story of the stag who allows the fox to lure him twice to the sickly lion's den, the second time to his doom. More suited to Aesopic terseness and pithy applicability is the eight-line fable "Divide and Conquer," which restates an old truth, that the wise trust friends rather than enemies. Another, "No Use Praying for a Robber," relates the tight morality story of a sick crow who can't pray for divine healing because he has robbed too many altars. A longer story that satisfies the style, length, and purpose of fable is "A Backfiring Strategem," the three-stage journey motif in which a donkey outsmarts himself by first collapsing under a load of salt and wasting it in a stream. On a second journey, to lighten his load, he deliberately tries the same ruse. By the third journey, the peddler bests the conniving donkey by loading him with sponges. On collapsing in the stream, the beast of burden soaks his absorbant pack and must then carry many times the original weight. A graphic example, the story provides the pictorial insight that bolsters the genre and benefits those who read it.

Babrius's stories of anthropomorphic gods lean more toward myth than fable as found in "Hope," a resetting of the story of Pandora, who released from Zeus's jar of good things all the world's blessings except Hope, which she captured by replacing the stopper. Another departure from simplistic piety is "Hero-Cult," the story of a pious sacrificer who wreathes the altars of a great man and daily prays for blessings. At length, the hero's spirit appears at midnight to differentiate between gods and heroes. Gods, he declares, are the givers of good. Heroes, on the other hand, specialize in causing human ills. The hero adds that by bestowing only one example of his gifts on the pious worshiper he can prove that his prayers should be directed to a god. The intent is clear: Babrius advises all to be careful what they pray for lest their prayers be answered.

As with most of the world's fables, *agon* or contest motifs appear sporadically in Babrius's fables, including "Borrowed Plumage," "Failure to Qualify as a Household Pet," and "Momus the Fault-Finder." In "The North Wind and the

Sun," a bit of competition in nature results in a pleasant moral that urges gentle persuasion over brute force. The fifteenth fable, "The Athenian and the Theban," pits the rival Greeks in a verbal comparison of two native heroes, Hercules and Theseus. Realizing that the divinity of Hercules outranks Theseus, a mere mortal, the Theban halts the exchange short of irreverence and declares, "So let Theseus be angry with us and Hercules with you Athenians." (Perry 1965, 27) An abbreviated and poorly stated fable, "Mediation à la Mode," pits dolphins against whales with a volunteer crab standing in the middle to referee. Other of Babrius's ill-conceived contest fables, including "Preposterous Leadership" and "The Heterogeneous Dogs," attest to his inability to maintain the taut faceoffs that competition motifs require.

The materials of Babrian fable blend humor with terror and a pathos that reflects anthropomorphic emotions as though they were natural to animals. The tale of "How the Kite Lost His Voice" is a simple matter of risk-taking to requite envy. The punishment is poetic justice: the kite—a type of hawk—imitates a horse neighing and loses his original voice. So too does the fox learn the wages of gluttony in "Deflation Necessary," which closes with his bloated body immured in the hollow of an oak. However, not all Babrian fables are so simply balanced, tit for tat, reprisal for fault. "The Toad Who Tried to Be as Big as an Ox" depicts a catastrophic loss—a mother toad grieving for her baby, which lies flattened under the ox's hoof; and "Close to the Law but Far from Justice" reprises the motif in a mournful mother swallow whose young are devoured by a serpent. Truth sometimes results in a fearful prediction, as in the words of the weary animal in "The Old Age of the Race-Horse," which warns youth not to boast of strength that they will lose in old age. A fable on early death, "The Old Bull and the Young Steer" reminds the young boaster of the danger in idleness. These examples attest to Babrius's attempt at Aesopic profundity and the resulting mediocrities that weaken his canon.

On the skillful end of the Babrian scale lie funny stories that appeal like anecdote, for example, the barbed exchange between mother crab and child in "Show Me How" and the dog's rejoinder to his master in "Always Ready to Go." Babrius also eases the less sanguine fables with spirited dialogue, for example, in "The Fox and the Crow":

> "Sir Crow, thy wings are beautiful, bright and keen thine eye, thy neck a wonder to behold. An eagle's breast thou dost display, and with thy talons over all the beasts thou canst prevail. So great a bird thou art; yet mute, alas, and without utterance."
>
> On hearing this flattery the crow's heart was puffed up with conceit, and dropping the cheese from his mouth, he loudly screamed: "Caw! Caw!"
>
> The clever fox pounced on the cheese and tauntingly remarked: "You were not dumb, it seems, you have indeed a voice; you have everything, Sir Crow, except brains." (Perry 1965, 97)

In "Mistaken for a Physician," a story containing a hint of subjective guile, Babrius has a spirit return from Hades to tease medical doctors who misdiagnose patients. The ridicule of doctors resurfaces in other stories, including "Doctor Wolf" and "Physician Heal Thyself," in which a frog falsely claims to know more about healing than Paean, doctor to the divine on Mt. Olympus. An action vignette, the hilarious unmasking in "The Weasel as Bride," contains a metamorphosis that ends abruptly on the wedding couch as the bride springs up to catch a mouse and the fabulist chortles that love gives place to nature. These sprinklings of mirth and satire relieve the advance of fable after fable professing nothing but advice to the guileless.

Overall, Babrian fable contains the wry counsel that ties the genre to folk wisdom, as found in the pragmatism of "The Unappreciated Weasel," "The Outcome of a Foreign Investment," and "Outwitting the Birds," the story of a farmer who calls for bread as a code word for his sling. An explicit sexual tale, "A Domestic Triangle," depicts a woman as outfoxed by her cuckolded husband, who then takes to bed the young man with whom she committed adultery. Scatology is a factor in "Unwelcome Attentions," the meetings between a dog and the statue of Hermes, who disdains a salute of canine urine, and in "The Rise of the Proletariat," which tells of a camel whose dung floats ahead of him as he crosses the river. Babrius relates the situation to a state run by its worst citizens. Less humorous and more perilous is "Better Lose the Ox than Catch the Thief," a land-based story that concludes with a drover locating his lost ox but discovering too late the danger of confronting the rustler, which is a lion. In "Hercules and the Ox-Driver," based on the adage "God helps those who help themselves," the god displays his annoyance by advising the shiftless seeker to apply some human effort before praying for divine aid. "The Oxen and the Butchers" reminds the victim that the peril at hand may be less fearful than an unseen calamity. A vignette heavy with agony reveals the pine tree split with wedges in "The Unkindest Cut of All," which ends with a reminder that pain caused by outsiders is less miserable than that brought on by kin. These examples display a spunk and validity that attest to the uneven quality of Babrius's fables.

Babrius follows the misogynistic philosophy that derives from Aesop and resurfaces in the antifemale ribaldry and jest of the Middle Ages. A disappointed wolf, in a glib put-down, claims that he fails to find food because he trusted a woman. In the same vein, the aforementioned "A Domestic Triangle" turns on an adulterous wife, whose husband repays her by bedding her lover. Babrius considers the turnabout just and makes no moral judgment against the two men for sodomy. A cynical tale of the old fool romancing two women results in the younger woman pulling out his gray hair and the older one tugging at the dark hair, thus leaving the hapless lothario with a bald head. A bit of anticlimax remarks that Aesop told the fable to show that women are as alluring and deadly as the sea.

To his credit, Babrius states well some of the folk-centered philosophy that colors the world canon of fable. "Man's Years," one of the strongest entries in his collection, compares the stages of human life to the horse, ox, and dog. In the first segment, humans tend toward haughtiness. In the second, the middle years, humankind grows practical and applies strength to toiling and reaping. It is the final stage that demeans, for elders grow like dogs: they become ill-tempered and fawn only when they expect a tidbit of food. Babrius concludes that humankind is "always barking, and he has no love for strangers." (Perry

1965, 93). As though sharpening the barb of his grim observation of old age, the speaker calls his student Branchus by name, perhaps to impress on him the weight of fable's contribution to wisdom lore.

Sources Cooper 1921; Duff and Duff 1982; Green 1965; Lang and Dudley 1969; Lesky 1966; Long, http://www.pacificnet.net; Perry 1952, 1965.

BABYLONIAN FABLE

In extant Mesopotamian writings, fable is not as common a literary genre as in Greek and Roman lore. It may consist of only about 100 individual texts from the eighteenth-century B.C.E. clay tablets derived from Nippur and Ur. A possible explanation for the rarity of fable is the high tone and style of Babylonian court literature, which learned editors collected as models of academic excellence. As was true in ancient China, the idea of preserving and honoring mere folktales may have seemed out of keeping with the veneration of the weightier epic, aphorism, and lyric, although one collection of aphorisms includes anecdotes and brief fables. Two exceptions are "The Elephant and the Wren," from *The Book of Achiqar* (ca. 2000 B.C.E.), and "The Snake and the Eagle." Both of these tales belong to the body of Sumerian *agon* or contest literature; they take the form of the *Streitgedicht* or dramatized debate between nature's rivals.

Unlike the Aesopic style of animal fable, the Babylonian fable embodies verbal contests between surreal creatures, beasts, or inanimate objects. Influenced by Semitic literature, fictional debate follows a standard motif: the exchange of points of view occurs before a god, who serves as judge. Composed to honor royalty of Ur's Third Dynasty, dating from 2000–1900 B.C.E., the varying texts were first published in an English collection, Samuel Noah Kramer's *Sumerian Mythology* (1944). Of his fragmentary epics, hymns, essays, proverbs, and myths, only a handful of fables survived entire to modern times: "The Tamarisk and the Palm," "The Fable of the Willow," "The Ox and the Horse," "Nisaba and Wheat," "The Fable of the Riding-Donkey," and "The Fable of the Fox," which appears to belong to a cycle of fox stories, one of the world's common beast motifs. Of this sextet, "The Fable of the Riding-Donkey" is in poorest condition, without a single complete sentence left intact.

"The Tamarisk and the Palm" illustrates the stiffness of Babylonian fable. The oral original dates to the early Akkadian period from 2300–2200 B.C.E. and is corroborated by a tablet in Middle Assyrian from around 1100 B.C.E. and a second tablet from around 1000–900 B.C.E. An opening line introduces the theme of jealousy by describing the newly appointed king's garden, in which he sets a tamarisk and a desert palm. The shrub, the primary speaker, brags to the palm that king and queen eat from dishes and goblets made from tamarisk. Elaborating on his importance, the shrub claims that the warrior and weaver make baskets and cloth from its fibers and that the temple exorcist purifies the air with tamarisk. In rebuttal, the palm names its many uses and mentions the fruit it produces. Although only the barest outline of the story remains, it appears to have influenced "The Assyrian Tree," a Pahlavi (or Iranian) fable, as well as a story by Callimachus and, perhaps, Strabo's *Geography* (ca. 20 C.E.), a nonfiction compendium that lists 360 uses for the palm.

Even less of "The Fable of the Willow" is extant. Fragments preserve a dispute between the tree and a laurel. (The translation *willow* remains in dispute and may refer instead to mulberry or poplar or to an assemblage of trees.) The concept of boastfulness persists, with the willow taunting the laurel for having shallow roots and thin foliage in contrast to the luxuriant willow. For the sake of argument, the laurel compares itself to the tamarisk, mountain ash, and palm, the purported king of trees. The motif of the boast fable continues the tradition of exalting strength, lordly deeds, and utility to the mighty.

Unlike Babylonian fables that limit characters to nature, "Nisaba and Wheat," which may date to 2000 B.C.E., applies the ritual contest to the goddess of grain. The wheat lauds her as "mistress of the underworld," a tradition that derives from the notion that plants rise through the soil but maintain a root structure in the nether world. Wheat questions why so powerful a deity would pick a fight with every plant and charges:

> You have created conflict and stirred up evil.
> You speak slander and utter libel,
> You have brought about hatred between the Igigi and the Annunnaki . . .
> You will anger the sage, you will destroy creation.
> (Lambert 1960, 171)

In the shreds of the tale that remain, the victory falls to Nisaba. The fable, composed in standard Babylonian dialect from the southern region, concludes with a *te deum,* or praise anthem, to the goddess for her significance to creation as a life giver and sustainer.

Taken from a series, "The Ox and the Horse" is a lengthy work housed in the library of Ashurbanipal, now the city of Sharquat, Iraq. Set during the annual flood, its lyric passages describe rampaging currents that water meadows and fields, initiating a period of fertile land and abundant calves and foals. The pair of contenders are naturally thrown together, as the opening lines indicate:

> It made the pasture flourish for cattle and produced luxuriant growth.
> The Ox and the Horse became friends,
> Their bellies were sated with the luscious pasture,
> In their pleasure they engaged in a dispute.
> (Lambert 1960, 177)

Researchers date this scrap of fable to the early Cassite period, ca. 1500 B.C.E., when horses were first bred and trained for human use. They became so valuable that they received meticulous care, a fact echoed by a related Middle Assyrian text. The horse, which is prized as battlefield transportation, counters the ox, whose hide provides leather for harnesses. Lording his brick-lined stall and his majesty in battle over the lifestyle of the humble ox, the horse pictures his rival as a menial dray fed on bran and led by a tether like a donkey. The modern reader is left to imagine the ox's comeback.

A sizable Akkadian story that prefigures Europe's extensive Reynard cycles, "The Fable of the Fox" exists in modern times from fragments too minute to reassemble. The texts derive from a Babylonian original from 1700 to 1600 B.C.E., two versions in Middle Assyrian around 1100 B.C.E., and nine from 600 B.C.E., the Late Assyrian period. The series surpasses the standard *agon* or contest literature in length and complexity. Unique to its text are extended images of impiety, conflagrations, seizing and tearing of flesh, thieving, sucking blood, and disembowelment. Complications in the story include a drought, an expedition, and a quarrel among three creatures—the fox, wolf, and dog. As is true of the beast fable, the characters revert to type, with the domesticated dog, a noble herder, countering attacks by the fierce wolf and cunning fox and the timorous cat and mongoose dreading the larger mammals. A judge, Samas, presides over a formal contest where the contestants make savage testimony followed by emotional cry:

> When the Fox heard [a call for the death penalty],
> He lifted his head, weeping to Samas.
> His tears came before the ray of Samas,
> "Do not arraign me, Samas, in this judgment."
> (Lambert 1960, 201)

Samas favors the fox, much as European stories centuries later center on the wiliest of forest prowlers.

In modern storytelling circles, self-taught anthropologist and platform performer Diane Wolkstein, professor of mythology at Sarah Lawrence College, has revived interest in world folktales, particularly Haitian lore, Sufi and Taoist stories, and Babylonian fable. A passionate, kinetic humanist and winner of the 1996 National Storytelling Association Circle of Excellence Award, she took as her mission statement a line from the medieval Persian romance *Layla and Majnun:* "Let me not be cured of love, but let my passion grow! Make my love a hundred times greater than it is today." (Miller and Snodgrass 1998, 296) The line presaged Wolkstein's nearly 20 years of researching and recasting stories. The pinnacle of her translations is the narrative poem of a Sumerian deity, Inanna, Queen of Heaven and Earth, and her consort, Dumuzi, the shepherd-king. Called the world's oldest love story, the epic was reshaped from scraps of cuneiform tablets that date to Abraham, the Old Testament patriarch who migrated west from ancient Ur. After immersing herself in the bits that survive, Wolkstein performed the *Cycle of Inanna* in June 1980 for the Mother Goddess Conference in Maine. In 1983, Wolkstein published the remains of Sanskrit lore, which she illustrated with drawings from Sumerian sculpture, bas-relief, and artistic patterns.

Sources Lambert 1960; Miller and Snodgrass; 1998; Perry 1965; Rosenberg 1997; Wolkstein and Kramer 1983.

 # BIERCE, AMBROSE

American frontier newspaperman, critic, columnist, poet, and writer of ironic fables with an element of grotesquerie, Ambrose Gwinett Bierce crafted a wealth of short, pithy stories for a collection, *Fantastic Fables* (1899). His earnest laceration of California's riffraff, felons, and scavengers earned him a lasting enmity for Swiftian satire directed against his enemies. Most of his narratives are emotionally jarring, as with "Man and Bird," a confrontation between a game bird and a shooter wielding a shotgun. At an impasse, the bird demands, "I am in it for you, but what is there in it for me?" (Komroff 1935, 455) Another lethal *agon* or contest story, "The Mirror," pits spaniel against bulldog. Their brief conversation ends with a smile from the bulldog, whose mouth is so full of sharp teeth that the spaniel keels over from fright. Many of Bierce's most popular tales defy his era's taste for realism by exploiting gothic style and affirm his reputation for flamboyance, psychological twists, and sardonic wit—all of which are evident in his self-revelatory fable "Fortune and Fabulist."

Bierce's background reflects the restlessness and risk-taking that sparked the American pioneering phenomenon. Born in 1842 in Meigs County, Ohio, he was the ninth living child of Marcus Aurelius and Laura Sherwood Bierce. In 1851, his family moved from a log cabin on Horse Cave Creek to a farm on Walnut Creek and later to Warsaw and Elkhart, Indiana. When the burden of overstrict Calvinism and endless land clearing and farmwork pushed him out on his own, he apprenticed with an abolitionist paper, the *Northern Indianian,* and educated himself through reading. An uncle, Lucius Verus Bierce, bankrolled him to Kentucky Military Institute, where Bierce studied military field strategy and cartography for a year until an arsonist destroyed the school. That incident, like events in his fables, has the finality of ill fate, one of Bierce's focal themes.

Bierce developed point of view from experiences as drummer for the Ninth Indiana Cavalry and from combat scenes he witnessed as a cartographer and field reporter. At the battles of Cheat Mountain, Missionary Ridge, Lookout Mountain, and Girard Hill, where he was decorated for rescuing a casualty during a siege, he developed an outlook strongly at odds with his former optimism, as displayed by a conversation between two dead soldiers in his fable "A Niggardly Offer." At the battle of Kennesaw Mountain in Tennessee, Bierce sustained a head wound that caused him recurrent pain, vertigo, and sudden collapse. At age 22, he resigned his post as brevet major to settle in Selma, Alabama, where he managed captured and abandoned properties; that done, he joined General William Hazen's expedition to seize Confederate cotton. A witness to the depredations of the military, he suffered depression at the sight of homelessness, hunger, and despair and at his role in further degrading the defeated South. Reflecting his increasingly cynical mindset, some of his fables refer to the military's penchant for the ridiculous, as in "The Tortoise and the Armadillo," Bierce's symbolic re-creation of the pointless battle between the historic ironclads, the *Monitor* and the *Merrimac.*

Along with Mark Twain and other writers and adventurers who fled west over the Rockies, Bierce accepted a job as engineering aide to map and inspect army fortifications from Nebraska to Fort Benton, Montana, a grueling journey through Indian country that he recounts in "Across the Plains." In California, he joined his brother Albert and worked as a night watchman at the U.S. Mint in San Francisco. To allay boredom, he drew political cartoons and edited the

News-Letter. Admirer Bret Harte, editor of the *Overland Monthly*, published his first ghost tale, "The Haunted Valley." Bierce pursued narrative and satire while reporting for the *Californian, Alta California, Golden Era,* and *News-Letter and California Advertiser.* A colleague of Bret Harte, Joaquin Miller, and Mark Twain, he earned the nicknames "The Devil's Lexicographer," "The Wickedest Man in San Francisco," and "Bitter Bierce" for the harsh cynicism of his short sketches. At the age of 29, he married Mary Ellen "Mollie" Day, daughter of a wealthy mining engineer. The family moved to London, where he published in *Figaro* and *Fun* and edited *The Lantern.* Under the pen name "Dod Grile," he published three collections of short works: *Nuggets and Dust Panned Out in California* (1872), *The Fiend's Delight* (1872), and *Cobwebs from an Empty Skull* (1874).

When asthma endangered his health, Bierce returned to California and another string of short stints. He served as editor, critic, and columnist for the *Examiner, Wasp,* and *Argonaut,* then left home to represent the Black Hills Placer Mining Company in Deadwood, South Dakota. When that job ended, he rode shotgun for Wells Fargo in the Dakota Territory. At an ebb in his fortunes, he holed up in a hotel and composed the first of a series of war pieces, "One of the Missing," which he sold to the *Wave.* In 1887, he signed on with William Randolph Hearst, a budding newspaper giant and strong supporter of Bierce's iconoclastic narratives. Bierce produced a column, "The Prattler," from his home in St. Helena and later from Aurora, California, where he controlled acute asthma attacks by avoiding city pollutants. He rose to national fame and earned a reputation as the Samuel Johnson of the West and arbiter of literary culture in the greater San Francisco area.

Bierce earned the nickname "Bitter" in middle age, when his style grew uncompromisingly acerbic and his outlook soured. After the death of his estranged wife and the loss of his sons from dueling and alcoholism, he retreated from his daughter. Immersing himself in solitude, he pedaled a bicycle into the hills and read Epictetus, drawing strength from classic stoicism. Often moody when he struggled for air, he adopted as a personal motto "Nothing matters," but he worked a steady schedule that refuted the claim. In the 1890s, he published the translation of a German romance, *The Monk and the Hangman's Daughter* (1892); satiric verse in *Black Beetles in Amber* (1892); two collections, *Tales of Soldiers and Civilians* (1891) and *Can Such Things Be?* (1893); and his Aesopic collection, *Fantastic Fables,* his only anthology devoted to the genre.

As an investigative reporter for Hearst Publications, Bierce journeyed to Washington, D.C., in 1900 as correspondent to the *Examiner* during hearings on fraudulant dealings by the Central and Southern Pacific railroads. To the delight of fans, he ridiculed entrepreneur Leland Stanford as "£eland $tanford" and lambasted the "Rail Rogues" who petitioned Congress to cancel their debts. On the side, he contributed thrillers and short fiction to the *New York Journal* and *Cosmopolitan.* Before retiring, he published poems in *Shapes of Clay* (1903); a collection of essays, *Shadow on the Dial* (1906); and *The Devil's Dictionary* (1906), a classic compendium of 500 sharp epigrams in the form of clever definitions. His final publication, *Collected Works* (1912), is a 12-volume anthology drawn from his entire career. In 1913, he toured major Civil War battlegrounds and, during the Mexican Revolution, drifted south of the Rio Grande to witness General Pancho Villa in action. Bierce was never seen again after the winter of 1913–1914. A last letter from Chihuahua, dated December 26, 1913, suggests that he sought a cavalier's death. He may have been shot in January 1914 at the siege of Ojinaga.

A comparison of Bierce's American fables with more bucolic works by Hans Christian Andersen, Gotthold Ephraim Lessing, and other European authors suggests an outlook warped by too long a camaraderie with frontier survivalism, violence, and war. A fair number of Bierce's titles—"The Wooden Gun," "The Discontented Malefactor," "The Lassoed Bear," "Two Footpads," and "The Ashes of Madame Blavatsky"—attest to his love of the outré, often chosen for bold exhibitionism rather than literary or philosophical significance. Concise to the point of truculence, his fables omit the *epimythium* and/or *promythium*, the framework introduction and formal moral preferred by stylists like Jean de La Fontaine and Jean de Florian. Instead Bierce stuck to clean, uncluttered narrative. Direct, unsettling situations place his characters in untenable face-offs, as found in "The Moral Principle and the Material Interest," "The Blotted Escutcheon and the Soiled Ermine," "Two Kings," "An Officer and a Thug," and "An Optimist." In the latter, two imperiled frogs contemplate their ill luck from the belly of a snake:

> "This is pretty hard luck," said one.
> "Don't jump to conclusions," the other said; "we are out of the wet and provided with board and lodging."
> "With lodging, certainly," said the First Frog; "but I don't see the board."
> "You are a croaker," the other explained. "We are the board."
> (Komroff 1935, 456)

The fable exemplifies a rhetorical device common to writers weaned on hard news reporting—the periodic sentence, which comes to rest on a hard fact.

At times, Bierce lightens his harsh perspective with playful musing, for example, "The Tail of the Sphinx," in which a dog discusses with his tail "an ambition to be as impassive as the Sphinx." (Komroff 1935, 459) In the fable "Wolf and Tortoise," the two beasts comment on the design of the tortoise's body. The wolf disparages the slow crawler, but the tortoise lobs back his earth-based optimism: "Providence has thoughtfully supplied me with an impenetrable shell." (Komroff 1935, 457) The wolf, unaccustomed to compromise, reflects, "It seems to me that it would have been just as easy to give you long legs." On the whole, Bierce avoids a sanguine view of nature, even when he allows himself to tease, for example, in "The Sagacious Rat." The jocular tone of the rat's invitation to a friend to accompany him to the corn bin conceals with courtesy a murderous opportunism. By allowing the friend to lead the way, the rat satisfies a prowling cat, which snatches up the friend and trots away.

Cynicism serves Bierce's fables, which depart from an Aesopic outlook to the tone and style of the American West as found in "Lion and Rattlesnake," the tale of a pair of carnivores on the prowl, and "The Crimson Candle," a cynical story of a faithless wife. In "The Lion and the Lamb," Bierce toys with the prophesy found in Isaiah 11:6 and upends the peaceable kingdom. The fabulist pictures the lion subverting universal felicity by dining on the village priest. In "The Rebellious Ant," Bierce focuses on the rebel who tires of common etiquette. To fellow ants who stop him in the act of carrying off a grain of wheat, the rebel offers an explanation of his surly behavior: "Sick of the hollow conventionalities of an effete civilization, . . . [I] returned to the simplicity of primitive life." (Komroff 1935, 465) When the greeters turn into road agents, the rebel, instantly reformed, grabs his grain, flees the scene, and resolves to adopt common courtesy as his modus operandi. The situation embodies the two-edged pragmatism of the Wild West. Bierce appears to have learned firsthand the danger of abandoning Eastern gentility in the face of the West Coast brigand, who prefers outright crime to pleasantries.

A favorite topic, lopsided justice, fuels several sardonic tales. In "The Man Plucking the Goose," the man allows the live goose his opinion, which the man ignores. Similarly, "The Tyrant Frog" turns upside down the relationship of frog and snake before inserting the view of the naturalist, who waits for the snake to swallow his dinner before collecting the snakeskin for his collection. In "The Disinterested Arbiter," a sheep observes the dispute between two dogs claiming the same bone. After he chucks the bone into a pond, the dogs demand an explanation. The sheep replies, "I'm a vegetarian." (Komroff 1935, 460) In a courtroom scene in "The Fox, the Duck, and the Lion," the contenders second-guess the lion, who will determine the ownership of a frog. The judge proves their assumptions wrong and, yawning from his boredom with the matter, advises that "the property in dispute has hopped away." (Komroff 1935, 460) Bierce can't resist a bit of anticlimax with the judge's fillip, "Perhaps you can procure another frog."

Whimsy is another of Bierce's approaches to fable, as found in the lion's discovery that he is good to eat in "The Revelation," one of Bierce's more ominous fables. The comic commentary of a pig reflecting on a drunk lying in a puddle provides a title for "The Ineffective Rooter." A parallel study of piggery powers "The Pig Transformed to a Man," a tale of magic that rewards a clean, learned pig by transforming it into a man. To the magician's chagrin, the man prefers the satisfactions of swinish behavior. For "The Opossum of the Future," the fabulist sets up a confrontation between the opossum and a snake that cuts off flight down a tree limb. Falling back on a history of dissembling, the opossum comments grandly: "My perfect friend . . . my parental instinct recognizes in you a noble evidence and illustration of the theory of development. You are the Opossum of the Future, the ultimate Fittest Survivor of our species, the ripe result of progressive prehensility—all tail!" (Komroff 1935, 461) Bierce's Calvinist upbringing provides the arch rejoinder. The snake, who claims strict scripture-based orthodoxy, rejects a scientific view. The fable halts abruptly, leaving the reader to guess the rest.

Bierce is less successful at the fool tale than at straightforward demonstrations of wisdom. He fails at comedy in "Two Horses," a confrontation between wild and domesticated horses, in which the latter falsely justify a need for bit, rein, and saddle. In "The Ass and the Moon" and "Sheep and Lion," Bierce hones the situations to a fine distinction. The foolish ass makes himself conspicuous by standing in front of the moon; the sheep boasts of being a noncombatant but allows himself to be bred for profit. In each instance, the soft edge fails to produce either a chuckle or "aha" response. More effective is "Philosophers Three," a sage example of animals fighting a flood. While the bear battles the flow and the fox hides in a hollow stump, the opossum declares, "There are malevolent forces . . . which the wise will neither confront nor avoid." (Komroff 1935, 459). He chooses instead to study the nature of his antagonist and play dead. A blend of wisdom and arch ridicule, "Dog and Doctor" contrasts the dog who buries a bone with a physician who buries a wealthy patient. Bierce pursues the cliché of the grasping professional who literally picks the meat from his clients until there is nothing left.

The savage dog-eat-dog situations in Bierce's most pointed stories move unrelentingly away from the survivalism of Uncle Remus's Brer Rabbit to a dire finale. Like the biological determinism at the heart of Jack London's Yukon adventure stories, Bierce's motifs give short shrift to wit as a protection of the weak. In "Cat and King," a retort to John Heywood's proverb, "A cat may look at a king," Bierce creates an ingenuous animal that prefers the king of mice to a human king. (Bartlett's 1992, 142) The sovereign is so taken with the cat's candor that he allows the cat to claw out the prime minister's eyes. Less confrontational is "The Sheep and the Shepherd," a resetting of "The Wolf in Sheep's Clothing," a model from Nikephoros Basilakis's *Progymnasmata* [Exercises] (ca. 1175). A sheep suffering from the heat joins a subdued flock and, anticipating a shearing, chastises them for cowering in the corner. The shepherd arrives, accepts the willing victim, and adds, "Mutton does not keep well in warm weather." (Komroff 1935, 468)

Sources Bartlett 1992; Bierce, 1963, 1977; Bierce, http://www-cgi.cs.cmu.edu; "Bierce Papers," http://sunsite.berkeley.edu; Ehrlich and Carruth 1982; Feinberg 1967; Grenander 1971; Gullette 1996; Kunitz 1942; Lamar 1977; Morris 1995; Snodgrass, *Encyclopedia of Frontier Literature* 1997, *Encyclopedia of Satirical Literature* 1997; Trent 1946; Wiggins 1964.

 # BRER RABBIT

A memorable, lovably vulnerable character from world fable, Brer Rabbit, the American adaptation of the West African trickster, thrives in the pages of Joel Chandler Harris's plantation vignettes. Well into the twentieth century, the famed rabbit remains active in Zora Neale Hurston's *Mules and Men* (1935), William Faulkner's narration, and the oral performances of Jackie Torrence and Gullah tellers Frankie and Doug Quimby. From Harris's introductory story, "Uncle Remus Initiates the Little Boy" in *Uncle Remus: His Songs and His Sayings* (1880), through original Harris stories and re-creations in children's literature, song, art, sculpture, and film, the wily rabbit remains perky, mischievous, and fleet of foot, never trusting too long the status quo. At his debut, he arrives in the second paragraph as Brer Fox crafts a trick. Before the fox can finish his sentence, "Brer Rabbit come a lopin' up de big road, lookin' des ez plump, en ez fat, en ez sassy ez a Moggin hoss [Morgan horse] in a barley-patch." (Harris 1982, 55) His self-satisfaction and the spirited impertinence of his rejoinders to the fox attest to his intention to remain alive and free without kowtowing to predators. The added fillip is his knavery, the willful pulling of pranks that keep him in close contact with his enemies to remind them that size and ferocity can't shield them from his annoying trickery.

The second of Harris's fables, "The Wonderful Tar-Baby Story," appears to have pleased audiences from its inception. A complex allegory that depicts the uppity rabbit enforcing his plantation manners on a small black boy, the story derives from an African situation in which a rabbit refuses to help dig a well, then defiantly roils and muddies the water. As a model of community oneness, the creation of a fetching female tarbaby ends the rabbit's thoughtless behaviors and holds him in check. Harris's version rewards the rabbit for meddling by sticking his all-fours to a glob of pitch. The meaning is clear enough and would cease with a suitable moral if the story were by Aesop. However, Harris, who aspired to more than simple beast fable, carries the situation beyond a one-on-one confrontation by leaving the rabbit in peril. As the smirking fox approaches, he can't resist chortling, "You look sorter stuck up dis mawnin'," a pun on the rabbit's hatred of snobbery. (Harris 1982, 59) Using the rabbit's discomfiture as a hook, Uncle Remus sends his young listener to "Miss Sally" and saves the episode of the rescue for another day.

Spooled out in lengths suited to a child's attention span, the stories of Brer Rabbit wind in and out of "Why Mr. Possum Loves Peace" and "The Story of the Deluge and Why It Came About," establishing the forest society with added details about Mr. Jack Sparrow, Mr. Dog, Brer Coon, Mr. Buzzard, Sis Cow, Brer Tarrypin, and Mr. Bear, all familiar Georgia mammals. In the rabbit's second appearance, narrated at the demand of the little boy, Remus declares that "in dem days Brer Rabbit en his fambly wuz at de head er de gang w'en enny racket wuz on han', en dar dey stayed." (Harris 1982, 62) A cheery, footloose denizen of the briar patch, the rabbit recovers from the tarbaby in a few days and returns to the neighborhood with the insouciance of a prominent community member and devoted self-promoter, his pose in "How Mr. Rabbit Lost His Fine Bushy Tail." The alter ego of old Remus, a subservient holdover from the Plantation South, the rabbit revels in his youth, vivacity, and freedom from intimidation and constraint.

Harris remains true to one aspect of fable—the constancy of danger, which lies in wait for the weak, simple-witted, and overconfident. Placing Brer Rabbit in the last category after a run-in with the fox, the teller depicts the rabbit's braggadocio. Like a strutting Mississippi gambler at a brothel, he puffs his cigar and impresses Miss Meadows's girls on the piazza, a vague company whom Harris never fully characterizes. The rewards of the rabbit's victory are sweet:

> Dey talk, en dey sing, en dey play on de peanner, de gals did, twel bimeby hit come time fer Brer Rabbit fer to be gwine, en he tell um all good-by, en strut out to de hoss-rack same's ef he wuz de king er de patter-rollers. [They talk, and they sing, and they play on the piano, the girls did, until soon it came time for

Brer Rabbit to go, and he told them good-by and strutted out to the horse-rack the same as if he was the king of the patrollers.] (Harris 1982, 71)

Never too content in one place, the rabbit must regularly adapt to new temptations and dangers by staying loose and keeping an eye toward his lair. In "The Awful Fate of Mr. Wolf," after repeated raids by the wolf on his den cost him peace of mind and some of his children, Brer Rabbit suffers bouts of cold chills and develops a human anger, cursing, growling, and setting out to build a wolf-proof home to thwart his stalker. When the wolf is safely stowed in a chest, the rabbit can wink at his reflection in a mirror, draw his chair up to the fire, chew tobacco, and call his litter to witness a cruel vengeance—scalding the wolf with boiling water through holes he has punched in the chest with a gimlet. The punishment grows from the elements with which nature has equipped the small, furry survivor: he has the sharp-pointed wit of the gimlet but relies on touches of villainy like the boiling water, which simmers in the pot until the rabbit is sure it is safe to inflict on a shackled enemy.

The social factor that sets Uncle Remus stories apart from fable from other eras and places is the adaptability of the rabbit to black plantation culture. As both anarchist and member of an integrated animal community, Brer Rabbit "howdies" and "'sponds" to greetings and gossips about his neighbors' latest episodes—the bear nursing the little alligator, the cow in the salad patch, the buzzard tricked by the terrapin, and Mrs. Partridge's fit. In "Mr. Wolf Makes a Failure," the rabbit asks about a mourner's gown and implies that he will visit the fox's house to sit up with the dead, a plantation custom expected of friends and kin. In "Mr. Rabbit and Mr. Bear," the rabbit plants a peanut patch, a valuable source of protein in the scant diet of plantation slaves as well as for farm families bereft of menfolk to plow and crop during the Civil War. Like the slave, a victim of forces beyond his control, the brash, willful rabbit is a comic Samson, who substitutes trickery and deceit for the strength needed to surprise and overwhelm the oppressive Philistines. To balance the stories with reality, Harris pairs episodes in which the rabbit is himself the victim, often of his own guile, as is the case with "Mr. Rabbit Finds His Match at Last" and "Mr. Rabbit Meets His Match Again." The juxtaposition of the rabbit's children, the focus of "A Story about the Little Rabbits," reemphasizes the vulnerability of small animals, especially their young, who were the ties that kept stronger adult slaves from fleeing the quarters and following the "drinking gourd," the Big Dipper that pointed the way north to freedom.

Overall, the suave, sassy Brer Rabbit is more than a survivor. His native wit and bold effrontery provide emotional release but expose him to reprisal. Determined to enliven his days, he declares "dey ain't no dull times wid him, kaze it look like he got sump'n n'er fer ter do every minnit er de day whedder he's at home or whedder he's abroad." (Brookes 1950, 66) Harris's insistence on a blend of escapism and roguery relieves the fable cycle of pity for the victim. Full of himself, Brer Rabbit departs to his private den to "lay down dar en de brier patch en roll en laugh twel his sides hurtid 'm. He bleedzd ter laff. Fox atter 'm, Buzzard atter 'm, en Cow atter 'm, en dey ain't kotch 'im yit." (Brooks 1950, 68) The characterization of the plantation scamp and hell-raiser lightens the mood and applies a veneer of wickedness that transforms Brer Rabbit from eluder of danger to strutter and braggart. The metamorphosis allies the trickster with human sinners whose character flaws are their undoing.

In the writings of Zora Neale Hurston, Brer Rabbit's name surfaces like an old friend—while courting Miss Saphronie or holding a convention of rabbits wearied of ducking and dodging hunting hounds. Situated among anecdotes and fables of Ole Massa and John Henry and the fool tales depicting rural people, the trickster stories of Brer Rabbit segue neatly into other animal company, including Brer 'Gator, Brer Hawk, and Brer Dog. The insouciant rabbit provokes the gator in a *pourquoi* incident that has Brer Rabbit tracking across the gator while he sleeps in the grass. To compensate for his discourtesy, the rabbit warns the gator that trouble will follow. When the gator falls asleep once more, the rabbit takes a fat pine knot and sets fire to the savannah. To the rabbit's rude snickers, the gator must test the circle of fire to find an escape. The story ends benignly: "Way after while he broke thru and hit de water 'ker ploogum!' He got all cooled off but he had done got smoked all up befo' he got to de water, and his eyes all red from de smoke." (Hurston 1990, 107) In *pourquoi* style, the story concludes with a description of the smoky hide, which remains the gator's outerwear forever.

See also Harris, Joel Chandler; Uncle Remus.

Sources Abrahams 1985; Bradbury 1963; Brookes 1950; Davis 1970; Dorson 1959; Ehrlich and Carruth 1982; Goss and Barnes 1989; Harlow 1941; Harris 1982; Hurston 1990; O'Shea 1996; Smith 1967; Snodgrass, *The Encyclopedia of Satirical Literature* 1997; *The Encyclopedia of Southern Literature* 1997.

 # BRITISH FABLE

Britain's folklore contains a number of fables among its extensive collection of fairy tales, fool tales and noodle stories, nursery rhymes, black dog tales, bogie and devil encounters, and historic ghosts and banshees. The traditional Aesopic fable of the British Isles owes its material to numerous sources. Although the loss of a text by Alfred the Great, the late ninth-century Anglo-Saxon king from Wessex, leaves a gap in scholarship, his work was a definite influence, mentioned by Norman-French poet and fabulist Marie de France. In the twelfth century, a delightful anonymous fable, *The Owl and the Nightingale* (ca. 1190), demonstrates in 1,704 lines the sophistication and metrical agility of the medieval *débat*, an intellectual exchange that reaches no conclusion but thoroughly airs opposing points of view. Attributed to Maister Nichole of Guldeforde [Master Nicholas of Guildford] of Portisham, who is named in line 147, the poem sheds light on late twelfth-century thought and logic. The fastidious nightingale accuses her opponent of transgressions against family. Specifically, she claims:

> Thu art lodlich an unclene;
> Bi thine neste Ich hit mene
> An eke bi thine fule brode:
> Thu fedes on hom a wel ful fode.

[You are loathsome and unclean;
Your nest is disgraceful
And also your large brood
Which you feed at home, a full family.]
(Bennett and Smithers 1968, 5)

To humiliating claims against the cleanliness of his nest, the owl retorts that the sweet-voiced nightingale absorbs herself in simpering love melody, which lures humankind to lust and adultery. A face-off between asceticism and art, the two points of view appear to debate the rise of courtly love verse, which contrasts the austerity of monastic traditions. The poet ends the exchange with the withdrawal of the birds and remarks, "Ne can Ich eu namore telle" [I can tell you no more.]

A tangible source of late medieval British apologue, or morality literature, is the era of Chaucer, which produced three fabulists—John Lydgate, John Gower, and Chaucer himself. An extensive fable collection published around 1390 was the work of Lydgate, a prolific writer who, like Chaucer, wrote original pieces blended with adaptations of material by Italian poet Giovanni Boccaccio, author of the *Decameron* (1353), and by Guido delle Colonne, a Sicilian judge who produced *canzone* and a history of the Trojan War. Lydgate was a prelate and poet from Newmarket. After taking orders with the Benedictines quartered at Bury St. Edmunds, he appears to have studied at the universities of Oxford and Cambridge and traveled across Europe before settling down to the post of prior of Hatfield Broadoak in Essex in 1423.

In his late sixties, Lydgate attained a pension as court poet. His published works include *Troy Book, The Siege of Thebes, The Fall of Princes, Daunce of Machabre,* and *London Lickpenny.* In the genre of fable, he restated Greek originals in *Isopes Fabules* (ca. 1398). Composing in the medieval tradition, he revealed his limited knowledge of the classics in lines 8–14, in which he describes Aesop as a Roman. He felt it necessary to explain in lines 31–35:

And, though I have no rethorik swete,
Have me excusyd: I was born in Lydgate;
Of Tullius gardeyn I passyd nat the gate,
And cause why: I had no lycence
There to gadyr floures of elloquence.
[And though I learned no rhetoric,
Excuse me, for I was born in Lydgate;
Of Cicero's garden I passed not the gate,
Because I had no opportunity
To gather his eloquent flowers.]
(Renoir 1967, 54)

Lydgate also produced moralistic and satiric animal lore in *Horse, Goose, and Sheep* and *The Churl and the Bird* (ca. 1390), a tale drawn from the *Gesta Romanorum* [Deeds of the Romans] (1324).

Lydgate's contemporary, John Gower, was a wealthy Kentishman of considerable leisure, learning, and intelligence and a friend of Chaucer. Less facile and urbane than Chaucer, he nonetheless embedded in his *Confessio Amantis* [Confession of a Lover] (1390) numerous jolly anecdotes, tales, and the fable

"Adrian and Bardus." A morality tale about a good-hearted rustic who aids a noble, it embodies the insincerity of the man in trouble who promises riches in exchange for succor. Gower contrasts the ingratitude of Adrian with the unfathomable generosity of an ape. The excess of Gower's hyperbole favors Oriental and Indian fable such as *A Thousand and One Nights* and *Panchatantra* by violating the logic and control of Aesopic lore, which tends to reward rescuers no more than one would expect from a normal earthly encounter.

A century later, folk wisdom gained wider audiences when it was transmitted to the printed page. The resultant body of British fables and exempla, or sermons, is a mishmash of classic Greek stories and local anecdotes, all marked by the idiosyncratic style and humor of Great Britain. "Belling the Cat" (ca. 1482), an anonymous rendering that resets an Aesopic story, details a secret conference between nobles concerning the arrogance of Cochran, a friend of James III. Lord Gray interrupts the complainers with the story of the mice who want to bell the cat but have no volunteer brave enough to do the job. Archibald, Earl of Angus, interrupts to offer his services, thus earning for himself the name of Archibald Bell-the-Cat. A vengeful retelling of "The Ant and the Cricket" allies the former with the king of Pismoules and the latter with the queen of the bumblebees. Entitled "The Bum Bee," the fable describes the queen's misery in a winter storm, when the king has no pity and sends her to gather honey. Six months later, when the king suffers a hunting accident in a summer rain, he petitions her for cover from the wet. She evens the score by dumping boiling water on him. The wry parody of marriage perpetuates a pervasive medieval tradition that recalls the bustling, assertive Wife of Bath and Dame Pertelote, the opinionated hen, in Chaucer's *Canterbury Tales*.

William Caxton, the Kentish translator and printer who introduced the printing press in England, published the work of thirteenth-century Italian scholar Francisco Accursius in translation under the title *The Boke of Subtyl Historyes and Fables of Esope* (1485), the first printed text of Aesop's fables and one of England's earliest cheap editions. A familiar fable, Aesop's fox and grapes appears in Middle English as "Of the Foxe and of the Raysyns." The composition is direct and simple: "As reciteth this fable of a foxe: whiche loked and beheld the raysyns that grewe upon an hyghe vyne; the whiche raysyns he moche desyred for to ete them. And whanne he sawe that none he myght gete: he torned his sorowe in to Ioye [joy]: and sayd these raysyns ben sowre." (Hobbs 1986, 34) Readers validated Caxton's work by placing it at the heart of the canon of educational literature as a reader for children.

According to William Roper's *The Life of Sir Thomas More* (1535), a letter from the sixteenth century establishes the use of fable in common discourse. Writing to Margaret Roper, Lady Alington, More's stepdaughter, repeats a pair of unusual fables told at court. The first, attributed to Cardinal Wolsey, tells of a land of fools that was deluged with rain. The few wise residents hid underground and expected to serve as an example to the simpletons who failed to take cover. Instead, the mud-covered fools congratulated themselves and taunted the wise ones. The second tale mocks the confessional, where the priest forgives the lion's bloody hunts, and makes no decision about the wolf's sins, yet

Frontispiece to Caxton's *Fables of Aesop*

Portrait of Edmund Spenser (1532–1590)

chastises the ass for devouring a blade of grass. The satiric edge proves that the subtlety of British animal fable was aimed more at adults than children.

The range of English fable profited from ties with the Continent, particularly Scandinavia, Belgium, and Holland. A manuscript by Danish cleric and historian Christien Pedersen contains *Aesop's Leyned og Fabler* [Aesop's Legends and Fables] (1556), which he produced for the masses after establishing himself at Malmø as a printer of the Bible and folklore. A contemporary, writer and mercenary Thomas Churchyard of Shrewsbury, collected verse and prose selections in *Churchyard Chippes* (ca. 1560) and *The Legend of Shore's Wife* (1563), the outgrowth of his sojourns in Scotland, Ireland, Belgium, and Holland. To the north of the British Isles, schoolmaster Robert Henryson of Dunfermline, Scotland, issued comic, pictorial versions of Aesopic stories, such as the "Taill of the Uplandis Mous and the Burges Mous" and "The Cock and the Fox" in *The Morall Fabillis of Esope the Phrygian, compylit in eloquent & ornate Scottis meter* (1570), which adapts to local idiom Heinrich Steinhöwel's fable collation. In a prologue, Henryson explains that fables of old are more than mere lessons in verse. He lauds the pleasant sounds as adjuncts to the ethical example, which passes into the human conscience through a subconscious immersion in character and action. Henryson's contemporary William Bullokar chose Greek fables as the working model for a simplified system of English spelling. The completed text, *Aesopz Fablz in Tru Ortography with Grammar-notz* (1585), is less a source of folklore than a curiosity. An innovative educator, John Brinsley, made similar use of Aesop as material for a children's reader, published in 1617 and reissued in 1624.

England's master allegorist, Edmund Spenser, composed resonant Aesopic models in *Mother Hubberds Tale* (1591), a pointed commentary in heroic couplets on his era and its politics. The four segments depict a fox and ape who live disguised and comment on behaviors and mores, as with this sketch from lines 891–914 disdaining the pitiful state of the gentleman at the court of Elizabeth I:

> So pitiful a thing is suitor's state . . .
>   Full little knowest thou that hast not tried,
> What hell it is in suing long to bide:
> To lose good days that might be better spent,
> To waste long nights in pensive discontent;
> To speed to-day, to be put back to-morrow;
> To feed on hope, to pine with fear and sorrow;
> To have thy prince's grace, yet want her peers';
> To have thy asking, yet wait many years;
> To fret thy soul with crosses and with cares,
> To eat thy heart through comfortless despairs:
> To fawn, to crouch, to wait, to ride, to run,
> To spend, to give, to want, to be undone.
> (Baugh 1948, 488)

However, Spenser pressed his luck with caricature too close to the original for safety. Court censors' suppression of *Mother Hubberds Tale* discouraged him from venturing again into blatant ridicule of England's powerful.

England's chief satirist of the Renaissance era, Ben Jonson, applied to characterization the medieval concept of the humors. Derived from Hippocrates's description of the four dominant body fluids—blood (jocularity), phlegm (indolence), yellow bile (envy), and black bile (anger)—and the crotchets, moods, and passions that overproduction, improper blend, and depletion cause in human behavior. In his bestial stage masterwork, *Volpone, the Fox* (1606), he displays the extremes of character. His cast functions according to inherent traits, from grump and grouch to sunny optimist, to warn the audience of unscrupulous behaviors common to the greedy, villainous deceiver. Imitating the more vengeful of medieval beast fables—namely, *Ysengrimus* and *Reynard the Fox*—Jonson illustrates how the protagonist dupes his prey.

Initiated by John Ogilby's slangy *Fables of Aesop, Paraphras'd in Verse* (1651), the golden era of English fable began in the mid-seventeenth century and lasted over 90 years. A safe expression of distaste for political and social unrest that accompanied the rise of the Puritans and the execution of Charles I, fable covered a broad gamut—from the experimental allegory in John Dryden's *The Hind and the Panther* (1687); Anne Kingsmill Finch, Countess of Winchelsea's *The Atheist and the Acorn* (1713); and John Gay's *Fifty-one Fables in Verse* (1727) down to the work of hacks who cranked out sixpenny pamphlets for the commoner's edification. Among the also-rans of England's opinionated fabulists were Charles Hoole, collector of grammatical examples in *Aesop's Fables in English and Latin* (1687); John Locke, who assembled the interlinear English-Latin collection, *Aesop's Fables* (1703); the anonymous author of *Fables, Moral and Political* (1703); and novelist Samuel Richardson, author of a Jacobite *Aesop's Fables* (1739).

By the Augustan definition, fable should bear a double meaning while accommodating its style and setting to nature. A succinct model from playwright Aphra Behn's *Aesop's Fables with His Life* (1687) demonstrates a proportion favoring moral as a third of the text:

The Crow with laden beak to tree retires,
The Fox to gette her prey her form admires,
While she to show her gratitude not small,
Offering to give her thanks, her prize lets fall.
Morall
Shun faithless flatterers, Harlots, jilting tars,
They are fooles hopes and youths deceitefull snares.
(Lewis 1996, 8)

The use of animals in the work pictures the intended lesson—the loss of the crow's prize, which falls to the flattering fox. The model created by Bernard de Mandeville, *The Fable of the Bees* (1729), achieved Behn's intent but so enraged readers that a vocal debate extended past Mandeville's life, providing a choice soapbox topic for preachers, politicians, and philosophers. Less abrasive are the gentle learning activities contained in Lady Eleanor Fenn's *Cobwebs to Catch Flies; or Dialogues in Short Sentences* (ca. 1783) and *Fables by Mrs. Teachwell* (1783), the educational readers and vocabulary builders that presaged the Victorian era's didactic fable schoolbooks. More grammarian and pedagogue than fabulist, Fenn, a Norfolk-born educator and social reformer, envisioned herself as the philanthropic anthologizer of utilitarian prose.

The growth of scholarly British folklore study began in the mid-nineteenth century. As represented in *A Dictionary of British Folk-Tales* (1971), an authoritative two-volume collection by Oxford scholar and folklorist Katharine Briggs, the publication of *Notes and Queries, The Gentleman's Magazine*, and *Athenaeum* led the way by reserving sections for the publication of oddments and suitable commentary. The tales themselves received serious study from the Folklore

Society, inaugurated in 1878, and reached a height of literary perusal from 1880 to 1910. The resulting emphasis on national lore of the British Isles details what critic Ronald Blythe has called "the homeliness and pain of bed, board, and grave," a somewhat overromanticized description for the simpler *agon* or contest demonstrated by "The Fox and the Hedgehog," "The Magpie's Nest," and "The Fox and the Magpie." (Briggs 1991, flap) Marked by imitations of birdcalls, "The Wood-Pigeon's Nest," a popular fable from the Isle of Wight, calls for gifted mimicry in oral tellings. The storyteller must pit the wood-pigeon's plaintive "That o'ooll do-o-o-o-o" against the sharp retort of the magpie's "No t'wunt, no t'wunt." (Briggs 1991, 127)

In Briggs's representative sample, the vying for power or prestige overrides humanism. A typically Aesopic struggle for eminence undergirds "The King of Birds," a competition text from Yorkshire about the tiny titmouse who bests the eagle by hitching a ride under his wings into the heavens. As the eagle floats aloft and gloats over his triumph, the titmouse then soars beyond him with a pert remonstrance:

> Tit, tit,
> Higher it,
> Tit, tit,
> Higher it.
> (Briggs 1991, 118)

From a more complex ethos come tales that typify competition as the struggle for survival. A fable paralleling Aesop's squeaking wheel, "The Tantony Pig" is a Somerset fable about a resourceful animal that faces execution. When hog-killing time approaches, the pig rings the bell that summons a clerk. Townsfolk are so impressed with its clever imitation of human behavior that they "'oodn't let 'en be bacon, so he runned round and eat up all their rubbidge for 'en grateful, and wur a Tantony Pig all his days." (Briggs 1991, 771) Less sanguine are the five-stanza fable-in-ballad death struggles "The Harnit and the Bittle" [The Hornet and the Beetle] from Gloucestershire and "The Frog and the Crow." In the latter, the crow lures the jolly frog from river to land, where the crow gobbles him up "there and then, O." (Briggs 1991, 110) Like the English ballads of Robin Hood's escape from the Sheriff of Nottingham and Rob Roy's scrapes with authorities, these defiances of death satisfy a folk need to supplant the peasant bed-to-churchyard destiny with glimmerings of hope and triumph.

Fables in dialect enrich the British canon with the uniquely energetic style, idiom, and delivery of commoners. In the thicker accents, as in "The Lion, the Leper, and the Tod" [The Lion, the Leopard, and the Fox], the story reads less like dialect than like a foreign language and requires an anglicized version for comparison and clarification. A brisk, readable idiomatic example, the Yorkshire brogue of "The Hare and the Prickly-Backed Urchin," gets off to a cheery start with "It war yaa Sunday mornin' i' Summer, just aboot t' time when t' buttery bushes blooms." (Briggs 1991, 113) Prefatory to the traditionally misaligned tortoise-and-hare race, the exchange between beasts moves at a spirited clip with these greetings:

"Noo mate, what cheer?" But t' hare raither fancied hissen, an 'stedd o' sayin': "Middlin', thankee, hoo's thysen?" he nobbut said, short like, "What's thoo doin' up here, all by thysen o' this fine mornin'?" "Oh, I's nobbut hevin' a stroll roond," said t' prickly-backt urchin. ["Now mate, what cheer?" But the hare rather fancied himself, and instead of saying "Fair, thank you, how are you?" he only said, short like, "What are you doing up here, all by yourself this fine morning?" "Oh, I'm just having a stroll," said the prickly backed urchin.] (Briggs 1991, 113)

In a less jocular vein, the two speakers of "The Farmer and His Ox" trade insults to no discernable purpose. The humor of the exchange lies in the fact that both man and beast speak the same untutored argot and repeat the phrase, "girt stupid vule [fool]." (Briggs 1991, 107) More detailed with barnyard wisdom is "The Yaller-Legg'd Cock'ril," an archetypal narrative power struggle between old hand and young upstart. After the old cock subdues the bumptious cockerel and the pigs devour the carcass down to the legs, the farmer reminds the other chickens, "Niver craw till yer spurs is grawn" [Never crow till your spurs are grown]. (Briggs 1977, 17)

Folk fable was the impetus for the emergence of a literary branch of the genre, which drew the likes of Alexander Pope, Robert Dodsley, Isaac Watts, Oliver Goldsmith, and Jonathan Swift. In a poem of six rhymed couplets, Pope composed a fool tale about two travelers vying for an oyster. Pope heightens the competition by introducing an abstract third party:

> While, scale in hand, Dame Justice pass'd along.
> Before her each with clamour pleads the laws,
> Explained the matter and would win the cause.
> Dame Justice weighing long the doubtful right,
> Takes, opens, swallows it before their sight.
> (Cooper 1921, 281)

In obvious glee at the fools' lack of caution, she instructs them to share the two halves of the worthless shell. A harsher remonstrance informs them, "We thrive at Westminster on fools like you. / 'Twas a fat Oyster—live in peace—Adieu." Pope's protégé, dramatist and critic Robert Dodsley, produced a critical essay on fable, the first of its kind, and a sheaf of original fables, *Select Fables of Esop and Other Fabulists* (1764), which includes an echo of Pope's oyster story. Transposing the situation to quarreling cats and a monkey as mediator, Dodsley ends with cruel comeuppance as the monkey gobbles the cheese in question before dismissing the court. The weakness of other models—"The Boys and the Frogs," "The Spider and the Silkworm," and "The Fly in Saint Paul's Cupola"—place Dodsley far below his betters in originality and taut narrative construction. Likewise, his aphorisms lack the sure-footed turn of phrase that was Pope's contribution to the Age of Enlightenment.

Felicity of expression marks the less pointed literary fables of England. Lacking Pope's rancor, Isaac Watts composed "The Sluggard" in *Divine Songs* (1720), an amiable verse discourse by a do-gooder hoping to inspire a layabout and backslider to arise, read his Bible, and weed his garden. In lively iambics, another poem from the anthology, "Against Idleness and Mischief," lauds the frugality and industry of the honeybee. Watts's naive meddling provoked Lewis Carroll to parody the poem in *Alice in Wonderland*. Goldsmith, who avoids the urbanity and grace of Pope for a more straightforward narrative, wrote "An Essay on Fable" in *Bewick's Select Fables* (1784). Among his beast lore are the wryly humorous "An Elegy on the Death of a Mad Dog" (1766), "The Lost Camel," a model of Sherlock Holmesian observation, and "The Spectacles," a winsome parable about the god Momus, who equips mortals with idiosyncratic vision from a satchel of eyeglasses, each tinted to a unique shade. A minor producer of the era's stock of fable, Jonathan Swift, master Irish satirist of the eighteenth century, penned two significant examples, "The Wasp and the Man," a poorly focused invective on the failure of humankind to profit from error, and "The Miser's Jackdaw," a witty exchange between a pinchpenny's bird and cat, who ridicule him for hoarding gold that he never uses. Swift appends a moral that expresses the satirist's credo: "Men are contented to be laughed at for their wit, but not their folly." (Komroff 1935, 238)

A more sedate style of writing appears in the *belles lettres* of the polite British Victorians. Irish poet Thomas Moore crafted a parental model, "The Young Lady and the Looking-Glass." The family's use of a mirror to alter a teenager's willful behavior creates more laborious tone and atmosphere than fable usually accommodates. However, Moore appends a saving grace—a six-line commentary that typifies the genre:

> Thus, Fable to the human kind
> Presents an image of the mind:
> It is a mirror, where we spy
> At large our own deformity:
> And learn of course those faults to mend
> Which but to mention would offend.
> (Cooper 1921, 285)

Less prescriptive are the refined stories of Margaret Scott Gatty. Published under the proper married woman's title of Mrs. Alfred Gatty of Burnham, Essex, she was a children's writer of *Aunt Judy's Tales* (1859) and editor of *Aunt Judy's Magazine* (1866–1873), which her daughters, Horatia Katherine Gatty and children's author Juliana Horatia Gatty Ewing, published until 1885. As was common for offspring of gentry, Gatty was educated at home and encouraged to produce literature, drawing, and calligraphy. Her writing career began in 1852 with *The Fairy Godmothers and Other Tales*, which she followed with four volumes entitled *Parables from Nature* (1855). Featuring the drawings of Holman Hunt and John Tenniel, illustrator of Lewis Carroll's *Alice in Wonderland*, Gatty's books were well received and widely reprinted and translated. Critics lauded her refined fables for their sweetness and reverence for nature. A model of Victorian decorum is "Night and Day," an *agon* or competition myth set in a primeval time when the two natural forces lash out in jealousy. Gatty pursues their differences with patience and appreciation for the qualities of each. Less rambunctious than the anonymous folk fables of the British Isles, the simmering feud motif boils down to a decorous conclusion, with the two competitors yielding to nature's demands.

See also Adams, Richard; Celtic fable; Chaucer, Geoffrey; Christian fable; Dryden, John; eighteenth-century fable; Gay, John; Hawkes, Jacquetta; Kipling, Rudyard; L'Estrange, Sir Roger; Mandeville, Bernard de; nineteenth-century fable; Orwell, George; Potter, Beatrix; Shakespeare, William; Shaw, George Bernard.

Sources Baugh 1948; Bennett and Smithers 1968; Briggs 1977, 1991; Cooper 1921; Crane 1932; Gatty 1869; Hobbs 1986; *The International Who's Who* 1987; Komroff 1935; Kunitz 1955; Lewis 1996; Meigs 1953; Noel 1975; Perry 1965; Renoir 1967; Smith 1900; Steinberg 1954; Ten Brink 1895.

 CELTIC FABLE

Celtic lore, among the oldest body of folk stories in Europe, belongs to an elaborate structure of myth and legend that captures in the wandering harper's metrics an ancient culture, ritual, and language. Unchallenged by the Roman invasions that adulterated and weakened British lore, the Celtic strand survived entire. It speaks through a runic script that dates to the preliterate druidic schools. The cult appears in the seven-volume *Commentarii de Bello Gallico* [The Gallic Wars] (58–52 B.C.E.), the war correspondence of Julius Caesar after his troops encountered Continental white-robed druid priests around 55 B.C.E. After Christian scribes established monastic settlements and began recording Irish vernacular stories in the eleventh and twelfth centuries, they produced vellum copies of the *Lebor Gabala Erenn* [Book of the Taking of Ireland] (eighth century), a sanitized, Church-sanctioned version of four widely spaced cycles:

- the mythological cycle of the semidivine gnomes, warlocks, magi, and fairy folk of pre-Gaelic pagan Ireland (1500 B.C.E.)

- the Ulster cycle of Cuchulainn's exploits and the tales of King Conor Mac Nessa of Ulster and Maeve, Queen of Connacht, from the first century C.E.

- the parallel Fenian cycle of the warrior-hunter Finn Mac Cumhaill—popularized as Finn Mac Cool—and his followers, lauded in third-century tales and ballads

- the historical cycle, namely, the ninth-century stories of the kings of Tara and of Saint Patrick

Less common to Celtic collections are straightforward Aesopic fables. One author of morality tales, the Welsh poet Siôn Cent, approached the classic genre in a dour reflection on morality around 1430:

Three lifetimes of a valiant-footed horse
For a man, and the life is short.
Three lifetimes of a man, nimble rover,
For a stag, keen leaper.
Three lifetimes of a stag, long-lived, long, lean,
For the blackbird of the wood, golden, proud, pretty,

Three lifetimes of the proud, pretty blackbird
For the oaktree above a fair soil.
Each one of these, a wheel's band,
Dies without warning.
(Breeze 1997, 142)

Obsessed with the inevitability of death, the verse departs from the heroic and magical story world for a somber reflection on evanescence, a subject that dominates the nature fables of the eighth-century Greek farmer-poet Hesiod and his successor, the late seventh-century B.C.E. soldier-poet Archilochus.

A more entertaining motif of Irish folklore is the traditional fool tale, a timeless folk story in which the unwise suffer at the hands—or beaks or fangs or claws—of smarter beasts. "The Cold May Night" embodies nature's punishment of fools in a cumulative tale about a miserably cold spring in which a crow eats an eagle's fledgling and steals its place in the warm nest. When the eagle returns and mothers the crow in the dark nest below, she comments on the uncommon weather. He surprises her by comparing the night to one years before. The mother, disconcerted by her clever young, follows his direction and visits the blackbird at the forge, a bull in a field, and the Blind Salmon of Assaroe before finding a witness to the earlier cold night. The salmon, like a jolly peasant roisterer, chaffs the eagle for being tricked by the clever crow, which devoured her babe and stole its berth.

The eagle is also at the heart of "The Fox and the Eagle," a standard revenge plot in which the eagle's snatching of two ducks during a time of famine results in a greater loss to the thief. Because the story hinges on food for the hungry rather than reward for the greedy, the turn of events serves nature's ends. At the close of the fable, the eagle carries off a third duck whose feathers conceal embers. After she inadvertently sets the nest on fire, the three ducks as well as the eagle's chicks fall to the ground, where the clever fox awaits. A similar end awaits the protagonist in "The Fox in Inishkea," the tale of a wily fox who boasts of tricking local people. Overconfident in his lair, he realizes too late that stalkers have cut the briar through which he swings out of range of dogs. Like his victims, he falls to the treacherous rocks below. A parallel tale, "The Magpie and the Fox," places the despoiler of nestlings in the power of the angry mother bird, who overfeeds the fox, then sics the hounds on him. Perhaps from their historic perspective as the prey of raiders and usurpers, the Irish relish revenge against the rapacious.

An Irish story that reprises the motif of the hare and the tortoise relies on less vindictive animal behaviors for its action. In "The Cat and the Dog," the dog challenges the cat for its place by the fire. The two run a race that puts the dog far ahead. When a beggar strikes the dog, precipitating a squabble with the angry animal, the cat takes advantage of their tiff and makes for home. According to *pourquoi* logic, she sits grinning by the hearth when the dog returns and keeps her spot to this day. A tale of innate qualities fuels "The Sow and Her *Banbh*," a brief exchange between mother and piglet, who reminds her that she will never stop thieving and risking flight from a pack of guard dogs. Wittier is "The Old Crow Teaches the Young Crow," a tit-for-tat between the wise elder and wiseacre young bird, who reminds his parent that danger exists in more guises than the old crow's simple lesson suggests. Satisfied that the young crow will survive the world's evils, the old crow urges, "Off you go. . . . You know more than myself!" (O'Sullivan 1966, 15) These fables examine animals in their normal settings and enliven nature's directives with anthropomorphic dialogue, the genius stroke of Aesopic fable.

As is common to more sophisticated post-Aesopic lore, Celtic beast tales may cluster into a cycle of episodes involving a focal animal. In "The Fox and the Heron," three strands form the text. In the opening segment, the fox advises the heron on how to trick the wrens into repaying a debt. A brief reprise of trickery enables the heron to get workmen to empty a pool in search of a purported lost purse. The heron profits by carrying off the eels that the diggers scoop up from the mucky bottom. The heron grows so enamored of her adviser that she marries him, but, true to his nature, he deceives her. The grim comeuppance to the fox is typical of Celtic glee in besting an opponent. As dogs rip the fox apart, he calls to the heron to fly down to his aid, but she abandons him to his doom.

Nineteenth-century engraving of "A Bard Reciting to Northmen"

Examples of less violent Celtic fable express a benevolent relationship among earthly creatures. "The Man Who Swallowed the Mouse" deals with a bizarre mishap and with a wise woman who suggests that he bait the mouse with plates of hot meat. "The Grateful Weasel" is a reward story about a man who holds a rat until the weasel can kill it. When his foot swells from rat bite, the grateful weasel carries healing leaves for the man to use as a poultice. A curious fable, "Two Women or Twelve Men," describes the training of three kit foxes. The sire takes the young ones to a house where voices indicate a spirited conversation. The first two foxes can't guess how many people are in the house, but the third proves worldly-wise. In the end, the old fox is pleased that one of his brood will cope well with humankind.

Sources Breeze 1997; Cross and Slover 1996; Curtin 1996; Dames 1992; Danaher 1972; Dillon 1968; Evans-Wentz 1994; O'Sullivan 1966; Rosenberg 1997; Squire 1994.

 # CHAUCER, GEOFFREY

For an after-hours author, Geoffrey Chaucer carries a heavy load of firsts: first literate author to compose in Middle English, first English poet to use heroic verse, first English humorist, and first poet buried in Poet's Corner of Westminster Abbey. His role as developer of Chauntecleer, one of fable's most resilient antiheroes, and of a *pourquoi* story about a white crow turned black links him to the lively beast lore of the eastern Mediterranean and northern Europe and to the cock who figures in the fables of Marie de France and later in Johann Wolfgang von Goethe's *Reineke Fuchs* and Edmond Rostand's bird play *Chantecler*.

Born on Thames Street, London, around 1340, Chaucer—the step-grandson of Richard, grandson of Robert of Ipswich, and son of vintner John Chaucer, all duty agents for the wine commission—enjoyed the privileges of the merchant class. He came of age at Aldgate on the city's northeastern edge and entered formal service as page to the countess of Ulster when he reached 17. In the family tradition of civil careers, he worked as a court officer under Edward III and served in the military. In 1359, during the Hundred Years' War, French invaders captured Chaucer and briefly held him for ransom.

A shrewd student of human motivation, Chaucer took advantage of professional and business opportunities and rose from valet to clerk, comptroller, and port authority. At the upper end of his advancement, he served as Kent's justice of the peace before being elected member of parliament and knight. He owed his steady advancement to ability and the favor and friendship of John of Gaunt, the duke of Lancaster, third in line to the English throne. Against the shifting currents of court politics, the poet's rise required competency in finance, diplomacy, and governmental and military intrigue. During this period, he translated the medieval satire *Roman de la Rose* [Romance of the Rose] (ca. 1280) and composed *The Book of the Duchess* (1369), written in honor of his patron's wife,

Blanche of Lancaster, and the first portion of *Legend of Good Women* (1386), dedicated to Anne of Bohemia. From the vantage point of a bureaucratic fishbowl, Chaucer could observe the faults of all social levels of English folk as well as outsiders drawn to the commercial houses of London. Posted seven times to France, Italy, and Spain, he experienced the humanistic fervor that fueled Italy's cultural renaissance. While on official business in Florence and Genoa, he read the classic works of poets Francesco Petrarch and Dante Alighieri and the tales of Giovanni Boccaccio, Italy's master storyteller.

On return to England, Chaucer married Philippa de Roet, the queen's lady-in-waiting, whose ties to court bolstered his own. They produced three children, Thomas, Elizabeth, and Lewis, and established a happy domesticity, interrupted frequently by his trips to the Continent. In 1374, Chaucer occupied an office on the Thames northeast of London Bridge near the Tower to oversee purchase of leather, wool, and wine for Richard II, Edward's successor. As was common in the upward spiral of men like Chaucer, he met opposition from enemies he had acquired during his rise; as a stress-reliever after office hours, he wrote *The House of Fame* (ca. 1370), *The Parliament of Fowls* (ca. 1377), a satiric competition fable in which male eagles compete for a choice female, *Troilus and Criseyde* (ca. 1385), and the first 24 of 120 entries in his chivalric framework narrative, *The Canterbury Tales*, including "The Nun's Priest's Tale," his comic fable of Chauntecleer and his wife, Dame Pertelote.

Prefatory to "The Nun's Priest's Tale," *The Parliament of Fowls* introduces a pervasive motif in beast lore—the bird congress, which dates to Aristophanes's farce *The Birds* and the medieval bird fable *The Owl and the Nightingale*. Typified as occasional verse, the 700-line verse fable, set in a dream framework, probes the love mystique of St. Valentine's Day. Chaucer follows the medieval assumption that the day was sacred to love because it was the mating time of birds. Tied to the 1381 courtship of Anne of Bohemia and Richard II, the poem satirizes social disorder in an era of top-down feudal control. In a vernal bower dotted with blue, yellow, and red blossoms and the flash of silver fins plying a nearby stream, the birds take their foreordained positions:

> That is to seyn, the foules of ravyne
> Weere hyest set, and thanne the foules smale
> That eten, as hem Nature wolde enclyne,
> As worm or thyng of which I telle no tale;
> And water-foul sat lowest in the dale;
> But foul that lyveth by sed sat on the grene,
> And that so fele that wonder was to sene.
> [That is to say, predatory fowls
> Sat highest, and the small birds
> That eat, as nature so inclines,
> Of worms and things of which I tell no tale;
> And waterfowl sat lowest in the dale;
> But fowl that lived on seed sat on the green
> That were so many, a wonder to be seen.]
> (Chaucer 1961, 314)

The benevolent conclusion speaks of the "blisse and joye" of the chosen couple and the birds' mating roundel that blesses their union. The picture of marital felicity welcomes summer and toasts "Saynt Valentyn."

Around 1385, Chaucer wrote the prologue to his intended masterwork, *The Canterbury Tales*, England's first major poem in Middle English, and mapped out most of the text of a cycle of stories, each to be narrated by pilgrims on a religious trek to Canterbury. The setting was the site of the martyrdom of Archbishop Thomas à Becket, whom henchmen of King Henry II had murdered in the cathedral in 1170 for limiting royal power over the Church and its tempting treasury and real estate. Within a year after John of Gaunt left for Spain, Chaucer lost both his civil post in the custom house and Philippa, who died in 1386. Critics believe that the poet compensated for loss of wife and job by channeling his energies into collecting and writing additions to the tales.

Four years later, Chaucer returned to court favor and, as clerk of the King's Works, oversaw the royal residences and properties. Formal retirement on June 4, 1400, preceded financial security during the reign of Henry IV and a sinecure as Somerset's deputy forester. During Chaucer's remaining five months, he completed *Treatise on the Astrolabe, Envoy to Scogan, Envoy to Bukton*, and *To His Empty Purse.* With royal permission, he settled in a rented home in the Garden of St. Mary's Chapel, Westminster, and, in his sixtieth year, rapidly declined both physically and emotionally. Shortly before his death on October 25, 1400, as plague stalked London, he had second thoughts about earthly frivolity. Still clinging to his manuscripts, he scrawled in longhand a six-sentence epilogue and muttered "Farewel my bok and my devocioun!" (Gardner 1977, 314) Never acknowledging his role in the standardization of the English language and the advancement of English poesy, Chaucer considered himself a hobby writer, but his peers—John Gower, John Lydgate, Thomas Hoccleve, Eustache Deschamps, and Thomas Usk—honored him as poet and storyteller.

Unnoticed by early literary historians, Chaucer received no affirmation for his preference of vernacular "Angle-ish" over French, the cultivated language, or Latin, the scholar's and prelate's choice. Later, however, for his trust in the instincts of ordinary folk and their ebullient language, he earned the sobriquet "the father of the language." It was his enthusiasm for the vivid, high-spirited "Angle-ish" that ennobled his tales, each told in a style appropriate to the fictional teller. Chaucer's skillful characterizations pose a droll, often satiric jab at the wealthy, educated, or privileged as well as the low-level conniver, mountebank, malcontent, and trickster. According to a contemporary, Oxford churchman Thomas Gascoigne, the poet regretted choosing themes of earthly passion over piety. In the twentieth century, biographer Marchette Chute considers *The Canterbury Tales* a lasting monument to Chaucer's earthy good humor and affection for English folk. Of his immortal canon she concludes: "He did not do it for approval or for money or for fame. He did it for love." (Chute 1946, 332)

Because Chaucer wrote for an elite social stratum who enjoyed the privileges of education and leisure, both necessities for pleasure reading, he composed entertaining tales that would appeal to people for whom a reading knowledge of Anglo-Saxon, French, and Latin could be assumed. His ability to

Portrait of Geoffrey Chaucer (mezzotint after a painting in the British Museum)

adapt the verse prologue, fabliau, courtly romance, short story, drama, and beast fable suggests that his own reading background and lingual skills were considerable. Likewise impressive was his command of Bible, philosophy, astronomy, medicine, geography, and European and Mediterranean culture. Locked in his personal book chest were 60 prime volumes, a valuable reference library greater than some medieval universities could boast. An unusual man endowed with

"The Wife of Bath" illustration from Chaucer's *Canterbury Tales*

an understated nobility and worldly knowledge, he was an admirable sire for English literature.

The most influential work from the Middle English period, Chaucer's *Canterbury Tales* (1387) is a *comédie humaine* and miniature of medieval literature. Fast-paced and drenched in ribaldry, it amuses and delights for its humor, wisdom, and intriguing panoply of English society. According to the prologue, on April 17 a motley party of 29 pilgrims of varying social levels assemble at the Tabard Inn in Southwark outside London on the south bank of the Thames to launch a 60-mile religious journey the next morning at dawn. Their itinerary aims for Canterbury, one of the period's holy centers, where they will seek cure at the shrine of martyr Thomas à Becket (1118–1170), whom Chaucer calls "the holy blisful martyr." (Chaucer 1961, 17) This framework supplies him with a variety of social points of view and literary styles. With both subtle and overt digs at his characters, he enhances caricature with small observations and ironies that later grow into major flaws. Harry Bailly, the Tabard's jovial manager and a mask for Chaucer, proposes that each pilgrim entertain and instruct the company by telling two tales on the way to Canterbury and two on the return. All travelers were to contribute to a free supper to honor the winner of the competition.

Chaucer's 3,446-line fable "The Nun's Priest's Tale" and a 361-line animal story, "The Manciple's Tale," follow other narratives that introduce the motifs of conflict, evil destiny, marriage, and the battle between the sexes, all themes central to the fables. The arrangement of tales depends on the drawing of straws to determine who goes first. The winner, the knight, tells a story of chivalric knights, which precedes the bawdy fabliau of Robin, a dissolute miller. The troop beds down for the night at Dartford and gets a late start on their pilgrimage. The host tries to keep the storytelling in motion and calls on the man of law, who relates a three-stage legend. Bailly turns to the prioress, Madam Eglantine, a prissy, self-absorbed sybarite who narrates a stock anti-Semitic miracle story. On the group's approach to the town of Rochester, the halfway mark of the trek, Bailly instructs the monk to tell a happier story, but the monk draws out multiple tragedies from history.

The introduction to fable tends toward impish good fun when, to end the litany of morbid tales, the knight calls for a cheery tale. Sir John, the nun's priest, promises to entertain and begins Chaucer's most popular story, the rollicking, suspenseful beast fable of Chauntecleer the rooster, set at dawn on a May morning in the enclosed chicken yard of a "povre widwe" [poor widow]. (Chaucer 1961, 202) To milk the story for its mock-heroic details, Chaucer applies the high-flown diction and cadencing of Homer's *Iliad* and Virgil's *Aeneid* and the chivalric conventions of Arthurian lore. In contrast to the humble, circumspect dairywoman, Chauntecleer preens in glory. Like Aeneas on the night of the sacking of Troy, he experiences prophetic dreams of a yellow beast with glittering eyes and a black brush of a tail; his wife, Dame Pertelote, a well-read, opinionated hen, scorns his whimperings and blames the foreboding vision on a superfluity of red bile. To corroborate her belief that dreams are worthless, she cites Cato, the Roman censor, and urges that her mate take an herbal laxative of worms for a few days, followed by a litany of digestive aids—centaury, fumitory, caper-spurge, and hellebore plus laurel, blackthorn, and ground ivy—to rid his digestive tract of an offending vapor. The self-prescription furthers the motif of the meddling wife and mocks people who diagnose and treat themselves when they aren't sure of the ailment.

Chaucer complicates the narrative by having Chauntecleer riposte with interlocking fables-within-the-fable, a series of incidents, including hagiography on the life of Saint Kenelm. The exempla, or sermons, allusive homiletic material appropriate to Sir John's priestly background, are intended to prove that dreams foretell the future. The couple's difference of opinion, common to medieval *débat*, suits Chaucer's overall theme of disunity between husband and wife. Sir John smooths over domestic strife by describing Chauntecleer's courtly flattery of Pertelote's red topknot, the standard gentlemanly discounting of a wife who oversteps her place. The clever switch turns from dark omens to the beauty of the hen's face. He concludes with an epigram, *Mulier est hominis confusio* [Woman is humankind's confusion], which Chauntecleer mistranslates as "womman is mannes joye and al his bliss." (Chaucer 1961, 203) Chaucer rounds out the scene with a temporary semblance of order: Chauntecleer, surrounded by seven adoring hens, treading the hen yard like a lion to locate a grain of corn.

The crux of the fable pits Chauntecleer against the fox, medieval literature's wiliest trickster. At the beginning of spring, Chauntecleer's family is enjoying fair weather as danger lurks nearby in the person of Sir Russel Fox, a murderer on a par with Judas Iscariot and Genelon, the turncoat of the French epic, *Chanson de Roland*. Chaucer heightens melodrama with an allusion to Launcelot du Lac, whose adultery with Guinevere brought down Arthur's Camelot. As introduction to the climax, Chaucer mourns in mock epic style:

> O Chauntecleer, acursed be that morwe
> That thou into that yerd flaugh fro the bemes!
> Thou were ful wel ywarned by thy dremes
> That thilke day was perilous to thee.
> [Oh Chauntecleer, accursed be that morn
> That you flew from the beams into the yard!
> You were well warned by your dreams
> That this day would imperil you.]
> (Chaucer 1961, 203)

Out of character to the fable is Sir John's digression to opinions by St. Augustine and Boethius. With an effort at restraint, the teller reminds himself, "My tale is of a cok," and the story continues.

After repeating to readers that women's advice was Adam's undoing in paradise, Sir John returns to the blithe morning stroll, during which the rooster serenades at large, "murier than the mermayde in the see" [merrier than the mermaid in the sea]. (Chaucer 1961, 204) Instinct warns him that the fox lurks on the periphery, but he harkens to flattery, an ironic touch linking Chauntecleer's folly to Eve's. Unlike the Aesopic fabulist, who aims for succinct narrative, the teller draws out the rooster's peril as Chauntecleer stretches his neck, closes his eyes, and crows for Sir Russel. The strutting pose approximates the vaunting heroes of classic epic who, like Achilles, fall victim to hubris, the deadly sin of pride.

The falling action precedes the traditional *epimythium*, or concluding moral, by drawing parallels to human folly. The action moves briskly toward the cock's doom as Sir Russel, clutching his prey about the neck, spirits him toward the grove. Chauntecleer's wives summon the widow and her daughters by raising a grand ruckus, the stock uproar of medieval peasant lore. Amid the rush and cries of "Out! harrow! and weylaway! Ha! Ha! the fox!" Chaucer embroiders the bumptious turbulence with military clarions:

> Of bras they broghten bemes, and of box,
> Of horn, of boon in whiche they blewe and powped,
> And therwithal they shriked and they howped.
> [They brought trumpets of brass and boxwood,
> Of horn and bone, in which they blew and pooped,
> And thus they shouted and they whooped.]
> (Chaucer 1961, 205)

The turn of fortune is pure Aesop: The fox, taken in by the canny fowl, takes his advice to sneer at the screeching peasant family. Once he spreads his jaws, the rooster leaps free and perches high in a tree. Chaucer accords to Sir Russel the honor of the moral:

> God yeve him meschaunce,
> That is so undiscreet of governaunce
> That jangleth whan he sholde holde his pees.
> [God give him ill luck,
> Who is so indiscreet of self-control
> That chatters when he should hold his peace.]
> (Chaucer 1961, 205)

Sir John belabors the moral with a call for vigilance against flatterers and closes with a biblical injunction from Saint Paul to accept moral teaching as personal instruction. As to fable, Sir John adds, "Taketh the fruyt, and lat the chaf be stille" [Take the fruit and leave the chaff] and closes with a pious call to the good to wait upon God's beneficence.

The remainder of Chaucer's stories vary in style and presentation but keep to the subjects he has introduced. At the high point of Chaucer's medley, Alice, the worldly wife of Bath, delivers a lengthy diatribe on women's liberation and the significance of sexual harmony. Chaucer satirizes jealousy as the group nears Sittingbourne by having Friar Hubert and the summoner tell unflattering tales about each other. By now at the edge of Southwark, the group listens to the lengthy story of the Oxford clerk, a shy man who tells a six-part story of the obedient Griselda, wife of Walter. The telling so affects the host that he wishes that his wife had been listening. In contrast to this story of a faithful wife, the merchant recites the story of January, the aged husband of May. The squire's incomplete story of Gawain, a knight of Arthur, introduces the romantic tale of four magic gifts. The merry, white-haired franklin balances heroic lore with a second romantic tale about Arveragus and Dorigen. The intense story seems so real to Bailly that he rails at the villain. The pardoner eases Bailly's outrage and relates a chilling allegory. The second nun launches a tale of St. Cecilia's martyrdom.

Bailly's neat plan of orchestrating stories to entertain and enlighten changes at Boughton-under-Blean, a forest five miles from a regular stopping place near Ospring, where a canon and his yeoman join the travelers. The yeoman humiliates the canon by telling a two-part story about a canon who deceives a gullible priest. A brief to-do over Roger, the drunken cook, precedes the manciple's Aesopic beast fable about Phoebus, a bloated *pourquoi* story that explains how a meddling white crow is forever stained black. A stereotypical tell-tale bird in the tradition of Sanskrit, Arabic, and European lore, the crow divulges an act of cuckoldry. The insult degrades Phoebus, the Greco-Roman god of light and creativity whom Ovid describes as living like an earthly man vulnerable to trickery and ruination. Phoebus slays his wife with one shot, then in regret, breaks his bow and arrows.

> "Traitour," quod he, "with tongue of scorpioun,
> Thou hast me broght to my confusioun;

Allas, that I was wroght! why nere I deed?
O deere wyf! o gemme of lustiheed!"
["Traitor," said he, "with scorpion's tongue,
You have brought me to disorder,
Alas, that I was born! Why am I not dead?
Oh dear wife! Oh jewel of joy!"]
(Chaucer 1961, 227)

The gabby crow, who is irate over being snatched featherless, is decked in black feathers and loses his sweet voice. The smug manciple speaks through Phoebus a warning about controlling wicked gossip. His *epimythium* exalts Aesopic fable with the advice, "Kepe well thy tonge, and thenk upon the crowe" [Guard your tongue and think upon the crow]. (Chaucer 1961, 227) Prefiguring Chaucer's eleventh-hour retraction, the epigram draws out the tension of a passing moment when the speaker must either commit thought to words or lose the opportunity.

See also Chauntecleer.

Sources Baugh 1948; Chaucer 1961, 1966, 1969, 1992; Chute 1946; Douglas 1948; Gardner 1977; Robinson 1957; Scott 1974.

 # CHAUNTECLEER

One of literature's enduring fictional beasts, Chauntecleer or Chanticleer, literally "Sing clear," is the exalted cock, a wry caricature of the self-deluding he-man of Geoffrey Chaucer's *The Nun's Priest's Tale* (1387) and of Edmond Rostand's play *Chantecler* (1899). An expansion of Aesopic animal lore, the parodied fowl and his misadventures draw on the conventions of European fable: vaunting pride, lurking predator, and lacklogic deterrents to stalkers. As watchman over the widow's hen yard, Chauntecleer glories in a magnificent call, crenellated red comb, lofty tail, and inky black bill. Decked with gold feathers, azure legs, and toes with lily-white claws, the rooster maintains a fine opinion of himself. For all his strut, he gave in to Lady Pertelote, his mate, when she was only a week old. As examples of vanity, the mated pair equate with Chaucer's fictional guildsmen and their wives, Madam Eglantine, the Wife of Bath, and the bantyish squire, all marked to varying degrees in character, speech, and tastes by the peacock's self-congratulation.

Chaucer perpetuates the droll parody of the macho man in the tiptoe grace of the rooster who temporarily reasserts his confidence. He copulates twenty times with his mate, then with a face as serious as a lion's, he strolls the yard and digs up kernels with his toes. To his one-word call of "chuk," the other six wives run to him, stirring his ego with their clucking blandishments. Blind-sided by his joy in the bright sun of May, Chauntecleer tumbles low from a shaft of fate, which Chaucer sharpens with a pseudo-chivalric comparison to Sir Launcelot du Lac, whose adultery with Queen Guinevere forms one of English literature's enduring tragic scenarios. The mention of her seducer would not have escaped the notice of the literati of Chaucer's day,

Edmond Rostand, author of the play *Chantecler*

nor does the modern reader fail to catch the deft undercutting of the rooster's vapid egotism.

Chaucer also compares Chauntecleer's situation to Adam's plight, deliberately belaboring the rooster's failure to heed his wife's warnings and the role of women in bringing woe to men. While the head wife lies in a hazy dust bath and her sister hens bask in the sun, Chauntecleer is gazing on a butterfly, a symbol of frivolity, when he meets his enemy, Russel the col-fox, and immediately jerks away in terror. The fox's soothing, ego-pleasing compliments to the rooster's voice immediately throw his victim off guard. In the springing of the trap, Chaucer compares the violent snatching of the rooster to the murder of Richard II. Epic shrieks rend the skies louder than when Troy fell and Rome burned. Chaucer drops his noble diction with the entrance of the widow and her daughters, who cry in frenzied peasant vernacular. The barnyard fills with Colle the dog, servants Talbot and Gerland, Malkyn the spinner brandishing a distaff, and a trail of animals—a cow and calf, hogs, ducks, geese, even a swarm of bees. Like Jack Straw and his followers, all raise a clatter of alarm.

The falling action of the beast fable returns to the high moral tone and elegant phrasing that Chaucer introduced earlier. Tricking the fox by turning vanity against his enemy, the vaunting, self-congratulatory antihero flees the scene in one graceful motion—he spreads his wings and alights in a treetop. He admits that he was wrong to fall for flattery the first time but seems, at least for the moment, to have profited from his near fatal error. The fox, too late smart, can only remark that the wise guard their tongue.

Some five centuries after Chaucer's *Canterbury Tales*, French romantic dramatist Edmond Rostand rejuvenated the image of Chaunticleer in his four-act verse drama *Chantecler*. An old-fashioned poet following in the wake of the Parnassian symbolists—Baudelaire, Rimbaud, and Verlaine—and oblivious to the stirrings of realism and naturalism, Rostand continued the tradition of French romance. A natural scholar of classic literature, he had established a place in world drama with *Cyrano de Bergerac* (1897), his masterpiece historical tragedy wrote for Benoît-Constant Coquelin, legendary comic star of the French national theater. For Sarah Bernhardt, the mistress of the French stage, Rostand composed sophisticated plays—*The Faraway Princess, The Woman of Samaria,* and the six-act historical drama *The Eaglet*. Also for Coquelin, Rostand wrote *Chantecler*, a witty, satiric animal fable, but the star died before the work was complete. Published in the June–September 1910 issues of *Hampton's Magazine*, the play appeared on stage, starring Sacha Guitry, but failed immediately.

Like Aristophanes's farce *The Birds*, the befeathered cast of *Chantecler* lists the stock figures of fable—Patou the dog, cat, toads, and rabbits plus a rogue's gallery of fowl, including the woodpecker, blackbird, peacock, nightingale, screech owl, pigeon, fighting cock, turkey, duck, gander, capon, warbler, heron, guinea fowl, pheasant, and assorted chickens. As the farm family's wagon rattles off to the fair, they leave behind an animal drama. The gathered fowl await the showoff of the barnyard:

> The One he is whose song is more an ornament to the landscape than the white hamlet to the hill! The One he is whose cry pierces the blue horizon like a gold-threaded needle stitching the hilltops to the sky! The Cock he is! When you would praise him, call him the Cock! (Rostand July 1910, 746)

With an impressive pedigree, Chantecler, son of a Gascon hen prized by Henry IV, hails from the neighborhood of Pau. His peers know him as the singer of song that "inspires, encourages, makes labor light, and keeps off birds of prey." (Rostand July 1910, 748)

Much of the humor of Rostand's rooster play is the epic crescendo of epithets and compliments before the hero appears on the garden wall. A Quixotic mimicker of knight errantry not too far removed from Cyrano, Chantecler spouts ornate verse to the rising sun before setting to rights the business of the day.

Among his self-important chores are limbering up the glottis and ridding his tail of flecks of eggshell. In Act II, his pomposity surfaces in self-serving remarks to the pheasant hen:

> Such a burden of responsibility treading upon me! . . . I feel the whole future depending upon an incomprehensible something which might perchance fail me! Do you understand now the anguish gnawing me?. . . I, for whom my born work remains a mystery, I, possessed ever by the fear of the morrow, am I sure of finding my song in my heart! (Rostand July 1910, 44)

Beyond a minuscule plot in which the night birds scheme to have the pheasant lure him to the forest into the grasp of a killer gamecock, the focus of Rostand's stage fluff is a reprise of the strutting fop, the preening ruler of the hen yard who trusts that nothing is so vital to the farm as the cock's cry to awaken the sun.

See also Chaucer, Geoffrey; Reynard the Fox.

Sources Baugh 1948; Chaucer 1969, 1992; Chute 1946; Enroth 1969; Gardner 1977; Gassner and Quinn 1969; Keates and Hornak 1994; Robinson 1957; Rostand 1910; Scott 1974.

 # CHRISTIAN FABLE

Because the education of the learned typically consists of traditional lore grounded in classical studies, authors have maintained well into the Christian era the value of fables as exempla and didactic lessons. Fables as models of discretion and right thinking derive from many sources, including the pagan stories of the Mediterranean, Zoroastrian, and Sufist lore, Gypsy tales, and Oriental stories adapted from Confucius and Buddhist jataka tales. Around 1000 C.E., Pope Sylvester II, born Gerbert of Auvergne, introduced Arabian learning in the story "Strike on This Spot," an Egyptian exemplum told by Caliph Abu-Bakr around 630 C.E. The fable of Dhun-Nun's discovery of the lost science of manufacture draws meaning from an inscription on a stone statue that instructs readers to "Strike on this spot for treasure." (Shah 1982, 55) Dhun-Nun succeeds where others fail because he studies the simplistic injunction and deduces that the spot is the end of the shadow, where he unearths a trapdoor and a cache of tools and instructions.

Additional Christian application of Aesopic fables derives from St. Gregory of Tours, who shunned the false fables of the pagans and substituted his own style, as in "The Boy and the Grapes" in Book IV of *The Miracles of St. Martin* (sixth century C.E.), and from Paulus Diaconus [Paul the Deacon] or Paul Warnefried, a Lombard who joined the Benedictines at Monte Cassino in the late eighth century C.E. and reprised three classic fables—"The Fable of the Sick Lion," "The Calf and the Stork," and "The Gout and the Flea." From the canon of rhymes, jingles, and earthy lyrics of the Rhineland comes "The Priest and the Wolf," an anonymous dilemma tale from the University of Cambridge collection that dates to 1000 C.E. The scenario is typical of confrontations between the priestly and profane, often with comic or satiric results.

Other models of folk verse derive from the Goliardic tradition. The exuberant secular verse cycle of *studentenlieder* [student songs] later known as the *Carmina Burana* [Songs of Beuron or Beuern] (twelfth century) was originally compiled and illustrated around 1230 and amended and added to until the early fourteenth century. It was recovered in Bavaria at Benediktbeuern, which lies between Innsbruck and Munich, but was not published until 1847. The identity of a few of the authors seems certain: Peter Abélard, Walter of Châtillon, Reinmar der Alte, Heinrich von Morungen, Walther von der Vogelweide, Otloh of St. Emmeram, Bishop Marbod of Rennes, Godfrey of Winchester, Godfrey of St. Victor, Dietmar von Aist, Neidhart von Reuenthal, and Der Marner.

A cultural curiosity, the *Carmina Burana* is comprised of crude, macaronic songs sung by wandering students to whom the fictional Golias or Guzzler served as champion and patron saint. Fleshed out with random profane verses, barroom ballads, ecclesiastical plays, hymns, crusader's anthems, rambunctious gaming and wooing songs, pastorals, dances, satires on church doctrine and practice, doggerel and animal noises, and jeering ditties, these diverse vernacular works credit minstrels, prelates, and troubadours for a widespread mob mentality sparked by an irreverent, raffish spirit bent on carnality and fun. Although rooted in Christian tradition, risqué lyrics sprang from the liberal arts that wandering students sampled during brief stints at major European universities. To earn their way from school to school, they juggled, entertained, riddled, and sang at banquets in a polyglot style that salted simplified phrases in liturgical Latin with bits of medieval French, Provençal, Greek, and Middle High German.

"Olim lacus colueram" [Once I Dwelt on the Lake], a popular segment in thumping trochaic tetrameter and feminine rhyme, dramatizes the dilemma of a spitted swan spiced and roasted on a rotisserie, anticipating the serving platter. Done to a turn, he moans:

> Eram nive candidior,
> Quavis ave formosior,
> Modo sum corvo nigrior;
> Miser, miser!
> [I was once whiter than snow,
> Shapelier than any bird you can name,
> Now I am blacker than a crow:
> Oh me, Oh my!]
> (Harrington 1925, 379)

In a droll testimonial and death plaint, the swan regrets that he has wasted his youth and, like a wandering student, embroiled himself in vice. Gnashing his beak, he expires to supply a delectable main course to chomping diners. Reprised in 1937 by composer Carl Orff, the fable, contained in "In Taberna" [In the Tavern], becomes the twelfth part of a cantata that features 25 of the initial collection of 350 lyrics. Although it lacks the "once upon a time" quality of fable, the scenario suits the definition of *fabula* in its compressed action, anthropomorphized animal protagonist, and didactic intent. It bursts the boundaries of fable by reaching beyond morality to drollery.

The spirited verse and prose tales of the thirteenth century enlarged and enlivened the canon of Christian fable. Westphalian clergyman Gerhard von Minden composed "Journey in a Well," a trickster tale set in a well with tandem pails. As the fox lures the wolf to uncertain peril at the bottom of the shaft, the returning bucket carries the fox back to safety. His cynical rejoinder clashes with models of Christian charity: "That's how it is in the world; one goes up and the other goes down." (Green 1965, 156) Von Minden struggles to square the theme with Christian principle by drawing a parallel between the weight of the animals and the enormity of their sins. An unlikely dust-off pictures the fox accepting his penance along with his freedom. Later in the thirteenth century, Petrus Alphonsus, a Christianized Jew and godson of Alphonse I, King of Aragon, collected Arab fables for similar purpose—to provide parents teachable models of probity for their children. Dotted with dialogue are "A New Use for the Gold-Brick Game" and "A Storyteller's Trick," a story-within-a-story told in the style of Scheherazade, along with "A Friend in Need Is a Friend Indeed," a dying father's advice on how to test true friendship. Devoid of the survivalism of purely literary fare, the stories create an artificial climate to nurture Christian tenets.

A contemporary of Petrus Alphonsus, Walter Map (or Mapes), a worthy chancellor of London, canon of St. Paul's, and archdeacon of Oxford appears to have written his own Goliardic entries in *De Nugis Curialium* [Nuggets from the Meetinghouse] (late thirteenth century), a miscellany of gossip and satire containing two verse fables, "The Dialogue between Water and Wine" and "The Dialogue between the Body and the Soul." In the latter, the body plays the part of the querulous sinner who pleads, "Dic mihi, si noveris, argumento clari, exeunt spiritu a carne quid sit caro? . . . Videtne? vel loquitur?" [Tell me, if you know, in clear logic, when the spirit leaves the body, what becomes of the flesh? . . . Does it see? or speak?] (Harrington 1925, 399) The spirit spares no anguish in describing the agony of souls doomed to the flames of hell. Such discourse was useful pulpit material to prelates facing a hardened citizenry for whom carnal pleasure was an antidote to everyday hardships.

The late Middle Ages perpetuated the tradition of Aesopic lore and folk fare alongside pulpit exempla. An English Cistercian monk, Odo of Cerinton (Cherington or Sherrington), collected fables in prose about 1200, most of which rely on Phaedrus and Reynard the Fox stories rather than Christian models. The best of the lot include "The Mice in Council," a reprise of "Belling the Cat," and "The Stupid Men of Willebeg," a fool tale about taxpayers who strap a bag of money about a rabbit's neck. A French prelate, Jacques de Vitry, made his reputation on preaching and rose from bishop of Acon in 1216 to cardinal bishop of Tusculum in 1227. Among his *Sermones Vulgares* [Ordinary Speeches] are "An Overconfident Astrologer," the tale of a sky-watcher who predicts the date of a king's death, "A Spoiled Horse," a folk fable, and "Penny Wise and Pound Foolish," a fool tale about a crafty boy whom Henry the doorkeeper instructs to buy a purse. The errand boy purchases a lesser bag and keeps half the money for himself, then learns that the doorkeeper had intended to give him the bag filled with money. Vitry's beast tale, "The Wolf's Logic," turns on the cynicism of a wolf who advises a lost lamb with specious logic: "Melius est ut comedam te quam quod mater tua amittat te" [It is better that I should eat you than that your mother should lose you]. (Harrington 1925, 426) Typical of Middle Ages misogyny is "An Ancient Saying Illustrated," which delights in the devil's quarrelsome wife, who gives her spouse such grief that he proposes returning her to her father. To his father-in-law's question, "Where is home?" the devil replies, "Infernus, ubi nunquam tantam discordiam vel molestiam sustinui" [Hell, where I never suffer such quarreling and misery].

As the Reformation battered entrenched Catholicism, ministers continued to put advice-laden fable to use in illustrative sermons. In the early sixteenth century, famed German minister and reformer Martin Luther translated fables into mundane anti-Papist homilies and pulpit illustrations. In "The Mouse and the Frog," the predominance of lesson to action tips the Aesopic model toward hard-line sermonizing. The fable's emphasis on trickery concludes with a warning to Christians: "Be careful whom you go about with. The world is full of treachery and falsehood. Anybody who has influence over another has him, as it were, in a sack. But treachery often strikes back at its own master." (Green 1965, 74) A more lethal story, "The Wolf and the Lamb," reminds hearers to avoid arguing with bigger, stronger adversaries. A familiar tale to readers of Aesop and La Fontaine, the story places in harm's reach a callow lamb, who takes issue with the wolf for accusing him of muddying the stream. The wolf's senseless retorts press him to rage. Luther abandons the story without a moral at the last line, which pictures the lamb torn to tasty bites. Himself a lamb during his hard-fought conversion of followers to Protestantism, Luther may have identified with the incautious neophyte who accused an aggressor of muddled logic.

Among late seventeenth-century Augustinian prelates, Abraham a Sancta Clara, an Austrian named Ulrich Megerle in his premonastery days, enriched his sermons with fables. Tinged with folk dialect, "The Young Fox and the Old Fox" contrasts mismatched animal voices with witty repartee:

> "Father, I want to fly."
> "You young dreamer," rejoined the old one, "what nonsense is this?"
> "Father I want to fly," repeated the young one.
> "You whipper-snapper," said the old fox, you've hardly got enough hair
> on your tail to wipe a blackboard, yet you want to fly!" (Green 1965, 69)

Reminiscent of an exchange between Daedalus and Icarus from Ovid's mythology, this discussion of flying leads to a bad end. To the oldster's concern, the bloody young flier remarks, "The flying . . . was as smooth as could be, Father. But the landing—why, the devil saw to that!" (Green 1965, 69) Sancta Clara's spirited give and take provides families with a model impasse between the old adviser and the young daredevil, a motif found worldwide in intergenerational quid pro quo.

A priest and storyteller of the early nineteenth century, Johann Peter Hebel, sometimes labeled a German Robert Burns, amassed folklore in his native Heidelberg. Through skill and determination, he achieved the rank of headmaster and overseer of the Evangelical Church. An influence on poets Johann Wolfgang von Goethe and Rainer Maria Rilke and on fiction writer Franz Kafka, Hebel wrote understated verse in the folksay of his homeland. In one example, "The Starling of Segringen," a barber teaches his pet bird clever phrases, but the bird prefers to utter the master's common epithets—"God's will be done," "Well, well, did you ever!" and "in company." (Green 1965, 95) Thus, when customers encourage the bird to perform, they hear the nettled Barber's cry of "You blockhead!" The jocular plot ends with the starling talking itself out of the bird-catcher's snare. Hebel, intent on warning the naive of dissolute companions, cannot pass up a "nota bene" [note well], which concludes "Many a young man who roams around rather than stay at home, has fallen into a snare 'in company' and never got out again."

A Christian apologist of the late nineteenth century, French poet Francis Jammes, a native of Tournay in the Pyrenees, celebrates folk communities in lyric free verse. He develops one of St. Francis's themes, humanity's cruelty to animals in *De l'Angélus de l'aube à l'Angélus du soir* [From Dawn Bell to Evening Bell] (1898). Worn and dejected, an aged cart horse collapses in harness and wings heavenward. At St. Peter's station, the horse asks about his departed mother. The horse's unselfishness wins him a place in heaven among departed animals. Jammes enlarges on the theme of earthly viciousness by naming as corroborative sufferers the wretched who had carried heavy stones, those who had circled merry-go-rounds all day, and the ones that perished needlessly in the bullfighting arena. In contrast to cold, pain, and weariness on earth, heaven's animals frolic and suckle their young in peace. They have no need to fear the world's cruelty, for "not one single human being was to be found in all this paradise." (Green 1965, 140) A benign fable, Jammes's kindly story omits the coal-stoked hell of conversion stories to encourage livestock owners and animal masters voluntarily to respect their four-footed brethren.

The best-loved Christian fables of the nineteenth century were written by social and historical novelist Charles Dickens, author of *A Christmas Carol* (1843) and *Christmas Books* (1852). At the height of his fame, Dickens was able to move readers as well as audiences at his lectures and public readings to repudiate sources of human misery by intense glimpses of poverty and the cruelties of such social institutions as orphanages, workhouses, corrupt law courts, and boarding schools. A meticulous researcher, he visited many of the locations that became settings for his books. He used his craft and humanitarian spirit to denounce corrupt officials, stony-hearted business leaders, and impersonal landholders and bankers. Through intensely melodramatic characterization, he ridiculed the vanity, materialism, and complacency of Victorian England and declared that greed and snobbery separated classes and enabled the privileged to overlook or ignore those suffering want, exploitation, and neglect.

Composed during one of Dickens's financial nadirs, *A Christmas Carol* appeared only five years after *Oliver Twist* (1838) and preceded Dickens's most popular novels—*David Copperfield* (1850), *A Tale of Two Cities* (1859), and *Great Expectations* (1861). In mid-October 1843, the author faced a 25 percent reduction in his journalist's salary of £200. Influenced by Washington Irving's *The*

An illustration from *A Christmas Carol* by Charles Dickens

Keeping of Christmas at Bracebridge Hall (1820), he wrote a story that elevates Christmas without glorifying the sectarian concepts of Christ, virgin birth, manger miracles, shepherds, magi, or angels. He completed the text of his first unserialized novella by the end of November—just in time for holiday publication—and expected the best-seller to earn £1,000. Although it was immensely popular in the United Kingdom and America, production costs reduced the profit to £250, which was not enough to quit his debts.

The marvel of Dickens's holiday fable is its growth into a December classic—a staple of drama, recitation, ballet, art, tableau, advertising, and silent enjoyment for celebrants of Christmas the world over. The story, a dramatic montage of Christmases past, present, and future, steals into readers' memories like a holiday carol. It's a rare person who can't quote Tiny Tim's toast, "God bless us, every one." Every Christmas season, millions of people watch one of numerous film versions. Others reread the tale of the emergence of love and open-heartedness in literature's darkest miser, Ebenezer Scrooge, whose reclamation from pinchpenny misanthrope to beneficent lover of humankind begins with four ghostly visits and concludes with a merry celebration and the good news that Tiny Tim will live. The reformation of Scrooge has become so much a part of world culture that his name equates with mean-spiritedness and greed just as the title resurrects hope of reclamation and redemption.

Not only a nonsectarian plea for generosity, the story also dramatizes the activities of two families observing traditions of Victorian England, where holly, roast goose, pudding, charity, religious ceremonies, parlor games, gifts, dancing, and hospitality entertained citizens and warmed their hearts. The growth of Dickens's fame as a holiday writer led to his publication of *The Chimes* the next year and to two magazines, *Household Words* and *All the Year Round*, which featured Christmas articles. To the end of his life, Dickens gave profitable annual readings from *A Christmas Carol*, expressing with drama, voice, and gesture the timeless charm of his fable.

The late nineteenth century produced additional Christmas fables, two of which were written by American poet and short fiction writer Henry Van Dyke. A Congregational minister in Newport, Rhode Island, and ambassador to Holland and Luxembourg from 1913 to 1916, he came from respectable Dutch stock and claimed a Princeton-educated physician as grandfather and a father who pastored the First Presbyterian Church of Germantown, Pennsylvania. Van Dyke's published sermons earned him fame, including a translation of the German romantic poet Friedrich Novalis's *The Blue Flower*, and two original Christmas fables: *The Story of the Other Wise Man* (1896) and *The First Christmas Tree* (1897).

Van Dyke's most popular work, *The Story of the Other Wise Man*, is a gauzy fabrication drawn on the inspiring figure of Artaban the Median, an astronomer and humanist of Ecbatana who accepts an invitation to join the Magi as they follow a pulsing star toward Bethlehem. The modern framework of the Christmas story is set among human ills, which Van Dyke pictures in graphic description that a parish minister would know firsthand:

> The year had been full of sickness and sorrow. Every day brought trouble. Every night was tormented with pain. They are very long—those nights when

one lies awake, and hears the laboring heart pumping wearily at its task, and watches for the morning, not knowing whether it will ever dawn." (Van Dyke 1923, xi)

The author pictures the hero as the consummate piddler, easily drawn into other people's troubles, even though he rides the great horse Vasda, which carries him rapidly toward his destination. The wandering mage chances to witness Herod's slaughter of the innocents, spends his lustrous pearl to rescue a girl from Macedonian soldiers, and arrives at Golgotha 33 years too late to pay his respect to the Christ Child, who is by then a grown man facing execution. Van Dyke concludes his fable with Artaban's death as he is caught up in the temblor that marks Christ's crucifixion. Near death, Arbatan hears a voice from heaven. Quoting from Matthew 15:40, Van Dyke cites Christ's words as though they were intended for the old mage: "Verily I say unto thee, inasmuch as thou hast done it unto one of the least of these my brethren, thou hast done it unto me." The citation serves both as *epimythium* and as a charge to Van Dyke's congregation.

Apart from the tales of the aforementioned learned authors, theologians, and preachers, Christian fable also claims folk origins. For example, the Romini of Ripanj, Yugoslavia, express their Gypsy traits in a dialogue between God and St. Peter entitled "How the Gypsies Became Musicians." The story uplifts the fate of a homeless people through the blessing of the fiddle, which God places on St. Peter's shoulders. Intended as a humanizing element in drinking halls where competition often led to violence, fiddle music served God's purpose to lift spirits and prevent quarrels. St. Peter, overjoyed that the fiddle had life-preserving powers, encouraged God to make more fiddlers. In the closing dialogue, God asks:

"But who could there be?"
"Let there be the Gypsies," answered St. Peter. "Let them amuse people so that they may not shed blood when they drink and make merry."
"Let it be so," said God.
And so it was.
(Tong 1989, 103)

The benevolence of the fiddle story typifies piquant, often wistful Gypsy fable, which ameliorates the harsh life of wandering outcasts who traditionally contend with prejudice and genocide.

In Volume 1 of *British Folktales*, folklorist Katharine Briggs records the peasant versions of brief encounters with Christ, a motif that also permeates the religious lore of Jews, Mormons, and Buddhists. In a Lancashire version, "Christ and the Peas," Christ calls on a poor woman and asks for food. To her reply that she cooks stones in her kettle to make her children think they are peas, he instructs her to lift the lid. She obeys and finds that the pot is indeed full of peas. A typical poor people's miracle, the story demonstrates obedience. Lacking a moral, the fable bears intrinsic worth by linking piety among the poor with an earthly reward for faith. Variations of the story alter the outcome from reward to punishment. An ominous wandering Christ tale from Gloucestershire, "The Owl Was a Baker's Daughter," turns a girl into an owl for being stingy with bread.

A contemporary of Van Dyke, North Carolinian William Sydney Porter, popular short fiction writer and creator of the surprise ending, is better known by his pen name, O. Henry. In 1895, he was convicted—and later exonerated—for embezzling $4,702.94. He fled to Honduras and South America, then returned to serve his sentence when he learned that his wife was near death from tuberculosis. For three years and three months, he bore #30664 on his shirt in the Ohio State Penitentiary in Columbus, where he worked in the dispensary. From his cell, he studied and pondered human dilemmas and published the first 14 of his 600 clever, episodic short stories and human interest vignettes.

At the beginning of the twentieth century, O. Henry produced a popular Christmas fable, "The Gift of the Magi" (1905). The simple story about two tender nobodies, Jim and Della Young, expresses O. Henry's forte—populist plots that celebrate forgivable shortcomings and endings based on an unforeseen zinger, the quick catch in the last lines that reveals a tidy change of heart or moral requital. Seeking for funds for the right gifts for each other, the penniless pair have no cash to spare and only two items to take pride in—Jim's gold pocket watch and Della's cascade of brown hair. The author chooses Della as his focus in this story of Christmas Eve penury:

> One dollar and eighty-seven cents. That was all. And sixty cents of it was in pennies. Pennies saved one and two at a time by bulldozing the grocer and the vegetable man and the butcher until one's cheek burned with silent imputation of parsimony that such close dealing implied. Three times Della counted it. One dollar and eighty-seven cents. And the next day would be Christmas. (O. Henry 1986, 360)

At Madame Sofronie's, Della swaps her hair for $20, but the fable ranges beyond her afternoon's shopping trip to ennoble and reaffirm the Christmas spirit.

With a mix of alarm and misunderstanding, O. Henry's double surprise carries the last half of the story to its end. The husband's inexplicable behavior at dinner implies fearful reprisal or, at the least, disappointment. After Della opens his gift of tortoise shell combs to adorn her short bob and he receives the platinum fob chain for his pawned watch, the two are left to meager chops for dinner and nothing to spare. Discreetly, the author withdraws from their domestic impasse to append his moral: "In a last word to the wise of these days let it be said that of all who give gifts these two were the wisest. Of all who give and receive gifts, such as they are wisest. Everywhere they are wisest. They are the Magi." (O. Henry 1986, 364) In concluding the short story in the style of a fable, the storyteller elevates his "foolish children" to symbols of Christmas love and selflessness. His well-matched duo, aptly named Mr. and Mrs. Young, extend the holiday theme to a prediction of marital harmony based on *agape*, the Greek concept of giving without thought of return.

An offshoot of Christian fable is a body of Mormonia, which reprises Protestant and Catholic pulpit material in the folk experiences of southwestern settlers. In 1956, Austin and Alta Fife attempted to dispel faulty notions about Mormonism by collecting a volume of Mormonia, *Saints of Sage and Saddle*, which follows the cult from Calvinist persecution in England across the prairies to the Great Basin of Utah. The study of Mormonism and its abhorrence of European mores opens on the epic trek west, which concluded July 24, 1847, with the arrival of the Saints in the Great Salt Lake Valley. The Fifes cite favorite marching songs: "Ye Saints Who Dwell on Britain's Shore," "And Should We Die before Our Journey's Through," and a salute to the handcarters, "As on the Road the Carts Were Pulled." Beloved fables of Christ in disguise reverberate through local collections with examples of lonely widows and hungry children whom the deity blesses for their obedience and faith. Additional southwestern animal stories and story-songs laud the tender-hearted who feed and water weary burros and toss crusts to the prowling lobo. The corpus of Mormon stories, tied to the barren and unforgiving desert, enhances Christian fables with the promise of blessing to those who persevere and who share their limited means with fellow outcasts and the poor and hungry.

One of the strongest strands of English fable in recent times comes from English fabulist Richard Adams, author of *Watership Down* (1974), *The Unbroken Web: Stories and Fables* (1980), and *Tales from Watership Down* (1997). In *The Unbroken Web*, Adams relates additions to English bird lore in "Why the Robin's Breast Is Red," a *pourquoi* story that belongs to the Christianized Arthurian canon. Set on Good Friday, the tale tells of the robin that made a nest near the gate of Jerusalem, where it witnesses the torment of Jesus on his way to execution on Calvary's hill. A curious bird, the robin, darting from bush to hedge, follows Jesus past the Stations of the Cross to Golgotha. As the crucifixion progresses to its barbaric conclusion, the robin tries to pull the nails from Jesus's hand and the crown of thorns from his head. A centurion stops a soldier from stoning the robin. In the end, Jesus blesses the bird. Adams identifies Longinus as the witness who retrieved Jesus's corpse and the savior of the robin, whom he transports to England to bring luck to people's houses. A beneficent story, it departs from heavier proselytizing common to the Middle Ages to connect compassion with good fortune.

See also Shaw, George Bernard.

Sources Adams 1980; Brick, http://www.willandcompany.com; Briggs 1991; Cantor 1994; *Carmina Burana* 1974; "Charles Dickens," http://cp-tel.net, http://www.mala; "A Christmas Carol," http://www.neurop2, http://www.susqu.edu; Curtius 1953; Dickens 1963; "Dickens Page," http://ernie.lang.nagoya-u.ac.jp; "Dickens Project: University of California," http://hum.ucsc.edu; Fife and Fife 1956; Giuliano and Collins 1986; Harrington 1925; Henry 1986; Kunitz 1942; "The Other Wise Man," http://www.spirituality.org; Parlett 1986; Raby 1997; Shah 1982; Snodgrass, *Encyclopedia of the Frontier Literature* 1997, *Encyclopedia of Southern Literature* 1997; Tong 1989; Van Dyke 1923.

 # CRUELTY JOKE

An offshoot of folly literature, the cruelty joke is by nature humorous, but it overlies a vicious hidden agenda. Usually rural in setting, as with the front porch stretchers Zora Neale Hurston recalled from Joe Clarke's jot 'em down store, it makes light of race and gender differences, illiteracy, spouse or animal abuse, misfortune, and physical imperfections or freakish conditions in humans and beasts, especially stuttering, harelip, slew foot, humpback, and squints. By setting up one group of characters as foolish and another as wise, the hard-handed jest implies that nonwhites, women, homosexuals, nonreaders, or handicapped people are, by nature of their condition, also fools and the perfect marks for tricksters, egotists, and con artists. A joke that is common to the vein of racial one-upmanship is "The Mule and the 'Highlife,'" a story recorded in Vance Randolph's *Hot Springs and Hell and Other Folk Jests and Anecdotes from the Ozarks* (1965). When the stranger steps in to speed up a colored man's mule, he applies a dollop of "highlife" under the animal's tail, causing it to bolt and shatter the wagon and disperse its contents over the countryside. The cruelty angle threatens the driver as well after he asks for a dose of the "highlife." Implicit in the humor of this type of fable is the menacing superiority of the stranger, whom the teller implies is a white racist itching to befuddle and possibly injure or kill both the black wagoneer and his mule.

Gender jests are another form of cruelty joke against a targeted group. Kenneth K. Krakow's *Georgia Place-names* (1975) repackages a lame tale of the kidnapper who uncovers a female victim too ugly to tolerate. In his cry of "Resack her!" is the makings of the place name Resaca, a town in Georgia. A subtler joke that requires hand gestures to complete is "The Last Word" from Marielle Glenn Hartsfield's *Tall Betsy and Dunce Baby: South Georgia Folktales* (1987), an *agon* or competition fable that pits husband against wife. As the couple argue the merits of knife and scissors to snip a piece of leather, the wife falls in the river and goes down for the third time. Her hand bobs to the surface to open her fingers in a sign of scissors, a V-shaped gesture that also stands for victory. The fable is a common example of husband-over-wife logic but shares the stage with its twin, the wife-over-husband scheme.

Often, the cruelty joke calls on a cast of simpletons who derive enlightenment from an outsider, the scenario that Mark Twain embroidered into his classic story "The Celebrated Jumping Frog of Calaveras County" (1867). Depending on the social thrust of the jest, the fools may range from the New England uplands to the agrarian South. Their rescuers are often members of groups who flaunt racial, cultural, or national superiority, for example, the European aristocrat visiting a clueless Vermont farmer or the Philadelphia Yankee interviewing hayseeds in Mississippi. When the locals control the plot, the outsider becomes the butt, as in the story of the testy carpetbagger whose horse refuses to pull the buggy until the Tennessee farm lad unties the bridle from the hitching post. A common subset of fable, the framework of the cruelty joke depends on a belief in superiority, whether stated, acted out, or implied.

Cruelty jokes based on physical deformity such as harelip or withered limb carry folk viciousness beyond the scope of enlightenment. In B. A. Botkin's *A Treasury of American Folklore* (1944), the story of a family with mouths skewed up, down, and sideways ridicules their efforts to blow out a candle. The intervention of a normal person provides the answer to their dilemma: to place the candle in the direction the face is twisted. Common to the fundamentalist South are jests at the expense of the lame-brained or long-winded preacher, who is

Poster for a Brooklyn lecture—Mark Twain and "The Celebrated Jumping Frog of Calaveras County"

usually cross-eyed, bald, deaf, or illiterate, as is the case with "The Preacher Who Couldn't Read," from Langston Hughes and Arna Bontemps's *The Book of Negro Folklore* (1958). The implication smears rural members of the clergy, who are stereotyped as too uneducated or too lazy to perform common labor yet too inept at pulpit oratory to succeed as ministers.

One wing of the cruelty joke canon victimizes the ministry itself minus any element of handicap, as is the case in Chapter 6 of Maya Angelou's *I Know Why the Caged Bird Sings* (1970) with the overly pious Reverend Thomas. As he expounds an energetic spiel, Sister Monroe is so filled with the spirit that she knocks his false teeth out of his mouth, leaving him to gum a suitable text: "Naked I came into the world, and naked I shall go out." (Angelou 1970, 36) A brief example of the fable proper is the ostentatious sermonizer who tries to add sound effects or live-action details, as demonstrated in "The Dove in the Loft" in Ray B. Browne's *A Night with the Hants and Other Alabama Folk Experiences* (1976). The foolish preacher's attempts to improve his sermon with the help of a rube or child, often hidden in the attic or under the pulpit floor, usually result in a humiliating incident, such as a fall, an untimely retort, or the intrusion of an animal into the church. The failure of the minister's ruse entertains the congregation at the same time it augments the theme of foolishness. A mildly sacrilegious jest at the expense of evangelicals is "Letters in the Sky," a motif replicated in J. Mason Brewer's *The Word on the Brazos: Negro Preacher Tales from the Brazos Bottoms of Texas* (1953). The requirement of a celestial revelation impels the congregation dimwit to declare that he saw the letters GPC aflame in the heavens. The boy interprets the letters to mean "Go preach Christ"; a disbelieving deacon refutes the interpretation and supplants it with "Go pick cotton." A story that stresses dialect as proof of ignorance is the deacon's encounter with bears, as told in Daryl Cumber Dance's *Shuckin' and Jivin': Folklore from Contemporary Black Americans* (1978). The deacon jumps into the stream rather than face bears, which approach from each end of the footbridge. To the preacher's suggestion that the deacon pray for deliverance, the victim replies that God is effective at "prayer meetin'" but not at "bear meetin'," a pun that taunts the overzealous who prefer piety to everyday gumption.

Law is also the source of rustic jest. A story with a legal element comes from Caleb A. Ridley's *The Southern Mountaineer* (ca. 1900). It involves the standard court testimony of a self-incriminating rube accused of cracking a neighbor's pot. The rube takes the stand to exclaim that the pot was already cracked when he borrowed it, it was whole when he returned it, and he didn't take it in the first place! Blended with racism and physical ungainliness is the ploy of the black man concealing a pig, found in Richard M. Dorson's *American Negro Folktales* (1967). To keep the sheriff from impounding the wayward pig, the black man dresses it in human garb. The sheriff, who is often the butt of country humor, falls for the gag but mutters as an afterthought that the fellow with the black man was uncommonly ugly.

Sources Angelou 1970; Brunvand 1996; Burrison 1989; Christiansen 1964; Curtius 1953; Dailey 1994; Hurston, *Dust Tracks on a Road* 1991, *Mule Bone: A Comedy of Negro Life* 1991, 1995; Ish-Kishor 1962; Krappe 1964; Polley 1978; Ross 1961; Shah 1975; Twain 1995; Weinreich 1988.

 # DRYDEN, JOHN

A versatile seventeenth-century satirist and fabulist and England's first literary critic, John Dryden startled his audience with *The Hind and the Panther* (1687), a bold narrative blending fable with religious apologia to reconcile the poet's conversion to Catholicism with the oppressive, antipapist Anglican views of his day. Still intent on religious matters, he also diverted readers with his last published work, *Fables Ancient and Modern* (1700), which intersperses original models with works paraphrased from classical fable. A student of the classics and emulator of Geoffrey Chaucer, William Shakespeare, Ben Jonson, and John Milton, Dryden excelled at proportion, clarity, and metrical precision. The prefaces to his works explain his views on wit and humor and list the criteria by which they should be judged. The impetus to his critical evaluation was, in part, his Puritan upbringing as well as his admiration for literature that balances reason with elegance. Because of the monumental influence of his writing, his era was known as the Age of Dryden.

Professional writing demanded much of Dryden, who rejected the patronage that supported poetasters and geniuses alike. The irony of his penury is not lost on literary historians whose admiration grew in proportion to the brilliance and profundity of Dryden's canon. Born August 9, 1631, in Aldwinkle All Saints, Northamptonshire, he completed Westminster School and earned a bachelor's degree from Trinity College, Cambridge. For two years, he served as clerk to Secretary of State John Thurloe. A royalist, Dryden matured during the Puritan-controlled Commonwealth and composed a reflective ode on Oliver Cromwell's death, *Heroique Stanzas* (1658). Two years later, at the fall of the religious cabal, with the publication of *Astraea Redux* and *To His Sacred Majesty*, Dryden welcomed Charles II, son of the murdered Charles I, and exulted in the restoration of monarchy and a favorable climate for the arts. A member of the Royal Society, he produced substantial, sober verse, including *Annus Mirabilis* (1667), a commentary on England's sufferings from bubonic plague, the Dutch War, and the London Fire of 1666, which gutted much of the city.

One of England's first freelance writers, Dryden earned a living from his publications plus the limited stipend from a minor inheritance. During the dizzying ebullience of the 1660s, he poured out witty stanzas and comic songs to flesh out farces and comedies, including *The Wild Gallant* (1663), *The Rival Ladies*

(1664), and *Secret Love, or the Maiden Queen* (1666). A shy man among the era's coffeehouse wits, he saved his sparkle for the repartee and dialogue of *Sir Martin Mar-All* (1667), *The Mock Astrologer* (1668), and *An Evening's Love* (1671). The high point of Restoration comedy, *Marriage à la Mode* (1673), abounds with his lighthearted characters, clever retort, and double entendre drawn from Molière's example. *The Indian Emperor* (1665), *Tyrannic Love* (1669), *Almanzor and Almahide* (1672), and *Aurengzebe* (1675), the last of the great rhymed stage epics, comprise his contribution to tragicomedy and heroic drama. He survived the scoffing of critics and met audience expectations with his greatest stage play, *All for Love, or the World Well Lost* (1678), a retelling of Shakespeare's *Antony and Cleopatra* (ca. 1605) reset in Restoration high tragedy. In 1668, Dryden published both *An Essay of Dramatic Poesy* and *A Defence of an Essay of Dramatic Poesy*, his learned discourses on the use of the rhymed couplet and the establishment of standards of diction for serious writing. In the last two decades of his career, he dedicated himself to satire with *Absalom and Achitophel* (1681), a biblical parody of failed Whig attempts to squelch an incipient Catholic branch of the royal genealogy of Charles II. Dryden followed with harsher ridicule, *Mac Flecknoe, or a Satyr upon the True-Blew-Protestant Poet, T. S.* (1682), an attack on a personal enemy, Thomas Shadwell.

During a period of self-study and redirection, Dryden withdrew to Devon to the home of his friend, Lord Clifford, for solace and solitude. He issued an unusually earnest fable in satire, *The Hind and the Panther* (1687), an amalgam of allegory and apologia, to defend his conversion from Anglicanism to Catholicism in response to the crowning of James II. For this difficult beast fable, Dryden's prodigious skill facilitated graceful dodges and feints, which take the form of symbol, antithesis, paradox, caesura, and a fable-within-the-fable in the story of the swallows and the martins. In direct exposition, he exonerates Catholicism in graceful hyperbole:

> A milk-white Hind, immortal and unchang'd,
> Fed on the lawns, and in the forest rang'd;
> Without unspotted, innocent within,
> She fear'd no danger, for she knew no sin.
> Yet had she oft been chas'd with horns and hounds
> And Scythian shafts; and many winged wounds
> Aim'd at her heart; was often forc'd to fly,
> And doom'd to death, though fated not to die.
> (Dryden n. d.)

Surrounding the delicate beast are symbolic beast-enemies: the bear (independent sects), hare (Quakers), buffoon ape (freethinkers), lion (king of England), buzzard (Anglican bishops), wolf (Presbyterians), false Reynard the Fox (Aryans), and bristling Baptist Boar (Anabaptists), a secretive skulker who masks his impurities with the "foam of sanctity." The harsh antipapist backlash that refused property and voting rights to Catholics appears in the abstract form of a black night: "Alone she came, no sleep their eyes to close:/Alone, and black she came; no friendly stars arose."

The work paints a brave front on a decision that cost the poet much gibing for his about-face to please the new papist king. In defense of his choice to convert, Dryden describes his personal quest for faith:

> O teach me to believe Thee thus conceal'd
> And search no farther than Thyself reveal'd;
> But her alone for my director take,
> Whom Thou hast promis'd never to forsake! . . .
> Be thine the glory, and be mine the shame.
> Good life be now my task: my doubts are done.

The poet confesses to thoughtlessness in his youth and adult errors in following "false lights." To elevate the prowling panther from unsavory company, Dryden casts him and, by extension, the established English church, as a "fairest creature of the spotted kind" whose faults and virtues are so entangled that no condemnation could ignore the good. A Platonic image views Anglicanism as a "[spirit] of a middle sort,/Too black for heav'n, and yet too white for hell." Like the medieval *Ysengrimus* and Edmund Spenser's *Mother Hubberd's Tale* (1591), Dryden's satire cut into tender sensibilities; the condescending tone stirred the wrath of devout Anglicans. A scathing retort in kind is Charles Montagu and Matthew Prior's *The Hind and the Panther Transvers'd to the Story of the Country Mouse and the City Mouse* (1687), a fable-for-fable riposte in Horatian style to requite Dryden's papist defense.

Dryden's reward came in his selection as England's poet laureate and the prestigious title of historiographer-royal in 1670. The pay of £200 was largely an honorarium, which was delayed by treasury incompetence or royal lapse. With the accession of William and Mary, Dryden lost his court appointment altogether in 1688 and was forced to move farther from town and to pay the double taxes levied against Catholics. Under hire of the count of Abingdon, he composed *Eleonora*, a poem to honor the dead countess, and worked at translation and stage scenario as a means of adding to a seriously declining income. At age 66, he published translations of Ovid, Juvenal, Theocritus, Horace, Persius, and Virgil. The latter netted a welcome £1,400 but failed to save the poet from a hard life of writing up to the last. Shortly before his death May 1, 1700, he retreated to Cotterstock to complete *Fables Ancient and Modern*, a jolly but unoriginal collection adapted from Chaucer, Boccaccio, Ovid, and Homer. A popular compendium of 18 classic tales and two originals, the work features Aesop's "The Cock and the Fox," Ovid's "Pygmalion and the Statue," Chaucer's "The Nun's Priest's Tale," and the medieval allegory "The Flower and the Leaf." Although he died a pauper, he is interred along with Chaucer in an honorable spot—Poets' Corner of Westminster Abbey.

Sources Baugh 1948; Bermel 1982; Brockett 1968; Burdick 1974; Crane 1932; Drabble 1985; Dryden, http://www.library.utoronto.ca; Eagle and Stephens 1992; Gassner and Quinn 1969; Highet 1962; Hornstein et al. 1973; Kunitz and Haycraft 1952; Lewis 1996; Magill 1958; Magnusson 1990; Person 1988; Pollard 1970; Roberts 1962; Van Doren 1936; Wilson 1965.

EIGHTEENTH-CENTURY FABLE

In the Age of Enlightenment, fable came into a well-deserved era of appreciation. Within refined circles, the eighteenth century was the heyday of coffee table fable books, particularly the extravagantly illustrated volume, which made the reading of these morality boosters more like entertainment and less like medicine. Literary historians rescued Aesop from earlier depictions of the halting, misshapen churl and recast him as a genial peasant, adviser to the mighty, and Western father of wisdom literature. In his *Spectator* essay, dated September 29, 1711, Joseph Addison champions the Aesopic genre as "the first pieces of wit that made their appearance in the world, and have been still highly valued not only in times of the greatest simplicity, but among the most polite ages of mankind." (Addison, Steele, 1907, 44) To express delight in fable, Addison appends to his essay a four-paragraph allegorical model on the relationship of two abstracts, Pleasure and Pain. On examining humankind, the two discover that "there was no Person so Vicious who had not some Good in him, nor any Person so Virtuous who had not in him some Evil." (Addison, Steele, 1907, 47) The fable concludes that pleasure and pain are "constant Yoke-fellows" and enlarges on the placement of souls in heaven or hell, depending on the preponderance of virtue or vice that marked the person in life. In harmony with the methodical style of Addison's day, this bland addition to the canon of world fable stresses philosophy and reason over diverting rhetorical touches, such as characterization and dialogue.

Producer of the era's best compendium of fable, *Fifty-one Fables in Verse* (1727), John Gay was the source of numerous prize editions that pleased young audiences for nearly a century. Later in the period, fable branched into literary fable—a longer, more complex genre prized by the Age of Reason, which esteemed logic and the workings of the mind. A paragon of the era's intense scrutiny of character is Christopher Smart's compilation of *Fables in Verse for the Improvement of the Young and the Old by Abraham Aesop Esq.* (1757), published by John Newbert. Less well known are John Hall Stevens's amusing *Fables for Grown Gentlemen* (1761), the sentimental stories of John Langhorne's *The Fables of Flora* (1771), the bowdlerized Aesopic stories of William Russell's *Fables Moral and Sentimental* (1772), the lightly satiric *Favole e Novelle* [Fables and Stories] (1782) of Italian historiographer Lorenzo Pignotti, and educator Sarah Kirby Trimmer's

"The coffee house orator"—inside an eighteenth-century London coffee shop

original stories, compiled in *Ladder to Learning* (1789) and *Family Magazine* (1788–1789). Disdainful of fairy tales, she preferred quality morality and wisdom literature and also provided teachers with advice in *An Easy Introduction to the Knowledge of Nature* (1780) and *The Oeconomy of Charity* (1787), a guidebook for superintendents of charity schools. In a period marked by declining educational standards and degeneration of public schools, these mildly instructive works retained their popularity through numerous printings.

Throughout Europe, the era proved favorable to the revival of ancient fable and to creative and innovative additions to the corpus, which jolted fable from its traditional confines into the broader span of literary fiction:

- In Germany, Johann Wolfgang von Goethe extolled the genre for imitating nature and for elevating morals. His signature contributions to fable include "Der Zauberlehrling" [The Sorcerer's Apprentice] and *Reineke Fuchs* [Reynard the Fox] (1792), a resetting of medieval stories in ballad form.

- Goethe's contemporary, impoverished teacher and playwright Gotthold Ephraim Lessing of Saxony, author of *Fabeln und Erzählungen in Reimen* [Fables and Stories in Rhyme] (1747) and *Fabeln: Drei Bücher* [Fables: Three Books] (1759), insisted on the spare, simple structure of the Aesopic form, which was morality in action.

- Another figure of the German romantic upsurge, moralist and hymnologist Christian Fürchtegott Gellert, also of Saxony, published *Fabeln und Erzählungen* [Fables and Tales] (1748), a collection of charming tales that disparaging critics labeled "verse *divertissement.*" One of Gellert's most intriguing allegories is "The Land of the Halt," an illustrative story of society's addiction to its faults. His expansion of the landscape of fable to abstract and philosophical concepts clashed with Lessing's simplicity, which allowed concepts to grow in the reader's mind without romanticism or symbolic extension.

- Less familiar than Goethe and Lessing, the German critic and theologian Johann Gottfried von Herder of Weimar, a leader of the *Sturm und Drang* [Storm and Stress] movement of the late eighteenth century, wrote and collected fables as models of his critical and philosophical theories. One of his more militaristic stories, "The Lion and the Bulls," offers graphic evidence of the divide-and-conquer concept, the winning strategy of Julius Caesar. The trick, founded on treachery and gossip, forces the bulls into fighting and suspicion. The lion's cynical trick suggests the political maneuverings of Herder's age, which tended to award the spoils to the most devious political manipulator.

- Herder's contemporary, August Gottlieb Meissner, author of "The Mouse and the Snail," excels at the intrinsic moral implicit in the trade-off between opposites. In another model, "Pride Goes before a Fall," a rush of action quickly stems the boasting of a unicorn, who lies dehorned after challenging a mountain as a means of impressing a raven. The raven retorts, "You have still to show me the proof of your strength, but proof of your foolishness . . . you have already given me unasked." (Green 1965, 130)

- In France, literary fable was known as the *conte philosophique* [philosophical story], the form of Voltaire's dystopic *Candide* (1759), a witty episodic satire of human foible and institutional excess.

- The British, too, developed a more erudite form, as modeled by Samuel Johnson's *The History of Rasselas, Prince of Abyssinia* (1759). Less memorable are Dr. Samuel Croxall's long-lived *The Fables of Aesop and Others Newly Done into English* (1722) and the collection of Robert Dodsley, published in 1761, a tedious work freighted with ponderous classical touches.

- A vindictive use of fable, Tomàs de Iriarte's *Fábulas literarias* [Literary Fables] (1782), served as a personal outlet for resentment and frustration and provoked pointed invective from Juan Pablo Forner, whose *El asno erudito* [The Erudite Ass] (1782) and unpublished lampoon "Los gramáticos chinos" [The Chinese Grammarians] carried on a literary squabble with Spain's most revered fabulist.

See also Gay, John; Goethe, Johann Wolfgang von; Iriarte, Tomàs de; Lessing, Gotthold Ephraim.

Sources Addison et al. 1907; Blackham 1985; Blain et al. 1990; "Brewer: Dictionary of Phrase and Fable," http://www.bibliomania.com; Briggs 1977, 1991; Cooper 1921; Creeden 1994; Green 1965; Hobbs 1986; Kohlschmidt 1975; Komroff 1935; Krappe 1964; Newbigging 1895; Steinberg 1954; Stephen and Lee 1922.

EXEMPLARY TALE

The exemplary tale or exemplum expresses a doctrine or illustrates a stern moral code, often through gentle self-mockery or humbling experience but never through bitterness or recrimination. Models of exempla from world lore span the globe, ranging from the many versions of the African-American tale "The Devil's Doing" and the Sufist Rumi's story of the blind men and the elephant to the southern con artist tale "The Clever Peddler and the Razor Straps" from Richard M. Dorson's *Jonathan Draws the Long Bow* (1946) and the Yiddish *moshl*, "A Bit of Herring, a Pinch of Salt, and a Morsel of Bread," the story of a jeweler who leaves a large town and finds contentment in selling everyday items to humble customers. For the convenience of the after-dinner speaker or writer searching for an appropriate exemplum, classical fable often falls into at least two of three characteristic segments. In some models, it tends to open with a *promythium*, or introduction, that may index the text among other bits of wisdom lore or may explain the author's intended application, such as a warning against pride or foolhardiness. An example from a fragment found on a classical papyrus directs the story to a particular audience: "To a man who is rich, and also a scoundrel, the following fable applies." (Perry 1965, xv) A prefatory directive from Book III of Phaedrus's fables declares, "Success invites many to their ruin." (Perry 1965, xv) In like manner, some fables conclude with an *epimythium*, the return to the teller's voice for a terse, sometimes gruff rejoinder or aphorism. In the absence of the initial summary or classification, the *epimythium* offers similar information at the story's conclusion. It is less common for the exemplum to contain all three elements—introduction, body, and concluding moral.

According to collector Thomas Newbigging, the genre of fable falls into three categories. The *rational fable* deals with people and deities, who may interact in a natural setting among ordinary flora and fauna. The *emblematic fable*, also called the Aesopic fable, chooses talking animals and plants as characters. The *mixed fable* blends characteristics of the rational and emblematic types. Along with the more complex beast epic, the original emblematic fable descended directly from the animal tale and, in its primitive state, bore an implicit gnomic message or proverb to explain a standard situation in human nature. A forerunner of the didactic fable, the animal tale is completely nature-oriented and carries an etiological purpose in that it illuminates cause and effect. Unlike Barney, Lassie, Smokey the Bear, Babar the Elephant, or Felix the Cat and other examples of modern anthropomorphism from picture book, video game, and Saturday morning cartoon, the characters of fable are unnamed, unadorned domestic and wild animals and the trees and plants of their milieu, which Joseph Addison classes as "Brutes and Vegetables." (Addison, Steele 1907, 45)

Long before Darwin surmised that humankind evolved from lower forms, the fable's creation of a symbolic relationship between animals and people reflected on the human penchant for appearing serpentine, vulpine, bovine, and simian. An example from the Yiddish fable "The Hen and Her Chicks" tells the simplistic story of a hen who asks her chicks one by one if they will care for her in old age. Because of a glib "Of course" from the first two, she drowns them both. The third answers pragmatically that by the time she is old, he will have to care for his own chicks. This chick she lets live by ferrying him to safety. In similar atavistic mode, the Finnish fable "The End of the World" tells of the hen who is hit on the head by an acorn and launches a panic that attracts three wild beasts—the bear, wolf, and fox. After these three tire of the mission of warning others and devour the hen and her barnyard companions, they cast eyes on each other. The fox snatches up his tail in a mock show of eating himself. When the bear and wolf imitate him, the fox dashes to safety, calling out, "You are fools to eat yourselves up, but I'd be crazier still if I stayed with you!" (Booss 1984, 590)

Exemplary fables tend toward interaction of peasants, townspeople, and animals and may carry a supernatural element, such as talking reeds, or outlandish details common to tall tales. An updated model, Isak Dinesen's "Babette's Feast" (1949)—written on a bet that she couldn't crack the American mass-circulation fiction market—substitutes the usual forms of magic with the clever kitchen wizardry of a skilled cook. Set in an isolated Lutheran colony in a sparsely supplied Scandinavian fishing village, the story opens the shallow world of Martine and Philippa, spinster daughters of a pious minister, through an epiphany of food. After extending fellowship to Babette, a refugee, the women invite aging friends to a meal that Babette turns into a sumptuous banquet. Dinesen contrasts the elements of the event by following a parsimonious prayer with the first dazzling course. The Dean speaks:

> May my food my body maintain,
> may my body my soul sustain,
> may my soul in deed and word
> give thanks for all things to the Lord.
> (Dinesen 1953, 35)

Beginning with sips of red Amontillado wine, the meal progresses from turtle soup to Blinis Demidoff [crepes stuffed Russian style], sparkling citrus quaffs of Veuve Cliquot 1860, "Cailles en Sarcophage" [quail in a tomb], and a light dessert of grapes, peaches, and fresh figs. The diners, too stunned to converse, grow light of heart as each morsel delights the palate and gladdens the digestion. A witty, propitious tale reconciling bliss and righteousness, Dinesen's story reaches its philosophical climax in Babette's evaluation of her financial failure: "Poor? . . . No, I shall never be poor. I told you that I am a great artist. A great artist, Mesdames, is never poor. We have something, Mesdames, of which other people know nothing." (Dinesen 1953, 47)

Dinesen reissued "Babette's Feast" in 1952 in a slick Christmas edition. In 1979, the story was the subject of an award-winning film, starring Stephane Audran as the sensual, sybaritic food lover who opens the hearts of fanatics to one of life's pleasures. On the screen, the unfolding of Babette's culinary achievement rejuvenates a village long soured on too much piety and self-denial.

The humorous situations of exempla serve writers of fiction with the bones of short stories. When dressed up with specific names, rounded characterizations,

Scene from the movie version of "Babette's Feast," 1987, directed by Gabriel Axel and starring Stephane Audran.

and place names, the story of the stolen child who bedevils his kidnappers becomes O. Henry's "The Ransom of Red Chief," a first-person narrative and southern classic published in *Whirligigs* (1910). Set in Alabama in a semirural town "flat as a flannel-cake, and called Summit, of course," the story of the kidnappers' comeuppance for snatching little Johnny Dorset ends in wry humor. The child's father, a "mortgage financier and a stern, upright collection-plate passer and forecloser" named Ebenezer Dorset shares a first name with Dickens's Scrooge, protagonist of the Christian fable *A Christmas Carol.* Dorset at first rejects a ransom letter offering "Red Chief's" return. (O. Henry 1953, 1144) At length, Father Dorset offers a counterproposal: "You bring Johnny home and pay me two hundred and fifty dollars in cash, and I agree to take him off your hands." (O. Henry 1953, 1151) The moral lesson to the kidnapper named Bill is clear: he accepts the trade and flees the unholy brat, crossing the "Central, Southern, and Middle Western States, and . . . legging it trippling for the Canadian border." (O. Henry 1853, 1152)

As vessels of religious precept, exemplary fables are a standard entry in Middle Eastern lore. Islam favors the exemplum, often in cryptic or enigmatic form. Sura 18 from the Koran (613 C.E.) offers an influential model to worshipers of Allah. Entitled "Al-kahf" [The Cave], it opens with an invocation, "In the Name of God, the Merciful, the Compassionate," and a psalm of praise. (Koran 1955, 316) Beginning in line eight, the story tells of a test of youths, identified with the seven Sleepers of Ephesus in Christian legend. Historically, the group of Muslims hid from Christian persecutors and died in the cave during the rule of the notorious emperor Decius around 245 C.E. Upon their return from hiding, the cave dwellers advise the true believer, "Take refuge in the Cave, and your Lord will unfold to you of His mercy, and will furnish you with a gentle issue of your affair." (Koran 1955, 317) The text predicts that the righteous shall obtain refuge in Eden, where "they shall be robed in green garments of silk and brocade, therein reclining upon couches—O, how excellent a reward! And O, how fair a resting-place." (Koran 1955, 320) A complex chapter, "The Cave" suggests motifs of resurrection and God's judgment, which is fixed in time but known to no one.

Also from Islam, a dervish manuscript, *Kitasb-i-Amu Daria* [The Book of the River Oxur], contains a teaching story of Uwais el-Qarni, founder of the Uwaisi or Solitary Dervishes. To illustrate the theme of patience, Uwais tells the allegorical fable "Wayfarer, Strangeness and Savetime." Like the wandering of Christian in John Bunyan's *Pilgrim's Progress*, the journeys of the three imperil them, in part, because of their methods of travel. After the Wayfarer takes a side road and is devoured by lions, Savetime searches for a shorter way and falls into quicksand, which halts his progress as he flounders in one spot. Proceeding alone, Strangeness stalks a party of wild beasts that hunt by day. The complex story-within-a-story explains how Strangeness observes unusual facts that enrich him. When he encounters Savetime, the former traveling companion learns of the caravansery of wild animals and, without absorbing the details of Strangeness's success, rushes into the hall of beasts and is devoured. As is true of wisdom lore, the story so involved disciples in its telling that they acquired a new appreciation for patience without realizing that they were being lectured.

As do other Mideastern religious sects, Jews value the exemplum as a teaching tool. The corpus of Yiddish *mesholim* consists of rabbinic lore told to elucidate a moral issue or exemplify a human foible. A southern exemplum that parallels the style and purpose of the Yiddish pulpit tale is "Drakesbill," a cumulative tale about a duck who tries to collect a debt from the king. The duck and his party of helpers—a ladder, fox, wasp nest, and brook—are so clever and effective that, not only does he collect the money, but he impresses the king's subjects, who oust the king and set Drakesbill on the throne. Implicit in the growing list of followers are hints that the duck's expedition will require such assistance as a ladder for climbing and water for putting out fire. The tradition of *mesholim* prepares the listener for a multistage conclusion drawing on the totality of experience that precedes the challenge. Attentive hearers who are most sensitive to prefatory episodes are most likely to profit from the fable and to apply its precepts to their own lives.

In addition to religious or educational use, exempla also entertain and satisfy the casual reader. A surprise best-seller in the American market, Richard Bach's fable *Jonathan Livingston Seagull* (1970) is an unassuming animal story that he claims resulted from a cyclical vision. Like Antoine de Saint-Exupéry, the author, a native of Oak Park, Illinois, and pilot in the U.S. Air Force during his twenties, combines his delight in flying with a love of writing. Rejected by numerous publishing houses, Bach's fable achieved the reader success that takes the jaded literary world by surprise. The story of a spunky seagull who dreams of flying for artistic self-expression rather than survival, the text follows the self-exile of a bird who learns to transcend physical limitation by challenging himself to exceed the usual expectations. His return to the earth-bound flock sets him further apart from mundane eat-to-live thinking. To a select group of students who share his desire, he confides, "Each of us is in truth an idea of the Great Gull, an unlimited idea of freedom . . . and precision flying is a step toward expressing our real nature." (Bach 1970, 103) In simple exhortation, Jonathan explains, "Everything that limits us we have to put aside."

Lauded as Buddhist mysticism and Christian allegory, the fable, like Isak Dinesen's "Babette's Feast," resounds with the themes of individualism and remaining true to self. As a mentor advises:

> The trick . . . was for Jonathan to stop seeing himself as trapped inside a limited body that had a forty-two-inch wingspan and performance that could be plotted on a chart. The trick was to know that his true nature lived, as perfect as an unwritten number, everywhere at once across space and time. (Bach 1970, 80)

With the simplicity of a bedtime story, *Jonathan Living Seagull* stimulates theological and metaphysical observation, including the author's vocal debate with critics who tried to dismiss the fable as pretentious fantasy repackaged as trumped-up Zen. A facile provoker of thought, it speaks to myriad levels and interests. Avoiding snide satire, it manages to question much of the materialistic world by returning to basic values and to those activities that satisfy intrinsically.

See also Christian fable; L'Estrange, Sir Roger; Rumi, Jalal ad-Din ar.

Sources Addison et al. 1907; Bach 1970; Booss 1984; Brunvand 1996; Burrison 1989; *Contemporary Authors* 1994; Cooper 1921; Dinesen 1953; Hobbs 1986; Ish-Kishor 1962; *The Koran Interpreted* 1955; Krappe 1964; Polley 1978; Ross 1961; Shah 1975; Thurman 1981; Watt 1994; Weinreich 1988.

FABLE

Close kin of the tale, parable, anecdote, and allegory, the fable is a timeless, fanciful literary genre that literary historians have labeled humanity's essence. In the second century C.E., the rhetorician Theon in his handbook *Progymnasmata* [Examples] defined fable as a *logos pseudos* or fictitious story dramatizing a truth. Longer than a metaphor and distinct from the genre of proverb, the fable accomplishes its end indirectly, through a limited set of actions performed by an equally limited set of primary characters. For example, from Mesopotamian lore, "The fox having urinated into the sea assumed aloud, 'The whole of the sea is my urine.'" (Perry 1965, xxxi) Similarly succinct is Francis Bacon's model in the essay *Of Vainglory* (1625), "The fly sate upon the axle-tree of the chariot-wheel and said, 'What a dust do I raise!'" (Perry 1965, xxxi) These two distinguishing traits of fiction, characters and action, set fable apart from more direct advice contained in bodies of wisdom lore, as found in the proverbs of Solomon and the Koran, Babylonian aphorism, the *Tao Te Ching*, or Confucius's sayings.

Less specific than the anecdote and briefer than the short story, the fable, according to Aristotle, is a terse, insightful *logos* or action that tends to have no specific setting other than nature itself. An example of a competition fable by the Arabian fabulist Lokman involves only two statements:

> A Doe once passed near a Lioness, saying, "I have many children in a year, and thou only hast in all thy life but one or two.
> And the Lioness said to her, "It is true; nevertheless, if it be but one, yet he is a lion." (Green 1965, 71)

Pregnant with implications about pride in quality, Lokman's story is complete in two sentences. Such understated exchanges were the standard for early Greek, Sanskrit, and Arabic fable, which left much to the reader's understanding. For the subtle audience, the implicit lesson resonated deeply within human perception, often coming to mind later as a rule of good conduct or an enrichment of law or religious principle. A second model, the Burmese fable "The Fisherman and the King's Chamberlain," originally collected in Maun Htin Aung's *Burmese Law Tales: The Legal Element in Burmese Folklore* (1962), tells of a royal doorman who demands half of the fisherman's reward for supplying the king with fish. To the king's surprise, the fisherman begs for 20 lashes and asks that half go to the chamberlain. The king is so moved by the fisherman's clever choice that he declares: "I order that the Chamberlain be dismissed for corruption and disloyalty, and the Fisherman appointed in his place." (Creeden 1994, 54) As is common in fable, the palace, chamberlain, and king are nonspecific examples of grafters in any bureaucracy. Although told in Burma, the story suits any high office and its attendant bureaucrats.

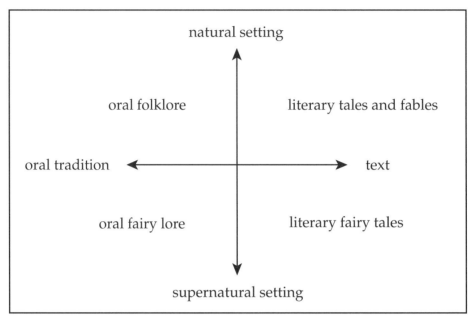

The settings and literary parameters of oral and literary folklore and fairy tales.

Often evolving from an action that occurs in a simple setting—in a deep wood, on a hillside, or along a stream—fable has no identifiable geography and no nationality. Time tends toward long years in the past, at the beginning of creation, or in the rule of an unnamed monarch, too far and too indistinct to fit into a specific biography or history, or as long ago as a mythic era "when the world was new," a hazy description from the Hmong fable "The Tiger Steals Nkauj Ncoom." (Livo and Cha 1991, 101) In its emergence on a spare canvas devoid of peripheral clues, fable stresses the dilemmas and choices of living beings, often animals acting like humans, gods interacting with earthlings, or simply animals interacting with each other. By conferring the power of reason and speech on beast characters, the fable creates a disarmingly whimsical transferral of advice or wisdom that delights readers as it instructs.

The purpose of the fabulist's extraction of action from real place and time is obvious—to focus on right thinking and ethical decision making. In *Plato and Platonism* (1893), Walter Pater refers to the didactic purpose of fable as "medicinable lies or fictions, with a provisional or economized truth in them, set forth under such terms as simple souls can best receive." (Newbigging 1895, 2) These purposeful fabrications, which the grammarian Aphthonius's *De Metris* [On

Metrics] (third century C.E.) calls "false discourse," arise from the substitution of beast for human, a distancing of the fabulist's didacticism that allows the reader a buffer zone between tender ego and remonstrance. By dressing up the animals in human interests and passions, the fabulist creates an air of naturalness that charms and amuses without weakening the salutary effect of quintessential common sense and wise counsel.

The defining factor in fable is the implicit or pictorial representation of truth. As La Fontaine describes the Aesopic apologue, its words are its body and the application its soul. An example rich in psychological compensation is the Greek fable "The Priest of Cybele and the Lion," the story of a eunuch whom a lion traps in a cave. By tapping his tambourine, the emasculated male surprises and terrifies the lion by creating an echo that reverberates throughout the underground chamber. The body of the story—the actions of the eunuch to rescue himself from the lion—suits the message implicit, that is, a clever would-be victim, using brains rather than brawn, can stave off a battle that he is certain to lose. But true to Aesopic style, the moral remains unstated, leaving to the reader to study the word picture for applicable precept.

As opposed to the aphorisms of Ben Franklin's Poor Richard, who urges the listener "Early to bed, early to rise, makes a man healthy, wealthy, and wise," the fable opts for a minuscule but engrossing drama that sticks close to nature, fact, and intuition. It sets up actors on a tiny stage to illustrate or elucidate an ethical principle, such as the folly of the greedy stock owner who kills the goose that lays the golden egg or the fool who ponders the sieve and doesn't know which holes to plug and which to leave open. Like the abstractions of algebra or the pawns on a chessboard, the actors in a fable are impersonal, as in the tiger and racehorse tales of western Australia. Within the confines of the great chain of being, each animal is its idiosyncratic self. Each performs an innate role—the stealthy fox stalks the unwary lamb, the witless peacock struts its gorgeous tail feathers, the monkey gazes at its reflection in a pool. Marie de France repeats Aesop's assessment of unchanging animal propensity in "The Grey Wolf," which concludes,

> Si sereit il tut dis gris lus,
> Fel e engrés, leiz e hidus.
> [A Grey wolf's what he'll be for aye,
> Mean and ugly, base and sly.]
> (Marie de France 1994, 178–179)

In G. K. Chesterton's words, all the animals "drive like inanimate forces, like great rivers or growing trees. . . . They cannot be anything but themselves." (*Aesop's Fables* n. d., ix) These certainties of nature become a large-scale animal alphabet that spells out human philosophic certainties—the self-incriminating behaviors that reveal inherent physical weakness and character flaws.

Other applications of fable speak to shrewdness or the ways of the world and may mock the hearer for ignorance or may instruct in methods of attaining personal satisfaction or security, as in the Sanskrit tale "The Apes Founding a City," in which city planners realize that they could easily be trapped within its walls. "The Wolf in Sheep's Clothing," a model from Nikephoros Basilakis's *Progymnasmata* (ca. 1175), describes the guile of the wolf who dresses in sheep-skin and is shut in with the flock at night. But when the shepherd reaches into the fold to select a lamb for dinner, by chance, he chooses the wolf. In this terri-fying scenario, Basilakis warns that assumed identities can confer new dan-gers, even on one who usually has little to fear. Another kernel of wisdom comes from "The Shepherd and the Butcher" (second century C.E.), as recited in a lec-ture by Maximus of Tyre. The lost lamb, after learning the professions of the shepherd and the butcher, wisely chooses to take up with the former. Less shrewd is the bull in a fable by Basilakis. The lion, fearing the bull's horns, flatters and charms his adversary into laying them aside. The unwitting bull makes the most lethal mistake in the animal world—he voluntarily becomes easy prey by abandoning his natural defense.

According to essayist Joseph Addison, fable flourishes during eras "when Learning [is] at its greatest Height." (Addison, Steele, 1907, 44) Compressed, limited in scope, and figurative rather than literal in character development, the fable is valuable to the writer as a straightforward narrative. Unlike fantasy, it clings to tradition yet offers a modicum of flexibility in style and content as the logic spools out to an inevitable conclusion. An example from French peas-ant lore is the tripartite story of a nameless old woodcutter, a narrative that falls into the classic three divisions. In the first episode, the woodcutter's wife scalds a prowling wolf by dumping a handy kettle of soup on its back. The pain proves a learning experience for the wolf, for, in two succeeding encounters, the wood-cutter has only to cry "Pour away, Jeannette! Pour away!" and the wolf flees the scene to avoid another baptism in boiling liquid. (Massignon 1968, 207)

The similarity of fables worldwide has left analysts with the so-called Aesopic question: How and why do these beast stories recur in different his-toric settings and eras, their contexts overlap, and their stereotypes remain con-stant? Translator P. F. Widdows, in his introduction to *The Fables of Phaedrus* (1992), summarizes the possibilities from three points of view. Psychologically, the stories appear to have devolved from a set of ideas and experiences com-mon to all periods when audiences reach a particular level of sophistication. Morphologically, fable reflects patterns of narrative structure that are held in common by all bodies of national literature. The third and least likely of expla-nations, diffusion, implies that the stories spread by some communication be-tween peoples, such as trading, cultural exchange, proselytizing, or conquering, and take on the characteristics and national mindset of the individual collector. Thus, the fox disdaining sour grapes might sneer at plums in China or prickly pear in the American Southwest.

The human cast of fable consists of similarly anonymous stock figures—the humble plowman, parson, or cottager of folklore and the predictable bumblers, sinners, and stooges of sermon, fabliau, and morality play. In many stories, these unindividualized human figures interact with ordinary beasts of burden and farm livestock. An example that contrasts human and bestial behavior is "The Charcoal Burner," the eastern European tale of a man who allows a bear, wolf, fox, and hare to warm themselves by his fire. He then kills them after they bring food to the house. Lacking the compassion of literature from the Christian Era, the story displays a self-serving logic that keeps the man alive and well fed at the expense of four dumb beasts.

Unacquainted with pat solutions and happy endings, the fable prefers a tone that leans toward a gloomy, unyielding naturalism, as found in Somadeva's *Tales from the Kathasaritsagara* (1994), which features interlocking survival stories and fool tales, and in the French fable "The Bear and the Beetle, or the War of the Animals," in which stinging insects overwhelm larger, fiercer mammals. Fables embrace common sense with overtones of shrewdness, as found in "The Fox and the Blackbird," a Greek fable in which a mother blackbird enlists a dog to take vengeance on a fox who eats the blackbird's young. As is common with fable, the hearer of the animal tale, safely removed from the stinging moral, knows many fools who fit the paradigm but has no reason to feel targeted for humiliation or criticism. Thus, the genre is a natural social outlet for the peasant underclass, who ridicule and lambaste their superiors through unflattering anecdotes couched as harmless, impersonal animal stories.

Worldwide, the canopy of fable shelters a field of specific subsets, which range from direct to subtle with tone variations from straightforward to cautionary, conspiratorial, humorous, and earthy:

- The *Aesopic fable* or *cautionary tale* in which animals, trees, and inanimate objects function as characters, for example, the French fable "The Four Friends," the story of a goose with a headache who finds a woman worse off than he and forgets the pain in his head while relieving the woman's suffering. A source of warning to exploiters is the Chilean fable "The Vixen," in which the title character tries to trick the monkey and, by her own guile, ends up a feast for dogs.

- The *exemplary tale* or *exemplum,* which expresses a doctrine or illustrates a stern moral code, often through self-mockery or humbling experience but never through bitterness or recrimination, as demonstrated by the destruction caused by avarice in Geoffrey Chaucer's *The Pardoner's Tale* and the worth of dreams in *The Nun's Priest's Tale* (1385). In the Age of Enlightenment, Samuel Johnson composed "The Fable of the Vultures," a philosophical condemnation of war through the eyes of a mother vulture. For selfish reasons, she delights in humans who readily slaughter and leave behind carcasses for her brood to eat. In the twentieth century, Rachel Carson introduced her environmental jeremiad *Silent Spring* (1962) through incidental fable, which describes a bucolic community blighted by a mysterious evil. Regarding the concept of environmental suicide, she concludes, "No witchcraft, no enemy action had silenced the rebirth of new life in this stricken world. The people had done it themselves." (Carson 1986, 490) As didactic learning experiences, these narratives remove the keen edge of censorship and admonition, thus educating the uninformed listener through example rather than rule or law.

- The *pourquoi story,* which explains the nature or existence of a phenomenon, for example, Joel Chandler Harris's account of "Why Mr. Cricket

Has Elbows on His Legs" from *Told by Uncle Remus: New Stories of the Old Plantation* (1905), New South Wales teller Peter Dargin's account of the creation of the Darling River, the chilling infanticide and cannibalism that mark the Hmong story "Why Monkey and Man Do Not Live Together," and the African stories "Pig's Long Nose and Greedy Mouth," "Why Hens Are Afraid of Owls," and "Why the Woodpecker Has No Song." In the latter, the woodpecker is shortchanged because of impatience. Thus, the *pourquoi* story fits the paradigm of fable by illustrating the pitfalls of human fault. The defining element to this explanation of nature is the extension of punishment to all animals of one species. Examples from platform storytelling include J. J. Reneaux's Cajun story "Why Alligator Hates Dog" and Carol Birch's original fable, "How the Rhinoceros Got Its Skin," an Afrocentric children's story in the style of Rudyard Kipling's *Just-So Stories for Little Children* (1902).

- The *explicit moral or allegorical tale,* as found in Rumi's Sufist teachings, Jacquetta Hawkes's "The Unites," and Paulo Coelho's *The Alchemist* (1988). As described by Joseph Addison, this form of ethical narrative employs as characters "Passions, Virtues, Vices, and other imaginary Persons of the like Nature" (Addison, Steele, 1907, 45), for example, Washington Irving's "The Devil and Tom Walker" (1824), an encounter between human protagonist and Satan in which the would-be victim must think up a ruse to halt Satan from snatching him off to the underworld. A southern example that mimics the allegorical tale describes two thieves hiding in a graveyard while they divide a load of stolen melons. A slave overhears them and reports to the master that it must be Judgment Day because God and Satan are choosing up corpses. The master investigates but is not swayed by the slave's misunderstanding. In the end, the master reclaims the melons stolen from his patch.

- The *instructive or edifying moral tale,* which entertains at the same time that it draws a parallel to guide or improve ethics or morality. The Finnish story "The Vain Bear" exemplifies a didactic narrative about egotism, a fault that violates society's code of behavior. The fox tricks the preening bear into sitting on a burning hay rick to turn his hair as flame red as the fox's pelt. A standard Afro-American moral tale, "Master John," makes a model of the slave who must concoct a lie to cover for his master's exaggerated tale of shooting a deer in the hoof and head with one shot. The slave quickly comes up with a cover—the deer was scratching its ear at the time. In private, the slave warns the master that on-the-spot prevarication of this quality is demanding work. Likewise clever is Manuel Komroff's "Cupid and the Lion," the closing model in his world collection *The Great Fables of All Nations* (1935). When the lion implores Cupid to end the fabulist's stereotyping of all lions as ridiculous, ungrateful, or evil, Cupid promises to climb on his back and shoot arrows at all the beasts of the forest to create a climate of love. The ingenuous baby divinity reminds the lion to bow low; the lion retorts, "And you remember also . . . that I am after all a Lion and that he who rides a Lion cannot dismount." (Komroff 1935, 487)

- The *fool tale,* a standard subset of Aesopic fables of logic and common sense, for example, Leo Tolstoy's "The Big Oven," "The Book," and "The Fool and His Knife." The third example is a two-stage test of a knife's cutting ability. Because it can't sever a nail or keep jelly from closing over the blade, the fool calls it worthless and discards it. The fool tale is found in many venues and describes the foolishness of the Irish workmen named Pat and Mike, the numskull stories of Australian yokels named Dad and Dave, the United States phenomenon of the little moron, and the universal search motif of an unmarried woman looking for a wise groom or a man seeking the perfect bride. The conclusion of searches for suitable mates is typically a test situation that the candidate fails. An example, "The Foolish Bride," demonstrates a pervasive motif found in *The Devil's Pretty Daughter and Other Ozark Folk Tales* (1955). In hard times, the bride squanders ham by slicing it and placing it directly on cabbages growing in the garden.

  Underscoring the obvious is the method of fool tales that enlighten the simpleton and end a dilemma. In a southern American example involving talking animals, the perky squirrel sits in an oak and looks down on the dim-witted bear who fears that an overhanging limb will blow down on his roof. The squirrel suggests a proactive solution: remove the limb before it becomes a hazard. The bear's gratitude becomes the squirrel's reward. A common variation of the animal fool tale shows the rabbit outwitting the bear by stealing meat from a slaughtered cow and leaving the tail for the bear. An added fillip at the end of the story pictures the bear within earshot of the rabbit's victory song. Quickly, the rabbit corrects the lyrics of his song to accord mastery to the foolish bear. In a less benevolent southern fool tale, "The Cat, the Monkey, and the Chestnuts," the foolish cat allows himself to be manipulated into removing chestnuts from the fire for the monkey to eat. The monkey crows his disdain for an animal so witless that he burns his paws without gaining any chestnuts for himself.

- Compounding the number of story types are variations of mode, which include the *chain story,* which interlinks events, each precipitating the next episode, as in "This Is the House That Jack Built" and the Japanese fable "Silly Saburo"; the *cumulative story,* which requires the repetition of a refrain, such as "The sky is falling" in the English fool tale "The Little Red Hen"; and the *compound triad,* which groups characters, actions, and/or events in threes, a common motif found in "The Three Sillies" and "Goldilocks and the Three Bears."

- The *cumulative story,* an expanded form of fool tale that moves from scenario to scenario, with each episode growing in intensity, humor, or threat. In the southern mountain story "Going to Squeetum's House," reported by

Elsie Clews Parsons in the *Journal of American Folklore* (1921), the fox tricks a housewife and takes her rooster. The trickery augments with the capture of a pig, then a child. Having ventured beyond the bestial realm, the fox overextends himself and falls prey to human vengeance. When he opens his sack to eat the child, he finds that a female trickster has replaced the child with a hunting dog, which gobbles up the fox. Just as the simple Aesopic story demonstrates an obvious truth, the cumulative tale develops at length the growing bravado of a fox who ultimately outsmarts himself.

- The *bawdy folktale* or jest, which imparts truths about amoral and immoral behaviors, usually at the expense of an adulterer or seducer. These tales were popular during the Middle Ages and remain in oral circulation as urban myth, such as cautionary tales about microwave ovens, human parts found in canned food, and the pet alligator grown to monstrous proportions in a city sewer system. Although pervasive and valuable as indicators of social rhythms and values, the bawdy folktale and jest rarely approach the level of literature. A ribald fable model from the Georgia Mountains comes from Vance Randolph's *Who Blowed Up the Church House and Other Ozark Folk Tales* (1952). Entitled "She Flunked the Fidelity Test," it describes the ruse by which a mature husband catches his young wife in adultery. He suspends a stone from the bedsprings and places a jar of cream directly below. When he returns from the fields, he discovers that the jar is full of butter.

- The *cruelty joke,* a humorous and sometimes scurrilous folk fable, usually rural in setting. A subset of the fool tale, the cruelty joke makes light of a physical imperfection or freakish condition and implies that handicapped people are also fools, for example, the stutterer in the well-worn joke about a sailor washed overboard. The only way the stutterer can alert the crew is to sing. He sets his words to a familiar tune: "Should auld acquaintance be forget and never brought to mind./The damned old cook fell overboard and is thirty miles behind."

Apart from its folk parent, the literary fable derives its name from the Latin *fabula,* a story, and usually turns on imaginative situations and dialogue acted out by one-dimensional animal characters that walk, talk, and scheme like humans. A popular example is Horace's "The City Mouse and the Country Mouse," which appears in volume two of his *Satires* (30 B.C.E.). A reprise in Eugenio Cirese's *Tempo d'allora, figure, storie e proverbi* [Time Gone By: Illustrations, Stories, and Proverbs] (1939), an Italian collection, resituates the characters in "The Palace Mouse and the Garden Mouse." Authors of fable rely on observation and the stereotypic qualities that each species has accumulated, such as the bloodthirsty wolves pitted against witless sheep in French and German tales, and the cunning fox that lurked in Babylonia's pre-Aesopic lore and Hebrew scripture. More general than the tale, parable, or allegory and less preachy than sermon, the literary fable is a light, generalized, often humorous text that bears a significant message. Pared down to a minimum of words and deeds, it narrates an undeniable certainty—a humanistic axiom that impels the hearer toward improved conduct and social or moral duty. Because of its anthropomorphic characterization, the literary tale's meaning lies far beyond the sum of its parts, as in the works of Antoine de Saint-Exupéry, Anne Bodart, and Jacquetta Hawkes. The meaning, implied by symbols and motifs, resides deep within surface detail, outside the voice of the adviser and apart from any obvious one-for-one explanation.

Set apart from other literary forms by its limitations, the fable emerges from homely, often rustic or barnyard imagery to create a never-to-be-forgotten connection with an encompassing truth. Any pragmatic use of fable requires more than a flash of recognition. Unlike a joke with a punch line or an allegory with an identifiable correspondence to a single human situation, the fable refers to a range of dramatic settings, such as different types of lies. It requires reflective interpretation and application to a broader realm of humanistic situations that shelter a cornucopia of vanities, frailties, and follies. Focused on a matter of general concern rather than a specific sin or shortcoming, the literary fable is a narrative device that is meant to provoke and channel concrete thinking toward that which is noble, exemplary, and estimable. Because of its rigid focus on a single action, it is suited to readers of limited attention span, even young children, who have become loyal fans.

In the genre's infancy, the simple Aesopic fable relied on familiar personae imbued with consistent traits: the wily fox, trembling hare, opinionated lion, lurking wolf, and patient donkey. In each case, character is fate—the dove stereotyped as always shy and fearful of predators and the owl wide-eyed and contemplative. In La Fontaine's preface to his 1668 volume, he comments on the applicability of bestial traits to humankind: "When Prometheus wanted to create mankind, he took the dominant quality of each beast, and from such diverse parts he made our kind; this work we call the microcosm. And so these fables are a picture in which each of us finds his portrait." (Hobbs, 22) As fable evolved with the writings of Phaedrus, Babrius, and Avianus, the moral picture of human foible moved to the foreground and eventually dominated the text, thus allying fable with satire, invective, and caricature.

To each self-incriminating action, the literary fabulist appends a moral tag, a stinger often pessimistic or resolute, leaving few alternatives for the outcome of foolish or hasty choices. Stated as a somber aphorism or snide adage, the concluding line could stand alone as sage or witty commentary on ignoble motivation, such as haste, self-pity, and vainglory. Beginning with Phaedrus and continuing through the writings of John Gay, moral statements moved to the opening line, thereby setting up an expectation that the action would justify the author's intent. In modern times, the moral almost always provides closure, as with these quippy, but thought-provoking models from George Ade's *Fables in Slang* (1900):

- If it is your play to be a hero, don't renig.

- Give the people what they think they want.

- People who expect to be luny will find it safer to travel in a bunch. (Ade 1900, 52, 74, 146)

In both arrangements—moral at the end and moral at the beginning—the literary fabulist chooses fable as a means of taking behaviors out of their normal context to teach virtue, censor vice, admonish wrongdoers, and model commendable behaviors. Simple and short, the stories lack leverage for grander purpose, such as heroic deeds and creative solutions. Gradually, literary fables have modernized and become more humanistic from a decidedly political, moral, or philosophical bent, for example, the French fable "The Wolf and the Fox in the Well," in which the wolf demands cheese and the fox convinces him that the reflection of the moon in the well is a wheel of cheese. The story concludes with the wolf's drowning—the standard play of the weaker animal seducing the stronger to its peril or doom by appealing to greed. Perhaps mimicking allegory or folktale, the literary fabulist does not tag the message onto the end like the tail of a dog, but, like Aesop, couches it in the action, usually as a choice of behaviors or responses that model the concept that self-destruction is inevitable to the would-be destroyer. As a contribution to wisdom literature, the literary fable stands apart as a succinct, muscular, and pithy narration unencumbered by excess detail. Unlike more ornate forms, it moves swiftly and cleanly to the heart of an issue. The best examples of these stories lead inexorably to a conclusion. As lean and purposeful as a geometry proof, a fable needs no elongation or embellishment. In his essay "Of Books," Montaigne names this vivid, essential, and profound meaning as the "first face" but indicates that other peripheral meanings bob to the surface as the reader takes time to ponder additional possibilities. (Newbigging 1895, 15)

Into the modern era, ancient and contemporary world fable has held steady in influence and readership. Loved by children and adults are the classics for bedside reading by Jacob and Wilhelm Grimm, Hans Christian Andersen, and Rudyard Kipling, all captured in Walt Disney animation, and the stories of Beatrix Potter, Richard Adams, and Kenneth Grahame. Appended to the world canon, *Jungle Beasts and Men* (1923) and *Gay-Neck: The Story of a Pigeon* (1927), by Dan Gopal Mukerji, an immigrant to the United States from India, epitomize the role of fable in complex fiction. Likewise seminal is the folk research of Robert E. Hayden and Ralph Ellison, who focused on simple folk wisdom for their contribution to the Federal Writers' Project of 1938–1942. Animal behaviors and morals enliven Antoine de Saint-Exupéry's *Le Petit Prince* [The Little Prince] (1943), Ernest J. Gaines's Louisiana folk base, J. R. R. Tolkien's Hobbit lore, Jacquetta Hawkes's *A Woman as Great as the World and Other Fables* (1953), and James Thurber's *Fables for Our Time and Famous Poems Illustrated* (1940) and *Further Fables for Our Time* (1956).

French utopist Michael Vendredi produced *Vendredi* (1967), a resetting of the fable of Robinson Crusoe; his German contemporary Wilhelm Scharrelmann composed timely wisdom lore, including "Deep Insight," an admonition to the proud, and "Dream behind Bars," a poignant cold war–era story of freedom and imagination. In the last quarter of the twentieth century, Samuel R. Delaney allied fable with science fiction in *Neveryona* (1986), the coming-of-age story of Pryn, who departs the mountains to see the world; Jacqueline Balcells produced a Chilean model, "The Enchanted Raisin" (1986); and Toni Morrison tapped fable for a stunning ghost story *Beloved* (1988), which earned her a Nobel Prize.

In the broader span of arts, literary fable undergirds and adorns mural, mosaic, dance, drama, and worship. Folkloric study lies at the heart of Scott Joplin's folk opera *Treemonisha* (1915), Marc Connelly's dialect play *The Green Pastures* (1929), and Langston Hughes's "Jesse B. Simple" cycle, published in 1957 as *The Best of Simple*, his *Book of Negro Folklore* (1958), coauthored by Arna Bontemps, and the comic play *Mule Bone*, a commentary on rural values composed during Hughes's collaboration with Zora Neale Hurston and delayed until its stage debut in 1991. Folk wisdom is the root of children's animal stories and cartoons, including A. A. Milne's Winnie the Pooh series, Babar the elephant, Paddington Bear, Snoopy and Woodstock, Garfield, Roadrunner and Wile E. Coyote, and the animated inner journey of Obblio and his dog Arrow, heroes of Harry Nilsson's animated film *The Point* (1985). In the latter, the round-headed child enlightens a narrow community by returning safely from exile and sharing his joy in adventure with his tormentors.

With the advent of multiculturalism in the 1980s and 1990s, readers young and old are becoming more familiar with native American trickster lore of Old Man Coyote, Caribbean stories of Anansi the spider, and the West African writings of Chinua Achebe. A spunky Louisianian, storyteller J. J. Reneaux taps traditional and contemporary ethnic folklore with emphasis on Deep South, Cajun, and Choctaw cultures. Her beast fables, such as the set-to of M'su Cocodrie, the alligator, against Bullet, the family dog, invigorate her anthologies and audiocassettes, which include the Anne Izard Storyteller's Choice winner *Cajun Folktales* (1992), *Why Alligator Hates Dog* (1995), recipient of the 1996 American Folklore Society's Aesop Accolade, and the audiocassette *Wake, Snake!* (1997).

Sources Addiso, et al. 1907; Ade 1900; *Aesop's Fables* 1968, 1993, n. d.; Afanasyev 1980; *Aristophanes* 1930; Aristotle 1921, 1931, 1946; Blackham 1985; Blain et al. 1990; "Brewer: Dictionary of Phrase and Fable," http://www.bibliomania.com; Briggs 1977, 1991; Brunvand 1996; Burrison 1989; Calvino 1980; Carson 1986; Connelly 1929; Cooper 1921; Creeden 1994; Dailey 1994; Davey and Seal 1993; *DISCovering Multicultural America*, http://www.galenet.gale.com; Feinberg 1967; Garland and Garland 1976; Gibb 1963; Green 1965; Harrington 1925; Harris 1955; Hobbs 1986; *The Interpreter's Dictionary of the Bible* 1962; Ish-Kishor 1962; Johnson 1970; Kohlschmidt 1975; Komroff 1935; Krappe 1964; Lambert 1960; Lang and Dudley 1969; Leach 1967; Lesky 1966; Livo and Cha 1991; Marie de France 1994; Massignon 1968; McGreal 1996; Miller and Snodgrass 1998; Naito 1972; Newbigging 1895; Palmer and Xiaomin 1997; Perry 1965, 1962, 1959; Pino-Saavedra 1967; Polley 1978; Raby 1997; Radice 1981; Reneaux 1992, 1995; Rosenberg 1997; Ross 1961; Shah 1975; Sherr and Kazickas 1994; Somadeva 1994; Steinberg 1954; Stephen and Lee 1922; Stinton 1979; Strayer 1989; Wallich 1994; Warmington 1938; Weinreich 1988; Widdows 1992; Willard 1967; Xenophon 1959.

FRENCH FABLE

The fame of French fable centers on the graceful verse of Jean de La Fontaine, but so limited an appreciation of the genre overlooks a long history of didactic animal lore. A 6,574-line Latin narrative poem, *Ysengrimus* (ca. 1150 C.E.)—an Ovidian mock epic by Magister Nivardus, a shadowy figure identified only as a Flemish teacher from Ghent, Liège, or Lille—provided a clarified source of animal epic, which had flourished in less decisive form from ancient times. The work is a colorful, long-lived translation of the anonymous Latin *Ecbasis Captivi* [Escape of a Prisoner] (ca. 940 C.E.). Composed in unrhymed elegiac form in seven books, the framework story projects an autonomous beast society devoid of the Aesopic stereotyping that predetermined individual animal behaviors. The action covers 12 episodes set late in the life of the dim-witted wolf Ysengrim or Isengrim, constable of Noble the lion-king, and Ysengrim's enemy, Reinard the fox, the trickster who cleverly turns predatory wolf into victim. In the poet's words:

> Reinardus varia spatians ambage meandi
> Callidus irritat ludificat querundem;
> Nam nunc multifido spiras curuamine tricans
> Anguis compliciti vincula cassa notat,
> Nunc obliquus ad hanc partemque incedit ad illam.
> Non redit aut prodit lineolasque terit,
> Sed numquam venturus eo, quo creditur isse;
> Dedalia fallax implicat arte chaos.

> [Reynard, making constant zigzags as he ran, cunningly exasperated and mocked the rustic. For at one moment, interweaving loops with many a twist, he imitated the redundant coils of a curled-up snake, while at another moment he darted off at a tangent to this side or that. He went neither backwards nor forwards in his little incursions, but he never arrived at the point he seemed to have been making for; with the art of Daedalus, the trickster wove chaos.] (Mann 1987, 220–221)

The fast-paced Latin version precedes two successful strands of trickster lore that reached their height in the French *Roman de Renart* and the German *Reinhart Fuchs* plus lesser contributions to beast literature, namely the Flemish *Reinaerts Historie*, Jacquemart Gielée's *Renart le Nouvel*, the Italian *Rainardo e Losengrino*, and the *Speculum Stultorum* [Mirror for Fools] (twelfth century) of a Canterbury monk, Nigel of Longchamps.

Historical and biographical landmarks within the text of *Ysengrimus* include mention of the monastery of St. Peter's south of Ghent, the Second Crusade of 1148, St. Bernard of Clairvaux, and Anselm, the bishop of Tournai from 1146 to 1149. Literary allusions derive from the Old and New Testaments, hagiography, church liturgy, and folklore, which the author smoothly phrases as epigrams, imagery, puns, and exempla. Enriched with farce and lively dialogue, the action reflects the trickster motif in which one animal conspires against another, a satire of rapacious twelfth-century church libertines who preyed on the unsuspecting European peasantry. In episode four, the wolf implores the fox to eat half of a ham he intends to snatch from a peasant. The fox tricks the man and returns to find that the wolf has eaten the ham, leaving the fox only a string. The fifth episode is a revenge tale in which Ysengrim the wolf, at the suggestion of the fox, dangles his tail in the water as a fishing line. Locals take advantage of the wolf and lop off his tail. In each match of wits, the trickster's complete trouncing of the mark leads to belly laughs consistent with the fool tale.

The victimization of Ysengrim continues in the next episode, in which four rams surround and gore him. A story-within-a-story describes the recovery of Rufanus, the lion whom Reinard cures by suggesting he wrap himself in Ysengrim's hide. A recounting of earlier episodes turns the tables on the fox by depicting him as the victim of his prey, a cock. Other episodes place the protagonists among a train of pilgrims and in the monastery of Blandigny. In the latter, Reinard leaves the wolf to the angry monks and slinks off to the wolf's den to violate his mate and her young. Episode VIII, a humorous fool tale, has the wolf making demands on a horse, who asks him to look at his foot. When Ysengrimus bends down, the horse lets fly with his hoof. A parallel to this episode finds the wolf attempting to devour Joseph the ram, who leaps into the wolf's open mouth. More examples of the wolf's gullibility place him at the mercy of the fox, Salaura the sow, and Carcophas the ass. The moral remains the same throughout—the smart underdog outfoxes the slow-witted bruiser every time. A condensed version that deletes satire and moralizing appeared in 1300 under the title *Ysengrimus Abbreviatus*, written perhaps by a prelate near Aachen.

Contemporaneous with the Ysengrimus and Reynard fable cycles is the work of Galterus Anglicus, chaplain of Henry II, who published a sheaf of 61 fables in 1175 known as the Lyons *Isopet* [Aesopics], which he rendered in elegiac form. The work was reissued in 1610 as *Romulus Niveleti* [Nivelet's Romulus], named for the compiler, Isaac Nèvelet, who collected beast stories in his *Mythologia Aesopica* [Aesopic Mythology]. Additional versions include a second *Isopet* by Gualterus Anglicus containing 64 fables, called *Isopet I* or *Isopet Avionnet* [Avianus's Aesopics], complete with introduction and epilogue. The 40 brief fables of the anonymous *Chartres Isopet* (late thirteenth century) contain a reprise of Alexander Neckham's *Novus Aesopus* [New Aesop], which concludes with a moral alternately named the sentence, exposition, or "essample" [example]. Literary histories assume the work was written by an unnamed priest from Île-de-France. A second version, *Isopet II*, derives from the same source and contains some longer fables.

The French contribution to medieval fable reached its height in the *Fables* (ca. 1189) of Marie de France. One of a series of *Isopets* or *Ysopets*, these renderings also flourished under the name *Avionnets* [Avianics], referring to the Latin recensions of Avianus in the fourth century C.E. Later eras produced additional fabulists, particularly Jean Baudoin, producer of *Les Fables d'Esope phrygien* [The Fables of the Phrygian Aesop] (1631). Two significant French translations of Marie's work appeared in the eighteenth century: Pierre Jean Baptiste Legrand d'Aussy's *Fabliaux ou contes du XIIe et du XIIIe siècles* [Fabliaux and Stories from the Twelfth and Thirteenth Centuries] (1779) and Marc Antoine René de Voyer d'Argenson's *Mélange tirés d'une grande bibliothèque* [A Mix Drawn from a Great Library] (1788). The late seventeenth century profited from the translations of orientalist and antiquarian Antoine Galland of Rollot, France, the adaptor of *Les Mille et une nuits* [The Thousand and One Nights] (1717) and *Les contes et fables indiennes de Bidpai et de Lokmam* [Indian Fables and Tales of Bidpai and Lokman] (1724). The early eighteenth century saw the creations of Antoine Houdard de La Motte, a poet and dramatist who wrote compendia of fables. A jolly dramatization, "The Clock and the Sun-Dial," pits a modern wind-up clock against the sun-powered sundial. The upstart ridicules the dial for dependence on the sun, but a dispersal of clouds reduces the boaster to shame. The sun, who rebukes the clock for being nearly an hour slow, suggests repairs and quietly remarks, "I speak but little—you call me slow—/But what I speak is truth." (Cooper 1921, 353)

A master of French fable, Jean-Pierre Claris de Florian succeeded La Motte as the era's popular novelist and dramatist. Born in Cévennes in 1755, he was influenced by Voltaire and Rousseau, the great voices of the eighteenth-century Enlightenment, and chose ethical themes as his metier. One example, an adaptation of the ancient world's golden mean, concludes "The Horse and the Colt," a wisdom tale reminding the prosperous to observe moderation. A second, "The House of Cards," uses a child's destruction of his younger brother's card stack to exemplify the difference between conquerors and founders of empires. Another, "The Husbandman and the Rats" describes the problem of false friends who share good times then disappear when a change of fate looms. Of such human propensities as gluttony, oppression, and ingratitude Florian says, "Most of us are aware of some of our defects, but to avow them is quite another matter; we prefer the endurance of real evils, rather than confess that we are afflicted with them." (Green 1965, 64) The protégé of the Duc de Penthièvre, Florian first produced romances and comedies, which earned him admission to the Académie Française in 1788. Critical response to his clever *Fables* (1792) ranks him below La Fontaine but well within the company of such world fabulists as the Spanish poet Tomás de Iriarte and English dramatist John Gay.

Following La Fontaine, the French master, into the tricky realm of court satire, Florian used fable as a vehicle of indirect mockery and criticism. Moving into dangerous territory in "The Apes and the Leopard," the fabulist describes a colony of apes at play in an innocent game involving identifying the paw that taps the blindfolded player. When the leopard turns the game to rougher fare, the wounded victim limps away from the field but restrains his outcry. To themselves, the other apes make their excuses and depart:

> But muttered to themselves upon the way:
> "Such games with princes are not safe to play:
> Under the velvet paw,
> Smooth as it looks, there always lurks a claw."
> (Cooper 1921, 357)

Alert to social differences that require some sacrifice for successful intercourse between the humble and their betters, Florian speaks of learning to bend the

Jean-Pierre Claris de Florian (1755–1794)

knee in another fable, "The Rhinoceros and the Dromedary." In "The Peacock, the Geese and the Diver," the latter rebukes snide geese for ridiculing the peacock's gawky legs and ill-tuned voice. In a pedantic tone, the diver makes a personal judgment of his own: "You have a voice and legs far worse than his,/ Without his brilliant dyes." (Cooper 1921, 358) In an era that saw the fatal conflict of French peasants and aristocracy rise to revolution, Florian produced "The Confident Parrot," the tale of the repetitive denial to the bird's fateful end, which comes with a cry of "It will be nothing." (Cooper 1921, 359) The best advice for surviving pernicious clashes of social class derives from the grandmother in "The Flying-Fish." She warns her child that, being neither eagle nor shark, the fish "must quietly follow a narrow path, swimming high near the air, and flying low near the water." (Cooper 1921, 361) The careful placement of innocents suggests the path that the fabulist himself may have chosen.

Florian approached the felicity and grace of La Fontaine's art with his refined sensibilities and penchant for creating animal frolics. "The Mole and the Rabbits" contrasts the dark world of the mole with a game of make-believe blindness. The rabbits, who play at blind-man's buff, amuse themselves like children:

> Rabbits! you exclaim, the thing is impossible. . . . He whom the riband deprived of light placed himself in the centre; the others leapt and danced round him, performing miracles; now running away, then coming close, and pulling his ears or his tail. The poor blind Rabbit, turning suddenly round, throws out his paws haphazard; but the flock quickly gets out of his reach, and he seizes nothing but air. (Green 1965, 63–64)

Florian focuses on generosity and fair play as the rabbits invite the mole to join their party. The rabbit's hesitancy at blindfolding the blind mounts to a fitting conclusion. The mole, who sees with other senses than vision, refuses to change the rules and demands a tight covering over his sightless eyes, even though sight is not his method of perceiving the world.

The French produced an early-twentieth-century fabulist in Jacques Anatole Thibault, the 1921 Nobelist who wrote under the pseudonym Anatole France. Educated both in religion and the classics at the Collège Stanislas, he maintained the open mind of the skeptic in a wide range of essays and novels. Both erudite and ironic, he excelled at the discursive grace for which La Fontaine was famous and contributed regularly to the journal *Le Temps*. His partisan novels countered contemporary mindsets, particularly responses to the Dreyfus case and other evidences of prejudice in courts, the church, and the military.

Best known for *Penguin Island* (1908), Anatole France skewered the inadequacies of human society, a theme that dominates his fables. In "Hurrah for the Penguins," a scene from the novel, the porpoise philosopher Gratien passes through Penguinia in an era that France characterizes as "the later Draconides." At rest in peace and serenity, Gratien enjoys the respite and innocently questions the tune the shepherd plays. A peasant boasts in a virulent display of chauvinism that the song is an antiporpoise war hymn that is so popular that little children learn it before they can speak. Gratien's probing scratches the surface of deep-seated hatred so groundless that it must embrace specious logic. To the peasant, enemy and neighbor are synonyms. As though warding off rebuttal, he snarls at Gratien, "Don't you know what patriotism is?" (Komroff 1935, 473)

Anatole France creates a clever series of observations from the dog Riquet, whose meditations parallel the style of the Roman stoic emperor Marcus Aurelius. In Canto XIII, the dog prays to his master Bergeret, god of courage, and lauds him for providing abundant meat and a warm fire. To Angélique the cook, Riquet offers veneration "in order that thou mayest give me much to eat." (Komroff 1935, 471) The satire of human adulation of deities produces humor in Canto XVI, in which Riquet considers divine the power to open doors.

France stretches a little thin the final cantos, in which Riquet invokes fear, the sacred and salutary emotion that keeps the dog alert to his enemies. In the summation of worries that beset the dog, he cowers from vehicles in the street, ragged men, and loud children, all of which he epitomizes as "hostile and dreadful things." (Komroff 1935, 472)

An unusual addition to the canon of French fables comes from the juvenilia of Anne Bodart, a clever, but self-consciously bright prodigy. Born in Brussels in June 1939, she got a start on writing from her poet father and novelist-playwright mother. Bodart was 14 when she began a collection, *Le Fourmi a Fait Coup* [The Ant Struck a Blow]. In 1956, Houghton Mifflin published the English version as *The Blue Dog and Other Fables for the French*, translated into English by Alice B. Toklas. From frequent rambles in the Forest of Soignes adjacent to the Bodart family home, the fabulist composed 17 somber vignettes that stress soul over heart. For models she drew on two favorite playwrights: William Shakespeare for nature and Jean Racine for structure.

Well versed in the works of Stendhal, André Gide, Albert Camus, Thomas Hardy, Leo Tolstoy, Fyodor Dostoyevsky, Rainer Maria Rilke, and T. S. Eliot, Bodart chose theater as her future metier, a focus that weights her fables with a stagy, precious artificiality. The unease and free-floating hostility of post–World War II existentialism colors her outré anthology in the temerity of stalking cats, the singularity of a blue dog dying in the snow, and the irony of an ant that lures a ring of rat thugs into dining on poison on the morning they intend to execute her. The ant returns to the safety of the kitchen, where the mistress of the house surmises that the ant was responsible for killing the three dead rats. Melodramatically, Bodart concludes, "She took the ant on the end of her nail, then she crushed it under her foot." (Bodart 1956, 7)

Naive questions of destiny and purpose reverberate through Bodart's spontaneous tales, which peruse a preponderance of four-footers—dogs, cats, rats, and a poodle sold because of his mistress's dream—plus an amorous coffeepot, a magpie, Robin Redbreast, a sage skilled in witchcraft, and a man who paints an infinite line down the middle of state-maintained roads. One of Bodart's favorites, "A London Night," revisits the death of Julius Caesar with theatrical overtones of anarchy and terror. In another cosmopolitan milieu, a dog named Feverish Paw dreams of having an anxiety attack in a department store, then awakens in a calm sitting room where a butler searches for a lost pair of gloves. In "The Poet," Bodart juxtaposes a human esthete with two rabbits who disapprove of his plucking a daisy. Overall, her aphorisms speak to austere, troubled lives freighted with apprehension and self-doubt: "There is not a life without its secret fear," "Rather death than such a life," "He who has not observed the earth has not known beauty," and "An unhappy animal, like an unhappy man, like an unhappy saint, learns much more quickly than someone blissfully settled in the midst of his happiness." (Bodart 1956, 27, 17, 20, 46–47)

Bodart tends to look down for her settings—to the road, table legs in a café, roots of a mountain ash, shadowy mouse hole, damp cellars, an ankle-high vision of humans in a salon, a rat-patrolled sewer, and hell itself. A skillful *pourquoi* story, "The Cat Who Wore Spectacles," accords equal citizenship to a cat, mice, and a bird within a household after the master gives them the power of speech. Out of place at table height, where the cat scratches with his pen a list of human faults, the animals return to floor-level babble after the sorcerer rethinks his experiment and restores their original voices. Bodart's tour de force, "A Thoughtful Minet to Shepherd Dog," is set in the Roman Hades. The cat exults in the kindness of the ferryman Charon and in a shrouded world where night vision comes in handy. The speaker recommends that the dog cling to the earth, with its warm sun, kennel, and rug to wrestle. With self-serving ingratiation, the cat urges him: "Beware of the thought of eternity, dog. It is so much better when one's life was a contemplative one, and you have always lived a worldly life." (Bodart 1956, 35) With an inscrutable gesture toward the mysteries of the underworld, the cat ends its discourse and signs off with "Vale," the Roman farewell.

See also France, Marie de; La Fontaine, Jean de; Reynard the Fox; Saint-Exupéry, Antoine de.

Sources Bodart 1956; Cooper 1921; Green 1965; Harvey and Heseltine 1959; Komroff 1935; Lerman 1956; Mann 1987; Massignon 1968; Nitze and Dargan 1950; *The Romance of Reynard the Fox* 1994; Steinberg 1954; Strayer 1989.

 # GAY, JOHN

Producer of a popular farce, *The Beggar's Opera* (1728), and the eighteenth century's best compendium of didactic lore, *Fifty-one Fables in Verse* (1727), John Gay wrote with skillful rhetoric and many a spot of humor. He rid fable of the obligatory appended moral, thereby freeing it of a weight that had tied it too severely to textbooks and sermons. A model of his spritely iambic tetrameter reveals a pointed satire within the action. At the crux of a truce between dog and wolf, the predator pleads his case:

> A wolf eats sheep but now and then,
> Ten thousands are devour'd by men.
> An open foe may prove a curse,
> But a pretended friend is worse.
> (Komroff 1935, 240)

Straightforward, lacking the subtleties of La Fontaine's urbane style, Gay allows the animal to speak clearly the object lesson—that human mutton eaters have no right to call the wolf a predator.

A witty, cultivated author, Gay was born to comfortable middle-class circumstances in Barnstaple, Devon, in September 1685. From a lackluster grammar school education, he accepted apprenticeship to a London silk mercer and draper. In 1712, he left trade and, as the duchess of Monmouth's scribe and protégé of the famed Scriblerus Club, developed a journalistic bent. The shift in careers was fortuitous, for journalism revealed Gay's gift for verse burlesque and mock epic. His climb from bourgeois beginnings was threatened after he invested unwisely in the South Sea Company and fell from court favor. The support of the duke and duchess of Queensbury carried him through the composition of *The Beggar's Opera*, a resilient stage farce that Bertolt Brecht and Kurt Weill reprised in 1928 as *The Threepenny Opera*.

Often teetering on the edge of public disapproval, Gay wrote in the style that suited the English court and dedicated his first volume to a young courtier, the duke of Cumberland, then six years old. Gay's perception of the character flaws that predominate among self-aggrandizers fuels "The Peacock, the Turkey and the Goose," a verse argument that concludes with the fabulist's personal observations:

Thus in assemblies have I seen
A nymph of brightest charms and mien,
Wake envy in each ugly face,
And buzzing scandal fills the place.
(Green 1965, 87)

A more genial verse confrontation between widely separated social strata, "The Man and the Flea" pits the main characters in a word battle over pride. To the human gush about glory and vast consequence, a dialogue in rhymed couplets awards the flea the last word. His parting shot charges that man's vanity outweighs logic and quips, "What, Heaven and Earth for thee designed!/For thee! Made only for our need,/That *more important Fleas* might feed." (Cooper 1921, 286) A second spirited fable, "The Boy and the Rainbow," describes the fool's efforts to locate the fabled pot of gold. In similar jaunty vein, Gay composed "The Hare and Many Friends," a longer fable about the hare's flight from pursuers and her pleas to other animals for succor. Politely spurned by horse, bull, goat, sheep, and calf, she is left only the pack of hunting hounds, an unlikely source of rescue. Such a lethal conclusion displays Gay's understanding of a world in which losers face the inevitability of destruction by the mob.

In unusual pairings, Gay pits mismatched competitors in "The Turkey and the Ant," a battle of words. The face-off opens with a melodramatic sally by the turkey, which curses man for preying on her species at Christmas and declares gluttony the worst of the seven deadly sins. The ant, on which the turkey and her brood intend to feed, retorts with biblical sobriety that sinners tend to be blind to their gross faults. A parallel battle, "The Farmer's Wife and the Raven," sets Gay's verse in a folk milieu, where the foolish marketer blames the raven for scaring her mount and causing her to smash a basket of eggs. The suave raven refuses to be spooked by her mouthings and calmly retorts, "Sure-footed Dun had kept her legs,/And you, good Woman, sav'd your eggs." (Cooper 1921, 292)

An undervalued quality in Gay's fables is his gift for realistic detail. In "The Wild Boar and the Ram," he places in the boar's comments a horror at the butcher's duties:

See, see, your murd'rer is in view:
With purple hands and reeking knife,
He strips the skin yet warm with life.
Your quarter'd sires, your bleeding dams,
The dying bleat of harmless lambs,
Call for revenge. O stupid race!
(Green 1965, 63)

The ancient ram gravely counters the boar's charge with an account of widespread violence—the ravages of human legal battles and war, for which the race of sheep supplies parchment for court suits and membranes for drums. A similar study of the demands of nature fleshes out "The Two Owls and the Sparrow," a blend of fool tale and advice motif. While reminding the owls that they can't live on the glory of their ancestry, the sparrow describes the place of the predator in the scheme of things:

John Gay (1685–1732)

Pursue the ways by Nature taught;
So shall yet find delicious fare,
And grateful farmers praise your care:
So shall sleek mice your chase reward,
And no keen cat find more regard.
(Green 1965, 176)

Less graphic than the former example, the sparrow's litany values the owl for keeping down the population of mice, who, if left unchallenged, would decimate the farmer's granary.

Gay's verse profits from his skill in theatrics. A model of high drama, "The Jugglers" depicts the skilled fingers of the professional huckster, who flips cards like winging birds, tosses about boxes, and tricks onlookers with legerdemain. In competition, the abstract figure of Vice performs her own sleight of hand, besting the senator, thief, dicer, and miser. Gay brings the one-sided contest to swift conclusion after the saddened juggler must own that Vice is a matchless rival. In a second allegory, the dramatic spiritual possession of a rake in "The Universal Apparition" leads the former wastrel from worldly temptations but gives him no peace in repose. More violent in action, "The Mastiff" drubs a bully for his life of fighting. In these and other antitheses, Gay investigates the opposing forces that pull and tear at the conscience and disrupt the comforts of gain. His effort to cultivate a young prince through fable failed: the wide-eyed child grew into Prince William, leader of a chilling slaughter of Scots in 1745 at the Battle of Culloden.

Sources Cooper 1921; Green 1965; Hobbs 1986; Komroff 1935; Lewis 1996; Snodgrass, *Encyclopedia of Satirical Literature* 1997.

GOETHE, JOHANN WOLFGANG VON

The leader of Germany's intellectual golden age, Johann Wolfgang von Goethe was poet, philosopher, dramatist, and scientist. His dabblings in art, physics, architecture, autobiographical fiction, and *belles lettres* produced a broad-ranged expertise in a variety of modes and genres, including fable and folklore. The only surviving son of Johann Caspar von Goethe, a wealthy Frankfort jurist and imperial councillor, Goethe was born August 28, 1749. He profited from the accomplishment of his mother, Catharina Elisabeth Textor, daughter of Frankfurt's mayor. She enlivened his imagination by teaching him the arts, theater, and skillful storytelling. Goethe and his sister Cornelia studied with their father at home and acquired refinement and cultivation in the arts, particularly conversation in European languages. He improved his knowledge of French through visits to marionette performances; by age eight he completed an epistolary novel composed in five languages. His enrollment in the University of Leipzig in 1765 was a mistake. So incensed was he with formal education that he turned disgust and rebellion into useful motivation for poems, plays, and his seminal work, *Faust* (1831), a classic study of human ambition, on which he worked for a half century.

While developing his lifelong love of writing and translation, Goethe followed transcendental precepts by drawing heavily on personal experience. After the rupture of a vessel in his lung during his late teens, he took to his bed and developed interests in mysticism, alchemy, astrology, and the occult, which influenced his considerable contribution to essay and wisdom literature. Taking up formal education in Strasbourg in 1770, Goethe freed himself from his father's confining discipline. Among lively companions, he fell in love, learned to dance and play the cello, and studied where his curiosity led, even to transmutation of souls, anatomy, and midwifery. Before he completed a law degree, he came under the influence of Johann Gottfried von Herder, a passionate Prussian poet and humanist who introduced him to *Volkslied* [German folklore], the Irish hero Ossian, and the verse of Homer, Pindar, and Shakespeare.

Relieved of more pedantic interests during the early years of his law practice, Goethe entered an era of introspection, his famous *Sturm und Drang* [storm and stress] period, a reaction against restrictive French classicism and against his own inflexible upbringing and the pettiness of his milieu. A whimsical fable from Goethe's mature poems and ballads, "Der Zauberlehrling" [The Sorceror's Apprentice] (1797) draws on an original by second-century Syrian fantacist, lecturer, and satirist Lucian (or Lycinus) of Samosata; the tale may have been repeated in "Isa and the Doubters," an eighth-century dervish tale of Jabir son of el-Hayyan, a Sufist and founder of Christian alchemy. The fable combines Goethe's perusal of folklore with a recurrent motif of the callow young man who must learn the penalties and consequences of power. In contrast to his unsuspecting naïveté stands the unnamed necromancer, an ominous, Merlinesque magus who prefigures Goethe's Faust. The fable recounts with first-person glee the mischief of a presumptuous lab boy. Rejoicing that the elderly wizard has turned his back, the boy trusts his memories of the spells and orgies he has observed and declares, "I'll do wonders, sha'n't I?" (Goethe 1871, 98) Optimistic to a fault, the apprentice mutters:

> Hear ye! hear ye!
> Hence! your spritely
> Office rightly,
> Featly showing!
> Toil, until with water clear, ye
> Fill the bath to overflowing.
> (Goethe 1871, 98)

The frayed broomstick, dressed in an old coat, jerks to attention at the boy's command, grabs a bucket, and marches off to the river. In compelling verse flow, the spell leaps out of control as the buckets splash more water than the tub can hold, spilling onto the floor and brimming every container.

Goethe's compassion for humanity takes palpable form in the guilt-laden apprentice, who quickly assesses his error in judgment and tries to amend it. His lame cry mocks his efforts:

> Stop, now stop!
> You have granted
> All I wanted.

Johann Wolfgang von Goethe, age 73, from a painting by Kolbe in the Goethe National Museum

Stop! Od rot it!
Running still? I'm like to drop!
What's the word? I've clean forgot it.
(Goethe 1871, 99–100)

The rush of waters, a symbol of the outpouring of recompense for even a small infraction, threatens to swamp the lad, who calls the broomstick the devil's child. Over the door and down the hall the waters pour while the apprentice

130

searches for a hatchet. As the situation threatens catastrophe, the boy calls on his master, who quickly restores order and reminds the broomstick who's in charge.

More fairy tale than fable, the story of "The Sorceror's Apprentice" bears elements of both. In the tradition of the characters of fable, the boy, like the necromancer, goes unnamed. The action, which remains free of subplots and lengthy moralizing, moves quickly from cause to conclusion. Smoothly Goethe carries the end of the dilemma into a deft reminder that boy, broom, and master have their places in the scheme of things. More kinetic than Aesop's simple barnyard fare, more dramatic than the *Panchatantra*, Goethe's tale is an object lesson to the bold *naif* that mere observation of a master's performance is not sufficient reason for pupil to replace teacher or to dare the master's powers, even for an unguarded moment alone in the master's lab. The resurgence of the story in the Grimms' fairy tales, Paul Dukas's symphonic poem *L'apprenti sorcier* (1897), and Walt Disney's first animated feature, *Fantasia* (1940), attests to the applicability of the apprentice's distress to universal youthful high spirits.

In his mid-twenties, Goethe formed a lasting friendship with Karl August, duke of Saxe-Weimar-Eisenbach and magnet for a growing center for artists, philosophers, and conversationalists. Their companionship led Goethe to a series of permanent posts on the duke's advisory board. Bureaucratic tasks, which were secondary to Goethe, did not sap his energies or interfere with his development as a lyric poet. He engaged in astronomy, geology, and a serious study of history. In his thirties, he reached a turning point: after shedding unpromising personal attachments and living in Italy and Sicily, he broadened his studies of ancient and Renaissance art and architecture and botany, which, when added to his knowledge of northern European literature, integrated for him the two halves of European literary traditions. At age forty, he withdrew from the European turmoil generated by the French Revolution and retreated to Weimar, where the duke provided a new residence. Goethe gave up travel for domesticity and established a common-law relationship with Christiane Vulpius, mother of his son August.

His love and faith in home and homeland confirmed, Goethe treasured German culture, as displayed by the literary journal *Die Horen* [The Seasons] (1794), a collection of epigrams in *Die Xenien* [Epigrams] (1794), and his profane bestiary *Reineke Fuchs* [Reynard the Fox] (1794), a decidedly German odyssey and popular contribution to the fox lore of Reynard, the hardy story cycle of the medieval European trickster. Embracing nature for intuitive instruction, the poet searched for universal truths drawn from the struggle for personal perfection. During the rise of Napoleon, Goethe's novels, plays, and translations demonstrated continued interest in human accomplishments. His treatise on color, an amalgamation of scientific theory and essay, attests to his unusual background in the humanities and sciences. The genius and breadth of his literary achievements drew visitors to his home from across Europe and the United States, with whom he sought a world literary accord. After his death on March 22, 1832, he was interred at Weimar alongside his colleague, Friedrich Schiller, and his patron, Duke Karl August.

A worthy legacy to world fable, Goethe's bestiary, *Reineke Fuchs*, remained popular in versions by Karl Joseph Simrock in 1846 and in Wilhelm von Kaulbach's edition of Goethe's verse. During England's Great Exhibition of 1851, Herrmann Plaucquet of Wurtemberg dispatched stuffed animals for a display depicting the German version of the Reynard canon. In 1853, Thomas James Arnold, a London police magistrate and amateur translator, released an English version based on a translation of Goethe's verse. By 1893, the story found a spot in the Kelmscott Press collection of fine works, as well as the Cranford Series and the collection known as Bohn's Standard Library.

Goethe's fox story opens at Whitsuntide with Noble the lion holding court. Of all the fawners on royalty, only Reynard the Rogue fails to attend. By way of explanation, the poet inserts an epigram: "An evil conscience shuns the light of day." (Goethe 1954, 2) In the standard beast competition, Sir Isegrim the wolf approaches the throne to complain of dishonor to his wife and his children's maimings, all "befouled and blinded by [Reynard's] filthy tricks." Echoes emerge from Hight Frizpate the poodle, but Tybalt the cat halts the tirade by claiming the stealing of the poodle's sausage as his own crime. The panther redirects the litany with a ponderous summary:

> No kind of crime but he doth exercise;
> Nought sacred is there in his impious eyes:
> His soul is fixed upon ungodly pelf.
> Although the Nobles, nay, the King himself
> Should suffer loss of health and wealth and all,
> And the whole State to hopeless ruin fall.
> (Goethe 1954, 4)

The hyperbole ranges out of bounds as the fox's reputation falls from rascal and villain to outright demon and threat to civilization. Epithets accrue to the fox in the Homeric style—ranging from sacrilegious thief to most dreaded of beasts, vile dissembler, and foul felon.

Goethe emulates the style of the *Panchatantra* by inserting story within story. When Badger, the fox's nephew, interposes a reminder that Reynard was once friend of Sir Isegrim, Badger elucidates the relationship with an episode in which the fox purposely stretched himself as stiff as a corpse before the arrival of the carter. Tossed up on the load for recycling, the fox worms his way into the pile of wares and tosses out fish for Isegrim. When Reynard jumped down to share the loot, he discovered that his pal had left bones and heads as the fox's half. The episode and its sequel, "The Countryman and His Swine," are typical of Aesopic fable in that the fox behaves like the *naif* by moving rashly into the deed without assuring his share of the take.

Goethe sets up the components of Reynard's trial in clear delineations of court order: the accusation precedes two summons, a trial, pardon, relapse, outlawry, journey, advocacy, second pardon, defiance, and battle. The cartoonesque procedure follows Reynard to the gallows, where he undergoes a last-minute change of heart and, feigning penitence, cries out, "Oh, aid me now, *Spiritus Domini!* [spirit of the Lord]" (Goethe 1954, 72) Hinting at a buried treasure, Reynard gets Noble's attention and enhances the moment by mentioning an assassination plot. Goethe adds a bold shot at the queen, who allows her imagination to run on at the thought of treasure, widowhood, and a possible remarriage. The misogynistic riff, typical of the medieval antifemale motif, serves Goethe as incidental humor rather than broader-based caricature.

Following the traditional motif of a pardon, Goethe dresses the fox in the pilgrim's robe and arms him with crucifix and staff, but his piety is short-lived. He soon dispatches to Noble the hare's head in a pouch. Ever the dupe, Noble bemoans his fate as Reynard's victim:

> He has deceived me—Me! his King and Lord!
> How could I trust the perjured Traitor's word?
> Oh! Day of shame! where shall I hide my head?
> Disgraced! dishonored! would that I were dead.
> (Goethe 1954, 118)

Illustration to Goethe's *Reineke Fuchs* [Reynard the Fox], 1794

To the distress of the court, as the king sinks in shame, Reynard thumbs his nose at legal proceedings.

The final battle finds the fox ready for action with tricks he learned from his aunt. He drags his oily tail in the dust and slaps the wolf with it. Their combat favors first one, then the other. While the wolf lies panting, Noble calls a halt and proclaims Reynard lord high chancellor. After the fox's return to his castle and family, Goethe interposes the fabulist's purpose:

> The truth with fables hath the Poet mixed,
> That Virtue in your hearts may be infixed;
> And you who purchase and peruse this poem
> May see the ways o' th' world, and learn to know 'em.
> (Goethe 1954, 248)

In cynical medieval fashion, the lengthy episodes of trickery, irreverence, and outright meanness end with the cry of the pious—"The Lord preserve us evermore. Amen!"

Sources Draper 1992; *The Encyclopedia of World Biography* 1973; Goethe 1871, 1954; Graham 1973; Hopper and Grebanier 1952; Kohlschmidt 1975; Mayer 1989; Rexroth 1969; Shah 1982.

 # GREEK FABLE

Historically, the Greek fable fits neatly into older and younger traditions: it preceded most of the fables of India, which it resembles in style and purpose, but was predated by Babylonian and Hebrew fables. An example from the land between the Tigris and Euphrates Rivers, the earliest Sanskrit fable, "The Snake and the Eagle," derives from the Cassite period, 1500–1200 B.C.E. This Sumerian-Babylonian-Assyrian composition of rhetorical wisdom lore eventually passed to the Hebrews and Greeks, who developed their own sophisticated models of the form created by their Babylonian forerunners. The Hebrew fable is least common and occurs in three instances in the Old Testament, two of which date to the tenth century B.C.E. It was the Greek fable that dominated the eastern Mediterranean world and developed the genre to a familiar didactic form in Western literature.

Beginning in the sixth century B.C.E., traditional Western fables clustered around the name Aesop, the father of modern fables. A legendary slave griot, Aesop and his history are clouded by the passage of time and subsequent faulty references. Numbering some 200 models, the Aesopic fable influenced generations of readers, storytellers, writers, artists, and thinkers, including Socrates, who was jailed under a capital sentence for impiety. As he is described in Plato's *Phaedo* (ca. 345 B.C.E.), the doomed philosopher whiled away his final days in prison by translating Aesop into verse. According to Addison, on the day of the philosopher's execution, after his keepers had removed his chains, Socrates sat rubbing his unfettered ankle and remarked "on the Nature of Pleasure and Pain in general, and how constantly they succeed one another. . . . If a Man of a

Illustration of a Hellenistic sculpture depicting Aesop, "the clever crooked Egyptian slave of Croesus's court, who gave advice in the form of fables."

good Genius for a Fable were to represent the Nature of Pleasure and Pain in that way of Writing, he would probably join them together after such a manner, that it would be impossible for the one to come into any Place, without being followed by the other." (Addison, Steele, 1907, 46)

By the second century C.E. the Aesopic fable had evolved fully as a literary genre. In the introduction to *Fable as Literature* (1985), H. J. Blackham relabels the emerging genre as *apologue* and characterizes it as a tactical maneuver intended to prompt original thought. More than didactic sermonette, the fable is a fictitious tale that acts out a self-evident principle. In Blackham's analysis, the fable is an open-ended experience. It begins with an idea that takes physical shape as an image that the author expresses through narrative. As metaphor, each fable is a brain exercise that invites exploratory rumination.

The Greeks who followed Aesop never forgot his example but never achieved his greatness. Some who composed fables were not natural fabulists but users of fable to achieve other literary ends:

- Homer employs a trickster tale in first person in Book XIV of the *Odyssey*. Beginning in line 459, Odysseus tests the loyalty of his swineherd Eumaeus by relating a war story about himself and Menelaus, although he conceals his identity by claiming to be a third party in the incident. While sleeping on marsh reeds on a windy, frosty night, the speaker regrets leaving his cloak behind. During the third watch, he inveigles Odysseus's assistance, which takes the form of a phony dream. A gullible volunteer jumps up and dashes to Agamemnon with the portent, leaving behind his cloak to warm the speaker.

- Hesiod, author of the fable "The Hawk and the Nightingale" (early seventh century B.C.E.), was a poet, cosmologist, and moralist who provided Greek textbooks the rapacious hawk as a model of expedience. So impressive is the work that contemporaries comprising the Hesiodic school imitated its cadence and motifs. Hesiod's career was surprisingly well rounded for a toiler of the fields. His store of aphorism, folklore, and local customs attests to a knowledge of the early Greek canon too thorough for a mere farmer. Over a rudimentary stock of images, however, rules the farmer's pragmatism, the stout hope of a man of faith and the fatalism of a survivor who has lived hard. Only moderately superstitious, Hesiod turned from the vicissitudes of fortune and founded his daily philosophy on husbandry and thrift. The solid Greekness of his ethical writings provided succeeding generations with firm underpinnings in mythology and god lore.

  Stoic and didactic to the point of fanaticism, the poet fought his ne'er-do-well brother for the appropriate portion of their father's estate. In court, Hesiod must have foreseen his loss when the judges sided with Perses, who had already bought their verdict. Speaking in the agrarian idiom of Balkan peasantry, Hesiod composed his *Theogony* (late eighth century B.C.E.) as a warning to inane men like Perses of the consequences of squandering land and a guide to appropriate times for tilling, cultivating, and harvesting. Like a true puritan, the farm poet allots himself times for pleasure but never in amounts that would jeopardize his establishment of a paying farm. His *Works and Days* (early seventh century B.C.E.), a priggish verse epistle, includes a treatise on the Five Ages of the World, the myth of Pandora's box, and "The Hawk and the Nightingale," Greece's oldest surviving literary fable. The tale, which precedes Hesiod's commentary on justice, follows the Aesopic model. It attests to the vigor, tension, and applicability of the genre, which may have been long established in earlier times. Briefly stated in eight sentences, the text appears in lines 202–221. Composed in first person, it opens with a didactic frame, commending "a fable for the barons" to Perses, a ne'er-do-well brother who should profit from their understanding by internalizing the message. (Hesiod 1973, 43) The story tells of a hawk who has apprehended a speckled nightingale with his claws. Still hale enough to squawk, the victim annoys her captor, who advises, "You shall go wherever I take you, for all your singing." Enjoying his mastery of a lesser bird, the hawk supplies the moral: "He is a fool who tries to match his strength with the stronger. / He will lose his battle, and with the shame will be hurt also." Lest Perses miss the point, the poet appends a warning that violence is hard enough on nobles. For a weak man like Perses, it is folly to practice strong-arm tactics.

- Archilochus, inventor of iambic meter, mismated metrics, the recitative, and the epode, produced memorable fables, "The Fox Avenging His Wrongs on the Eagle" (ca. 650 B.C.E.) and "The Ape and the Fox," which features an unlikely camaraderie between an ape and a fox. Archilochus leaves a corpus of fragmentary verse on a wide range of topics and three vernacular fables, the most familiar cited in the *Proverbs* of the rhetorician Zenobius (ca. 130 C.E.): "The Fox knoweth many things, the Hedgehog one great thing." (Edmonds 1931, 175) According to Gnaeus Lentulus Gaetulicus, a first-century C.E. Roman army commander and poet, an aura of scandal and dishonor clings to Archilochus's name:

  Here, by the seashore, there lies
  Archilochus, whose Muse was
  Dipped in viper's gall, who stained
  Mild Helicon with blood. The
  Father knows it, mourning for
  His three daughters hanged, shamed by
  Those bitter verses. Stranger
  Tread softly, lest you rouse the
  Wasps that settle on this tomb.
  (Radice 233)

  Valerius Maximus notes in *Memorable Deeds and Sayings* (31 C.E.) that conservative Spartans suppressed Archilochus's books as harmful to impressionable young readers. To the poet's credit, his workaday language and steady rhythms influenced the playwright Aristophanes and poets Pindar, Callimachus, Catullus, and Horace.

- Aeschylus, the first of the Western world's three founders of tragedy, employed fable in a scrap of Libyan lore from *Myrmidones* [The Myrmidons]. Like Aesop and Hesiod, he tells as illustration "The Eagle and the Arrow," a bitterly ironic fable in which the eagle regrets that he dies from a projectile fletched with feathers from his own wings. The playwright speaks directly to his audience in the eagle's moans, "Thus, not by others, but by means of our own plumage, are we slain." (Aeschylus 1936, 425) Late in the seventeenth century, English poet Edmund Waller reprised the fable in the second stanza of "To a Lady Singing a Song of His Own Composing," a love plaint that rues:

  > That eagle's fate and mine are one,
  > Which, on the shaft that made him die,
  > Espied a feather of his own,
  > Wherewith he wont to soar so high.

  Parallel to the fable, the poem muses on Chloris's recitation of Waller's verse and exults that "with this spell / Of my own teaching, I am taught." (Lamson & Smith 1942, 1068).

  In *Agamemnon*, a tragedy of the *Oresteia*, Aeschylus incorporates a fable in the chorus's musings on upbringing. The brief narrative, "The Man Who Reared a Lion's Cub," builds tension by describing the cub's suitability as a pet: "Gentle it was in the prelude of its life, kindly to children, and a delight to the old. Much did it get, held in arms like a nursling child, with its bright eye turned toward his hand, and fawning under compulsion of its belly's need." (Agamemnon 1936, 63)

  True to its instinctive nature, in adulthood, the fierce pet wreaks ruin on the man's flocks and defiles the house with blood. The human family shrinks from greater carnage and weeps bitterly. The chorus concludes, "A priest of ruin, by ordinance of God, was it reared in the house," a parallel to Ilium's welcome of Helen, the prince's bride whose pursuers rain hellish punishment on her adoptive homeland. These two models display not only Aeschylus's skill with the genre of fable, but also his reverence for illustrative exempla as repositories of noble and enduring truths.

- Book I of Herodotus's *Histories* (ca. 425 B.C.E.) features a prose fable, "The Fisherman Pipes to the Fish," a witty rejoinder from Cyrus who disdains ambassadors seeking concessions. He describes a fisherman who pipes for fish in hopes of luring them ashore. Giving up on music, he turns to a net to haul them in. The fish begin to leap about. He reminds them, "It is too late to dance now: you might have danced to my music—but you would not." (Herodotus 1961, 71)

- Sophocles's *Ajax* (ca. 451 B.C.E.) contains two brief fables in the scrap between Menelaus and Teucer. Menelaus leads off with the story of a bold man who urges a ship's crew to sail during the stormy season. When the tempest rages, the man cowers under his cloak and lets the crew trample him. Menelaus concludes his parable, "And so with thee and thy fierce speech—perchance a great tempest, though its breath come from a little cloud, shall quench thy blustering." (Sophocles 1936, 213) Teucer's riposte is a fool tale that pictures a man triumphing in his neighbor's woes. Teucer sees himself in the reproachful man who warns the fool, "Do not evil to the dead; for, if thou dost, be sure that thou wilt come to harm." (Sophocles 1936, 214)

- Aristophanes's acerbic comedy *The Wasps* (422 B.C.E.) contains "Aesop and the Bitch," "The Sybarite," and "The Sybarite Woman." The first story serves the character Philocleon, who tries to demonstrate intelligence with his Aesopic remark. He puts into the mouth of Aesop a non sequitur to a barking dog:

  > Oh you bitch! you bitch!
  > If in the stead of that ungodly tongue
  > You'd buy some wheat, methinks you'd have more sense.
  > (Aristophanes vol. 1, 1930, 539)

  Philocleon continues with "The Sybarite," a brief dramatic moment when a friend observes an inexperienced driver who has fallen from his chariot and fractured his skull. The friend suggests, "Let each man exercise the art he knows." (Aristophanes vol. 1, 1930, 541) The third story, "The Sybarite Woman," is a brief folk tale about a pot that testifies against the woman who broke it. In a harsh retort, she urges, "If you would leave off calling friends to witness, / And buy a rivet, you would show more brains." (Aristophanes, vol. 1, 1930, 541)

  Eight years later, Aristophanes incorporated in his stage farce *The Birds* (414 B.C.E.) "The Eagle and the Beetle," the story of the beetle that seeks revenge against the predatory eagle by destroying its eggs. Even though the eagle flies to Olympus and lays her eggs in Zeus's lap, the beetle overcomes the bird by fouling the god's face, causing him to leap up and dump the eggs to their destruction. The fable attaches to Aesop's peril at the hands of the Delphians, who violated the sanctuary of the Muses' shrine and apprehended the fabulist to drag him to the place of execution. A second fable from *The Birds*, "The Crested Lark Burying Her Father," is a farfetched explanation of the lark's oversized crest. Because the father died before the world was created, the lark had no earth in which to entomb him and, on the fifth day of her search for a burial place, interred him in her head.

- Plato's *Phaedo* (mid-fourth century) features a prose fable on "Pleasure and Pain" in which Socrates rubs his leg after the removal of a chain. He ponders the two abstracts, which seem to dog humanity with both blessing and suffering. Congenially, he surmises, "If Aesop had thought of them, he would have made a fable telling how they were at war and god wished to reconcile them, and when he could not do that, he fastened their heads together, and for that reason, when one of them comes to anyone, the other follows after." (Plato 1947, 209–211) A similar abstract pairing comes from Plato's *Symposium*, which explains Eros's nature as the blend of his parents, Plenty and Poverty. Another nature story, "The Cicadas" in *Phaedrus*, is a charming *pourquoi* explanation of the frail insect that appears to sing and to live, like the Muses, without need of food or drink. *Alcibiades* contains an animal story, "One-Way Traffic into the Lion's Cave," which Babrius repeats. In Plato's version, the scant remark has the fox commenting to the lion that the tracks go in one direction just as money enters Lacedaemon but never exits.

- Book II of Xenophon's *Memoirs of Socrates* (mid-fourth century B.C.E.) incorporates "The Sheep and the Dog." In reply to Aristarchus's claims that the women of the house believe that he lolls in idleness, Socrates tells a story set in a time when beasts could talk. The sheep rebuke the master for feeding a dog that supplies nothing. The dog, who reminds them that he keeps away wolves, earns new respect in place of their carping.

- Demosthenes of Athens told the fable of "The Wolf and the Shepherd" (mid-fourth century B.C.E.) to King Philip, who had demanded Athens's ten most learned citizens during a time of danger to the populace.

- From the mid to late fourth century B.C.E., Aristotle featured several prose fables in his work: Stesichorus tells "The Horse and Stag" and "The Fox and Hedgehog" in Book II of *Rhetorica*. In the former, Stesichorus uses the trickster tale to warn the Himerans about the rider who promises to aid the horse against the stag. The man cleverly gains the horse's confidence, then enslaves him. Stesichorus warns the unwary, "You too . . . take care lest, in your desire for revenge on your enemies, you meet the same fate as the horse. By making Phalaris military dictator, you have already let yourselves be bridled. If you let him get on to your backs by giving him a bodyguard, from that moment you will be his slaves." (Aristotle 1946, 1393b) The second model is a finely detailed fable that Aesop related to the Samians about a trapped fox who was also covered with ticks. When the hedgehog offers to remove the ticks, the beleaguered animal rejects relief in fear of a hungrier swarm of ticks, who will drain him completely of blood. At a demagogue's trial, the philosopher concludes to the people of Samos: "This man will do you no more harm, for he is rich. But if you kill him, others will come who are still hungry, and they will go on stealing until they have emptied your treasure." (Perry 1965, 504)

    In pursuit of logic, Aristotle cites other Greek fables. In Book II of *Meteorologica,* an Aesopic story, "Aesop at the Shipyards," fleshes out a discussion of why the sea is salty. In the original telling, Charybdis, the sucking whirlpool, twice swallowed the sea. The first time, the mountains appeared; the second time, the islands. Aesop warns a ferryman that a third gulp will swallow the seas entirely. In Book III of *Politica*, Aristotle refers to Antisthenes's cynical story, "The Lions and Hares." The familiar moral demonstrates that the weaker animals may propose change, but it is the clawed, fanged lions who retain force on their side.

Another text, *Historia Animalium* [The Story of Animals], contains "The Eagle Once a Man," an exemplum of animal lore about the eagle's hooked beak, which gradually curves inward until the bird starves to death. The tale elucidates Aristotle's statement that the eagle was once a man who had wronged his friend.

- Demetrius Phalareus, an Athenian philosopher exiled in Alexandria, merely collected fables into *Aesopia* (ca. early third century B.C.E.), a single scroll without enhancement or development which Demetrius intended for use by writers, historians, and speakers. Although the work has not survived, it was an apparent touchstone for fabulists Babrius and Phaedrus as well as Plutarch, Dio Chrysostom, Lucian, and Themistius and receives mention by third century C.E. biographer Diogenes Laertius.

  A politician by profession, Demetrius was born around 350 B.C.E. One of the Peripatetics, he served the Alexandria library as its first director. He was driven from Athens in 307 B.C.E., came under the protection of Ptolemy Soter, and rose to some significance in Egypt's state affairs. Demetrius's writings include history, ethics, and politics. Although none of his texts survives, a list of his works appears in the *Lives and Opinions of the Eminent Philosophers* (ca. 320 C.E.), the notable source work of Diogenes Laertius.

- A restless, brilliant court poet, critic, encyclopedist, and reference librarian, Callimachus (also called Battiades) composed over 800 titles in varied prose and prose forms and left substance of 120 volumes of the Greek canon orderly and accessible. As a fabulist, Callimachus composed an easy type of tale that flowed naturally to its conclusion with no heavy-handed thrust toward a moral. The opening entry of his *Epigrammata* [Proverbs] (ca. 270 B.C.E.) tells the story of a stranger seeking advice from Pittacus of Mytilene, one of the Seven Wise Men of ancient Greece. Tempted by two offers of marriage, the stranger cannot choose between a woman of equal station and a wealthy woman from a prestigious family. Pittacus urges the man to follow a group of boys playing at tops. One of the boys cries out, "Keep your own rank," a reference to the path the restless spinner etches in the dust. The stranger departs with an answer to his quandary. More anecdote than fable, the story demonstrates the facile elegance and charm that Callimachus imparts to didactic narrative and exemplifies his willingness to deviate from rigorous rules of literary genre. A briefer fable indicates the poet's familiarity with the terse, pedagogical Aesopic form. In his eighth epigram, Callimachus tells of a boy who adorns his stepmother's burial monument in hopes that death has gentled her nature. In keeping with the stereotype of the acerbic, controlling stepparent, the poet describes the stone as toppling over on the hapless boy and crushing him. To this starkly catastrophic tale, the poet cautions the parentless, "Ye step-sons, shun even the grave of a stepmother." (Callimachus 1955, 143)

Callimachus's use of fable in the *Iambics*, a true *satura lanx* or collection of tasty pieces he may have added over his career, follows traditional Aesopic form. In Book IV, he employs a specific subset of fable, the *agon* or literary debate between rivals, for "The Laurel Tree and the Olive," which he claims to have derived from ancient Lydian lore. In the 90-plus lines—surviving fragments found on the Oxyrhynchus papyrus, which was discovered west of the Nile at the beginning of the twentieth century—the poet describes the boasts of two overproud trees on Mt. Tmolus in European Turkey. A thornbush interposes a request for peace and receives the laurel's rebuke for being presumptuous. The miniature drama suggests the poet's position as librarian in a civic institution, where pretentious, squabbling bureaucrats disdained his opinions.

- Early in the first century C.E., Dio Chrysostom's orations drew on two versions of "The Owl and the Birds," a portentous *pourquoi* story in which the owl warns the birds of birdlime or mistletoe in oak trees, the sowing of flax seed, and the fletching of arrows for the bow, each of which bode ill for flying creatures. Because they ignore her warnings, the birds suffer the effects of birdlime, nets, and arrows. Too late made wise, they continue to revere the owl, who has given up advice and calls out her lament for their heedlessness. Another fable, "The Musical Dogs," is a jovial spoof of lyre players. According to the story, most of the animal kingdom listened peacefully to Orpheus's music. Only the dogs tried to master the art. After they turned into human beings, the lyre players retained some of Orpheus's art, but a preponderance of canine behavior. A model of poor logic, "The Eyes and the Mouth" tells of the eyes' jealousy when the mouth enjoyed honey. The man ends the quarrel by putting honey on the eyes, which feel the sting and deduce that honey is really acerbic. In each model the fabulist demonstrates an astute placement of wisdom literature and its pithy morals.

- Plutarch, a Greek philosopher and biographer of the early second century C.E., frequently expressed subtle human concepts in fables such as "The Privilege of Grief," a *pourquoi* story that accounts for the purpose of sorrow and tears. In *De Capienda ex Inimicis Utilitate* [Concerning Learning from One's Enemies], Plutarch tells the story of the Satyr and Fire to illustrate the need to appreciate fire, which can burn the incautious. On the other hand, the fabulist expresses the glory of light and heat and the magic of fire in the hands of the artisan.

    Plutarch composed *Questiones Convivales* [Festive Inquiries], a nine-book dialogue on learned table conversation. Among his models is the survival fable "The Fox and the Crane," sometimes cited as "The Fox and the Stork," which was reprised by Jean de La Fontaine. A compendium on the conversation of seven wise men repeats "The Wolf and the Shepherds" and "The Dog's House," a fable explaining the wisdom of winter and the profligacy of summer. The dog, who must huddle in a ball in winter, resolves to build a warm house. In summer, however, he

Plutarch (A.D. 46–120)

reverses the decision made during warm weather because the work seems unnecessary. Another fable in this collection, "The Moon and Her Mother," expresses the quandary of a mother who can't weave a gown for her daughter because the daughter is constantly changing shape. More esoteric than models used by Aristophanes and Aristotle, Plutarch displays the broad motifs that open the mind to conjecture.

In *Vitae Decem Oratorium* [The Lives of Ten Orators], Plutarch tells of Demosthenes's fable, "The Shadow of an Ass," a brilliant tour de force that the orator related to noisy Athenians. The story begins with the quarrel between the driver and the man who had hired the ass. Because both want shelter from the sun in the animal's shadow, they debate who has the right to the shade. When Demosthenes stopped in mid-fable, the Athenians demanded that he finish. Pointedly, he retorted that they want to hear an animal fable but have no time for a speech on crucial matters. In his *Aetia Graeca* [Greek Causes], Plutarch narrates "Aphrodite and the Merchant," a *pourquoi* story of Aphrodite's advice to the captain Dexicreon to carry a cargo of water. When the sea grows calm, the captain profits by selling fresh water to stranded merchants. With the profits, Dexicreon establishes Aphrodite's cult in Samos. A brief fable of the runaway slave illuminates *Conjugalia Praecepta* [Precepts of Marriage], a sympathetic piece that reflects his warmth and personal experience. The story describes how the owner chases the slave into a mill, where he exults that the pursuit ended in the perfect place.

Plutarch's *Praecepta* [Precepts] contains "The Wren on the Eagle's Back," a common *agon* or competition motif that depicts the wren as riding on the eagle's shoulders, then dashing ahead at the last moment to win the race. In Plutarch's *Life of Themistocles*, he quotes his subject's fable "The Feast Day and the Day After." Also in the competitive mode, the story tells of a quarrel between the two abstracts as to which was better. The Day After boasts that his events lack the bustling and strain of the festival day. The Feast Day retorts that the Day After is indeed more relaxed, but its tranquillity depends on contrast with the vigor of the day before. The *Life of Aratus* cites "The Cuckoo and the Little Birds," a nature story about chicks that avoid the cuckoo out of fear that he will grow into a hawk.

- The prolific Syrian fantacist, lecturer, and satirist Lucian (or Lycinus) of Samosata utilizes fable as illustration, for example, "The Dancing Apes," which explains how a viewer ends the mockery of apes dancing by tossing nuts among them, which they retrieve in an untidy scuffle. Lucian incorporates in his Attic dialogue *Hermotimus* (ca. 175 C.E.) "The Man Who Tried to Count the Waves," a lyric Aesopic story. The protagonist bewails losing count of the passing waves until Profit appears and urges him to forget the past and begin counting the waves of the future. In *Cynicus*, Lucian tells of "The Boy on the Wild Horse," an illustration of boldness gone wrong. After the horse sets off with the boy clinging to his back, there is little choice for the boy to do but go wherever the horse takes him.

A haunting addition to Lucian's stories is "The Sorcerer's Apprentice," a dialogue story immortalized through variations and retellings. The fable of the impetuous young understudy recurs through the Middle Ages and in the Romantic Age before reaching its height in Germany's golden age. A lively addition to the poems of Johann Wolfgang von Goethe, the story prefaced his invention on the mad scientist motif, which spawned his masterwork, *Faust* (1831).

- Contemporary with the works of Lucian are the orations of Aristides, a Mysian orator and scholar who composed teachings he received in a dream from the healer Asclepius. In his orations, Aristides cites "The Mouse and the Oyster," an unusual pairing that describes how the hungry mouse pokes its head into an oyster shell in search of food. The incautious mouse finds himself trapped after the shell snaps shut. The motif of physical trap parallels that of similar body parts in a vise in Native American stories of the trickster rabbit or coyote and in monkey stories from the *Panchatantra*. In each instance, the fable warns of foolish actions that imperil the body or, by extension, a political or social position, such as allying with dangerous forces or trapping a political body between the elements of conjoined forces.

- Around 250 C.E., the biographer Diogenes Laertius composed a lengthy source work on Greek philosophers. One of his wittiest pieces, translated by Dudley Fitts as "Tauromancy at Memphis," describes the prophetic powers of a bull:

> At Memphis the horn'd bull told our friend
> Eudoxos of his approaching end.
> That is the story I have heard.
> But lest you think me so absurd
> As to believe that bulls can chatter
> Or bull-calves either, for that matter,
> Hear what happened: the prophetic brute
> With its long wet tongue lapped the fine new suit
> Eudoxos was wearing, as much as to say
> Your demise is arranged for this very day.
> Whereas our friend obligingly
> Went home and died. Age? 53.
> (Radice 1981, 282)

A blend of arch anecdote and fool tale, the stanza demonstrates Diogenes's adept inventiveness in turning fable to satiric ends.

- In the late third century C.E., Themistius, a Greek philosopher and cultured but derivative rhetorician from Paphlagonia, produced an oration for his father. In Book 32, he cites a resilient story, "The Creation of Man." The fable quotes Aesop's account of Prometheus mixing tears with clay to make human forms. Thus, the fable indicates that weeping is indigenous to human makeup. Themistius adds that humans should do their best to control their tears with soothing sleep and self-admonition, both of which are effective antidotes to grief.

- Near the middle of the fourth century, Gregory of Nazianzus, a Cappadocian theologian, composed graceful moral poems containing "The Origin of Blushes," a *pourquoi* fable. He explains how God differentiates between the wicked and the just by staining the cheeks of the good with red, which rises with their shame. Women especially suffer the infusion to mark their weaknesses. The truly wicked display no mark of shame because of their insensitivity to moral flaws. The story, typical of more flexible pulpit fare, serves numerous sermon topics.

- In a collection of speeches, Himerius, a Greek rhetorician of the late fourth century C.E., quotes "Apollo, the Muses, and the Dryads," one of Aesop's fables. The story tells of the god's performance on his lyre and the enjoyment of the muses and dryads until the latter frolic out of control. Mount Helicon rebukes the nymphs in a human voice and reminds them that Apollo's musical powers are manifold. In his *Eclogue*, Himerius tells of the advent of Eros, who allies the preservation of humankind with vulgar passion, the source of procreation. The paradox demonstrates the sophistication of late Greek literary fable, which deviates from the trite mythic elements of pre-Christian models.

- In Nikephoras Gregoras's *Byzantine History of 1204–1359*, the fable of the black cat approaches the ambience and pithy good humor of northern European models. The story depicts a shoemaker's white cat who faithfully caught one mouse per day. After she fell into a pot of blacking, the mice assumed that she had taken priestly orders. Fearlessly, they ran amok. The cat doubled her intake to two mice per day, leaving the mice to wonder why black fur made her twice as savage as when she was white. The implications were not lost on urbane readers, who welcomed satire of religious exploitation and excess.

See also Aesop; Phaedrus.

Sources *Aeschylus* 1936; *Aristophanes* 1930; Aristotle 1921, 1931, 1946; Bowder 1982; Callimachus 1955; Durant 1939; Edmonds 1931; Flaceliere 1962; Hadas 1954; Hammond 1992; Herodotus 1961; *Hesiod* 1973; *Hesiod and Theognis* 1973; Kitto 1951; Lamson and Smith 1942; Lang and Dudley 1969; Lesky 1966; Perry 1965; Plato 1947, 1960; Radice 1981; Snodgrass, *Greek Classics* 1988; Sophocles 1936; Xenophon 1959.

GRIMM, JACOB AND WILHELM

Folklore became a legitimate science after its elevation by two German ethnographers, mythographers, and philologists, the brothers Jacob and Wilhelm Grimm, a working partnership whose stories earned the praise of such diverse admirers as George Bernard Shaw, Charles Dickens, C. S. Lewis, and Margaret

Atwood. Known collectively as the Brothers Grimm, the two German librarians and college professors collected the most popular and revered compendium of children's fairy tales and fables of the mid-nineteenth century. Their devotion to stories of enchantment, witches, gnomes, and fairy folk preserved much Teutonic lore that might otherwise have vanished. Together, they authored the three-volume *Kinder und Hausmärchen* [Children's and Household Tales], entitled in English *Grimm's Fairy Tales* (1812, 1815, 1822), containing the signal works of children's fantasy—"Hansel and Gretel," "Cinderella," "Rumplestiltskin," "The Bremen Town Musicians," "The Elves and the Shoemaker," "Sleeping Beauty," "Tom Thumb," and "Snow White and the Seven Dwarves." In 1822, the duo also published a seminal commentary on comparative folklore, one of many articles and treatises that established their status as experts in the field.

The brothers were born in Hanau, Germany, a year apart, the second and third of the nine children of Dorothea Zimmer and attorney Philipp Wilhelm Grimm. In 1796, Jacob became head of household after his father's death and the loss of three siblings. Jacob and Wilhelm lived with an aunt while studying in Kassel. In 1802, Jacob Grimm entered law school at the University of Marburg; Wilhelm, who was weakened by heart disease, followed the next year. At the ages of 20 and 21, they were so impressed by Clemens Brentano and Achim von Arnim's two-volume folk poetry *Des Knaben Wunderhorn* [The Boy's Magic Horn] (1806–1808) that they began collecting their own *Märchen* [folklore]. As novelist Thomas Mann described their immersion, they were "romantically inspired lovers of German antiquity who listened to fairy tales from the lips of the people and collected them conscientiously." (Tatar 1987, xiii–xiv) Their obsession with antiquarian delights was compromised by their mother's death in 1808, when the brothers had to take mundane jobs at the Kassel library to support their remaining siblings.

The duo lived together, even after Wilhelm's marriage in 1825 to Henriette Dorothea Wild. The brothers achieved a working synergy, with Jacob providing the scholarly brilliance and Wilhelm supplying the practical skills of order, composition, and presentation and upgrading subsequent editions of their work. By their late twenties, they had completed two volumes of tales, the most popular in the German language, containing a total of 156 entries. Following their issuance of the sixth edition, the contents grew to 200 stories and 10 legends. By 1819, publication of the two-volume *Deutsche Sagen* [German Legends] (1816, 1818) earned them honorary degrees and positions among distinguished company at the University of Göttingen and, in 1841, at the University of Berlin.

In addition to their famous children's stories, the Brothers Grimm published jointly *Altdeutsche Wälder* [Old German Forest] (1813, 1815, 1816), *Der arme Heinrich von Hartmann von der Aue* [Poor Heinrich by Hartmann von der Aue] (1815), *Lieder der alten Edda* [Lays from the Elder Edda] (1815), *Irische Elfenmärchen* [Irish Fairy Tales] (1826), *Reinhart Fuchs* [Reynard the Fox] (1834), and the A–F entries to the 32-volume *Deutsches Wörterbuch* [German Dictionary] (1852–1960). Although they differed in focus and depth of scholarship, the collaborators were considered interchangeably as "Grimm" in discussions of German linguistics,

GRIMM, JACOB AND WILHELM

Jacob and Wilhelm Grimm

philology, folklore, and medieval studies. On his own, Jacob Grimm completed
a monumental four-volume *Deutsche Grammatik* [German Grammar] (1819, 1826,
1831, 1837), which proposed Grimm's law, the pattern of consonant shift in
Germanic languages that clarified the linguistic mutation that occurred when
language branches drifted away from the parent stem, as with the Latin *pisces*
and *pater* and the English *fish* and *father*. He also wrote *Deutsche Rechtsaltertümer*
[German Legal Antiquities] (1828), *Deutsche Mythologie* [German Mythology]
(1835), and the two-volume *Geschichte der deutschen Sprache* [History of the German Language] (1848). Wilhelm Grimm produced *Altdänische Heldenlieder,*

Balladen und Märchen [Old Danish Heroic Lays, Ballads, and Folktales] (1811), *Über deutsche Runen* [On German Runes] (1821), and *Die deutsche Heldensage* [The German Heroic Legend] (1829).

Unlike classic fabulists, their medieval and Renaissance imitators, and a contemporary, Johann Lessing, the Brothers Grimm insisted that fables thrive on expansion and detail, often quirky happenings out of keeping with nature. Literary historian Ben Perry describes their outlook: "What was for Lessing the soul of fable, namely its brevity, was looked upon by Grimm as its death." (Perry 1959, 20) The brothers' interest in elaborate fairy tale far overshadowed simple fable in their *Märchenbuch*, which includes the standard animal dominator-victim motifs in "Cat and Mouse in Partnership," "Wolf and Man," "Wolf and Fox," and "Fox and Cat." One quaint example of Aesopic didacticism, "The Mouse, the Bird, and the Sausage," presents in fanciful style the theme of family dissension. The odd triad keeps house, with the bird collecting wood, the mouse running the household, and the sausage cooking and dipping his blunt body into the broth to give it flavor. The felicitous division of labor ends after the bird grows discontent outside the home and insists on taking an indoor job. As is common to the Grimms' lore, violence overwhelms domestic harmony and results in the death of sausage and mouse, leaving the bird to fend for himself. At the bird's death, the story ends abruptly, its characters all used up. The implicit moral leaves the reader to deduce that a harmonious division of labor requires some compromise and that quarreling and jealousy upset the status quo, often at terrible expense to all parties. Twentieth-century critics and children's reading specialists deplore the casual reference to violence, mayhem, and death that permeates the fable, as well as the rest of the collection, but the Brothers Grimm apparently saw no reason to bowdlerize texts to shield young minds from lurid detail.

Other examples involve violence on a greater scale. A story of mismatched animals, "The Wren and the Bear," escalates from an insult to the wren's chicks and humble nest into a war in the animal kingdom. In jolly, mock heroic style, the wren summons his troops from the flying creatures and commences battle:

> He called not only the birds both large and small, but also the gnats, the hornets, the bees, and the flies. . . . When the day broke, all the four-footed animals came rushing to the spot where the battle was to take place. They came with such a trampling that the earth shook. The wren and his army came swarming through the air. They fluttered and buzzed enough to terrify one. (Grimm n. d., 38)

Though outsized by the offending bear, the wren tricks the advancing army by having bees sting the fox's leg. Because he lowers his tail, his followers assume that the war goes against them. At their flight from combat, the fabulists restore order but withhold a total truce until the bear apologizes to the birds. Perhaps catering to young needs with a whimsical ending, the story downplays war and saves its strongest statement for the sin of rudeness, which must be redressed by true contrition.

A third fable that demonstrates the Grimm brothers' emphasis on discontent as a forerunner of ruin is "The Straw, the Coal, and the Bean." Like "The

Mouse, the Bird, and the Sausage," the plot turns on an unusual triad who meet at the hearthside and determine to save themselves from the dinnertime fire by running away. Their disjointed companionship ends at a stream, where the coal crosses the water by walking across the floating straw. In midstream, the ember sets fire to the straw and, with its destruction, expires in the water. In a surprise twist, the fabulists rescue the lone bean by turning his part of the fable into a *pourquoi* story. After he splits his sides laughing and a wandering tailor sews him up, the story ends with a harmless conclusion, "As he used black thread, all beans have a black seam to this day." (Grimm n. d., 215) Typical of folk pragmatism, the ending appears uninfluenced by the two preceding deaths, one by conflagration and one by drowning.

In a preface to the second edition, Wilhelm Grimm states that he preserved collected lore in its natural state, but that he touched up expressions where necessary for meaning. In his letter to Goethe in January 1816, Grimm commented on the authenticity of *Children's and Household Tales:* "They represent, without any additions by other hands, the characteristic poetic views and attitudes of the common people, since only a strongly felt need was ever the occasion for composing them." (Peppard 1971, 70) He insists that his collected works contain no embellishments and that they are intended to please and instruct on their own merit. Through felicitous translation, the Grimms' collected stories and fables delighted the French and English and influenced other folklorists in similar scholarly compilations. In the Americas, the Grimms' anthologies became household items among German settlers and reached a height of popularity in the United States with the Walt Disney films *Snow White and the Seven Dwarfs* (1937) and *Sleeping Beauty* (1959). In 1962, the Oscar-winning MGM film *The Wonderful World of the Brothers Grimm* starred a top-heavy cast of Laurence Harvey, Claire Bloom, Buddy Hackett, Terry-Thomas, Russ Tamblyn, Yvette Mimieux, Barbara Eden, Jim Backus, Otto Kruger, Arnold Stang, and Walter Slezak. Although poorly received by critics, the film biography helped establish in the public's estimation the international reception of the Grimms' lore.

Sources Addison et al. 1907; Gág 1936; Green 1965; "The Grimm Brothers," http://nova.med.nyu.edu; "The Grimm Brothers Home Page," http://www.pitt.edu; Grimm 1972, n. d.; Lüth 1982; McGlathey 1988; Meigs 1953; Peppard 1971; Perry 1959; Ranke 1966; Tatar 1987.

HAMILTON, VIRGINIA

One of America's revered children's authors, Virginia Hamilton has a feel for native lore and its power over contemporary audiences. Born and reared in Yellow Springs, Ohio, she came of age in an area that once served as a waystation on the Underground Railroad, a stopping place for fleeing slaves who mapped their way north by the Big Dipper, their starry "drinking gourd." The daughter of musician Kenneth Jones and Etta Belle Perry Hamilton, she profited from local lore and the tellings of imaginative parents, who soothed her fears with tall tales and animal stories. She graduated from Antioch College in 1955 and from Ohio State University three years later, ready to begin a writing career that never strayed from the tales of night runners and doughty animals who stayed one leap ahead of capture. Before becoming a professional writer, she attended the New School for Social Research. Following a brief sojourn in New York, she and husband Arnold Adoff returned to her quiet hometown to establish a family.

Hamilton's outlook reflects the life experiences of her parents. Her father ran gambling parlors in mining towns and farmed the rich Miami Valley in Ohio. Her mother, the eldest child of fugitive slave Levi Perry, grew up in the oral lore of the antebellum South. From these divergent ties, plus the melancholy lyrics of her Aunt Leanna and the folksay of her Uncle King, Hamilton evolved a narrative base for a prolific young adult canon, which includes some 30 titles. Significant to their inventive plots are the tales and mythology of America's black culture, especially the garnered lore of the plantation housekeeper, who toiled "from dayclean to daylean" [from dawn to dusk]. (Hamilton 1995, xiii) Broom or ladle in hand, the black kitchen mistress entertained the master's children with riddles and word games, then returned home to the cabin fireside to delight her own children with stored-up narrative treasures.

Long burdened by distrust and fear of the dark, Hamilton has credited her gambler's instinct and the optimism of the wanderer with the productivity of her nighttime work schedule. Content with her industry, she has earned awards for three decades of publications. *Zeely* (1967), an American Library Association (ALA) notable book, won the Edgar Allan Poe Award for best juvenile mystery and a Nancy Black Memorial Award. *The House of Dies Drear* (1968) won an ALA Award, the Mystery Writers of America Edgar Award, *School Library Journal* "Best of the Best Books," and the Ohioana Book Award. *The Planet of Junior Brown* (1971) achieved both the ALA Award and National Book Award and was named a Newbery Honor Book. In ensuing decades, Hamilton has added the Regina Medal, Hans Christian Andersen Medal, Boston Globe-Horn Book Award, Laura Ingalls Wilder Medal, National Council of Teachers of English Choice Book, and the Coretta Scott King Award, all conferred on *The People Could Fly* (1985).

A promising source of black parody of the ruling slaveowner, *The People Could Fly* pairs stories with commentary in which Hamilton accounts for the dialect, narrative style, transmission, and purpose of plantation animal tales. For a Gullah moral for "Bruh Alligator and Bruh Deer," she presents the line in standard English, then appends its melodious low-country version:

> Dat w'ymekso ebbuh sence de 'greement mek, w'enebbuh dog run'um, buh deer tek de ribbuh en' buh alligettuh lem'lone, en' w'en de beagle' come 'e ketch'um, but ef buh deer ebbuh come duh ribbuh bidout dog dey att'um, him haffuh tek 'e chance. [That is why ever since their agreement, whenever dog hunts, brother deer takes the river and brother alligator leaves him alone, and when the beagle comes, he catches him, but if brother deer ever comes to the river without a dog after him, he has to take his chances.] (Hamilton 1995, 30)

The recital of the Gullah original reflects the writer's impossible task of translating pure verbal folk music into intelligible paper-copy English. Thus, the author explains that the ideophonic demands of animal voicings and inarticulate cries are as much responsible for the success of fable as is the bow to a viola serenade or heel taps to a buck and wing.

Within Afro-American lore, Hamilton highlights a resilient folktale, "He Lion, Bruh Bear, and Bruh Rabbit," which has made its way over Africa, Europe, and the Americas in the wake of technological advancement. In the guise of the droll griot, Hamilton relates the animal fable as an edifying entertainment for the young. In typical fable form, the smallest animals conspire to rid themselves of a prevailing terror by introducing the lordly lion to Man, whose roar comes, not from an overproud throat, but a gun. Downsizing the he-lion's self-promotion of "ME AND MYSELF, ME AND MYSELF," the animals bring peace to the forest, which is occasionally riffled by a subdued mutter of "Me and Myself and Man." Hamilton, a master of understatement, concludes, "Wasn't too loud atall." (Hamilton 1995, 5, 12)

One of a growing breed of pro-female fabulists, Hamilton dedicates *Her Stories: African American Folktales, Fairy Tales, and True Tales* (1995) to the mothers, grandmothers, aunts, and great-aunts who maintain the traditions that emerge from history and personal experience: "They let us know they stood for us. Talking, they combed our hair, rocked us to sleep, sang to us, told us tales of then and now—and tomorrow. They worried about us. They hoped for us and showed us the way. They cared." (Hamilton 1995, v) In retrospect, Hamilton admires the gentling gestures and facial reassurances of the female folktellers of her childhood. In the shine of their eyes and the play of their smiles, she finds a security that carries over into everyday life.

Security is the theme of Hamilton's pastoral tale "Little Girl and Buh Rabby," a benign animal fable that depicts the garden-raiding trickster in a harrumph of female disapproval—"Him, stand-up ears, tail, big ole feet." (Hamilton 1995, 3) Within the confines of the family vegetable plot, the unnamed girl-child immures the rabbit. After the father stuffs him in a gunnysack and suspends him from a prickly honey locust tree, the rabbit's fate appears sealed, but his wiliness fools the wolf, who soon is jammed into his place. The comic turn-about tale with its motif of the false message concludes with the wolf taking the ten stinging blows of the switch and the rabbit once more roaming free, the fabulist's evidence that humankind may win a single battle, but the long war between gardener and predator never ends.

A better glimpse of the matriarch's domestic control enhances "Lena and Big One Tiger," a comeuppance plot that pits a picky maiden against a four-footed shape-shifter who woos her in human guise. Impressed by fine buggy and sable horse, Lena marries in haste, then regrets the strictures of Big One's house, where she languishes for three days without food in the company of a dried carcass and a snoopy fly. The intervention of Jacob, a family friend, restores Lena to her family, but not until there has been a mystical tit-for-tat between the two males who fight for supremacy. Big One, angry that his domain is threatened calls "Whoga, whoga, whogalor, da humbarnorta, sundundilly?" Nonplussed, the stalwart rescuer replies, "Coo me sormber norty sundundilly indelarun." (Hamilton 1995, 8) When the masculine power struggle ends, the bride accepts the woeful truth that the tiger deceived her because of her boast that she would have no mate with scars. Hamilton balances this fearsome warning with "Miz Hattie Gets Some Company," a grandmotherly *pourquoi* story of a lone householder, owner of the first mouser. At story's end, the timorous female returns to security and contentment with Purralee the cat soft as a cushion on her lap.

Sources Abrahams 1985; *Contemporary Authors* 1994; Hamilton 1985, 1995.

 # HARRIS, JOEL CHANDLER

Chief among nineteenth-century fabulists is Joel Chandler Harris, the Atlanta-based editor and peacemaker who amassed the largest single collection of Afro-American folklore. From local beginnings, he created over 220 whimsical beast allegories to ameliorate the economic and social turmoil of the Reconstruction era, which his black persona characterizes as "befo' de war, endurin' er de war, en atterwads." (Brookes 1950, 3) Harris exemplifies the ease with which some white and black tellers exchanged native lore. In dialect, he exclaimed: "It's mighty funny 'bout tales. . . . Tell um ez you may an' whence you may, some'll say tain't no tale, an' den ag'in some'll say dat it's a fine tale. Dey ain't no tellin'." (Brookes 1950, unnumbered) Obviously at ease with African-American material and performance style, he set his series of fables far from slavery in a never-never land where firelight flickers and no outside force threatens.

Uncle Remus fables are long-lived in part because they appeal to the humble as well as the mighty. Mark Twain attested to their quality: "Uncle Remus . . . and the little boy and their relations with each other are bright, fine literature, and worthy to live." (Brookes 1950, 40) Lauded by Edith Roosevelt, who put her children to bed by reading them Uncle Remus stories, Harris delighted in dinner at the White House. His host, President Theodore Roosevelt, observed, "Presidents may come and presidents may go . . . but Uncle Remus stays put." (Remus 1982, 7) The president's family and other fans, including Walter Hines Page and Andrew Carnegie, identified the mild-mannered white newspaperman and raconteur with his fictional mouthpiece—Uncle Remus, the kindly old storyteller, a composite of several plantation models. Through Harris's skillful patois, the elderly former slave touched readers of all ages by personalizing West African fable and anecdote shared in a pure, innocent setting. Harris profits from the selection of a blackface persona endowed with antebellum charm and Old World wisdom. Rather than pose as objective ethnographer of the Uncle Remus stories, Harris took the role of the aged African griot addressing a young audience, whom he later identified as a fictive version of the real Joe Harris.

The premiere newspaper column—Brer Fox's invitation to dine with Brer Rabbit—introduced characters and situations that became a way of writing and a mask for the remaining quarter century of Harris's career. His familiarity with the smart-mouthed rabbit suggests a fictional compensation for his own shyness and wretched stuttering, which left him cotton-mouthed and panicky in public settings. Of his terror, he confessed: "I am morbidly sensitive. . . . It is an affliction—a disease. . . . It is worse than death itself. It is horrible." (Harris 1982, 9–10) To fans, he refused to recite or read aloud, opting instead to do his talking with a pen. Safely concealed behind paper and ink, Harris added to American myth with two compilations of stories, *Uncle Remus: His Songs and His Sayings* (1880), an anthology of proverbs, a story of the war, nine songs, 21 character sketches, and 34 brief fables averaging three pages in length, and *Nights with Uncle Remus: Myths and Legends of the Old Plantation* (1883), containing 71 stories. The second volume mixes middle Georgia dialect with coastal patois by introducing Daddy Jack, a true African, Gullah-speaking narrator. The complex dialect and its elisions and arcane spellings preserved a rare form of West African dialect but inhibited the popularity of the work among outsiders.

A rare episode in the latter volume describes how the self-effacing Harris joined a group of blacks one night at a railroad platform where the group perched on cross ties to watch for an incoming train. In a restrained voice, he told the tarbaby story, first published in 1879 and followed with "Brer Rabbit and the Mosquitoes." In the dark, black admirers called out "He's a honey, mon!" and "Gentermens! Git out de way, an' gin 'im room!" (Burrison 1989, 21) Without overt competition, the stories, jests, and vocal gestures of fellow tellers added to Harris's stock and found their way into publication when rephrased by the fictional Uncle Remus. Although Harris did not have enough light to take notes, he valued "this friendly curtain" of darkness as a beneficial condition easing inhibitions among the amateur tellers and implied that the night session also negated differences in race, education, and social status. (Burrison 1989, 21)

Wise to the complexities of human relations, Harris soothed postwar instability by narrating gentle beast fables that eased the disaffection between races and conferred honor on rural, earth-based tales and songs, many of which folklorist Florence Baer's *Sources and Analogues of the Uncle Remus Tales* (1981) traced to Africa. To the former slave's ear, the stress on fleetness of foot and trickery recalls the slave's milieu, from which the only release was flight. An added benefit, the interest of children in the Uncle Remus tales, boosted him to world fame as aphorist and collector of didactic lore about winsome animal characters who learn to coexist. Critics enlarge on local praise by crediting Harris with ennobling the American underclass, authenticating primitive vernacular, perpetuating Negro folklore, and validating black culture; but Harris knew a greater truth—the stories existed among natives in North and South America and in Egypt, Arabia, India, and Siam. Early on, the creator of Uncle Remus realized that his material was universal.

Harris came from an unpromising rural situation. Born December 9, 1848, in Eatonton, a backwoods crossroads in central Georgia, he was the illegitimate son of seamstress Mary Harris. Literary histories make no record of the Irish laborer who abandoned Harris's mother during pregnancy. She gave her scruffy, red-haired son the best beginning she could afford. Circumstance limited his home and education to a cottage and the local dollar-a-month subscription school, both paid for by a compassionate landlord. To supplement classroom work, each night she read aloud to young Joe from Oliver Goldsmith's *The Vicar of Wakefield*.

By age 13, Harris had developed into a shy, stuttering, inquisitive lad. While reading a Milledgeville newspaper at the post office, he read a want ad for a printer's devil. He arranged an apprenticeship in Putnam County and boarded nine miles from home at Turnwold Plantation with Joseph Addison Turner, editor of the *Countryman*, a weekly literary journal established March 4, 1862. Composed in the sedate style of the *Tatler* and *Spectator*, forerunner of the modern magazine, Turner's periodical emulated British satirists Joseph Addison, Richard Steele, and Oliver Goldsmith and achieved a circulation of 2,000. For a rural four-pager cranked out on a hand press, Turner's prospectus was ambitious: "This paper is a complete cyclopedia of the History of the Times—The War News—Agriculture, Stock-Raising—Field-Sports—Wit—Humor—Anecdote—Tales—Philosophy—Morals—Poetry—Politics—Art—Science—Useful recipes— Money and Market Matters—Literature—Gen'l Miscellany." (Harlow 1941, 83) Harris's job was the bottom level of journalistic endeavor—the selection of filler from volumes of François La Rochefoucauld's maxims and *The Percy Anecdotes*. With experience came the courage to submit original two- and three-line items.

In adulthood, Harris looked back on the apprenticeship as a poor man's introduction to the liberal arts and the basics of editing and composition. In breaks from the work of the printer's devil, he read books from the manor's ample library and the South's best news sources on events of the Civil War. He published regularly under the pen names of "Marlowe" and "Tellmenow Isitsoornot." Still in need of acceptance and parenting, he formed friendships with three slaves, Uncle George Terrell, Uncle Bob Capers, and Old Harbert, whom he endeared to himself by aiding a runaway slave. On serene evenings among friends while savoring fresh gingersnaps and yams baked in hearth ashes, he absorbed a treasury of beast stories and morality tales of Kaffir, Rhodesian, and Hottentot origin told in the grandfatherly style of the West African griot. In reflection of his fireside introduction to oral narrative, he characterized those plantation nights as "unadulterated human nature," richly grounded on a universal humanity and logic. ("Joel Chandler Harris" 1996, n. p.)

In May 1866, in the financial upheaval following General Sherman's destructive march to the sea, Turner lost his fortune and his paper. Displaced from the *Countryman*, Harris typeset for the *Macon Telegraph*, then accepted an assistant editorship on the New Orleans *Crescent Monthly*. Among the writers who clustered around Louisiana artists, he encountered humorist Mark Twain and Louisiana local colorist Lafcadio Hearn. In the autobiography *Life on the Mississippi* (1883), Twain reflects on Harris's physical attributes and demeanor:

> He was said to be undersized, red-haired, and somewhat freckled. He was the only man in the party whose outside tallied with his bill of particulars. He was said to be very shy. He is a shy man. Of this there is no doubt. It may not show on the surface, but the shyness is there. After days of intimacy one wonders to see that it is still in about as strong force as ever. (Twain 1990, 306)

Twain admires Harris's "fine and beautiful nature" and his genius as America's master of black vernacular. Twain got a chuckle from a flock of children, who approached the embodiment of Uncle Remus and were shocked at his white skin. To counter their dismay, Harris read aloud the tarbaby story.

From 1867 to 1870, Harris's advancing career resettled him in Forsythe, Georgia, as editor of the *Monroe Advertiser*. In Savannah, William Tappan Thompson replaced Turner as mentor while Harris covered the Georgia legislature for the *Morning News*. During his sojourn on the coast, he married Esther "Essie" LaRose, daughter of a steamboat captain of French-Canadian ancestry. Harris's final move placed him in a fortuitous role on the *Atlanta Constitution*. In summer 1876, an outbreak of yellow fever forced him to flee the coast with his wife and two sons, Julian and Lucien. The Harris family settled inland in Atlanta, the city most intimately connected with his development as essayist, polemicist, and teller of the Uncle Remus fables. As editor and adviser to Henry W. Grady, dynamic proponent of the New South, for the next quarter century, Harris produced columns and editorials that helped shape the newspaper's conciliatory policies. Domesticated and content at Wren's Nest, his country estate, he lovingly referred to himself as a farmer and his home as Snap Bean Farm. Now a museum and garden on Atlanta's outer edge, the property has become a literary shrine on a par with Thomas Wolfe's Asheville boardinghouse and William Faulkner's Rowan Oak.

A chance reading of an inaccurate article—William Owens's "Folklore of Southern Negroes" in *Lippincott's Magazine* (December 1877)—impelled Harris to publish a rebuttal, "Negro Folklore: The Story of Mr. Rabbit and Mr. Fox, as Told by Uncle Remus," published July 20, 1879. The event coincided with the

Joel Chandler Harris

withdrawal of federal troops from Atlanta, a test of the shaky reunification that bound black and white in the beginnings of an egalitarian society. Because Harris revered West African dialect and narratives that his friends had shared on Turnwold plantation, he pursued an avocation—compiling, arranging, and preserving beast fables, some of which he located among Daufuskie Island storytellers living near Hilton Head on the north Georgian coast. A subsequent serendipity brought Uncle Remus to the world: in 1879, Harris had to substitute for columnist Sam W. Small who had been supplying the Sunday edition with dialect vignettes composed under the fictional persona of Uncle Si. In his mid-fifties, Harris turned his writing from state politics and economic news to the lore he had heard from the genial old slaves he loved in childhood. An immediate success, the unembellished stories received a thousand inquiries and an offer of a book-length anthology from Appleton, a New York publisher. Numerous papers reprinted the weekly stories, notably the *New York Evening Post*, which Harris applauded for spreading an underappreciated form of Americana. Harris gathered the tales into subsequent anthologies: *Daddy Jake the Runaway and Short Stories Told after Dark* (1889), the story of the slave's flight and 13 additional stories plus one fable of "Crazy Sue"; the 16 stories in *Uncle Remus and His Friends* (1892); *Told by Uncle Remus* (1903); *The Tar-Baby and Other Rhymes of Uncle Remus*, (1904), which contains 27 verse folk tales; and *Uncle Remus and Brer Rabbit* (1906), comprised of 11 stories, 5 of which are delivered in verse.

Harris's purpose in posing as the black narrator of oral African fable launched much critical surmise and rebuttal about a fictional speaker who seemed much too happy as a plantation menial. The obsequious old man was depicted as dropping by the newsroom to panhandle and offer homespun wisdom, for example, in an opinion from "Race Improvement." Remus declares, "W'en freedom come out de niggers sorter got dere humps up, an' dey staid dat way, twel bimeby dey begun fer ter git hongry, an' den dey begun fer ter drap inter line right smartually; an' now . . . dey er des ez palaverous ez dey wuz befo' de war. Dey er gittin'on solid groun', mon." (Harris 1982, 200) By way of introduction, Harris asked readers with no background in plantations and blacks to imagine the nightly visits of a small child to a venerable old negro storyteller who retains from slavery the pride and prejudices that were a natural outgrowth of the system. In "A Story of the War," Harris softens the old man's image by calling him "Daddy" and depicting him as exceptionally tall but well bred, "his hat in one hand, a carriage-whip in the other, and an expectant smile lighting up his rugged face." (Harris 1982, 178) The old man is so devoted to his owners that he shoots a Yankee liberator who takes aim at his master.

Not all readers are prepared to accept Harris's literary vision of the benevolent old darky spinning stories of resourceful animals. Some literary analysts declare Harris an altruist and archivist eager to preserve Afro-American lore as a gesture of reparation to former African slaves. Others insist that he lacked ethnographic and philological fervor and hoped only to entertain and enlighten readers of the *Atlanta Constitution* with refurbished Aesopic tales. Throughout the academic furor, Harris maintained the guise of the *naif* and, in his life and letters, as reported in *Joel Chandler Harris, Editor and Essayist* (1918), quipped, "To know that you are ignorant is a valuable form of knowledge, and I am gradually accumulating a vast store of it." (Brookes 1950, 35) His understated preface to the 1880 volume publicly settles his stake in the issue of authenticity: "It would be presumptuous in me to offer an opinion as to the origin of these curious myth-stories; but, if ethnologists should discover that they did not originate with the African, the proof to that effect should be accompanied with a good deal of persuasive eloquence." (O'Shea 1996, 4) Thus, to remain well outside academic wrangling, Harris, assuming the mask of the genteel southern gentleman, shied away from any connection with folk scholarship or literary ambition. Indeed, in 1886, he groused, "People persist in calling me a literary man, when I am a journalist and nothing else." (Harris 1982, 10) A decade later in a letter to Ambrose Bierce dated July 16, 1896, Harris declares himself merely a "cornfield journalist." (O'Shea 1996, 3)

An underrated by-product of Harris's first compendium is the wealth of southern tradition that derives from the black slave's syncretism of Christianity with survival smarts. The author's preface draws attention to the rhythm of a revival hymn, a southern relic that storyteller Richard Chase characterized as "the sundown voices of the Negroes . . . singing their sacred songs." (1955, x) The eight-line stanza, first published in the *Atlanta Constitution* on January 18, 1877, rejoices in the retribution of Judgment Day:

> Oh, what shill we do w'en de great day comes,
> Wid de blowin' er de trunpits en de bangin' er de drums?
> How many po' sinners'll be kotched out late
> En fine no latch ter de goldin gate.
> > No use fer ter wait twel ter-morror!
> > De sun must n't set on yo' sorror,
> > Sin's ez sharp ez a bamboo-brier—
> > Oh, Lord! fetch de mo'ners up higher!
> (Harris 1982, 161)

The smugness of fundamentalism, when restated in underclass vernacular, seems an appropriate pose for a slave who is otherwise prevented from displaying hatred and contempt for a supercilious master. Like their Aesopic forerunners, these sentiments edge into impudence with the nuance of "De wheels er distruckshun is a hummin'." The revival singer—like the resourceful, undersized Brer Rabbit of Uncle Remus's tales—can chortle in private as white enslavers lose sight of heaven, the symbolic final resting place of the righteous.

Harris did not limit himself to the Remus format. His familiarity with a variety of character types, social milieus, and dialects is obvious in stories published in *Harper's, Saturday Evening Post,* and *Century* and became the basis for *Mingo and Other Sketches in Black and White* (1884), *Free Joe and Other Georgian Sketches* (1887), and *Daddy Jack the Runaway, and Other Stories Told after Dark* (1889). Outside animal fable, Harris published 20 volumes, including *Gabriel Tolliver* (1902), a contemplative review of the Reconstruction era; novels, *The Romance of Rockville* (1878) and *Sister Jane, Her Friends and Acquaintances* (1896); short story collections, *Tales of Home Folks in Peace and War* (1896) and *On the*

Wing of Occasions (1900); *The Story of Aaron* (1895); *Little Mr. Thimblefinger* (1894) and *Mr. Rabbit at Home* (1895), both diversions for children, the latter containing the *pourquoi* story "Why the Bear Is a Wrestler"; and a fictional autobiography, *On the Plantation* (1892), which he serialized and syndicated in national newspapers for $2,500. Overall, Harris included devil tales, hauntings and ghost stories, superstition, and myths and origin stories such as "Why the Moon's Face Is Smutty," "Why the Guineas Stay Awake," and "Why Mr. Cricket Has Elbows on His legs." In these, the author allowed himself to range beyond the plantation to tribal and racial origin, world deluge, and the workings of the universe.

The framework, too, alters after the initial stories. In the 1905 volume, Harris replaced the original little boy with the son, a pale, vitiated child who lacked the puerile impishness of the original. The teller comments on a different generation robbed of spunk "by that mysterious course of discipline that some mothers know how to apply." (Harris 1955, 580) More than ever, the nameless child needs sessions with the wise griot, who remarks, "Honey, you look so much like Brer Rabbit dat I bleedz [obliges] ter laugh. . . . You look like Brer rabbit when he tryin' fer ter make up his min' whedder ter run er no." (Harris 1995, 582)

Ever witty and ready to poke fun at human weakness, Harris displayed skill with folksay that resulted in a collection of dialect apologue:

- Too menny fr'en's spiles de dinner.

- Bad news is soon tole.

- 'Twon't do ter give out too much cloff fer ter cut one pa'r pants.

- Fine um what you will en w'en you may, good chilluns allers gits tuck keer on.

- Like settin' a mule fer ter trap a hummin'-bird.

- Troubles is seasonin'.

- De vittles wat's kumerlated widout enny sweatin' mos' allers gener'lly b'longs ter some yuther man by rights. (Harris 1982, 221)

- Hit look lak sparrer-grass, hit feel lak sparrer-grass, hit tas'e lak sparrer-grass, en I bless ef 'taint sparrer-grass.

- Ez soshubble ez a baskit er kittens.

- Lazy fokes' stummicks don't git tired. (Snodgrass 1990, *passim*)

- Ef youer gwine ter copy atter yuther folks, copy atter dem w'at some 'count.

- She had a tongue wid salt en pepper on it.

- Fool fer luck, en po' man fer chillun.

- De word went 'round an' when it come back ter whar it started, it ain't look like itse'f.

- When de spoon want anything it hatter go ter de bowl. (Brookes 1950, *passim)*

- Licker talks mighty loud w'en it gits loose fum de jug.

- Hongry rooster don't cackle w'en he fine a wum.

- Youk'n hide de fier, but w'at you gwine do wid de smoke?

- Watch out w'en youer gittin' all you want. Fattenin' hogs ain't in luck. (Bartlett 1992, 536)

At age 52, Harris, well known to the reading public, resigned from the newspaper in 1900 and devoted his time to freelance writing. In his last year, Harris, in collaboration with his son Julian and editor Don Marquis, issued more tales in *Uncle Remus's Magazine* (1907), which attained a circulation of 200,000. The journal merged with *Home Magazine* after the author's death from nephritis July 3, 1908. Posthumous editions of his folklore—*Uncle Remus and the Little Boy* (1910), *Uncle Remus Returns* (1918), *The Witch Wolf: An Uncle Remus Story* (1921), and *Seven Tales of Uncle Remus* (1948)—feature original drawings by Harris's illustrator and friend, Arthur Burdette Frost, to whom Harris dedicates the second edition of *Uncle Remus: His Songs and His Sayings.*

Friends and admirers mourned Harris's passing with simple ceremony at the family plot in Westview Cemetery, where he, his wife, mother, and children are interred near Joel's friend and colleague, Henry Grady. Alongside the grave is a marker of Georgia granite and an inscription:

> I seem to see before me the smiling faces of thousands of children—some young and fresh and some wearing the friendly marks of age, but all children at heart—and not an unfriendly face among them. And while I am trying hard to speak the right word, I seem to hear a voice lifted above the rest, saying, "You have made some of us happy." And so I feel my heart fluttering and my lips trembling and I have to bow silently, and turn away and hurry back into the obscurity that suits me best. (Harlow 1941, 276)

The sentiment reflects the times and regional experience that Harris embodies and the demeanor of a genuinely unassuming southern fabulist. In the lobby of the Atlanta *Journal-Constitution*, he shares honors along with author Margaret Mitchell and columnist Don Marquis, creator of "archy" the cockroach. Scholars draw a greater understanding of Afro-American fable from Emory University's collection of Harris's private papers, correspondence, and manuscripts.

Critical studies of Uncle Remus fables and of their African beginnings indicate that Harris did more than transmit folklore through cadence and altered spelling: his inventive style and perception of slave duplicity broadened the pithy trickster tales into recognizable story-length plots and provided a valuable insight into the slave's world view. Walt Disney enlivened the stories with color visuals in the double Oscar-winning *Song of the South* (1946). The first film to blend human and animated characters, it grossed millions on successive showings, halted only briefly during the race-conscious 1960s. In the cartoon segment, the mischievous, fleet-footed meddler, Brer Rabbit, and his animal pals

A film still from *Song of the South* by Joel Chandler Harris, starring James Baskett as Uncle Remus.

accompany Uncle Remus down a country road, sing "Zip-a-Dee-Do-Dah" and act out the famous Tarbaby story, initiated by the voice and wide eyes of James Baskett, who plays the lovable Negro narrator. The story follows Harris's debut, "Brer Rabbit, Brer Fox, and the Tar-Baby," derived from West African trickster lore and published November 16, 1879. After the screen version of Uncle Remus educates his young listener about the rabbit's self-sufficiency, he spins out the humorous Tarbaby incident, in which the rabbit's curiosity and stubbornness nearly land him in the predators' cookpot. Stalked by Brer Fox, the rabbit is unaware of the snare and comes "pacin' down de road—lippity-clippity, clippity-lippity—dez ez sassy ez a jay-bird" but well armed with the instinctive briar-patch survival skills of his breed. (Harris 1952, 548)

The plot of Harris's most anthologized story demonstrates an amalgam of universal beast lore and traditions of a captive people. A proponent of plantation courtesy—an outdated obeisance and coping mechanism that made bondage bearable—Brer Rabbit insists that the silent Tarbaby reply to his greeting. Further refusal ignites the rabbit's temper. Blows to the Tarbaby's body stick the rabbit, forepaw and hind foot, to the unblinking figure. To the boy's questions about how Brer Rabbit eludes the fox, Uncle Remus hedges, "He mout, en den agin he moutent. Some say Jedge B'ar come 'long en loosed 'im—some say he didn't." (Harris 1982, 10) The suspense is the hallmark of the plot, which turns on a persistant tension between large carnivores and their smaller, wiser quarry, who flourish from a blend of impudence and cunning. The surface story entertains, but the complex strategy of Brer Rabbit's plots satisfies by reshuffling a plantation hierarchy that relegates the bottom layer to blacks. As the bard explains in *Nights with Uncle Remus,* "Well, I tell you dis, ef deze yer tales wuz des fun, fun, fun, en giggle, giggle, giggle, I let you know I'd a-done drapt um long ago." (Harris 1982, 25)

See also Brer Rabbit; Uncle Remus.

Sources Bartlett 1992; Bradbury 1963; Brookes 1950; Burrison 1989; Davis 1970; Dorson 1959; Ehrlich and Carruth 1982; Harris 1952, 1955, 1982; Harlow 1941; Lester 1988, 1994; O'Shea 1996; Smith 1967; Snodgrass, *Encyclopedia of Satirical Literature* 1997, *Encyclopedia of Southern Literature* 1997; Twain 1990; Wilson and Ferris 1989.

 # HAWKES, JACQUETTA HOPKINS

An unusual source of fable is the perceptive naturalism of archeologist-anthropologist Jacquetta Hopkins Hawkes of Cambridge, England. A twentieth-century relief from the insipid Victorianism of the previous generation of fabulists—Mrs. Scott Gatty, Alice and Phoebe Cary, and Charles Kingsley—Hawkes avoids the starch and pomp of Edwardian drawing-room fare, sticky-sweet children's fantasy, and the moralizing of Aesopists to find her own oblique sophistication and delicately modernist point of view. Stylistically, she profits from scientific training. Her evocative, earth-based tales range from tight apologue to utopian myth and expansive prophecy, which transcend the lesson-making of mundane morality tales. Overall, her collection balances precise observations of nature with parallel sardonic humor and evocative studies of the human condition.

Born in 1910, the daughter of Sir Frederick Gowland Hopkins, O.M., Hawkes was the cousin of poet Gerard Manley Hopkins, also a nature lover. She was educated at Perse School and Newnham College, Cambridge, and pursued her profession at digs throughout the British Isles, France, and Palestine. When World War II intervened, she turned to civil service as principal of the Post-War Reconstruction Secretariat and United Kingdom principal and secretary of UNESCO. An altruist of high character and reliability, deserving the public's trust, she was named a life trustee of Stratford-on-Avon, Shakespeare's birthplace, at age 75 and continued to advise tourist boards on festivals celebrating England's ancient beginnings. Her extensive writings include *Early Britain* (1945), *A Guide to Prehistoric and Roman Monuments in England and Wales* (1951), and *A Woman as Great as the World and Other Fables* (1953), a compendium of 18 fables imbued with morality, discernment, and satire.

Hawkes's 18 animistic fables vary in texture, length, and setting. A lyric *agon* or confrontation fable, "Land, Water and Wind" exemplifies her expansive world knowledge and appreciation of nature's fine-tuning. In a pointless squabble, a stag confronts a shark, inciting broad claims concerning the importance of land and sea. The two are hushed by a whisper from the pines as the wind adds a third perspective:

> Because I have no boundaries but am free to blow forever round this space-hung ball, I am almost without being. I am invisible and can only make my presence known by bending the vegetation or roughening the water; I can only speak with the lips of the leaves and the falling waves. Be thankful that each one's bay is the other's headland, for otherwise there would be neither bay nor headland; without the contending of one against the other, both would lose all character and virtue. (Hawkes 1953, 36)

Vanishing into a hush, the wind can barely utter its envy. As quiet settles over the two combatants, they carry newfound wisdom back to their natural habitats. In these and other stories from the animal kingdom, Hawkes deftly analyzes the workings of nature. Long training in laboratory and field work conditioned her to value environment as nature's control and as an end in itself.

In "The Wren," a traditional competition scenario about the election of a king, the fabulist overlays the narrative with translations of bird and animal calls—the hen's repeated "Wot, wot, wot," the tree frog's thrumming "Natt, natt, natt," and, from the crow, a ragged shout of "Squorko." (Green 1965, 48) An invention on one of Aesop's fables, the story pits bird against bird to see which can fly highest. The wren hitches a ride on the eagle, then surpasses his flight and chirps "King am I! King am I!" but earns the jibes of his fellows for scheming. (Green 1965, 49) Hawkes inserts a three-paragraph fable-within-a-fable with a *pourquoi* note accounting for the owl's nocturnal habits. The fable concludes with the birds' impasse: the wren earns the title of hedge-king for his boast of "King am I!" and the lark, ignoring the birds' protracted squabble, contents herself with the sunrise. Wise in her immersion in nature, she calls, "Oh, how lovely! how lovely! Oh, how lovely, how lovely!" (Green 1965, 50)

Anticipating the utopian exodus of rabbits in Richard Adams's *Watership Down* (1972), Hawkes composed a gem of a fable that expands the genre with complex themes and journey motifs derived from Homer and Anglo-Saxon folk epic. Her heroic company, a community of beavers, wearies of their small island domain and longs for "Other Island," the ideal homeland. The structure of the story carries the adventurers far away over salt water in a homemade craft powered by waggling beaver tails. The mission, like expeditions headed for the New World, requires suffering and sacrifice in the loss of fresh fish for food and the drowning of oarsmen swept overboard. On the survivors' return, Hawkes contrasts their disillusionment in the anticipated perfect world with their rapture in the seer's made-up stories. Bedraggled and short-tempered, they settle in for an evening of banqueting and recitation. The elder comments enthusiastically on the storyteller's powers and promises the adventurers that they will be magically transported to distant climes. A forgiving story, Hawkes's beaver fable poses a benign contrast between the hardy dreamers who actualize their ideals and the storyteller who demands no more exertion than relaxed body and willing ears.

With another epic fable, "The Great Fish," Hawkes blends nature lore with the creation of a mythic forebear, the one salmon who refuses defeat. The story, reminiscent of Hawaiian fable about the shark, follows the cyclic struggles of the fish upstream and over obstacles to their spawning grounds. Amid fast-flowing glacial runoff, the migrators, one by one, give up their fight against the current and choose a bed for their young. Hawkes ennobles the hard-headedness of the one fish whose persistence plunges him repeatedly into a tall cataract. At the fish's inevitable death, the author carries his example far into the future, when all fish learn from their forebear's example. A model of universal wisdom lore, the story depicts him reduced to a backbone feathered with spiny ribs and concludes with the paradox of the individualist-turned-martyr: of all the fish who swim upstream, only the daring adventurer attains immortality.

Hawkes's artful fables range over a broad landscape—a walled garden, a city of cats, a plantation, and a beautiful fountain that crumbles from one slip of a clumsy bullock that wandered into a dainty garden enclosure without intending harm. In another antithesis, "The Garden Seat," a bed of yellow alyssum overtakes a bench and consumes the rock garden itself, shutting out visitors entirely. A variation on the Roman fable about the body parts' quarrel with the stomach, "The Weevil and the Chestnut Tree" focuses on the destruction of the tree's parts for the delight of the insidious weevil. In the end, the greedy insect destroys a whole tree, a vast feast of wood pulp that far exceeds his need. In a contrasting mood, the title story depicts the rebellion of a titanic woman against the wind, who has been her all-consuming, domineering lover. Intrigued by solitary delights, the protagonist can gaze at her body in the bath and roll among the clouds in an ecstasy that derives from self-pleasure. Parallel to the woman's overthrow of an oppressor, "Elopdatery"—a word maneuver based on "tadpole" spelled backwards—pictures the frog community suffering from a draconian law that reduces their number to one pair. In each whimsical examination of proportion, the matter of place echoes the necessary rigidity of biological placement and questions human individualism and its challenge to nature.

Hawkes enhances the tension created by her probing fables through deft juxtaposition of stories. Two ominous perusals of nature, "Export and Die" and "Death and the Standard of Living," speak through symbolism the author's doubts about human ambition. The first fable depicts the greed of penguins willing to trade their eggs for sacks of fish. A neatly contrived miniature of the free market system winds down to the scruffy remains of a civilization in shambles. When the overseers attempt to return the penguins to the natural order, a rout ensues, with young penguins splashing the spokesman and an older female fouling his feet with excrement. The second story about the surreal corruption and decline of a lovely girl follows the protagonist through an escalating bloat of fashion—overlarge purses crammed with makeup, tight shoes and dresses, and outsized hats and corsets that overwhelm her human qualities. The story ends at the grave after the woman confronts the image of the girl she once was. Without a cry, the clotheshorse sinks into oblivion, covered by a winding sheet of fashion and a layer of crumbling earth. In both fables, the slide to destruction is direct and swift, but a whiff of regret pervades the finale of each, revealing the author's reluctance to subdue a subjectivity that undercuts her scientific bent.

In Hawkes's literary cosmos, creatures, for all their curiosity and striving for something better, do well to remain where nature intends them. From a pontifical point of view, she creates human strictures in "The Poet, the Woman and the Wall," a melodramatic fable that echoes the failed love of Pyramus and Thisbe, a Greek myth about a pair of lovers separated by a wall. The fable turns on the spontaneous love match between a poet and a beautiful married woman who meet at the court theater. The fabulist gives the star-crossed pair a single moment face to face before separating them forever—she imprisoned like Rapunzel in a tower for her adulterous intentions and he self-exiled at the foot of the structure to sing endless canticles to his lady fair. With a brief ironic twist on the romance of unattainable union, the fable ends with the "woman [experiencing] an even loftier exaltation than before" and the poet reaching heights of classic lyricism.

Lucid, yet distant, Hawkes's ironies deepen from questions of character and appropriate behavior to the whims of fate. In "The Couple Who Lived and the Couple Who Died," she painstakingly contrasts two marriages and narrates the surviving couple's faithfulness to the friends who died in the bloom of love. In an unexpected lurch from melancholy, the fable concludes with the elderly husband stroking his wife's hand and gazing with revulsion at her knotty veins. The either-or motif appears to power "The Three Women," a story in the tradition of the king's search for a wife, which dates as far back as the *Panchatantra*. In Hawkes's revisionist telling, a god attempts to create the perfect woman by wedding obedience and restraint to passion. Departing from the usual "lady or the tiger" choice, the fable swamps an unsuspecting third party, the potential brides' handmaiden, who has no notion of vying for the position of consort to a god. Redolent with feminist irony, the story pretends to glory in the girl's suitability, but Hawkes inserts her doubt that a patriarchal marriage is meant to please the wife.

In a departure from typical fable settings and characters, Hawkes poses her longest entry, "The Unites," an intriguing utopian myth that depicts struggle on earth through the observations of God's messenger. In her insightful vision, Hawkes describes how "the Messenger had come close enough to Men during the centuries he had remained among them to understand something of their anguish, their wish for peace." (Hawkes 1953, 101) The messenger is enthralled with the beauties of nature at dusk, then dismayed by the depraved, sac-like beings who have evolved over time. A fragment of an inscription, "Unites the Human Race"—a phrase from the first stanza of "The Internationale," the Communist workers' anthem—gives the story its title and reflects on the irony of humanity's mechanistic hell on earth, generated in part by atomic power.

Hawkes's contrast of a failed majority with a small pocket of survivors lifts the fable from jeremiad to vision. In the style of the utopist masters—George Orwell, Aldous Huxley, H. G. Wells, Ayn Rand, and Yevgeny Zamyatin—she rebuilds the narrative in the opposite direction, toward a pastoral contentment. In a miniature monarchy, replete with the failings of earlier eras of human history, live a people who destroy their society by overthrowing and enslaving the advanced Unites, then consuming themselves in civil war. In describing the survivors, the messenger is disappointed in their fallacies and cruel actions and declares, "Many of those present were still only beginners in humanity and had little understanding of words and feelings." (Hawkes 1953, 165) With painful awareness of human weakness, he asks God, "Must the best and the worst always flourish together among Men? I fear it may be so, dear Lord." Still drawn to the clash of hope battling despair, the messenger requests that God dispatch him once more to earth to observe the unfolding drama.

The rare amalgam of scientist and fabulist, Jacquetta Hawkes maintains enough severity and edge in her tone to force readers to make their own value judgments about situations that are far from obvious at first glance. Her strength as a writer appears in the meticulous study of details, both of inanimate and animate nature. In "The Unites," she speaks through the Sage, the unnamed savant and historian who lectures surviving earthlings on humanity's decline and helps them to anticipate the future. With the controlled passion of the scientist, he insists, "To feel responsibility for those below, to devote oneself to those above. That should be Man's inalienable gift, one of the gifts distinguishing him from beasts and insects." (Hawkes 1953, 169) Riposting to the arrogance of misguided humanity, Hawkes speaks through the Sage her perception of human intellect among earth's priorities: "Those great men who have been put at the head of society are as grains of dust at the foot of the colossal mystery of this universe." She enlarges on the concept of hubris with a bit of the stargazer's advice: "Look, my friends, through the depths of the starry sky above you and take it as a symbol of the mystery that dwarfs us all." To its detriment as a fable, Hawkes's overlong, overly ambitious tale has the makings of a novel. Like H. G. Wells's *Time Machine*, it takes on the whole of human history, yet, in a refined, even flow of narrative, it embodies her view of the fabulist—a humanist whose wisdom chips away at the follies that doom human progress.

Sources Butcher 1953; Dobrée 1953; Fremantle 1953; Green 1965; Hawkes 1953; Matthews 1953; Shattock 1993.

 # HISPANIC FABLE

Hispanic fable reached the North, South, and Central America and the Caribbean in a form that reflected European values, themes, and settings. Carried by soldiers, adventurers, and priests, these illustrative tales passed into the lore of native tellers whom Spain conquered between 1591 and 1621 in a rapid racial and cultural amalgamation. Motifs fit the cultural outlook of confluent lore:

- As curriculum of convent schools, which provided acculturation for native peoples, Tomás de Iriarte's fables demonstrated the teller's strong moral and ethical intent.

- Fool tales and popular *corridos*, the folk ballads arising from current events, expressed the contempt and envy of nonwhite peoples for the ignorant *gringo*, the perennial white dupe.

- Unadorned trickster lore such as "Rabbit and Fox" and "Rabbit and Coyote" used irony and satire to laud native people for their survival of conquest, genocide, and despair. The sturdy often are depicted as humble burros or wily goats, the doughty animals that thrive in Mexico's rugged Sierra Madres. A popular trickster of anonymous Hispanic lore is Judge Coyote, the rascal of Mexican fiction who permeates folk fable as far north as Colorado and south to the Latino enclaves of Central and South America. In the episode of Rabbit and Rattlesnake, the rescuer saves the snake from a crushing rock. Rattlesnake rewards him by claiming him for his dinner. Upon Rabbit's appeal to Judge Coyote, the sly trickster maneuvers the snake back under the boulder and rebukes him: "You are the great villain of the *animalitos*. . . . Now you have your reward for trying to eat Señor Rabbit after he treated you with kindness." (Creeden 1994, 81) A familiar balance of opportunism with deception, the story suits the Mexican sense of justice.

An unusual source of Spanish fable, "The Carol of the Birds," a gentle Christmas ballad recorded in English by the Robert Shaw Chorale, sets up a community of birds as its cast. The amicable procession follows the Star of Bethlehem to the Christ Child's bed. Each responds to the miracle of divine birth as its nature dictates: leading the way, the kingly eagle enters with praise and proclamation; in his shadow, the sparrow, a spirited, but less impressive bird, declares a cause for jubilation. The list of feathered callers wings in and out of the haunting strains, a melodic minor rich in harmony and graceful phrasing. After the robin, cuckoo, and quail embarrass themselves by vying for the virgin's attention, the fabulist turns to closure. In the final two lines, the barn owl takes his turn, but finds the scene too radiant for a night flier's eyes. Blinded by brilliance, he speeds homeward to the safety of darkness. A subtle song-fable, the cortege of visitors from nature parallels the biblical seekers—regal magi alongside tattered shepherds and a sublime chorus of angels. The folk fable's shift in point of view from human social groups to animal classes and subclasses reprises the Aesopic intent to represent in animal bodies the foibles of humanity.

Hispanic-American contributors to America's folk base regularly draw on fable, much as the Greco-Roman lyric and dramatic authors placed apologue throughout their canon. The purveyors of incidental fable range from Gabriel Garcia Márquez's magical realism, as displayed by *One Hundred Years of Solitude* (1970), the *llanista*, or ranchland, fiction of Rudolfo Anaya, Southwest-based author of *Bless Me, Ultima* (1972), and collected lore of Américo Paredes, native of Brownsville, Texas, president of the American Folklore Society and author of *Uncle Remus con Chile* [Uncle Remus with Chile] (1992), to the works of Chilean journalist Jacqueline Balcells and Peruvian novelist Isabel Allende. While living in Paris, Balcells composed in French "The Enchanted Raisin" (1986) for her children. Since its appearance in Spanish and English, the fable has become a staple in modern collections of apologue.

Opening in "once upon a time" style, the transformation tale focuses on an unnamed mother of "three absolutely unbearable children." (Balcells 1996, 478)

While the father travels on business, their misbehavior gradually shrinks the attractive mother into grandmotherly decrepitude, but the children continue thinking up willful pranks:

> "Let's take the feathers out of the pillows!"
> "Let's pull out the dog's fur!"
> "Let's cut off the cat's ears!"
> "Let's dig a hole in the field for the gardener to fall into!"

After the mother turns into a raisin, the story pursues a humorously overstated "evil stepmother" motif. Balcells inserts an internal moral at the height of danger, when the hungry children, locked in the attic, "realized with surprise that they hadn't fought, whined, or played pranks for a long time." (Balcells 1996, 481) Charged with a child's sense of justice, the story concludes with the rejuvenation of the shriveled mother from a soak in the children's tears. Without explicit moralizing, Balcells illustrates the value of shared misfortune and challenge in restoring order and good behavior.

Balcells's contemporary, Isabel Allende, uses fable as a binding factor in *La casa de los espíritus* [The House of the Spirits] (1982), an international best-seller that has been called the "Gone with the Wind" of Chile. The novel and its film version boosted her to fame as the leading female author of Latin America. In Chapter 4, she inserts a pivotal beast fable, with which Pedro García entertains his grandson, Pedro Tercero, and Pedro's friend Blanca, the child of Esteban Trueba, Pedro's arrogant *patrón* and the owner of Tres Marías, a sizable plantation. The story is an obvious allegory on the colonial social order by which the landed gentry exploit poor native workers. In the action, a fox makes a nightly raid on a henhouse to steal eggs and devour baby chicks. To save their domain, the hens, symbols of grassroots rebellion, organize a reprisal. Descending on the fox, they peck him severely and rout him from the coop.

Allende depicts Blanca Trueba as laughing at the entertaining story and young Pedro as stony-faced and pensive. Unlike the aristocratic Blanca, who has known the best of the best, Pedro has lived the hardscrabble existence of the plantation drone and perceives that the storyteller has a greater purpose in the story. In Allende's words, "He spent the whole evening absorbed in thought, ruminating on the story of the fox and the hens, and perhaps that was the night the boy began to become a man." (Allende 1982, 141) When Pedro Tercero grows into a volatile revolutionary, he popularizes the fable as a subversive cantina ballad that characterizes the peasant intent to rid themselves of enslavement to the aristocracy. In subtle Aesopic style, he subtly instructs the underclass to be patient and to trust their growing union to defeat the colonial foxes who enrich themselves on the proceeds of peon labor. Through the singer, the old storyteller's fable remains alive throughout the novel and foreshadows the inevitable clash between rising socialism and entrenched moneyed interests. By the time Pedro Tercero reaches his mid-thirties, he is an astute anarchist who "[sings] of life, friendship, love, and also revolution." (Allende 1982, 309) Allende's empowerment through fable returns to the genre's humble beginnings. By placing the beast tale at the heart of her nationalistic novel, she

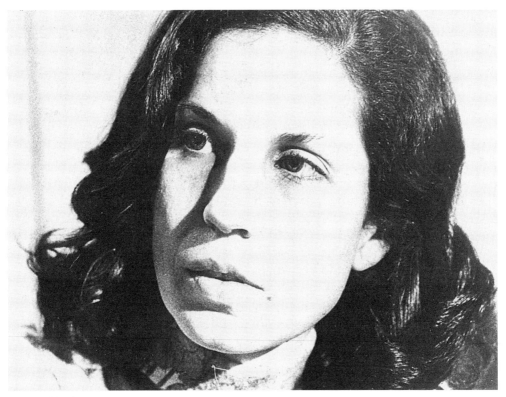

Isabel Allende

accords to the humble the respect they merit for persevering against overwhelming elitism. Allende's tribute to her homeland was filmed in 1993 in a screen saga starring Meryl Streep, Jeremy Irons, Glenn Close, and Vanessa Redgrave. A well-matched pair, Winona Ryder as Blanca and Antonio Banderas as the storysinger-turned-rebel, provide the romantic element.

Beyond polemics, simple expressions of Hispanic fable entertain bilingual and Anglo audiences through the platform performances of skillful storytellers:

- A twentieth-century bilingual *cuentista*/folkteller, David Gonzalez preserves Latino folklore from Cuba, Puerto Rico, the Caribbean, Mexico, and the Dominican Republic and composes original didactic pieces. An unusual solo theater, infused with song, dance, comic energy, and imagination, draws on ethnic costumes in day-glo colors. His intention is to create fables to teach listeners about trust, courage, work, and faith. His repertoire for *Run It Down: The Stories, Music and Poetry of David Gonzalez*, a two-hour stage tapestry, and other presentations includes "The Man Who Could Make Trees Sing," "The Beat of My Heart," "Chango and the Power of the Drum," and "The King of My Heart/*El Rey del Agua*," the story of a small girl and a magic goldfish.

- Another bilingual teller, Californian Olga Loya, preserves vivid tales from Mexico, Cuba, Guatemala, Yucatan, Nicaragua, Colombia, and Puerto

Rico in her repertoire, which is published in *Momentos Mágicos/Magic Moments* (1997). Among her 15 Hispanic/English fables are a trickster tale, "How Monkey Tricked Crocodile," and a *pourquoi* story, "How People Came to Be," from the Mayan Popol Vuh.

- A gifted contemporary raconteur who preserves the southwestern United States blend of Hispanic lore with Native American fable, Arizonan Joe Hayes relates bilingual fables from Pueblo, Navajo, Tohono O'odham, Hopi, Snohomish, and Latin American sources. His beast fables, trickster stories, ecology and nature lore, *pourquoi* stories, and tall tales employ gesture, facial contortion, and nonverbal clues to demonstrate Hispanic vocabulary. Since 1979, he has performed beast stories at the Wheelwright Museum of the American Indian and at educational and professional venues throughout the United States. His *No Way, Jose!/De Ninguna Manera, José!* (1986) presents a beast fable about how the rooster José gets to his Uncle Perico's wedding; the evocative Tohono O'Odham tale about how the Sky God gave the rattlesnake its fangs appears in *Soft Child: How Rattlesnake Got Its Fangs* (1993). Other of Hayes's children's fables include *The Day It Snowed Tortillas* (1982); *Coyote &* (1982), source of "Coyote & the Turkey," "Coyote & the Rabbit," "Coyote & the Mice," "Coyote & the Locust," "Coyote & the Rattlesnake," "Coyote & the Turtle," "Coyote & the Quail," and "Coyote & Horned Toad"; an anthology, *Everyone Knows Gato Pinto: More Tales from Spanish New Mexico* (1992); and *The Butterflies Trick Coyote* (1993). In 1996, he collected "Rain," "The Gum Chewing Rattler," "Valgame Dios!" "One Day, One Night," "Sky Pushing Poles," "Yellow Corn Girl," "The Earth Monster," "Yellow behind the Ears," and "The Cricket" in *Here Comes the Storyteller*. For disseminating Hispanic and Native American lore, Hayes has won both the Arizona Young Readers' Award and designation as a New Mexico Commission on Higher Education Eminent Scholar.

See also Iriarte, Tomás de.

Sources Allende 1982; Balcells 1996; Blackham 1985; Blain et al. 1990; "Brewer: Dictionary of Phrase and Fable," http://www.bibliomania.com; Brunvand 1996; Burrison 1989; "The Carol of the Birds" 1953; Cooper 1921; Creeden 1994; Dailey 1994; *DISCovering Multicultural America*, http://www. galenet.gale.com; Green 1965; Hayes 1993; Hobbs 1986; Komroff 1935; Leach 1967; Loya 1997; Miller and Snodgrass 1998; Newbigging 1895; Paredes 1970; Pino-Saavedra 1967; Polley, 1978; Rosenberg 1997; Ross 1961.

 # HURSTON, ZORA NEALE

An ebullient folklorist and Florida regionalist from the 1920s and 1930s, Zora Neale Hurston rose to prominence as one of W. E. B. Du Bois's "talented tenth," the gifted leaders of an African-American cultural revolution. She became so well known and revered as foremother of black female folk writers that the name

Zora suffices without a surname. A prominent ethnologist, trained by Franz Boas, America's foremost anthropologist, she ventured into fable, spiritualism, and folk analysis as well as novels, short stories, and folk drama. In addition to writing the first American feminist novel, she was the first black author to collect African-American and Caribbean folklore. But like Jacquetta Hawkes and Virginia Hamilton, Hurston lacked name recognition as a folk anthologist until the surge of interest in feminism in the 1970s. Like author Joel Chandler Harris and storytellers J. J. Reneaux and Gayle Ross, she studied regional lore in dialect along with ritual, customs, and social structure, thereby enriching and legitimizing a segment of black lore often passed over or discounted as the stories of the least literate segment of the American South and the Caribbean isles.

Born on January 7, 1891, in Notasulga, Alabama, Hurston deliberately obscured her age and birthplace to accommodate wishful thinking. To appear a decade younger than she was and to conceal the shame of completing a high school diploma at age 26, she claimed to have been born in 1901, in Eatonville, an encapsulated black community in Polk County, Florida, on Highway 4 only a few miles north of Orlando between Maitland and Winter Park. During her years as a folklorist and compiler, she came to value her Florida homeland as "a place that draws people—white people from all over the world, and Negroes from every Southern state surely and some from the North and West." (Hurston 1990, 1)

Despite inadequate formal education, the Hurston family boasted a proud lineage, including an alderman and three-term mayor of Eatonville, the first incorporated, self-governing black town in the United States. Described as an optimist and irrepressible showoff in "How It Feels to Be Colored Me" (1928), Hurston transcended the financial instability. Always conscious of the family's need, she appreciated the work of her mother, seamstress and teacher Lucy Ann Potts, who eked out cash money to supplement the work of husband John Hurston, a semiliterate mulatto sharecropper from Alabama. In an autobiography, *Dust Tracks on a Road* (1942), Hurston describes the family hardships borne by the children of a poorly paid minister of Zion Hope Baptist Church, who supplemented two jobs with a third, carpentering. The Hurstons lived on ample farmland dotted with a barn, vegetable patch, citrus and guava groves, chickens, and fragrant cape jasmine. During her six years at Hungerford School, Zora demanded recognition as the fifth of a family of eight and played hide and whoop, chick-mah-chick, hide and seek, and other inventive games. From her mother, she received home schooling at parsing and long division but treasured most the lessons in self-fulfillment and exhortations to "jump at de sun." (Hurston 1991, 13)

The exhibitionism that pushed Hurston to center stage in childhood prefigured a swift rise to greatness. In an era of beatings, lynchings, and oppression of southern minorities, she claimed not to mind being black, preferred self-esteem to the pose of "tragically colored," and disdained "the sobbing school of Negrohood." (Lyons 1990, 102) Her formal education left raw edges but valued community lore as a homemade college curriculum. In 1904, she quit school to keep house and babysit for her brother, Dr. Bob Hurston, a Memphis physician. In place of classes, she studied the trickster tales, cruelty jokes, and fool tales that emanated from the porch of Joe Clarke's neighborhood store, where idlers swapped stretchers, boasted, teased, sang, recited episodes of tricksters High John the Conqueror (or John de Conker) and Daddy Mention, and enlivened their exchanges with such cynical self-pitying quips as "laughin' to keep from cryin'" and "I have been in sorrow's kitchen and licked out all de pots." (Maggio 1992, 302)

The peak of Hurston's childhood trauma occurred after her mother's sudden death from a lung ailment in 1904, when John Hurston disrupted the balance of power by marrying Mattie, a woman Zora despised enough to threaten with a hatchet. In her early teens, she became a lifelong wanderer after Reverend Hurston parceled out her siblings to other families and dispatched her to a Jacksonville boarding school. He was so annoyed by her hostility that he wrote the headmaster to suggest that the administration adopt Zora. Within months, she fled, working for $10 per week as maid and seamstress to an itinerant Gilbert and Sullivan road show. While the troupe performed British light opera in Baltimore, she took additional jobs as barbershop manicurist and nightclub waitress. Boarding with her sister, Sarah Hurston Mack, in 1918, Hurston earned a high school diploma from the Morgan Academy, the beginning of her life as a scholar and researcher. Already 27 years old, she enrolled at Howard Prep School before attempting Howard University, the "Negro Harvard," in Washington, D.C. For the next six years, she studied literature under some of the era's notables—critic Alain Locke, linguist Lorenzo Dow Turner, and poet George Douglas Johnson. Slowed but unhindered by an undiagnosed chronic intestinal complaint, she completed an associate degree and published her first fiction, "John Redding Goes to Sea" (1921) in *Stylus*, Howard University's literary magazine.

In the era of flamboyant flappers and the black renaissance, Hurston, a budding artiste, rose to fame in Harlem, New York, and gloried in the exuberant eclecticism of Seventh Avenue. In 1928, she announced: "[In Harlem] the cosmic Zora emerges. I belong to no race nor time. I am the eternal feminine with its string of beads. I have no separate feeling about being an American citizen and colored. I am merely a fragment of the Great Soul that surges within the boundaries." (Hurston 1985, 1652) As mentors, she adopted singers, painters, sculptors, writers, and revolutionaries and earned her living as research assistant and companion. She absorbed the uniqueness of black novelists Jessie Redmon Fauset and Margaret Walker, critic and anthologist Arna Bontemps, painter Aaron Douglas, sociologist Charles S. Johnson, actors with the Krigwa Players, and poets Claude McKay, Sterling S. Brown, Jean Toomer, and Langston Hughes. Her own works—"Drenched in Light" (1924) and "Spunk" (1925)— found places in Alain Locke's anthology *The New Negro*, followed by a burst of folk-based creativity the next year: "Sweat," "The Gilded Six-Bits," "Muttsy," "Possum or Pig," "The Eatonville Anthology," and three plays, *The First One, Spear,* and *Color Struck*. The last two plays won drama awards from *Crisis* and *Opportunity* magazines. For her elaborate revue, *The Great Day*, she melded work lyrics, revival sermon, and spirituals with juke joint dancing and blues. Although it ran only one day on Broadway, January 10, 1932, Hurston successfully recast the play at Rollins College a year later under the title *From Sun to Sun*.

On scholarship to Barnard College as the first black female to enroll and to earn a B.A. degree, Hurston became the first member of the Negro Historical Society Fellowship to research the *Clothilde*, the last slave galley bearing Africans to the United States. In 1930, she collaborated with poet and literary lion Langston Hughes and coeditor Wallace Thurman on a short-lived literary quarterly called *Fire!!*, an outlet for black writers. Hurston and Hughes worked on a three-act comedy, *Mule Bone*, which adapted "The Bone of Contention," her comic folk fable derived from Florida folk rhythms. Hurston and Hughes completed only the third act. The coauthors abruptly ended their partnership after he accused her of reissuing *Mule Bone* under her name and retitling it *De Turkey and De Law*. It was not performed until February 1991, when a revival of her early contributions to the Harlem Renaissance secured a place on the stage at New York's Lincoln Center.

At Columbia University, Hurston, recently divorced from a seven months' marriage to musician and medical student Herbert Sheen, chose scholarship over domesticity. In an era that preceded the validation of folklore as a discipline, she sought two brilliant teachers—anthropologists Ruth Benedict and Franz Boas—to guide her fieldwork. At their suggestion, she returned to Eatonville to study the black settlement outside St. Augustine, Florida. In field notes, she exulted in folksay, which she termed the "pot-likker of human living." (Maggio 1992, 261) Supported by patron Charlotte Osgood "Godmother" Mason, a white heiress, Hurston spent the early depression era driving her car to backwoods locales. After researching articles on black lore, she published them in Nancy Cunard's *The Negro, An Anthology* (1934). Southwestern song gatherer Alan Lomax honored Hurston's interest in southern lore by labeling her "probably the best-informed person today on Western Negro folklore." (Lyons 1990, 66)

Folklore was only a portion of Hurston's immense field of interest. The only female folklorist studying the American South, she overturned the prevailing theory that ethnologists should divorce themselves from home and peruse exotic or unknown cultures, as did Paul Radin, researcher among North American forest Indians, and Margaret Mead, student of Samoan society. Posing as "Zora, Queen of the Niggerati," scorner of the "Negrotarians and the Astorperious set," Hurston produced earth-based spectacles of the "lowly down under," blending down-home verse, songs, spirituals, and griot lore at black colleges and New York's Harold Golden Theatre. (Hurston 1981, 7) As a contribution to the era's pan-African movement, her treatise traces the amalgamation of American, Caribbean, and African traditions. Insightful articles appeared in the *Journal of Negro History, World Tomorrow,* and the *Journal of American Folklore*, each brimming with her vigorous dialect stories. An example from "Why de Porpoise's Tail Is on Crosswise" demonstrates the felicity of her language: "De Sun went zoonin' on cross de elements. Now, de porpoise was hanging round there and heard God what he tole de Sun, so he decided he'd take dat trip round de world hisself. He looked up and saw de Sun kytin' along, so he lit out too, him and dat Sun!" (Hurston 1995, 837) This and other stories demon-

Photograph of Zora Neale Hurston, taken in Eatonville, Florida, by Alan Lomax, 1935.

strate, with no need for peripheral commentary, Hurston's affinity for exuberant oral lore. The momentum of her spirit, originality, and innovation
undergirded the formation of a drama department at Bethune-Cookman College in Daytona Beach. Apart from scholarly endeavor, she wrote a play, *Singing Steel* (1934), and a novel, *Jonah's Gourd Vine* (1934), based on her parents'
lives. Her buoyant productivity extended into the late 1930s with more stories;
two novels, *Moses, Man of the Mountain* (1939) and *Their Eyes Were Watching God*

(1937), a reclaimed treasure brought to prominence in the 1970s; and two volumes of southern and Caribbean games, hoodoo, fables, and folklore entitled *Mules and Men* (1935) and *Tell My Horse* (1938), published in England as *Voodoo Gods: An Inquiry into Native Myths and Magic in Jamaica and Haiti.*

From an intimate acquaintance with front-porch storytelling, Hurston returned home—where she was "just Zora to the neighbors"—to compose an ambitious, compelling collection of beliefs, wisdom lore, and rituals along with comedy, fool tales, cruelty jokes, and animal fables. (Hurston 1990, 2) In *Mules and Men*, her emergence from black humor and passions resulted in a bred-in-the-bone familiarity that she called "the map of Dixie on my tongue." (Hurston 1990, xv) Already in her mid-forties, she was far enough divorced in time and experience from front-porch Eatonville to relive its canon of fables while deconstructing their sources and purpose through an academic objectivity she called the "spy-glass of Anthropology." (Hurston 1990, xvii) Unlike W. E. B. Du Bois, whose *The Souls of Black Folks* (1903) maintained the historian's demarcation between lore and learning, Hurston showed no hesitancy to glory in the animal stories and trickster tales of the southland. Less reticent than southern memoirists and novelists William Wells Brown and Charles Chesnutt , she displayed no qualms toward folksy wit and stories. As though taking notes on her girlhood, she reflected on a fabulist's haven—a homeland still in touch with the antebellum plantation system yet newly introduced to emancipation and the hope of self-actualization.

Reflecting the joy she found in story sessions, Hurston wrote with first-person authority the definitive study of southern fable. In her introduction, she claims: "From the earliest rocking of my cradle, I had known about the capers Brer rabbit is apt to cut and what the Squinch Owl says from the house top." (Hurston 1990, 1) Her self-deprecating fable of the preacher who looks for a divine sign concludes in the bray of a plow mule, which bawls, "Wanh-uh! Go preach! Go preach! Go preach!" (Hurston 1990, 22) The story reaches an Aesopic conclusion that the failed minister should get a job plowing, which was his divine calling all along. In typical cycle, the story sets off a series of preacher types—the revivalist who wins converts with a .44 Special, the leader of prayer meeting at "Macedony" Baptist Church, a folksy Christ who creates his church from the rocks collected by Peter and the eleven other disciples, and a creation fable that pictures blacks "stretched out asleep on de grass under de tree of life." (Hurston 1990, 30) In a put-down of rich whites, Hurston pits moneyman John D. Rockefeller against inventor Henry Ford. In standard *agon* or competition motif, Rockefeller plans to build a solid gold road around the world. Not to be outdone by wealth alone, the clever inventor promises to buy the road and put his famed tin lizzies on it. In a stanza from black juke lore, Hurston sneered:

> Oh de white gal rides in a Cadillac,
> De yeller gal rides de same,
> Black gal rides in a rusty Ford
> But she gits dere just de same.
> (Hurston 1995, 843)

Hurston's familiarity with the history of investor Rockefeller and automaker Ford exemplifies her self-assurance in a nation that exalted wealthy white males and relegated to unimportance the saucy black woman at the bottom of the social ladder. Out of order and committed to disorder, she dared taunt and demystify her betters in song and fable.

The fresh fervor and verve of Hurston's fables depart from the sweetness of Uncle Remus to the piquance and world-weariness of adult fare. Her narratives cover woofing or aimless talk, juking and jiving, court battles, and testifying for the Lord. She includes competition stories about men vying for the same sweetheart, morality tales about people who fish on Sunday, and a rascal story of a judge who compares the odor of a black defendant with the smell of a goat. Hurston is adept at the fool tale, for example, the incident of an educated girl who can't spell the clucking noise by which a plowman summons a mule and the anecdote about the man cheated of a gold watch he found lying in the road. Hurston's scenarios picture dogs, snakes, turtles, gators, and skeeters in natural habitats alongside humble folk in the acts that round out the day—saddling a horse, cooking a meal, treating sore joints, making a trade, telling lies, and even peeking up Ole Miss's drawers, which the speaker later admits are hanging on the clothesline.

With no effort at self-censorship, Hurston includes a wide span of texts, from tales of gamblers, grifters, and adulterers to stories of families trying to feed too many children, the creation of male and female, face-offs against the devil, and a brag story about the wind and the water. Her protagonists range from the anonymous Marys and Ellas to the familiar Box-Car Daddy and John Henry, a standard laboring-class hero who compares with the Jewish hero Daniel and the northwestern phenomenon of Joe Magarac. In his workday glory, John Henry rises above abysmal back-wearying day labor to a fierce pride, as captured in the lyrics of a standard folk paean:

> John Henry told his Captain,
> Man ain't nothing but a man,
> And 'fore I'll let that steam drill beat me down
> I'll die with this hammer in my hand,
> Die with this hammer in my hand.
> (Hurston 1990, 251)

In contrasting comic stories of John the lazy fieldhand, the same black persona becomes the antihero of plantation days who falls for the massa's trick of speaking with the Lord's authoritative voice. Terrorized, John hides under the bed, then makes a break to the field. His wife, in admiration for her husband's swift flight from perdition, exclaims to her brood, "You know de Lawd can't outrun yo' pappy—specially when he's barefooted at dat." (Hurston 1990, 72)

During Hurston's sojourn among practitioners of Louisiana-style gris-gris, a form of black magic, the reverend Father Joe Watson, familiarly known as the Frizzly Rooster, initiated her into the voodoo priesthood, a theatrical public role that required her to dress in outlandish ritual regalia. The far-fetched narrative of *Mules and Men* includes particulars of the initiation. Although Sterling

Brown, Richard Wright, Alain Locke, and a few vocal critics accused her of coarseness, caricature, and naïveté, other contemporaries lauded her masterwork of dialect, primitivism, arcana, conjure plants and herbal medicine, word games, and human sexuality. In particular, they admired a talented female's confrontation with academic patriarchy and her establishment of authority on a subject she had obviously viewed up close.

Hurston's later writings strayed further from fable and folk sayings to more complex lore. From Haiti she migrated to Jamaica in 1936 on successive Guggenheim fellowships to document African and Bahamian obeah, or voodoo, practice. Over a period of seven weeks in 1937, she recovered from a lapsed love affair by sheltering once more in Haiti to write her most famous fiction, *Their Eyes Were Watching God*, a fount of black English and universal themes interweaving patriarchy, racism, sexism, and ageism into a satisfying novel of self-actualization. A contemporary of Margaret Mitchell's Scarlett O'Hara, heroine of *Gone with the Wind* (1936), Hurston's Janie fought similar rounds with patriarchy, paralleling Scarlett's allure, self-reliance, and emancipation from male dominance. At the end of the 1930s, Hurston wed Albert Price III, a graduate student at Columbia University 25 years her junior, but left him to tour Florida with Alan Lomax in search of music for a Library of Congress collection and to write *The Florida Negro* for the Works Progress Administration and the Federal Theater Project. In summer 1939, she taught drama at North Carolina Negro College in Durham and returned to a rocky domestic scene. The marriage foundered in 1940 after Price, like Hurston's first husband, forced her to choose between research and home. On a Rosenwald fellowship, she combed South Carolina, Louisiana, Alabama, Haiti, the British West Indies, and Jamaica for material for novels. At home both in academia and in the field, she collected anecdotes and songs that elucidated her target—racial delineations among quadroons, octoroons, high yellows, and full-blooded blacks.

The early 1940s saw the divergence of Hurston's career from pure research to more creative writing and reflection. In 1941, she lived in California with friend Katherine Mershon while composing *Dust Tracks on a Road*. Her evocative memoir races along in snatches of conversation, song, and verse marking rhythmic work, snacks of parched peanuts and meals on fried rabbit, and volatile exchanges:

> The pay night rocks on with music and gambling and laughter and dancing and fights. The big pile of cross-ties burning out in front simmers down to low ashes before sun-up, so then it is time to throw up all the likker you can't keep down and go somewhere and sleep the rest off, whether your knife has blood on it or not. (Hurston 1973, 2714)

Pulsating with impulsive, primeval actions, the work rounds up a panorama of native epithets and terms—store-bought, coolin' board, straw-boss, pushee and pullee, barracoon, jook, grass-gut cow, and "git my switchblade and go round de ham-bone looking for meat." (Hurston 1973, 2715)

During the preliminaries to World War II, Hurston's emotional ambivalence marred her autobiography, which won an Anisfield-Wolf Award. In the mid-

1940s to early 1950s, she published an occluded novel about poor whites, *Seraph on the Suwanee* (1948), as well as a dwindling number of fables, tales, articles, and profiles for the *American Mercury, Saturday Evening Post, Southern Literary Messenger, Negro Digest,* and *American Legion* magazine and reviewed for the New York *Herald Tribune.* Profiles of her career appeared in *Who's Who in America, Twentieth Century Authors,* and *Current Biography.* Her fortunes bobbed up once more with a major coup—a cover story about Hurston in the February 1943 *Saturday Review*—followed by a distinguished alumna award from Howard University and several weeks of pure research in the black neighborhoods of British Honduras. Nearing retirement, she fled the big city scene, where educated blacks tended toward elitism, self-promotion, and snobbery, and retreated to Belle Glade, Florida, which reminded her of the gentler, less competitive Eatonville of her childhood.

Depleted by poverty, obesity, and ulcer and gall bladder attacks, in 1948 Hurston weathered public vilification from a false accusation of abusing a retarded boy, a fiasco that the *Baltimore Afro-American* sensationalized. She took refuge in researching Latin texts by Josephus, Livy, Eusebius, Strabo, and Nicolas of Damascus for a biography, *The Life of Herod the Great.* Before a downturn ended her career, she supported herself as story consultant for Paramount Pictures, scriptwriter for a Cincinnati radio station, freelance journalist for the *Pittsburgh Courier,* writer for the *Encyclopedia Americana,* librarian at Patrick Air Force Base, columnist for the *Fort Pierce Chronicle,* and substitute teacher in Fort Pierce, Florida. At a financial ebb, she sold little fiction and was evicted from her home in Eau Gallie, Florida. She roused an uproar in 1954 by denouncing northern liberals who pushed for desegregation. She countered that the closing of all-black schools would demoralize Negro students by divesting them of black teachers and a pro-African curriculum. Sick, weary, and unemployable, she sank to meager domestic work in Rivo Alto, near Miami, and lived on welfare. Late in October 1959, she entered the Saint Lucie County Welfare Home in Fort Pierce to recuperate from a stroke and died there of hypertensive heart disease on January 28, 1960. County authorities buried her unclaimed remains in an anonymous plot in a black graveyard, the Garden of the Heavenly Rest.

During the 1970s, a period that revived interest in storytelling, the Harlem Renaissance, and black feminism, Hurston's work rebounded to prominence. Unself-conscious in their re-creation of black lore, her dialogues, fables, and essays began to appear in textbooks and anthologies. Her enthusiasm for folklore energized more polemical black writings with a coarse, often bawdy delight in the spontaneous joy of human society. Publishers scrambled to reissue her novels and plays; curators and archivists collected her papers and memorabilia at the University of Florida. In August 1973, novelist Alice Walker, author of *The Color Purple,* marked Hurston's grave to honor the extraordinary female pathfinder as a southern genius. With the assistance of novelist Toni Cade Bambara, critic Helen Hunt Washington, biographer Robert E. Hemenway, and historian Henry Louis Gates, Jr., Walker introduced Hurston to a new generation of readers with "In Search of Zora Neale Hurston" (1974), published in *Ms.,* and composed the foreword to Robert E. Hemenway's *Zora Neale Hurston:*

A Literary Biography. Walker's most influential memorial is a collection, *I Love Myself: When I Am Laughing . . . and Then Again When I Am Looking Mean and Impressive: A Zora Neale Hurston Reader* (1979). Other posthumous publications include *The Sanctified Church: The Folklore Writings of Zora Neale Hurston* (1981), *Spunk: The Selected Short Stories of Zora Neale Hurston* (1985), and *Mule Bone: A Comedy of Negro Life* (1990). In 1990, PBS's *American Playhouse* featured a 90-minute biography, *Zora Is My Name*, starring Ruby Dee and Louis Gossett, Jr. In February 1991, 60 years after its composition, *Mule Bone* was produced on Broadway. In 1993, a book collector found among sorority memorabilia from Howard University a lost Hurston play, "Spear," and an essay, "The Ten Commandments of Charm," along with a story, "Under the Bridge." Toni Morrison, Maya Angelou, Susan Straight, Ntozake Shange, and other late twentieth-century authors have proclaimed their debt to her scholarship, collected lore and wisdom, and sparkling southern vernacular.

See also Brer Rabbit.

Sources Abrahams 1985; Asante and Mattson 1992; Blain et al. 1990; Blair 1944; Blankenship 1931; Bloom 1986; Boas 1990; Davidson and Wagner-Martin 1995; Haskins 1996; Hemenway 1977; Hine 1993; Holloway 1987; Hooks 1997; Howard 1980; Hurston 1981, *Mules and Men* 1990, *Their Eyes Were Watching God* 1990, *Dust Tracks on a Road* 1991, *Mule Bone: A Comedy of Negro Life* 1991, *The Complete Stories* 1995, *Zora Neale Hurston: Folklore, Memoirs, and Other Writings* 1995; Lewis 1981; Low and Clift 1981; Lyons 1990; Maggio 1992; Meckler 1996; Nathiri 1991; Pierpont 1997; Ploski and Williams 1989; Porters 1992; Rampersad 1986; Rubin 1982; Sheffey 1992; Sherr and Kazickas 1994; Snodgrass, *Encyclopedia of Southern Literature* 1997; Walker, 1979, 1983; Wall 1995; Washington 1987; Wilson and Ferris 1989; Witcover 1991; Yates 1991; "Zora Neale Hurston" http://www.ceth.rutgers.edu; "Zora Neale Hurston" http://www.detroit.freenet.org.

ILLUSTRATORS

From the begining of printed text, fable has challenged the book illustrator. The concept of drawing a situation that particularizes both the action and moral has made the illustration of fable one of the crowning achievements of literary graphics. By the end of the fifteenth century, over 20 illustrators had produced individual editions of Aesop's animal lore. Three who published in the 1470s— Domenico di Vivaldi, Ernst Voulliéme, illustrator of the Ulm text, and Liberale da Verona—outclassed earlier and later competition with simplicity and attention to the central incident. Vivaldi's metal cuts, which may have been complete by 1476, are the least familiar to modern readers. Voulliéme's woodcuts, the first distinctive German illustrations, appeared in Augsburg and were prized by readers of *Aesop's Life and Fables* (ca. 1477), collated by humanist physician Heinrich Steinhöwel from the works of Avianus, Rimicius, and Bracciolini Poggio. A frontispiece captures the storyteller in peasant guise, his hand lifted in admonition, his body lame and twisted, and his torso covered by a smock, the garment of the servant class. In depicting a fox admiring grapes, the Voulliéme edition achieves an altered perspective by minimizing the small-nosed fox while enlarging four bunches of grapes bulging with clear circlets of juicy pulp. Likewise magnifying simple animal characters, Voulliéme's drawing of the grasshopper and ant places the two characters face to face in the foreground of a walled city and between two gnarled stumps and a boulder. The roughness of the ground detail emphasizes the winter setting, which gets at Aesop's focus—the absence of greenery that threatens the frivolous grasshopper with starvation.

Voulliéme portrays his grasp of fable in the quick studies he makes of primitively sketched animals. The connection of the mouth of the predator to the headless torso of a crane speaks at a glance the dramatic thrust of "The Wolf and the Crane." Detail is limited to V-shaped flecks, the distinguishing feature of "The Peacock Complains to Juno about His Voice" and "The Fox and the Stork," and less imaginative circles that adorn the beast for "The Panther and the Shepherds." The body of the serpent in "The Snake Fatal to the Compassionate Man" is devoid of incidental markings, as are the two-dimensional characters of "The Ant and the Fly." Likewise simple, yet enhanced by foreground drawings of dandelion and lily of the valley is the face-off between beasts in

"The Wolf and the Lamb, which implies the predator's advantage by placing the wolf above the lamb, as it meekly laps at a stream. Publishers extended their own peculiar form of compliment by plagiarizing Ernst Voulliéme's work, which was the most copied of the era.

Less refined is the work of Verona, also known as Liberale di Jacopo dalla Brava, a miniaturist and panel painter named for his hometown. After studying the works of Mantegna and Cremona, he published original choir book illuminations in ornate, calligraphic style and painted "The Lamentation over the Dead Christ," a fresco in the Cappella Bonaveri in Sant'Anastasia. Verona's Italian edition of *Aesop's Fables* (1479) features rough, heavy-handed woodcuts marked by short, incisive strokes as though carved with a knife. The drawings reside in textured frames composed of fine, evenly spaced braid. Within this controlled exterior, the creatures of "The Hart, the Sheep and the Wolf" live out their instinct-driven behaviors. Unlike Ernst Voulliéme's towering backdrops, Verona's human buildings keep to a minimum while emphasizing leaves, coarse undergrowth, pelt, and bristling tail. An artistic duplication centers "The Dog and His Shadow," which parallels the animal in profile with an obscured mirror image in the flowing stream below the bridge. The drawing of meaty haunches in his jaws appears crude in contrast to the treetops, studded portals,

Illustration by J. J. Grandville for *Fables de La Fontaine,* "The Wolf and the Lamb"

and tiled roof of the church behind. The starkness of contrast sets Aesopic lore within the rules of nature, even though intrusive human habitation encases the view.

A contemporary volume from Naples, *Aesop's Life and Fables* (1485), departs from raw woodcut with delicate border design, fanciful beasts, and sparkling energy, which complement the narrative action. In "The Frogs Who Wanted a King," the unidentified illustrator echoes the wrestlings of the animal kingdom with a human wrestling scene in the scrolled arch and capital that heads the drawing. Within a double framework of rococo braid, acanthus leaves, and rosettes, Jupiter leans from a wreathed sun to cast doom on the frogs. In their haste for a king, they quiver in fear of a snarling, long-tailed heron. The fowl resembles a regal gryphon that might ornament a coat of arms. Contrasting with the fierce bird are the naked backsides of a half dozen frogs, five of whom crouch in a near-human pose while the sixth appears to slink away like the doomed medieval sinners in Hieronymus Bosch's *Hellmouth*. A companion drawing of "The Lion and the Horse" repeats the heavy frame and capital. Within the borders, a debased lion with outstretched clawed feet and piteously human face falls to the sharp rear hooves of the horse. The contrast of the richly flowing lion's mane and tail with the stylized mane and scattered tail of the horse suggests a deeper reading of the fable: the energetic horse, unburdened by the expectations that encumber the "king of beasts," scampers away from the would-be predator and from his apothecary's tools, which stand at center of the foreground.

A similar style in woodcut, the anonymous *Aesopo Historiado* [Historic Aesop] (1497) from Venice, mimics the Naples volume with a single frame, composed of open acanthus leaves, vines, and urns in balanced presentation. The capital, a battle scene of seven naked warriors entering combat with spears, swords, and outstretched shields, surpasses the Italian forerunner in grandeur, suggesting the capital friezes of fifth-century Greek temple architecture. At the heart of "The Rat, the Frog, and the Kite," the artist pictures a stylized moment of action as the frog plunges toward the bottom of the river to drown the rat just as the kite dives from the sky to devour them both. To the left, the artist poses rat with frog cartoon-style to show the two in conversation before the conflict. The heaviest texturing of this picture draws attention from the walled medieval city, trees, and river foliage to the coursing stream, its heavily roiled waters suggesting struggle in nature. The same volume depicts a more serene confrontation for "The Frog and the Ox." Composed to depict the conversational element, the illustration contrasts the bloated frog in profile to the angular pose of the ox, which displays spine, arched tail, and rounded ribs and horns. As with "The Rat, the Frog, and the Kite," the drawing features heavy detailing of the current and stylized greenery among the cattails but appends a simpler frame of mythological figures blowing horns above scrollery of urns, vines, trifoliate plants, and stylized four-footed beasts.

The late Renaissance evolved a uniquely refined approach to fable. Etching produced a lighter, lacier quality suggesting freehand art. Enhanced detail work and shading permitted greater control of perspective. A Roman edition, *Fabulae*

Centum [One Hundred Stories] (1565), presents a cluttered, unsophisticated array of animals, plants, and trees in clumsy perspective. Depicting "The Eagle and the Fox," an uneven fable that lacks the usual taut construction of Aesopic narrative, the illustration loses control of the climactic moment, when the eagle's nest catches fire and the hatchlings fall to the ground to be devoured by the fox. More artistic is "The Fly," a drawing overwhelmed by indoor geometry with nature relegated to a simplistic window view. The depiction of the fly as she drowns in a pot of stewing meat conveys no tension. The artist is so consumed by the task of drawing hearth, fire, and mantle that the purpose of the fable takes second place.

The woodcut of the Venice edition of *Cento Favole Morali* [One Hundred Moral Fables] (1577) stands out for its emphasis on action rather than style. Using heavy crosshatching to suggest the intricacy of hair and bristle for "The Ass and the Boar," this unnamed artist, emulating Titian, chooses a stark black frame to encase a fearful moment as the witless ass draws the anger of a crouching boar with snout uplifted and bared tusks. Paralleling the fable's internal clash is a sheaf of heady stalks that bristle and sway with the wind. Similarly fearful is the imminent impact depicted in "The Wolf and the Lamb," a black-edged print that displays one of the most familiar of animal confrontations in art. The wolf stands poised at the water's edge while the innocent lamb minces from the undergrowth with delicate feet turned outward as though leisurely unaware of looming death.

A touchstone of Aesopic illustration, Marcus Geeraerts's edition, *De Warachtighe Fabulen der Dieren* [The True Fables of Animals] (1567) highlights naturalistic animal behaviors and habitats. Geeraerts (or Gheeraerts), a Flemish painter and engraver, specialized in religious and animal subjects. His skill at incorporating animals into a worldly milieu is evident in "The Fox and the Goat," a story that touches on the human frailty of looking before leaping. Geeraerts captures the encompassing human background of walled city, boatman, and smokestack. An ominous cloud echoes the plight of the grim-faced goat, which thrusts absurdly weak and knobby forelegs to the top of the well while the sleek, unsympathetic fox gazes down. In a multifaceted drawing of "The Hares and the Frogs," Geeraerts sets up a turmoil in nature, as hares, with ears pricked for danger, flee the tossing boughs and frogs leap for cover in the brook. Attention to detail, pose, and membership in the group gives each hare and frog individuality and highlights its singular contribution to the composition.

Seventeenth-century English fable compendia featured several distinct styles. A Bohemian engraver and etcher from Prague known for "Views of London," an architectural panorama of London after the Great Fire of 1666, Wenceslaus (or Wenzel) Hollar mimicked Geeraerts in *Aesopics, or a Second Collection of Fables* (1668) by returning to elegance and detail work in his two editions. For "The Two Crabs," Hollar sketches a Turneresque sky and harbor scene with minutely textured city, ships, and lighthouse set against the focal animals, which dominate the bottom half of the scene. The chiaroscuro tells the tale: Light clouds contrast the scuttle of large and small crab making their way over the sand. Much more dramatic is the furor of the trapped king of beasts in "The Lion and the Mouse." For the fearful moment when the lion realizes its danger, Hollar again overtops his drawing with clouds, a craggy hillside, and horsemen and hounds pursuing a lion. In the foreground to the left, the muscular lion struggles within the diamond-patterned net. Its tail stands at the alert and jaws growl its apprehension. Almost out of sight to the far right, a mouse no larger than the bob on the lion's tail chews into the dark cords that bind the lion to a stump. The effect of Hollar's foreshortening enhances the lion's dismay, an open-jawed pose less dreadful than dreading.

In the late seventeenth century, cartoonist Francis Barlow was inspired by Dutch cartoonists to complete an illustrated grammar text, a polyglot juxtaposition of single fables in English, French, and Latin. In response to complex political maneuverings, he produced richly textured caricature, the best of which adorned playing cards that were sold uncut as broadsides. In 1687, his shaded drawings for *Aesop's Fables with His Life* edged even further from self-conscious artistry to a more inviting verisimilitude, as demonstrated by a woeful glimpse of perjured liars vomiting the identifiable contents of their stomachs before a saint and Aesop himself, who perches in the foreground with hands raised in the act of illustrating his oral narrative. The frontispiece perpetuates the vision of Aesop as a dowdy hunchback, whom Barlow surrounds with a wide array of beings ranging from adder, frog, and oppossum in the lower left to the broad-antlered moose and braying camel on the diagonal corner. At the heart of the view are the peaceable shapes of lion, ibex, ram, horse, and gesturing monkey, with roosting peacock overhead and smiling fox in the lower right corner. For "The Fox and the Crane," Barlow balances the tit-for-tat fable that depicts the crane outfoxing the fox by serving his guest from a long-necked vase accessible only to a long-beaked bird. The composition anchors the hungry fox in the lower foreground and the crane above. Clearly dividing the picture by the vase at center, Barlow enlarges the crane's advantage by depicting him with feathered wings outspread and steely eye on his rival. Charged with bestial emotion is "The Dog and the Ox," another imbalance of power that pictures the yapping dog in the manger and the ox lowering its horns and charging. To heighten the impression of impending doom, Barlow dots the barn floor with nine delicate chicks and a hen who wisely keeps her distance.

Also in the late 1600s came the first illustrated text of Jean de La Fontaine's fables, completed by François Chauveau, an influential illustrator who had studied his predecessors and knew the field. An unusual symbolism emerged in 1677 in a French edition featuring the etchings of Sébastien Leclerc, which connect individual fables to statuary in the formal *Labyrinte* at Versailles. These depictions are made more valuable by the fact that the sculptures themselves have not survived to modern times. The turns and twists, each marked by a balletic fountain representing an individual fable, suggest the complex didactic purpose of fables, which lead human steps through the maze of dilemmas and choices. For "The Fox and the Carved Head," Leclerc sets a fallen sculpted head under the uplifted paw of a fox, which cranes upward and spouts water from its mouth. The composition places the figure at the bottom quarter of the drawing and dwarfs it with the dense sculpted hedge that separates two garden alleys overarched with evergreen branches. In contrast to the symbolism of the forking alleyway is the winding path of "The Swan and the Stork," a graceful grotto sculpture linking both birds with arching water spouts. This pairing of fowls echoes the theme of the fable—the fragility and limited earthly life of living things. One of the sparest of texts appeared in 1697, when Rabbi Moses ben Eliezer Wallich of Worms produced a derivative volume, *Sefer Meshalim* [Book of Fables], containing 34 illustrated fables. The simple woodcuts boxed in by a heavy black frame display light texturing and wooden poses of animal, plants, and peasants involved in obvious endeavors. In Fable XVII, a mouse tiptoes up behind a sleeping lion in a two-dimensional drawing that is functional but primitive. Other entries, such as fables XXV and XVI, which depict human interaction with animals, stiffly demonstrate action but lack the subtleties of facial expression, gesture, and pose that color the better fable collections of the Renaissance and seventeenth century. One fable, an extensive study of desire and infidelity, exceeds the cardboard gracelessness of previous works by violating perspective to such lengths that its purpose is unclear.

Improvements in illustrative technique mark the work of the last three centuries. In 1722, Elisha Kirkall produced passable metal cuts for Samuel Croxall's *Fables of Aesop and Others.* Petite and prettily encased on four-cornered matting, the oval vignette for "The Lioness and the Fox" pairs the conversing animals without the menace of deadlier confrontations. The fox, which is light in body and wits, faces a disgruntled lion, a chesty, prick-eared beast that reminds the fox that quality outvalues quantity. Far superior to Kirkall in depth, clarity, and subtlety is the work of Jean-Baptiste Oudry, a tapestry designer, painter, and animal painter. Oudry established his reputation by painting Arcadian settings, which were favored as paneled decor for elegant homes. A member of the Royal Academy, he numbered among his clients the French court, Peter the Great, the prince of Mecklenburg-Schwein, and the queen of Sweden. Oudry produced original designs for the Beauvais tapestry works, including illustrations of Molière's plays and La Fontaine's fables, and scenes from the hunts of Louis XV for Gobelins tapestry factory, which he served as inspector general. His book illustrations adorn editions of Miguel de Cervantes's *Don Quixote* and *La Roman comique*. His drawings, set against the lush Regency background, complement a four-volume set of La Fontaine's *Fables Choisies* [Selected Fables] (1755–1759). For "The Viper and the File," Oudry encases the serpent's attack on the metal file in a clock boutique. Around the sinuous body of the viper stand ornate table and floor clocks and a large selection of watches. The grandeur of the storefront, with its coat of arms above the open door, emphasizes the triviality of the snake, which occupies less than a tenth of the composition. Similarly replete with extravagant scrollery and elegance is the setting for Horace's "The Town Mouse and the Country Mouse," one of the most popular fables of all time. Atop a corner of a dinner table, centered with a lavish epergne lit by two four-branched candelabra, the two mice face each other over an empty place setting. Rather than the high drama of the chase, Oudry chooses a quiet moment that precedes the attack of the cat. To relieve the drawing of stuffy arrogance, Oudry casually drapes a napkin over a chair and a second serving cloth on the adjacent banquet at the base of two wine bottles. As a balance, he heightens chiaroscuro by directing an ominous shadow over the right half of the composition. The looming darkness enhances the fable, a wisdom tale that warns the social climber of the dangers of urbanism.

The nineteenth century maintained much of the Aesopic tradition of earlier illustrators, but with uneven success. For example, in an anonymous etching for "Les Loups et Les Brebis" [The Wolves and the Sheep] (1806), the artist separates strikingly similar wolves and dogs for the consummation of a treaty guaranteeing safety to the sheep, which browse the grassy yard in the background. Unlike the energetic works of Barlow, Geeraerts, and Hollar and the splendid detail of Doré and Oudry, this illustration misconceives fable as a static, predictable literary form. Such a limited understanding of the genre compromised the reader's perceptions and blunted the fabulist's moral point.

By the Victorian era, book illustrators overshadowed the humble fabulist with technological advancement. Artists chose from lithography, photogravure, etching, and multiple forms of engraving. Thomas Bewick, illustrator of *The History of British Birds*, *The History of Quadrupeds*, and *The History of British Fishes*, was a proponent of a stolid form of wood engraving on the butt of a hardwood block. His early works include woodcuts for *Gay's Fables* (1779) and *Select Fables of Aesop and Others* (1784), for which he produced a pleasant cameo depicting "The Crow and the Pitcher." Less inspired than his forebears, Bewick ranges from ferns to wildflowers and crow feathers but lacks perception and energy. Assisted by his son and partner, Robert Elliott Bewick, he accomodated revisions in fable collection with *Aesop's Fables* (1818). Contrasting the polite but dull compositions of the Bewicks, Samuel Howitt infused fable with tension and stark realism in his etchings for *A New Work of Animals Principally Designed from the Fables of Aesop, Gay and Phaedras* (1811). In a violent scene that anticipates Alfred Tennyson's "nature red in tooth and claw," Howitt hurls a pack of slim, deadly hunting hounds at their prey for "The Stag and His Antlers." The crux of the fable—the stag's inordinate pride in his rack—dominates the illustration, which contrasts the vicious eyes and flashing teeth with the stag's long, soft neck and protruding tongue, both prized by the hurtling hounds.

In the 1830s, Georges Gouget and J. J. Grandville produced subtle beasts for fable illustrations. In deftly controlled engravings for *Fables de La Fontaine* (1833–1834), Gouget pictures four sneering foxes ridiculing a tailless brother in "The Fox without a Tail." The hurt expression on the maimed fox's face establishes the fabulist's intent. The illustration for "The Ape and the Dolphin," a stylized pairing of two unlikely companions, engulfs the ape with lowering sky, listing two-masted ship, and wide expanse of ocean, which the ape attempts to escape. A more facile artist, Grandville, pseudonym of Jean Ignace Isidore Gérard of Nancy, France, mastered the merger of human face and animal frame. Forerunners of John Tenniel's drawings for Lewis Carroll's *Alice in Wonderland*, Grandville's human-beast figures in the 70 panels of *Les Métamorphoses du jour; ou, les hommes à têtes de bêtes* [Present-day Metamorphoses, or Men with Heads of Beasts] (1829) anticipate the distortions and fantasy art of the Dadaists and

Illustration by J. J. Grandville, "The City Rat and the Country Rat"

surrealists. He was widely renowned as lithographer, illustrator, and political cartoonist for two popular journals, *La Caricature* and *Le Charivari* [The Tease]. For *Fables de La Fontaine* (1838), Grandville adapted his satiric style to suit anthropomorphic animal behavior, such as the droll view of six stags overwhelming with kindness their dying fellow. Coursing with energy is "The Hare and the Tortoise," for which Grandville depicts the undershell tracings of the tortoise as it hurls its body over the finish line. Unusual touches include a milestone topped by a mole, who appears to judge the race. From the rear, an elongated hare stretches its forelegs and gallops around the final turn several lengths behind his doughty opponent. A clever collaborator with the fabulist, Grandville internalized the height of dramatic action in fable's miniature canvas and poured his artistry into the confrontation at the core of the tale.

Less predictable than the work of Gouget and Grandville is Charles Henry Bennett's *The Fables of Aesop and Others Translated from Human Nature* (1857), which he wrote and illustrated with animal-headed human characters. A jovial cartoonist and equal to Grandville, Bennett exaggerates foibles in "The Frog and the Ox" through the flaring eyes and outthrust chin of the ox and the pompous strut of the frog. To place the fashionable duo in time and place, he dresses them in spiffy frockcoats, vests, and top hats and embellishes their sartorial splendor with canes, foulard, and stick pin. A similar droll drawing accompanies "The Dog in the Manger," which juxtaposes an irate mastiff/butler with a bull, which appears at the foyer of a fine home ostensibly in the pose of errand boy.

The crown of nineteenth-century fable illustration belongs to French painter and lithographer Gustave Doré. Born in Strasbourg, he gained public notoriety as caricaturist for the weekly *Journal pour Rire* [Journal of Laughter]. Doré achieved greatness by illustrating French works, beginning with François Rabelais's *Oeuvres*, the anonymous Hebrew folk fable *The Wandering Jew*, and Honoré de Balzac's *Les Contes drolatiques*. Doré's superb taste in European masterpieces and his feel for poetic imagery undergird his mature work—Dante Alighieri's *Inferno, Purgatorio*, and *Paradiso*; the Bible; Miguel de Cervantes's *Don Quixote*; John Milton's *Paradise Lost*; and Alfred Tennyson's *Idylls of the King*. A collector's item is Doré's 1868 edition of *Fables de La Fontaine*, a vivid blend of satire and wickedness that echoes the menace of his brilliant illustration of Dante's *Inferno*. A magnificent example of Doré's gift is "The Mice in Council," populated by some 60 mice in varied poses. As the presiding mouse extends a cord and bell in his paw, the timid council shrinks from the job of "belling the cat." Doré excels in high drama and shadowed menace, the lurking fear that links his drawings to potential violence and evanescence.

The next generation of Aesop illustration produced cartoonist and illustrator Walter Crane of Liverpool, son of portrait artist Thomas Crane and student of pre-Raphaelite giants Dante Gabriel Rossetti, John Millais, and William Morris. The creator of toy books, Crane carried fable illustration to a new era with photoetching for editions of Edmund Spenser's *Faerie Queene* and *The Shepheardes Calendar, The Frog Prince*, and Edmund Evans's books of nursery rhymes. For *The Baby's Own Aesop* (1886), Crane stressed fauna over flora. His view of teeming animal life energizes "The Birds, the Bears, and the Bat." Stretched from lower left to upper right in sharp diagonal, the conjoined animal kingdom ousts the startled bat, a turncoat that lifts its feeble wings in token of the comeuppance he receives from angry animals. In a swirling nature collage, the artist captures "The Wind and the Sun" in a three-color print featuring *supra* a vigorous horn-blower forcing a gale against the back of the wayfarer, and *infra*, the youthful sun overheating the wayfarer, who must doff his cloak and flee for shade.

Crane's technique influenced artists Alexander Calder and Arthur Rackham, who illustrated J. M. Barrie's *Peter Pan, Tales from Shakespeare, The Wind in the Willows*, the stories of Hans Christian Andersen, and *Aesop's Fables* (1916). Rackham's style is whimsical and lively, envigorated with intriguing side notes and possibilities left to the imagination. For "The Moon and Her Mother," a chastened stripling of a moon cringes before the long-nosed human seamstress, who moistens her thread and brandishes a needle in preparation for a daunting task. Unshadowed by greenery, Rackham's big-eyed, rough-textured personae of "The Owl and the Birds" stand like individuals in conference, with the owl fallen silent left of center and the crow tilting its head askance as if doubtful but still attentive to its mentor. Rackham is unequaled in texture, the cohesive factor of "The Fisherman Piping," "The Fir Tree and the Bramble," "The Man and the Satyr," "The Shipwrecked Man and the Sea," and "The Two Pots," which features a detailed toby mug staring down a copper pot graced with delicate *repoussée*. In "The Frogs Ask for a King," 13 frogs in frolicsome postures swing, dive, climb, dance, and converse. Athwart the whole is the diagonal log that forms their playground. Against its warty surface lap quivery wavelets in the stream, a contrast to the vertical tufts of weeds at top and the rounded pebbles below. The completeness of the scenario illustrates an essential element of fable— the cohesion of individual habitats within nature.

Rackham accords each story its essence. His humor gets the better of drama for "The Blackamoor" and "The Two Pots," both steeped in humanity's gift for sin and error. He tweaks both beasts of "The Lion, Jupiter, and the Elephant" by rolling the two sets of eyes upward toward a dot of a gnat. For "The Goatherd and the Goat," the artist conceals the actors in silhouette against a white landscape. For texture, he grounds the scenario in a few dozen pebbles and lifts skyward the tops of spruces. A more acute depiction of confrontation appears with "The Cat and the Cock," which pits a keen-clawed black cat against the devastated cock, elegant in elongated neck feathers and ribbons of tail feathers but obviously at a disadvantage on its own extended nails. The drama of evil cat eyes admiring its prey contrasts with the wisps of pin feathers that attest to a battle for survival. Rackham's forces of nature teem with promise or lurk in wait for victims, as detailed in the menacing postures of "The North Wind and the Sun" and the abject pose of a fallen trunk in "The Oak and the Reeds."

Calder, an American kinetic sculptor from Pennsylvania, is the father of the air-stirred mobile, which preceded his interest in wood and wire toys in the shape of circus animals. His coil-spring line abstractions enliven *The Fables of Aesop According to Sir Roger L'Estrange* (1931), which he interprets in pseudo-primitive style. For "The Wolf and the Crane," the illustrator departs from nature with a diagonal alignment of bird reaching into the beast's throat. In a violation of perspective, Calder displays the complete outlines of overlaid paws and reveals the offending bone deep within the wolf's gullet. Less forbidding is the cross-eyed beast in "The Camel and the Driftwood," which is gracelessly posed with knees knocking and ragged tail adroop. In each vignette, animal vulnerability complements fable's standard themes of violence within the animal world.

In a departure from European masters, American illustrators have produced an idiosyncratic style of fable illustration. The touchstone, Arthur Burdette Frost, provided line drawings for the 1896 revised edition of Joel Chandler Harris's initial anthology, *Uncle Remus: His Songs and His Sayings* (1880), replacing the original work of Frederick Stuart Church and J. H. Moser and following the cartoonesque inadequacies of Church and William Holbrook Beard in *Nights with Uncle Remus* (1883) and Edward Windsor Kemble in *Daddy Jake, the Runaway* (1889). In the preface and dedication to the reworked flagship edition, Harris comments on the effect of animal fables on young readers:

> Phantoms! Children of dreams! True, my dear Frost; but if you could see the thousands of letters that have come to me from far and near, and all fresh from the hearts and hands of children, and from men and women who have not forgotten how to be children, you would not wonder at the dream. And such a

dream can do no harm. Insubstantial though it may be, I would not at this hour exchange it for all the fame won by my mightier brethren of the pen—whom I most humbly salute. (Harris, 1955, xxxi)

In gracious Georgia gentleman style, Harris anticipates that Frost's work will broaden the appeal of the initial collection: "Because you have breathed the breath of life into these amiable brethren of wood and field. Because, by a stroke here and a touch there, you have conveyed into their quaint antics the illumination of your own inimitable humor, which is as true to our sun and soil as it is to the spirit and essence of the matter set forth." (Harris 1955, xxxii) This generous but astute explanation of the illustrator's role in producing fable for public consumption honors Frost and his predecessors. In conclusion, Harris adds, "The book was mine, but now you have made it yours, both sap and pith. Take it, therefore, my dear Frost."

Skilled in the central goal of fable, Frost captures the jaunty human pride and self-incriminating chutzpah in the profile view of Brer Rabbit, who steps out in style, with cane in left hand, right hand on hip, and head and ears aligned above erect posture. Counter to the immaculate collar, overalls, and ramrod backbone is the animal's fulsome tail, which he forfeits forever in the *pourquoi* story "How Mr. Rabbit Lost His Fine Bushy Tail." Previous to the second edition, Frost had illustrated *Uncle Remus and His Friends* (1892), which varies the poses of the famous trickster to show him seated in a relaxed but wary conference with the wolf and atop a stone with forepaws on knees as he leans into the task of warning his five babes of the dangers that lie ahead. In the latter drawing, which appears in "Why Brother Wolf Didn't Eat the Little Rabbits," Frost carefully delineates innocence on the soft paws and rounded noses of the children as opposed to the sharp face and ready hoppers of their sire. The background, a Georgia streambed crosshatched with undefined bramble, echoes the stern lesson the father delivers without overdramatizing potential harm in nature. In a subsequent story, "Brother Fox Still in Trouble," Brer Rabbit leans forward, forepaws on knees, ears perked, eye glistening, and whiskers a-twiddle in a pose of readiness, the very attitude he inculcates in his youngsters.

By 1905, the Harris sequel, *Told by Uncle Remus* (1905), allies Frost's fine-lined crosshatching with a starker style by coillustrator J. M. Condé, whose influence marks "Why Mr. Cricket Has Elbows on His Legs." In few strokes of the pen, Condé's drawings depict a caricature of the negro before the fireplace, his open-mouthed children in inane pickaninny pose behind him. At the end of the story, the father stands in amazement, his garments in tatters. The perky headrag, melodramatic gestures, and open, white-rimmed mouths of husband and wife mimic the demeaning Jim Crow minstrel figures that dominated theatricals and publications of the era. In contrast, Frosts's drawings, particularly those that illustrate "When Brother Rabbit Was King," adorn the creatures with more dignity and individuality than Condé's vaudeville puppets. The change to J. M. Condé in two brief collections, *Uncle Remus and Brer Rabbit* (1907) and *Uncle Remus and the Little Boy* (1910), proves that Condé is at fault for the vitiated, ill-favored animal portraits that obscure the focus of Harris's fables. For *Uncle Remus Returns* (1918), Frost reprises former triumphs by fleshing out his animal poses with subtlety and wry humor, the hallmarks of the chiaroscuro that augments the drawing accompanying "Impty-Umpty and the Blacksmith." Obviously better at preserving decorum than Condé, Frost proved his use to American fable with a wealth of illustrations that enhance Harris's sweet-natured tale-telling and collation of Gullah and West African lore.

In the 1920s, the Japanese tradition of kamishibai, literally "paper drama," rose to popularity on streets and byways. A storyteller/candy vendor, armed with storyboards mounted on a small handlebar stage, bicycled through the residential area and villages to relate serialized fables and fairy tales to draw buyers for his wares. Each story evolved from static, overdramatized scenes depicted cartoon style. After entrancing young fans with the crudely drawn, but memorable events of "The Monkey and the Crab," "How the Years Were Named," "The Tongue-Cut Sparrow," and "The Mouse's Wedding," the teller packed his illustrations and departed midstory, leaving his audience a-tingle for the next clak-clak of his wooden clappers. The simplistic story drawings held juvenile viewers until the mid-1950s, when television began to supplant the itinerant storyteller. In the 1990s, the demand for multicultural fable restored the kamishibai tradition to use, this time in the hands of parents, child care givers, teachers, and librarians.

"The Cricket and the Rat"

The height of twentieth-century American fable derives from the blend of words and spare, linear art by humorist-illustrator James Thurber, author of *Fables for Our Times* (1940) and its sequel, *Further Fables for Our Time* (1956). Deft at the clean-line sketch, he overcame blindness with a Zeiss loop—defense plant headgear and goggles fitted with magnification—to draw the furrowed brows of little men hesitating in the presence of amorphous glowering females who hover like virulent jellyfish. These regrettable man-to-woman stare-downs occur under the watchful gaze of oversized dogs, whose gelid pose captures them in the act of silent but intense disapproval and dismay. In *The Last Flower* (1939), a pictorial forerunner of Thurber's infatuation with fable, the purity of line enhances the bold gesture—oversized marching feet and hawk-eyed, Hitleresque demagogues haranguing each other. After the results of World War XII return civilization to its cycle of one man, one woman, and one flower, Thurber retreats into the sparest of cartooning techniques, a primitivism both naive and subtle. Of the Zeitgeist that spawned his wistful cartoon fable he remarked, "A species living under the threat of obliteration is bound to produce obliterature—and that's what we are producing." (Morsberger 1964, 41)

The retro style of two other American illustrators, Antonio Frasconi and Joseph Low, departs from detailed line drawing to old-style woodcut and linoleum cut, both mimicking Renaissance anthologies. Frasconi, an American immigrant from Buenos Aires, Argentina, won numerous awards for graphic arts, including the 1955 American Institute of Graphic Arts Book of the Year for *Twelve Fables of Aesop* (1954). For "The Fox and the Crow" in *9 Aesop's Fables* (1953), Frasconi chooses whimsy and sprightliness over grim drama. He enlarges the two pairs of eyes to stress the telling moment when the foolish crow drops his chunk of cheese to the bushy-tailed fox below. Sheltering the scenario is a stylized tree marked by crosshatched trunk, knotty limb, and carefully outlined leaves. For "The Jay in Peacock's Feathers," Frasconi delights in the humor of a scraggly jay shedding the peacock finery he wrongfully wore and the mirthful audience of peafowl that deride his foolishness. Frasconi's contemporary, Joseph Low, the high-spirited illustrator of *Aesop: A Portfolio of Color Prints* (1963), enjoys the jest of "The Lion in Love" by capturing the beast's discomfiture. With claws in the foreground and teeth behind, the frail beast stares aghast from the composition, its scraggly mane a match for a sparse-haired tail. In the same primitive style, Low draws the focal animal for "The Cock and the Pearl." Less dynamic than other drawings, Low's cock appears alert and perky as it demonstrates its wisdom in preferring nourishing grain to a jewel. These muscular figures complement the twentieth century's recensions of Aesop, Bidpai, and *The Arabian Nights* and the Disneyesque screen confections that characterize the core fables in *Fantasia* (1940), *Song of the South* (1946), *The Jungle Book* (1967), *The Little Mermaid* (1989), *Aladdin* (1992), and *The Lion King* (1994).

See also Saint-Exupéry, Antoine de; Potter, Beatrix; Thurber, James.

Sources *Aesop: Five Centuries of Illustrated Fables* 1964; *Aesop's Fables* 1968, 1993, n. d.; Eisenstadt and Tamaki, n. d.; Harris 1955; Hobbs 1986; Lewis 1996; Mackay 1973; Massignon 1968; Morsberger 1964; *Something about the Author* 1988; Thurber 1940, 1987; Wallich 1994; *Who's Who in American Art* 1976; Widdows 1992.

IRIARTE, TOMÁS DE

A dramatist and fabulist of Spain's golden age of poetry, Tomás de Iriarte (or Yriarte) y Oropesa produced simple didactic fare that was frequently translated into English. Versions of his work appeared in *Blackwood's Magazine* and illustrated elementary school textbooks for two centuries. Born September 18, 1750, in Orotava, Tinerife, Canary Islands, he was the student of a scholarly uncle, Don Juan de Iriarte, and attended *tertulias* [social clubs] that brought him into the literary circle with dramatist and poet Leandro de Moratin and satirist José de Cadalso Vasquez. A significant figure of the Spanish Enlightenment, the fabulist settled in Madrid and rose to prominence as a state scholar. Succeeding his uncle as a civil employee, Iriarte served the secretary of state as translator of French drama for the Spanish stage and was promoted to archivist for the War Department. In addition to literary pursuits, he is best known for translating the 476 hexameters of Horace's *Arte Poética* into 1,065 Spanish verses and for writing a neoclassic best-seller, *La Música* (1779), a didactic poem that went through three printings in its first year.

Clouding Iriarte's reputation is a series of political and literary controversies that embroiled Ramón de la Cruz and the poet Meléndez Valdés in extensive but petty wrangling. A sour-tempered satirist and polemicist, Juan Pablo Forner, lambasted Iriarte's *Fábulas literarias* [Literary Fables] (1782) with pointed invective, *El asno erudito* [The Erudite Ass] (1782), and an unpublished lampoon, "Los gramáticos chinos" [The Chinese Grammarians]. A year later, Iriarte riposted with *Para casos tales suele tenor los maestros oficiales* (1783), a cryptic title that precedes an explanation—For Such Cases the Official Masters Usually Hold: A Critical-Parenthetical Letter or Pathetic Exhortation, Which Eleuterio Geta [Iriarte's pseudonym] Wrote to the Author of the *Fabulas Literarias*. This protracted and unprofessional dust-up resulted in public humiliation: Forner was officially silenced and the Catholic Inquisition denounced Iriarte for his disrespect to the pope in the fable "La barca de Simón" [Simon's Boat]. Some eight years later, about the time of his death in Madrid on September 17, 1791, Iriarte's reputation became mired in controversy during a literary dispute with a colleague, Basque poet and fabulist Félix María Samaniego. After his anonymous antireligious attack on Iriarte aroused Catholic officials, calumny from the attack attached to both writers' names. Two years after Iriarte's death, Samaniego was confined to house arrest in a monastery near Laguardia, Spain. Biographer Cotarelo y Mori sorted out the shameful legacy a century later in *Iriarte y su época* [Iriarte and His Epoch] (1897).

Chief of Iriarte's contributions to world literature are the fables, a facile collection of 76 verse beast tales composed in meters and styles suited to the truths he wanted to illustrate. He composed the lot, one by one, in reply to personal enemies and detractors. The totality covers a series of topics—criticism, study of classic models, clarity and diction, beauty and utility, and simplicity. Iriarte's sophisticated narratives espouse his own literary philosophy and denigrate those of certain contemporaries. A graceful, unassuming animal story, "The Ass and the Flute," satirizes lucky fools like the ass, which by chance snorts into the musical instrument, thus blowing a single uninspired note. In similar vein, "The Cathedral Bell and the Hermitage Bell," "The Goose and the Goldfinch," "The Ivy and the Thyme," and "The Bear and the Monkey" all treat the subject of display of talents. The first, a mockery of the hermit who longs for fame, contrasts the constant tinkling of the hermit's bell with the single toll of the cathedral bell. The fabulist concludes with an eight-line moral:

> Of true merit and excellence, many men try,
> By grave airs and long faces, the place to supply;
> And think that their wisdom is surely inferred
> From their seldom vouchsafing to utter a word.
>
> Indeed, it is true, in a general way,
> Asses may not be known if they never should bray,
> And for a wise animal safely may pass;
> If one opens his mouth, then we know he's an ass.
> (Yriarte 1855, 16)

Equally disdainful, "The Bear, the Monkey and the Hog" speaks directly to the issue of reputation and advises mediocre performers, "Authors, who seek a noble fame,/Mark well the moral of my verse!/That's bad which worthy judges blame;/What bad applaud, is worse." (Yriarte 1855, 7)

Iriarte's focus on the artist's trials holds firm through numerous object lessons, for example, the pointless boasting in "The Frog and the Hen," the value of quantity over quality in "The Two Thrushes," and the need to be valued in "The Jeweller and the Lace-Maker." The bitter tone of "The Ivy and the Thyme" enhances the clash between the climber and the modest writer. To the ivy, which boasts of rising quickly by clinging to a majestic oak, the thyme has wise advice: if the tree is felled, the ivy will fall to ruin, where thyme will shade its burial place. Obviously angered by poseurs whose rapid grasp of high court approval depends on the power and prestige of the patron, Iriarte reviles the spineless fawner. His prediction that the oak will fall to the woodsman's ax parallels the chancy court promotion that may precede an unforeseen tumble, bringing down the courtier along with clients and hangers-on.

Edging closer to his own trade with "The Sword and the Spit" and "The Goose and the Goldfinch," Iriarte mocks the unpredictable nature of translation, which can turn "noble swords to vulgar spits." (Yriarte 1855, 95) To the pathetic goose that tries to imitate the mellifluous goldfinch, Iriarte adds the hissing onomatopoeia that mimics the poetaster's chagrin at failure to duplicate poetic expertise. Iriarte's insistence on good work habits fuels a challenge match, "The Ant and the Flea," which contrasts the proficiency of the two insects. The diligent ant displays her job of carrying heavy loads in granary and dormitory. To her obvious dedication to hard labor, the flea mutters agreeably:

> Ah, yes, undoubtedly;
> I grant it; certainly. O, so I see!
> 'Tis plain. I think so, too, myself. Of course.
> All right. I understand. There's better and there's worse.
> (Yriarte 1855, 20)

When it comes his turn to perform, he quickly dispenses with the busy ant, claiming, "I've an engagement now. Another day/We'll think on it." (Yriarte 1855, 20)

With controlled annoyance, Iriarte flaunts his subjectivity in repeated spewings at those who offend or rival him. His professional griping fuels the bloated moralizing of "The Duck and the Serpent" and "The Bustard," a jab at artists who steal from others' works. Digging into his pack of personal animosities, Iriarte creates "The Linnet and the Swan," a lengthy, vitriolic swipe at the rival who rests on claims from the past. To the snooty swan, the linnet replies:

> With boundless curiosity we all—
> All other voices by silent wonder shackled
> Should listen to that harmony divine,
> Which boasts far greater fame than mine;
> Though none of us, as yet, hath ever heard.
> (Yriarte 1855, 33–34)

Iriarte carefully restates his moral in the final sestet by instructing coxcombs who cheat the audience by competing with real talent.

In contrast to fables displaying heavy-handed acrimony, Iriarte wrote more graceful *agon* or competition pieces, such as "The Silkworm and the Spider," in which the exchange between rivals ends with a smiling reminder from the silkworm that her spinning, although tedious and slow, endures long after the spider web is swept away. Likewise controlled and universal is the exchange in "The Two Rabbits," the classic argument over trifles unsuited to time, place, or provocation. The didacticism of "The Frog and the Frogling" is another model of Aesopic style. As the frogling learns from examining tall reeds that have been knocked to the ground, pompous exteriors often conceal an insubstantial interior. By refraining from appending a message to his detractors, Iriarte carries out the true Aesopic purpose of fable—the creation of universal lessons in light situations drawn from nature.

When directing his focus to dramatic presentation of a moral or ethical subject, Iriarte succeeds at the kind of fable that Aesop and Jean de La Fontaine mastered. The nattering of "The Goat and the Horse" expresses Iriarte's love of music, which the horse enjoys as part of his earthly pleasure. Smoothly suited to place and time, "The Owl" is another case in point. The implications of the bird's nocturnal behavior create an ominous atmosphere as he profanes a church by a nocturnal flight toward the lamp suspended over the Virgin's shrine. The fabulist describes the audacity of the interloper, which swoops toward the cache of oil but veers away from a light too intense for his lidless eyes. The scenario departs from the more vengeful fare that forever links Iriarte's canon with a penchant for vendetta. However, the majority of Iriarte's fables—such as "The Rich Man's Library," "The Rope-Dancer," and "The Connoisseurs"—remain studded with confrontation, a guiding principle that separates his style from the more congenial writings of Native American fabulists, Aesop, Bidpai, La Fontaine, and Ivan Krylov.

Sources "Anthology of Spanish Poetry," http://www.ipfw.indiana.edu; Cooper 1921; Komroff 1935; "La Poesía de los Siglos de Oro," http://www.geocities.com; Ward 1978; Yriarte 1855.

JEWISH FABLE

Jewish lore, one of the world's touchstones of wisdom literature, is rich in parable, anecdote, and fable. The Torah, which Christians call the Old Testament, contains several fables, markedly contrasting in style and context. An example from Hebrew lore appears in Judges 9:8–15, composed in David's time, approximately 925 B.C.E. The brief prophetic fable is a pulpit maneuver by Jotham, king of Judah, who relates the story to the citizens of Shechem from the pinnacle of Mount Gerizim around the twelfth century B.C.E. Jotham chooses a simple nature tale as an exemplum and indirect denunciation of Abimelech, the illegitimate son of Gideon and a murderous power-monger whom the people have unwisely elected as their ruler. The fable speaks of talking trees that elect first the olive, then the fig, vine, and bramble as lord over all trees. After the first three candidates decline and opt to retain their production of oil, sweet fruit, and wine, the bramble characterizes the dangers of naming a peer as lord: "If in truth ye anoint me king over you, then come and put your trust in my shadow: and if not, let fire come out of the bramble, and devour the cedars of Lebanon." The fable particularizes the menace of the lowly briar, which offers no shade and constantly threatens to erupt in wildfire. In true fable fashion, the image opens the minds of Jotham's hearers to the insidious threat of a morally bankrupt wheeler-dealer such as Abimelech, who had amassed a campaign chest from a temple treasury, hired ward heelers to disperse a stable base of voters, and swept into victory. As Jotham predicted, Abimelech's three years of rule preceded a mass revolt, a civic wildfire that the king could not control. Unsuccessfully fighting the conflagration, Abimelech fell to his own devious methods on the outskirts of Thebez, where, like flame, he was stamped out, leaving behind desolation for Shechem.

A similar fable of thistles and cedars occurs in II Kings 14:9 after Amaziah, king of Judah, summons Jehoash, Israel's able king, for a parley around 790 B.C.E. The situation, which bristles with foreboding, illustrates the difference between confidence and brashness. Jehoash must deal with a foolhardy, war-proud king who has assaulted Edom near the southern end of the Dead Sea and threatens a similar foray into Israel. For the sake of analogy, Jehoash insults the arrogant upstart with a rebuff stated in compact fable form: "The thistle that was in Lebanon sent to the cedar that was in Lebanon, saying, Give thy daughter to my son to wife: and there passed by a wild beast that was in Lebanon, and trode down the thistle." Rephrased almost verbatim in II Chronicles 25:18, composed around 400 B.C.E., the message strikes directly at Judah's monarch, a lowly bramble who dares to equate itself with a cedar. Jehoash is a god-centered king who alludes to his majesty as a cedar and to his might as a wild beast. Fearless before taunts, he makes no effort to conceal his contempt. Moving from illustrative fiction to political situation, Jehoash adds, "Thou hast indeed smitten Edom, and thine heart hath lifted thee up." He departs from all pretense of diplomacy to insist that Amaziah "tarry at home."

In contrast to this open-access tale from nature that invites application to numerous hierarchical situations, a more restricted fable appears in II Samuel 12:1–6, a biographical study compiled around the sixth century B.C.E. The story tells of one particular sinner—the rich man who seizes the poor man's lamb. Narrated by Nathan, Jerusalem's court prophet during the early tenth century B.C.E., the story is a deliberate thrust at David, ruler of a united kingdom and despoiler of Bathsheba, wife of Uriah the Hittite, a man who served honorably in David's army. To enlarge on David's moral infraction, Nathan contrasts a rich man with many flocks and herds and a poor man, who kept a ewe lamb, hand-fed it, and loved it as a household pet. As an enhancement of the animal's importance to the poor owner's children, Nathan adds, "It did eat of his own meat, and drank of his own cup, and lay in his bosom, and was unto him as a daughter." The story reaches its crux with the arrival of a traveler, for whom the rich man spares his own flock and kills and dresses the poor man's pet lamb.

Nathan's beguilingly clear-cut fable strikes to the heart of its intended victim—a king who is accustomed to delivering judgments from the bench to settle strife among his subjects. According to essayist Joseph Addison, Nathan's coup was "to convey Instruction to the Ear of a King without offending it, and to bring the Man after God's own Heart to a right Sense of his Guilt and his Duty." (Addison & Steele 1907, 44) Enraged at the unidentified rich man in the fable, David leaps up and demands, "As the Lord liveth, the man that hath done this thing shall surely die: And he shall restore the lamb fourfold, because he did this thing, and because he had no pity." With courtly aplomb, Nathan has his hearer where he wants him. To the vulnerable hypocrite on the throne, the prophet retorts, "Thou art the man." Unlike the expansive story lines of Aesopic lore, Nathan's verbal mousetrap catches David unaware, shocking him with the enormity of his crimes against Bathsheba and Uriah.

The drama of fable-within-history offers a rare glimpse of apologue as pricker of conscience. Maneuvering beyond the universality of fable, Nathan gets personal. He omits the neatly understated aphorisms of Greek fable to thunder, "Wherefore hast thou despised the commandment of the Lord, to do evil in his sight?" Ominously he ticks off David's crimes—having Uriah killed in battle and usurping his wife—then foretells the downfall of the royal house. True to the prophet's rebuke, the prediction that "the sword shall never depart from thine house" reverberates through the adulterer's residence and kingdom, costing him the lives of four sons and the rape of his daughter Dinah. With the narration of a simple fable, a somber Hebrew tragedy is set: Yahweh, the avenging deity, allows the king to live but robs him of domestic peace and political accord. At a crucial moment for the crown, David loses Absalom, the beloved son who dares to lead a revolt against the father and usurp his father's harem. Pursued by Joab, David's commander in chief, the royal youth dies in tragic powerlessness—like Ariadne from Greek myth, he is suspended by his shoulder-length hair from an overhanging tree limb. Absalom dies with multiple darts piercing his torso, leaving the king to wail in II Samuel 18:33, "O my son Absalom, my son, my son Absalom! would God I had died for thee, O Absalom, my son, my son!" The composite picture of Nathan's warning and David's punishment for deception and murder places fable in an unusual position—at the climax of the inevitable conflict between Hebrew priest and arrogant king.

The tradition of fable as ethical illustration and precept occurs throughout the eastern Mediterranean, particularly in Greece, India, Syria, and Egypt. Among Hebrew scholars in Talmudic and Midrashic literature, prose and verse fable was particularly useful as a source of wisdom and moral instruction. The canon of Jewish fable demonstrates stronger Indian influence than Greek. Although some are anonymous, a few are identified by date and author:

- Around 960 B.C.E., fable served Solomon, the prestigious judge and monarch of Jerusalem, who relied on apologue as a method of dispensing justice in his law courts and as exempla in books of wisdom literature, which appear in the Bible as Proverbs, Ecclesiastes, and Song of Solomon. The most famous of his courtroom stories is the anecdote about the two women claiming the same baby in I Kings 3:16–28. Solomon's name became so much a part of justice fables that the Solomonic character appears in lore as far away as Malaysia.

- Aesopic lore influenced pulpit lore round the first and second century C.E. with Johannan ben Zakkai's fox stories. In 117 C.E., Joshua ben Hananiah cited Aesop's "The Lion and the Crane" as a means of soothing a Jewish gathering that challenged Hadrian's refusal to rebuild the temple. In the second century, Akiba expressed the importance of scriptural study by telling "The Fox and the Fishes." During that same era, Rabbi Meir composed some 300 fox fables, of which only three are extant.

- Rabbi Joshua ben Levi's contribution, "The Serpent, Its Tail, and Head," is a brief wisdom tale that deprecates the foolish follower who would supplant a true leader. By depicting the snake's trials—falling into a ditch and tearing its body on thorns—Rabbi ben Levi establishes his contention that no sensible head should be led by a tail.

A vigorous segment of Jewish literature is comprised of folklore in Yiddish, a literary language that, like English, dates from the 1380s, when Jewish peasants settled among German-speaking people. As with other amalgamations of people, language, and customs, Yiddish is a nexus of intersecting folkways, scripture, wisdom literature, and idiom. One of the genres that found favor both with German locals and the Jewish hierarchy was fable. In 1697, Rabbi

Moses ben Eliezer Wallich of Worms produced *Sefer Meshalim* [Book of Fables], a valued text that survives in two copies, housed in Oxford and Amsterdam. A third was destroyed with an entire Hamburg library in World War II. Wallich's collection of 34 fables is a charming *divertissement* that offers insight into Yiddish literature. The fables in Wallich's anthology display both the Aesopic and Arabic traditions. According to his introduction, Wallich drew on several sources:

- the 119 Aesopic stories in the *Mishlei Shu'alim* [Fox Fables] (ca. early thirteenth century), an anthology compiled by a French Jew, Berechiah ben Natronai ha-Nakdan, who was influenced by the medieval Reynard the Fox cycle and the lyrics of Marie de France.

- from Asian sources, Isaac ibn Abi Sahula's *Meshal ha-Kadmoni* [Ancient Parable] (thirteenth century), a complex framework of stories written in the Arabic *maqama* style, which orders illustrative stories under five themes—reason, repentance, advice and readiness, modesty and humility, and reverence.

- the earthy, good-natured, and lightly ironic fables of *Kuh Buch* or *Ku-Bukh* [Cow Book] (1555), a collection of 35 models of farm-based animal lore published in Verona by Abraham ben Mattathias. A student of commonalities of Jewish life, the author of the *Kuh Buch* models his work on the Italian *facetiae* of the late Renaissance and dresses lore in the peasant tastes and amusements of the times, particularly those entries that treat human foibles.

Not mentioned in Wallich's list is a non-Jewish compendium in Middle High German, Aesopic stories entitled *Der Edelstein* (mid-fourteenth century), by Ulrich Boner, a Dominican friar from Basel. It was first showcased in 1461 as one of the first books printed in the German language.

Wallich introduces his collection with a straightforward explanation of style and purpose. Presenting "good Yiddish" language and appropriate illustrations, his stories precede a moral that teaches listeners how to conduct themselves. In jocular but pious voice, Wallich adds:

> Therefore come all you men, women, and maidens and inspect this handsome book. You won't flee from it. And do buy it. When you read what is in it, your heart will rejoice. You won't begrudge the money. And do it soon. May God quickly send us the Messiah. Amen, may his will be thus. (Wallich 1994, 1)

In a lengthy preface, Wallich declares that writing the book subjected his intellect to a needle-sharp study of ethics, the "hard morsels" he chewed upon to the exclusion of weather, wind, wife, child, deaf, blind, singing, piping, rain, snow, and other commotions. In the wracking style of Ecclesiasticus, he warns that all, whether male, female, young, pious, rich, or poor, should turn from evil advice to embrace the morality of his fables, which, like roses, flowers, and honey, delight while they instruct. At least half of the preface urges upright Jewish behaviors. Wallich enlarges the book's worth with sensuous imagery: "Velvet and silk do not adorn like this book . . . like spices trickling down."

An engraving of a Jewish scholar reading fables from a Hebrew text.

(Wallich 1994, 4) As his selling spiel winds down, he adds that his book should be used as a text "to teach the children that God will grant you [and] . . . to pass the time." (Wallich 1994, 5) He concludes with a prayer for God's blessing.

After the lengthy buildup, the body of fables proves as informal and conversational as the chatty preface. Each concludes with a brief restatement of the moral in the language of one-on-one tutoring. For example, Fable II moves toward a five-sentence homily that encases the aphorism like a kernel in a walnut shell: "A man who does not know himself is surely a fool." (Wallich 1994, 11) Subsequent lessons browbeat the reader with obvious, clumsily stated conclusions:

- One should pay no attention to evil talk. (Fable XVI)

- Happy is he who has a loyal heart and steadfastly remembers the good done him. (Fable VII)

- With many shepherds the sheep are badly tended. (Fable XII)

- He who steps forth with unfettered spirit and also with cleverness can win every battle. (Fable IX)

- One should prefer short rations in peace to a king's bounty in misery and wretchedness. (Fable X, a resetting of the ubiquitous "City Mouse and Country Mouse" of Horace)

An irksomely antifemale motif in one of Wallich's fables repeats misogynistic medieval notions that women are lustful, loquacious, and tricky. In Fable XIX, the fabulist opens on a pathetic grieving widow mourning beside her husband's tomb. Guilelessly, she shares food with a man who guards the corpse of a hanged felon on a nearby gibbet. Without preface, the guard urges her, "Listen to me and I'll relieve you of all your sorrow. You needn't be ashamed; take me for your lover." (Wallich 1994, 45) The fable takes a ghoulish turn: the day following a night of lovemaking, the two discover that someone has removed the hanged man from the gallows. The widow urges her lover to exhume her husband's remains and suspend them in the felon's place. To accentuate the woman's lewd, disloyal behavior, Wallich emphasizes that she takes a young man to replace her husband. In the appended sermonette, Wallich reviles "faithless women whose behinds are always itching." (Wallich 1994, 46) His 12-sentence exegesis grows quickly out of proportion to the elements of the fable and ignores completely the role of the guard in initiating the roadside romance. Like a sour scold, Wallich presses his case that "evil women instigate much wickedness and much evil results from them."

Only slightly less antifemale is Fable XXX, a two-pronged story that exhorts both husband and wife for their foolishness and treachery. The tale of a pious Jew and his whorish mate, the fable grows tedious with lengthy description of his daily attendance at temple and her pretense of slavish devotion to cooking and homemaking. The gullible old fool fails to see that she uses food as both coverup and compensation for lecherous frolics with a younger man. When the lover urges her to steal from her husband and elope, she gladly departs, leaving behind a befuddled and cuckolded temple-goer who learns too late the dangers of naïveté, piety, and complacency. Wallich's moral reminds women to be honorable and men to observe their homes more carefully. The story has the emotional force of a situation that Wallich has perhaps known or experienced and blows out of proportion to establish his case. As an addendum, he notes, "Everything is appropriate to its own time; there should not be too much of anything, but everything in proper measure," a restatement of Horace's *aurea mediocritas,* the Latin "golden mean."

Jewish fables from more recent times include the works of Joel Bril Loewe, Judah Ben-Zeeb, Baruch Lindau, Shalom Cohen, Mordecai Aaron Günzburg, Judah Löb Gordon, Abraham Paperna, Judah Steinberg, humanist Elie Wiesel, and storyteller Peninnah Schram. Wiesel, a Romanian survivor of the Holocaust and the foremost ethicist and peacemaker of his time, is revered for moral candor and graceful but compelling polemics. He learned Hasidic lore from the family storyteller, his maternal grandfather Reb Dodye Feig. Steeped in the dark conflicts of realistic narrative, Wiesel has acknowledged the value of fable and parable in his compelling writings: *La Ville de la chance* [The Town beyond the Wall] (1962), *Les Portes de la forêt* [The Gates of the Forest] (1964), *Le Chant des morts* [Legends of Our Time] (1966), and the drama *Zalmen; ou, La Folie de Dieu* [Zalmen; or, The Madness of God] (1968). In personal testimony of the difficulty of writing about Jewish struggles in his autobiography *All Rivers Run to the Sea* (1995), he comments: "To write is to plumb the unfathomable depths of being. Writing lies within the domain of mystery. The space between any two words is vaster than the distance between heaven and earth. To bridge it you must close your eyes and leap. A Hasidic tradition tells us that in the Torah the white spaces, too, are God-given. Ultimately, to write is an act of faith." (Wiesel 1995, 321) He expands on the difference between the literary and ethical dimension and declares, "The truth I present is unvarnished; I cannot do otherwise." The extent of Wiesel's published parables, articles, speeches on the persecuted, and ethical and biblical teachings earned him the 1986 Nobel Peace Prize and the admiration of world leaders of many faiths.

A New York storyteller and student of Wiesel, Peninnah Schram specializes in legends, parables, and folktales from biblical, Talmudic, Midrashic, Hasidic, Ashkenazi, Sephardic, Yiddish, and Israeli sources. Her performances of Judaic wit and wisdom from Lithuanian and White Russian anthologies stress the fool and trickster mode and episodes in the life of Elijah the Prophet. A National Storytelling Association leadership award winner, Schram, a dynamic voice for humanism, relates practical human knowledge about how to live and die, which she derived from her father, a cantor and collector of biblical and Midrashic lore. Following her mother's advice to be *klug* (smart/wise) and to apply *hob sekhl* (common sense), Schram adopted a tradition found in Kabbala: read the literal sequence of events, learn the lesson or moral, shape the events in personal language, interpret the story as it applies to life, and understand why the totality appeals to the teller. Labeled the "Queen of Jewish Storytellers," she considers herself a *shelihah tzibur* [messenger of the people] and has broadened her outreach from small groups to national conventions, television, radio, audiocassette, and print, including *Jewish Stories One Generation Tells Another* (1987) and *Eight Tales for Eight Nights: Stories for Chanukah* (1990).

Sources Addison et al. 1907; Blackham 1985; *Contemporary Authors* 1994; Creeden 1994; Freedman 1983; *Holy Bible* 1986; Jeffrey 1992; Komroff 1935; Kreuzer 1995; Landman 1948; Schram 1987, 1990; Shah 1982; Wallich 1994; Wiesel 1995.

 # JUST-SO STORIES

The appeal of *Just-So Stories* (1902), the most Aesopic of Rudyard Kipling's lore, rests on the author's blended point of view as an English child born in India and come to fame as a journalist and storyteller at the height of the British Raj. The *pourquoi* style amuses curious children, as do Kipling's original pen-and-ink illustrations, which he drew for his daughters, Josephine and Elsie, and for visiting cousins who joined the family storytelling sessions. Several sources influenced the series. The question-and-answer technique is perhaps a derivative of the Uncle Remus stories of Joel Chandler Harris, whom Kipling knew and admired. Critics suggest that his approach to changes in animal shape and behavior is a twist of the evolutionary theories of Jean Lamarck, French army officer and naturalist whose *Philosophie zoologique* (1809) and *Histoire des animaux sans vertèbres* [Story of Invertebrate Animals] (1822) are forerunners of Charles Darwin's concept of natural selection.

The narrator, the voice of Kipling, entertains an unnamed child whom he calls "My Best Beloved," with a series of 12 fanciful tales about the nature of ten animals and the creation of the first letter and the entire alphabet. The opening story, "How the Whale Got His Throat," sets the tone with a blithe preface that describes the whale's diet: "He ate the starfish and the garfish, and the crab and the dab, and the plaice and the dace, and the skate and his mate, and the mackereel and the pickereel, and the really truly twirly-whirly eel. All the fishes he could find in the sea he ate with his mouth—so!" (Kipling 1974, 7) The whale, at the suggestion of the clever 'Stute Fish, swallows the shipwrecked mariner, who is floating on a raft east of Newfoundland and south of Greenland. The Hi-ber-ni-an Mariner uses his suspenders, raft, and jackknife to carve and fit a grating in the whale's throat and stop the whale from swallowing anything but very small fish. By dancing and upsetting the whale's insides, he forces the whale to set him free in Ireland, his native land. From the beginning narrative, Kipling strings together these hypnotic episodes with alliteration and his unnamed listener's gleeful anticipation of the chain of events that forever alters human and animal behavior.

Kipling's art rests on the core flaw of Victorian thinking—that humanity stands at the center of creation. With a blend of verse and prose, "How the Camel Got His Hump," set at the beginning of time, explains why all the animals work for humankind. The camel, when asked to do his part, only mutters, "Humph!" The Djinn of All Deserts listens to the complaints of the disgruntled horse, dog, and ox, and promises to make the camel do his part. When a hump appears on the camel's back, the speaker moralizes:

The Camel's hump is an ugly lump
  Which well you may see at the Zoo;
But uglier yet is the hump we get
  From having too little to do.
(Kipling 1974, 23)

The misbehaving camel "Humphs" himself and tries to catch up the three days the other animals have worked but never learns to mind his manners. Thus, the fabulist segues neatly into the focus of Victorian children's literature, the moral lesson. By robbing the camel of its autonomy, he forces it into a chain of enslaved images marching in lockstep to the voice of the nursery storyteller.

Ever attuned to geography, Kipling moves to a setting on an island in the Red Sea for "How the Rhinoceros Got His Skin." The rhinoceros, which robs a Parsee of his cake and upsets his stove, is the obvious cause of trouble. During a heat wave five weeks later, the Parsee gets his revenge on the rhinoceros, which leaves his pelt on the beach while he bathes in seawater: "He went to his camp and filled his hat with cake-crumbs, for the Parsee never ate anything but cake, and never swept out his camp. He took that skin, and he rubbed that skin just as full of old, dry, stale, tickly cake-crumbs and some burned currants as ever it could *possibly* hold." (Kipling 1974, 25) The rhinoceros returns and puts on his skin. Kipling expands on his rubbing and itching, which stretches the skin and precipitates a permanent bad temper. The story ends with the Aesopic dichotomy of conclusions: the ill-tempered rhino is marked for life and the long-suffering Parsee descends from his palm tree, moves away from the rhino, and returns to his orderly life, a model well suited to late nineteenth-century decorum.

With remarkable felicity, the story of "How the Leopard Got His Spots," set in the African grassland, speaks in childishly unthreatening tones of the law of the jungle. Downplaying the recurrent element of slaughter, Kipling enhances the instructional value of the fable with data about the terrain, rocks, grass, and indigenous animals. The plot explains natural camouflage. The potential victims of a leopard and an Ethiopian hunter gradually migrate from the high veldt to a shadier place and are spotted and striped by their new environment: "The Giraffe grew blotchy, and the Zebra grew stripy, and the Eland and the Koodoo grew darker, with little wavy grey lines on their backs like bark on a tree trunk; and so, though you could hear them and smell them, you could very seldom see them, and then only when you knew precisely where to look." (Kipling 1974, 33) The natural protection of spots and speckles frees them from danger. The wise baboon advises the Ethiopian to follow the game and to "change as soon as you can." The hunter alters his own skin to a dark brown/ purple/slate color, then causes the leopard to change his spots by stippling the leopard's torso with five small black marks made with the tips of the Ethiopian's fingers. With their new camouflage, the duo return to their hunting and live happily ever after, content with nature-imitating markings. The fabulist's tone maintains equanimity as if to prove to young listeners that altering nature need not cause fuss or pain or even brief inconvenience. Folding up like a neat portfolio, the story moves from exposition to end with purpose in mind and, like a tidy maiden aunt, dusts off the conclusion with a minimum of hullabaloo.

Kipling's "The Elephant's Child," the quintessential child's curiosity tale, combines Aesopic morality and the aphorism about crocodile tears with *pourquoi* method. Relatives and other jungle animals often spank the young animal for asking questions about the crocodile's dinner. Despite constant punishment, the little elephant sets out for "the great grey-green, greasy Limpopo River" and continues to ask his question. (Kipling 1974, 45) The story reaches an impasse common in Eastern lore, especially in fables derived from the *Panchatantra*. When the elephant encounters the crocodile, he gets his nose trapped in strong jaws and stretched out of shape. He waits for the flesh to shrink, but the Bi-Coloured-Python-Rock-Snake advises him to adapt to his new trunk by plucking fruit and grass, spraying water and mud, and swatting flies and obnoxious people. Kipling allows the long-suffering child a modicum of vengeance when he returns home. Using his long trunk, he punishes all the animals that had spanked him. The moral is benevolent. Asserting control, Kipling declares that from that day, the animals stopped spanking others.

Following his pattern of interspersing prose stories with reflective poems and ditties, Kipling inserts an untitled 20-line poem about his "six honest serving-men," a reference to six familiar abstracts—the journalist's questions of what, why, when, how, where, and who. The fable describes how the news writer's team of questions covers land and sea, east to west, over the reporter's work day. Kipling personalizes the poem in the final seven lines with a prod at "a person small," his daughter Josephine, whom he accuses of asking ten million questions, which include "One million Hows, two million Wheres/And seven million Whys!" (Kipling 1974, 56) The light tone avoids the standard moral and bids his daughter to continue probing the world. Even though Kipling was an outspoken opponent of women's rights, his encouragement of his daughter is a refreshing nod to a young female with obvious intellect. She died before the book was completed, yet her presence inspires and impels the paternal storyteller to continue his narrative.

Averse to the human foible of discontent is the story of the fractious beast in "The Sing-Song of Old Man Kangaroo." Because he begs the Big God Nqong to make him different from the other animals and more popular by five o'clock in the afternoon, Nqong inaugurates a chase scene by summoning Yellow-Dog Dingo to chase the kangaroo, who flees like a hare. Again, Kipling takes the opportunity to educate readers, this time on the terrain of Australia: "He ran through the desert; he ran through the mountains; he ran through the salt-pans; he ran through the reed-beds; he ran through the blue gums; he ran through the spinifex; he ran till his front legs ached. He had to!" (Kipling 1974, 60) Over ti-trees, the tropics of Cancer and Capricorn, and over the Wollgong River, the duo runs until five o'clock, by which time the kangaroo has developed short front legs and strong rear legs from hopping out of the way of the dingo. Out of sorts with his treatment, the kangaroo stops complaining to avoid subsequent chasing. Thus, Kipling accounts for the two beasts' mutual dislike. He closes with a poem declaring that, if the reader trotted all over Australia, he would develop similar legs and would "be a Marvellous Kid!" (Kipling 1974, 65) Beneath this genial avuncularity lies a speaker known to the Victorian world—the missionarying didact who dispenses a ripe world wisdom.

For a fable of cooperation, Kipling moves to the Amazon River, where the Jaguar learns from his mother how to eat the Hedgehog and the Tortoise. The setting and situation follow the author's pattern of juxtaposing exotic beings and places with the ever-present domestic scene of knowing parent instructing neophyte offspring. To escape being eaten, the victims confuse the newcomer with contrary information about their respective hard shell and prickly spines. After they curl themselves up and swim for exercise, they metamorphose into pinecone shapes. Mother Jaguar renames the new creatures for "The Beginning of the Armadillos." Kipling caps his seventh fable with a nose-to-nose confrontation of the turtle turning into a long-tailed armadillo and the hedgehog sprouting the same carapaced tail. The jocular verse that serves as coda declares: "I've never seen a Jaguar,/Nor yet an Armadill—/O dilloing in his armour,/And I s'pose I never will." (Kipling 1974, 79)

Perhaps the most touching of entries are Kipling's eighth and ninth fables, which depart from animal lore to explain the evolution of literacy. "How the First Letter Was Written" and "How the Alphabet Was Made" together tell the story of Taffimai Metallumai, a Neolithic child identified as "Small-person-without-any-manners-who-ought-to-be-spanked," who tries to help her father Tegumai Bopsulai send a message to her mother Teshumai. To draw a pictograph on birch bark, she uses a stranger's magic shark's tooth and plunks into a familiar childhood work pose—prone on her stomach with legs in the air. By the time she has created a symbolic message for the stranger to carry to Taffy's mother, Taffy has begun an alphabet. In describing the action, Kipling digresses to lampoon self-important tribal bureaucrats:

> Head Chief, the Vice-Chief, the Deputy and assistant Chiefs (all armed to the upper teeth), the Hetmans and Heads of Hundreds, Platoffs with their Platoons, and Dolmans with their Detachments; Woons, Neguses, and Akhoonds ranking in the rear (still armed to the teeth). Behind them was the Tribe in hierarchical order, from owners of four caves (one for each season, a private reindeer-run, and two salmon-leaps, to feudal and prognathous Villeins, semi-entitled to half a bearskin of winter nights, seven yards from the fire, and adscript serfs, holding the reversion of a scrapped marrow-bone under heriot. (Kipling 1974, 87)

A subplot involves the stranger, who speaks only Tewara. The chief thanks Taffy for inventing picture-language but suggests that she not send messages by outlanders who can't explain her meaning. For maximum educational value, Kipling's concluding poem connects Taffy to the aboriginal Britons who settled Merrow Down.

In the sequel, Kipling crafts a *pourquoi* story about the next stage of writing, in which Taffy develops a phonetic alphabet. She works diligently to imitate 33 natural shapes, pictures, and sounds, such as an open mouth, the hiss of the snake, the drying-pole, the curve of the river, and the shark's tooth, which Kipling illustrates with line drawings. He concludes that after thousands of years, "Hieroglyphics, and Demotics, and Nilotics, and Cryptics, and Cufics, and Runics, and Dorics, and Ionics, and all sorts of other ricks and tricks" become the ABCs, which Kipling's "Best Beloved" must learn. An appended version of the alphabet explains that A is an elk tusk, B a beaver, C an oyster shell, and so on to Z, a Z-snake. Unlike the coolly objective Aesop, Phaedrus, Avianus, and Babrius, Kipling adds a five-stanza poem that yields to a subjective glow in admiration of his own Taffy, an obvious daddy's girl.

The remainder of Kipling's *Just-So Stories* returns to earlier mode. The final three fables merge fairy tale with *pourquoi* mode for animal stories of a crab, cat, and butterfly. In the tenth fable, one of the least successful of the collection, the Eldest Magician responds to complaints by man that the tide runs down the river twice a day and upsets his peaceful life. When the Eldest Magician investigates, he learns from the daughter of the man in the moon that King Crab causes the difficulty when he hunts for food. To punish "The Crab That Plays with the Sea," the Magician causes the crab's shell to soften 1 month out of 12, but he protects the crab by allowing him to hide in holes and under rocks and weeds in the sea or on land and by providing pinchers for claws.

Kipling's eleventh fable is a skillful humanistic story of compromises that turns to a time when civilization had converted neither wild beasts nor wild humankind. The cave family—comprised of a man, a woman, and a baby—subdues the dog, the horse, and the cow, but the woman is unable to domesticate the protagonist of the story, "The Cat That Walked by Himself." After the woman gives birth, the cat ingratiates himself by tickling and entertaining her infant and by chasing away mice in exchange for free access to the cave and plenty of milk to drink. The family accepts the free-spirited ways of the cat in exchange for his help. Kipling enhances the theme of feline independence with a black-on-white drawing of a lordly, self-satisfied cat strolling a boulevard of trees that lean far out of his way.

The concluding blend of fairy tale and fable, "The Butterfly That Stamped," turns to the Semitic world for a story about pride, anger, and control. Like Scheherazade of *A Thousand and One Nights*, Kipling illustrates the difficulty of the protagonist of "The Most Wise Sovereign Suleiman-bin-Daoud—Solomon the Son of David" in handling his harem of wives. Still entertaining his "Best Beloved" with pro-female stories, Kipling focuses on a woman as wise as Taffimei in Solomon's beautiful wife, Balkis. Declining to use his magic ring, Solomon ponders the quarreling wives who make his life miserable. Balkis, who loves Solomon and worries about his perplexity, hides in the garden to observe him. A butterfly asks Solomon's help in impressing the butterfly's wife. When the butterfly stamps his foot, Solomon twists his ring and causes his palace to disappear. At a second twist, the palace reappears. To subdue his wife, the butterfly uses the event as proof of his strength; Balkis, quick to adapt Solomon's magic, explains to the quarreling harem that Solomon has the power to do terrible things to punish them if they don't make peace. The timorous wives tiptoe amicably back to the palace. Solomon is duly impressed with his lovely, pragmatic wife and enjoys peace once more. Kipling depicts the male-female relationship as a matter of trickery and control, an indisputable fact that

Balkis both understands and accepts. A reflection of the coping devices of women in the patriarchal world of England and its subject nations, the story is dismaying proof of how little progress the women of Kipling's day had made against powerlessness and manipulation.

Overall, Kipling negates the harsher lessons of the natural world—the great preying on the small and the need for constant vigilance, which permeates Aesopic fable. The *Just-So Stories* turn on humor and a Victorian smugness that separates the good children at the teller's feet from the naughty creatures of each tale. From an adult point of view, the teller imposes on his fictional landscape the typically British insistence on propriety and control. Thus, the animal characters enjoy their just rewards, and animal society, set to rights in the end, maintains order.

To draw his bright listeners into the cadence of his voice, Kipling salts the lines with cumbersome geographical terms and demanding diction, chosen as much for their sound and rhythm as for their meaning. Drifting toward the never-never land of fairy tale, his fables find goodness and promise in natural habitats and distribute models of obedience, courtesy, and respect for others as lessons to his "Best Beloved" and his young readers. In primeval home settings, he situates the irrepressible Taffimai, the neolithic equivalent of his own Josephine, whose curiosity locates a worthy subject for intellect and who invents the concept of symbolic letters that stand for sounds and words. Equally nonthreatening is Balkis's story, which overlooks masculine powermongering as demonstrated by Solomon's need for trophy wives, a scenario that flourished in parts of the British Empire in Kipling's day. In a male-centered world, it is the woman who originates a method of controlling competition among his concubines. In paternal style, Kipling reshapes the cosmos to suit the children at his knee. He gentles the deadly jungle scene with poetic justice, a child's equivalent of law and order, and assures his "Best Beloved" that Daddy's stories can explain away most of the world's evils, even polygamy and the denigration of women.

See also Kipling, Rudyard.

Sources Bauer 1994; Bradbury 1996; Brookes 1950; Commire 1978; Dobreé 1967; Eagle and Stephens 1992; Ehrlich and Carruth 1982; Gillman 1996; Green 1971; Gross 1972; Islam 1975; Kemp 1988; Kipling 1893, 1917, 1931, 1974; Kunitz 1942; Kirkpatrick 1978; Maddock 1975; Magill 1958; Moss 1982; Orel 1989; Paffard 1989; Rao 1967; Roby 1982; Seymour-Smith 1989; Sheppard 1978; Stewart 1966; Weygandt 1939.

 # KIPLING, RUDYARD

The product of two diverse cultures in Asia and Europe, Joseph Rudyard Kipling was himself a two-sided anomaly. To the adoring public, he became Edwardian England's raconteur, myth-maker, bard, and balladeer. At his height, "If" and "Recessional" (1897) were his best-loved lyric poems and are still anthologized as stirring examples of courage and pacifism. In his private moments in the last two decades of his life, he developed the dark, troubled outlook of the misanthrope. Overall, he remains the era's proponent of duty, responsibility, and heroic action, but a major portion of his enduring fame derives from the fables he composed for his pampered daughters. A beloved child himself in the early years, Kipling was born in Bombay, India, on December 30, 1865, the son of Alice Macdonald, a Methodist clergyman's daughter, and John Lockwood Kipling, a professor of architectural sculpture who taught at the Bombay School of Arts and managed the Lahore Museum. Kipling's introduction into Hindustani exoticism and animal lore began in the nursery with his favorite storytellers, the native ayahs who adored him. He grew up bilingual and at times favored Indian influences over British.

The end of idyllic childhood was Kipling's first introduction to realism. At age six, he and his little sister Beatrice, "Trix," passed into the care of a brutal pair of relatives in Southsea. While he educated himself to become a journalist in the suffocatingly prim milieu of Hope House in Portsmouth, he suffered taunts for myopia, battled a sadistic son of the household, and puzzled over the hostility of his foster mother, who hated him for his wit and precocity. By 1877, his nerves frayed, Kipling suffered a breakdown. He cautiously analyzed the precarious situation of living among people who despised him: "It demanded constant wariness, the habit of observation, and attendance on moods and tempers; the noting of discrepancies between speech and action; a certain reserve of demeanour; an automatic suspicion of sudden favours." (Sheppard 1978, 92) He edited the school paper for the United Services College, a snobbish institution for the children of civil servants, but elected not to enter a university. On his return to India, he worked as a journalist from 1882 to 1887 for the Lahore *Civil and Military Gazette* and spent the next two years editing the Allahabad *Pioneer*. He gained recognition for insights into the Anglo-Indian lifestyle, appreciation for the common soldier, and a collection of witty stories, fables, and verse.

Undated photograph of Rudyard Kipling

In 1886 Kipling published his impressions of the Anglo-Indian world in *Departmental Ditties and Other Verses*, which preceded a prodigious outpouring of works on the British Empire, all published in 1888— *Baa, Baa, Black Sheep; Soldiers Three; In Black and White; Under the Deodars;* and *Plain Tales from the Hills*, which introduced his colonial Three Musketeers, Ortheris, Mulvaney, and Learoyd. Two narratives from the early period established his fame as a writer of classic short fiction: *The Phantom Rickshaw*, containing "The Man Who Would Be King" (1888), an adventure story about two British soldiers who travel back in time by venturing into Afghanistan, where a primitive tribe reveres Alexander the Great, and "Without Benefit of Clergy" (1891), a soulfully sad, romantic dirge about a bureaucrat in the British Raj who marries a native woman, then sinks silently into the bachelor soldier's life after an epidemic steals her away. By the early 1890s, Kipling completed a classic volume of verse, *Barrack Room Ballads* (1892); two more story collections, *Life's Handicap* (1891) and *Many Inventions* (1893); two novels, *The Light That Failed* (1890) and *Tha Naulahka: A Story of West and East* (1892); and a travelogue, *Letters of Marque* (1891), covering an assignment that took him to Japan, California, New York, and England. His success, though considerable in India, did not extend to England and the United States until after his marriage in 1892 to an American, Caroline "Carrie" Starr Balestier. After their four-year tenure at his in-laws' estate in New England, Kipling built a new house, Naulahka, and, while touring the area, became a close friend of Mark Twain and a fan of Joel Chandler Harris's Uncle Remus fables.

While Kipling was establishing himself as a family man in Brattleboro, Vermont, he followed the pattern of Harris, Lewis Carroll, Beatrix Potter, Oscar Wilde, and Robert Louis Stevenson by creating entertaining oral stories for a specific audience. The impetus for his shift to children's fable arose from his daughters—Josephine, born in 1892, and Elsie, four years younger. Although he still published adult fiction in *Ladies' Home Journal*, wrote a verse anthology, *The Seven Seas* (1896), and an adventure novel, *Captains Courageous* (1897), serialized in *McClure's Magazine*, he had begun a collection of animal tales that complement the beloved Mowgli stories, *The Jungle Book* (1894) and *The Second Jungle Book* (1895). The whimsical children's lore that he composed to intrigue and delight his own daughters was an intimate exchange that a cousin, Angela Mackail Thirkell, remembers sharing with the Kipling girls:

> The *Just-So Stories* are a poor thing in print compared with the fun of hearing them told in Cousin Ruddy's deep unhesitating voice. There was a ritual about them, each phrase having its special intonation which had to be exactly the same each time and without which the stories are dried husks. There is an inimitable cadence, an emphasis of certain words, an exaggeration of certain phrases, a kind of intoning here and there which made his telling unforgettable. (Gross 1972, 118)

His secret was synergy—the ability to voice his fables with the edge of the aphorist and the pleasure of the dispenser of tales. Beneath the mantle of wisdom lay a genuine warmth and ease with a young audience, a milieu safe from the onerous tangle of Anglo-Indian affairs.

During the 1890s, Kipling's popularity and income reached their peak. After the family fell ill with influenza and whooping cough in February 1899, he was weakened by disease, then devastated by Josephine's death, which occurred on March 6, 1899, but was kept secret until he was strong enough to bear it. Fans coveted his autographs and collected outside his hotel while he recuperated. Among family, the storytelling sessions were put aside while he grieved. Upon his return to England, he lived in Maidencombe, Devon, where he first conceived the idea of writing parables to educate children. They first appeared as *Stalky & Co.* (1899), a rollicking collection of narratives derived from the unruly pals of his boarding school years. Of this era, *Kim* (1901) is considered Kipling's masterpiece, possibly the best of his entire canon, and remains a classic story of the torment borne by children of two worlds. After moving to Rottingdean, East Sussex, the current home of the Kipling Society, he continued to travel to world hot spots and served as a correspondent for the *Friend* in the Boer War.

In a swirl of combat and colonial uproar, Kipling sorted through his "just-so" tellings of Josephine and Elsie's favorite animal fables and collected them for *Just-So Stories for Little Children* (1902), which immortalizes Josephine as Taffimai, the creator of the alphabet. For lovers of Kipling, the stories preserve both fiction and original art, two illustrations per story. The captions elucidate the pleasant landscapes and wholesome characters he chose for the idyllic fables, in which all turns out well. He wrote under one drawing, "This is the Parsee Pestonjee Bomonjee sitting in his palm tree . . . he has a knife in his hand to cut his name on palm trees. The black things on the islands out at sea are bits of ships that got wrecked going down the Red Sea but all the passengers were saved and went home." (Gross, 1972, 118) The stability and universality of his fable text balances the tenuous fireside circle, raising for Josephine a monument of delightfully incantatory tales.

Kipling, along with his wife and two remaining children, John and Elsie, settled in a mossy, gray stone house built in 1654 at Burwash, a secluded section of Sussex, where he lived the remaining years of his life out of close contact with the adoring public. After the publication of verse in *The Five Nations* (1903), short fiction collected in *Traffics and Discoveries* (1904), and another children's adventure, *Puck of Pook's Hill* (1906), he became England's first recipient of the Nobel Prize for Literature, conferred in 1907. The inscription accompanying the award lauds his powers of observation, originality, imagination, and perceptive character delineation.

In 1917, Kipling published *A Diversity of Creatures*, a compendium of story, memoir, and verse that delineates his respect for fable. The best example from the lot, "The Legend of Mirth," accounts for good humor in Raphael, Gabriel, Michael, and Azrael, the four stodgy archangels. On their return to heaven:

> O well and roundly, when Command was given,
> They told their tale against themselves to Heaven,
> And in the silence, waiting on The Word,
> Received the Peace and Pardon of The Lord.
> (Kipling 1917, 333)

In "The Fabulists," Kipling offers a verse definition of fable and expresses regard for Aesop. The first stanza declares:

> When all the world would have a matter hid,
>   Since Truth is seldom friend to any crowd,
> Men write in fable, as old Aesop did,
>   Jesting at that which none will name aloud.
> And this they needs must do, or it will fall;
> Unless they please, they are not heard at all.
> (Kipling 1917, 381)

The remaining four stanzas speak in abstracts of Folly, Sloth, and Fear and sink into an occluded pessimism, his legacy from World War I and the loss of his 18-year-old son in combat. Sorrow intensified Kipling's need for privacy and moved him toward hard-edged statements of truth, even though he doubted that temporal-minded readers cared for universal concerns.

Kipling's other postwar writings are marked by his interest in Asia, the sea, and civilization as a whole. In 1931, he published *The Humorous Tales of Rudyard Kipling*, which contains "Moti Guj—Mutineer," a genial, once-upon-a-time sort of fable about an elephant's distress during the absence of his mahout, and "The First Sailor," a *pourquoi* story of Nobby the sailor that originated in a 1918 speech to naval officers. In the latter, humor arises from the author's reduction of invention to trial and error and happenstance:

> Then they [the sailor and his wife] wanted to go home. They had lost the North Foreland in the morning haze; they had lost their heads; they would have lost their paddles if those hadn't been lashed. They had lost everything except the instinct that told them to keep the sun at their backs and dig out. They dug out till they dripped—the first human beings who had ever come back from the End of the World. (Kipling 1931, 42–43)

After Nobby evolves the sail, he realizes "he [has] mastered the second of the Two Greatest Mysteries in the world—he understood the Way of a Ship on the Sea." (Kipling 1931, 46) His gifts, according to the High Priest, are neither fame nor wealth—only wind, sun, sea, and the ship that carries him. The remainder of the anthology includes prose and verse fables about democracy, colonialism, cattle breeding, the military, and journalism—the collected oddments from an energetic, focused life.

Kipling's unfinished autobiography, *Something of Myself* (1937), was published posthumously following his sudden death from a perforated ulcer in London on January 18, 1936. His ashes were buried between Thomas Hardy and Charles Dickens in Poet's Corner of Westminster Abbey, where Kipling's public—both dignitaries and faithful readers from many countries—mourned and eulogized him. Attached to his name were eight honorary doctorates from prestigious English and French universities, the Order of Merit, the Gold Medal of the Royal Society of Literature, and election to the Athenaeum and the French *Académie des Sciences et Politiques*. Comment by General Sir Ian Hamilton in the London *Observer* notes that his death placed a full stop on the period when war was romanticized and the empire's expansion a duty.

Kipling's vast outpouring of articles, stories, sketches, and verse falls into many categories—brooding demon tales, dashing good war tales, lyric pacifism, and nostalgic views of old India. On the downside, an onslaught of anticolonialism in cartoon, verse, and prose mocked the racist jingoism of Rudyard Kipling's poem "The White Man's Burden," published in *McClure's Magazine* in 1899 as a tribute to England's civilizing mission among the darker races. On the positive side, Kipling's vigor, restlessness, and gift for re-creating ambience compare favorably with E. M. Forster's multiracial novels, the war stories of Ernest Hemingway, Alfred Tennyson's sonorous verse, and the romance and sensitivity of Katherine Mansfield. Kipling is perhaps best loved for his children's stories and fables, particularly those that detail the lives of English children growing up in British India. His mastery of narrative, symbol, unity, and genteel humor earns him a place among the great storytellers of all time.

Kipling's stories and adventures have frequently graced the screen, including the Cary Grant-Douglas Fairbanks version of *Gunga Din* (1939), Errol Flynn's starring role in *Kim* (1950), and the mythic tragicomedy *The Man Who Would Be King* (1975), starring Sean Connery and Michael Caine as army pals negotiating the mountains of Afghanistan. *The Jungle Book*, the most popular of Kipling's children's books, appeared in 1967 as an animated feature film starring Sabu and produced by Disney Studios. It has also been performed and published by platform storyteller Jackson Gillman. In 1995, another teller, Jim Weiss, recorded four of Rudyard Kipling's *Just-So Stories*—"Mowgli's Brothers," "Red Dog," "Tiger, Tiger," and "The Spring Running."

See also Just-So Stories.

Sources Bauer 1994; Bradbury 1996; Brookes 1950; Commire 1978; Dobrée 1967; Eagle and Stephens 1992; Ehrlich and Carruth 1982; Gillman 1996; Green 1971; Gross 1972; Islam 1975; Kemp 1988; Kipling 1893, 1917, 1931, 1974; Kirkpatrick 1978; Kunitz 1942; Maddock 1975; Magill 1958; Miller and Snodgrass 1998; Moss 1982; Orel 1989; Paffard 1989; Rao 1967; Roby 1982; Seymour-Smith 1989; Sheppard 1978; Stewart 1966; Weygandt 1939.

KRYLOV, IVAN ANDREYEVICH

Finding felicity in apologue after attempting other genres, fiction writer Ivan Andreyevich Krylov [or Krilov] produced Russia's most memorable milestone in the history of fable. An affable, good-natured fabulist, he avoided the vitriol of the subjective fabulist and looked beyond personal grudges to craft sage tales to meet the needs of a wide audience. For his perspicacious collection of hundreds of models of wisdom lore, he enjoyed over a half century of success. With the tact and skill of a master, he supplied intrinsic morals for his own tales, which Russian children memorized and recited, including "The Quartet," an amusingly satiric conversation among four nonmusical beasts that perform a muddled musicale. For his lasting contribution to reader enlightenment, he was dubbed the "Russian La Fontaine." European translations spread his influence, as did English translations in *Fraser's Magazine*.

A Muscovite born in poverty on February 13, 1769, Krylov received minimal schooling and seemed doomed to clerking in the mercantile trade, which he entered at age nine. In his solitude, he began writing in grade school, producing opera, comedy, and high drama by his teens. In his late twenties he achieved recognition as a media satirist, but his work was suppressed when his wit conflicted with bureaucratic sensibilities. A satirical journalist and critic, he wrote plays that attained some success in production but not in print. In 1805, he started translating Jean de La Fontaine's fables, which inspired him to compose his own moral tales. At 38, he settled into disciplined writing of his chosen genre and produced a remarkable collection—nine anthologies of original fables, published from 1809 to 1843. The first volume, *Basni* (1809), brought him to the attention of the tsar, who extended patronage and a do-nothing job at the St. Petersburg library. Krylov remained on staff until age 71 and used his free time to complete eight more volumes of verse fable. Much honored and beloved by readers, he received the nation's accolades for his personal touches to the fables of Aesop and La Fontaine and for his epigrammatic endings, for example, in "The Magpie and the Raven," in which the latter sneers, "Anybody who chatters as much as you do is bound to tell a few lies." (Green 1965, 191)

The pragmatism of Krylov's choice homilies applies to a number of commonplace situations, such as his disdain for the busybody, who makes no more progress in his rushing about than a squirrel on a treadmill, and his amusement at the witless borrower who chops off his sleeves to patch a ragged elbow. A common subject in Asian lore, particularly the *Panchatantra*, is the training of a leader, the focus of Krylov's "The Education of the Young Lion." The fabulist speaks through the musing of the lion king, who realizes that princes profit less from specialists than from generalists who know the needs and concerns of their native land. In "The Inquisitive Man," the fabulist's knowing smile at the man's concern for small details is enough to round out a genial recital of the wonders of the Museum of Natural History. Another plainspoken model, "The Cask," tells of a neighbor's return of a borrowed vat smelling so strongly of oil that it must be burned after scalding, airing, and scrubbing fail to remove the taint. To strike home the human meaning, the fabulist speaks directly to parents and reminds them that early defects may spoil the youth for the remainder of life. With "The Rain Cloud," the fabulist lauds generosity to those who most need it, suggesting perhaps the fine gifts that favor-seekers press on aristocrats, who have so much finery that additions to their trove are little appreciated.

By emulating the diction of the commoner, Krylov taps into the energy and mirth of the Russian peasant, as in "The Pebble and the Diamond," which dispenses a smart comeuppance to the social-climbing pebble that longs to become a royal jewel. Krylov's characters demonstrate the peasant stodginess, logic, and sense of fairness he observed among rural folk. Models of his respect for Russia's simple beginnings include "The Pike and the Cat" and "The Leaves and the Roots." The latter is a pleasant yet pointed reminder that the rising leaves and twigs may reach into the heavens for praise and prestige, but they cannot deny the source of their strength—the unseen root system that feeds the whole tree. Without rancor, Krylov states, "With every spring new Leaves are born; but if the Roots once perish neither [the leaves] nor the tree can live at all." (Cooper 1921, 398) In the same agreeable but firm tone, "The Two Flies and the Bee" stresses the value of one's native land and the contentment and comforts of a stable home. The bee tells the two flies who intend to emulate Sir Parrot and emigrate to an appealing clime that they are shirking daily tasks and warns, "It matters not where you're abiders,—/None profit by you, save the Spiders." (Cooper 1921, 401)

Krylov's feel for nature and his gift for description undergird much of his moralizing. In "The Ass and the Nightingale," he builds up his case against the ass's criticism by praising the beautiful song of the Russian nightingale:

> The Nightingale began to display her art, whistling in countless ways, with long-drawn, sobbing notes, and passing from one song to another. At one time she let her voice die away until it was like the distant echo of the wind among the reeds; at another, she poured forth a shower of tiny notes, like the ripple of running water. All nature stopped to listen to her song: the breezes died down; the other birds were hushed; the cattle and the sheep laid themselves silently down upon the grass. (Cooper 1921, 404)

The fable, thus elevated to winsome praise, thumps to earth with the ass's ignorant comment that the nightingale should take lessons from the cock. Krylov's ear for the crass, inappropriate remark turns verbal irony into a cutting gibe at the amateur critic. Other models express examples of foible through understatement, a rhetorical device that graces the simple *agon* or competition plot of "The Farmer's Horse and His Dog," and drollery, the controlled style of humor that drives "The Elephant and the Pug Dog." When wisdom requires a harsher retort, as in the concluding riposte in "The Boastful Geese," Krylov builds tension, then polishes off the brief exchange with repartee suited to the situation. To the geese's claims of honorable ancestry, the passerby notes, "Let your fathers sleep in peace—they received their reward. But you, my friends, are fit only to be roasted." (Cooper 1921, 410)

The wit and sizzle of his epigrammatic lines demonstrate the shrewd pragmatism of the survivor and the cynic's interest in vices, especially those of the bureaucracy. For "The Cuckoo and the Eagle," Krylov restates the aphorism about silk purses and sow's ears with the eagle's remark, "I am a King, but I am not God. . . . to make a Nightingale out of a Cuckoo—that I cannot do." (Cooper 1921, 410) The action of "The Sheep's Petition" tweaks the legal machinery that purports to defend the weak. After the sheep press their case again the wolves, Leo the King roars his decision:

> If any Wolf shall any Sheep offend,
> Said Sheep with leave said Wolf to apprehend,
> And carry him before the nearest Bear
> In the Commission of the Peace—and then
> Such order as the matter may invite
> Be duly made—and Heaven defend the right!
> (Cooper 1921, 398)

The humor of the situation appears in the absence of cases against the wolves, who "now graze, it is to be inferred/(How this agrees with them I have not heard)." Tongue in cheek, the fabulist moralizes: "If rogues defraud, or men in power oppress—/Go to law instantly and get redress."

The strength of Krylov's narrative is his ability to let characters condemn themselves through foolish comments and actions, as with the monkey who smashes the spectacles that would restore his vision and the pig who gripes about the use of the term "swinish" to characterize dirt and untidiness. In "The Elephant in Favor," a bristling court ponders the traits that endear the elephant to the lion king. The fox, who values a bushy tail, finds it odd that the elephant has no brush; the bear notes that the elephant lacks claws. The ox wonders if the king mistook tusks for horns. The self-adulating ass, a standard figure of ridicule in world fable, expresses his fatuous wisdom by braying, "If it had not been for his beautiful long ears, he would never have got into favor!" (Cooper 1921, 411) Likewise, the smaller conversant in "The Eagle and the Spider" expresses his pretensions just as a gust of wind sweeps him and his web to perdition. Needing no moral to enhance the animals' inane comments, Krylov allows the evidence to speak for itself.

Sources Cizevskij 1971; Cooper 1921; Green 1965; Komroff 1935; Krylov 1927; Steinberg 1954.

 LA FONTAINE, JEAN DE

The author of a masterwork, *Fables choisies* [Selected Fables] (1668), Jean de La Fontaine made the first major contribution to the Western segment of the genre since Aesop and earned for himself the renown of a Homer or Shakespeare. Like playwright Molière, La Fontaine was a strong voice for the return to nuance and nature in poetry, a movement that countered the extravagance, artificiality, and absurd conventions of the *précieux* [affected] school of thought, which aimed to please an effete group of courtiers and patrons. Under the direct control of Louis XIV, La Fontaine acquired a familiarity with the brief but lusty animal tale and developed its inner tension and vivid verisimilitude in *vers irréguliers,* an amalgam of prose and poetry. In subsequent collections published in 1678, 1679, and 1693, La Fontaine advanced his command of fable form and achieved freshness and depth at the same time that he incorporated a subjective outlook and experience. His purpose remained light and unsullied by grim didacticism. As he stated in "Discours à Mme. de la Sablière":

> La bagatelle, la science,
> Les chimères, le rien, tout est bon; je soutiens
> Qu'il faut de tout aux entretiens.
> [A bauble, a skill,
> Fancies, nothings, all is good; I hope
> Above all to entertain.]
> (La Fontaine 1995, 240)

His words center him in the seventeenth-century French social sphere, ever joyous, poised, and free of cant to pursue his motto, "Diversité c'est ma devise" [Diversity is my watchword]. (La Fontaine 1995, vii)

La Fontaine's life story describes a man unlikely to influence the reading and character of French youth. Born July 8, 1621, in the northeastern Champagne region at Château-Thierry, France, he enjoyed an affluence markedly different from the purported slavery of Aesop and Uncle Remus. The grandson of a merchant and the first of two sons of Françoise Pidoux of Poitiers and her third husband, Charles de La Fontaine, a middle-class bureaucrat, La Fontaine appears to have been a diligent if dreamy student who scorned teachers. With the encouragement of a father who also loved books, he completed primary classes at the local school on the rue du Château before transferring in 1641 as a novice to the Congrégation de l'Oratoire in Paris and the Saint-Magloire school for further education. Among the spiritually inclined, however, he felt compelled to admit that he could be neither priest nor zealot, perhaps because of his *mauvaise grâce* [wicked tendency], which he regretted late in life for its endangerment of his immortal soul. (Mackay 1973, 25)

After separation from religious training in 1642, La Fontaine returned home and, under the influence of his cousin, opted for music and worldly literature, especially the epic verse of Virgil, Terence's plays, and Honoré d'Urfé's pastoral novel *Astreé*. Following the death of his mother in 1643, La Fontaine gave himself to serious study and imitation of the masters, taking as his model the epicurean verse of Horace and joining a youthful group of poets at the *Table Ronde*. Ever the charmer, La Fontaine disconcerted his family by dressing in fashionable coats and boots, frequenting gaming tables and cabarets, and courting attractive women. Naturally self-serving, erratic, and lazy, he frittered away his time but pleased his father by studying law for two years in Paris and by marrying an heiress, 14-year-old Marie Héricart, at La Ferté-Milon on November 10, 1647. Although he quickly tired of her and dallied with the abbess of the Benedictine convent at Ardennes, Marie bore him a son, Charles, in October 1653, whom the father devalued with the same insouciance he applied to all aspects of married life.

As did his grandfather and father, La Fontaine used the inheritance he gained from his mother's estate to buy the office of *conseiller du roi et maître des eaux et forêts* [king's counselor and inspector of waterways and forests] in 1652, which he retained until retirement in 1671 at age 50. His duties were minimal, requiring that he inspect woodlots and enforce game laws. Following his father's death at a difficult time in the family's finances, he inherited both the post of *capitaine des chasses* [captain of the hunts] and his father's debts, which distracted him from his literary pursuits. Supported by patrons, he settled in Paris and contemplated literary masters, who influenced his writing style. In his formative years, he assiduously produced drama and verse as conscientious models rather than creative masterpieces—a ballet, *Les Rieurs du Beau-Richard* [The Laughter of Handsome Richard] (1665), a disappointing opera, *Daphné* (1682), and three plays, *L'Eunuque* [The Eunuch] (1654), *Climène* (1671), and *Adonis* (1658).

At the halfway point in his life, La Fontaine abandoned his pose as "le papillion du Parnasse" [the butterfly of Mount Parnassus] and mellowed into a contemplative professional writer. (La Fontaine 1995, vii) In 1657, he entered the protection of Nicolas Foucquet, France's treasury superintendent and the client of La Fontaine's uncle Jannart, and was commissioned to extol the beauties of Foucquet's estate at Vaux-le-Vicomte. Four times a year, in exchange for a quarterly allowance and all the solitude his work demanded, the poet paid his patron in ballades, madrigals, odes, sonnets, and dizains honoring the family, friends, or members of court. The alliance ended disastrously in 1661 with Foucquet's arrest and permanent exile for embezzlement. The shock of the king's displeasure forever tinged La Fontaine's writing with a somber-sad awakening to earthly impermanence.

Engraving of Jean de La Fontaine in the company of his contemporaries, Boileau, Molière, and Racine.

A penniless persona non grata, La Fontaine withdrew to Paris and cultivated the friendship of Molière, Jean Racine, and Nicolas Boileau, thus forming a quartet of the late seventeenth century's finest *litterateurs*. Following the example of the social poet, La Fontaine thrived from an alliance with Godefroy, Duc de Bouillon, and his wife, Marie-Anne Mancini. He enjoyed the patronage of Marguerite of Lorraine, the Grand Condé Louis II, and the Contis and Vendômes. La Fontaine's late works continue his interest in experimentation, ranging from *Les Amours de Psyché et de Cupidon* [The Loves of Psyche and Cupid] (1669) and the sexually explicit *Contes et Nouvelles en vers tirées de Boccace et l'Arioste* [Stories and Novels in Verse Drawn from Boccaccio and Ariosto] (1671) to *La Captivité de Saint Malc* (1673), a libretto for Lully's opera *Daphné* (1674), *Poème du Quinquina et autres ouvrages* [A Poem in Quinine and Other Works] (1682), and *L'Astrée* (1691), a lamentable three-act tragedy.

At the height of his productivity, La Fontaine bucked the trends and gave up writing for stage and salon and set out like a new-age *jongleur* to produce *Fables choisies*. For models, over a 45-year period of composition, he drew on classical texts, primarily Aesop. A longtime admirer of Greek and Roman classics, La Fontaine exclaimed:

> Térence est dans mes mains; je m'instruis dans Horace
> Homère est son rival sont mes dieux du Parnasse.
> [Terence is in my hands; I learn from Horace;
> Homer and his rival are my gods of Parnassus.]
> (Mackay 1973, 14)

Without violating his source, La Fontaine restated Aesopic, Phadrean, Avianian, and Horatian fables along with Sanskrit lore of Bidpai and some medieval tales. The resulting compendium was a fresh, daring concept—a sheaf of 124 innovative fables divided into six sections and dedicated to the dauphin. The opening line speaks the poet's hopes for his work: "Je chante les héros dont Esope est le père" [I sing the heros of whom Aesop is the father.] (Nitze and Dargan 1950, 302)

La Fontaine championed the concept of painless education for a prince in whom the king placed high hopes of intellect and wisdom. By way of literary example, the French fabulist admired Aesop for subtlety—the ability to impart advice without arousing suspicion in the reader. To round out the king's daily example of governance, the fabulist followed Socrates's example and proposed a variety of illustrative stories acted out on a fictional canvas. In "Le Bucheron et Mercury" [The Woodcutter and Mercury], La Fontaine termed his collection

> Une ample comédie en cent actes divers,
> Et dont la scène est l'univers.
> [A full comedy in 100 diverse acts
> Of which the stage is the universe.]
> (Mackay 1973, 12)

Throughout, gods, men, and animals play equal roles. The purpose of these miniature ethical scenarios was to instill good habits before the prince could be corrupted by inevitable court vices.

During La Fontaine's rise as a *fablier*, he advanced from epicurean *libertin* to realist, as demonstrated by an overtaxed peasant's suicidal intent in "Death and the Woodman" and a gesture toward feckless destiny, the theme of the market jaunt in "The Pig, the Goat and the Sheep." For financial support, La Fontaine lived on the property of an admirer, Madame Marguerite de La Sablière, an amateur astronomer and cultivated salon-keeper who admired his candor and sincerity. In exchange for some of his best verse, which he addressed to the fictional "Iris," she introduced him to philosophers, writers, scientists, and scholars and opened her home to his friend and admirer Charles Perrault, author of *Histoires ou Contes du temps passé* [Stories or Tales of Long Ago] (1697), better known as *Contes de ma Mère l'Oye* [Mother Goose Stories], source of "Little Red Riding Hood," "Sleeping Beauty," "Puss in Boots," "Hop o' My Thumb," "The Fairies," "Cinderella," and "Bluebeard." Before La Sablière's conversion at a severe religious house for incurables, La Fontaine had produced his second volume of fables. He remained her friend and dependent and resided in her little house near the Rue St. Honoré, allowing her to reform his worldliness until her death in 1693.

Despite harsh criticism by the court of Louis XIV for his libertarian thinking, devotion to solitude and nature, and defiance of the church, La Fontaine survived official disapproval and remained true to the subtle criticisms of power in his fables, particularly "The Sick Lion and the Fox" and "The Lion, the Wolf, and the Fox." At the age of 62, he compensated for the loss of his patroness by entering the Academie Française, which became the focus of his declining years. Among the members, La Fontaine was happy to find bibliophile Olivier Patru, an arbiter of style and taste and an authority on fable. Still shy and absent-minded, La Fontaine entered the debates of his fellows, which evolved into the classic squaring off of ancients against moderns. Although combative in matters of art, he was a natural friend-maker and enjoyed the approval of professionals, artists, and the clergy. Extolled among the literati, he basked in the favor of François La Rochefoucauld, Charles de Saint-Évremond, Madame de Sévigné, and Madame de La Fayette. Impaired by rheumatism and senility, he lived with a housekeeper who excused the wayward dalliances of his youth and declared him as simple and guileless as a child. On April 13, 1695, two years after denouncing his prurient short fiction as *contes infâmes* [infamous short stories] and lauding his blameless fables, La Fontaine died in Paris and was buried among great writers in Père la Chaise cemetery near friends and fellow playwrights Jean Racine and Pierre Corneille.

Under the influence of Phaedrus, Plato, Abstemius, Aphthonius, Babrius, Plutarch, and Nicholas Nèvelet's *Mythologia Aesopica* (1610), La Fontaine produced in all 240 facile verse fables of a surprising diversity, complexity, realism, unity, and scope. In a reflection on his source from Phaedrus, the Roman adapter of Aesop, La Fontaine declares,

> On ne trouvera pas ici l'élégance ni l'extrême brièveté qui rendent Phèdre recommendable: ce sont qualités au-dessus de ma portée. [Neither the elegance nor the extreme brevity that are so appealing in Phaedrus will be found here: Those are qualities beyond my scope.] (Widdows 1992, xviii–xix)

The fabulist elaborates that he brings to his verse tales an original strength—the lively wit that suits the French language in the same way that pithiness suited Phaedrus's Latin, which derives its terse elasticity from the era of the playwright Terence.

The flow of fable from the pen of La Fontaine reprises traditional themes in the sprightly, unencumbered line peculiar to the seventeenth century. In the familiar fox and grapes story, the fox makes his tart, succinct "sour grapes" remark, which twentieth-century American fabulist Edward Marsh translates: "They're green," said he, "and fit for snobs to munch." (Green 1965, 15) The equally familiar exchange between ant and grasshopper reads like an exchange between burghers in a Paris market

> When fair, what brought you through?
> I sang for those who might pass by chance—night and day, an't you please.
> Sang, you say? You have put me at ease. A singer! Excellent. Now dance.
> (La Fontaine 1954, 13)

The addition of human speakers makes no change in diction and tone, for La Fontaine's animals speak the idiomatic commonalities of humankind. An example from "The Old Man and the Ass" demonstrates the balance of speakers:

> The old man said, "Quick, we must fly."
> The saucy vagabond asked, "Why? For fear I'd be bowed down by two and their weight?"
> "By no means," the man said while hastening toward the gate.
> The ass said, "But how does all this affect me? How should I care whose ass I am! French donkeys have an epigram: A master is one's enemy."
> (La Fontaine 1954, 125)

The ready retorts produce memorable epigrams as terse as "Choose wisdom, even in an enemy" and as supple as "Love quails at times; although it can make fear cower." (La Fontaine 1954, 182, 224)

Drama was La Fontaine's first love. For the fables, he developed the momentary confrontation to a height of theatricality. For "The League of Rats," better known as "Belling the Cat," he inserts a rhetorical question to the lurk of the cat, "What foresight would avail?" implying that warning would aid his prey. (La Fontaine 1954, 316) The story progresses as Madame Silverskin the mouse consults a ponderously eminent rat who had never "dreaded a cat nabob/Teeth, paws, or claws of tom or tab." With a curtsy, she departs while the conference determines an antidote to Raminograb, who "makes mice his special food." The audience's frisson gives way to false courage, marked by calls of "Up! To arms. Rush to our friends' defense!" Buckling on armor and stuffing cheese into haversacks, the would-be cat conquerors resolve "to win or throw their lives away." In the chivalric platitudes common to war lyrics, the gay and valorous undercurrent swells to the expected height, which tumbles groundward as "Old Rough" approaches. At one growl, the assemblage slips away, "convinced of a rat-hole's worth." As La Fontaine had intended, the story delights while it implants the image of the superb plan that no committee member has the courage to push through to completion.

Undated illustration of Jean de La Fontaine

Over the four and a half decades of composition, La Fontaine's poetic line varied from octosyllabics and Alexandrines to three- and four-syllable lines in varied meter to enliven the text and free it of pedantry. Above all, his work maintained an *"air agréable,"* a lightness of tone that dominated the writings of his era. (Mackay 1973, 194) To wrench fable free from its traditional sermoniz-ing, he created a revolutionary form that restates overt didacticism with a subtler moral reflection drawn from observation of nature and human behavior. Of particular note are books 7–11, a mature, nonpreachy triumph of language that he intended for adult readers. Introduced in 1668, his 12 books of fables began appearing in print and continued in production through 1694, shortly before his death. By 1673, Molière was citing "The Ass's Skin" and "The Cock and the Fox" in Act II, Scene 11 of *Le Malade imaginaire* [The Imaginary Invalid]. In 1683, Lady Harvey had suggested the stories of Reynard the Fox, from which La Fontaine derived *Le Renard anglais* [The English Reynard], which he dedicated to her.

The second volume of *Fables Choisies* (1678) preceded the stand-alone Book XII, a collection of 24 fables, of which 10 were reprised from earlier editions. These works derive from new sources, particularly readings in Plato and Lucretius's *De Natura Rerum* [On the Nature of Things] (60 B.C.E.). A quarter of La Fontaine's new material comes from the East Asian fables of "the wise Indian Bidpai." (Mackay 1973, 204) François Bernier had introduced La Fontaine to the mythology and lore of India in *Livre des Lumières* [The Book of Lights] (1644), which David Sahid of Ispahan translated into French with commentaries by Gilbert Gaumen. More varied and serious than his Aesopic collection, the anthology demonstrates La Fontaine's contemplative nature, a seriousness of purpose, and an awareness of the natural voice of living things. As he explained in the epilogue of Book XI, with a comment that anticipates the transcendental concept of the oversoul (Mackay 1973, 205):

> Car tout parle dans l'univers;
> Il n'est rien qui n'ait son language.
> [For all things speak in the universe
> There is nothing that has not its own language.]

In "Discours à Mme. de la Sablière," a passionate rebuttal of Descartes's claims that animals are robotic, La Fontaine ridicules the notion that "la bête est une machine" [a beast is a machine], each creature wound up like a watch, with gears and wheels moving the mechanism,

> La première y meut la seconde
> Une troisième suit, elle sonne à la fin.
> [The first moves the second,
> A third follows suit to chime the hour.]
> (La Fontaine 1995, 240)

Embroiled in polemics, La Fontaine carries his argument to extremes and invites his fictional Iris to read on for proof.

Stylistic change reveals the poet at the threshold of *vers libre* [free verse] in its appeal to the reader through excision of adornment in favor of a well-plotted logic. In "Deux Rats, le Renard et l'Oeuf" [Two Rats, the Fox, and an Egg], La Fontaine continues his defiance of Descartes by first conceding that animals don't think and respond in human fashion, but recoiling from the idea that they operate on a blind clockspring, devoid of feelings of pleasure or the will to survive. In lieu of Descartes's theory of animal automatism, the poet envisions a double soul in nature, the first stage being the fundamental spirit found in all—the wise and foolish, infants and idiots, and animals. The more refined level of spirit, which rises above the baser emotion, human beings share with the angels. Based on a conception of animal instinct and human will, La Fontaine amasses ample cause to castigate human villains for discourtesy, ingratitude, cruelty, and aggression, for which they have no justification. Calling on the wisdom of Cicero's *De Senectute* [On Old Age] (44 B.C.E.), La Fontaine reminds the proud that death cannot be denied. Whether princes or commoners, all beings, he declares, anticipate their demise from their first breath to their last, a reflection of his contemporaries' reaction to the death of Louis XIV's infant son in 1672 and a freak carriage accident that killed a curé who accompanied a corpse.

La Fontaine profited from an economy of language and understated realism. A sympathetic example that draws on the fabulist's days as supervisor of forests is "L'Homme et son Image" [The Man and His Reflection], in which an elderly woodcutter complains of multiple miseries—hunger, fatigue, and the demands of his wife and children, soldiers, taxes, creditors, and forced labor. From unpleasant memories of school, La Fontaine writes "L'Enfant et le Maître l'école" [The Child and the Schoolmaster], which deplores the scolding tongue of the pedant. Less critical are glimpses of rural life, which he describes in fables about the swallow who warns sailors of inclement weather and the lark who encourages her children to rest themselves and enjoy their comfortable nest. Other bird stories tell of the charitable dove, a cockerel, and a peacock with its rainbow of a hundred silken shades resembling a jewelry shop. Animals in these fables seem much at home in their habitats, as with the long-legged heron on the riverbank and the carp and pike sharing a pool. "Le Lièvre et les Grenouilles" [The Hare and the Frogs], a close study of timorous people, regrets that the fearful never enjoy a morsel in peace because they are cursed with fears that disturb their sleep and quail at "Un souffle, une ombre, un rien" [A breath, a shadow, nothing at all].

Much of the fabulist's facility with situation and tone derives from the narrative command of Giovanni Boccaccio, the fourteenth-century Italian master he most admired. La Fontaine also internalized the frivolities of François Rabelais, the seriousness of Niccolò Machiavelli and Torquato Tasso, and the classic grace of Ovid. Very much his own man in his own time, La Fontaine enhanced original verse with good-natured narration, sparkling joie de vivre, and a disarmingly expressive style. He enriched the spare Aesopic fable with conversational diction and touches of elegy, idyll, lyric, and epistle. His characterization varied to suit his intent, including mythic heroes, farm folk, and domestic and farm animals common to the French countryside. Like Aesop and Horace, he chose rural settings for his miniature animal dramas, but his intent was to upbraid the snobbery and elitism of his era. Less a satirist than a humanist, La Fontaine avoided keen-edged invective and weighty didacticism by stressing his private thoughts, wisdom, and inoffensive conclusions about human affairs.

He left unpublished the last of his *Contes et nouvelles en vers* [Tales and Novels in Verse], the spicy carnal stories that embarrassed his sober years yet solidified his popularity. In 1821, C. A. Walckenaer published the *Oeuvres Complètes de La Fontaine* [The Complete Works of La Fontaine], which were reissued twice in the nineteenth century and again in 1942. Apart from dramas, court tributes, and verse romances, his fables remain classics of world literature, perhaps more for the clever caricatures of different animals than for the political and social controversies they represent. French schools revere his stories for their sage recreation of compact life scenes. A tribute to his skill is the resurgence of interest in his fables during the Romantic era, especially the writings of an admirer, Russian fabulist Ivan Andreyevich Krylov, and of imitators, notably poet and playwright Antoine Houdart de La Motte, author of *Fables* (1719), and Archbishop François de Salignac de La Mothe-Fénelon, both of whom wrote tedious court verse. Later fans include poet Paul Valéry, novelist André Gide, and playwright Jean Giraudoux.

Critics consider La Fontaine a master of control who managed his literary characters like shadow puppets on a screen. Concealed by the action and understated ironies of his charming *contes*, the writer disclosed little of his manipulation, preferring to let the animals act out a host of human situations and attitudes. His works proved so popular with all ages and levels of society that public schools ousted religious didacticism and replaced it with his fables. One of the lasting encomia to La Fontaine comes from a personal letter from the earl of Chesterfield to his godson. Written in 1764, the letter lauds the French fabulist by contrasting the fluffy Mother Goose lore of Charles Perrault to La Fontaine's sturdy, sensible tales.

See also illustrators.

Sources Cooper 1921; Harvey and Heseltine 1959; Hobbs 1986; "Jean de La Fontaine," http://www.callisto.si.usherb.ca; "Jean de La Fontaine," http://www.metdanse.com; "La Fontaine," http://www.argyro.net; La Fontaine 1954, 1965, 1995; Mackay 1973; Massignon 1968; "Musée Jean de la Fontaine," http://perso.wanadoo.fr; Nitze and Dargan 1950; Steinberg 1954; Widdows 1992.

 # LATIN FABLE

As is the case with most Latin texts, the Greek prototype guided fabulists who perpetuated the tradition of producing anonymous compendia marked only by the name Aesop. Quintilian's *Institutio Oratoria* [Oratorical Instruction] (ca. 96 C.E.) exalts these works as suited to primary education because of their clear, unadorned language, which serves as models for student imitation in oral and written Greek. Independent Roman fables derive from the writings of Ennius, Lucilius, Horace, Livy, Philo Judaeus, Plutarch, Romulus, and Lucan.

- Writing in the mid-second century B.C.E., Quintus Ennius, the father of Roman epic poetry and the most prominent poet of the early age, composed drama, epic, satire, epigrams, and epitaphs as well as fables.

- Born to the Equestrian rank around 180 B.C.E., Gaius Lucilius, satirist and fabulist, produced 30 books, of which most are lost. He preferred an urban setting for its atmosphere of learning and opportunity and the stimulus of two of Imperial Rome's best poets, Petronius and Lucan. Within a patrician circle, Lucilius enjoyed the stimulation of professionals, military leaders, and politicians. Like all well-educated Romans, he was a student of Greek classic writings. As a dabbler in meter, he perfected hexameter for his criticisms of Roman society's materialism and smug self-possession, which he observed firsthand. He chastised private and public pecadillos in burlesque and parody, as found in the remains of his bumptious fool tale. The protagonist is a dolt who chooses to spite his adulterous wife by using a polished sherd to amputate his genitals. The scurrilous tale demonstrates Lucilius's skill at drollery.

Out of a rogue's gallery of villains, Lucilius appears to have despised pinchpennies in particular. A fool tale about Aulus the miser describes a tight-fisted father who drowns his child to save him the cost of raising it. In neat epigram, Lucilius smirks, "The only family a miser needs is money." (Radice 1981, 257) Another miser tale reprises an exchange between Asclepiades and a mouse. When the miser dismisses him from his humble home, the mouse replies, "My good friend, Asclepiades, I shall cost you nothing, I want only bed, not breakfast." (Radice 1981, 261) Other scraps of fable indicate a vigorous, rollicking beat and sometimes raw verbal acuity, as found in the beginning of a story about a well-endowed ram. Lucilius's crisp, wickedly rich satire remained in vogue throughout Rome's history and influenced Quintilian, Cicero, Tacitus, Juvenal, and Horace.

- Rome's most eloquent lyric voice, Quintus Horatius Flaccus, better known as Horace, dominated the first century B.C.E. with epistles, odes, epodes, satire, and belles lettres. Among his contributions is the fable "The City Mouse and the Country Mouse."

- A minor author, Philo Judaeus, an immigrant Jew from first-century Alexandria, composed an essay on language in which he cites a humorous *pourquoi* story from Callimachus accounting for human talkativeness. The fable claims that, during the golden age of Cronus, humans and animals shared language. Because the animals make demands on Zeus during the rule of Olympian gods, the gift of language falls to humans alone. Thus, individual human voices resemble the ass, parrot, and fish.

- Philo's contemporary, Marcus Annaeus Lucanus, a brash but derivative epic poet of the mid-first century C.E., wrote fable as well as epigram and lyric verse.

As the genre developed into more sophisticated rhetoric, it occurred with frequency as incidental fable in the writings of skillful Roman speakers and historians.

- A powerful example derives from Book II of Rome's first history, Livy's *Ab Urbe Condita* [From the Foundation of the City] (ca. 14 C.E.). The historian repeats the story of an imaginary mutiny of body parts that Menenius Agrippa reputedly related to a Roman mob during the political crisis of

494 B.C.E. Chosen by the senatorial party for his general appeal, Agrippa addresses a clutch of deserters on the Sacred Mount. To illustrate the folly of revolting against the government, he introduces the setting of his fable as a time when body parts had individual thoughts and language to express them. He contends that the parts of the body resented having to feed the lazy stomach. The cabal of discontented members plots to carry no food to the mouth. The mouth refuses to accept food or the teeth to chew. Agrippa concludes,

> But alas! while they sought in their resentment to subdue the belly by starvation, they themselves and the whole body wasted away to nothing. By this it was apparent that the belly, too, has no mean service to perform: it receives food, indeed; but it also nourishes in its turn the other members, giving back to all parts of the body, through all its veins, the blood it has made by the process of digestion; and upon this blood our life and our health depend. (Livy 1971, 142)

The story, an ancient favorite in the Aesopic tradition, may date to 1250 B.C.E. Its action offers an implicit truth—that a cooperative effort as important as nourishment requires the work of all participants. When any individual fails to perform a specific task, the entire organism atrophies and loses its ability to function. Livy adds that the wedge between commoners and bureaucrats was lifted and negotiations begun toward an agreement. As a result of Menenius Agrippa's clever narrative, the ruling party avoided chaos and commoners acquired the first set of popular tribunes, who protected citizens against the excesses of consuls and the senatorial class. The story returns to classic literature in William Shakespeare's Roman tragedy *Coriolanus* (ca. 1608–1610), Act I, Scene i.

- Rome's professional fabulists—Phaedrus and Babrius in the first century C.E. and Lucian a century later—took the genre to new heights. The Hellenized Latin verses of Babrius, which existed in secondhand medieval accounts, were first read in the original in 1843, when they were discovered on Mount Athos, the holy mountain of the monks of St. Basil in northeastern Greece.

- The author of *Noctes Atticae* [Attic Nights] (ca. 180 C.E.), Aulus Gellius was a conscientious amateur encyclopedist and tireless fact-finder. Although his master work, *Attic Nights,* is at times tedious and pedestrian, the value of Gellius's compendium to literature is his recovery and preservation of extracts, citations, and fables that would otherwise be lost to subsequent generations. In cosmopolitan Roman style, Aulus Gellius sifted the Greco-Roman world for its philological excerpts and cultural treasures. The final work filled 20 books, which he left to his children. Of the 19 surviving volumes, the introduction and epilogue are missing, but the remaining text is in good form. It was first published in Rome in 1469 and served the Middle Ages, when his oddments of learning were in vogue.

In a protracted prologue, Aulus Gellius introduces his jottings as a haphazard arrangement of "anything worth remembering . . . whatever took my fancy, of any and every kind, without any definite plan or order; and such notes I would lay away as an aid to my memory, like a kind of literary storehouse. (Aulus Gellius 1946, xxvii) He intends to keep his miscellany at hand to draw on for needed terms and topics. He chooses the title as a reminder of the long winter nights he spent at a country estate outside Athens and disdains the florid titles of similar compendia, such as Tapestry, Torches, Honeycomb, and the Fruit Basket. He admits to his limitations of form and elegance and names the setting rather than choosing some loftier title. He adds a quotation from Heracleitus that learning does not make a scholar.

In the twenty-ninth entry of Book II, Aulus Gellius inserts an observation on Aesop and describes him as wise for teaching salutary thoughts through fable rather than the stiff, dictatorial essays of philosophers. As a model of Aesop's wholesome, succinctly developed *fabulae*, Gellius chooses a complex story from the tetrameter verse *Saturae* [medley] of Quintus Ennius. In the fable, the mother lark leaves her nestlings in the ripening field even after the farmer has called his friends and relatives to help with the reaping. Only when the farmer and his sons prepare to harvest by themselves does the lark move her nest. Aulus Gellius savors the poet Ennius's version of the moral: "Hoc erit tibi argumentum semper in promptu situm:/Ne quid expectes amicos, quod tute agere posses." [This adage ever have in readiness:/Ask not of friends what you yourself can do.] (Aulus Gellius 1946, 229)

- Early in the third century C.E., Claudius Aelianus, called Aelian, a rhetorician and chief, composed *Historia Animalium* [Animal Stories], a compendium of excerpts and anecdotes on animal behaviors. He relates "The Ass and the Snake Called Dipsas," a *pourquoi* story derived from Greek creation myth that accounts for the snake's thirst and long life.

- In 315 C.E., Aelius Festus Aphthonius, the rhetorician of Antioch, retranslated 40 verse fables to prose and wrote a scholarly dissertation on the genre, which Christian anthologists had revered for use as pulpit exempla.

- Book II of Diogenes Laertius's *Vitae Philosophorum* [Lives of the Philosophers] (third century C.E.) introduces a passage about Sophocles relating "Aesop to the Corinthians," a story meant to epitomize virtue as timeless. With oratorical gravity, the speaker exhorts the residents of Corinth, "Judge not virtue by popular standards." (Perry 1965, 503) In the preface to *Popular Proverbs*, Diogenes Laertius also cites a dilemma tale, "The Fisherman and the Octopus," which depicts a shivering fisherman choosing between freezing in the water to capture the octopus or staying warm and letting his children starve. The story had appeared nearly eight centuries earlier in two Greek sources—Timocreon's lyrics of the late fifth century B.C.E. and a victory ode by Simonides of the mid-fifth century B.C.E.

- Decimus Magnus Ausonius, a poet and court tutor during the Emperor Valentinian's reign in the mid-fourth century C.E., returned prose fable to verse; Julianus Titianus, his contemporary, translated verse fables into prose.

- A barely identified Roman poet who flourished in the early fifth century C.E., Avianus (also Avianius or Avienus) is best known for a sheaf of 42 elegiac fables. Tentatively identified with Postumius Rufius Festus Avienus, author of *Aratea Phenomena* and *Aratea Prognostica* [The Phenomenae of Aratus and The Predictions of Aratus], *Ora Maritima* [The Maritime Shores] and *Descriptio Orbis Terrae* [Description of the World], Avianus was elevated to a minor authority on geography and science and fable during the Middle Ages. However, the contrast of these scholarly works with the fables questions the alliance of the two bodies of work under one author. A final judgment seems unlikely, in part because the collection of fables is corrupted by the addition of ponderous *promythia,* or introductions, and anticlimactic *epimythia,* or morals, of which only a few appear to be original.

  Avianus appears to have profited from a quality education in the classics. He was born around 380 C.E. into a prestigious old family in Volsinii in northern Latium, an established territory in west-central Italy on the Tyrrhenian coast. A descendent of the Stoic philosopher Musonius Rufus, teacher of Epictetus, Avianus achieved the rank of proconsul of Africa and Achaea. Although he lived within the Christian Era, the poet addressed the tastes, rituals, and attitudes of pagan culture. He employed classical elements of Virgil and Ovid as adornments, although he lapses into ignoble Latin and at times overplays picturesque details. Markedly wordy and inferior in tone and control to the works of his predecessors, Phaedrus and Babrius, who could state fables in four to six lines of verse, the overblown fables of Avianus remain central to the corpus of world fable, in part because they reprise some of Babrius's lost works.

  Prefacing his collection, Avianus dedicates his work to Macrobius Theodosius, the African praetorian prefect and author of *Saturnalia,* in which Avianus is mentioned. The poet appends a dedicatory letter in the editorial "we" embracing fable as the genre he chooses to *nostri nominis memoriam mandaremus* [entrust the memory of our name]. (Duff and Duff 1982, 680–681) He justifies his selection of a flexible class of literature because it combines the best of opposites: "In these [fables], fiction, if gracefully conceived, is not out of place, and one is not oppressed by the necessity of adhering to the truth." Avianus expresses his debt to Aesop and declares that Socrates and Horace were both users of *fabulae* as literary "expressions of life." In a brief assessment of the value of fable, Avianus concludes that his stories delight the imagination, exercise mental faculties, relieve tension, and provide an awareness of the whole course of human endeavor. He adds that, to accomplish his aims and provide suitable maxims, he has animated beasts, birds, and such inanimate objects as pots, amphorae, and a soldier's trumpet.

Avianus is relegated to low status among fabulists, yet his work exceeds that of Babrius in its unity and development. As opposed to the thin actions that support heavy morals in his predecessor's fables, Avianus's tales seem amply stated. A worthy model is "The Soldier Who Burned the Weapons," a glimpse of the retired warrior who honors his vow to sacrifice on a holy pyre the weapons that he carried to war and to jettison also those that he collected from fallen adversaries. A trumpet interrupts his pious action and demands a reprieve on the grounds that it served in a noncombatant capacity and "only mustered the weapons of war with wind and note." (Duff and Duff 1982, 743) The angry soldier tosses the trumpet into the flames more vigorously than he had his armaments. His justification is logical: the trumpet is guiltless of attack but is more cruel in its power to turn men into killers.

Avianus appears to have used the standard Aesopic text of his day. The difference between Avian lore and the original *fabulae* is a marked expansion, either to include more detail or to enhance the classic Roman style. The results are unwieldy and out of character for standard animal lore. Avianus dares to pad his lines with ornate phrases stolen from Ovid and Virgil, which stand out as inappropriate and patched in among less lofty images. For example, in his opening *fabula*, "The Nurse and Her Child," he describes how the child allowed heavy slumber to overtake tired limbs, and the wolf, waiting in vain to devour the child, returns to the lair with wasted cheeks and jaws drawn and emaciated. The result is a contrived artificiality that mocks the simplicity of Aesop and Babrius.

In the heavily illustrated Spanish anthology, *Las vida del Ysopet con sus fabulas hystoriadas* [The Life of Aesop with his Fables] (1489), Chapter 7 contains 27 fables attributed to Avianus and obviously derived from Babrius, including extant stories and some that are now lost. Like Aesop, Avianus follows the characteristic pattern of describing the behaviors of both domestic and wild animals, including "The Farmer and His Obstinate Ox," "The River Fish and the Sea Fish," and "The Pig without a Heart." Likewise common are the wolf, tortoise, bird, lobster, crayfish, frog, crane, peacock, ape, and crow. In addition, he depicts interactions with villagers, a doctor, country folk, a traveler, a satyr, the imaginary tigride, and the gods Jupiter and Phoebus Apollo, who walk on earth among humankind to learn more about their weaknesses and foibles. Inanimate objects also come to life, as in "The Pine Tree and the Turkey Oak"and "Of the Storm and the Pot."

Avianus's themes and morals perpetuate folk logic. A chilling example, "The Covetous Man and the Envious Man," describes the two praying for their heart's desire. The story concludes with the ironic switch on the man who chooses to go second. After asking for double what the envious man asks, the covetous man receives twice the request for a blind eye. Thus, poetic justice accords him a life in darkness. Less fearful is the fool tale "The Boy and the Thief," which displays the trickster's wit. The boy convinces the thief that a golden pitcher has slipped from its tether into the well. The thief, after removing his cloak and shinnying to the bottom of the well, finds nothing. On his emergence from the well, he discovers that the boy has slipped away with his cloak. Wiser by the loss of his garment, the thief remarks that the fool deserves to lose who thinks that a golden vessel lies hidden in clear water. In L'Estrange's words, "Some thieves are ripe for the gallows sooner than others." (Perry 1965, 533)

Avianus warns about believing foolish females and cautions against excesses of pride, the great sin that plagues the ancient world. His situations hinge on vengeance, envy, conceit, and disharmony. His mundane morals, imitating Aesop's style and settings, lack the grace and facility of the master. Overburdened with sermons to the detriment of wit, Avianus's logy aphorisms urge:

- Learn, however, that the deities are not swayed by indolent vows; bring the gods to your help by acting yourself.

- In vain we resist the mighty and . . . it is by slow degrees that we surmount the fury of their menaces.

- Let anyone who believes in a woman's sincerity reflect that to him these words are spoken and that it is he whom this lesson censures.

- No one should covet another person's goods lest he lose what he formerly possessed quietly.

- It was better to go alone than ill accompanied.

- Anyone elated with newfound glory pays a just penalty in hankering after what is too high for him.

- No one can win victory by an advance guard of threats.

An obvious theft from Aesop is the inferior warning that "A bird in the hand is worth more than a vulture on the wing," a distant second to the more familiar and memorable "A bird in the hand is worth two in the bush." (Aesop 1993, 186) More felicitous on the tongue and to the brain is the last line of "The Weeping Lad and the Thief," which advises, "Fortunate is he whom the perils of others renders cautious and wise." (Aesop 1993, 188)

See also Babrius, Valerius; French fable; Phaedrus.

Sources Aesop's Fables 1993; Aulus Gellius 1946; Bowder 1980; Cooper 1921; Duff and Duff 1982; Hadas 1954; Hammond and Scullard 1992; Krappe 1964; Lang and Dudley 1969; Livy 1971; Mantinband 1956; Perry 1965; Radice 1981; Warmington 1938.

LESSING, GOTTHOLD EPHRAIM

A German dramatist and critic, Gotthold Ephraim Lessing is also renowned for *Fabeln* [Fables] (1759), his memorable addition to the Western canon of folk tales. The son of a Protestant parson, he was born January 1, 1729, in Kamenz, Saxony, and advanced from grade school in Meissen to Leipzig University, where he pursued a degree in theology. At the age of 20, obviously unsuited to a pastorate, he left formal study for a reporting job in Berlin, freelanced as a translator and ghost writer, and involved himself in stage productions. During the development of his literary style, he published *Beiträge zur Historie des Theaters* [Contributions to the History of the Theater] (1750) and *Literaturbriefe*, a series of critical epistles that he polished to perfection. In his prime, he served General Tauentzien as secretary and used his ample leisure to read the classics.

Lessing's development as a fabulist derived from a strong background in theater. In 1767, he worked at Hamburg Theatre as critic-in-residence and published *Die Hamburgische Dramaturgie* (1769), a vehicle for his drama interpretations and commentary on the oppressive rule of French theater. As librarian at Wolfenbüttel at age 41, he lost an annoyingly rancorous edge. He was briefly married to Eva König, who died in childbirth. Returning to the competitive literary fray in 1778, he published *Wolfenbüttelsche Fragmente eines Ungenannten* [Anonymous Fragments from Wolfenbüttel] (1778), a rationalist attack on Lutheran fundamentalism, particularly the belief in scriptural inerrancy. When he was forced to desist, he produced *Nathan der Weise* (1779), a paean to tolerance.

According to literary historian Ben E. Perry, Lessing's style honored the Greek and Roman fable, which was a literary invention intended to convey a didactic moral, the intended ethical purpose. Attempting to improve on Jean de La Fontaine's graceful stories, which he felt were too pretty and too closely allied to social manners, Lessing returned to the structure and universal themes of Aesop's fables, as displayed by "Dressed in Strange Feathers," a brief, brutal story of a crow who is picked bald by angry peafowl after he struts in a coat made of their feathers. A felicitous example, "Friendship without Envy," allies a peacock and nightingale, pairing beauty of feathers with musical song. Unlike the Brothers Grimm, who expanded animal stories with details, Lessing treasured classical fable for its tight, brief narrative and an air of *ipse dixit* [the thing speaks for itself].

For his original tales, Lessing crafted a rigidly terse form, for example, the simple exchange in "The Ox and the Calf," in which the young calf's boasting discloses a callow egotism, and a single comment in "The Wild Apple Tree," in which the rose bush chides the bitter apple for glorying vicariously in the honeybees' industry. "The Sparrow and the Ostrich" reaches the height of economy of words—an implied dialogue reduced to one sentence: "You may boast as much as you please of your strength and size," said the Sparrow to the Ostrich, "but you will never be so good a bird as I am; I don't fly far, 'tis true, and that only by starts; yet I do fly, and you cannot do any such thing." (Komroff 1935, 285) In each brief tale, the fabulist appears to state the situation and rush directly to some climactic point without developing even a minimum of details along the way. At times he seems eager to foist his judgment on the reader, as in "The Fox and the Mask," the tale of a fox contemplating a Greek theater mask. With spiteful glee, Lessing snickers, "Everlasting talkers! perverters of our most innocent thoughts! The fox knew you." (Komroff 1935, 283)

The quick take that results from Lessing's compression is the "aha" experience of intrinsic moral, as found in the five sentences of "The Sparrows," in which the birds misjudge a refurbished chapel as useless after a new application of plaster immures the birds' nests in the chinks. One entry, "The Blind Hen," dramatizes the symbiosis of a blind digger and rapacious hanger-on who exploits her companion's handicap; the motif of self-enrichment recurs in "The Wolf and the Shepherd," in which both parties mourn the loss of a flock of sheep but for distinctly different reasons. In some instances, the succinct wording of Lessing's apologue produces too much ambiguity, as with "The Bramble," which reveals a will to destroy without developing motivation. In most instances, however, the visual and behavioral cues tell the tale, as in a droll commentary on religious faith found in the *pourquoi* tale, "The Donkeys." Annoyed that the master beats them, the mild-mannered drays petition Jupiter for redress. He makes no effort to upbraid the driver for insensitivity. Instead, the god toughens the donkeys' hides to weary the master's arm from repeated lashing. Too willing to accept aid of any sort, the donkeys claim the god both merciful and wise and withdraw from his throne room rejoicing.

Lessing is adept at the fool tale. He creates both the wry put-down, for example, "The Bear and the Elephant," and advice to the young, the crux of "The Old Stag and the Young Stag." In the former story, which mocks the dancing style of two awkward, lumbering animals, Lessing dramatizes the difference between looking foolish and feeling foolish. In the latter fable, the inexperienced stag learns that danger lurked in the bow and arrow long before the invention of the shotgun. In a second archery story, "The Archer and His Bow," the fabulist builds on the archer's demand for embellishments to be etched on a prize ebony bow and saves to last the obvious fault—deep carving weakens the wood until it snaps. An unusual pairing of folly and wisdom, "Solomon's Ghost," departs from the realism of fable. The ghost, which confronts an aged plowman sowing grain in the heat of the day, reminds the old man: "'Thou hast learnt but the half of thy lesson,' pursued the Spirit. 'Go once more to the Ant, and she will teach thee to rest in the winter of thy existence, and enjoy what thou hast earned.'" (Komroff 1935, 290) Another instance of supernatural intrusion in fool tales turns "Jupiter and the Horse" into a *pourquoi* story. To the horse's meddling with creation, Jupiter agrees to all suggestions and transforms the senseless horse into an odd-shaped mutation, the hump-backed forerunner of the camel. The amalgamation of fool tale and *pourquoi* story reminds the complainer that God may take too literally a foolish request in answering a prayer.

Lessing's fool tales tend toward the rude confrontation of unequal parties. When two birds face off in "The Peacock and the Rooster," the cock disabuses the peafowl of pride by accusing him of being a worthless combination of paint and feathers. A subtler put-down in "The Lion and the Hare" pictures the lion creating a hypothetical case to prove that a harmless animal can terrify a larger beast with an awkward noise, as in the oink of a pig alarming an elephant. The hare misapplies the example to his race's fear of dogs. Another model of specious logic, "The Wolf, a Hero," compares differing points of view. The young wolf looks upon his father's demise as a suitable death after his elder parent challenged 200 such enemies. The fox makes a less flattering delineation when he asserts that the wolf preyed on simple sheep and asses all his life but met his match in his first attack on an ox. In stating these inequities in nature, Lessing maintains both directly and indirectly fable's traditional championing of the weaker animals against tyranny by the strong.

In his contemplation of human folly, Lessing applies animal behaviors to mundane situations, as in parallel observations of the reindeer and eagle on flight in "The Ostrich." Lessing's version of the fox and grapes, entitled "The Bunch of Grapes," pictures the sparrows feasting on grapes that the fox has spurned as sour. The fabulist adds, "No fox ever jumped up at them again." (Green 1965, 58) At the end of "The Goose," he ridicules the pretentious fowl for mimicking the graceful swan and exclaims, "How many Geese there are, without wings, who, because of similar pretentions become a laughing stock to their neighbours." (Cooper 1921, 433) A subtler exchange pits the gluttonous pig against the oak. Outraged that the snuffling snout routed out acorns without speaking a word of thanks, the oak upbraids the pig. The pig cleverly retorts that he would show gratitude if he thought the tree dropped its fruit solely on his account. Lessing's reversion to such commonsense conclusions returns his fables to their folk roots, which he found in his readings of Aesop and Bidpai's *Panchatantra*.

It would be a disservice to Lessing to imply that his work was wholly derivative. His choice of characters and situations broach new possibilities in anthropomorphism, as with "The Statue of Brass" and "The Fairies' Gift," a familiar motif on the subject of natal gifts. One ingenious scenario derives from the sniping of rival game tokens in "The Knight in Chess." A commentary on pride, the three-sentence fable depicts the old knights' complaints because two young players replace a lost knight with a specially marked pawn. At the knight's cry of "Mr. Upstart," the players retort, "Silence! Does he not give us the same service as you do?" (Komroff 1935, 291)

Another of Lessing's experiments with the genre is the linkage of fables into a multisectioned beast cycle. A seven-part study of human relationships with an animal predator, "The History of the Old Wolf," begins in the animal's dotage with an appeal to the first shepherd for an adequate retirement portion. The shepherd, savvy to the wolf's past history, retorts, "You and avarice never yet had enough." (Komroff 1935, 294) The dickering continues in the second and third segments, which call by name Montano, a third shepherd of the wolf's acquaintance. In each case, the wolf finds the men still smarting over past forays into their flocks. Lessing interrupts the fourth shepherd's sober retort with an insider's joke: To the beginning of an epigram, the wolf interrupts, "You are beginning to moralize. Farewell!" (Komroff 1935, 296) As a whole, the cycle illustrates how hard-hearted men drive their old nemesis to extremes. Because the wolf attacks their children before he can be exterminated, the wisest of the seven shepherds regrets that he gave the elderly predator no opportunity to improve. A commentary on recidivism, the cycle applies to efforts to rehabilitate criminals and suggests that the wolves of society will always require cautious handling, but that they deserve some pity and trust. A second beast cycle, "The Beasts Striving for Precedence," ponders the natural pecking order of the animal kingdom and the role of humankind in nature. Less episodic than the wolf cycle, the four-part story bristles with long-held suspicions. In the end, the lion maintains his superiority over lesser beings and, trailing the elephant, tiger, bear, fox, and horse, withdraws from the controversy. In harmony with the fabulist's commentary on egalitarianism, the ape and donkey, the dregs of the animal kingdom, quibble the longest and are the last to withdraw from the assembly.

Sources Cooper 1921; Goring 1994; Graham 1973; Green 1965; Hobbs 1986; Komroff 1935; Krappe 1964; Perry 1959; Steinberg 1954.

L'ESTRANGE, SIR ROGER

The collector of 500 "little stories" in an illustrated compendium entitled *Fables of Aesop and Other Eminent Mythologists: With Morals and Reflexions* (1692), Sir Roger L'Estrange realized the significance of his work to education. In an admonition to the adult reader composed in 1699, he said, "For *Children* must be Ply'd with *Idle Tales*, and *Twittle-Twattles;* and betwixt *Jest* and *Earnest, Flatter'd,* and *Cajol'd,* into a *Sense*, and *Love* of their *Duty.*" (Hobbs 1986, 33) He intended to lighten the more didactic stories with gaiety, vigor, and a touch of the risqué. A major contributor to the fable-as-exemplum school of thought, L'Estrange was a pragmatist as well as didact. In the exuberant preface, he questions the importance of fable to moral education: "This Rhapsody of Fables is a Book universally Read, and Taught in all our Schools. . . . The Boys break their Teeth upon the Shells, without ever coming near the Kernel. They learn Fables by Lessons, and the Moral is the least part of our Care in a Child's Institution." (Hobbs 1986, 18) His collection opens on a frontispiece in which the hump-shouldered Aesop stands amid his beasts, whom the artist gathers in an odd mélange of disproportionate poses. Aesop points with his quill to a parchment that reads "Utile Dulci" [sweet use], the pragmatist's watchword. (Lewis 1996, 75)

A Catholic Tory and Stuart propagandist from Hunstanton, Norfolk, who sided with the monarchy during the English Civil Wars and Commonwealth, L'Estrange was both admired and despised for political as well as professional reasons. He was arrested as a royalist spy in 1644 during a cabal to seize Lynn, Norfolk, from Puritan forces and spent four years in Newgate Prison before escaping to Holland. After obtaining pardon from Lord Protectorate Oliver Cromwell in 1653, L'Estrange landed a political appointment as surveyor of the imprimery, which empowered him to license and superintend the press and to eradicate freelancers who maligned the government. Chief among his adversaries was John Milton, a Puritan apologist against whom L'Estrange issued *No*

Blinde Guides (1660), a pert slap at the sightless epic poet who authored *Paradise Lost*. L'Estrange's loyalty to the Crown earned him a knighthood for discrediting the Popish Plot, a scurrilous underground effort to malign Jesuits for allegedly conspiring to kill Charles II.

For financial reasons, L'Estrange turned his energies to pamphleteering. His newspapers—*Intelligencer, News,* and *Observator*— brought him more controversy than money. After losing his post in 1688 following the overthrow of James II, L'Estrange bolstered his income with translation, which was ready money for a graceful writer of his talents. In addition to Seneca, Cicero, Josephus, Erasmus, and Quevedo, L'Estrange produced a popular version of Aesop's fables rendered in titillating style. For his effrontery to public taste, as demonstrated by the urinating duo in "The Donkeys Make a Petition to Zeus," he acquired literary rather than political enemies. A rival, fabulist Dr. Samuel Croxall, author of *Fables of Aesop and Others* (1722), accused L'Estrange of inserting papist sentiments in stories and of corrupting minors. Croxall's crotchety conservatism provided ammunition for satirist Samuel Richardson, who belittled Croxall's criticisms as petty and exaggerated.

From a lifetime of close scrapes, L'Estrange developed a mastery of the terse, somewhat cynical survival tale, for example, "The Sleeping Dog and the Wolf" and "The Cocks and Partridge," a pairing of a single partridge with a pen of fighting cocks. After the feisty roosters drive her from their feed, she takes offense that she has been spurned as the stranger in their midst. It is only after the cocks rend each other's flesh that she realizes her good fortune, for the fighters were kinder to her than to their fellows. A parallel survival tale, "The Farmer and His Dogs," describes the desperation of the starving stockman, who slaughters for food his sheep, goats, and oxen. The dogs, who realize the importance of the oxen to their master, a plowman, evaluate their own situation and determine that they must flee if they want to remain alive. In the same vein, "The Travellers and the Bear" describes how two wayfarers flee a bear. One shinnies up a tree; the other pretends to be a corpse. After the bear snuffles the pretender, it departs, leaving the duo unharmed. The traveler in the tree asks what the bear had whispered. His companion replies, "Don't travel in company with friends who fail to stand by you in time of danger." (Perry 1965, 432) L'Estrange profits from adding humor to his survival lore, as found in "The Young Goat and the Wolf as Musician," in which a doomed kid tricks a wolf into playing the flute for a preexecution dance. Because the piping summons dogs, the wolf gives up plans to eat the kid and remarks that he should stick by his career as butcher and leave piping to musicians.

L'Estrange was capable of more complex studies of human guile, as found in the depiction of a life of crime in "The Thief and His Mother" and snide sacrilege of "The Traveler's Offering to Hermes," in which the traveler devours dates and walnuts and leaves the god pits and shells as an offering. In "The Youngsters in the Butcher's Shop," two boys plot a scam. When confronted for theft, the boy who steals the meat, then puts it in his coconspirator's pocket, is able to say he doesn't have the meat. The other of the duplicitous pair can safely claim that he didn't steal it. The butcher, who exceeds the two in experience and wisdom, reminds them that it is easy to deceive a man, but the gods are not so easily tricked. Equally smug is the final line of "The Ape and the Fox," a story about the fox's envy of the ape king. After tricking the ape into a trap, the fox sneers that the ape has shown himself less than a suitable king.

Like predecessors in the genre, L'Estrange varies animal characters with human and mythic figures. For "Hermes and Tiresias," the fabulist pits the god against the famed Greek clairvoyant, who interprets Hermes's description of a crow's movements as proof that Hermes's theft of cattle is known to heaven. On a human level, a less successful fable, "The Ill-Tempered Wife," details a similar situation of a husband getting the best of his fractious wife. In "The Camel Who Wanted Horns," a creation situation involving a carping camel, the fabulist depicts the god Zeus losing his temper and awarding the complainer both horns and cropped ears.

Sources Hobbs 1986; Lewis 1996; Perry 1965.

 # MANDEVILLE, BERNARD DE

An eighteenth-century parodist, translator, and pamphleteer, Bernard de Mandeville used fable as his primary mode of literary expression and published *Some Fables after the Easie and Familiar Method of Monsieur de la Fontaine* (1703), which includes two original fables, "The Carp" and "The Nightingale and the Owl." A negligible piece of hack work, the fables rephrased the French master in English doggerel as a ready source of income while Mandeville established a paying medical practice. He followed with more imitation: a translation of Paul Scarron's burlesque into *Typhon or the Wars Between the Gods and Giants* and *Aesop Dress'd or A Collection of Fables Writ in Familiar Verse* (1704). Mandeville expanded a third venture in fable, a sixpenny quarto entitled "The Grumbling Hive, or Knave turn'd Honest" (1705), into *The Fable of the Bees or Private Vices, Publick Benefits* (1714), the controversial work for which he is best known. An ambiguous 408-line mock epic verse, the antiutopian treatise takes the form of allegory to account for the collapse of organized society after worker bees falter from human failings.

Degreed in philosophy, Mandeville was well prepared for intellectual discourse. Born in 1670 in Dort, Holland, he was educated at an Erasmian school in Rotterdam and at the University of Leyden, where he completed a specialty in nervous disorders. In 1699, having acquired proficiency in English, he settled in London, where he married an Englishwoman. An outgrowth of his practice was his *Treatise of the Hypochondriack and Hysterick Passions* (1711), which he expanded in 1730. Apart from professional treatises, he wrote dialogues, verse, and philosophical musings. His radical tract, *The Virgin Unmasked* (1714), calls for state-run brothels and the liberation and education of women. Subsequent musings, *Free Thoughts on Religion, the Church, and National Happiness* (1720), defends deism; a later work, *An Enquiry into the Origin of Honour* (1732), peruses the subject of self-esteem. His erudition and wit earned the respect of Benjamin Franklin and other radicals of the Enlightenment. Critics, who were confused by his tongue-in-cheek doggerel or who differed with his belief that luxury and affluence benefit mankind, refuted his verse argument. Alexander Pope made him the butt of satire and public humiliation, as did numerous other learned contemporaries. To these repudiations Mandeville replied with an apologia, *A Letter to Dion* (1732). However, substantial voices, including Daniel

Defoe, Dr. Samuel Johnson, Robert Browning, and David Hume, acknowledged his ready wit, pungent satire, and subtlety.

Mandeville's contribution to fable is a 408-line allegorical poem in the style of Menippean satire. It depicts his belief that moral weakness is inevitable to humanity. In his opinion, the only way to attain earthly perfection is through a restructuring of human nature. When his original doggerel resurfaced as *The Fable of the Bees*, the lively bits of controversy stirred readers to a more sophisticated awareness of vice. In the tyrannical world of the hive, the bees live "in Luxury and Ease" while subscribing to monarchy rather than the less dependable democracy. The aspect of Mandeville's fable that outraged his contemporaries is a deviation from Juvenalian satire and from the satiric norms of the age. In the preface, he purports to explain how people use vices as a means of transforming themselves into acceptable members of society. He introduces his milieu in an unassuming opening stanza composed of six rhymed couplets in iambic tetrameter:

> A Spacious Hive well stock'd with Bees,
> That lived in Luxury and Ease;
> And yet as fam'd for Laws and Arms,
> As yielding large and early Swarms;
> Was counted the great Nursery
> Of Sciences and Industry.
> (Mandeville 1989, 63)

The poem eases into a direct comparison with human society in the second stanza, which compares a hive to a town. The success of the hive, Mandeville insists, derives from "Lust and Vanity," a source of employment and financial success. (Mandeville 1989, 64) Some of the bees are entrepreneurs, some laborers, and some clergy, who "want no Stock, but that of Brass, and may set up with a Cross." He categorizes the hive's vice mongers as

> Sharpers, Parasites, Pimps, Players,
> Pick-Pockets, Coiners, Quacks, Sooth-sayers,
> And all those, that, in Enmity
> With down-right Working, cunningly
> Convert to their own Use the Labour
> Of their good-natur'ed heedless Neighbour.
> (Mandeville 1989, 64)

In a surprising blast at his era's civility, the poet declares that all trades contain a modicum of dishonesty and insists that "No Calling was without Deceit."

Subsequent stanzas of Mandeville's verse fable enumerate with Chaucerian glee the failings of professions that contribute capital to a successful society. First, he singles out attorneys who encourage lawsuits and anticipate a good return as their hourly fees accrue. In the second example, physicians cherish fame and profit over patient well-being. The third mark, priests, earn their stripes through four of the Seven Deadly Sins—"Sloth, Lust, Avarice and Pride." (Mandeville 1989, 65) The profits elevate the higher echelons, who live well-fed, pampered, and otiose. The litany continues, rank by rank, including the military, monarchy, and bureaucrats. The poet reaches his height of vitriol with a view of blind Justice, whose scales dip with bribes and whose punishments fall hardest on the poor. He concludes that no part of society is free of fault and blames avarice as the chief vice. The paradox of the piece claims that, for all its evil, sin is the "Wheel that turn'd the Trade." (Mandeville 1989, 68)

As a microcosm of human life, the hive, symbolizing a small town, abstains from "Engines, Labourers, Ships, Castles, Arms, Artificers, Craft, Science, Shop, or Instrument." Rebel bees overthrow the cohesiveness of the hive and begin to emulate humankind by taking up human foibles and vices. Their number includes entrepreneurs, lawyers, physicians, priests, soldiers, and kings. At length, fairness, as symbolized by the traditional blindfolded woman holding up the scales of justice, gives way to bribery, vice, and cunning deceptions. The cause of so great a change in the bees' social order is avarice, "That damn'd ill-natur'd baneful Vice."

Mandeville's vigorous parody pretends to vilify the domination of hive life by epitomizing hypocrisy, laziness, and profligacy, all of which portend certain ruin. In actuality, the theme of this often misread poem is the necessity of vice, which serves the community and civilization through the utilitarian virtue of self-interest. The society grows so depleted of willing laborers that defeat seems inevitable. The faithful one-tenth stand their ground and defeat their enemies. Many thousand die in the conflict. The rest, determined to "avoid Extravagance," fly "into a hollow Tree, Blest with Content and Honesty." Without vice and hypocrisy he claims, ingenuity would languish. Extolling synergy, the combined efforts of workers toward a common goal, the poem lauds an eighteenth-century pantisocracy, the total social leveling in which citizens attain equality through cooperation.

The unassuming fable incensed men of the stature of Anglican bishop George Berkeley, clergyman Isaac Watts, logician William Warburton, philosopher Francis Hutcheson, and critic John Dennis. Ministers thundered sermons against Mandeville; author John Brown penned a nasty retort comparing Mandeville to Thomas Hobbes, materialistic author of *The Leviathan* (1651). John Wesley was so outraged that he composed in his diary, "Till now I imagined there had never appeared in the world such a book as the works of Machiavelli. But de Mandeville goes far beyond it." (Mandeville 1989, 8) Mystic William Law riposted with *Remarks on Mandeville's Fables of the Bees* (1723), a caustic retort that won more kudos than had Mandeville's satire.

The stir caused by the publication in 1723 tossed Mandeville into the center of extensive public quibbling. In July, the grand jury of Middlesex declared the satire a public nuisance. Later that month, the *London Journal* published a vicious attack signed by the pseudonym Theophilus Philo-Britannicus, a self-proclaimed lover of England who castigated the immigrant Mandeville. Two weeks later, Mandeville answered his critics in the same journal with "A Vindication of the Book," an essay he published that same year in pamphlet form. In its final appearance in 1724, *The Fable of the Bees* grew into a volume to which Mandeville appended two essays: "An Essay on Charity and Charity-Schools" and "A Search into the Nature of Society." As the controversy continued its rumble, Mandeville brought out *The Fable of the Bees, Part II* (1729), in which he declared himself interested in truth concerning the nature of humankind and society. The work anticipates his sequel, *Enquiry into the Origin of Honour, and the Usefulness of Christianity in War* (1732). Decades after his death, Mandeville remained a *cause célèbre* throughout Europe and was translated, read, argued, and despised.

    Sources Crane 1932; Drabble 1985; Johnson 1968; Magnusson 1990; Mandeville 1989.

MARCH, WILLIAM

Writing under an abbreviated form of his real name, William Edward March Campbell produced a respectable corpus of short stories, a popular novel, *The Bad Seed* (1954), as well as a collection of fables. Published posthumously, his apologues preserve the tension and format of traditional Aesopic lore at the same time that they examine twentieth-century ills. Less urbane than Thurber's collection, the March anthology is comprised of fool tales, beast stories, barnyard wisdom, war stories, graveyard jest, and *agon* or competition plots replete with a hard-eyed realism that refuses to blink. Much of March's wisdom derives from his personal good fortune and his observation of World War I and the international jitters and mounting intolerance that preceded World War II. The reenactment of age-old enmity and strife he depicts in fable through the ongoing struggle between the fictional Bretts and Wittins.

    Although he lived his adult years in plenty and privilege, March grew up in humble circumstances. Born September 18, 1893, in Lockhart, Alabama, he was the son of Suzy March and John Leonard Campbell, an itinerant sawmill worker. March traveled from job to job with his family and began work as a laborer at age 14. Because he lacked both a secure home and uninterrupted education, he had to work nights to finance and prepare for a year at Valparaiso University and another at the law school of the University of Alabama. Departing from a legal clerkship with a New York law partnership, he served in the Marines during World War I at Mont Blanc, Soissons, Verdun, and Belleau Wood, some of the bloodiest dots on the war map. He earned a Navy Cross, Croix de Guerre with Palm, and Distinguished Service Cross. The damage his lungs suffered from gas compromised his health, but his emotional stability was the greater victim of his war experience, as seen in his philosophical questions in fables that establish a human tendency toward conflict, inhumanity, and violence.

    March's financial success as a founder and vice president of operations for the Waterman Steamship Company preceded travel in England and Germany and early retirement at age 45. Already a successful author with his war masterpiece, *Company K* (1933), derived from a letter-diary to his sister Margaret, he comforted a battered psyche through a freelance writing career, begun in the mid-1930s with short fiction published in *Esquire, Yale Review,* and *Good Housekeeping* and anthologized in *The O. Henry Prize Stories* and *The Best American Short Stories* series. March's interest in character issues and compromises fuels his study of psychological disturbance, *The Looking Glass* (1943), a satiric fable, *October Island* (1952), and *The Bad Seed*, an examination of inherent evil set close to home in Mobile. The latter was the impetus of Maxwell Anderson's horror play that was filmed two years after March's death, on May 14, 1954, at his home in New Orleans. The cinema melodrama was a vehicle for Patty McCormack and Nancy Kelly, who earned Oscar nominations along with photographer Harold Rosson and costar Eileen Heckart.

Over two summers, William T. Going edited March's short works, which the author had compiled in 1938 from 125 submissions to *Accent, Kansas Magazine, The Prairie Schooner, Rocky Mountain Review, Tanager, University Review, Old Line, New York Sun*, and *New York Post*. Issued posthumously as *99 Fables by William March* (1960), the final cut of Aesopic narratives features a large variety of animal characters—the traditional crow, jackal, peacock, bees, donkey, stags, ram, and rabbit along with the less common mockingbirds, polecat, lovebird, gull, woodchuck, badger, and snapping turtle. These ironic stories, which March's publisher originally rejected, draw on classic situations from Phaedrus, the Bible, fairy tales, and John Bunyan's *Pilgrim's Progress*. Less embellished than the works of Jean de La Fontaine and John Gay, they mirror the sharp irony and self-mockery of the *Fantastic Fables* of Ambrose "Bitter" Bierce, another American fabulist who struggled with disillusion.

March encases his works in a clever framework that links modern models to the Greek originals. In "Aesop and King Croesus," the slave Aesop relates a fable-within-a-fable to the citizens whom Croesus intends to tax. Yielding to unfair taxation, the people withdraw in tears at an unavoidable increase in tribute. The fabulist archly concludes that they acknowledge Aesop's story, "since the fable is, and always has been, the platitude's natural frame." (March 1960, 2) Returning to Aesop in the ninety-seventh entry, March composes "Aesop's Last Fable," a retelling of the Phrygian sage's violent death during a business trip to Delphi. With an ironic twist, March explains that locals tire of Aesop's tendency to answer straightforward questions with fables rather than with simple replies. In the midst of Aesop's third explanatory fable, the Delphians hustle him to a cliff and hurl him over the brink to the rocks below with a curt explanation that the moral "is so obvious that it needs no elaboration." (March 1960, 197) The next entry, "Iadmon and Aesop," illustrates how the old man's martyrdom to the genre of fable may have elevated him in the Delphians' estimation and spurred them to treasure his sayings. The final fable quivers with March's snide mirth by personifying Truth as a rubbery, shapeless old woman who can be stretched well beyond her bounds.

March's adaptation of animal truths follows the tradition that grounds most of the world's fables. The questioning screech owl, insulted rabbit, thin-skinned elephant, self-absorbed turkey hen, and intransigent possum speak and act their human faults with the imperfect reason of human thinking and mindset. The snapping turtle who mistakes a vine for a snake epitomizes a stubborn refusal to compromise that is the very stuff from which Aesop crafted his originals. The moral, too, echoes the master's objectivity in judging untenable defects. When the turtle dies while holding fast to the vine, his friends speak his epitaph: "Sometimes it's hard to tell the difference between strength of character and plain stupidity." (March 1960, 121) Such caustic observations remind readers that, just like foolish beasts, humankind suffers for its vanities, as demonstrated by the unwise bird of paradise who perches too close to a rainbow to display his colors to best advantage, by the terrier who thinks he takes his mistress for a walk, and by the worm who comments to the poet, "The perfection of man was assuredly made for the pleasure of worms." (March 1960, 9)

It is obvious throughout that a preponderance of March's animal scenarios reflects the most pressing dilemmas and resultant despair and self-delusion inherent in the human situation. A droll commentary on human values, "The Hangman and the Hero" depicts the hangman's position at the outer rim of social respectability. In response to his denigration of the tortoise, the animal replies with a discreet gibe: "Perhaps if our brains could accept contradictions without conflict, we wouldn't have remained tortoises for a million years, as we have, but would have developed into something as powerful as man, who rules the universe." (March 1960, 133–134) A more poignant vignette about the condition of the world derives from "The Magician and the Mole," a satire on forcing a recluse to face reality. Similar in tone is "The End of the World," a commentary on point of view. The only member of the Brett nation to escape general slaughter is near the end of his tether. At the sight of his sorrow, cowering in terror that the world is ending, the animals congregate in consternation and, as one, remind him that for the animal kingdom, life has changed little since the demise of the Bretts. Reaching beyond the scope of the forest, March's ambiguous conclusion leaves the reader much to ponder, not the least of which is the conundrum of overreaction versus underreaction.

Overall, March's revamping of Aesopic situations revitalizes traditional animal stories, as with the doom of the trusting specialist in "The Doctor and the Hippopotamus," a new treatment of "The Stork and the Frog," and the clever con game in "The Grasshoppers and Their Wealthy Neighbors," a reprise of Aesop's "The Ant and the Grasshopper." At the tag end of the latter, March glibly reminds the reader that "Those who have nothing are anxious to share it." (March 1960, 77) A deft recasting of classic fable occurs in "The Queen and the Woodcutter's Wife," which turns topsy-turvy the wisdom of the city mouse and the country mouse, also the wolf in sheep's clothing, which March reenacts as "The Doubting Ducks," in which a fox swims like a duck. The additive that separates March from Aesop is the time in which March collected his wisdom and the impending cataclysm that awaited his contemporaries in the Holocaust and a second world war. March maintains an intense interest in life and death issues, as with his bald re-creation of terror in a doomed beast in "The Philosophical Lead-Ram" and the incautious familiarity between dominant and recessive species in "The Guinea Fowl and the Farmer." For "Man and His Natural Enemy," March enacts a raw-rimmed criticism of scholastics whose admiration of human civility fails to evaluate plentiful evidence to the contrary. As the oppressors converge on a runaway slave, they halt at rhododendron bushes in the park and tear him to bits. March's castigation of the professor's rosy view suggests that the author witnessed the slide of Europe's elite thinkers into a willful myopia while fascist thugs banded together to stalk the unwary.

The dynamics of March's selection are personal, for he stresses commonplace situations that gall him. For "Good News and Bad News," he ridicules the perennial bearer of sorrowful tidings. He chortles in private at the vanity of "The Identical Crows" and reminds the reader, "When things are equally black, there's little profit in drawing distinctions." (March 1960, 82) His experience with war enhances the wisdom of "The Sheep and the Soldiers," which concludes that "A comedian finds everything amusing except a joke on himself." (March 1960, 15) With a touch of cynicism, March accounts for the panther outsmarting the woodcutter and reflects that some people are more easily fooled by compassion than greed. In a lighter vein, the author chortles at the egotistical gull who believes he caused an earthquake and ridicules the old man in "The Shepherd and His Monument," in which the elderly egotist opens himself to public scorn while trying to prove to mockers that he was handsome in youth. These perusals of pervasive defects and quirks ally March with fable's standard themes and motifs but tip his satire toward the caustic end of the humor scale.

Of all types, March obsesses most on corrupt women. For "The Criminal Female," he narrows his remarks to the misogynistic moral, "Any crime is permitted a female if she remembers to do it in the name of love." (March 1960, 13) Similarly disdainful of women is "The Fisherman and the Hen," which concludes, "An old hen will put up with anything if you'll give her a little affection now and then." (March 1960, 172) More blatant misogyny ends "The Pious Mantis," in which the worshipful insect beheads her mate, then settles into a prayerful pose. March opines, "There is no creature more cruel in her heart than a pious woman." (March 1960, 189) Although he gives no autobiographical clue to the frequent chiming on misogyny, the recurrence of negativism suggests bad experiences with relatives or a wronged love affair.

Settings range across an appropriately varied landscape—a cabbage patch, barnyard, jungle, beehive, merchant's garden, palace audience room, spare mountaintop, and an ascetic's cave. A succinct commentary on the paradox of religious faith is "The Miracle," which March places on the slope of an exploding volcano. With a piquant portrait of the detached observer, who bears a strong resemblance to the fabulist himself, March denotes the role of miracles—both real and sham—in affirming godhood. The backdrop of a courtroom enhances the droll comedy of a mink talking his way out of punishment for killing hens. A juggler's tent at the fair is the setting for a mildly comic confrontation between a farm lad and two ladies in hats that block his view of the stage. Juxtaposed is the story of the proud queen who walks only on carpets that lead to the palace door. In this pairing, March segues directly from the boy's ironic social situation to the ominous reminder to the queen—and the reader—that no carpet can stop human flesh from its natural deterioration into dust.

The subjects and themes of March's apologues are both universal and timely to the late 1930s, particularly the savagery in "The King and the Bright Young Men," "The Mongoose and the Cobra," "The Wasp and the Caterpillar," and

"The King and the Outcast." With "The Strangers" and "The King and the Out-cast," March demonstrates the plight of society's misunderstood underclass, an indirect reference to Jews, Gypsies, Mormons, homosexuals, and other vic-tims of Hitler's Reich. Militarism and oppression fuel a deadly war in "The Elephants and the Antelopes," the menace of warmongers in "The Nightingale That Listened to Men," and the overthrow at the heart of "Wild Horses," all drawn from the mounting tyranny of Adolf Hitler over Germany. "The Mon-key Hill" contains a subtle message that squabbling European nations may delay too long in making peace and fall prey to an external threat. "The Panthers, the Leopards, and the Jaguars" exemplifies the oversimplified "us vs. them" men-tality that forced European factions into difficult corners. Another form of power struggle underscores "The World and Its Redeemers," "The Prophets and the Mountains," and "The Miracle," all on the theme of encroaching religious zeal-otry. Intent on expressing the terrible hatreds and animosities that no veneer of goodness or altruism can mask, March composes fables that display human behavior in its most puzzling extremes. "The Dog and Her Rival" leads to a moral: "Love can be the most dreadful disguise that hate assumes." (March 1960, 81) Near the end of the collection, "The Slave and the Cart Horse" lauds the compassion of a whipped slave for a strained dray animal. When the man and his wife rise above their own misery to pity the animal, March moves to an ambiguous conclusion: "No man can see his own misery clearly, and that is God's great mercy to us all." (March 1960, 183)

March's selection of small dramas attests to his humanism and his skill as a raconteur. A model of literary acumen is "The King and the Bright Young Man," a fable that draws on subjective analysis of storytelling as a means of determin-ing human talent. Among less intense fables lie small gems deriving from March's personal observations. In "The Tears of the Rich," a master rationalizes callous disrespect for a valued mule who is too old to serve. Depriving the animal of a well-earned retirement, the master turns him out in the wilds. The mule, misreading his master's anguish, chooses to remain silent rather than defend his position and trouble the master. On behalf of the dumb animal, March speaks an aphorism well suited to social disregard for the needy: "There's no sight in the world so moving as the rich contemplating their own ruin." (March 1960, 103) Paired with this fable is "Dishonored Prophets," a sardonic but real-istic scenario in which the successful prophet teaches a neophyte how to couch prophesy in terms that will please all. March weaves the moral into the prophet's discourse: "A prophet with honor is one who repeats the things that others already believe." (March 1960, 106) Near the end of the collection appears a tenderhearted contrast of crassness and nobility. In "The King and the Nature of Man," March sets up a hypothetical situation in which a king tests 50 prison-ers by making them face beheading. Their behaviors range from cursing, shout-ing, and senseless violence to prayerful resignation and squabbling over meaningless honors. Out of the 50, the single act that impresses the king is a soldier's plea that a friend's sentence be rescinded. When the king learns that the soldier is willing to sacrifice himself for the doomed friend, he lowers his head and says nothing while pondering whether to laugh or cry. A rare bit of depth for the fable, the scenario reveals a fabulist who doesn't profess to have all the answers.

March's skill at aphorism derives from straightforward expression of worldly wisdom, for example, "Those with nothing to say need many words to say it" and "Liars often conform strictly to the truth." (March 1960, 95, 41) The moral tags proceed directly from typical Aesopic situations:

- To geese who live well in the midst of weekly beheadings of their fellows, the only response to carnage is disinterest. In token of their inaction, March concludes, "Disaster is something that happens to others." (March 1960, 89)

- At the inevitable death of two stags who clash horns and die entangled, the author notes, "Make hatred your business and you guarantee your own destruction." (March 1960, 25)

- The dun-colored field mice and hedgehog elude the hunter, leading the fabulist to conclude, "The obscure escape and remain forever the same." (March 1960, 47)

- To an old cow who rejects the idealism of youthful heifers, March concludes, "It's better to be surprised than disappointed." (March 1960, 67)

In true Aesopic form, March chooses to let some fables demonstrate their wisdom without the addition of a cleverly phrased explanation, as is the case of domesticated animals accepting their fate in "The Wolves and the Work Animals," the foolish behavior inherent in "The Widow and Her Son," and the lacklogic vengeance demonstrated by "The Magician and the Peasants." A contemplation of morality at the heart of "The Woodchuck and the Old Bones" sets the fabulist's concern in a graveyard. After digging his home between two ancient monuments, the woodchuck reads a pithy quatrain about the warrior's valor and the maiden's loveliness. The woodchuck's response is appropriate to his understanding of evanescence. Like the reader of modern fable, he is moved by the miniature dramas implied by the paired epitaphs, but he can think of no rejoinder, no epigram. Stretched out in the sunshine, he murmurs only, "Well!" (March 1960, 88)

Sources Ehrlich and Carruth 1982; Garraty 1955; March 1960.

 # MARIE DE FRANCE

The versatile trouvère and creator of an anthology of Norman-French animal fables, Marie de France is one of the strongest voices of the Middle Ages and of all women's literature. Because her canon is shrouded in supposition and erroneous criticism, the order and authenticity of her works is at best an educated guess. It is likely that she first produced *Lais* (ca. 1160), a 12-part series of contemporary biographical *roman courtois* [courtly romance] and fairy tales in rhymed octosyllabic couplets that derive from the cycle of Breton *contes* [stories]. She dedicated her urbane short romances to a noble king, who was either

Henry II, William the Conqueror's great-grandson and husband of Eleanor of Aquitaine, or their son, who succeeded to the English throne in 1170. The miniature romances were suited to the Breton harp, which roving gleemen strummed as they sang to entertain Norman and French courts. A boon to the *lai*, her gracile touch enhanced above physical action or didacticism the underlying psychology, characterization, and intense emotion of unhappy, unfulfilled people. Though highly personalized, her subjective involvement in the telling remains controlled, as shown by the conclusion to the story of Equitan:

> It all happened just as I've told you.
> The Bretons made a *lai* about it,
> About Equitan, his fate,
> And the woman who loved him so much.
> (Marie de France, *Fables*, 1994, 202)

At the end of a 35-year career, Marie wrote *L'Espurgatoire de Seint Patriz* [The Purgatory of St. Patrick] (ca. 1189), a somber 2,300-line Latin legend based on *Tractatus de Purgatorio Sancti Patricii* [Treatise on St. Patrick's Purgatory] (ca. 1189). For a pre-Dantean journey into hell, the Irishman Owein enters a nether world through a fissure on Station Island in County Donegal, Ireland, to atone for his sins.

A pioneer poet in the Norman-French language, Marie is unique among women of the Middle Ages for success in publication and the influence of her finesse and refined sensibilities on European literature. She was born in Normandy or Île-de-France and lived outside her native land at the court of Henry II. Literary historians picture her at the royal chateaux at Guyenne and Anjou among a sparkling company of Gascon knights, troubadours, and the epic poet Chrétien de Troyes. Her identity, concealed under a nom de plume, remains a mystery. A farfetched explanation of her writings surmises that a male scribe added her name to an original manuscript. Marie's proud self-introduction in the epilogue of her fables has puzzled generations of medievalists:

> Me numerai pur remembrance
> Marie ai num, si sui de France.
> Put cel estre que clerc plusur
> Prendreient sur eus mun labur.
> [I'll give my name, for memory:
> I am from France, my name's Marie.
> And it may hap that many a clerk
> Will claim as his what is my work.]
> (Marie de France, *Fables*, 1994, 256–257)

In her romance of Guigemar, she identifies herself as "Marie, ki en sun tens pas ne s'oblie" [Marie, who in her time should not be forgotten]. (Marie de France, Fables, 1994, 4) Her clearly expressed desire to remain known suggests that she may have chosen anonymity for reasons of personal necessity or even safety. The intriguing possibilities of her identity have led literary historians to consider a number of capable contemporaries named Mary: the bastard daughter of Geoffrey IV of Anjou and half-sister of Henry II, who became Abbess Mary of Shaftesbury in Dorset; Abbess Marie of Reading; Marie de Meulan, the daughter of Waleran de Meulan (or Beaumont) of the Vexin and wife of the land-rich Baron Hugh Talbot of Cleuville; Marie de Champaigne, daughter of Eleanor of Aquitaine who became patroness to Chrétien de Troyes; and Marie, daughter of Matilda and Stephen of Blois, King of England, who was countess of Boulogne, wife of Matthew, son of the Earl of Flanders, and eventual prioress of Lillechurch and abbess of Romsey in Hampshire. The absence of surnames or other specifics to identify these four possibilities suggests the difficulty of pinpointing particular women.

During an age that offered few opportunities for creative females, Marie de France developed into a refined, educated writer who mastered both English and Latin. She was well read in Old French and Anglo-Norman romances as well as the amorous works of Ovid and the drier Latin grammarians. Apparently she preferred to remain unmarried and, as was the custom with spinsters from prestigious families, may have retired to a convent late in life. She claims "Soventes fiez en ai velle" [I have often stayed awake at night working] but that she was in no way impeded in her scholarship. (Buck 1992, 786) A source of her 102 fables, Henry Beauclerc's English version of the Latin *Romulus* and *Phaedrus* translated by King Alfred the Great, is lost. Of her own version of the fables she states:

> M'entremis de cest livre faire
> E de l'Engleis en Romanz traire.
> [I undertook to write this book
> And to translate the English into French.]
> (Marie de France 1986, 15)

The fact that her collection derives from the Aesopic tradition is revealed in the term *Ysopet* or *Isopet*, a descriptive generalization that ties them to their Greek source and names the French component of European Aesopic lore. Of the total, some are Eastern in origin, reflecting a reading of the *Panchatantra* as well as the works of Bracciolini Poggio, Abstemius, and the English Cistercian monk, Odo of Cerinton (Cherington or Sherrington). Also familiar to Marie were *Roman de Renart* (ca. 1250), *Le Roman de la Rose* (ca. 1280), and world folktales from Germany, Russia, Italy, Serbia, Arabia, and Hebrew colonies of the Middle East. At least 40 of her fables derive from *Romulus Nilantii*, a Latin text published by Frédéric Nilant and later known as *Romuli Fabulae Aesopiae* (1709), a popular collection of Phaedrus's fables. Others appear nowhere before her manuscripts and suggest that she collected and recorded parts of an oral tradition in vogue in her day from the war stories brought home by veterans of the Crusades. She dedicated the anthology to her patron, Count William, an admirably chivalric supporter who may have been William of Mandeville, Earl of Essex, or Guillaume Longespée, Henry II's illegitimate son. Of early copies of the work, 23 survive from the late Middle Ages, as compared with only five of the *Lais*.

Marie's *Fables* (ca. 1189) is a collection of 103 tales, some of which are so far removed from the Aesopic tradition that they are known as *fabulae extravagantes* [fanciful stories]. Her prologue opens with a salute to well-read readers who treasure the moral teachings of such philosophers as Aesop and Romulus. Beginning with Aesop, she restates some of the most memorable: "The Cock and the Gem," "The Dog and the Cheese," and "The Sun Who Wished to Wed." Her *modus scribendi* begins the nature tale with action and moves directly to a climatic scene and moral, usually confined to no more than four lines. Her strength in epigram lies in concise, clear advice:

- Veü l'avums de humme e de femme:
  Bien e honur mut poi prisent;
  Le pis pernent, le meux despisent.
  [We've seen with men and women too:
  They neither good nor honor prize;
  The worst they seize; the best, despise.]
  (Marie de France, *Fables*, 1994, 32–33)

- Ki plus coveite que sun dreit,
  Par sei memes se recruit.
  [Those who desire more than is just
  Will be undone by their own lust.]
  (Marie de France, *Fables*, 1994, 42–43)

- Cum plus est fort, pis lur fet:
  Tuz jurs lur est en mal aguet.
  [The stronger the lord, the worse their fate:
  His ambush always lies in wait.]
  (Marie de France, *Fables*, 1994, 46–47)

One of her most skillfully worded entries, "The Preacher and the Wolf," maintains its parallel turns of phrase through an extended dialogue concluding in a warning that the tongue often betrays secret thoughts. In a rapid give and take, the preacher begins teaching the wolf his letters:

'A' dist le prestre; 'A' dist li lus,
Que mut ert fel e enginnus.
'B' dist le prestre, 'di od mei.'
'B' dist li lus, 'jo l'otrei.'
'C' dist le prestre, 'di avant.'
'C' dist li lus, 'a i dunc itant?'
['A' said the preacher; 'A' wolf said,
Who very crafty was, and bad.
'B' said the priest, 'say it with me.'
'B' said the wolf, 'and I agree.'
'C' said the preacher, 'say it o'er.'
'C' said the wolf, 'are there yet more?']
(Marie de France, *Fables*, 1994, 216–217]

Although the wolf can't recite the ABCs, he is quick to spell lamb. With a nimble switch to moral, the fabulist declares, "With many men you'll find / Whatever's topmost in their mind / The mouth lets slip," a medieval forerunner of the Freudian slip.

A distinct precursor to Giovanni Boccaccio and Geoffrey Chaucer, the liberal subject matter of Marie de France's fables champions female characters who grasp independence as they elude powerlessness and victimization. Her deities depart from the traditional Jupiter to Juno and showcase the feminine abstracts Destiny, Wisdom, the Creator, and an all-encompassing *la deuesse* [the Goddess]. With lissome grace, Marie displays a warm sensitivity toward the female in "The Wolf and the Crane," "The Lamb and the Goat," a paean to the foster mother who nurtured another's young, and the rape victim in "The Fox and the Bear." In "The Mouse and the Frog," Marie inserts her own details, picturing the female mouse sitting on the doorstep smoothing strands of whiskers and combing them with her tiny feet. The mouse, one of Marie's strong female characters, makes no apology to the visiting frog for being a landlady and boasts, "Bien est en ma subjectïun" [All is under my control]. (Marie de France, Fables, 1994, 36–37) With self-assurance suited to her station, the mouse claims ample grain garnered from the peasants' leavings. At the height of the frog's treachery against the trusting mouse, the victim refuses to die quietly and lets out a cry that summons the kite to rescue. With some satisfaction, Marie belabors the moral, which warns traitors that, in snaring their victims, they often imperil themselves. The forthright strength and verve of her female personae belies the myth that medieval women were docile and dependent. Two parallel strong females are the survivor in "The Wolf and the Sow" and the rescuer in "The Lion and the Mouse." In the former, the fabulist showcases mothers who protect their young from predators; on the other hand, in the latter, Marie chooses to moralize on the poor rather than on the plight of women.

The medieval spirit is strong in Marie's fables, as expressed in her gestures to monarchy in "The Eagle, the Hawk, and the Doves" and "The Birds and the Cuckoo," a serious court scene in "The Lion and the Fox," honor owed to the lord in "The Peasant and the Oxen," pious submission to God in "The Rich Man Who Wished To Cross the Sea," a domestic squabble turned violent in "The Peasant and His Contrary Wife," and settling of a feud by combat in "The Wolf and the Beetle." She frequently instructs her readers on the seven deadly sins, a pervasive paradigm of evil that provides the crux of "The Dragon and the Peasant," "The Fox and the Dove," "The Blacksmith and the Axe," "The Monkey and Her Baby," "The Vole Who Sought a Wife," and "The Wolf and the Sheep." In fairness to humankind, the fabulist offsets her sympathy for women with the prevailing misogyny of the Middle Ages, which fuels "The Peasant and His Cantankeorus Wife" and "The Peasant and the Snake," one of the most protracted and ominous fables in the collection. In a period when the church formalized diatribes against woman as the offspring of Eve, corrupter of Eden, Marie versified "The Hermit and the Peasant," which supplants Eve with a disobedient male. Counter to the tale runs "The Pregnant Hound," an Aesopic story about the freeloading bitch who begs shelter until she delivers pups, then refuses to move on. Further distancing Marie from devout feminism are the conniving females who deny their adulteries in "The Peasant Who Saw Another with His Wife." Its companion piece, "The Peasant Who Saw His Wife with Her Lover," culminates in a chill warning that women possess more craft and falsehood than the devil's inventions. The moral mirrors the pervasive search for witches throughout Europe, where predominantly female suspects were publicly tortured and murdered for complicity with Satan.

In addition to misogyny and witch-hunts, other inequities dominate Marie's selections, which often mourn the suffering of the weak and destitute, as in the standoff in "The Lion, the Buffalo, and the Wolf," bribery in "The Peasant and His Jackdaw," false justice in "The Monkey King," and a threat to innocent babes in "The Fox and the Eagle." A poignant one-on-one story, "The Dog and the Ewe," presents courtroom drama at its seediest—the testimony of a wolf and kite to support the dog's false statement that the ewe owes him a loaf of bread. After the callous judge finds for the plaintiff, the ewe's fortunes rapidly decline:

> I chiens i vient, sa leine en porte,
> E li escufles d'autre part,
> E puis li lus, trop est li tart
> Que le chars fust entre eus destreite.
> [The dog was there, her fleece to strip.
> The kite came for his share of fleece;
> The wolf was anxious for his piece.
> They could not wait her flesh to eat.]
> (Marie de France, *Fables,* 1994, 42–43)

Overall, the fabulist's literary clashes suit the Middle Ages in that they tend to pit rich against poor and powerful against powerless, a focus of the feudal period.

Sources Bishop 1965; Buck 1992; Cantor 1994; *Catholic Encyclopedia*, http:// www. knight.org; Krappe 1964; Marie de France 1986, 1994; Massignon 1968; Nitze and Dargan 1950; Strayer 1989.

 # MEDIEVAL FABLE

In the Middle Ages of the Western world, the traditions of European fable continued in varied collections, translations, recensions, and imitative writings:

- the fables of Paulus Diaconus [Paul the Deacon], a Lombard monk, historian, and scholar from the mid-eighth century, who tells of "The Calf and the Stork," a bland comparison of animal needs, and "The Flea and the Gout," a witty *pourquoi* story that accounts for the presence of biting fleas among the poor and gout among the self-indulgent rich.

- an anonymous rewriting of the Avianian fables, called the *Novus Avianus* [New Avianus] (ca. 1100).

- Bishop Walther or Galterus Anglicus, Henry II's court priest and versifier of the Romulus fables (late twelfth century), an anonymous Latin collection the author claims to have translated from Greek for his son Tiberius.

- Alexander Neckham (or Neckam or Nequam), a grammarian and author from St. Albans who lectured in Paris and became a school principal

Illustration to *The Fables of Bidpai*, "Lion, King of Animals."

in Dunstable. After rising to the post of abbot of Cirencester in 1213, he wrote *Novus Avianus* [A New Avianus] and *Novus Aesopus* [A New Aesop] (ca. 1215), both adaptations of traditional fables in Latin. A case of self-incriminating humor, "The Vulture and the Eagle" tells of a vulture that poses as an eaglet and lives in comfort as the eagle's child. When the mother bird remarks on a terrible storm, the vulture pipes up that he's seen worse storms in his day. The eagle realizes that a young bird should not have so long a memory and chucks the vulture out of the nest.

- Baldo, a twelfth-century collector of a subsequent *Novus Aesopus.*

- Nivardus of Ghent, author of *Ysengrimus* (1148), an antimonastic satire in the form of a beast epic about a hypocritical wolf-monk.

- a grab-bag collection, *Gesta Romanorum* [Deeds of the Romans] (1324), a misleading title for a collection of tales and oddments borne west with crusaders returning from the eastern Mediterranean and printed in 1473 on the earliest form of movable type. Probably intended as religious instruction, the anthology contains fables gleaned from Sufist stories, the Koran, the Arabic *A Thousand and One Nights*, and the Persian *Tuti Nameh* (ca. 1300). The *epimythia,* or morals, often inadequate or ridiculously inapplicable, indicate the haphazard compilation of the fables, which nonetheless provided material for Geoffrey Chaucer and survived into the Renaissance to influence Shakespeare and his contemporaries. Common to the texts are unidentified kings who serve as models of royalty, as found in the fool tale "The Ridiculous Donkey." Other fables name real monarchs, as with "The Lady of Comfort," a fable about the Roman emperor Vespasian and the daughter he renamed because of her beauty, and "A Dove Warns the City," which is set in the reign of Henry II. A somber postmortem around the tomb of Alexander the Great lists the sententious observations of philosophers who take advantage of the king's absence to muse on the strength of death against a mortal world leader. Additional mention of Dionysius, Theodosius, and Fulgentius tag individual tales to particular eras.

- In the mid-thirteenth century, Dominican friar and encyclopedist Vincent de Beauvais (or Vincentius Bellovacensius), produced his own fables in *Speculum Majus* [A Greater Mirror], a satiric compendium commissioned by King Louis IX.

- Anticipating the compendia of Giovanni Boccaccio and Geoffrey Chaucer is an oriental cycle, *Historia Septem Sapientum* [The Seven Wise Men], attached to the canon of Johannes of Alta Silvia near the end of the twelfth century. A graphic entry, "The Dog," tells of a man who leaves a dog to guard his son and returns to find the dog's mouth filled with blood. Without realizing that the dog has killed a menacing snake, the man slaughters the faithful guard dog.

During a period dominated by Bible reading and disputation about scriptural matters, fable rose in importance to a key form of instruction. Fabulists made a decisive move from short illustrative tales to cycles and epic. An original narrative style flourished from the pen of Marie de France, a twelfth-century Norman-French writer, who published a compendium of fables around 1189. Her addition to the Western canon of allegorical narrative prefaced new interest in beast fable, a longer animal tale composed of suspenseful and often satiric episodes in which a villain stalks a potential victim or victims. At the core of this era of beast epics stands its wiliest protagonist, Reynard or Renart the Fox, whose lore is collected in the *Roman de Renart* [Stories of Reynard], which parodied the courtly verse that rose to prominence alongside feudal combat stories.

German lore evolved its own fable in the lore of an irrepressible jester and practical joker. Named for the "owl in the mirror," a wise reflection, the medieval Tyl [or Till] Eulenspiegel (originally named Dylulenspegel) survived in stories centered on the German town of Brunswick and composed in the fashion of a *volksmund*, a people's literary effort. A cycle of scatological fool tales about the sophomoric young picaro from Kneitlingen, Saxony, the stories begin chronologically with his baptism, after which his godmother drops him in a muddy pool and then washes him clean again in a kettle all in the same day. Symbolically passed from the font to earthly muck and into human cleansing, the renowned *wunderkin* is a rascal and showoff from toddlerhood and dedicates himself to a human waywardness that finds him lacking in polish but amply blessed with insight into pretense. Whether mooning a tormentor, sticking out his tongue, or feeding his widowed mother on stolen bread, he applies guile and pragmatism to the problem of living among mockers.

The focal characteristic of Till is that he, like a mirror, takes images and exaggerations literally. When the baker he works for charges him to sift by moonlight, Till dusts expensive flour into a lighted spot in the courtyard. After he is hired to stand in a tower and sound an alarm for the enemy, he waits until the field is overrun, then declares that he doesn't need to sound the bugle for any more enemies. Because the king asks Till to get the best shoes for his horse, Till demands gold horseshoes and silver nails. After the duke banishes him from his land, Till buys a cartful of soil and proclaims it his own land. Wandering over Magdeburg, Lüneburg, Erfurt, Nuremberg, Bamberg, and beyond, he carries his witless literalism to Rome, Leipzig, Paris, Ueltzen, and London and appears in court, tower, city hall, scaffold, pigsty, bedchamber, even an Easter pageant. In each instance, Till finds occasion to scandalize and upbraid the rich and self-important.

To the end, the outrageous behavior of Till reeks of feces, his favorite recompense for the unwary. Near the conclusion of his rambles, purportedly at age 60, he lies ill at Mölln, where an apothecary treats him with a purgative. Because the house is locked, Till has no toilet. His solution is typical of his literal thinking: "He was full of worry and need, so he went into the pharmacy, shitted into one of the books, and said, "The medicine came from here. It ought to be returned here. That way the pharmacist doesn't lose anything. I can't pay

Illustration to *The Fables of Bidpai,* "The Tortoise and Two Ducks."

for it anyway." (*Till* 1995, 184) Bemused to be dumped at the hospital of the Holy Ghost, Till tries to fathom why he prays for the Holy Ghost to enter him instead of vice versa. The puns and wordplay reach their height at his death-bed, where his mother attends him:

- In answer to "where are you sick," he replies, "between the bed-box and the wall."

- In request of a sweet word, he replies "honey."

- When his mother asks for sweet advice to remember him by, he urges her to defecate downwind to keep the odor from her nose.

- In repenting his sins, he confides to the priest the three pranks he didn't get to carry out.

Even his wake is made ridiculous by a sow and piglets let loose in the hospital. Because of an error, his corpse is carried to his grave upside down, with his posterior sticking up, much as it obtruded throughout his life. Another mishap causes him to be buried standing upright. The stone over him reads, "Don't move this stone: let that be clear—Eulenspiegel's buried here. Anno domini MCCCL." (*Till* 1995, 191) Above his epitaph is the glyph of owl and glass.

A focus of *Schwankbücher* [jest-books] written in low German, the vagabond buffoon became so real in the late Middle Ages that his fictional remains are interred in a grave in Mölln, Schleswig-Holstein, marked with his death date of 1350. The city maintains his legend in annual festivals. The crux of Eulenspiegel lore is an ongoing confrontation between the clever rustic and the condescending burgher, priest, and noble. In 1500 the series first appeared in print in the towns of Brunswick and Augsburg in anecdotal broadsides. These scurrilous tales were set in towns to ridicule known figures who deserved public or political deflation. The cycle reached stasis in print form in the high German *Ein kurtzweilig Lesen von Dyl Vlenspiegel* [An Amusing Book about Till Eulenspiegel] (1515) and, in English, *Here beginneth a merye Jest of a man that was called Howleglas* (ca. 1560). Tentatively attached to author Hermann Bote, the original text conceals in questionable acrostic the writer's name.

As a model of peasant trickster, the protagonist of medieval *fabliaux*, Till is an impudent lout whose mystique endears him to the lowly. His canon, like Geoffrey Chaucer's *The Canterbury Tales* and William Shakespeare's Falstaff plays, provides a glimpse of the commonalities of town life in late medieval Germany. The wide-eyed innocent, Till takes the lowly, messy jobs—carrying messages, sweeping the barber shop, cleaning pelts, hawking religious relics, tending the sanctuary, and apprenticing to the shoemaker, brewer, and furrier. Inadvertently, he appears to ridicule and dupe the pompous, pretentious, and villainous elements of society. To boast his roguish pranks, he takes charcoal or chalk and draws the owl and mirror over a door much as the fictional Zorro lashes out a three-slash Z. Till's name suggests an indecent pun on "Ul'n speghel" [wipe the ass]. Other interpretations tie his name to the owl as the devil's familiar.

Still admired in the Renaissance and beyond, Till Eulenspiegel's legend underwent subsequent metamorphoses. Belgian author Charles de Coster, from Munich, Bavaria, turned his pranks into polished French in *La Légende de les aventures héroiques, joyeues, et glorieuses d'Ulenspiegel et de Lamme Goedzak au pays de Flandres et ailleurs* [The Glorious Adventures of Tyl Eulenspiegel and of Lamme Goedzak of Flanders and Other Places] (1866), a Rabelaisian story of a Flemish folk hero on a par with the English Robin Hood and with Voltaire's Candide. Resituated in the sixteenth century during the Catholic Inquisition, the hero avenges his father, whom zealots burn at the stake for heresy. For championing liberty, the book was lauded as the "Bible of Flanders" and "a breviary of freedom." In 1928, Gerhart Hauptmann extended the cycle with an epic narrative, *Till Eulenspiegel.* The Eulenspiegel phenomenon includes woodcuts by Hans Baldung Grien and a fresh, joyous orchestral suite, *Till Eulenspiegels lustige Streiche* [Till Eulenspiegel's Merry Pranks] (1895), written by Richard Strauss, who, like de Coster, was from Munich. On a par with Sergei Prokofiev's *Peter and the Wolf* and Paul Dukas's *The Sorceror's Apprentice*, the work is an evocative blend of symphonic devices to reflect the bumbling fool and his misadventures.

See also British fable; Chaucer, Geoffrey; Chaunticleer; Christian fable; Marie de France; Reynard the Fox.

Sources Blackham 1985; "Brewer: Dictionary of Phrase and Fable," http://www.bibliomania.com; Briggs 1977, 1991; Cooper 1921; Creeden 1994; Feinberg 1967; Garland and Garland 1976; Harrington 1925; Hobbs 1986; Kohlschmidt 1975; Komroff 1935; Krappe 1964; Marie de France 1994; Newbigging 1895; Raby 1997; Rosenberg 1997; Steinberg 1954; Strayer 1989; Williams 1978.

 NATIVE AMERICAN FABLE

Native American lore is rooted in self-discovery. For the wise seeker, communion with nature provides the quiet introspection and observation that prefaces insights and a profound change of behavior and character. A model from Hawaiian fable is the survival tale of Mikololou, the familiar journeyman shark of the Ka'u district of Hawai'i. While visiting Pearl Harbor with a school of shark friends, Mikololou is snared in a net and left to die in the heat. His spirit survives in his tongue, which children toss into the sea. In an alternate version in Thomas G. Thrum's *Hawaiian Folk Tales: A Collection of Native Legends* (1907), a dog devours the tongue, leaps in for a swim, and is transformed into Mikololou. Rejuvenated by seawater in both tellings, Mikololou survives and escapes the treachery of fishermen. Hawaiians, in admiration of the wily shark, derive from his story a proverb, "Mikololou lived through his tongue," a reminder that escape may come from unlikely sources. (Nakuina 1994, 72)

Native American fable can derive its wisdom from winners or losers, a theme of Canadian Mohawk poet Pauline Johnson's "The Cattle Thief." One Lenape story from *The White Deer and Other Stories Told by the Lenape* (1995), "Three Boys on a Vision Quest," demonstrates how human flaws can precede suffering and doom. When the three seek a glimpse of the future, they encounter Manitou, the pervasive Algonquin divinity of eastern forest tribes, who communicates with individuals through dream state or trance. To the first, he grants the wish to hunt; to the second boy, he grants the powers of a warrior. The third, who foolishly wishes for women to like him, is destroyed by women. For moral instruction, teller Warren Longbone appends two straightforward admonitions: "One is to not be greedy when you ask for something, and the other is to not ask to be more than you can be." (Bierhorst 1995, 76) In the spare, austere style of native storytelling, the fable offers no second chance, no reprieve. The *epimythium* arrives too late to help the third seeker, but preserves the example of his faulty thinking.

Extending to all Lenape, pre-Columbian fable warned of the dangers of European adventurers. In "The First Land Sale," the Delaware accept trinkets and tools for which they have no use and witness a white man kidnapping a native girl and departing. Still trusting, they confer with the white man upon his return and agree to sell land as big as a cowhide. The devious settler trims the skin into one continuous narrow string and stretches it around a large parcel of land. The sardonic fable concludes, "So he began to cheat the Indians first jump. And he's still doing it." (Bierhorst 1995, 106) The story, retold myriad ways by tribes across native America, embodies the comfortless truth that Indians are fated to be cheated and cozzened out of their birthright. This folkloric motif of trickery and displacement is the focus of Conrad Richter's young adult classic *The Light in the Forest* (1953), which is set on the Lenape land that whites seized and built into Pittsburgh, Pennsylvania.

Indian beast lore forms a core "aha" experience in New World literature by reminding European newcomers that human pride can distort the sacred interdependence of all earth's beings. An example of Menominee nature lore, "The Catfish and the Moose," recorded in the anthropological papers of the American Museum of Natural History, concludes with a simple moral precept: "It is wrong to despise any living thing, no matter how small and humble it appears to be." (Cooper 1921, 472) According to folklorist Harold Courlander, the wise Hopi have from early times felt a close alliance with the earth. Speaking a Uto-Aztecan language, these seminomadic gatherers of the San Juan Valley traversed an extensive terrain and followed watercourses in their search for wild seeds, berries, and small game. For pleasure and instruction, they made up stories along the way to enshrine and ennoble their experience. The Ojibwa, too, tell stories that illustrate useful deductions about nature, for example, "The Three Cranberries," a model story about the green cranberry's natural camouflage in a spruce tree. Such stories permeate the Plains lore collected and translated by Paul Radin, who recorded the Winnebago hare cycle, Wakdjunkaga satire cycle, and Assiniboine and Tlingit trickster myths.

A prominent element of Indian fable is the *pourquoi* story, which establishes the logic that undergirds nature, as in the Pueblo stories "The Coyote and the Crows" and "Grandma Spider" and the Blackfoot myths "How the Old Man Made People" and "How the Thunder Made Horses." These nature-based stories often rely on foolish behaviors, for example, the Cherokee favorite "Why the Bears Have Short Tails." This fable turns on the trickery of the fox, who cons the bear into sitting on ice and dropping his tail into the fishing hole as a lure. Children relish the buildup to the bear's leap from his cold seat and gleefully exult that his tail remains behind, frozen to the ice. A similar audience participation story, "The Wildcat and the Rabbit," requires listeners to gobble like turkeys and drum like the rabbit. More lyrical and less rambunctious is a Miwok story of the measure worm's patience and perseverance, the motif of "The Measure Worm Rock," which Stephen Powers recorded in *The Overland Monthly* in the early 1870s to account for the name of a landmark, *Tutochanula*, which mimics the native name for the inchworm.

Gathered from petroglyphs, hula, and kahunas or storytellers and published in G. W. Kahiolo's weekly newspaper *Ka Hae Hawai'i* (1861), Abraham Fornander's *Collection of Hawaiian Antiquities and Folklore* (1919) and Thomas G. Thrum's *Hawaiian Folk Tales: A Collection of Native Legends* (1907) and *More Hawaiian Folk Tales* (1923), island myth contains episodes in fable form. Thrum's epic of Kapo'i includes the story of Kapo'i of Kahehuna, Honolulu, who steals seven owl eggs while he searches for thatch. Shortly before roasting them in ti leaves, he hears the owl's voice demanding the eggs. Out of pity for the bird, Kapo'i returns the eggs. His reward is instruction on where and how to build a temple and altar. Because the king threatens to execute Kapo'i for violating an edict against erecting temples, the owls gather for a raid on the place of execution and peck and scratch the king's minions. The *pourquoi* story ends with Hawaiians deifying owls and valuing nature over human pride. Like the fables of Aesop, the rescue motif depends on the natural defenses of small animals, which triumph over human treachery.

In addition to aggressor-victim lore, much native lore relies on learning from mistakes, for example, the incautious fish who allow the mink to manipulate them into a fight in the Menominee tale "The Mink, the Pike, and the Pickerel." A witty fool tale, the Cherokee story of the rabbit who tries to squeeze a drop of cooking fat from his thin haunch represents the flip side of straightforward wisdom lore and demonstrates how folly generates its own lessons, often couched in good-natured comedy and debasement of the unwise. Sometimes borne to extremes of humiliation, these instructive stories tend toward elements of mastery. The Eskimo story "The Owl and the Lemming," which anthropologist Franz Boas collected from the Baffin Bay area, expresses the natural antipathy of creature for creature and concludes with the burrowing lemming kicking a footful of dirt in the face of the looming owl. Such expressions of comeuppance are common to Native American lore, which values humorous put-downs as natural adjuncts to instruction.

Twentieth-century lore preserves through Native American stories a wise appreciation of nature's cycles. The best known of Native American fabulists is Abenaki teller and author Joseph Bruchac, an entertaining moralist and culture instructor. His autobiography, anthologies, videotapes, and audiocassettes foster harmony with nature as they reaffirm native identity in a Europeanized society. With hand drum and rattle, the gently reassuring teller reshapes organic entities that date to the beginnings of human life and perpetuate the lore of Gluscabi, the Abenaki creator. Since the beginning of his career in the mid-1960s, he has assumed the native role of "wampum keeper" or storyteller and celebrates the Learning Circle, which impels his hearers to observe, remember, and share. For his true-to-tradition writings, he has earned the 1996 American Folklore Society Aesop Accolade and the New York Library Association Knickerbocker Award. His considerable addition to the Native American fable canon, written in part with ecologist Michael J. Caduto and Cherokee teller Gayle Ross, places him at the forefront of modern fable writing.

Bruchac's reverence for preliterate history echoes a similar appreciation in other native narrators. A Hasinai storyteller of the Caddo nation, Dayton Edmonds, of Omak, Washington, relates wisdom stories, legends, and nature lore. He learned from his grandfathers, both priests of the peyote religion, the ancient traditions of native moundbuilders, healers, advisers, and practitioners of the sacred art of the storykeeper. In 1979, Edmonds had a mystic experience when he discovered an eagle's wing feather. Since then, he has entertained a wide variety of audiences and published four anthologies, videos, and an audiocassette, *A Storyteller's Story*, which contains a modern coyote tale and traditional wisdom.

Similarly faithful to Native American lore is Cherokee teller Lloyd Arneach, 1992 chair of the Georgia Governor's Council for Native American Concerns and senior Native American adviser for "Festival of Fires" at the 1996 Olympics in Atlanta. Arneach tells the vision stories of puberty plus creation myths, *pourquoi* stories, and benevolent fables that explain the necessity for morals, manners, and self-improvement. Born in the Great Smoky Mountains of North Carolina, he heard stories from his parents and tribal elders, who used fable as a form of discipline. These traditional stories, which collector James Mooney recorded in *Myths of the Cherokee* (1900), were the impetus for Arneach's children's book *Animal's Ball Game* (1992). In his *pourquoi* story "How the Mink Got His Dark Coat," he stresses the instinctive thievery of the mink, which is the cause of the other animals' decision to toast him in a fire. A more devious trickster story, "The Possum's Tail," describes the proud opossum, who allows the cricket to groom his lustrous tail fur. The cricket's haphazard snips rob the possum of his glory, leaving him bare as a lizard and grinning with embarrassment.

A Kiowa collector and author, Matt "Sitting Bear" Jones blends Plains Indian creation stories with beast fables and tales of cultural identity. His comic, kinetic re-creations of traditional Indian lore hinge on animal characterizations, which he enhances with ceremonial dress and jewelry. A great-hearted performer, he assumes the person and behaviors of native tricksters, such as the possum or coyote, acts out the parts, and alters his voice to emulate the creatures and their emotions. A native of Wichita, Kansas, and fellow of the Center for Great Plains Studies, Jones has worked in television production, acted in movies, and contributed fables to *Native America in the Twentieth Century: An Encyclopedia* (1996).

From the British Columbian tradition of the Nootka, storyteller Johnny Moses promotes spiritual and healing medicine through morality tales and nature lore. His performances reprise the art of the shaman who uses illustrative stories, dreamscapes, and symbol to express cosmic truths. Under the traditional name of Whis-tem-men-knee or Walking Medicine Robe, Moses serves as tribal ambassador by performing tales of ants, bears, and coyotes in eight native languages. His characterizations range from the Grandmother Tree to the Crow and Octopus Lady. In print, sign language, web site, and lecture, he promotes Sisiwiss spirituality and wholeness, the themes of *Medicine Teachings of the Earth*, his introduction to the power of the Creator, and in the focus of his contribution to the anthology *Ghostwise, A Book of Midnight Stories* (1997).

A traditional troubadour, Texas storyteller and singer Gayle Ross—winner of the 1997 National Storytelling Association Circle of Excellence, 1996 American Folklore Society Aesop Accolade, and 1996 Anne Izard Storytellers' Choice Book Award—maintains that human speech evolved because people had to have a way to communicate and share experience. Her blend of traditional and original fable transcends nationality and culture by stressing intrinsic humanism. A distant relative of Cherokee chief John Ross, she learned animal lore in childhood from her grandmother, a local storykeeper. To rescue native culture from extinction and misapplication by the uninformed, she has performed, recorded, and published creation myth, *pourquoi* stories, and nature fables. Available in print are "The Bird That Was Ashamed of Its Feet," "Daughter of the Sun," and a full range of rabbit trickster lore: "Flint Visits Rabbit," "Why Possum's Tail Is Bare," "Rabbit Escapes from the Wolves," "How Deer Won His Antlers," "Why Deer's Teeth Are Blunt," "Rabbit Helps Wildcat Hunt Turkeys," "Rabbit Goes Duck Hunting," "Rabbit and the Tar Wolf," "Bear Dines with Rabbit," "Rabbit Steals from Fox," "Rabbit Sends Wolf to the Sunset," "Rabbit Dances with the People," and "How Rabbit Tricked Otter," the subject of a best-selling children's book and audiocassette.

See also storytelling; trickster.

Sources Ancient O'ahu: Stories from Fornander & Thrum 1996; Arneach 1992; Bemister 1973; Bierhorst 1995; Bruchac 1993, 1994, *The Boy Who Lived with the Bears and Other Iroquois Stories* 1995, *Dog People: Native Dog Stories* 1995, *Native Wisdom* 1995, 1996; Bruchac and Caduto 1990, 1991; Burrison 1989; Cooper 1921; Courlander 1971; Cuevas 1991; Edmonds 1994, 1995, 1996, *The Farmer's Three Sons* 1997, *The Gift of Fire,* 1997; Emerson 1997; Feldmann 1965; Fraser 1968; Jones 1994; Kame'eleihiwa 1996; Lummis 1992; Marriott and Rachlin 1975; McGregor 1998; Miller and Snodgrass 1998; Moses, http://www.hometownet.com, 1992; Moses and Goldie 1992; Nakuina 1994; Patterson and Snodgrass 1994; Radin 1972; Ross 1994, 1995.

NINETEENTH-CENTURY FABLE

In the nineteenth century, the creation of literary fable and scholarly collection and criticism of folk models dominated a new age for the genre. Europe's Romantic era produced a worthy successor to Jean de La Fontaine—Russian fabulist Ivan Andreyevich Krylov, whose nine collections of fables and translations of La Fontaine's tales influenced generations of Russian schoolchildren, including painter Marc Chagall. Krylov's contemporary, Ivan Turgenev, composed the rare first-person fable, "Only a Sparrow." Observing a sparrow offering herself to an alert hunting hound, the speaker takes pity on the bird, who confronts the great dog to save a fallen chick from the nest. The anecdote encases Turgenev's belief that love outweighs the fear of death. A fellow Russian, novelist Leo Tolstoy, wrote an array of fool tales and animal fables to entertain and enlighten the children of his family's estate. A favorite ironic tale, "The King and the Falcon," expresses the need for gratitude after a falcon saves a king from drinking poisoned water. Equally somber are the mortal situations of "The Mouse Who Lived under the Granary" and "The Gnat and the Lion," both concluding a series of boasts with appropriate justice to the boaster. A test of wisdom, "The Raven and His Young" reveals the survival instincts that cause a father raven to save the most honest of his three young. In these and other examples, Tolstoy expressed his sympathy for humble folk and his understanding of human weakness.

The nineteenth century was a high point in academic analysis of fable as a focus for linguistic, nationalistic, and ethical study. Folklore established legitimacy with the work of two German collectors and philologists, the brothers Jakob and Wilhelm Grimm, authors of the three-volume *Kinder und Hausmärchen*, commonly known as Grimm's Fairy Tales (1812, 1815, 1822), a seminal work of comparative folklore, and of *Reinhart Fuchs* [Reynard the Fox] (1834), a perpetuation of medieval animal lore. A Scottish contemporary of the Brothers Grimm, historical novelist Sir Walter Scott introduced textural criticism by tracing individual versions to their parent text. Johann Heinrich Pestalozzi—a Swiss educational innovator and founder of the Swiss International Village, a residential orphanage and farm school for children of all nationalities, applied fable to such professional treatises as *How Gertrude Educates Her Children* (1801). These animal stories solidify his theories in narrative, for example, "The Old Bear in the Tree," a somber fool tale about a parent who dies while setting a bad example for his young. At the beginning of the twentieth century, a Glasgow native, Sir James George Frazer, a respected folklorist, classicist, and professor of anthropology at Liverpool and Cambridge universities, published in 12 volumes his comparative treatise, *The Golden Bough: The Roots of Religion and Folklore* (1911–1915) and *Folklore in the Old Testament* (1918), both forerunners of serious psychological, sociological, and religious research by twentieth-century theoreticians Bruno Bettelheim, Paul Radin, Emile Durkheim, Carl Jung, and Joseph Campbell.

Nineteenth-century fable also thrived in satire, political essay, and artistic illustrations—a topsy-turvy presentation in which familiar stories took second place to elegant artistry. The contrast of purpose and vehicle is greater than at any other era of fable production, as shown by these creators and collectors:

- Polemicist and free thinker William Godwin added to the canon *Fables Ancient and Modern* (1805), a forerunner of the modern coffee table collection cleverly illustrated by William Mulready. Godwin's fellow English fabulist, Dr. John Aikin, composed some innovative stories that perpetuate the nature-nurture controversy. One example, the story "Nature and Education" creates an artificial scenario in which the two abstracts discuss the growth of firs and oaks. A labored story, it exemplifies the meager efforts of second-raters like Aikin to apply abstract logic to natural settings and characters.

- Among illustrated verse editions are Richard Scrafton Sharpe's funny limericks in *Friends in a New Dress* (1807) and Jeffreys Taylor's *Aesop in Rhyme, with Some Originals* (1821).

- Andreas Fay, the "Hungarian Aesop," produced *Fables* (1820), an appealing collection of succinct stories that includes "The Caterpillar," a simplistic *agon* or competition story that ridicules the caterpillar for his inane boasts.

- Dutch bureaucrat and satirist Eduard Douwes Dekker, an influential iconoclast publishing under the pseudonym Multatuli, protested his

Engraving of Sir Walter Scott

country's imperialism over the nation of Java. A clever lampoon of the industrial era's grim commercialism colors "Life in the Heights," a fable about a butterfly that spurns the crush of the lowlands for the untouched shoots and blossoms that flourish far above the muddy cart tracks of the valley below.

- Dekker's contemporary, Austrian dramatist and lyricist Franz Grillparzer, produced a creation fable, "Momus the Mocker," which tells of a faultfinder's ridicule of Jupiter's first bull. An ungraceful example of didacticism masked as fable, the story is little more than the god's irritated retort to Momus, who chattered senselessly in the presence of the deity.

- In the mid-nineteenth century, the misanthrope Arthur Schopenhauer included in his philosophical writings the fable of "The Porcupines." Stated as a *pourquoi* story, the animal tale depicts porcupines who try to snuggle against the cold. The closest distance they can arrange without risking spiny quills in their flesh is a space the philosopher equates with common courtesy.

- The classic work of the times, Gustave Doré's dynamic 1868 edition of *Fables de La Fontaine*, provided a touchstone by which later illustrated fable compendia were judged. Contemporaneous with Doré's publication was the resurgence of animal fable as an integral element of children's literature. One contributor, Ludwig Bechstein, a German librarian and author of children's stories, penned *Tales*, a mid-nineteenth-century collection of amusing fables that draw on medieval Reynard the Fox stories. The most significant addition to children's folklore is the resetting of West African fable in the gently humorous tales of Uncle Remus, the unassuming Reconstruction era editorials of Joel Chandler Harris. In the American West, Ambrose Bierce produced a more vitriolic tale.

Passing from adult shelves to the nursery and classroom, the genre issued from the pens of the giants of juvenile literature. One of the most successful in southern Europe, Italian collector Domenico Comparetti, rivaled northern European folklorists to become the Italian Grimm. He compiled a general assortment of material for *Popular Italian Tales* (1875), but the promise of more volumes faded. A year earlier, his peer, Carolina Coronedi-Berti, had compiled an anthology in the Bolognese dialect. In Tuscany, Gherardo Nerucci collected lore of his native region in *Sessanta novelle popolari Montanesi* [Sixty Popular Tales from Montale] (1880). In 1881, Pietro Pellizzari collected stories in the Apulian dialect for *Fiabe e canzoni popolari del contado di Maglie in terra d'Otranto* [Popular Fables and Songs from the Country of Maglie in Terra d'Otranto]. A Sicilian contemporary, Giuseppe Pitrè, a physician and folklorist who drew on a large staff of collectors, made his own compilation for a four-volume collection of 300 entries for *Fiabe, novelle e racconti popolari Siciliani* (Sicilian Fables, Stories and Popular Tales] (1875).

Parisian fabulist Hilaire Belloc established a distinct yoking of witty story with drawing in *The Bad Child's Book of Beasts* (1896) and *Cautionary Tales* (1907).

An emphasis on the physical details of the beast's shape and behavior dominates the essayist's *A Moral Alphabet* (1899), an upbeat bestiary that juxtaposes insect with mammal and snail and waterbeetle with pig and elephant. Composed in light verse, some of the fictional situations reflect the grim imbalance of animals and their natural predators. The bear devours the staunch hunter, leading the fabulist to the moral: "Decisive action in the hour of need/Denotes the Hero, but does not succeed." (Green 1965, 166) On a whimsical note, the ill-fated gnu gains a reprieve from the Boers, who stumble over the animal's ungainly name. The pause is time enough for the gnu to flee. Anticipating Rudyard Kipling's child-pleasing *Just-So Stories for Little Children* (1902), the moral speaks directly to the storyteller's audience: "Child, if you have a rummy kind of name,/ Remember to be thankful for the same." (Green 1965, 167)

Additional models of innovative drawing and fable production flourished throughout Europe:

- Wilhelm Hey's stories and Otto Speckter's lithographs in *Noch fünfzig Fabeln für Kinder* [Fifty More Stories for Children] (1837)

- Wilhelm Busch's *Max und Moritz* (1865)

- Lewis Carroll's *Alice in Wonderland* (1865) and *Through the Looking-Glass and What Alice Found There* (1871)

- Rudyard Kipling's *The Jungle Book* (1894–1895)

- Joseph Jacobs's *The Fables of Aesop* (1889), a reprise of early classic sources hyped as "Phaedrus with trimmings." (Perry 1965, xxxiii)

- Kenneth Grahame's animal adventures in *The Wind in the Willows* (1908)

- Beatrix Potter's *The Tale of Peter Rabbit* (1893), *The Tale of Squirrel Nutkin* (1903), and *The Tale of Samuel Whiskers* (1908), and her return to Aesop and Horace for *Johnny Town-Mouse* (1918) and several unpublished fables in the classic tradition.

Near the end of the nineteenth century, the formal study of fable by Australian folklorist Joseph Jacobs lent a cachet to the genre through erudite treatises on the *Panchatantra*, William Caxton's versions of *Aesop's Fables*, and *Reynard the Fox*.

See also Andersen, Hans Christian; Bierce, Ambrose; Christian fable; Grimm, Jacob and Wilhelm; *Just-So Stories;* Kipling, Rudyard; Krylov, Ivan Andreyevich; Potter, Beatrix; Wilde, Oscar.

Sources Blackham 1985; Blain et al 1990; "Brewer: Dictionary of Phrase and Fable," http://www.bibliomania.com; Briggs 1977, 1991; Calvino 1980; Cooper 1921; Creeden 1994; Dailey 1994; Feinberg 1967; Garland and Garland 1976; Green 1965; Grimm n. d.; Harris 1955; Hobbs 1986; Kohlschmidt 1975; Komroff 1935; Krappe 1964; Leach 1967; Marie de France 1994; Newbigging 1895; Perry 1959; Polley 1978; Rosenberg 1997; Ross 1961; Steinberg 1954; Stephen and Lee 1922.

ORIENTAL FABLE

Parallel to the compilation and discussion of Semitic and Mediterranean fables was the accumulation of Sanskrit beast fables in the *Panchatantra* [Five Chapters], a compendium of Indian folk wisdom begun in the fifth century B.C.E. The meandering framework story was perhaps mutually influential on the Greek version of the genre through interchange of stories along trade routes. These pivotal Hindu entries, accredited to Bidpai, are available only through Arabic translators, who collected the animal stories in the *Kalilah wa Dimnah* (mid-eighth century C.E.). The recension takes its title from the pair of jackals who serve as advisers to the lion king. The work survives in numerous versions, including the thirteenth-century Latin translation of John of Capua, which influenced Ibn Zafar's *Consolation Philtres for the Man of Authority* (1154), a collection of wisdom lore introduced by a set of fictitious characters.

A uniquely Indian fable derived from Buddhist lore in the form of birth stories of Buddha from the fifth century B.C.E. is the jataka—literally a "nativity story"—a scriptural morality tale that recounts one episode from the sage's previous animal lives. Scenes from these pictorial fables adorn relic shrines of Sanchi and Amaravati and of Bharhut, which date them to the third century B.C.E. The Indian poet Aryasura composed one version, *Jatakamala* [Garland of Birth Stories] (200 C.E.), a collection of 550 stories that the nineteenth-century critic Rhys Davids elevates to the most significant of ancient folklore anthologies. In each of these narratives, the exemplary purpose must link with some incident in the Buddha's life. However, as demonstrated by "The Otters and the Jackal," a fool tale about two quarrelers who are cheated by a referee, piety does not exclude wit, humor, and comedy from the texts.

Unlike the typical Aesopic animal tale, which carries an implicit message, the jataka bears an explicit moral appended to the text.

- In "The Discontented Ox" from the *Munika Jataka*, for example, the lesser ox learns that envy of the pig is unwarranted because their owner is fattening him to kill and serve at a family wedding feast. When he realizes the pig's fate, the discontented ox remarks, "It is better a hundred-fold to content ourselves with the food we get, even though it be only grass and straw, for it is a pledge that our lives will not be cut short." (Cooper 1921, 234)

- That altruism is not always beneficial. In the fabulist's words, "With every intention of doing good, the ignorant and foolish succeed only in doing harm." (Cooper 1921, 235)

- A version of Rumi's popular "The Blind Men and the Elephant" appears as "The Judas Tree," in which four princes of Benares study the tree, but each sees it in a different season. The wise king understands that each son's limited experience results in partial understanding of the tree's size, color, texture, and shape.

Intended to glorify and sanctify the Buddha, jataka fables permeated religious discourse throughout the formative years of Buddhism. The style and motivation of these illustrative tales influenced later Indian lore, medieval Christian sermons, Geoffrey Chaucer's *Canterbury Tales* (1387), and the writings of Renaissance storyteller Giovanni Boccaccio and fabulist Gian Francesco Poggio, and flourish in the essence of Rudyard Kipling's three children's collections—*The Jungle Book* (1894), *The Second Jungle Book* (1895), and *Just-So Stories for Little Children* (1902).

Additional western Asian lore, collected from the shepherds of the steppes and dervishes in teahouses as well as from courtiers in mosques and caravanserai, displays the ageless moral teachings of myriad storytellers, each embellishing and individualizing stories from the past. Somadeva, a Kashmiri Brahmin, compiled traditional Sanskrit lore in *Kathasaritsagara*, an anthology presented to Queen Suryamati in 1070. A veritable chapbook of myth, legend, tale, anecdote, riddle, and epic, it contains some animal tales and fables. In the seventh book, *Saktiyasas*, Somadeva narrates the typically brief wisdom stories: "The Wicked Wife," "The Cuckolded Husband," "The Princess with the Parrot," and "The Bull Frightens the Lion," a direct link to "The Monkey Who Pulled out the Wedge," a featured admonitory episode from the *Panchatantra*.

In contrast to the pervasive expression of fable over most of the world, some ancient Asian literatures contain no fable. Chinese writers spurned the barnyard wisdom stories for demeaning humankind as beasts. Rather than the Aesopic lore found in Europe, native tellers preferred human-centered folk morality tales, for example, "The Pear Seed," the story of a hungry man who is hauled before the king for stealing a pear. To establish his relative innocence, he offers a magic seed that will grow a golden pear, but demands a guiltless person to plant it. One by one, the king's courtiers demur because of illicit behaviors. In Chinese tradition, the brief tale establishes a memorable truth about justice and the degree of guilt that all people share.

The late evolution of Oriental fable follows a different path from the European, African, and American canon yet has influenced much of world lore with its charm, grace, and wisdom. Because of its tradition of morality and wisdom literature, China remained devoid of true beast fable until the fourth and sixth centuries C.E., when Buddhist priests imported jataka tales and fables from the *Panchatantra* by way of Indian Buddhism. Put to didactic use, these religious tales, collected under the title *Po-yü ching*, express difficult doctrines. Similar to Europe's eternal battle between Ysengrimus the wolf and Reynard the fox, the interaction of Monkey and Pigsy, protagonist and antagonist of Buddhist monkey tales, forms a cycle of satiric anti-Taoist stories that demean weak, idle, and grasping officials and prelates. One hearty trickster tale, "Fox Outfoxed," tells of a man who meets a fox disguised as a human. The fox divulges that his chief fear is the dog; the man replies that he fears money. After the man sets his dog on the fox-in-man's-clothes, the fox runs away, but returns to pelt his aggressor with bags of money. The story ends humorously with the man crying in terror of more bags of loot lobbed through the air. The story's trickster parallels Uncle Remus's Brer Rabbit, who pulls the same reverse psychology by claiming to fear the briar patch.

Secular Chinese lore reflects the pervasive nature stories that crop up worldwide. An example of river lore is "The Bittern and the Mussel," a standoff between two stubborn combatants who are easily snatched up by a fisherman and carried home for his dinner. A wisdom tale, from Chiang-Yi, "The Fox and the Tiger," depicts the fox as the arch deceiver. At a crucial moment, the tiger places himself behind the fox, who convinces him that the Lord of Heaven ordained a place of honor for the fox. The foolish tiger, impressed by the other animals' disappearance at sight of the fox, misconstrues fear as obeisance. More pointed in its ordering of animals is "The Locust, the Beetle, the Goldfinch, and the Hunter," an illustrative tale that epitomizes the stalker of each. The hunter, who has no natural predator, slips into a ditch, thus startling the goldfinch he intends to shoot. The rapid disappearance of beetle and locust proves the moral that to be too intent on advantage opens the fool to unseen dangers. Another animal tale, "Why the Dog and the Cat Are Enemies," uses *pourquoi* logic to end a story about the cat's perpetual harassment of the dog. This story parallels the ubiquitous motif of animal antipathies that echoes throughout Native American anthologies.

Similar to other national fables, the Chinese demonstrate a reverence for the wisdom that comes from observing and profiting from the behaviors of models in nature. An example from the eighth century is "Cats and Parrots," an anonymous one-line story laden with mirth at human folly: "Early in the eighth century the usurping Empress Wu taught cats and parrots to drink from the same dish, but her belief that she had brought about the millennium was very soon shattered." (*Adventures* 1970, 298) The extreme brevity of the fable forces the reader to search for meaning, which lies in the implication of the last verb. The empress's hopes crash to earth along with the feeding dish. On a larger plane, the story suggests a sobering thought—that human aggrandizement is built on tenuous ground.

Even later to produce fables were the Japanese. Their *Nihon-shoki* [Chronicles of Japan] (ca. 750), *Kohi-ki* [Ancient Records] (ca. 750), and *Konjaku Monogatari* [Tales, Ancient and Modern], a compendium of realistic tales of the Heian period, supposedly composed by courtier Minamoto Takakuni around 1075, are laced with Aesopic fables in which the small and weak use their heads to outfox larger, less acute predators. One example, "A Cat-Hater," is the straightforward story of a resourceful tax collector who subjects the cat hater to a meowing chorus of cats to force him to pay up. A more complex Japanese fable, "The Monkey's Gratitude," departs from obvious cause-and-effect action to a complex interaction between human characters and beasts. After a woman releases the monkey's paw from a clamshell, the monkey snatches her baby and hides it in a tree. Villagers threaten the monkey until they realize that it wards off an eagle that wanted to steal the baby.

Like haiku, Japanese didactic stories are brief but laden with paradox that hint at the meaning of Zen Buddhism. This spare form of Japanese lore attained its peak in the thirteenth and early fourteenth centuries. The introduction of European thought and learning to Japanese culture occurred in the sixteenth century, when Jesuit missionaries imported Aesop's wily animals, a parallel to early Japanese exempla. As a genre, Japanese fable sought the Zen goal of *satori* or enlightenment, the slow dawning of wisdom from experience. An example from a sutra or model of human experience is the story of the man and the vine. Dangling over a precipice with a tiger lurking above him and another tiger awaiting his fall below, the man clings to the vine. As two mice gnaw at the vine, he reaches for a strawberry and marvels at its sweetness. Like Aesopic lore, the implication for human existence lies in the action—the moment of sensory pleasure in the midst of precarious earthly life.

The Western storyteller's conduit for Oriental literature has been the Middle East, through which fables and proverbs have passed on the caravans traveling from China, India, and Afghanistan to the Ottoman Empire. By its connection with Europe, the thin link of eastern Turkey across the Bosporus to its western half has become the loom of history threaded with the many-colored strands of European and Asian lore. Retold by Turks, Kurds, and Armenians, stories from Far Eastern culture have come to life through Islamic tellers, each adapting and shaping where necessary to suit the experience of their listeners, as is the case with Oriental lore in *A Thousand and One Nights*, the most enduring of eclectic anthologies. To remote villagers lacking mail service, libraries, and schools, a vast network of puppetry, riddling, recitation, and kamishibai storytelling has remained a standard form of communication and edification, especially during the high holy days of Ramadan. The Turkish potpourri of lore covers the spectrum of world stories: some about the supernatural, others more pragmatic, enigma fables, fool tales, exempla, bandit lore, and anecdotes.

See also Rumi, Jalal ad-Din ar.

Sources *Adventures in World Literature* 1970; Babbitt 1940; Blackham 1985; "Brewer: Dictionary of Phrase and Fable," http://www.bibliomania.com; Cooper 1921; Creeden 1994; Dailey 1994; Green 1965; Hobbs 1986; Komroff 1935; Krappe 1964; Lang and Dudley 1969; Leach 1967; Livo and Cha 1991; McGreal 1996; Naito 1972; Newbigging 1895; Palmer and Xiaomin 1997; Rosenberg 1997; Shah 1975; Shah 1982; Somadeva 1994; Steinberg 1954; Walker and Uysal 1966; Werner 1995.

 # ORWELL, GEORGE

England's foremost fabulist of the modern era, George Orwell developed animal fable into keen-edged beast lore. Treasured for nonconformist patriotism and dystopian satire, *Animal Farm* (1945), he challenged the limited parameters of Aesopic beast lore by producing the definitive antitotalitarian novel to follow World War II. Born Eric Arthur Blair on July 23, 1903, in Motihari, Bengal, he was the son of Ida Mabel Limouzin, Anglo-French daughter of a teak merchant, and Eric Blair, Sr., a narcotics agent. At age four, he and his two sisters, Margaret and Avril, returned to England, where he entered Eastbourne's St. Cyprian's Boys' School. Homesick and friendless, he despised the petty elitism and favor-currying inherent in the English boarding school system. In his memoir *Such, Such Were the Joys* (1953), he describes language and literature as his escape, especially the satire of Jonathan Swift and the Indian exotica, fables, and *bildungsroman* of Rudyard Kipling, who, like Orwell, was a child of the empire.

During World War I, Orwell remained a pacifist and socialist on international issues while working in social service. He describes his role as sergeant in the Burmese police in *Burmese Days* (1934), in which he pictures himself as an unwilling "pukka sahib." His most anthologized essay, "Shooting an Elephant" (1950), is a first person characterizing the burden of a white man in the unenviable position of peace officer over an alien district of southern Burma. By January 1927, he grew so disillusioned with British racism that he resigned from the imperial police force and took up writing under the pen name George Orwell.

Influenced by Jack London's dystopian treatise *The People of the Abyss* (1903), Orwell followed the pattern of working menial jobs in pub kitchens to observe up close Europe's laboring class, which he pictures in *Down and Out in Paris and London* (1933). While completing *A Clergyman's Daughter* (1935) and *Keep the Aspidistra Flying* (1936), he held down a dismal teaching post at Hawthorne High School for Boys in Hayes, Middlesex, and clerked part time in a Hampstead bookstore. After marrying journalist Eileen O'Shaughnessy in 1936, he managed a pub and grocery store in Wallington, Hertsfordshire. During this mercantile period of his career, a venture into humorless polemics, *The Road to Wigan Pier* (1937), led him to view politicians as untrustworthy and dishonorable.

Orwell's career weaves in and out during periods of peace and military madness. As Europe entered the tense malaise that preceded World War II, Orwell joined Spain's POUM [Partedo Obrero de Unification Marxista], a Marxist Republican militia fighting Generalissimo Francisco Franco and fascism. While serving as war correspondent at the Aragon front, Orwell took a sniper's bullet in the throat in June 1937. Recovered from paralysis and aphasia, he wrote antifascist pieces until a Communist purge forced him and his wife northeast to safety across the Pyrenees Mountains. His passionate anticommunism reached its height in *Homage to Catalonia* (1938). His first successful novel, *Coming Up for Air* (1939), expressed a sincere joy in returning to sanity in England's heartland. In the bucolic setting of a Hertfordshire farm, he raised hens and grew vegetables until Nazi bombings drove him out. While developing longer works, Orwell produced a wartime literary column, "As I Please," for the *London Tribune*. He collected his pre–World War II polemics in *Inside the Whale and Other Essays* (1940) and *The Lion and the Unicorn: Socialism and the English Genius* (1940). No longer content with a benign humanism after axis powers overran Eastern Europe, he sought a commission in the army, which declared him ineligible because of consumptive lungs. He opted for the national militia, served the BBC as their Indian editor, edited the left-wing *Tribune*, and made antitotalitarian broadcasts overseas.

During the dark mid-1940s, Orwell composed *Animal Farm*, a beast fantasy that incorporates his farming experiences with wartime journalism. The unflinching antiauthoritarianism of his prose was a hard sell, but the finished work was worth the effort to locate a publisher. The novel's rustic simplicity conceals a hellish reprise of world experiments in fascism and communism. The era and its stories compromised his weakened condition and cost him permanent bad health. While polishing *Dickens, Dali, and Others: Studies in Popular Culture* in 1946, he suffered a worsening of tuberculosis and the loss of his wife, who died unexpectedly during a hysterectomy.

Orwell was driven to complete his final opus. Frequently bedfast and cognizant that his lung ailment was terminal, he elected to keep his adopted infant, Richard Horatio, and to continue writing. With the help of a sister, the family settled off Scotland's west coast at Barnhill on Jura, Argylls, a windswept, isolated island of the Inner Hebrides. In January 1949, before hospitalization at a sanitarium in Gloucestershire, England, he finished *1984*, a dispirited dystopian classic originally titled *The Last Man in Europe*. During a brief rally in strength, he lambasted the indignities of the English boarding school system, a topic that had nagged him throughout his adult years. Within months of his death, he wed Sonia Mary Brownell and prepared to retire to a Swiss sanitarium when lung hemorrhaging sapped his strength. On his deathbed, he composed both his will and an understated epitaph:

> Here Lies
> Eric Arthur Blair
> Born June 25th 1903
> Died January 21st 1950

His collected essays, polemics, and letters, published in 1968, filled four volumes. Both *Animal Farm* and *1984* were filmed: the first in 1955 as an unsuccessful cartoon diatribe, the second the same year starring Michael Redgrave and Edmond O'Brien. A new version filmed in 1984, starring John Hurt and Richard Burton, deviated from Orwell's antitotalitarian intent.

See also Animal Farm.

Sources Buitehuis and Nadel 1988; Crick 1980; *DISCovering Authors* 1993; Ferrell 1988; Gardner 1987; Miller 1989; Orwell 1946; Reilly 1989; Snodgrass, *Encyclopedia of Satirical Literature* 1997.

PANCHATANTRA

A model of the concept of *niti* or prudent conduct, the *Panchatantra* (or *Pañca-Tantra)* [Five Chapters or Formulas]—alternately identified as *Pancakhyanaka* [Five Short Narratives]—was composed around the third century C.E. from a tradition of Asian fables that parallels and possibly predates the Phrygian lore of Aesop. Begun in oral tellings, the interlinking stories and anecdotes, which include the fables of the Arabian fabulist Lokman (also Lukman or Lokmam or Loqman) (ca. 1100 B.C.E.) found eager listeners in the atria of temples, princely palace chambers, market squares, and the shade of village banyan trees. Tellers ranged from the skilled raconteur to local elders, pious holy men, and everyday narrators. Performers of the native stories sang and piped while mimes and dancers acted the parts. Borne on caravans like treasured silks, spices, and gems, fables from the *Panchatantra* traveled west across Afghanistan and Turkey and across the Bosporus to Europe. A valued commodity, it was the first Indian literature to reach Western cultures.

Ostensibly the work of Brahmin teacher Visnu Sarma or Vishnusharman, a revered teacher of Mahilaropya in southeast India, the collected stories are sometimes credited to Visnugupta Canakya, author of the *Arthasastra*. The body of the *Panchatantra* covers the five elements of courtly policy as defined by the philosopher Kautilya in the third century B.C.E. These topics are universal elements of a full life—gaining friends, losing friends, war and peace, losing property, and personal conduct. A phenomenon in world wisdom literature, the *Panchatantra* influenced Western thought long before mass distribution and was available in print in the major European and West Asian languages by the seventeenth century. Traces of Indian themes and motifs appear in the work of numerous fabulists, for example, the fables of Marie de France and "The Princess and the Pea" from Hans Christian Andersen's stories.

The text of the *Panchatantra* exhibits stock prose and verse parables and animal fables from Indian classics: the *Hitopadesha* [Book of Common Advice] and the Arabic and Persian branches of holy *jatakas* [nativity stories], illustrative stories derived from the incarnations of the Buddha. Alternately known as *The Fables of Bidpai* (also Vidyapati or Pilpay), these Sanskrit tales are the spoken lessons of the savant Bidpai, whose task it is to disseminate *artha* [world wisdom]. The Indian counterpart of the fabulist Aesop, Bidpai is the official court title of the narrator, who produces fable and exemplum as a form of instruction to three callow princelings. Aphoristic in style and tone, the framework of stories lauds native wit over cooperation. Characterization is limited to animals that behave like humans, in the fashion of the animal-headed deities of Egyptian mythology, which bear little resemblance to actual bestial behavior. Like the mismatch of Reynard the fox with his dupe Ysengrimus, the hero jackal contrasts with his cunning the stupidity of slower-witted beasts. A paean to "looking out for number one," the stories countenance self-preservation as a necessary philosophy for the wise survivor.

The body of Indian fables may have accumulated in Kashmir from 100 B.C.E. and is believed to be one of only two compendia to survive the fire that destroyed the great library of Alexandria, Egypt. These collected tales entered the Persian canon around 570 C.E. after court doctor Burzoe translated them into Pahlavi (or Pehlevi), the literary middle Persian language. Of the original Sanskrit and Persian, nothing remains except a Syrian version, *Kalilag wa Dimnag,* and the Arabic equivalent, *Kalilah wa Dimnah*, which blends *Panchatantra* stories with Persian and Manichean folk fables. The latter was translated around 750 C.E. by Ibn al-Muquaffa, a Zoroastrian court scribe and author of *Khwataynamak* [The Book of Kings], a popular Persian mythology. The amusing fable collection was named for the pair of jackals—the scavengers Kalilag/Kalilah and Dimnag/Dimnah—who advise the impulsive lion king. The work, which influenced Spanish lore in the late eleventh century, survives in a cycle of translations and transcreatons:

- the *Kalilah wa Dimnah,* translated into graceful Persian verse (mid-tenth century) by court singer and versifier Rudaki, father of Perso-Isamic poetry

- the sole Greek version, *Stephanites kai Ichnelates* (eleventh century)

- an influential Hebrew translation of the *Panchatantra* by Rabbi Joel (twelfth century)

- *Hitopadesha* or *Hitopadeca* [Good Advice] (twelfth century), a shortened version of the *Panchatantra*

- John of Capua's *Directorium humanae vitae* [Guide for Human Life], a Latin translation of the Arabic branch of Indian lore (thirteenth century), and a subsequent Latin version translated by Raymond de Béziers (fourteenth century)

- the first print version, *Das Buch der Beyspiele* [Bidpay's Book], completed in Germany in 1483

- a Persian translation of cyclic or framework fables, *Anwar-e Suhayli* [The Lights of Canopus] attributed to mystic Hoseyn Wa'ez-e Kashefi of Herat and illustrated by Mogul painters in naturalistic style at the court of Akbar (ca. 1500–1505)

- an Elizabethan English translation, Sir Thomas North's *The Morall Philosophie of Doni* (1570), taken from Antonio Francesco Doni's Italian version, *La Moral Philosophia*, published in 1552

- the Turkish *Hümayun-name* (seventh century)

Thus, available throughout Europe from the eleventh century, Bidpai's *Panchatantra* influenced fable form and style but received less credit than the Greek Aesop and his followers. In some instances of incorrect attribution, stories that derive from Bidpai are mislabeled as Aesopic or classic Greek.

Keyed specifically to Asia, episodes of the *Panchatantra* take place in identifiable cities and geographical locales, for example, "The Monkey Gardeners," a humorous fool tale set in Benares. Other locales range from the Deccan and Brahman forests to Behar, Brahmaputra, the Godavery and Ganges Rivers, and the Mandara Mountains. The anthology includes beast dialogue and argument involving pigeons, tigers, jackals, and black snakes along with human characters, as in "The Brahman and the Pans." The fabulist establishes character with appropriate epithets, including Fierce-Heart the lion and Golden-Skin the Mouse, an admonitory tale set in Champaka featuring the combined wisdom of two beggar priests who outwit a brazen mouse that eats from a begging bowl. Drawing from everyday situations, the stories feature typical Indian characters—the Brahmin, washerman, potter, hermit, Hindu ascetic, and royalty—as well as the nameless thief, a standard villain in all fable.

The text of the *Panchatantra* is a *nitisastra* or training manual that opens on the erudition of Brahmin scholar Visnu Sarma, who identifies himself as 80 years old and free of worldliness. His only pride lies in the education of the reigning king's doltish sons—Vasu, Ugra, and Ananta—whom the tutor trains at their father's command for the demands of *nripanitisastra* or governance. Sarma's method is to remove the boys from the royal setting and take them home with him. There, over a period of six months, he expatiates on the broad array of problems and dilemmas he sets before his inexperienced pupils. The various situations call on wisdom of all kinds—from family and home, society, politics, and practical discrimination of right from wrong or savvy from foolish. These court essentials comprise a worldly wisdom intended to equip the ideal king for *realpolitik* and the greater realm of ethical conduct.

In Book I, the Estrangement of Friends, the framework begins with an unassuming "once upon a time" and continues through stories within stories to explain how the jackal destroys a friendship between the lion and bull. In the beginning, a merchant prince named Varhamana muses on wealth and decides to travel to the distant town of Mathura. On the way, he abandons his bull, which becomes hopelessly mired down. On recovery, however, he flourishes and meets the lion king and his extensive retinue. Among the followers are a pair of jackals who relate "The Monkey and the Wedge," a popular didactic beast fable about meddling. After the monkey loses his genitals when the wedge slips out of a log and the two sides clap shut, the male-centered story concludes that a wise person is careful to mind his own business.

The loose spooling of stories within stories moves effortlessly forward, never halting for too much linkage or heavy didacticism. Jewels of fable emerge whole and perfect in their style and purpose, for example, the story of Bellowing Bull, attendant to Fine Tooth, merchant of Prosperityville. A simple action, the story hinges on the attendant's audacity in sitting in the high priest's chair while the master is engaged in entertaining the king. Hauled out by the scruff, Bellowing Bull despairs and berates himself for suffering public humiliation. The proverb expresses his quandary: ranting over an insult is pointless. "The chickpea may hop up and down frantically; but will it crack the frying pan?" (Sarma 1993, 39) Less sanguine is the trickster tale, "The Crow and the Flamingo." In Bidpai's telling, the naughty crow costs his neighbor his life after the crow drops a pebble in the mouth of a sleeping bowman, then flies away. The archer awakens, sees only the flamingo, and shoots him dead. Quick to point out a character-enhancing human parallel, the fabulist notes, "Be sure you're not making common cause with a scoundrel." (Green 1965, 116)

As with all fable, the *Panchatantra* sets its wealth of stories outside reality, for example, the story of two geese that hold a stick between them to which a turtle clings for transportation to a better habitat and the tale of the jackal that falls into a vat of blue dye and names himself king of animals. In the allegorical style of John Bunyan's *Pilgrim Progress*, place names such as Honey City and people like Shining Power suggest any place that seems too good to be true and any king who flaunts his dominance. Royal subjects tend to be witless or belligerent drones, as found in the allegorical names Dull, Smart Aleck, Little Simple, and Wheelbearer. Paralleling Aesop, the Asian narrator transposes human figures into animal forms. The figures identify easily with human foibles: the proud lion king, faithful mongoose, wily jackal, egotistic lapwing, pompous donkey, intrusive monkey, and fierce crocodile. The narrator's frequent framing of aphorism links individual fault with warning and counsel. For example:

- The ass, who bemoaned the loss of his tail, was in far greater affliction when he saw himself without ears . . . whoever he be that takes no reason for his guide, wanders about, and at length falls. (Komroff 1935, 133)

- 'Tis easy to acquire wealth . . . but a difficult thing to expend it well. Riches many times prove fatal. (Komroff 1935, 147)

- What is bred in the bone will never come out of the flesh; neither can anything come out of a vessel but what is put into it. (Komroff 1935, 160)

- Princes are like serpents; formed coil upon coil, encased in smooth, sinuous scales; cruel, tortuous in movement, menacingly fierce, savage, yielding only to magical arts. (Sarma 1993, 23)

- A horse, a weapon, a text, a lute, a voice, a man and a woman—they perform ill, or well, according to who masters them. (Sarma 1993, 27)

- The weak, if wary and mistrustful, can easily withstand the strongest; the strong who are foolish and trustful, may be overthrown by the weakest. (Sarma 1993, 33)

- Until you possess full information about someone's conduct, lineage, strength, make no alliance with him. (Sarma 1993, 361)

- In union there is strength, a favorite aphorism of Mohandas Gandhi, a world-famous Indian nationalist leader and proponent of passive resistance. (Cooper 1921, 209)

The narrator, retaining his air of wisdom and good intent, concludes with a restatement of his treatise's purpose and motivation: "A good and true poet aims to be of service to others here in this world, and to lead the way to the World of Eternal Light, as the wise and learned declare." (Sarma 1993, 435) Overall, these early animal tales expound themes of patronage, self-reliance, adaptability, ingenuity, guile, and pragmatism. In the *Kalilah wa Dimnah*, the Arabic translator alters the original stories to include a trial and punishment for the trickster Dimna. Like the harsh endings to Aesopic fable, Dimna must starve to death for his treachery, a punishment arising from stringent Islamic morality codes.

In current times, the *Panchatantra*, called the mother of Asian folklore, proves as resilient as the ancient lore of the Greeks, Hebrews, and Babylonians. In 1914, Johannes Hertel's version prefaced a lifetime of work on the corpus with a tribute to some 200 versions available in 50 languages. He praised the collection's emergence in all civilized nations and its triumph over language, custom, and religious bias. A 1925 version by Arthur W. Rhyder returned to the original Sanskrit text for maximum accuracy. In the late twentieth century, Parisian storyteller Abbi Patrix perpetuates Indian lore in bilingual French and English performances for radio, film, and theater. Drawing on masks, mime, and theatrics, he presents "Le Compagnon" [The Companion], a solo stage piece adapted from *Tales from Norway*, and "The War of the Crows and the Owls," an Indian story from the *Panchantantra*, which he has recorded on audiocassette.

See also Oriental fable.

Sources Banerji and Chakraborty 1991; Beck, http://www.west.net; Cooper 1921; Cowen 1989; Green 1965; Komroff 1935; Hobbs 1986; Krappe 1964; Lang and Dudley 1969; McGreal 1996; Miller and Snodgrass 1998; Patrix 1995; "Sanskrit Literature," http://www.connect.net; Sarma 1993.

 # PHAEDRUS

The first Latin author to translate the works of Aesop from Greek, Phaedrus (or Phaeder, the French equivalent) is, in style and substance, more sparkling entertainer than sober moralist. Far from a master of the genre, he declares in Book IV of his fables his obligation to Aesop with a straightforward delineation between originator and adaptor: "Invenit ille, nostra perfect manus" [He invented the form; my hand perfected it]. (Perry 1965, 336–337) Critics revere Phaedrus for separating fable from the typically Greek element of didactic aphorism or wisdom lore into an independent, amusing literary genre more suited to the court Latin of the early empire. Until his time, anthologizers amassed fables essentially for utilitarian purpose—to be used as reference repositories, much like apothegms collected in Bartlett's *Familiar Quotations* or handbooks consulted by sermonizers, historians, and after-dinner speakers as sources of light anecdote, satiric models, or exempla. Like myth, fable attained the rank of literature only by virtue of being rendered as poetry. In prose, it was merely raw anecdote. In the urbane style of the playwright Terence, Phaedrus published five artistically composed books of approximately 150 verse fables to be enjoyed as literature. His instincts proved right—his books became first-century best-sellers.

The fables themselves, composed in succinct lines of iambic senarii or six-foot lines, demonstrate the Aesopic beast lore typical of Phaedrus's Greek predecessor. Less composer than editor and innovator, Phaedrus cannibalized the *Aesopia* (ca. early third century B.C.E.), a slim volume of fables compiled by Demetrius Phalereus, a learned Athenian philosopher, orator, and antiquarian exiled to Alexandria near the end of the fourth century B.C.E. Although the subject matter is not original, Phaedrus's clarity and simplicity are a refreshing break from the weighty, sober-sided reports, speeches, elegies, and essays of his day. His themes, motifs, and *pseudapologi* or stylized morals, which ridicule the social and political foibles of the Roman Empire's early years, appear to have been read among the powerful and raised a stir when their gibes hit on a painful truth. Although Seneca and other learned critics of the day ignored Phaedrus's facile versions, readers adored them.

Phaedrus's origins pay tribute to the self-styled satirist. Born a slave around 15 B.C.E. in Thrace on the Black Sea, in modern Bulgaria or Romania, where Aesop may have lived, he claimed in the prologue to Book III to have been born on the Pierian Mountain of Thessaly, the home of the Muses and of the mythic singers Linus and Orpheus. Perhaps the son of a schoolmaster, as conjectured by biographer and Italian scholar Attilio de Lorenzi, the fabulist was well educated, possibly in Italy, in the Roman province of Macedonia, or both. Manumitted in boyhood, he may have come to Rome in 11 B.C.E. as part of the retinue of General Lucius Calpurnius Piso Frugi, who returned victorious from quelling a two-year revolt in Thrace. It is conjectured that Phaedrus's fluency in Greek and Latin made him a likely *paedagogus* or school companion, a job for a slave entrusted with the welfare and protection of a noble's son to and from class. As such, Phaedrus may have attended Lucius, the grandson of Augustus, Rome's first emperor, during sessions at the school of Verrius Flaccus on the Palatine and, simultaneously, enriched his own education by listening to lectures and observing drills and recitations.

Elevated beyond his original status in Thrace, Phaedrus spent his adult life in Rome and at Tiberius's summer villa at Cape Misenum near Naples as a freedman attached to the imperial staff. At the imperial library, he had access to Aesop, not in the original, but true to the original example, which he termed in Book IV "fabulis quas Aesopias, non Aesopi" [Aesopic, but not by the name Aesop]. (Perry 1965, xxxiv) With an unhindered view of palace peccadilloes, he gathered anecdotes and incriminating situations that made for witty fable. For example, in the opening entry of Book V, he maligns Demetrius Poliorcetes, mistakenly identified as "the Phalerean," a self-absorbed Athenian tyrant who enjoyed the fawning of sycophants. When confronted by a mincing, eyelash-batting catamite, Demetrius demands to know the name of the obvious homosexual in his audience. His attendants provide the name of the famous author Menander, a giant among playwrights well known for his comedies. Demetrius quickly downshifts, muttering "Homo . . . fieri non potest formosior" [No man could be comelier]. (Perry 1965, 352)

Phaedrus's ease among royals apparently ended when he was in his mid-forties. About 31 C.E., Books I and II of his *Fabulae Aesopiae* angered Lucius Aelius Sejanus, an influential palace janizary and manipulator of the emperor Tiberius, Augustus's successor. Notorious for conniving and paranoia, Sejanus had been praetorian prefect since 14 C.E. and perhaps had seen Phaedrus rise in notoriety for derisive humor. From Phaedrus's animal stories, Sejanus inferred taunts and parodies of his enlarged position at court. After he reestablished Tiberius at an estate in Capri on Italy's west coast, he either had the books confiscated or their publication suppressed. In a self-serving act, Sejanus, when accused of poisoning Tiberius's son Drusus, pressed false charges that led to the banishment of other members of Tiberius's family. Although Sejanus was found out and executed for sedition, Books III–V of Phaedrus's fables remained out of favor until Tiberius's death in 37 C.E. or perhaps even into the reigns of Claudius or Nero, Rome's third and fourth emperors. Impaired by old age, Phaedrus lived long enough to enjoy limited literary renown as Aesop's imitator. Martial and Avianus were the first writers to comment on the empire's own fabulist. Writing over a half century after the contretemps that silenced the clever fables, Martial, in Book II, verse 20 of his *Epigrammata* (ca. 85 C.E.), speaks of "inprobi iocos Phaedri" [the jokes of wicked Phaedrus]. ("Martial *Epigrammiton*," n. p.)

Unlike Horace, Ennius, Lucilius, Lucianus, Avianus, and other Latin authors who only dabbled in fable, Phaedrus limited himself to the one genre, which suited his style and didactic ends. He transposed the stories from Greek prose into incisive, concentrated stanzas of Latin iambics, of which 94 are extant. His most famous stories are familiar situations to readers of Aesop: the lion's share, the purses of faults that hang before and behind the carrier, the fox who spurns sour grapes, and the ape judge who makes a mockery of jurisprudence. Phaedrus's fables remained in vogue throughout Europe and Britain into the Middle Ages. Showcased in a popular compendium known as *Romulus* (tenth century), the mythical founder of Rome, 34 of Phaedrus's works survived in prose translation. Niccolo Perotti and his son Pyrrhus, fifteenth-century humanists, reproduced the Latin fables for the church and simplified them as a text for Niccolo's nephew. In the eighteenth century, a manuscript of 64 stories nearly doubled the world's collection of Phaedrian fable. In 1760, translator Christopher Smart's *Poetical Translation of the Fables of Phaedrus* rendered 64 Latin models in octosyllabic couplets and issued them in a reader for students. Smart intended that the young Latin student "by this explanatory version and parsing index will get the drift of the author's meaning, learn his syntax, and make a better progress in the tongue than he would by a mere prose translation, which is rather too great a help." (Widdows 1992, xxii) A subsequent discovery in the Vatican archives produced another 30 Phaedrian fables, which were published in 1831, bringing the total to 94.

The organization of Phaedrus's five books is simple and orderly. Beneath the title *Phaedri Augusti Liberti Fabularum Aesopiarum* [The Aesopic Fables of Phaedrus the Freedman of Augustus], the author inserts a modest four-sentence prologue crediting Aesop as his source but claiming the style as his own. Phaedrus characterizes the poems as "polivi versibus senariis" or "polished in senarian verses," a description of the six-foot meter common to the stage, which, to the English speaker, tends to fall into easy, readable double ranks of threes. The thirteenth line of "The Frogs Asked for a King" demonstrates the tendency of six-foot lines to break into halves after the third beat: "Pater deorum risit atque illis dedit" [The father of the gods laughed and granted them (a sliver of wood)]. (Perry 1965, 192–194) The poet enhances the separation by the internal rhyme of two verbs, laughed and granted. However, the enterprising poet does not allow the overall rhythm to fall into rockinghorse tedium. He inserts lively conversations, as found in "The Wolf and the Lamb," a portentous exchange freighted with implications for the weak who inadvertantly encounter the strong. To the wolf's two direct questions, the lamb provides plausible answers establishing innocence:

> "Cur" inquit "turbulentam fecisti mihi
> Aquam bibenti?" laniger contra timens:
> "Qui possum, quaeso, facere quod quaereris, lupe?
> A te decurrit ad meos haustus liquor."
> Repulsus ille veritatis viribus
> "Ante hos sex menses male" ait "dixisti mihi."
> Respondit agnus "Equidem natus non eram."
> "Pater hercle tuus."
> ["Why," said he, "have you stirred the water where I am drinking?" Fearfully, the woolly one ventured: "Pray, how can I, wolf, be guilty of the thing you charge? The water flows from you downstream to where I drink." Stymied by the strength of truth, the wolf exclaimed, "Six months ago you cursed me." "Indeed," replied the lamb, "at that time I was not yet born." "Well then, I swear, it was your father."] (Perry 1965, 190–193)

Thus, the first fable concludes in a swift, violent death that derives from nature's natural enmity between the lamb and the predatory wolf. Phaedrus appends a single *epimythium,* or moral, directed to similarly predatory people "qui fictis causis innocentes opprimunt" [who invent false charges by which to oppress the innocent]. (Perry 1965, 192–193)

The remaining 30 fables of Book I cover the standard Aesopic range of animal situations in natural settings: a strutting jackdaw and a peacock, the dog carrying a haunch of meat as it crosses the river, and a complex story involving a cow, nanny goat, sheep, and lion. In the sixth entry, Phaedrus introduces "Ranae ad Solem" [The Frogs Complain against the Sun] with a nod to the master, Aesop, who selects the fable to suit a wedding party at the home of a thief, who is his neighbor. The fabulist's sly jest warns that the sun's injustices are bad enough while he is a bachelor. The frog speaker names the sun's slights against earthlings, then concludes rhetorically, "quidnam futurum est si crearit liberos?" [What will happen if he has children?]. (Perry 1965, 198–199)

Not all Phaedrus's efforts are so facile or neatly balanced. "Vulpis ad Personam Tragicam" [The Fox before the Tragic Actor's Mask], which is limited to a one-line story and a one-line *epimythium*, lacks the subtlety and conversational tone of more pungent fables. The eighth fable, "Lupus et Grauis" [The Wolf and the Crane], demonstrates a worse pattern in Phaedrus's style: it opens with a tedious, overlong *promythium*, or introduction, that extends for three clauses: "This is directed to those to whom Luck has granted honor and glory, but who has denied them common sense." The ninth fable, "Asinus et Leo Venantes" [The Ass and the Lion Go Hunting], encumbered with another of Phaedrus's pedestrian forewords, prefaces a series of three fables that limp into action on verbose prefatory remarks. Briefly, Phaedrus breaks the pattern with Fable 14, "Ex Sutore Medicus" [From Cobbler to Physician], a clever drama about an impostor posing as a doctor. The fable winds down to a keen jab at his gullible clients.

Phaedrus's style in Book I approaches artistry with Fable 18, "Mulier Parturiens" [The Women Giving Birth], a folk yarn tipped with earthy humor. To the anxious husband urging the laboring pregnant wife to recline on their bed, she caustically replies that it seems unwise to lay her troubles on the place where they were conceived. The pun on *conceptum* [conceived] elevates the fable a step above more mundane rhetoric. In contrast, subsequent stories—"Canes Famelici" [The Famished Dogs], "Canis Fidelis" [The Faithful Dog], "Canes et Crocodile" [The Dogs and the Crocodiles], and "Rana Rupta et Bos" [The Frog Who Burst Herself and the Cow]—revert to the plainspoken, unadorned, often violent nature lore that began the book. Near the end of the collection, Phaedrus resorts to the *agon* or contest fable, a dramatized debate between rivals in nature. Popularized in the Babylonian lore of 1800 B.C.E., the resilient form remains vivid in "Asinus Inridens Aprum" [The Ass Insults the Boar], a ribald one-upsmanship in which the ass compares his penis to the boar's snout. The final two fables—"Ranae Metuentes Taurorum Proelia" [The Frogs Fearing the Battle of the Bulls] and "Milvus et Columbae" [The Kite and the Doves] echo the fabulist's sentiment that safety for lesser animals is an uncertain commodity.

Phaedrus's second work varies in size and style from Book I. Opening on an extended *prologus*, the author again defers to Aesop as the progenitor of fable and states the purpose of Aesopic fable: "quam corrigatur error ut mortalium acuatque sese diligens industria" [that the mistakes of mortals may be corrected, and that a close study of fable may sharpen the wits]. Phaedrus asks that the repetition of old fables may stand on its own merits and promises to retain the spirit of the *senis* [old man]. Phaedrus announces his intention to add to the master's fables for the sake of variety and hopes that the reader will graciously accept his additions. With a slick segue, he closes with a recommendation for brevity and leads into the theme of generosity, the subject of his first fable, "Iuvencus, Leo et Praedator" [The Bullock, the Lion, and the Robber].

The remaining seven fables and epilogue lack a clear organization and purpose. To the opening animal fable, Phaedrus adds two stories about human folly, the second a pointed retort that Aesop makes to a man who stanches a dog bite with bread and tosses the blood-soaked crust to the dog to deter it from further attack. Aesop upbraids the victim with a sensible comment: "Don't let any more dogs see you doing this, lest they devour us alive when they learn that guilt is rewarded in this way." (Perry 1965, 237) Unlike the verbose maxims that mark the wisdom of Book I's fables, Phaedrus slices the maxim to four words—"Successus improborum plures allicit" [The evildoers' success lures many others]. The unusual gesture of hurling bloodied enticements to a dog may underlie a developing situational satire in Phaedrus that alarmed the evil Sejanus, who had ample reason to fear verse aimed at the bloodthirsty.

With Fable 4, Phaedrus returns to beast lore, then sets a subsequent fable in a contemporary time and place. In "Tib. Caesar ad Atriensem" [Tiberius Caesar to a Flunky], set at the royal country house at Misenum, an overdressed house servant makes a show of watering down the dusty path the emperor treads. By way of rebuke, Caesar accuses the man of simulating real labor and warns that emancipation will require much more work than a mere show of busyness. Juxtaposed to this vignette of a cynical, glib emperor is the fable about a turtle whom the eagle and crow smash against the rocks. The two fables serve as alternate views of the powerless: the ingratiating servant and the helpless turtle. In both instances, the victims, man and turtle, have little hope of extricating themselves from the grasp of the mighty. Hard on Fable 7 comes "Muli Duo et Latrones" [The Two Mules and the Thieves], an echo of the previous situations that ends in mutilation of a pack animal. Phaedrus notes that the mule loaded with barley is spared, but the overproud bearer of treasure is a clear target for thieves. The final fable, "Cervus ad Boves" [The Stag Confronting Oxen], sounds once more the warning that the master will watch carefully over his possessions.

Book II closes on an unsuccessful subterfuge that perhaps laid Phaedrus open to imperial criticism. With an epilogue flaunting the statue that Athenians raised to the slave Aesop, Phaedrus, obviously courting praise, flagrantly struts his own accomplishments and sets himself up for a fall. He states that, since he couldn't be the father of fable, he wrote fables, not out of envy of the originator, but out of emulation. (Perry 1965, 248) In an overstated defense of his second Aesopic collection, Phaedrus rather shakily summons cultivated readers to enjoy his efforts on the grounds that by elevating a homegrown poet, Latium can match the literary excellence of Greece. He envisions the alternative to praise—the disaffection of *rabulis* [ranting lawyers] who carp at their betters. Should such ill fortune fall on the fabulist, he stands ready to accept exile until Fortune is shamed by such a verdict.

For whatever reason—either inadvertently self-inflicted or wrongfully thrust upon him by Sejanus—a backlash against Phaedrus suppressed his last three fable collections, which contain 55 stories or over half of his canon. The silence in the interim cost Rome the joy of classic works of native literature. Composed after Sejanus's fall in 31 B.C.E., Book III, which opens on Phaedrus's dedication of his fables to an unknown Eutychus, introduces a worthy addition to Roman lore and a substantial amount of autobiographical commentary about the fabulist. Phaedrus complains that Rome's haughty literary circle shuns him, and he archly compares his gift of fables to the Greek spy Sinon's presentation of the Trojan Horse to King Priam. The purpose of this ploy appears in the explanation: the slave fabulist, who dares not speak directly about the foibles of the upper classes, projects his criticisms onto their actions in impersonal fables. The genre suits Phaedrus, who describes Aesop's literary footpath as an expanding highway broadened by topics springing from Roman society. In a stinger aimed at the departed Sejanus, Phaedrus notes that people who find themselves ridiculed on the pages of fable fall victim to their own bad consciences. Posing as the *naif*, the fabulist claims to have no particular object in mind but rather to aim his maxims at humanity in general. With a self-important flourish, he draws his prologue to a close by noting that he, more than the outsiders Aesop and Anacharsis, a sixth-century Scythian prince, should acquire everlasting fame and glory for his works, even though he remained a Thracian outsider and never achieved Roman citizenship.

The skill of the preliminary books appears newly honed in Book III, which transcends the confines of Aesopic form. Phaedrus composes clever fables, yet chooses an obscure but curious offering for the initial entry. Permeating "Anus ad Amphoram" [The Old Woman Addresses the Wine Jar] is a wistful longing. After inhaling the rich aroma of lees at the bottom of an empty amphora, she murmurs, "O suavis anima, quale in te dicam bonum antehac fuisse, tales cum sint relquae!" [Ah, sweet ghost, how good you must have been before, whenever your remains are so excellent!]. (Perry 1965, 258–259) The moral deliberately conceals the fabulist's purpose with the comment that people who know him understand the reference. Scholars conjecture that he may have been suffering the onset of old age, which he refers to in the epilogue with *"nam vita morti propior est cotidie"* [For life is each day nearer to death]. (Perry 1965, 292–293) A politically motivated alternative suggests that he regrets the downfall of the Roman republic, which collapsed with the death of Julius Caesar in 44 B.C.E. and was supplanted after a decade-long civil war by Caesar's nephew Octavius, who had proclaimed himself Emperor Augustus before Phaedrus was born.

The collection of animal subjects in Book III returns to the classic fable mode with "The Fly and the Mule," "The Wolf to the Dog," "The Cockerel and the Pearl," "The Panther and the Shepherds," and "The Dog to the Lamb," a troubling tale about a newborn animal whose mother, in Roman tradition, exposes it and leaves it to die. A mélange of beasts and humans extends from ordinary discourse to outré confrontations between cicada and owl and a wasp's judgment over bees and drones, but the majority of topics refer to people, many of whom are identified as historical figures. In Fables 3, 5, 14, and 19, Phaedrus pictures Aesop himself, referring to him as "naris emunctae senex" [an old man of keen discernment] and relishing his quick-witted rejoinders to fools and busybodies. (Perry 1956, 262–263) Phaedrus also lauds Socrates's loyalty to true friends and remarks, "Vulgare amici nomen sed rara est fides" [Common is the name of friend, but rare is loyalty]. (Perry 1965, 270–271) The entry loses its grasp of fable and audience by Phaedrus's hasty, intrusive exclamation that, if he could equal Socrates's fame, he would gladly suffer his death, a savage state execution by hemlock poisoning for allegedly misleading youth by defaming the gods. The comment is obviously self-serving in that Phaedrus, who was a palace servant rather than a teacher, risked nothing that approached the self-sacrifice of Socrates.

In answer to critics who accuse Phaedrus of foreshortened or sparse fables, the fabulist composes "The Poet, on Believing and Not Believing." The 60-line verse introduces a grim crime scenario with reminders of the wretched deaths of Hippolytus and Cassandra, one a suicide and the other a murder victim in Greek mythology. The action of the fable describes a character who, like William Shakespeare's Othello, falls under the evil influence of another character. The freedman who slanders the man's wife sets off a chain of events that ends with the man's murder of his son and the subsequent suicide of the man and trial of his wife before Rome's Centumviral Court. Phaedrus cites *divo Augusto* [the divine Augustus] as the Solomon-like judge who determines that the woman deserves no blame but rather pity for being deprived of son and husband in one fearful night. (Perry 1965, 274–275) Perhaps referring to an actual murder-suicide, Phaedrus expounds that perplexing human strivings tend toward different ends.

A succession of more succinct and edgier prefaces, texts, and morals lifts Book III to the forefront of Phaedrus's literary offerings. The appearance of the bees and the drones before the claims court in Fable 13 exemplifies a clever on-the-spot separation of sheep from goats. By ordering the bees and drones to create test hives to determine who originated the hive in the oak tree, the wasp who serves as judge precipitates the drones' refusal. A well-stated fable in true Aesopic form, it neglects to add the customary moral. However, other texts supply Book III with memorable maxims. From applying Aesop's morals to his own time, the Roman fabulist could state with authority:

- "Solet a despectis par referri gratia" [Those who are scorned usually pay in the same coin]. (Perry 1965, 260–261)
- "Successus ad perniciem multos devocat" [Success invites many to their ruin]. (Perry 1965, 264–265)
- "Quam dulcis sit libertas" [How sweet is liberty]. (Perry 1965, 266–267)
- "Id demum est homini turpe quo meruit pati" [What is truly shameful to a man is what he deserves to suffer]. (Perry 1965, 278–279)
- "Noli adfectare quod tibi non est datum [Don't strive for a talent that has not been given]. (Perry 1965, 288–289)

Phaedrus also sets before the reader curiosities, such as the conundrum "Periculosum est credere et non credere" [It is dangerous alike to believe and not to believe], and the occasional frivolity, particularly "The Cockerel and the Pearl," which ends with a dedication to those who don't appreciate the fabulist. (Perry 1965, 272–273)

Comprised of 26 fables, Book IV takes up the subject of the epilogue in the preceding book, which claims that Phaedrus ended his work to leave for others some fables for restating. To Particulo, the unidentified dedicatee, the fabulist asserts that his new compendium features new themes. Treating once more a blend of human, animal, and divine subjects, the text includes a popular proverb, "The Mountain in Labor," and two of Aesop's oft-cited fables, "The Lion King" and "The Fox and the Grapes." The latter, translated by Christopher Smart, presents Phaedrus at his best:

> An hungry fox with fierce attack
> Sprang on a vine, but tumbled back,
> Nor could attain the point in view,
> So near the sky the bunches grew.
> As he went off, "They're scurvy stuff,"
> Says he, "and not half ripe enough—
> And I've more reverence for my tripes
> Than to torment them with the gripes."
> For those this tale is very pat
> Who lessen what they can't come at.
> (Widdows 1992, xxiii)

This rendition in couplets of iambic tetrameter demonstrates the concise, taut dramatic scene at the heart of fable and the fabulist's quick leap to a didactic maxim, which Smart marks with an idiomatic twist in the final phrase.

Throughout Phaedrus's fourth book, Aesop himself reappears. As counselor and judge, he narrates the sage fable "On the Fortunes of Men" and settles the matter of "The Enigmatic Will," which leaves to three dissimilar daughters the requirement to pay a large sum to their mother. Adjacent to small treasures of fable, such as "On the Faults of Men" and "The Fox and the Goat," Phaedrus inserts the witty "The Bearded Nanny Goats," a send-up of Ennius's parody of Euripides's *Medea*. He also includes the frail fables "The Evils of Wealth" and "The Serpent at the Blacksmith's," both unsuccessful in dramatic tension and elucidation of philosophy. In a show of virtuosity, Phaedrus rallies with two clever survival tales about the poet Simonides and supplies "The Thief and His Lamp" with three unrelated maxims, all drawn from the theft of light from Jupiter's holy altar.

Phaedrus's final collection of ten fables displays the uneven array of narrative. The allegorical fable "Time," which departs true fable form, turns on an extended metaphor rather than standard narrative. "Prince, the Flutist" also violates the usual form and brevity to describe the arrangement of the Roman theater and the ejection of an egotist from the stage. A poorly worded beast fable, "The Bull and the Calf," precedes the final animal story, "The Old Man and the Hunter," which completes Phaedrus's output without an epilogue. With a brief spark of wit, the fabulist rounds out the story of the old dog who has lost his grip with a timely remonstrance: "quo fuimus lauda, si iam damnas quod sumus" [Praise me for what I was, if you condemn me now for what I am]. (Perry 1956, 368–369) With an obscure comment to Philetus, a character or colleague heretofore unmentioned, Phaedrus implies private reasons for his last fable.

A coda to Phaedrus's canon derives from Perotti's appendix, a transcription of 30 additional fables from a manuscript now lost. These five additional books extend the canon with the same irregular mix of woods lore in "The Beaver" and "When the Bear Gets Hungry," the short story of "The Widow and the Soldier," myths about Mercury, Jupiter, Prometheus, Ixion, Sisyphus, the Danaides, Juno, and Venus, historical reference to Aesop, Socrates, and Pompey the Great, and a prophesy spoken by Apollo's oracle. Overall, the combined canon of Phaedrus plus Perotti's appendix provides the reader an anthology of folk wisdom, prevailing misogyny, comic episode, biographical anecdote, animal lore, and glimpses of the classical Mediterranean world in theater, law court, birthing chamber, inn, marketplace, and doctor's office. Phaedrus gives in to a bemused curiosity about all facets of life and maintains the pessimist's belief that the weak always remain victims of the strong and the humble must bow to the exalted.

Restated by Jean de La Fontaine, seventeenth-century French versions— "Le Loup et le Chien" [The Wolf and the Dog], "Le Vieux Chat et la jeune Souris" [The Old Cat and the Young Mouse], "Les Deux Pigeons" [The Two Pigeons]— published in 1694, retain their witty twist and appropriately virtuous morals, which French schoolchildren still inscribe in their copybooks to memorize and recite. In a generous gesture of goodwill for his reliance on Phaedrus's anthology, fabulist La Fontaine declared himself incapable of imitating the elegance and brevity implicit in the Latin language. Modestly, he claimed, "J'ai cru qu'il fallait en recompense égayer l'ouvrage plus qu'il n'a fait" [I believed that I should cheer up the work more than he did]. (La Fontaine 1954, n. p.)

Sources Bowder 1980; Hadas 1954; Hammond and Scullard 1992; Komroff 1935; Krappe 1964; La Fontaine 1954; Lewis 1996; "Martial *Epigrammiton*," http://www.gmu.edu; Perry 1952, 1965; Stinton 1979; Widdows 1992.

 # POTTER, BEATRIX

The creator of Peter Rabbit, Helen Beatrix Potter is a perennial favorite among classic writers and illustrators of children's animal stories. The child of Helen Leech and barrister Rupert Potter, she was born July 28, 1866, in South Kensington and enjoyed the substantial wealth that her family received from their inherited shares of the Lancashire cotton industry. Nonetheless, she was a solitary, unhappy child who grew up under conventional middle-class standards in the upstairs nursery at Bolton Gardens and, with her younger brother Bertram, was tutored by governesses. She relished weekends at the family's country estate in Cumbria and visits to her paternal grandmother at Camfield Place, Essendon, where she was free of strict parental supervision and the monotony of the nursery. Like novelists Charlotte and Emily Brontë, Potter read widely at will from English classics, including the fables of Jean de La Fontaine. She taught herself to draw and paint and kept a private menagerie of rabbits, field mice, hedgehog, and snails to study and draw. With the encouragement of one nursemaid, she made trips to the Natural History Museum to sketch biota.

On her own, she learned to dissect animal specimens and to classify fossils and fungi.

Doomed to spinsterhood, Potter willingly accepted her father's domination. In 1891, to entertain Noel Moore, a former governess's son recovering from scarlet fever, she began composing story-letters about her pets, which she illustrated in muted pastel watercolors. These anecdotal missives presaged the bunny families and bucolic beasts that spawned an English literary phenomenon. She presented one scholarly paper on natural habitats, "The Germination of the Spores of Agaricineae" (1897), to the Linnean Society of London. In 1901, she published privately 250 copies of her best-seller, *The Tale of Peter Rabbit*, and followed the next year with *The Tailor of Gloucester*, which features drawings of a real cottage in Gloucester, and, in 1903, *The Tale of Squirrel Nutkin*, with drawings she made on holiday at Herbert's Island, Keswick.

During the preliminary stages of her career, Potter's expectations remained guarded. To her friend Freda Moore she wrote:

> Your mouse-book is not printed yet; but the coloured edition of Peter Rabbit is ready, & I think it is to be in the shops this week; if there are any book shops about Wandsworth you must look, whether it is in the windows. The publisher has sold more copies than he printed (6,000) so he is going to print another edition at once. (Potter 1966, 48)

Encouraged by the Frederick Warne publishing house, she produced 24 additional titles over a span of 30 years, each child-sized to make it easy for children to hold and read. Financial independence preceded liberation from her father

A poster for the MGM movie *Peter Rabbit and Tales of Beatrix Potter*, performed by dancers of the Royal Ballet.

and a short-lived betrothal to Frederick Warne's son Norman, who died within months from leukemia. Her parents were relieved at the end of her engagement, for they ranked Norman a tradesman, a status below the Potters' social rank.

On her own, Potter purchased a seventeenth-century property, Hill Top Farm, Westmoreland, the rustic setting of *The Pie and the Patty Pan*. Reveling in independence and creative zest, she reached a peak of creativity in her thirties and forties with publication of *Jeremy Fisher* (1906), *Tom Kitten* (1907), *Jemima Puddleduck* (1908), *Samuel Whiskers, or the Roly-Poly Pudding* (1908), *Ginger and Pickles* (1909), *Mr. Tod* (1912), and *Pigling Bland* (1913). The courtesies of village life and the importance of responsibility and discipline, the focuses of her animal tales, reflect Victorian civility, which flourished among well-bred people into the Edwardian era. On the pragmatic side, she learned the exigencies and cycles of farmwork and married a local attorney, William "Willie" Heelis. With his concurrence, she bred Herdwick sheep and, in 1930, became the first female president of the Herdwick Sheepbreeder's Association.

In 1918, Potter, immersed in the demands of livestock, turned from creative animal lore to pure Aesopic fables for *The Tale of Johnny Town-Mouse*, a retelling of Horace's popular "The Town Mouse and the Country Mouse." She continued in the genre with *The Tale of the Birds and Mr. Tod* (1919) and *Grasshopper Belle and Susan Emmett* (1919), the latter easily identified as adaptations of Aesop's "The Ant and the Grasshopper." These late efforts proved so profitable and satisfying that Potter also completed *The Tale of Jenny Crow*, a blend of five ancient fables. Set in the town of Hawkshead in the Lake District, *The Tale of Johnny Town-Mouse* pictures elements of Potter's life—her plowhorse Diamond, the cook, her husband's golf clubs, and architectural trimmings and ironwork. She dedicated the story to "Aesop in the shadows" and, in Aesopic style, revealed to young readers the importance of table manners, deference to guests, and self-restraint. (Potter 1989, 318) At the climax of the contrast between town and country, she speaks through the countrified Timmy Willie: "When it rains, I sit in my little sandy burrow and shell corn and seeds from my Autumn store. I peek out at the throstles and blackbirds on the lawn, and my friend Cock Robin. And when the sun comes out again, you should see my garden and the flowers—roses and pinks and pansies—no noise except the birds and bees, and the lambs in the meadows." (Potter 198, 325). The contentment of the country mouse is no doubt Potter's contentment, a low-key enjoyment of rural life that permeates her canon. She seems pleased to speak from experience in the *epimythium,* or moral, which declares, "One place suits one person, another place suits another person. For my part I prefer to live in the country, like Timmy Willie." (Potter 1989, 330)

At Potter's death at Sawrey on December 22, 1943, some 4,000 acres of her Lake District properties passed into the National Trust, a tribute to her support of England's green space and wild animals and birds. Her fables thrived in numerous translations, including Latin, and survive in calendars, stuffed animals, fabrics, pottery, filmstrips, audiotape, videotape, and an MGM film, *Peter Rabbit and the Tales of Beatrix Potter* (1971). Editor Leslie Linder deciphered and published *The Journal of Beatrix Potter 1881–1889* (1966), which fed world interest in the writer's formative years. Cottage crafts flourish from re-creations of lightly stippled miniatures and oval vignettes of Squirrel Nutkin, Benjamin Bunny, Mrs. Tittlemouse, Mrs. Tiggly-Winkle, Tabitha Twitchit, and Flopsy Bunnies, her anthropomorphized animal family. A collection of Potter's watercolor prints is housed in the Tate Gallery in London; the National Book League of London and the Rare Book Department of the Free Library of Philadelphia house her manuscripts and memorabilia.

Sources "Beatrix Potter," http://www.cyberramp.net; Blain et al. 1990; Drabble 1985; Ehrlich and Carruth 1982; Hobbs 1989; Linder 1971; MacDonald 1986; Potter 1966, 1989; Shattock 1993; Taylor 1989.

 # *POURQUOI* STORY

The *pourquoi* story, a component of narrative that is both fable and myth, explains the nature or existence of a phenomenon. Examples include the Toba Indian tale from Argentina "How Man Learned to Make Fire," the aboriginal explanation of "How the Dingo Came to Australia," and the Algerian version of "How Mankind Learned to Make Bread." A positive cosmic story overlaid with the cooperation and creativity of early tribes comes from the Jicarilla Apache, who prize the emergence myth "How the People Sang the Mountains Up." A benign tale, it explains how the gods, animals, and people sang to make the mountains grow toward heaven's two lights, the sun and moon, the source of earthly strength. In such models, the explanation myth celebrates creation at the same time that it enumerates the essentials of human existence and rejoices in the oneness of humankind with all nature. A Christian version, German poet Helmut von Cube's "The Spider," gives a labored account of the insect's struggles among fiercer animals, then focuses on her salvation at the end of a sticky thread that becomes transportation, home, and lair. With a lyrical fillip, the fabulist concludes, "Ever since then the spider has been spinning her nets—terrible, like the earth, and wonderful, like Heaven." (Green 1965, 174)

A parallel strand of *pourquoi* stories varies by texture, tone, and motivation to illustrate the necessary punishments of human weakness. The human tendency toward disorderly conduct, crime, and anarchy colors an intriguing universal focus in primitive thinking—the texture of the moon's surface or the "man in the moon." In a mild example of challenge to authority, the Lillooet of British Columbia see the lunar shapes of the frog sisters, who washed onto the moon's surface during a heavy rain. The abnormal weather results from the despair of the beaver, who wept uncontrollably over their rejection of his proposal of marriage. The Urubu of South America picture the stark face on the moon as the marked features of a man who shirked his responsibilities to family and ran away to hide his shame. In a Tatar tale from the Altai region of Siberia, the moon polices the earth by snatching up a wicked cannibal who was in the act of pulling fruit from a hawthorn bush. The resulting figure on the moon's surface models the old man caught red-handed, still clinging to the bush. The Masai of Kenya account for the man in the moon with a story of domestic violence. After the sun and moon marry and part after a domestic spat, the sun blazes with shame, but the moon remains petulant and sports the results of spousal violence—a misshapen mouth and only one eye. In the Old Norse tale in Snorri Sturluson's *Edda*, Mani the Moon ends child abuse by rescuing Hjuki and Bil, two overworked children who parallel Jack and Jill in the English version. Still clinging to the bucket and pole they used to fetch water, the pair live at rest in the sky. As is true of folk narrative, the various explanations reveal more about tribal values than about the cosmos.

Pourquoi stories display the concerns and hopes of individual figures whose actions affect a species, from Joel Chandler Harris's account of "Why Mr. Cricket Has Elbows on His Legs" in *Told by Uncle Remus: New Stories of the Old Plantation* (1905) to the chilling infanticide and cannibalism that mark the Hmong story "Why Monkey and Man Do Not Live Together" and the African stories "Pig's Long Nose and Greedy Mouth," "Why Hens Are Afraid of Owls," and "Why the Woodpecker Has No Song," the result of the bird's impatience. Examples from current platform storytelling include Peter Dargin's account of the creation of the Darling River in New South Wales, J. J. Reneaux's Cajun story "Why Alligator Hates Dog," and Carol Birch's original fable, "How the Rhinoceros Got Its Skin," an Afrocentric children's story in the style of Rudyard Kipling's *Just-So Stories* (1902). A dominant thread is a fault or evil that must be quelled or requited, as in "Why Frogs Croak in Wet Weather," a Korean *pourquoi* story of filial disobedience, and the Creek fable of "How Bat Won the Ball Game," in which the winged bat is excluded from four-legged mammals and has to prove himself worthy of a place on the team. Thus, the *pourquoi* story fits the paradigm of fable by illustrating the pitfalls of human defect, which range from the minor faults of the tattler to wife and child abusers and the horrendous felons who stalk and devour humankind. The defining element to this explanation of nature is the extension of punishment to all beings of one species, for example, why all beans are striped, why goats can't climb trees, and why no jellyfish has a shell.

Sources Green 1965; Ingpen and Hayes, *Folk Tales & Fables of the Americas & the Pacific* 1994, *Folk Tales & Fables of Asia & Australia*, 1994; Livo and Cha 1991; Miller and Snodgrass 1998; Reneaux 1992, 1995; Ross 1994, 1995.

 RENAISSANCE FABLE

Fable suited the spirit of the Renaissance, an explosively exuberant era of humanistic learning and discovery. After the introduction of printing, the fable became popular reading material and was found on bookshelves all across Europe:

- In Italy, Maximus Planudes, a Greek Orthodox monk, scholar, and theologian from Constantinople who served as emissary to Venice in 1327, produced a collection of 150 Greek fables. His compendium includes tales from the *Panchatantra* and restatements of an inferior copy of Aesop's work. The anthology passed to Rinuccio Thesalo (or d'Arezzo), who, supported by Cardinal Antonio Cerdá of Mallorca, translated the work into Latin and added some tales of his own under the title *Las fabulas de Remicio* [The Fables of Remicio].

- In the mid-fifteenth century, a Florentine humanist, Gian Francesco Bracciolini Poggio, produced the risqué *Liber Facetiarum* [The Book of Witticisms], a satiric collection aimed at lay priests and monks. The volume contains the ribald, earthy "The Miller, His Son, and the Ass," "Teaching an Ass To Read," "The Rustic Seeking to Cross a River" and "The Fox and the Woodcutter" and Planudes's Greek translations of Aesop, which Accursius published around 1480.

- Painter, architect, and engineer Leonardo da Vinci published original fables early in the sixteenth century. Still a popular genre at the end of the century, the fable remained strong in the didacticism of Caravaggian novelist Giovanni Francesco Straparola, author of 74 licentious folk stories in *Le Piacevoli Notti* [Pleasant Nights] (1553), the succinct fables of Laurentius Abstemius (mid-sixteenth century), the 400 tales of Giulio Landi, which were issued in a popular anthology in 1575, and the work of Lorenzo Vallo (or Laurentius Valla), late fifteenth-century Italian humanist, classicist, and apostolic assistant to Pope Nicholas V. In addition to translations of works by Aesop, Xenophon, Herodotus, and Thucydides, Vallo wrote *De Elegantia Latinae Linguae* [On the Elegance of the Latin Language], a writer's handbook.

- According to Swedish folklorist Carl von Sydow, Scandinavia—home of Icelandic sagas and the collected fairy tales of Hans Christian Andersen and the Brothers Grimm—has its place in the history of fable. From a manuscript by Danish cleric and historian Christien Pedersen came *Aesop's Leyned og Fabler* [Aesop's Legends and Fables] (1556), which he produced after establishing himself as a printer of the Bible and old folklore at Malmø.

- Britain's Renaissance contribution to fable attaches more to printing than to composition. In 1485, William Caxton, who introduced the printing press in England, published Accursius's book in English under the title *The Boke of Subtyl Historyes and Fables of Esope,* the first printed text of Aesop's fables and a long-lived influence on children's literature. Scottish teacher Robert Henryson's lively *The Morall Fabillis of Esope the Phrygian, compylit in eloquent & ornate Scottis meter* (1570) adapts the work of Heinrich Steinhöwel's collation, a richly illustrated work in vernacular German entitled *Aesop's Life and Fables* (ca. 1477). An oddity among the lot is William Bullokar's *Aesopz Fablz in Tru Ortography with Grammar-notz* (1585), a model of reformed English spelling. An innovative educator, John Brinsley made similar use of Aesop as material for a classroom reader, published in 1617 and reissued in 1624.

- Like other Mediterranean nations, Spain revered Aesop and the treasured stories of the *Panchatantra.* In 1251, King Alfonso X commissioned a translation of the Arabic *Kalila wa Dimna,* retitled *Calila e Digna* in Spanish. From *Fabulae* [Stories] (ca. 1220) of parson Odo of Cheriton [or Sherington], an influential spicy treasury translated from Latin in the thirteenth century, the Spanish reprised *El libro de los gatos* [The Book of Cats]. In the fourteenth century, Juan Ruiz of Hita interpolated 24 Greek fables into *Libro do buen amor* and Don Juan Manuel did the same for *Conde Lucanor.* In the early fifteenth century, Clemente Sénchez blended Aesopic material into *Libro de los exenplos por ABC* [A Book of Examples of the ABCs]. In 1489, German printer Johan Hurus produced the first print copy of a Spanish compendium, *Las vida del Ysopet con sus fabulas hystoriadas* [The Life of Aesop with his Fables], illustrated by 200 woodcuts that picture life in medieval Europe. A popular reader, it colored the thinking and speech of children and influenced writers novelist Miguel Cervantes, playwright Lope de Vega, and fabulists Tomás de Iriarte (or Yriarte) and Félix María Samaniego, a devoted Basque poet who composed *Fábulas morales* [Moral Fables] (1781) for students. An enduring classroom classic in Spain, the anthology continues to influence curriculum for elementary students. A fabulist from Tenerife, Canary Islands, and student of a scholarly uncle, Iriarte settled in Madrid, where he served the secretary of state as translator. Although his name is embroiled in the politics of his day, he is best known for translating Horace's *Arte Poética* [Poetic Art] and for writing *La Música* (1779) and *Fábulas literarias* [Literary Fables] (1782), a facile collection composed in meters suited to each tale.

- In Germany, Joachim Liebhard, later known as Camerarius, a college professor and classical scholar, published a fable collection for classroom use at the University of Tübingen. His *Äsop* (1476), printed in Spain, contains "The Grateful Ant," a wordy revision of a fable focusing on the value of good deeds. Johannes Pauli's *Schimpf und Ernst* (1522) repeats eight fables later as the popular *Kuh Buch* or *Ku-Bukh* [Cow Book] (1555), a Yiddish collection of 35 models of animal lore published in Verona by Abraham ben Mattathias. Martinus Montanus, a Strasbourg native and collector of anecdotes, published a collation of medieval lore in 1560. One of his stories, "Grace at Meals," wrests humor from the squirrel's outfoxing the fox by tricking him into praying before devouring his quarry. More popular among family readers than pulpit collections and miscellanies were Burkhard Waldis's 14 stories in *Esopus* [Aesop] (1548). A contemporary of Waldis, Robert Stephens, printed an augmented version of Planudes's fables in 1546, an era when vendors hawked cheap chapbooks on street corners.

- Holland claims its part in the canon of fable with the work of teacher Erasmus Alberus, author of *Fabeln* [Fables] (1534), who saw the genre as a means of sugar-coating moral instruction for students. An influential text of fables, Martin Dorp's 500 entries in *Phaedrus* (1513) comprise one of many classroom aids commissioned by the Dutch government. The consensus of educators regarding the usefulness of fable appears strong over a century later, in 1626, when Daniel Heinsius produced another Dutch fable compendium. Developing from spare print stories, the genre of fable blended with emblems to produce symbolic moral stories.

- Switzerland, too, added its creativity to the corpus of fable. Around 1330, a Dominican friar and teacher, Ulrich Boner of Berne, reprised the fables of Avianus and Walther in *Edelstein*, an influential text and one of the early print versions, which by 1461 placed fables in the hands of the ordinary reader. In 1610, Swiss editor Isaac Nicholas Nèvelet issued several hundred fables in *Mythologia Aesopica* [Aesopic Mythology], yet another version of the Greek fables plus 40 of Ausonius's stories, 40 by Aphthonius, 42 by Babrius, and 36 anonymous entries. Composed in paired versions in Greek with Latin translation, this volume is the most complete of the Aesop corpus and derives much of its material from the works of Galterus Anglicus. The *Mythologia Aesopica* ranked alongside scripture as the most widely read book of its day and was a strong influence on the work of Jean de La Fontaine.

A contemporary of Nevelet, Neapolitan soldier Gian Alesion Abbattutis, Count of Torone, writing under the pseudonym Giambattista Basile, compiled 50 dialect stories for *Il Pentamerone* [The Pentameron or Entertainment for the Little Ones] (1637), translated by Sir Richard Burton in 1893. To please a discriminating audience, Basile stocked his baroque framework anthology with folk plots from Oriental tradition and European tastes, including Italian versions of "Babes in the Wood," "Cinderella," "Rapunzel," and "Puss-in-Boots." Given by turns to carnality, coarseness, joy, and wonder, he adorned all with outrageous humor, effusive phrasing, domestic detail, and rural exuberance. Unlike more literary folklorists, Basile took his text of fable, fairy tales, and fantasies directly from oral versions. He grouped them into five books, each trailing a didactic epilogue. The stories range from delightful happily-ever-after plots to "The Face," a spare fable about a princess who tempts fate by boring through her tower prison with a bone to seek her lover.

Late Renaissance and seventeenth-century European writers dipped into classic sources to augment the Aesopic fable with subtler, more sophisticated conflicts and themes. François Rabelais added fable lore to *Gargantua and Pantagruel* (1562); William Shakespeare did the same to *Coriolanus* (ca. 1605) with reference to Menenius Agrippa's "The Belly and the Parts of the Body." Most famous of the revised fables are Edmund Spenser's "Mother Hubberd's Tale" (1591) and John Dryden's verse fable *The Hind and the Panther* (1687), a weightier narrative based on theological disputation. A minor publication in terms of popularity is *Fables of Aesop Paraphras'd in Verse* (1665), the work of Scottish printer and cartographer John Ogilby, tutor to the children of the earl of Strafford and surveyor of London following the Great Fire of 1666. Lest he be thought a fool, Ogilby made a defensive prefatory statement that even Socrates translated fables. Among Augustinian friars, Abraham a Sancta Clara, an Austrian satirist from Kreenheinstetten formerly known as Ulrich Megerle, animated his sermons with fables. He imported fables from world sources to Vienna as part of his position as court preacher. A popular contemporary of Sancta Clara is translator and journalist Sir Roger L'Estrange, author of *Fables of Aesop and Other Eminent Mythologists* (1692), an anthology of over 500 tales.

A high point in the evolution of the fable occurred in the late seventeenth century with the collected fables of Jean de La Fontaine, whose Aesopic *Fables choisies* [Selected Fables] (1668) precede a quarter century of his original narratives that ridicule bureaucracy, monarchy, religion, and the moneyed middle class. In contrast with the delight of La Fontaine's works run the weighty thoughts of John Locke, who glorified the role of the school as the hand that writes on the *tabula rasa*, the blank slate of the child's mind. In *Some Thoughts Concerning Education* (1693), he rejected the frivolous fairy tales but defended the more substantial logic of Aesop and Reynard the Fox and corroborated the belief that picture books lure young readers to uplifting texts much as honey masks a loathsome tonic. A staple in school text, emblem book, and political pamphlet, these fables teased the creative urges of artists Chauveau, Jean-Baptiste Oudry, J. J. Grandville, and Gustave Doré, perhaps the most famous of Aesop's French illustrators.

See also L'Estrange, Roger; Shakespeare, William.

Sources Blackham 1985; Blain et al. 1990; "Brewer: Dictionary of Phrase and Fable," http://www.bibliomania.com; Briggs 1977, 1991; Calvino 1980; Cooper 1921; Creeden 1994; Dailey 1994; Green 1965; Hobbs 1986; Komroff 1935; Krappe 1964; Leach 1967; Marie de France 1994; Newbigging 1895; Rosenberg 1997; Steinberg 1954.

REYNARD THE FOX

The allegorical Reynard the Fox is a furry rogue who became so common and popular a figure in European bourgeois folklore that he appears in cathedral embellishment, children's songs and ditties, the Bayeux Tapestry, and a roundel of stained glass at Holy Cross Church in Byfield, Northamptonshire, in which he wears a crown and leers triumphantly as he throttles a goose. Created by French poet Pierre "Perrot" de St. Cloud in northeast France between 1174 and 1177, Reynard is primarily a humorous diversion,

> Tel chose dire
> Dont je vos puisse fere rire,
> Quar je sai bien, ce est la pure.
> [Such things to tell
> Whereby, I know, laugh you may,
> For that forsooth is the way of truth.]
> (Nitze and Dargan 1950, 67)

The canvas on which Reynard appears is a cameo of medieval France, realistic in details of stuffy courts as well as outlying hedgerows, heaths, farmsteads, monastic retreats, and the fox's own stronghold of Maupertius. The imaginatively robust character of Reynard faces the wolf Isengrin or Ysengrim, the king's multilingual marshal, in an intricate, muscular mock heroic. A thoroughly orchestrated fable and counterreligious allegory, the work depicts the two beasts as barons, subjects of Noble the lion. In the irreverent and cynical Gallic spirit, this satire of the *le roman courtois* [courtly romance] of twelfth-century French feudalism turns on a long-running feud between the fox and his perennial dupe, the wolf. Key to the fable's belly laughs is the fox's failure to outwit a series of intended animal victims—Tibert the cat, Tiécelin the crow, Bruyant the bull, and Chauntecler the cock, the protagonist of Geoffrey Chaucer's *The Nun's Priest's Tale* (1385).

In a segment focusing on the theme of justice, Reynard must defend himself against the charge of taking advantage of Dame Hersent, the wolf's mate, after she became stuck in a burrow while hunting with her husband. The barons assemble on Ascension Day for the assizes to hear her testimony, which she renders before the bailiff can round up the accused. According to the poet,

> Her struggles had been to no avail.
> Ysengrin grabs her by the tail
> And pulls on it with might and main
> Until Hersent is in such pain
> That Ysengrin in anguish tries
> To make the hole a larger size.
> (Renard 1994, 270)

The ribald seduction scene precedes arrest and a plenary session, at which Ysengrin accuses his enemy of having "pissed on my cubs, pulled out their hair,/ Saying that they were bastards born." (Renard 1994, 271) His wife, cringing and blushing on the stand, swears vociferously to God and his saints that Reynard is indeed a rapist but did nothing to her that he wouldn't do to his own mother. The cast offers a full range of speakers, male and female, including Chauntecler's enraged wife Pinte, who swoons prettily in the manner of court ladies whose delicacy deflects accusations that tend to sully their reputations.

Reynard's indubitable Reynard heightens his eventual flight from justice. Chauntecler, Pinte, "layer of great eggs," and three other wives, bearing a dismembered chicken on a bier, press their accusations. (Romance 1994, 9) Revelation of the sufferings of the victim, Lady Coupée, Pinte's sister, pushes Reynard deeper into culpability. The court proceedings halt for proper interment and a vigil. The poet adds an epitaph:

> Upon this plain, beneath this tree,
> There lies Pinte's sister, named Coupée.
> Reynard, grown ever wickeder,
> With his teeth made grim work of her.
> (Romance 1994, 11)

With a deft bit of melodrama, the text notes that Pinte and Chauntecler revile the fox so virulently that viewers "might well have been moved to deepest pity." The poet leaves the ambiguity of whom to pity—Pinte weeping for her mangled sister or Reynard, who has yet to face his incensed accusers.

For maximum burlesque of medieval legalism, St. Cloud elongates the court scene with calls for Reynard's apprehension. Bruin's arrival at Maupertius coincides with the fox's enjoyment of a fine French lunch of bacon, peas, and seven cents' worth of honey in the comb. The description of dining on beef with green grape sauce forms a fable on pretense and hard-heartedness. In the face of lavish procedures, which feature the ritual removal of the lord's sleeves before hand-washing, the fox contrasts the meal of a peasant, who holds a crust of bread on his lap, where dogs snatch at it. The picture of greedy-fisted aristocrats and servants flinging bones to the poor concludes in a grim moral: "Stewards, cooks: they're all cast in the same mould. The lords get little of some things that those thieves have in abundance—they should all be burnt and their ashes scattered to the wind!" (Romance 1994, 12)

The text takes on mock-epic extravagance after lion-king summons Reynard to court with an official letter that asks him to bring only the rope for a noose. On his arrival at court, the melodrama rises with the barons' outraged cries. To their claims, Reynard admits his sins, which he embellishes with boasts that magnify his guilt. The king calls on the bumbling Monseigneur the Camel of Lombardy, a papal legate dispatched from Constantinople, to debate the logic of the claim that rape is not a felony when the perpetrator truly loves the victim, in this case, a nobleman's wife. The decision, couched in Latin clichés, is ominous: the camel believes "Res ipse loquitor" [the thing speaks for itself]. Reynard pleads to make a pilgrimage, then rips off his cross, wipes his behind with it, and sneers at the court as he scoots into his castle, which is supplied for seven years' of siege. Intended for oral delivery, the narrative reads well and builds the type of crowd-pleasing suspense that marks a classic recitation piece. Although the text skewers the upper echelons of society, its delicious raciness

"The Fox Flattering the Chicken," from *Roman de Renart* [Story of Reynard the Fox], Bibliothéque Nationale, Paris

pleased a mixed audience of cultivated aristocrats, both male and female, and their attendant clerics.

From 1174 to 1250, ensuing generations of French satirists added 28 strands to the original story to stress the sexual aggression of the rapacious rising middle class against the ineptitude of the declining aristocracy. In risqué folk tradition, the tapestry of fox lore, known as *Roman de Renart* (ca. 1250), relates to the kernel story independent tales of villainy, rowdiness, and impertinence. The scenarios vary yet anchor to the courtly milieu: "The Siege of Maupertius," "Reynard the Dyer—Reynard the Minstrel," "Reynard and the Eels," and so forth. Independent composers link these varied additives mainly by the involvement of Reynard, alternately known as Reynard the Red, the arch-deceiver, universal trickster, or plotter of all wickedness, all drawing on theatrical epithets for Satan. Their epimythia decline to succinct morals known as *proverbes au vilain* or folk sayings, the style of epigram that suits essentially rural lore, for example, from Galterus Anglicus's fable:

> Let him who seeks folk to ensnare
> And do them harm himself beware
> Lest he in his own trap be caught.
> Then cry: "Ah, woe is me! I ought
> Not to work others' injury!
> It's right the harm should come to me
> And that I, once my trap is set,
> Should fall myself into the net.
> (Romance 1994, 254–255)

As in other parts of the Reynard canon, this *epimythium* maintains the convention of the fox's amorality and submersion in rationalization and self-pity, qualities that suit his defiant behavior even in the extremes of danger.

Like Geoffrey Chaucer's Canterbury pilgrims, the figures in French fox lore lampoon all players of medieval society, from the king and his toadying prelates to the petty squabbling nobility, crass parish clergy, moneyed landowners, and debased villeins. Ultimately caught in the segment known as "The Judgment of Renard," the fox gives up his ladder of lies and escapes the pillory by agreeing to journey overseas to the Holy Land to work off his sin. When he is far enough away to shuck the pilgrim's tunic and badge, he thumbs his nose at Noble. The king dispatches the court standard-bearer, Tardif the snail, at the head of a pursuit party. Additional scenes show Reynard under siege in *Chastel Renard* and disguised as a wandering harper. In others, he faces Ysengrim in combat, searches for a wife for Noble, and joins Bernard the ass and Belin the ram on a pilgrimage to Rome. Ultimately, instead of confessing, he gobbles up a confessor and overthrows Noble. An anticlimactic sequel describes the feigned death of Reynard. The animals take their places in his elaborate funeral cortege, which halts abruptly with his resurgence and flight with Chantecler tucked under his arm. Like a matinee cliffhanger, he grasps immortality and provides future writers with additional opportunities to revive his lengthy canon with new tellings.

The parody at the heart of Reynard's canon ridicules the gluttony, impiety, and lechery of revered medieval figures at all levels, from urbane clergy to bestial serfs. The fox's rambunctious forays upset the order of Noble's self-important court and seneschal Brichemer the stag. The pastiche is a mockery of the Round Table and Sir Kay, King Arthur's manager, as well as a parody of the court of Charlemagne. Self-important court attendants also imitate the pomposity of the courtiers who clustered around Louis VII, who was king when St. Cloud wrote his travesty. Without serious acrimony toward individuals, the author intends to spoof standard figures, such as the thin-skinned strutter, befuddled councilor, fickle lady love, and worthless chamberlain. Reynard's attack on Dame Hersent parallels the high court romance of the deflowering of Guinevere, Elaine, and Isolde. In mock-heroic style, the charge of marauding hounds parodies Homer's catalog of warriors, each called by an aristocratic title and led by the lance-toting Baron Roenel. Throughout, Reynard remains a comic figure, brash and unrepentent. As fable insists, he acts out the plan of nature that makes him the loner and eternal enemy of wolf and cock.

A resilient folk motif, the Reynard corpus expanded into peripheral lore. Throughout the last decades of the thirteenth century and into the fourteenth, additions to the Reynard series stretched and reshaped the tone and focus of the animal satire, including these:

- the Latin *Ysengrimus* (1148), published in Ghent.

- contemporary with St. Cloud's fox stories, Heinrich der Glîchezaere's Alsatian series, *Reinhart Fuchs* (ca. 1180), which commits to verse the early adventures of the fox. The text parallels traditional episodes and appends original fables. The tone of the German Reynard departs from the lighter humor of French lore to a serious, potentially tragic mode, which reflects the mindset of a moralist rather than satirist. The didactic purpose is clearly the presentation of the deception, lies, and evil that permeate the medieval world.

- a Franco-Italian version, *Rainardo e Lesengrino* (ca. 1200), in which the fox acts out the rape and judgment in a setting south of the Alps.

- a parallel cycle from Flanders and Holland, *Van den Vos Reinaerde* (ca. 1250), an uplifting comic version that avoids the dour clerical moralizing that had clouded the fox's story. *Reinaert de Vos* (ca. 1250), a popular Flemish text that outshone French and German models, is signed only by the name Willem.

- Contemporaneous with the low country fox, England, too, had its hedge lore, which fueled the anonymous *Of the Vox and of the Wolf* (ca. 1250) and Chaucer's battle between the fox and the proud cock Chaunticleer.

- A distant reprise of Reynard's adventures appears in the eastern Mediterranean, composed by diplomat and soldier Philippe de Novare as a component of *Mémoires*, in which he conceals real adversaries under animal names.

- In 1261, Rutebeuf of Champaign, a trouvère and author of the acerbic, Faustian *Miracle de Thèphile*, added to the fox canon *Renard le Bestourné*, a harsh satire of mendicant friars. In the pro-Reynard tradition, the poet begins,

  > Reynard is dead, yet lives in style;
  > Reynard is base, Reynard is vile,
  > But Reynard reigns.
  > (Romance 1994, 256)

- Around 1270 appeared *Couronnement de Renart* [The Coronation of Reynard], a broad-based travesty on the political situation in Flanders between old and new money. A contemporary, Baldwinus Juvenis or Baldwin the Young, made a Latin translation of the Reynard cycle.

- Jacquemart Gielée (or Gelée) of Lille added *Renart le Nouvel* (1288), a cynical moral satire on the decline of chivalry and Christian virtues in which Reynard becomes the adversary of Noble.

- A former priest's exhaustive compendium of Reynard stories, *Renart le Contrefait* [Reynard the Many-Sided] (ca. 1340), distorts the fox into a demon and corrupts the animal motifs with digressions on history, politics, customs, and curiosities.

- The sustained parody suffered under the hands of a Flemish recensionist, who composed *Reinaerts Histoire* (ca. 1370), a loose arrangement of jolly fox fables.

- England's first printer, William Caxton, exalted fox lore at his Westminster press with *The Historye of Reynart the Foxe* (1481), a popular rendering that reprises the mid-thirteenth century Flemish text by Willem. In defense of Willem's text, Caxton commented: "I have not added ne mynusshed [minused] but have folowed as nyghe as I can my copye which was in dutche, and by me Willm Caxton translated in to this rude & symple englyssh." (Goethe 1954, vii–viii) The text remained long in circulation with Caxton's second setting in 1489 and a subsequent 1494 edition by Richard Pynson, a Norman-French printer.

- In Gouda, Holland, in 1479, the Dutch printer Gheraert Leeu added a prose compendium, *Die Hystorie van Reynaert die Vos* [The History of Reynard the Fox]. In 1485, printer Jacob Jacobszoen van der Meer reprised the text in Delft. Two years later, he issued a reprint with glossary by Hinrek van Alckmer or Heinrich von Alkmar. Two rhymed rescensions, *Rienaerts Histoire* and *Reinke de Vos* appeared in 1498 at Lübeck. A High German translation was printed in 1544 at Frankfurt; Hartmann Schopper's Latin version was complete in 1567. However, neither of these upgraded bestiaries outshone the original Low German best-seller, which survived three centuries of reprints.

- In 1654, John Shirley upgraded Caxton's bestiary with *The Most Delectable History of Reynard the Fox, Newly Corrected & Purged from all grossness in Phrase & Matter*. Three decades later, the text was amended to *The Shifts of Renardine, the Son of Reynard the Fox* (1684). A Dutch version, *The Most Delectable History of Reynard the Fox* (1676), enlarged the original. As also, augmented and inlarged with sundry excellent morals. (Romance 1994, xi)

- The English, late arrivals in the long history of fox lore, valued *The Crafty Courtier: or the Fable of Reynard the Fox* (1706), an English version of Kaspar Schoppe's Latin fox cycle.

- Reprised in 1752 in High German by Johann Christoph Gottsched, a conservative scholar and logician from Königsberg, a loftier version preceded Johann Goethe's classic *Reinecke Fuchs* (1794).

- Still viable in the nineteenth century, Reynard lore entered English doggerel from Low German as translated by D. W. Soltau in 1826. Samuel Naylor continued the tradition with *Reynard the Fox, a renowned Apologue of the Middle Age, reproduced in Rhyme* (1844). E. W. Holloway added his classic touch with *Reynard the Fox, a Poem in twelve Cantos* (1852).

See also Chaucer, Geoffrey; Goethe, Johann Wolfgang von.

Sources Bishop 1965; Cantor 1994; Goethe 1954; Harrington 1925; Nitze and Dargan 1950; *The Romance of Reynard the Fox* 1994; Strayer 1989; *Ysengrimus* 1884.

 # RUMI, JALAL AD-DIN AR

A teller of educational fables, Jalal ad-Din ar-Rumi or Mawlana [Our Master], a thirteenth-century Iranian theologian and mystic poet, wrote fables to enlighten disciples. He composed wisdom lore with such clarity and precision that it influenced the *Gesta Romanorum* [Deeds of the Romans], the folk tales of Danish teller Hans Christian Andersen, and the plays of William Shakespeare. The supreme master of Persian verse, he produced the epic encyclopedia of mysticism, *Masnavi-ye Ma'navi* [Spiritual Couplets], an adjunct to the Koran. The work, which is devoid of the dogma and formalism of orthodox Islam, was the impetus to the Mawlawiyah, order commonly called the Whirling Dervishes, seekers of otherworldliness and perfection.

A key story in Rumi's encyclopedia, "Three Pieces of Advice," tells of a man who captures a bird and lets it go free in exchange for three valuable admonitions. After the man hears the first two maxims, the bird squawks out a surprise—a claim that it contains jewels. At the man's demand for the rest of the advice, the bird replies, "I told you not to worry about what had been lost, and not to believe in something contrary to sense. Now you are doing both." (Shah 1982, 132) As is typical of fool tales, the bird humiliates the man and leaves him to ponder that a fool is the victim of his inborn restrictions and, therefore, unsalvageable. Among dervishes, the story attained value for opening young minds and preparing them to learn from unusual events and experiences.

Rumi's life, like the story of the advice from the bird, was filled with experiences that enlightened and prepared him for the role of wise man and mentor to others. The son of iconoclastic theologian Baha ad-Din Walad, he was born September 30, 1207, in Balkh, Ghurid, in what is now Afghanistan. At age 11, he was swept up in a mass exodus before Mongol invaders and fled with his family to Nishapur, Iran. Under the tutelage of Persian sage Farid od-Din'Attar, he acquired the first of his considerable Sanskrit lore from Attar's *Asrarnama* [Book of Secrets] and moved into the chain of descent that passed authority from one sage to another. Migrations to Mecca and other stopping places concluded in Laranda in Anatolia, where Rumi's family came under the beneficent rule of the Seljuq Turks. At Konya, Rumi followed his father on the staff at the madrasah, a learned consortium, where he taught religion. In 1232, Rumi studied Iranian theories of mysticism with Burhan ad-Din Muhaqqiq, his father's disciple. Rumi extended his knowledge through journeys to Syrian Sufist enclaves, led by Islamic philosopher Ibn al-'Arabi.

In 1244, Rumi met Shams ad-Din of Tabriz, a self-styled dervish who humbled him, separated him from the stodginess of academe, and altered his thinking about divinity. From late November into January 1245, the two departed from society to study together. The intensity of their relationship outraged Rumi's family and students, who ousted Shams. Rumi's sincere distress forced his oldest son, Sultan Walad, to return Rumi's spiritual catalyst from Syria. Shams remained on the edge of respectable society until 1247, when he was murdered, probably by Rumi's sons or jealous disciples. Rumi found solace in Salah ad-Din Zarkub, a goldworker in the local marketplace. Like American Shakers, charismatics, and glossolalists worshiping in unknown languages, Rumi danced to the ringing of Salah's hammer and wrote verse in tribute to rapture, through which he attained sublimity by fragmenting self, withdrawing from imperfection and passions, and uniting with Allah, god of Islam.

The loss of a mentor inspired Rumi to turn from theology to mystical verse. Writing under the pseudonym Shams, he composed 30,000 verses and many *ruba'iyat* or quatrains on the theme of love, loss, and yearning. Set to the music of drum, flute, or paddles of a water mill, individual poems delight in natural settings and spontaneous dance. Collected as *Divan-e Shams* [The Collected Verse of Shams], his dithyrambic lyrics, innovative language, rhapsodic images, and pulsing cadences express an ecstasy that is both spiritual and erotic. Beyond the narrow interpretations of scripture, Rumi reached for *fana*, the revered state of union with God that satisfied his longing for peace, purity, spirituality, and truth. Through seven allegorical vales—quest, love, understanding, detachment, unity, bewilderment, and extinction—he reached for emerging sainthood and exaltation of the almighty.

Under the influence of a third love, Husam ad-Din Chelebi, Rumi's Diiya' al-Haqq [Ray of Truth], the poet completed *Masnavi-ye Ma'navi* (ca. 1270), an evocative miscellany flecked with gem-like epigrams, anecdotes, tales, and fables. As expressions of how God works through the spirit, the stories inspire hearers to private mental pictures and subconscious associations. An allegory crucial to Rumi's message tells of a discipline who knocks at the teacher's door. When the hermit asks his name, the seeker replies "It is I." The hermit sends him away to prepare more fully for learning. At the end of a year, the seeker returns with the right answer. No longer an individual personality, he identifies himself as the master. The hermit gives up his place to the seeker, who has departed from the distractions of worldliness to enter a radiant, mystical state of truth.

Among Rumi's 26,000 ghazals or couplets is "The Caged Bird," a fable about a Persian merchant whose caged bird, out of longing for home, sings only of freedom. Gifted with speech, the bird begs to accompany her owner to her forest homeland and to fly free once more. The merchant refuses but agrees to carry a message to the bird's family that she is safe in a cage. To his amazement, a wild relative of his bird hears the message and falls dead. When the merchant returns home with news of the odd occurrence, the merchant's bird collapses. When he reaches for her crumpled body, she suddenly flits away. Her retort explains the puzzling death of the forest bird: it acted out the ruse by which the caged bird could gain her freedom. A teaching tale common to Sufi instruction, the story plants deep in the intriguing plot a lesson that stimulates and enlightens disciples. In the clever overthrow of an oppressor, the story bears hope to all victims of physical and emotional imprisonment. For the Sufist, implications of other forms of psycho-spiritual confinement—bias, bad habits, inhibitions, and pessimism—expand the story's application to suit the individual hearer. Among religious explications of the story, it symbolizes the death of self that must precede a true knowledge of God.

A puzzling fable, "The Horseman and the Snake," contains a dark allegory applicable to the role of savant in society. It depicts a bizarre incident in which a mysterious horseman stops to help a man who swallows a venomous snake in his sleep. To save the sleeper from certain death, the horseman lashes him and forces him to swallow rotten apples and great gulps of water. When the terrified victim finally vomits up the water, apples, and snake, he realizes that his tormentor is actually a savior. The horseman's enigmatic explanation is directed at the unwary: "If I had told you, you would not have believed. Or you would have been paralyzed by fright. Or run away. Or gone to sleep again, seeking forgetfulness. And there would not have been time." (Shah 1982, 140–141) The answer accounts for the impulsive extremism of the Sufi, who bear at heart a compassion for the unknowing and paradoxically save them by lashing them awake with zealous teachings.

The most famous story from Rumi's Sufist exempla is "The Blind Ones and the Matter of the Elephant," an illustrative example that ministers and teachers have reduced to the blind men and the elephant. Set in Ghor, a city of sightless inhabitants, the story takes on ominous proportions from the exposition, which describes the elephant as a mighty siege animal encamped with hostile troops in the desert. To timorous men eager to assess their danger, tentative touches give fragmented information. To the hand groping the animal's upper head, the ear felt like a broad, rough rug. To the hand at the trunk, it was a "straight and hollow pipe, awful and destructive." (Shah 1982, 25) To the rear of the animal, other hands touch legs and tail, reaching hasty conclusions that an elephant is like a pillar or a rope. Moving from incident to universal application, Rumi concludes, "The created is not informed about divinity. There is no way in this science by means of the ordinary intellect." The value of Rumi's model has become a classic warning of hasty judgment or judgment based on faulty or incomplete information.

Rumi's influence on narrative, like that of Aesop, recurs in fables that name him as sage or teacher, such as "The Merchant and the Christian Dervish" in Aflaki's collection *Munaqib el-Arifin*, the lives of early dervishes (1353). The story elevates Rumi to magician by giving him the power to create telepathic images to prove to a seeker that, to end a streak of ill luck, he must seek forgiveness of a Christian dervish. Another Rumi original, "The Dog and the Donkey," tells of a man who learns animal language and earns the beasts' disdain for interrupting where he is not welcome. The enigmatic fable, devoid of *epimythium,* or appended moral, was repeated in the collection of Majnun Qalandar, an outcast whose thirteenth-century recitations marked him as a raving savant.

At his death, Rumi left as disciple his love Husam, then Sultan Walad, founder of the Mawlawiyah or whirling dervishes, whose spiritual search finds expresses in physical ecstasy. Sultan Walad also immortalized Rumi in biography. In addition to his great verse anthologies, Rumi left collected dialogues, *Fihi ma fihi* [There is what there is], letters, and the legends that arose from his symbolic teachings and poems, which R. A. Nicholson translated into English from 1925 to 1940. Rumi's tomb under the Green Dome has become a museum and *tekye* or shrine, where an annual revival throbs with ritual music and dancing.

Sources Ghazali 1964; *Letters of a Sufi Master* 1969; McDermott 1997; Nicholson 1950; Schimmel 1975, 1982; Shah 1982; Snodgrass 1995; Waley 1993.

 # SAINT-EXUPÉRY, ANTOINE DE

A distinguished daredevil pilot, mystic, and wistful, introspective humanist, Antoine de Saint-Exupéry, known familiarly as "Saint-Ex," lived the passionate life of a dreamer turned doer. His love of flying and of the stories he could relate about storms over the desert and rescues from the deep made him welcome among clutches of barnstormers and supporters of the French Resistance, which he helped organize. A devotion to duty and country balances his passion for solitude in the clouds, which echoes Herman Melville's romance with the deep and anticipates Arthur Clarke's reverence for outer space. Born in Lyons, France, on June 29, 1900, to Jean Cesar and Marie Boyer de Fonscolombe de Saint-Exupéry, Saint-Exupéry lived under the restrained circumstances of aristocrats fallen on hard times. His schooling was limited to l'Ecole Bossuet and Lycée Saint-Louis, a naval preparatory academy. The right age to serve in World War I, he readied himself for a naval appointment but failed the entrance exam to officer candidate school. Service as a draftee in the French Army Air Force in 1921 rerouted him to the Avord air training center and introduced him to flying, which became his true home.

Military training preceded employment as a *pilote de ligne* [commercial flier] for Aéropostale in 1926, when Saint-Exupéry pioneered night flights ferrying cargo from Toulouse to Morocco, Mauritania, and Dakar, then to Brazil and Patagonia, and over the Andes chain to Buenos Aires, Argentina. In the third year of his career, he received the Legion of Honor Award for peacefully negotiating a volatile Moroccan faceoff between Spaniards and Moors. After breaking into print with a first novel, *Courrier sud* [Southern Mail] (1928), he produced a best-seller, *Vol de nuit* [Night Flight] (1931), which earned him the Prix Femina. In scenes that merge death in the skies with the ineffable loveliness of the heavens, Saint-Exupéry displays what critic André Legarde terms a *méditation constante* [true meditation], the source of his work's cohesion and worth, which reached its height in his unfinished *Citadelle* (1948). (Lagarde and Michard 1973, 489) During France's development of technical improvements to aeronautics, he served as a test pilot and tinkerer. When injuries compromised his ability to fly, he departed temporarily from his wife, Consuelo, to take a post as foreign correspondent and cover the beginning of the Spanish civil war for *L'Intransigeant* and the 1937 siege of Madrid for *Paris-Soir*.

French author and aviator Antoine de Saint-Exupéry

Personal observations of world events inspired Saint-Exupéry to write autobiographical essay, the mode of *Terre des hommes* [Land of Men, retitled in English *Wind, Sand, and Stars*] (1939), on which André Gide advised him. Clean, spare prose and dedication to humanism won Saint-Exupéry the Grand Prix from the Academie Française. A narrow escape during his military service during World War II sent him through Portugal to safety in the United States. Retiring to the reserves as a captain decorated with the Croix de Guerre for reconnaissance flight during the Battle of France, he recounted *Pilote de Guerre* [War Pilot, called *Flight to Arras* in the English version] (1942) from a stockpile of memorable events and musings. A model of French patriotism, the expatriate aviator settled in the village of Northport, Long Island, and toured the United States speaking and writing about the need for cohesion among forces battling fascism. The shift in interests appeared on his passport, which altered his profession from aviator to *homme de lettres* [man of letters].

In 1943—a year before his mysterious death in the crash of a photographic mission for Free French Forces over Provence only weeks before the liberation of Paris—Saint-Exupéry composed a lyrical fable, *Le petit prince* [The Little Prince], an autobiographical fantasy that captures his intense love of freedom. The dedication honors a friend, Leon Werth, at the same time that it expresses the author's idealism: "I ask the indulgence of the children who may read this book for dedicating it to a grown-up. I have a serious reason: He is the best friend I have in the world. . . . If all these reasons are not enough, I will dedicate the book to the child from whom this grown-up grew. All grown-ups were once children—although few of them remember it." (Saint-Exupéry 1943, 5) A controlling motif, the balance of child-like wisdom against earthly suffering expresses the author's tenuous truce with a dangerous world. The fable captures the pervasive insecurity and dread of Europe at war.

The strength of the genre guaranteed Saint-Exupéry's immortality in its winsome, minimalist story of a downed pilot who encounters an extraterrestrial in the Sahara Desert. The petite prince speaks his intimate knowledge of soullessness:

> I know a planet where there is a certain red-faced gentleman. He has never smelled a flower. He has never looked at a star. He has never loved any one. He has never done anything in his life but add up figures. And all day, he says over and over, just like you: "I am busy with matters of consequence!" (Saint-Exupéry 1943, 27)

Certain of his right to rage, the child-philosopher rails against pride and concludes, "But he is not a man—he is a mushroom!" He requests a sketch of a sheep, which requires a muzzle to keep it from eating his only flower, a rose. Key to the fable's theme is the prince's love of roses, which the fox tells him are valuable for the care they require. It is the fox who delivers the salient advice to the rose lover: "It is only with the heart one can see rightly; what is essential is invisible to the eye." (Saint-Exupéry 1943, 70)

Inklings of the fabulist's motivation necessitate the bizarre motifs and settings of *The Little Prince*, which pictures the pint-sized savant befriending the adult earthling and reintroducing him to the delights of childhood. According to his dedicatory remarks, the fabulist intends to banish the cold and misery of France under Hitler through literary consolation. For the prince, choices are simplified by his dedication to duty and his preference for the small joys that color his life on a minuscule asteroid. His mode of travel—a flock of birds—suits a simple lifestyle. Ensuing wise commentary rejuvenates the pilot, who comes to value the boy over his own concern that his supplies may run out before he can repair the plane and return to civilization. In a poignant scenario, the prince yields to the bite of a snake to release him from an earthly body. The pilot hesitates to leave the flushed child and reminds himself, "One runs the risk of weeping a little, if one lets himself be tamed." (Saint-Exupéry 1943, 81)

A touching child's view of the afterlife infuses the last scenes with hope. Before dying, the prince begins distancing himself by reuniting the pilot with the stars: "For some, who are travelers, the stars are guides. For others they are no more than little lights in the sky. For others, who are scholars, they are problems. For my businessman they were wealth. But all these stars are silent. You—you alone—will have the stars as no one else has them." (Saint-Exupéry 1943, 85) The child's gift of a unique star empowers his friend to look upward and seek laughter, the only bit of evidence that the soul has found its home. With the self-assured wisdom of a graybeard, the prince adds, "And when your sorrow is comforted (time soothes all sorrows) you will be content that you have known me." A sincere expression of friendship, the child's farewell speaks a world knowledge far greater than his years.

Six years pass between the first 26 chapters and its conclusion. The fable grows wistful as the pain of loss lessens with time. In a soliloquy, the pilot divulges that he has concealed his friendship with the little prince. Among adult acquaintances, the man masks downheartedness as fatigue. In the end, the battle between hope and despair gives place to joy in the cosmic mystique. Still debating the question of whether the sheep has eaten the prince's only rose, the pilot accepts the child's philosophy for its simplicity—the necessity of responsibility and the value of friendship. With an enigmatic fade, the story ends on a single challenge to maturity: "No grown-up will ever understand that [the survival of the rose] is a matter of so much importance!" (Saint-Exupéry 1943, 91) Speaking through the stranded aviator, Saint-Exupéry sides with beauty and fragility. He envisions heaven as the irrepressible laugh of the child-spirit that wings from star to star across the night sky.

Whimsically warm, reflective, and transcendent, *The Little Prince* compares in original art and characterization with the fantasy of Lewis Carroll's *Alice in Wonderland* (1865) and the mystic fancy of Maurice Maeterlinck's *The Blue Bird* (1909). Through the tempering of adult thoughts in a child's words, the story endears with a blend of innocence and altruism. Like Richard Bach's wise fable *Jonathan Livingston Seagull* (1970), Saint-Exupéry forces the frail action to hoist a monumental metaphysical load—the belief that art and life must merge to reach fruition. The fable was the subject of an overproduced Lerner and Loewe musical filmed by Paramount in 1975. The cast, starring Richard Kiley, Joss Ackland, and Steven Warner, features the dancing of Bob Fosse and Gene Wilder, who plays the fox. The title song, "The Little Prince from Who Knows Where," was nominated for an Oscar and won a Golden Globe Award.

Sources Grigson 1963; Lagarde 1973; Magill 1958; Ryan 1995; Saint-Exupéry 1943, 1975; "St. Exupery," http://www.westegg.com; *Twentieth Century Literary Criticism* 1979, 1995.

SHAKESPEARE, WILLIAM

An actor, theatrical producer, and playwright who drew on English traditions as well as the standard stories, tales, and fables common to a classical grade-school education, Shakespeare epitomizes the pragmatism of the English Renaissance. From Giovanni Boccaccio's *Decameron* alone, the playwright drew elements of *All's Well That Ends Well* (ca. 1604), *Cymbeline* (ca. 1608–1610), *A Winter's Tale* (ca. 1610–1611), and *Two Gentlemen of Verona* (ca. 1613). Among other sources are John Gower's *Confessio Amantis* and Geoffrey Chaucer's *The Canterbury Tales*, both influences on *The Taming of the Shrew* (ca. 1589); *A Thousand and One Nights*, a source for *The Taming of the Shrew* (ca. 1589); Apuleius's *The Golden Ass*, background material for *A Midsummer Night's Dream* (ca. 1593–1595), the Greco-Roman fable that undergirds *Coriolanus* (ca. 1605–1609), and *Gesta Romanorum*, which supplied details for *Pericles* (1606–1608). The biblical and mythical images, history, folklore, and adages that were common knowledge in the mid-sixteenth century permeated Shakespeare's stage and poetic works, demonstrating an intelligence open to curiosities and literature from all parts.

Born April 23, 1564, in Stratford-on-Avon, Shakespeare grew up in a folk milieu and studied at a Latin grammar school. His formal education may have ended at age 13, when his father, a local glover, suffered a financial reversal. There remains little historical data from his youth, but Shakespeare was obviously well read and well versed in England's literature and folk tradition, such as the yearly St. George's Day pageant in Stratford, plant myths, and common nostrums. Because of his family's misfortune, he received no university training and, in 1584, settled his wife and children at his father's house and set out for London for a career in acting, then considered a shady, insubstantial calling, particularly for a married man.

In London's thriving theatrical milieu around 1587, Shakespeare was a popular, talented stage professional despite a late start. He enjoyed the challenge of show business, in part because he knew what playgoers liked to see, hear, and experience during a performance—suspenseful narrative, romance, spirits, murder, faraway settings, and the downfall of royalty. His wide-ranging plots and settings reflect the Renaissance interest in universal matters and in human concerns, including love, treachery, family, loyalty, success, and failure. His use of rhetorical devices indicates a command of poesy and humor. The addition of incidental satire to nearly all the plays proves that he did not overlook the human capacity for folly and stupidity. A model of classic fable adorns the tragedy *Coriolanus* (ca. 1608–1610), the downfall of a graceless, cheerless public figure unsuited to the political demands of a confrontation between leaders and followers. The text derives from Plutarch's *Life of Coriolanus* (ca. 110 C.E.), which repeats a fable found in Book II of Livy's *Ab Urbe Condita* [From the Foundation of the City] (ca. 14 C.E.). In Act I, Scene i, the recitation of the fable of the body parts and their rebellion against the belly suits the playwright's demonstration of the seriousness of anarchy. The protagonist's friend and adviser, the worthy Menenius Agrippa, approaches a company of rash, mutinous citizens with his wise story as a sop to their growing outrage. An elderly statesman and nonconfrontational public speaker, he introduces his homily with a stout warning:

> For your wants,
> Your suffering in this dearth, you may as well
> Strike at the heaven with your staves as lift them
> Against the Roman state, whose course will on
> The way it takes, cracking ten thousand curbs
> Of more strong link asunder than can ever
> Appear in your impediment.
> (Shakespeare 1974, I, i, 66–72)

To Agrippa's declaration that Rome's governors care for the plebeians like children, the citizens scoff and retort, "Suffer us to famish, and their store-houses cramm'd with grain; make edicts for usury, to support usurers; repeal daily any wholesome act establish'd against the rich, and provide more piercing statues daily to chain up and restrain the poor." (Shakespeare 1974, I, i, 79–86)

Shakespeare's skill at storytelling implants narrative within narrative, enhancing the use of drama with fable. To a tense situation already stoked with images of food and famine, he depicts Agrippa in the act of launching a "pretty tale" and acknowledging that it may already be familiar to members of the mob. The citizens are in no mood for fables, yet they tolerate the telling. Agrippa, who shares the aristocratic disdain for commoners, begins in standard fable style with "a time when all the body's members / Rebell'd against the belly." (Shakespeare 1974, I, i, 96–97) The accusations parallel the citizens complaints—that the stomach was a vast black hole in the center of the body and that it lay "idle and inactive," a contrast to the other organs, who "see and hear, devise, instruct, walk, feel, and mutually participate, did minister unto the appetite and affection common of the whole body." (Shakespeare 1974, I, i, 102–105). Agrippa draws out the story with the belly's smiling and taunting, anthropomorphic characteristics that his audience could recognize in their current situation.

Shakespeare alters Livy's straightforward narration by having a citizen contribute observations on the dramatic story. At length, Agrippa reins in his impatient hearers and returns to the teller's role. As a model of class warfare, Shakespeare appends dialogue from the "most grave belly" to his accusers. In its own behalf, the belly claims to be "the store-house and the shop / Of the whole body." It cautions the limbs to remember how nutriment flows from stomach to circulatory system, heart, and brain, "through the cranks and offices of man, / The strongest nerves and small inferior veins." (Shakespeare 1974, I, i, 137–138) To assure the mob's understanding of the allegory, Agrippa allies senators with belly and the plebeians with the mutinous body parts. Genially,

Scene from a 1935 stage production of *A Midsummer Night's Dream*

he halts for an open-ended response by asking, "What do you think,/You, the great toe of this assembly?" (Shakespeare 1974, I, i, 154–155)

The addition of Coriolanus, a victorious Roman general, to the scene augments the role of fable in Shakespeare's text with comparisons drawn from Aesop: "Where he should find you lions, finds you hares;/Where foxes, geese." (Shakespeare 1974, I, i, 171–172) The noted warrior, lacking the graces of an orator, swings back to Agrippa's imagery with his contention,

> . . . your affections are
> A sick man's appetite, who desires most that
> Which would increase his evil.
> (Shakespeare 1974, I, i, 177–179)

Coriolanus's disaffection for working-class Romans resounds in his brief retort, "Hang 'em!" Thus, Shakespeare contrasts the patient teller of fables with the brashly judgmental Coriolanus.

Sources Bentley 1961; Boyce 1990; Campbell 1943; Chute 1949, 1951; Gassner and Quinn 1969; Lanier 1978; Miller 1989; Muir and Schoenbaum 1971; Sandler 1986; Shakespeare 1974.

SHAW, GEORGE BERNARD

An eccentric genius from Dublin, Ireland, George Bernard Shaw—known as the "Man of the Century," or simply G. B. S.—dominated the critical and theatrical worlds at the end of the nineteenth century and well into the twentieth. Brash and judgmental over a 70-year career, he wrote voluminously, covering such varied issues as women's rights and Hitler and fascism. The author of numerous witty comedies—*The Philanderer* (1905) and *Pygmalion* (1912)—he composed a theatrical fable, *Androcles and the Lion* (1912), based on a tenth-century Roman story by the anonymous fabulist Romulus. Prefaced in subsequent editions by a treatise, "On the Prospects of Christianity" (1915), the play expresses Shaw's unorthodox religiosity. In his tentative apologia, he acknowledges, "I am ready to admit that after contemplating the world and human nature for nearly sixty years, I see no way out of the world's misery but the way which would have been found by Christ's will if he had undertaken the work of a modern practical statesman." (Shaw 1951, 9) Thus, he transforms the simple fable of a tender-hearted animal lover into a complex stage satire of Christianity put to the test during the religious persecutions of Rome's decadent empire.

Shaw, who came from a troubled household, was amply educated in controversy and compromise. Born on July 26, 1856, the only son and last of three children of George Carr, an alcoholic and unsuccessful corn factor, and singer and operatic coach Lucinda Elizabeth Gurley Shaw, he understood the hardships of the poor Protestant in Ireland. In early childhood, he suffered the silences and disagreements common to unhappily mated parents. A gifted reader but a mediocre student in all subjects except composition at the Wesleyan Connexional School, he was tutored by his uncle, the Reverend George Carroll. At age 15, after his father's desertion, Shaw worked as cashier and realtor before accepting the fact that he couldn't make a go of business in Ireland. In 1876, he resettled his mother and sister Lucy in London and supported them by clerking for a telephone company. While his mother taught school, he continued his education with self-directed study in the British Museum reading rooms. From delivering soap-box orations in Hyde Park, he advanced to reporting for the London *Star, Pall Mall Gazette*, and *World* under the witty pseudonym Corno di Bassetto [trumpet of the little bass]. An assertive commentator and opinionated reformer, he devastated opponents with strong, clear essays on war, women, education, propriety, racial bias, temperance, vegetarianism, vivisection, vaccination, and the vagaries of the British stage and English spelling. After establishing himself as art, music, and drama critic for *Saturday Review*, he left journalism for novel writing. In 1882, he embraced Marxism and for two decades wrote and edited tracts for the atheistic Fabian Society. As speaker, tractarian, and polemicist, he set new standards of morality and taste.

Tall, red-haired, and abstemious, Shaw corresponded with female intellectuals but shied away from intimacy with women. His platonic marriage with Charlotte Frances Payne-Townshend in 1898, an Irish heiress, improved his tenuous health. On her money, he settled in Hertsfordshire, where he perfected drama as his most effective medium. His command of oratorical mode undergirds a

George Bernard Shaw

vigorous blend of criticism and humor that held his audience spellbound. Through the satire of *Arms and the Man* (1894), he debunked the glories and pretensions of militarism. His best-received comedy, *Man and Superman* (1905), featured a popular historical figure, Don Juan. To depict anti-Christian persecution during the Roman Empire, Shaw blended a popular fable with comedy, dialectic, irony, and whimsy in *Androcles and the Lion*.

Latin fable supplied Shaw with one of the genre's most common confrontations—a meek, undersized man facing a terrifying carnivore. In the original, the lion suffers from a thorn in his paw, which a gentle shepherd extracts. The story moves from forest to city after both beast and man fall into the hands of the Romans, who condemn the innocent shepherd to death in the arena by wild beast. The "aha" situation reduces the story's tense confrontation as the lion recognizes the kind man who relieved him of pain. At story's end, both man and beast receive pardon. Shaw chooses to ignore the simple ending, in which the man returns to his pastoral setting and the lion to the forest. For the stage, a grander fantasy pairs the unlikely mates—Tommy the lion with Andy the Christian—in a whimsical waltz before applause that bursts from the amphitheater, the usual scene of human torment and mangled remains.

Shaw's popularity took a giant leap forward in his next comedy, the complex *Pygmalion* (1913), also drawn from classic literature. In the matchup of Henry Higgins and Eliza Doolittle, Shaw staged the miscommunication common to male-female relations while he touted the importance of speech and grammar to social acceptability. In 1925, two years after his successful *Saint Joan*, he received the Nobel Prize for Literature, which he donated to the Anglo-Swedish Literary Foundation. Smug and vainglorious from his sudden spurt of fame, he made a world tour in 1933 and gathered encomia from adoring fans, even Americans, whom he claimed to abhor. The first filming of *Pygmalion* earned him an Academy Award in 1938. He died from hip injuries suffered in a fall on November 2, 1950. In 1952, Howard Hughes produced a stage-bound cinema version of *Androcles and the Lion*, scripted by Chester Erskine. Originally cast with Harpo Marx as Andy and Rex Harrison as Caesar, the final list of personae featured Alan Young as the Greek tailor along with Jean Simmons, Maurice Evans, Elsa Lanchester, Gene Lockhart, and Victor Mature. Two years later, *Pygmalion* was reworked as *My Fair Lady*, a musical stage romance that earned five Oscars and three Oscar nominations after its filming in 1964.

See also *Androcles and the Lion*.

Sources Bermel 1982; Brockett 1968; Gassner and Quinn 1969; Green 1965; Grigson 1963; Hill 1978; Holroyd 1989; Hornstein et al. 1973; Kunitz 1942; Magill 1958; Shaw 1951.

 # STEVENSON, ROBERT LOUIS

Like fellow storytellers Rudyard Kipling, Beatrix Potter, Oscar Wilde, and Lewis Carroll, Robert Louis Stevenson composed stories for a live and demanding audience as well as for general publication. His love of entertaining children derived in part from his own dismal childhood. Though weak most of his days from chronic bronchitis or tuberculosis, he traveled the world and lived an active life, partially inspired by his literary hero, Daniel Defoe. His memories of boyhood pursued him through adulthood, during which he actively shucked off Victorian constraints and lived the carefree bohemianism that he created for fictional characters. Born November 13, 1850, to Thomas and Margaret Balfour Stevenson, he was a precocious, coddled only child whose wealthy parents and nurse indulged his whims. A half-hearted student at Edinburgh University, he followed family tradition and studied first civil engineering, then read law at the office of Skene Edwards and Gordon. However, against family wishes, Stevenson decided to forgo the rigors of engineering or courtroom work for writing. Early on, he won a silver medal from the Royal Scottish Society of Arts for an essay on lighthouses. A combination of raffish companions, a fling with a prostitute, and liberal political opinions estranged him from his Calvinistic father, who was so domineering that he continued charging his son a penny for each slang utterance until Stevenson reached his twenties.

As he developed individuality and independence, Stevenson began writing travelogues and published *An Inland Voyage* (1878) and *Travels with a Donkey in the Cevennes* (1879). While visiting Fontainebleu in 1876 to strengthen weak lungs, he had met Fanny Vandegrift Osbourne, a married art student 11 years his senior and the mother of 11-year-old Lloyd and 18-year-old Belle. Despite his father's disapproval of the match, Stevenson pursued his love to the United States, lived and wrote for a time in Monterey, California, and, following her divorce from Samuel Osbourne and Stevenson's collapse from another bout of lung infection, married Fanny in San Francisco in May 1880. They settled in a cabin near the Silverado Mine on Mount St. Helens northwest of Calistoga, where he wrote *The Silverado Squatters* (1883). Broken in health and lacking adequate finances, he faced a bleak outlook. He reconciled with his father and obtained enough family money to relieve his penniless state, yet was unable to devote himself wholeheartedly to work because of continued bad health. At one time he wrote articles for the *Californian* for $2 each. He visited numerous spas and clinics in Europe and sailed aboard the schooner *Casco* among the Society Islands for 18 months.

In 1887, the financial picture shifted after Thomas Stevenson died, leaving his son comfortably well off. While residing in Davos, Switzerland, with his wife and stepson Lloyd, Stevenson entertained the boy with the episodic narration of *Treasure Island*, his first critical success, which earned him a lasting place in young adult literature but only £30 in cash. Like much of his work, critics praise the story for its mastery of high adventure, realistic details, and general appeal, but they cannot avoid pointing out a lack of polish and underlying thematic weakness. Later publications, however, reveal an evolving maturity, especially *The Master of Ballantrae: A Winter's Tale* (1889). Stevenson was working on another adventure novel, *The Weir of Hermiston*, on the day he died.

Stevenson is known for work in a variety of genres, from *The New Arabian Nights* (1882) and the perceptive poems of childhood in *A Child's Garden of Verses* (1885) to essays for *Scribner's*, the "Skye Boat Song" (1896), and the chilling

Robert Louis Stevenson

novella *The Strange Case of Dr. Jekyll and Mr. Hyde* (1886), a wildly successful morality fable that passed into the English language as "Jekyll-and-Hyde," a description for a schizoid personality. The work immediately sold 50,000 copies in England and 200,000 pirated copies in the United States, which earned the author fame but no royalties. His most popular adventure tales—*Treasure Island* (serialized from July 1881 to June 1882 in *Young Folks* magazine under the title of "The Sea Cook or Treasure Island" and published in book form in 1883) and *Kidnapped* (1886), set on the Argyll Islands west of Scotland—made him famous on both sides of the Atlantic. Other popular titles by Stevenson include *The Body Snatcher* (1885), *The Merry Men and Other Tales and Fables* (1887), *The Black Arrow* (1888), "The Bottle Imp" (1888), and "The Enchantress" (1989), a recovered short story his stepson had suppressed. After trying Saranac Lake, New York, and California's Napa Valley for salutary climate, the author spent his last years with his wife, mother, stepson, and stepdaughter at Diamond Head, Hawaii, then at Vailima, his plantation house in Samoa. His output reached its height and supplied him with more money than he had dreamed of making from writing. He enjoyed the sea air, farmed, and sailed the schooner *Equator* from Hawaii to his home. Adoring natives, whom he championed and defended against imperialism, dubbed him "Tusitala" [teller of tales] for his narrative skill. At his sudden death from cerebral hemorrhage in 1894 at age 44, native pallbearers carried his remains to a grave on Mount Vaea, marked by a romantic epitaph: "Under the wide and starry sky/Dig the grave and let me lie." (Eagle 1992, 83)

A study of Stevenson's letters has helped to delineate between the instant success of action stories for children and the popularized notion of the white exploiter among unsuspecting savages, a view that literary historians have discredited in recent years. At present, Stevenson is better known for sensitive poetry, psychological insights into moral dilemmas, and a mastery of original suspense, mystery, and horror tales. *Treasure Island, Dr. Jekyll and Mr. Hyde,* and *Kidnapped* have often been filmed or retold in cartoon form and are categorized among the most solid and universal of children's classics.

Among Stevenson's surprisingly ample canon of plays, travelogues, novels, short stories, essays, tales, poems, diaries, and memoirs, a small collection of 20 fables, published posthumously as *Fables* (1896), receives little commentary from critics, who tend to focus on adventures and poems. Using the confines of fable as a literary challenge, he began accumulating models in a variety of modes, including conventional fable, legend, and mystic tale, and promised Longman a manuscript by 1888. The great shift in his lifestyle distracted him from the projected work, which was left incomplete at his death.

The posthumous collection is an unusual sheaf of mature philosophical abstractions that muse over Stevenson's wanderings and seekings and his vacillation between bold runaway and penitent apostate. The first fable, "The Persons of the Tale," opens on familiar territory about the time that Stevenson completed Chapter 32 of *Treasure Island*. The drama derives from a conversation between Long John Silver and Captain Smollett recorded during a lull in their jobs as fictional characters. Talk heats up to a fierce competition for the author's respect. Smollett declares, "It's common sense, that what is good is useful too." (Stevenson 1905, 8) He and Silver come to the conclusion that virtue and villainy, the yin and yang of behaviors, form a balance to flesh out a full human profile. Rather than sign off on a moral, Stevenson carries the speakers to a surreal awareness of the author, who calls them back to their fictional task by opening his inkpot to begin Chapter 33.

Stevenson follows with two dramatic scenarios on the subject of looming catastrophe. The first is set at sea where a captain and crew debate appropriate action to take while a ship is sinking. The crux of the story is a disagreement between the unnamed captain and First Lieutenant Spoker over whether Spoker should shave or go to a watery grave with a stubbly face. The philosophic captain notes, "Life, at any moment and in any view, is as dangerous as a sinking ship; and yet it is man's handsome fashion to carry umbrellas, to wear indiarubber overshoes, to begin vast works, and to conduct himself in every way as if he might hope to be eternal." (Stevenson 1905, 13) Stevenson's stroke of black humor carries the prototypical Aesopic fable far from its original succinct form and conniving animal characters. The fable concludes with the captain maintaining his composure, asking for a cigar, and blowing up the ship "with a glorious detonation." The second story of the pair, "The Two Matches," pictures a smoker ponderings the possibility of striking a second match, lighting his pipe, and setting ablaze the dry California woods. The author brings the conjecture to a moot point when the smoker tries unsuccessfully to strike the second match. The theme of this oddly existential fable—solitude and thought pushed beyond sense—appears to derive from Stevenson's years as an invalid, when thought games were his daily challenge.

Skilled at a broad range of literary modes, Stevenson relieves his fable collection of predictability with a variety of diction, settings—castles, kirks, and huts on stilts—and dramatis personae, from the high to the lowest, from crones to seers, with a preponderance of ordinary folk. His juxtaposition plays story against story, as with the jump from a debate between a sick man and would-be rescuer to "The Devil and the Innkeeper," a witty folk narrative that engages the two in debate over innate evil. The innkeeper's decision to hang his adversary concludes the sophistry by which the devil eludes punishment. The tenth fable, "The Man and His Friend," places a quarreling twosome before "the great white Justice of the Peace," who finds the complainer guilty of foolishness in choosing so untrue a man for friend. (Stevenson 1905, 40) An unsubtle warning to those who challenge the status quo, "The Citizen and the Traveller" is set at a marketplace, where defiant citizens murder the stranger who threatens their delusions. Less dire is "The Distinguished Stranger," which criticizes a world order that places vertebrates above trees, which the alien admires above humans and cows as "the people with green heads." (Stevenson 1905, 47) The eleventh fable, "The Reader," debates righteousness and impiety in a fable-within-a-fable, which concludes with the judgmental reader tossing an impious book into the fire. Intent on silencing the Calvinistic echoes in his soul, Stevenson hones the narrative down to an unsettling mental image, "The coward crouches from the rod/And loathes the iron face of God." (Stevenson 1905, 54)

"The Transformation in Dr. Lanyon's Office," illustration from *Dr. Jekyll and Mr. Hyde*

At least three of the fables are set in Samoa, Stevenson's chosen homeland. "The Carthorses and the Saddlehorse" presents a dramatic confrontation between two worlds, with each side misconstruing the fundaments of the other. The sixteenth fable, "Something in It," jeopardizes a single-minded missionary, who, upon testing the truth of the island's pantheon of gods, concludes, "But if these tales are true, I wonder what about my tales!" (Stevenson 1905, 53) At the end of a seriocomic sojourn in Samoan hell, the missionary returns to land, having refused to drink the kava that symbolizes compromise in his traditional faith. Without hesitation, he rings the bell for services and continues disseminating questionable theology to islanders. Stevenson's moral—a caricature of the indomitable evangelist teetering on a pinpoint of truth—suggests a real proselytizer from the author's South Sea experience.

Unlike Aesop and his followers, Stevenson undergirds his didactic stories with a heavy subjectivity. A droll commentary on useless philosophical debate fuels "The Penitent," a brief fable that reflects Stevenson's personal differences with his Calvinist parents. The author pursues his disdain for Protestant zeal in "The Yellow Paint," a jolly send-up of the inflated promises that come with contrition and baptism, and "The House of Eld," a thin allegory that names the emotional price the author paid for rejecting his family's faith. Set among worshipers of the Roman gods Jupiter and Vulcan, the narrative reveals the semblance of atheism and the galling self-castigation that protagonist Jack inflicts on himself when he returns from a challenge match against sorcery. Stevenson replicates the framework of old-style fable in his six-line verse *epimythium*, which reminds the would-be iconoclast that chopping down the old tree (religion) risks the lives of parents, whose hearts and bones are encircled by the roots (orthodoxy). The author concludes that the tree topples, groaning like a mandrake, the fabled mandragora herb shaped in stem and root like a human torso with appended legs that suffer when wrested from the soil.

In succeeding visions of the search for truth and harmony, Stevenson questions his personal path from Scotland's harsh piety to carefree island mores. In "The Four Reformers," he collects four unidentified debaters who meet "under a bramble bush" to discuss how to change the world. (Stevenson 1905, 38) They ponder abolition of marriage, God, and work, then confront the standard flaw in rebellion—what to put in place of familiar human structures. The weakest of Stevenson's 20 philosophic fables, the brief dialogue thins out to a timorous list of unthinkably bold steps—to abolish the Bible and law. The third reformer reaches the unlikely conclusion that total reform would abolish humankind. An uneasy litany of quest stories—"Faith, Half-Faith, and No Faith at All," "The Touchstone," "The Poor Thing," and "The Song of the Morrow"—mirrors the self-doubt that marred the author's attempt at happiness on a Pacific isle. As Aesop warned, "To change place is not to change one's nature."

Sources Calder 1980, 1981; Eagle and Stephens 1992; Ehrlich and Carruth 1982; Maixner 1981; Nickerson 1982; Rankin 1987; "Robert Louis Stevenson," http://www. halcyon.com; Rubin 1995; Saposnik 1974; Skow 1995; Stevenson 1905; Swearingen 1980.

STORYTELLING

Storytelling is an elemental art. It originated in preliterate society at firesides, oases, forest glades, and streamsides, where communities paused to share their past in anecdote, eyewitness accounts, and formulaic stories that mesmerize and charm. Central to the storyteller's success is a talent for telling matched to communities for whom an evening of stories is the normal end of the workday, whether led by the puppeteers of Java, string tellers of Zaire, sand tracers of Walberi, Australia, Sufi masters, or the Maître Conte [master storyteller] of Haiti. The value of oral transmission is the immediacy and inventiveness of the telling, which is as much acting and mime as literature. No transmitter repeats a story exactly. No translator can retain the music and cadence of the original transmission. Thus, such story cycles as the *Panchatantra*, *Tales from the Kathasaritsagara*, Aesop's fables, *A Thousand and One Nights*, Jataka tales, Jamaican Anancy trickster tales, High John the Conqueror, Daddy Mention, and Uncle Remus's Brer Rabbit stories turn into lore, the accrescence of detail and surmise that carries the totality forward into later settings and recensions.

The kinetics of storytelling accommodate the audience physically and historically by expanding or condensing, suiting the version within certain parameters to contemporary tastes, sensibilities, maturity, and needs. For example, the dilemma tale of Senegal, Togo, and Gambia presents a complicated plot requiring a blend of pragmatism, social ethos, and morality. The story of three sons who wander the world and return in a year to compare their wealth concludes with the three joining their powers to revive their father from the grave. At the crux, the teller turns the solution over to volunteers from the audience with the question, "Now which of these three sons has performed the best?" (Abrahams 1993, 115) Other models of dilemma lore pose character assessment or ethical judgment involving who gets the bride, who should be king, who rates the glory, or who deserves to be executed. Composed in the past and resolved in the present, the oldest of these plots are ever fresh, relevant, and stirring.

The role of teller has varied over time, but has always adapted to human affairs and learning. Whether worldly, wise, pedantic, rigidly orthodox, or cynical, the storyteller—who may answer to the title of harper, griot, minstrel, seanachie, kahuna, scop, or *rhapsodes*—often presents fable and other forms of wisdom lore with no comment, thus allowing the narrative, out of its own tension and resolution, to instruct or chasten. The session may begin with what Turkish tellers call the *tekerleme*, a nonsense jingle, for example, "When the camel was a town crier and the cock was a barber, when the sieve was in the straw and I was rocking my mothers' cradle." (Walker and Uysal 1966, 10–11) Another method is a familiar invocation—"Listen, my children," "Cric? Crac!," or "A story, a story! Let it go, let it come"—and formulaic closure, as in the Ghayan, *"ray ras,* the story is over." (Abrahams 1993, 299, 165) Above all, tellers trust their material, which they craft with attention to motivation and the sparest of details and limited cast of characters, seldom numbering over three. The action is swift and precipitate, rarely encompassing more than the passage of a day.

By giving speech to inanimate trees, rocks, and beasts, the storyteller presents impersonal wisdom that suits any setting.

Not all of the storyteller's involvement is objective. A professional necessity for beast fable is the creation of idiosyncratic animal voices, human cries and cackles, and the soughing of wind and water. In the lively telling of the Ghayan story "All the Little Animals," the presenter must alternate between straightforward text and the rabbit's hunting song, which thrums:

> Gbevevevevevevevel
> *My dogs don't hunt with bells, sic 'em. Big Lion*
> *Hyena, it will get in my eyes,* tendee vem
>   *It will get in my eyes,* tendee
> *It will get in my eyes,* tendee vem
>   *It will get in my eyes,* tendee
> *The little animals have all died,* tendee vem
> (Abrahams 1993, 164)

A soothing mother ostrich's call enlivens the Masai story "Whose Children?" with repetitions of

> Sweet, fat children
>   Follow me.
> Sweet, fat babies
>   Follow me

offset by distress cries of "Lion stole my children. Help! Help!/Lion stole my children. Help! Help!" (Creeden, 1994, 106) Such artful voicing lifts storytelling from a distinct literary form to performance art. A modern example comes from aboriginal teller Eustan Williams of the Githavul Tribe who relates "Dirrangun at Tooloom," the *pourquoi* story of a clever old woman who hid Australia's water. At the hag's demise, the teller represents the cries of the old woman as her fig tree collapses, freeing two streams to become the Clarence and South Rivers. A second water story, "Dirrangun at Baryulgil," related by Lucy Daley of the Bunjalung tribe, requires mouth and throat noises to imitate the drifting mists and gush of a sacred spring. At the height of the tale, when Dirrangun realizes she can't stop the flow from a broken dam, she shouts a curse that adulterates the water with salt, then throws herself into the path of the stream, which turns her to stone. Aboriginal teller Percy Mumbulla, an elder of Wallaga Lake, New South Wales, must make similar noises to re-create animals' squawks of "Gook-gook, gook-gook" for the story "Doonootes" and the cry of the harpooner and the slap of the orca's tail on the water for "The Whalers."

The late twentieth century saw a renaissance in English-language actor/tellers as well as in native tellers of other languages. Modern tellers range over the gamut of narrative venues:

- early childhood specialists Rafe Martin, Margaret Green, and Norma Livo

- Caribbean tellers Ken Corsbie, Grace Hallworth, Louise Bennett, and Paul Keens-Douglas

Engraving based on a nineteenth-century painting by C. Gregory, titled "Folk-Lore"

- African-American tellers Jackie Torrence, Frankie and Doug Quimby, Rex Ellis, Mary Carter Smith, Adisa Bankole, and Charlotte Blake Alston

- Cajun performer J. J. Reneaux

- Jewish storykeepers Diane Wolkstein, Jim Weiss, and Nancy Schimmel

- bilingual tellers Joe Hayes, Olga Loya, Folke Tegetoff, David Gonzalez, and Michael Parent

- Native American fabulists Matt Jones, Gayle Ross, Lloyd Arneach, Johnny Moses, and Joseph Bruchac.

- Hawaiian tellers Jeff Gere and "Uncle Charlie" Maxwell

An American favorite, Pleasant De Spain, delights listeners with such creative fables as "Frog Swallows Ocean," "Rabbit's Tail Tale," "The Savage Skylark," "Cardinal's Red Feathers," "Starfire," and "The Grizzly Bear Feast." In the griot tradition, Rex Ellis recites African and African-American fables intended to teach right behaviors in young listeners. A professional platform teller and vibrant preserver of Australian fable, Peter Dargin, from Dubbo, New South Wales, specializes in traditional Australian lore, outback adventures, and Jack the Jolly Swagman stories. Dargin's numerous publications and public performances feature "The Swagman's Stone Soup," a classic fable worldwide that exalts community and cooperation. Dargin's local material centers on creation stories about the Darling River, an Australian version of Rumi's Sufi tale "The Six Wise Men and the Elephant,"and "Kabungada the Pelican," an outback classic

Cherokee storyteller Gayle Ross

that explains the geological origin of opals. In the view of D'Jimo Kouyate, a Senegalese griot, the common bond of these and other practitioners is the power to give back the fragments of culture that have been forgotten, misplaced, lost, or stolen.

To confer oral heritage, some raconteurs blend oral skills with the sounds of musical instruments and rhythm enhancers, such as the African griot's strum of the kora, the Japanese itinerant teller's wood clappers, Brother Blue's snapping fingers, Mary Carter Smith's cowtail switch, and the ching and sway of Ellaraino's bangles and hoop earrings. In obeisance to high-energy cadencing, Rex Ellis plucks the mbira, the African thumb piano; Patrick Ball prefers the Celtic harp; Adisa Bankole drums the phrasing that structures his narrative; Shanta masters words with a backdrop of reed zither, sitar, and shakere; Mauian teller Uncle Charlie Maxwell depends on the plunk of the koa guitar. To a slap on the tambourine, Gullah teller Doug Quimby emulates the labors of dockworkers:

> Peh me, peh me,
> Peh me ma munie doun . . . HUNH
> Peh me or go to jayul,
> Peh me ma munie doun . . . HUNH!
> [Pay me my money down. Pay me or go to jail.]
> (Goss & Barnes 1989, 489)

The alliance of narration with rhythm and melody creates a multiple sensory image—the tripartite brain impulses that secure the fabulist's message through eye, ear, imagination, and body rhythms.

In modern tradition, raconteurs experiment and recast age-old stories with verbal brilliance. An innovative storykeeper in the Aesopic tradition, Heather Forest crafts material from beast fables, the animated strands of human experience, which she relates with original guitar music and ideophonic effects. Like the Celtic minstrel, she savors the kernel of universal wisdom at the core of classic fable. In an interview for *Sing Out*, she confided: "When I'm telling an old story I get a chill up my spine thinking that I'm touching tongue with the same story that someone might have told a thousand years ago. I feel that it's a message that someone long ago felt that this was important enough to save." (Keding 1995, n. p.) Her fresh retellings highlight words that convey a metaphoric glimpse of human nature, the central image of "King Solomon and the Otter," "The Lion and the Rabbit," and her version of "Stone Soup." Forest's expertise at sound and rhythm has earned her the high honors reserved for the teller—an American Booksellers Association Pick of the List, *Storytelling World* Anthology Award, and, in 1997, entry into the National Storytelling Association Circle of Excellence.

Other examples of successful storytelling include collectors of fable and lore from varied sources. Canadian performer Dan Yashinsky has amassed traditional wonder tales, medieval satire, and fool tales to recite in a variety of venues. Of Jewish, Romanian, Turkish, and French ancestry, he came of age among immigrant tale tellers before studying the master fabulists—Geoffrey

Chaucer, Scheherazade, Giovanni Bocaccio, and Homer. To perpetuate the fabulist's role in modern times, in 1978 to 1979, Yashinsky founded the Toronto Festival of Storytelling, the Storytellers School of Toronto, and "1,001 Friday Nights of Storytelling," North America's longest-running weekly session. In 1990, he won the City of Toronto Book Prize for *Tales for an Unknown City*. A publishing success story and multiple award winner with similar enthusiasm for wisdom lore, Jim Weiss and Greathall Productions thrive on a variety of myth, drama, fairy tale, and fable. His preference in Aesopic lore leans toward "The Crow and the Pitcher," "The Lion and the Mouse," and "The Tortoise and the Hare" and Horace's "The City Mouse and the Country Mouse." He has earned repeated rewards for his recorded performances, including Aesopic *Animal Tales* (1990), *Arabian Nights* (1990), *The Jungle Book* (1995), and *A Christmas Carol and Other Favorites* (1996).

See also Adams, Richard; Harris, Joel Chandler; Hurston, Zora Neale; Native American fable; *A Thousand and One Nights*.

Sources Abrahams 1993; *Aesop: Five Centuries of Illustrated Fables* 1964; Bancroft 1994, 1995, 1996; Creeden 1994; Dargin 1991, 1997; De Spain 1994, 1996, 1998; Emerson 1997; Forest 1982, 1989; Goss and Barnes 1989; Hurston 1981; Keding 1995; Mbitu and Prime 1997; Miller and Snodgrass 1998; Somadeva 1994; Walker and Uysal 1966; Weiss, *Animal Tales* 1990, *Arabian Nights* 1990, 1995; Yolen 1986.

 A THOUSAND AND ONE NIGHTS

From an Islamic frame of reference comes the Middle Eastern phenomenon *Alf Laylah Wa Laylah* [A Thousand and One Nights], a secular storybook that opens and closes with pious prayers and praise to Allah. No other Oriental or Middle Eastern work has had a greater impact on European thought or been translated so rapidly into all Western languages. The final collection is a widely appreciated and emulated body of interlocking vernacular folksay, didactic fable, anecdote, jest, and fairy tales by tenth- and twelfth-century writers in Baghdad and by eleventh- and fourteenth-century Egyptian authors. It has its nucleus in *Hazar Afsanah* [A Thousand Tales] (ninth century), a Persian storybook translated into Arabic. The final collection, completed over seven centuries, places in a charming framework Indian, Persian, and Arabian lore accumulated from a broad range of times and places, including India, Iran, Iraq, Egypt, Turkey, and Greece. According to fragmentary background, Ibn an-Nadim claims that Abu 'Abd Allah ibn 'Abdus al-Jashyari intended to compile 1,000 popular stories but died in 942 C.E. with only 480 complete. Rounding out the collection, later editors appended more stories in an effort to achieve the original goal.

Of particular delight are segments of the *A Thousand and One Nights* that triumph in worldwide popularity:

- the roc or rukh, a legendary bird large enough to abduct elephants

- Ali Baba and the Forty Thieves

- Alá al-Din [Aladdin] and the Magic Lamp, the story of a boy living with his widowed mother. By summoning the power of a magic lamp, he acquires wealth, property, and a royal wife

- jinn stories of supernatural spirits who take human and animal shape

- the Seven Viziers or the Seven Sages, part of the Sinbadnameh or Sinbad cycle, a framework narrative about a king who engages the mentor Sindbad to instruct the royal prince

- the seven voyages of Sinbad the Sailor

- Jewish stories of "The Sultan and His Three Sons," "The Angel of Death," and "Alexander and the Pious Man"

Scheherazade intriguing her husband with stories

The impetus to the collection is its pivotal theme—a male-centered social code and savage patriarchy displayed in the barbarism of an Iranian sultan, Shahriyar, who distrusts women. To rid himself of imagined female treachery, he enjoys a different virgin wife each night and slays her at sunrise. The social and religious implications of his paranoia affect the entire kingdom, for none of his mates can produce heirs if they are not allowed to live. The long string of dead wives ends with the stories' narrator, Scheherazade, the daughter of his vizier. An accomplished, spunky survivor, she has read widely from books, annals, biographies, fables, and legends. Like Islamic women of the Middle Ages, she acquires knowledge to ready her for the responsibility of a home, husband, children, and household staff. She must prepare her mind for the important work of educating the royal children and advising them on matters of behavior and mores, religious faith, mate selection, and work. A civilizing influence on all society, the king's consort sets the tone of the royal family, including arousing her husband's sexual desire to procreate more children.

A forerunner of the Renaissance woman, Scheherazade is equal to the task of humanizing her deranged husband and restoring the sanctity of life. Her knowledge of history, philosophy, and the arts and sciences is so complete that she can recite passages by heart. To break the three-year cycle of slaughter that might end her life and that of her sister Dynyazad, she insists on marrying the king and tells him delightful stories, each left unfinished until the next night.

The holy context of her narrative harmonizes religious beliefs, customs, and superstitions with the moral order of Islamic society. The sultan is so charmed that he stays her execution for a thousand and one nights. In the end, after remaining married two years and nine and a half months to the same woman, he abandons his harsh perception of womanhood and embraces his artful wife and nighttime entertainer. Translated from Arabic to Persian around 850 C.E., the collection survived in loose form until the eighteenth century, when an Egyptian editor turned the stories into a unified work.

At the beginning of the mélange of bawdy, exotic, and tantalizing fare is a simple rural story, "The Donkey, the Ox, and the Farmer." A fool tale about an ox who lets a donkey manipulate him with bad advice, the story turns on the ox's pretended ill health. The wise farmer, who knows the donkey's tricks, forces him into the ox's harness and works him for two days. Relying on the ox's gullibility, the donkey restores him to interest in work with a warning that the farmer will kill him if his vigor doesn't soon return. The second bit of advice so fills the ox with enthusiasm that the farmer falls down laughing at his jubilation. Less sanguine is "Aiming Too High," the story of a sparrow that tries to carry off a ram. For his conceit, the shepherd rips his wing feathers and ties his legs together. To his children, the shepherd snorts, "That is someone who wanted to make himself equal to a creature greater than himself." (Green 1965, 145) Well suited to Arabian philosophy and a rigid system of social caste, the warning grows out of predemocratic society. Thus, the fable fits advice lore that reminds the ambitious to content themselves with the standard life pattern.

The twelfth of the collection's sixteen cycles or episodes is "The Hedgehog and the Pigeons," a framework narrative in the style of the *Panchatantra* that opens on the trickster hedgehog's greed for dates. Disguising himself as a monk on retreat, he claims to have renounced the world 30 years before. Within the deceiver's narrative is a brief fable of the farmer who neglects to sow his fields because he doesn't want to risk failure. The pigeon internalizes the exemplum and shakes down a year's supply of dates, which the trickster steals. The story satirizes the glib preacher who, after impressing others with his piety, easily dupes them. In retort, the pigeon tells his own admonitory fable about two thieves who unintentionally poison themselves. At this point in the narration, the audience interrupts: "Oh Scheherazade," said the king, "these fables are not only edifying, they're delightful. Let me hear some more." (Zipes 1991, 427) The sequence proceeds with "The Tale of the Thief and His Monkey," which interlocks with "The Tale of the Foolish Weaver." Unlike the clear divisions between Aesopic lore, the intricacy of Scheherazade's stories is like an alluring palace with atria opening onto side chambers, niches, and gardens, each with its own savor and mystique. With family, duty, and self-preservation uppermost in her mind, she draws Shahryar into "The Wily Dalilah and Her Daughter Zaynab," a complex trickster story of two female survivors who survive capture, torment, and near crucifixion while outwitting the males of Baghdad.

The sequence comes to closure with "The Marriage of King Shahryar and Scheherazade." Presenting her three little sons to the king, the storyteller prostrates herself at his feet to beg a reprieve for the sake of the royal children. The obeisance highlights the book's raison d'être—the salvation of Scheherazade and of the king, whose arrogant despotism abates through newfound humility, right thinking, and ethical actions. Shahryar's compliments reflect the author's reverence for stories: "I found you chaste, pure, ingenuous, and pious! May Allah bless you and your father and mother and their root and branch!" (Zipes 1991, 577) Scheherazade's reply wishes long life, dignity, and majesty to the king and, by extension, to her stories. Wilting from exertion, she adds, "But telling all these tales can be exhausting, and listening can be tedious, and what I have told is sufficient warning for the man with good sense and also sufficient admonishment for the wise." Cleansed of his misogyny and distrust, Shahryar praises her as the means by which God saves humankind from oppression and slaughter. The grand preparations that conclude the work contrast the simple, unadorned fare of Aesop, Babrius, Avianus, and Jean de La Fontaine, for the king is so imbued with narrative that he bubbles over to his brothers about Scheherazade's clever "proverbs, parables, chronicles, pleasantries, quips, jests, stories, anecdotes, dialogues, histories, and verses." (Zipes 1991, 579) The mirrored joys of the resolution derive from the marriage of Scheherazade's sister to Shahryar's brother, a parallel misogynist who also murdered his wives one by one after copulating with them. The bounty of the wedding scene spreads to the king's subjects, who profit from Scheherazade's wise counsel. The ultimate good spools out worldwide in the stories that the king's scribes set down in 30 volumes.

Drawing on a Syrian manuscript, French translator and Oriental scholar Antoine Galland retold in a 12-volume collection *Les Mille et Une Nuits, contes arabes traduits en français* [The Thousand and One Nights, Arabian Stories Translated into French] (1708), which stimulated European curiosity about Islamic culture and literature. One of many works to reach ordinary readers, the anthology was available in cheap copies for home use and in bowdlerized versions for schoolchildren. In 1888, Sir Richard Francis Burton, Oxford-trained linguist, adventurer, author, and translator of Basile's *The Pentamerone* (1893), the *Kama Sutra* (1883) and other Oriental works, published in ten volumes an unexpurgated translation of *The Book of the Thousand Nights and a Night: A Plain and Literal Translation of the Arabian Nights Entertainment*. Critics accuse him of misappropriating much of the work of John Payne's modestly successful *The Book of the Thousand Nights and One Night* (1884), Totaram Sháyán's *Hazar Dastan* [The Thousand Tales] (nineteenth century), and Hermann Zotenberg's *Histoire d' Alá al-Din ou La Lampe Merveilleuse, Texte Arabe* [The Story of Aladdin or the Wonderful Lamp from the Arabic Text] (1888). The stories influenced William Shakespeare's *Taming of the Shrew* (ca. 1589), Alfred Tennyson's "A Recollection of the Arabian Nights," the work of American muralist Maxfield Parrish, who illustrated an edition of the *Arabian Nights*, and the music of Russian composer Nikolai Rimsky-Korsakov, who in 1888 showcased the "Scheherazade Symphonic Suite," simultaneously with the newly published translations of the stories. In addition, numerous twentieth-century movies are based on the stories, including *Ali Baba and the Forty Thieves* (1943), *Sinbad the Sailor* (1947), *Ali Baba and the Forty Thieves* (1954), *Ali Baba and the Seven Saracens* (1965), *Sinbad and the*

"Open, Sesame"

Ali Baba and the Forty Thieves

Eye of the Tiger (1977), and Walt Disney's Academy Award–winning animated version of *Aladdin* (1992), featuring the voice of Robin Williams.

Sources *Adventures in World Literature* 1970; Blackham 1985; "Brewer: Dictionary of Phrase and Fable," http://www.bibliomania.com; Cooper 1921; Creeden 1994; Dailey 1994; Green 1965; Hobbs 1986; Komroff 1935; Krappe 1964; Lang and Dudley 1969; Leach 1967; McGreal 1996; Newbigging 1895; Rosenberg 1997; Shah 1982; Somadeva 1994; Steinberg 1954; Zipes 1991.

THURBER, JAMES

A taciturn, difficult man, essayist, cartoonist, and playwright James Thurber was, nonetheless, one of the foremost humorists of the mid-twentieth century and the prize fabulist of the era in both the United States and Britain. The stereotypical middle American, he became the heartland's voice, an astute creator sometimes confused in the reader's mind with the muddling antihero trapped in wakeful somnambulism and accompanied by his partisans, Thurber's sad-eyed, resolute dogs. Grown pessimistic to the point of despair in his last decade, Thurber limited his satire to a spare landscape of contemporary figures—bloated husbands, shrewish wives, and the glib, knowing dogs who observe their disgruntled, unfulfilling marriages. The languor and malaise of his subjects belie the vigor and intensity of his psychological probings into domestic dilemmas, which critics Alistair Cooke, Malcolm Cowley, John Updike, Dorothy Parker, and T. S. Eliot admired for tension and accuracy. In exultation, the *New York Times* labeled Thurber "a Joyce in false-face." (Thurber 1940, flap) The height of Thurber's creativity is *Fables for Our Time and Famous Poems Illustrated* (1940), an anthology containing 28 original illustrated fables, favoring the familiar mouse, lion, and wolf of Aesop along with a bloodhound, unicorn, scorched moth, and "The Scotty Who Knew Too Much," modeled after his own dog, Jeannie. A sequel, *Further Fables for Our Time* (1956), presents 37 of Thurber's fables for the *New Yorker* and ten additions, which add to hens, lions, and foxes a new cast featuring a godfather and godchild, "The Lady of the Legs," and a chipmunk and its mate.

Thurber was a writer and scribbler from childhood. He was born December 8, 1894, in Columbus, Ohio, a geographic touchstone for his classic story "The Night the Bed Fell." The second of the three sons of Mary Agnes "Mame" Fisher and Charles Leander Thurber, he was influenced by his mother's vaudeville-inspired pranks and his father's ill-paid political career, which kept family finances near the breaking point. After Charles Thurber accepted the job of assistant to a congressman in 1901, the family settled in Falls Church, Virginia, for two years. In a backyard mishap, James was blinded in the left eye by his older brother William, who shot him with an arrow while playing William Tell. The disaster was exacerbated by his mother's brief infatuation with Christian Science, which caused her to delay treatment until the eye was beyond reclamation. On return to Columbus, the Thurbers continued to scrimp along on spotty income and eventually moved into the home of grandfather William Fisher.

Educated at Sullivant School, Thurber was a self-starter. He taught himself to use the family Underwood typewriter and wrote his first poem, "My Aunt Mrs. John T. Savage's Garden at 185 South Fifth Street, Columbus, Ohio," at age 13. From East High in Columbus, he moved on to Ohio State from 1913 to 1919, where he wrote for the university paper, the *Ohio Lantern*, and the literary journal, the *Sun-Dial*. Without announcing a departure from class, he coasted for a year to watch Charlie Chaplin movies and Westerns and to read independently. He spent the war years as code clerk in the Department of State in Washington, D.C., and in the American embassy in Paris. As a city hall reporter and reviewer for the Columbus *Dispatch*, state correspondent for the *Christian Science Monitor* and the Paris and Riviera editions of the *Chicago Tribune*, he enjoyed post–World War I Paris with wife Althea Adams. In his first separation from the American ethos, he evolved a detachment that powered his later career in satirizing the miasmas of everyday life.

By 1926, Thurber had abandoned journalism and established a permanent literary home more suited to his talents. Fortuitously, he chose the *New Yorker*. Although he helped set the magazine's tone and direction, he at first felt hemmed in by the job of managing editor. To revive his quirky humor and conversational pacing, he shucked off administrative constraints and took refuge in light verse, casual pieces, and "Talk of the Town," the urbane column that suited his penchant for witty, contemplative commentary. For literary companionship, he joined a coterie of town wits who frequented the Algonquin Hotel and drew murals for the Cafe Français at Rockefeller Center and for Tim Costello's Third Avenue Saloon, a popular after-hours haunt.

In ten-minute intervals, Thurber sketched rudimentary cartoons as an offhand outlet for nervous energy. The first professional treatment of his doodlings resulted in 1931 after his supportive officemate, essayist E. B. White, retrieved a crumpled scrap tossed into the wastebasket and submitted it to the art department for publication. The drawing prefaced a lifetime of complex, enigmatic drawings. He gathered them into compendia devoted to tremulous males and Wagnerian females—both disturbingly reminiscent of his dismal first marriage—and to dogs, whom he depicted as critics of humankind's folly. He won the American Cartoonists' T-Square Award in 1956 but relegated cartooning to the distant edge of his creative hours as an adjunct to satire and parody. Because he undervalued his scribblings, only 40 of the original panels survive.

By 1933, Thurber had resigned from fulltime employment to freelance and exhibit his art in one-man shows. He wrote chiefly for the *New Yorker*, which paid him from $200 to $400 for his submissions and continued publishing his work for over three decades. After roaming England, Bermuda, and California, he settled on an annual migration from Connecticut to various addresses in Greenwich Village with Helen Muriel Wismer, a magazine editor and his second wife. He assembled some of his best pieces to complete *The Middle-Aged Man on the Flying Trapeze* (1935). A work habit of late-night prowlings gave place to a regular schedule of nocturnal writing. His book-length publications include his own compendia and the illustration of five books by other people on dogs, fashion, etiquette, and etymology. In 1939, Thurber collaborated with

Elliott Nugent to produce a play, *The Male Animal*, and achieved lasting fame for a six-page short story, "The Secret Life of Walter Mitty." From frequent selection for textbooks and anthologies of humor and satire, Walter Mitty, the droll fantasizer, added his name to the English language as a synonym for bemusement and woolgathering.

In the late 1930s, Thurber quailed at the emerging cataclysm in Europe and complained that "there was no God watching over the sorrowful and sinister scene, these menacing and meaningless animals." (Morsberger 1964, 34) He engrossed himself in fable, a light, pithy literary genre well suited to his touch and need. As World War II took shape in Europe, he found plenty of subjects for fable, including characters that resemble Mussolini, Hitler, Jewish internees, and jack-booted female emasculators. An early attempt, "The Bright Emperor" (1932), displays Thurber's intense distaste for women, especially those who connive, wangle, or bluster their way into control. In the text, a little girl subdues a king with presents. A favorite in textbooks and models of satire, his updated Little Red Riding Hood depicts the sturdy young protagonist as a gun-toting moll who shoots the wolf. He concludes, "It is not so easy to fool little girls nowadays as it used to be." (Thurber 1940, 5) Counter to the hooded heroine Thurber appends the grim, gloating wife in "The Unicorn in the Garden," whose clever husband circumvents her attempt to have him committed. To females in his audience who plot their mates' undoing, Thurber quips, "Don't count your boobies until they are hatched." (Bernstein 1975, 308)

In the mid-1940s, before his sight fogged permanently into blindness, Thurber lived in Cornwall, where he wrote *My World—and Welcome to It* (1942), "The Catbird Seat" (1943), *Men, Women and Dogs* (1943), and *The Thurber Carnival* (1945). His allegorical fairy tales—*Many Moons* (1943), *The Great Quillow* (1944), his Ohioana Medal–winning *The White Deer* (1945), *The Thirteen Clocks* (1950), and *The Wonderful O* (1957)—entertain both children and adults by contending against time-honored villains in multitiered satires of Adolf Hitler, Joseph Stalin, and Joseph McCarthy's repressive House Un-American Affairs Committee (HUAC). Although Thurber predicted his investigation by HUAC, at the end of the 1940s, fate brought him instead Columbia University's Laughing Lions Award for humor and honorary doctorates from Kenyon College and Williams College. His frustration with publishers fueled "File and Forget" (1953), which characterizes a disaffection for office trivialities. Nonetheless, in this same period, he extolled mid-life contentment at his colonial estate, establishing that he intended to relax with boules, ball games on the radio, a sizable wine cellar, poodles, *Huckleberry Finn*, and friends.

Misfortune clouded Thurber's declining years, which were a mixture of career triumphs and personal disasters. Occasional blackouts limited his driving. By 1950, he lost vision in his remaining eye from cataract and trachoma. In subsequent years, he struggled with the malaise that accompanied a toxic thyroid condition and published his increasingly negative satire, which even Roger Angell, his editor at the *New Yorker,* often rejected. Thurber rallied in 1953, when the Ohioana Library Association awarded him its Sesquicentennial Medal and Yale University granted him an honorary LL.D. In 1957, he won the American

Library Association's Library and Justice Award for *Further Fables for Our Time* (1956); in 1958, he was honored with an invitation to *Punch*'s Wednesday gathering. Two years later, he received a Tony for *A Thurber Carnival* (1960), a Broadway smash that starred Paul Ford, Peggy Cass, and Tom Ewell. In 1961, Ohio State honored him for "Meritorious Service to Humanity and to Our Alma Mater." Embittered and alcoholic, he died of pneumonia following surgery to relieve a blood clot.

In retrospect, Thurber's contributions to fable class him among giants of world literature—Aesop, Phaedrus, Horace, and Jean de La Fontaine. Preceding his major fable collections were hints of genius, particularly *The Last Flower: A Parable in Pictures* (1939), a pictorial fable of World War XII. Appropriately, he developed the text cartoon style in 51 frames, which took him two hours. He dedicated the somber work to his daughter in hopes of a better world. The near annihilation of gentility and beauty from the earth results in an ennui in which "human beings just sat around, doing nothing." (Thurber 1987, 322) A renaissance prefaces Thurber's focus on a single couple and a flower, forerunners of another buildup of civilization and the oppressive cadence of marching feet, launched by self-appointed "liberators." The second apocalypse returns the cycle to another man, woman, and flower. The book's fragile optimism strikes a shaky balance with grim foreboding and apocalyptic humor. Still applicable at the end of Thurber's life, *The Last Flower* survived the war era to apply to protracted cold war tensions and the ban-the-bomb mania of the 1960s, a downhill slide he jokingly referred to as "carpe noctem" [seize the night]. (Morsberger 1964, 42)

In the same vein as his doomed blossom, *Fables for Our Time*, an innovative restatement of Aesop and Horace, parodies the inanity and brutality of humankind, an appropriate subject for the year 1940. Opening on a zany parody of Horace's "The City Mouse and the Country Mouse," he brings sustained humor and lucid criticisms of contemporary life to the misadventures of "The Mouse Who Went to the Country," a jab at misaligned transportation systems that sour the city mouse on bucolic destinations. Thurber's moral speaks the cynicism of the city dweller: "Stay where you are, you're sitting pretty." (Thurber 1940, 3) The third fable, "The Two Turkeys," probes the wisdom of cultivating contentment and concludes that feisty young malcontents may suffer the demise of the contender ("Moral: Youth will be served, frequently stuffed with chestnuts"). (Thurber 1940, 7) Less reassuring is his prediction that Nazism will swamp the docile European Jew, the obvious victim of "The Rabbits Who Caused All the Trouble." To those who refused to take seriously the menacing madman in Germany, Thurber penned a new, grim version of the Little Red Hen, whom he martyrs, then vindicates: "For the heavens actually *were* falling down. Moral: It wouldn't surprise me a bit if they did." (Thurber 1940, 71)

Throughout Thurber's succinct fables, the action finds its target in the tidy aphorism that graces the end. In Aesopic style, he dispatches manipulative promoters ("Moral: If you live as humans do, it will be the end of you"), unimaginative Babbitts ("Moral: There is no safety in numbers, or in anything else"), and the contentment of the deluded ("Moral: Who flies afar from the sphere of our sorrow is here today and here tomorrow"). (Thurber 1940, 10, 13, 19) With facetious lightheartedness, he tosses in contemporary conundrums—the lone male who can't find his studs and suspenders after his wife leaves him, bus schedules that don't apply on weekends, hasty divorces, teetotalers who become egregious bores after going on the wagon, and self-serving demagogues who devour the meek. To satisfy his animus, he pursues a private war against bossy, vindictive females with "The Lion Who Wanted to Zoom" and "The Stork Who Married a Dumb Wife." Yet, he manages to parody his own Walter Mitty self with the timorous, tormented old gentleman in "The Green Isle in the Sea," who finds a former haven too blighted and leafless to shelter him from incoming bombers, a touch that wrests Aesopic form from its setting on the ancient Mediterranean rim and, eerily, anticipates Japan's daylight attack on Pearl Harbor only months after his book's initial success.

Stylistically, Thurber's command of fable is right on target. The action moves as relentlessly toward doom as a cataract over a cliff. His diction echoes the times and reads as clearly as kudos from the dress circle at the St. James, as hard-nosed as a caption from Dick Tracy. His scenarios are replete with the same violent retribution that colors the fables of Aesop and La Fontaine. "The Seal Who Became Famous" drowns; "The Scotty Who Knew Too Much" ends up trounced and lodged in a nursing home; "The Owl Who Was God" gets himself and his disciples hit by a truck; the protagonists of "The Sheep in Wolf's Clothing" are set upon by wolves and killed. Black humor anchors his motifs in the adult realm with glimpses of chilling reprisals, for example, the dust-off from the jilted wife in "The Crow and the Oriole," who departs with a new man, leaving her husband a two-line farewell urging him to "find some arsenic in the medicine chest." (Thurber 1940, 46) Fine-honed and unforgiving, his plotlines award the boob and the braggart their just deserts, as demonstrated by the egotistic focus of "The Elephant Who Challenged the World," in which the great beast falls to the treachery of a diligent termite.

With a wordsmith's apt grace, Thurber rephrases the balance of nature in droll onomatopoeia and brilliant puns. His self-important speckled hen consoles herself with "clucking and cut-cutting and cadawcutting." (Thurber 1940, 57) When the foxes devour the orioles, their leader turns into the self-congratulating, blood-soaked liberator. The moral intones, "Government of the orioles, by the foxes, and for the foxes, must perish from the earth." (Thurber 1940, 53) To the shiftless, girl-chasing beaver named Al, Thurber delivers the spoils, noting, "It is better to have loafed and lost than never to have loafed at all." (Thurber 1940, 55) His update of the race between the tortoise and the hare ends in disaster for the Aesop-quoting tortoise and a choice mixed metaphor: "A new broom may sweep clean, but never trust an old saw." (Thurber 1940, 61)

In the sequel, *Further Fables for Our Time*, Thurber tires of his cowering, ego-shriveled men and, like Mark Twain in his last years, wields an acerbic satire. Disappointed in the somber, but unrelenting idealism that undergirded his essays, Thurber, like a knight facing impossible odds, established a rationale for his fables by claiming to be "intensely dedicated to opposing the perilous wrongs and injustices of this bad earth." (Morsberger 1964, 31) Witty, barbed, and well aimed, these caustic observations of Eisenhower-era quandaries leave behind the home and barnyard of Aesop's day to examine the trends, neuroses, and dirty politics that lie at the heart of society's malaise. Satisfyingly accurate, the fables skewer the collapse of justice in "The Trial of the Old Watchdog," deride the acquisitive generation with a sassy child bearding her parent in "The Father and His Daughter," which follows a line drawing of a fierce confrontation between a determined little girl and an out-of-control father. In "The Bat Who Got the Hell Out," Thurber lambastes ushers hawking an evangelist's book entitled *You Can Be Jehovah's Pal*. In "The Cat in the Lifeboat" and "The Truth about Toads," Thurber's unblinking gaze lights on his own weakness—alcohol—which cost him friends and led to embarrassing word battles, posturing, fracases, and ejections from bars and nightclubs.

Thurber's ability to enliven straightforward text with slang, impertinent dialogue, and a spectacular demonstration of sibilance, onomatopoeia, archaism, repetition, and deliberate mixed metaphor rewards the sophisticated reader, who comes to expect zestful drollery. In the new batch of fables, Thurber refers directly to the masters, Aesop and La Fontaine, and flaunts his skill with lucid rhetorical devices, as with the pun on *Die Fledermaus* in "The Bat Who Got the Hell Out" and slang in "The Truth about Toads." In the style of Lewis Carroll's "Jabberwocky," Thurber employs onomatopoeic portmanteau words such as "flugger" in "The Clothes Moth and the Luna Moth" and "flobbering" in "The Sea and the Shore." The last, a contemplative piece on the hierarchy that impedes equality between the sexes, features Thurber's spare line drawing of a disturbingly empty, expressionless lemming gazing at nothing. Playful word games result in "mousy-wants-a-corner, hide-and-squeak, one-old-cat, mouse-in-boots" and "posse cat" for "The Foolhardy Mouse and the Cautious Cat" and a guilt-ridden guinea pig in "The Bragdowdy and the Busybody" who becomes "national president of the Daughters of Ambitious Rodents." (Thurber 1956, 11, 13, 63) Thurber's flair for restated allusions and clichés crops up regularly in such *mots justes* as "copy cat on a daily paper," "playing leap-bear," "son of a vixen," "an old wolves' tale," "ne'er-do-anything," "gloomy-go-sorry," and the dour one-liner, "a thing of beauty is a joy for such a little time." (Thurber 1956, 54, 47, 44, 26, 55, 29) Well versed in literature, Thurber manages words and implications with aplomb. A cynical merger of aphorism with Bible injunction notes that "Finders are not their brothers' keepers." (Thurber 1956, 111) The tour de force of poetic allusion, "The Rose, the Fountain, and the Dove," reprises lines from William Shakespeare's *Macbeth*, William Wordsworth's "She Dwelt among the Untrodden Ways," John Keats's "Ode on a Grecian Urn," and Thomas Gray's "Elegy Written in a Country Churchyard."

The moral tags in *Further Fables for Our Time* take on a new edge. Thurber's world-weary comment on the demise of a weed reminds, "*Tout*, as the French say, in a philosophy older than ours and an idiom often more succinct, *passe*." (Thurber 1956, 17) In "The Butterfly, the Ladybug, and the Phoebe," an act of cannibalism precedes the reminder, "She who goes unarmed in Paradise should first be sure that's where she is." (Thurber 1956, 10) A jab at human self-immersion declares, "The noblest study of mankind is Man, says Man." (Thurber 1956, 69) One of the most salient of aphorisms from this collection allies wordplay and wisdom for "It is wiser to be hendubious than cocksure," the conclusion of Thurber's version of "The Goose That Laid the Golden Egg." (Thurber 1956, 98) The moral shares the page with a flint-eyed rooster glancing over its shoulder as if ruing its folly.

In Thurber's hands, rhyme becomes a meaningful tool in the concluding lines, which tie up individual tales with the succinct, orderly grace of a bow on a package. Clever couplets conclude "The Daws on the Dial" and "What Happened to Charles," which epitomizes with a journalist's rejoinder, "Get it right or let it alone. The conclusion you jump to may be your own." (Thurber 1956, 30) A well-favored couplet mocking religious charlatans states, "By decent minds is he abhorred who'd make a Babbitt of the Lord," an allusion to Sinclair Lewis's hollow Rotarian. (Thurber 1956, 22) A second couplet composed in Burma Shave style and tone reminds, "Where most of us end up there is no knowing, but the hellbent get where they are going." (Thurber 1956, 28) At the end of a modern setting of "The City Mouse and the Country Mouse," Thurber observes "This is the posture of Fortune's slave: one foot in the gravy, one foot in the grave." (Thurber 1956, 112) Likewise somber is the gloomy, unfunny end to "The Cat and the Lifeboat," which asks, "O why should the spirit of mortal be proud, in this little voyage from swaddle to shroud?" (Thurber 1956, 59)

Some of Thurber's sallies teeter and fall flat. The last lines of "The Rose, the Fountain, and the Dove" and "The Philosopher and the Oyster" border on nostalgia, an inappropriate motive for the staid, hyperrealistic Aesopic genre. Likewise out of sync is "The Weaver and the Worm," a contrived piece that abandons subtlety in favor of a burdensome didacticism. In "Tea for One," "The Tigress and Her Mate," and "The Bachelor Penguin and the Virtuous Mate," Thurber returns to his overstated hobbyhorse, the unfulfilled love match and the female's coldhearted manipulation of the male, a personal battle that he waged too often in public. Similarly ineffective is a limp derision of greed, "The Godfather and His Godchild," which establishes no clear motive or purpose in the child's desire to break the old man's glasses and spit on his shoes. Least successful is the wordy moral "Fools rush in where angels fear to tread, and the angels are all in Heaven, but few of the fools are dead," an underdeveloped aphorism that tries too hard and accomplishes too little. (Thurber 1956, 14)

Tone, Thurber's master touch, also wavers in the second volume of fables. He spotlights a snide, hurtful one-upmanship between gossips in "The Lover and His Lass," in which self-important parrots ridicule the lovemaking of two hippos. Armed with cheeky, wry fillips, the fabulist allows himself to wing too close to his middle-age doldrums in "The Bluebird and His Brother," which philosophizes, "It is more dangerous to straight-arm life than to embrace it" (Thurber 1956, 31) A surprisingly graceless end to a flirtation between the clothes moth and the luna moth plunks to earth with the fizzle of a cigarette stub dunked into cold coffee. The story concludes with the world-weary assertion that "Love is blind, but desire just doesn't give a good goddam." (Thurber 1956, 35) Yet, Thurber recovers a few pages later with five versions of one of the Western world's most familiar pairings, "The Fox and Crow." The fourth version concludes with the fox's urbane tercet: "'I submit this cheese in evidence, as Exhibit A, and bid you and the criminal a very good day.' Whereupon he lit a cigarette and strolled away." (Thurber 1956, 45)

In fables intended for the post–World War II generation, Thurber wars on frivolous technology, the Iron Curtain, and HUAC. For "The Grizzly and the Gadgets," he takes on air freshener, clever door chimes, and a trick cigarette box and launches a tantrum that overturns Thoreau for the comment "Nowadays most men lead lives of noisy desperation." (Thurber 1956, 94) A stagy depiction of world tyranny empowers "The Bears and the Monkeys," in which the bears resemble the beleaguered Soviet Russians of the post-Stalin era. In defiance of reckless warmongering, Thurber reprises the king of the jungle competition in "The Tiger Who Would Be King," which rightly advises, "You can't very well be king of beasts if there aren't any." (Thurber 1956, 125) The rumor-mongering and sacking of a fellow mongoose in "The Peacelike Mongoose" is a vehicle for the fabulist's hatred of McCarthyist red-baiting. With justifiable bitterness, Thurber dredges up the creative world's enmity against insiders who trump up charges of leftist sympathizing and complicity with Communists: "Ashes to ashes, and clay to clay, if the enemy doesn't get you your own folks may." (Thurber 1956, 86)

Well into the 1990s, waves of demand for Thurber's work as cartoonist, librettist, and satirist have preceded reissued volumes of essays, cartoons, and personal correspondence. His wife and editor introduced *Thurber and Company* (1966) and helped to compile *Selected Letters of James Thurber* (1981). Harper and Row reprised his opinions in *Collecting Himself: James Thurber on Writing and Writers, Humor and Himself* (1990). Amply suited to stage and screen, productions of his writings cover a half century and include a choreographed version of *The Last Flower* (1959). The 1960s and 1970s saw continued Thurber successes with several disc recordings, particularly Broadway Production's *A Thurber Carnival* (1960), the cast of which Thurber joined for 88 performances of the skit "File and Forget"; Sheldon Leonard's television comedy *My World and Welcome to It* (1969–1970), starring William Windom as Thurber; the films *The Battle of the Sexes* (1960) and *The War between Men and Women* (1972), featuring Barbara Harris and Jack Lemmon; and a 1960 film and 1972 filmstrip of *Many Moons*, which was also animated in 1975.

Sources Bernstein 1975; Chapman, http://ils.unc.edu; Corbett, http://www.bookwire.com; Feinberg 1967; Grauer 1995; "James Thurber," http://us.imdb.com; Morsberger 1964; Rosen 1995; Sherwin 1996; Thurber 1940, 1956, 1987; "Thurber's World (and Welcome to It)!" http://home.earthlink.net.

 # TRICKSTER

As old as the enduring folktales of most primitive tribes and as recent as Richard Adams's *Watership Down* (1972) and its sequel, *Tales from Watership Down* (1997), trickster lore embodies the core purpose of fable—to delineate methods by which victims triumph over predators and bullies. Within the face-off between ill-matched adversaries lie the underpinnings of human behavioral patterns, both social and political. In the American Southwest, it is the amoral coyote who trounces assorted predators; in France and Germany, the fox consistently dupes the dim-witted wolf; in the central Pacific, the shark is king; the east Africans of Zanzibar, Mauritius, and Madagascar claim a human trickster, Abunuwas; among the Bantu of central Africa, the hare bests his enemy, the hyena. In a beloved African story cycle, the weak-limbed spider Anansi portrays the extreme pairing of a quick mind with a nonthreatening body. From the Hausa lore of northern Nigeria comes the story "Spider and the Lion," an unlikely matchup of weak with strong—Africa's most ingenious insect against the king of the jungle. Like a clever wrestler, the spider turns the lion's greed against him, causing his own momentum to lay him low. With a well-placed hint that he can change the colors of animal pelts, Spider soon has the lion stripping pelts from a dead cow, running into trees, and lying meekly before Spider, who trusses him with leather thongs. Eager to assist in the color-changing process, the lion stretches his limbs and notes, "It's loose here too . . . I can still move my back legs. Surely you ought to tie them tighter than that." (Arnott 1963, 28) As suspense builds, Spider springs his vengeance by branding the tethered lion with hot skewers. When the lion falls totally into his captor's power, Spider boasts, "If I hear again that you are following me, you'll regret it as many another animal has done. And what's more, I am in charge of the bush now and all animals have to obey me, so don't you forget it!" (Arnott 1963, 31)

The trickster achieves a height of curiosity and mischief in Native American lore. Anthropologists Paul Radin and Franz Boas studied the trickster in his usual incarnation—as a male called Old-Man or Old Man Coyote, the name by which the Brulé Sioux and Shoshone knew him. As the ancient wise one, he shares the literary traditsion of Moses, Merlin, Uncle Remus, and the modern wise man, Obi-Wan Kenobi, mentor to Luke Skywalker in *Star Wars*. To others, the trickster took a variety of shapes and names:

- He was Azeban the raccoon to the Abenaki.

- To the Arapaho, he was Iktomi the spider.

- The Catawba called him One Tail Clear of Hair, a reference to the opossum's bare tail.

- The Kiowa revered him as Saynday, a blend of hero and villain.

- The Micmac or Wabanaki of Nova Scotia knew him as Glooskap the frog, who taught Indians to fish, hunt, tan, weave, and attach beaded artistry to their crafts.

- The Penobscot called him Gluscabi, a variant of Glooskap.

- The Lakota Sioux told stories of the trickster hare.

- The Nootka or Tanaina made him a two-legged beast—Chulyen the crow or Guguyni the raven.

- The Ojibwa told stories of Nanabozho or Wenabozho the hare, whose powers of trickery challenged the natural world.

- The Passamaquoddy paired Gloskap with a devious uncle, Mikchich the turtle.

- The Yupik knew trickster fables about Amaguq the wolf, the shape-shifter who could alter appearance and size at will.

Under whatever name, the trickster's reprehensible character manifests itself in obstinence, lying, gluttony, and violence, either in pranks that humiliate humankind or chicanery that disconcerts the creator. To balance his meanness, he often outsmarts himself, causing pain and embarrassment by ripping his ears or tail or trapping his head or paw in a narrow-necked jar or his genitals in a vise. In a simple example, the action is the old trick of "I made you look," the modus operandi of the rabbit who wagers half his possessions that he can jump over the mark before the fox. The trick of pointing toward a crow in the sky gives the rabbit enough time to outjump the fox, who seems unusually dull-witted to have fallen for so obvious a gag.

Hawaiian lore from O'ahu presents the island's preliterate past through epic and fable that feature the deceptions and guile of the *kolohe* or trickster.

- The outsider Kane'opa flees O'ahu and joins forces with the king of Kaua'i to overthrow cannibal spirits known as akua so the islands are fit for human settlers.

- In the Ko'olau section of O'ahu, the deceiver Kaulu is the mythic tamer of wild places and thief of food from the gods who matches powers with the cannibal daemon Haumea and the gluttonous rat Mokoli'i. A tragic parallel to Kaua'i, Kaulu from Wai'anae, Maui, completes the Promethean task of locating islands for pioneers to settle, slowing the progress of the sun across the heavens, and stealing fire.

- In one trickster episode, the devious pig Kamapua'a—a deity and shape-shifter featured in an anonymous epic in the Hawaiian-language newspaper *Ka Leo o ka Lahui* (1891)—locates eight canoes loaded with calabashes of pork, fish, sugarcane, poi, gourds, bananas, and fresh water. He waits until the paddlers eat their fill from two canoes and drop off to sleep before devouring all the food from the remaining six canoes. He abstains only from the pork, which he considers his brother. When the paddlers awaken, they find excrement and urine befouling their stores. Their inquiry turns to the untouched pig, which is proof that Kamapua'a is responsible for robbing them of food.

More akin to mythic nature heroes than characters from fable, these stories express the values of courtesy, fairness, charity, courage, and generosity integral to the island chain's social ethos. Largely ignored by colonial curricula, the stories survive in the *kahuna* or storyteller's oral sessions, as well as hula, art, jewelry, songs, and verse. A symbol of chaos, such trickster cycles as the Hawaiian pig hero Kamapua'a never reach stasis. Variances in the deceiver's fate depend on extent of guile, evil intent, and circumstance. For example, in the Amakosa story "Is It Right That He Should Bite Me?" the jackal, normally intent on some greedy end, assists the helpful white man by replacing a rock over an ungrateful snake and leaving it to get out as best it can. From the same people comes "Saving the Rain," in which the lion shaves and greases the jackal's tail in preparation for dashing his brains out on a stone. The quick flight of the jackal saves his hide, but he must avenge himself by convincing the lion that he must prop up an overhanging crag or else be crushed. The jackal exits the story content, leaving the quavering lion to starve and die. A tit for tat, the Igbo come-uppance story, "Tiger Slights the Tortoise," exonerates the tortoise's trickery in repayment of the tiger's slight. More lethal is the Fipian "Treachery Repaid," a sinister African tale in which both hare and jackal agree to kill their mothers. Scattered among narrative lines is the repeated verse of the hare, who sings at the burrow entrance:

> Mother open the door-o
> I am not like that Jackal-o,
> Who killed his mother-o,
> He of the long tail-o!
> (Abrahams 1993, 219)

The contrast of blithe verse and murderous intent heightens the suspense. At fable's end, both mothers are dead and jackal and hare part company permanently.

Trickster stories need not end in a one-for-one battle of wits. The Ghanian fable "Spider and Squirrel," a contest of diehard rivals, resettles the score between Spider and his victims in a surprising turn of events. After he takes Squirrel to court to wrest his stash of corn, a rainstorm temporarily halts Spider's family from enjoying their wrongful gains. A crow spreads his wings to shelter the grain. When the storm passes, the crow claims the unattended corn, which it carries away in its claws. The teller concludes, "You might think that Spider would have learnt a lesson from this, and would have given up his thieving ways, but I am sorry to say that in no time at all he forgot about it and was soon up to his tricks again." (Arnott 1963, 67) And so the cycle spins on.

Literary scamps like the spider crop up in folk songs, wisdom lore, sand art, ivory carvings, temple mural, basketry, dance, mime, and every anthology of world fable:

- The most familiar example, Aesop's race between the tortoise and the hare, dramatizes the tug of war between competing animals, usually of widely varying skills and strengths.

- Central to Yoruba stories are parallel tricksters—Etu the antelope in "The Antelope in the Moon" and the tortoise in "Tortoise and the Palm Tree," "How Tortoise Grew a Tail," and "Tortoise's Last Journey," a sacrifice story that elevates the trickster to sanctity in the Osanyin healing cult.

- A powerful model from Sufi lore is the clever caged bird who outwits her master and gains her freedom in storyteller Rumi's thirteenth-century collection of Persian teaching tales.

- A pervasive hero/villain, Anansi (or Anancy) the Spider enlivens the Caribbean lore of Paul Keens-Douglas and Grace Hamilton. Anansi parallels the Zandian spider Ture, hero of "Spider Outwits the Rich Woman," who terrorizes a human by threatening to look down from his perch in the tree and cause everybody to die.

- Another local pair, Iwa and the orphaned scamp Maui, frequent Hawaiian stories.

- Perhaps the least threatening and most annoying is the tricky rabbit of West Africa, Georgia's Sea Islands, Plains and Southwestern Indians, and plantation beast fable.

- Ti Malice, the Haitian trickster, enriches himself through mischief, which forms the plot of New York storyteller Diane Wolkstein's Creole fool tale "Bouki Dances the Kokioko" (1997). Malice cajoles Bouki the rooster into dancing, a reprise of the trick of Sir Russel the col-fox, nemesis of Chauntecleer in Geoffrey Chaucer's "The Nun's Priest's Tale" (ca. 1387). While Bouki's eyes are shut, Malice makes away with his sack filled with 5,000 gourds, but his wickedness is balanced with fun. The arch punch line of the Haitian favorite—"If you have no sense, put your sack on the ground and dance"—draws all into the circle. (Wolkstein, *Storytelling*, 1997, 13)

- A pervasive Plains figure, coyote is the beneficent trickster who drives away winter. In a Kootenai *pourquoi* story collected by anthropologist Franz Boas in 1914, coyote aids humankind by joining the lynx and grizzly bear. Coyote's meddling produces an end to 12 months of cold weather and initiates spring, his gift to the world. Similarly, other tribes tell the same episodes, but alter the trickster to raven, mink, bluejay, and hare.

- In Europe, the irrepressible trickster is the fox, who roams the text of Aesop, Babrius, Phaedrus, Marie de France, Geoffrey Chaucer, and Jean de La Fontaine. The latter crafted stories in which the fate of the conniving fox varies. In "The Goat in the Well," the scheming fox misleads the goat, then chides him for his gullibility. Freed from the deep shaft, the fox chortles that anyone so stupid deserves to suffer. Implicit in Aesop's smirking fox is his willingness to overlook his own peril in the well in a rush to heap abuse on a weaker animal. The lessons implied by the fable are manifold, not the least of which is a study of the twisted thinking of nature's self-appointed critic. In a humorous reversal, La Fontaine pictures the fox's less able companion, the wolf, dressed in human smock in "The Wolf Turned Shepherd." The audacious trickster falls so short of fooling his intended victims that the denizens of the neighborhood nab him and give him a deserved drubbing. A satisfying requital, La Fontaine's fable restores the human wish that all connivers meet their just deserts.

Overall, the fox maintains an unstable balance of wins and losses. Pitted against a fool in "The Fox and the Raven," La Fontaine's fox effortlessly steals the bird's cheese by flattering him into opening his beak; in "The Fox and the Stork," however, the fabulist proves that the trickster is not always the winner of every match, even against a wobbly bird like the stork. In another setting, "The Sick Lion and the Fox," the wary fox survives because he discerns that the tracks leading to the lion king's cave are all incoming. La Fontaine takes the fox's side by stressing that his caution spares him a cruel death. Thus, deceit seems like only one aspect of a complex personality that has been stereotyped as totally dishonest and malicious. Likewise aware of the fox's strengths, Jean-Pierre de Florian, a protégé of La Fontaine, depicts the fox's bold effrontery in "The Silkworm," in which the fox sees through the rival spider's fault-finding with a straightforward reminder that "Madam spins too." (Cooper 1921, 362) This fox, unlike more blatant deceivers, demonstrates the world-wise skills of patience, observation, and cool retort.

In many guises, tradition tends to glorify the trickster's conniving. Ivan Andreyevich Krylov's fable "The Three Moujiks" lauds the clever diner who involves his table mates in contrived news of a war with China, then devours the soup and porridge while they wrangle over politics. In a peasant setting, Krylov creates "The Fox as Architect," an uncomplicated tale about a fox that builds the lion a hen yard and adds a small hole by which the fox can rob his client. In *Uncle Remus Returns* (1918), Joel Chandler Harris's griot champions the world's prototypical deceiver and justifies his devices: "Ef I ain't mighty much mistaken, honey, you wanter know how come Brer Rabbit kin outdo de yuther creeturs when he ain't got no tushes [tusks] ner no claws, an' not much strenk' . . . Well, dat's de ve'y identual thing dat de tales is all about." (Brookes 1950, 63) The statement exonerates the trickster—whether spider, hare, fox, hackal, or tortoise—and lifts him from the level of the mountebank to survivor.

Over the full range of world literature, the anomalous trickster animates and amuses at the same time that he manipulates and menaces his quarry and ultimately destroys them. La Fontaine blends horror and humor in "The Cormorant and the Fishes," a studied decimation of a fish pool from which the fish willingly depart into the bird's mouth after he tricks a crayfish to warn other pool dwellers that the fisherman is near. Safe in a tarn near the cormorant's nest, the fish swim happily, oblivious to the bird's plan to devour them one by one for his daily meals. In the *Panchatantra* and Somadeva's *Kathasaritsagara*, the quippy, curious monkey is the star trickster and self-mutilator in the focal story, "The Monkey Who Pulled Out the Wedge," a painful learning experience that costs him his genitals. An austere entry in the cycle, "The Jackal and the Drum," pictures the jackal as he examines a wondrous sound-producing instrument. He tells a series of interlinked stories about a number of tricksters, beginning with "The Crab Who Killed the Crane" and "The Hare Who Tricked the Lion," both survival tales in which tricksters must use their wits to save their lives. The series continues with "The Bedbug and the Flea," "How the Camel Was Tricked," and others that turn on the necessity of using intelligence to avoid being devoured by larger beasts.

From the Carolingian era come the life-or-death fables of Paulus Diaconus, an eighth-century monk and historian from Lombardy. Before serving at the court of Charlemagne around 780, Paulus wrote a life of Gregory, a book of homilies, and "The Sick Lion, the Fox, and the Bear." Based on a fierce triad, the tale expresses the malicious trickery of the fox, who bests the two stronger animals. After the animals assemble to console the ailing king of beasts, the bear denounces the fox for neglecting the king. The court responds by condemning the fox to immediate execution. On learning of the sentence, he dresses in a ragged cloak and scuffed shoes and pretends that he has wearied himself in search of a doctor to cure the lion. He ends the lie with dire therapy: the lion is to wrap himself in a bear pelt. Desperate for relief, the lion immediately has the bear beheaded and skinned. The fox chortles at the expense of the bear, who was the cause of the fox's dilemma. The same animal triad is the cast of "Farmers Three," a beast fable from Finnish lore. The action relies on inequalities of intelligence among the bear, wolf, and fox, who clear land, burn stumps, shift rocks, and plant grain. The fox, who maneuvers to avoid the most dangerous and cumbrous chores, returns for the harvest. Magnanimously, he offers to accept the smallest portion because his body is smallest. To the bear, he awards the straw, to the wolf the chaff. Keeping the grain heads for himself, he contrives to fool his fellow farmers once more.

The trickster is crucial to the fables revered by African slaves and transferred to the Western Hemisphere as models of living by one's wits in an unfair society founded on human bondage. Prized in black Africa for satire, the stories of the untrustworthy spider of Sierra Leone, Liberia, and Ghana or the fun-loving tortoise in Benin, Yoruba, and Nigeria reduce to metaphor the problems and ambiguities inherent in the social order. An example from Yoruba lore is the tortoise's theft of the gods' calabash of wisdom. In his haste to bring home a treasure, the foolish tortoise dashes the awkward calabash to the roadside, thereby scattering shards of wisdom over the earth. The trickster's purpose is to use his negative impulse to turn disorder to advantage—by stealing the coconuts, eluding the alligator, or making the camel look ridiculous. Carried from varying strands along Africa's western coast, these victim-over-master stories culminate in the tricky Brer Rabbit and and the human slave tricksters, High John the Conqueror and Daddy Mention. The ultimate underdog, according to storyteller Steve Sanfield, John served his purpose as the repository of hope for slave populations whose evening entertainment included episodes of John's trickery.

One of the most successful of modern fabulists, Richard Adams, reprises world trickster motifs in *Watership Down*, which embroiders his novel-length animal epic with fable in frequent storytelling sessions. His mythic character El-ahrairah and pal Rabscuttle provide comic relief in the form of rascal tales rich in survival themes. A droll creation story in Chapter 6 occurs after the rabbit god Frith made the world. At Frith's command to bring order and discipline to the animal kingdom, the beasts hold a caucus. He allots each animal some of the fierce accoutrements that endanger the smallest and least fierce of animals. As a result, the digging claws and piercing fangs of the badger and fox make life chancy for the small-framed rabbit. When the blessing of animals reaches El-ahrairah, he hides in a hole from the god and asks him to bless his bottom, which protrudes from the burrow. Frith replies: "Very well, I will bless your bottom as it sticks out of the hole. Bottom, be strength and warning and speed forever and save the life of your master. Be it so!" (Adams 1972, 37) Afterward, the rabbit's tail shines like a star and his back legs grow long and powerful. The progeny of El-ahrairah remain swift runners and diggers to preserve their race against a host of enemies.

As Adams moves back to the flight of rabbits from twentieth-century Sandleford Warren, his epic hero, Hazel, prays to El-ahrairah for protection. The interweaving of El-ahrairah lore uplifts Hazel's story at frequent intervals. In Chapter 12, the exodus motif depicts El-ahrairah plotting to lead his people from the marshes of Kelfazin, a boggy land to which rabbits are ill-suited. Prince Rainbow declares that El-ahrairah must prove himself honest. El-ahrairah suggests stealing King Drazin's lettuces and employs Rabscuttle, his lieutenant, to infiltrate the palace and spoil food in the king's larder. El-ahrairah disguises himself and visits the king, who suffers a churning stomach. The trickster, pretending to be the chief physician, diagnoses the problem as Lousepedoodle infestation. When the captain of the guard declares that the rabbits are mustering for war, Drazin orders him to dump the deadly lettuces at the marshes. Thus El-ahrairah wins a bet that he can get the king to deliver greenstuff to him. The stream of tricks continues, including El-ahrairah's gulling of Hufsa, a spy and tattler, whom El-ahrairah discredits. In each incident, El-ahrairah, bolstered by Rabscuttle, is equal to the task.

In the final fable, Adams varies the structure of his trickster lore to parallel a twentieth-century threat of rabbit extinction. In the story of King Darzin's scheme to pen the rabbits in their holes, El-ahrairah and Rabscuttle reprise the epic trek to the underworld to confront death. After fleeing to the Black Rabbit of Inlé, the duo enters a fearful stone warren. Adams depicts the deadly game-playing of the trickster in matches of bob-stones, which cost El-ahrairah his whiskers, tail, and ears, the meager protections that save rabbits from predators. Deep in the pit of dead souls, a scaled-down rabbit trickster sheds completely his deceptions and deliberately exposes himself to white blindness to carry it back to earth and infect Darzin's troop. The Black Rabbit is so moved by El-ahrairah's noble gesture that he promises to save the warren. Lord Frith, in token of the trickster's great-hearted devotion to his people, restores his tail, whiskers, and ears. The story suits the final episode of animal storytelling, for El-ahrairah is no longer the amusing rascal. His emergence as savior recasts him as a mythic hero on a par with the Babylonian Gilgamesh, the Greek Odysseus and the Roman Aeneas.

Modern tellers of trickster lore reprise these standard ruses in the rambunctious stories performed live and in concert. Among the best received are Cherokee teller Gayle Ross, Abenaki savant Joseph Bruchac, and Cajun storyteller J. J. Reneaux. According to Reneaux, bayou dwellers maintain the underdog's admiration for jokes and pranks, even when the jokester suffers from a misfiring trick. Usually African or Native American in origin, Reneaux's stories appeal to humor and insight. One example, "The Theft of Honey," a tale of the tricky *lapin* [rabbit] who hoodoos the boastful *bouqui* [fox] out of his honey by pretending to run home to welcome a new godchild. The typical fillip comes at the end, when the rabbit plays the comforter and shares his syrup with the loser, after which they nap in the shade. Reneaux concludes, "Bouqui twitched and trembled in his sleep, but Lapin slept like a *bébé* and had sweet dreams—sweet as honey." (Reneaux 1992, 30)

See also Anansi; Brer Rabbit; Reynard the Fox.

Sources Abrahams 1993; Adams 1972, 1997; *Ancient O'ahu: Stories from Fornander & Thrum* 1996; Arnott 1963; Bierhorst 1995; Brookes 1950; Cooper 1921; Crafts 1996; Emerson 1997; Goss and Barnes 1989; Green 1965; Hurston 1981; Jones 1995; Kame'eleihiwa 1996; Lester 1988, 1994; Mbitu and Prime 1997; Miller and Snodgrass 1998; Patterson and Snodgrass 1994; Reneaux 1992; Sanfield 1996; Somadeva 1994; Thompson 1969; Wolkstein, "Bouki Dances the Kokioko" 1997, *Bouki Dances the Kokioko: A Haitian Story* 1997.

UNCLE REMUS

A voluable alter ego for Joel Chandler Harris, a sweet-natured Atlanta reporter, editor, and columnist for the *Atlanta Constitution*, Uncle Remus talked his way from the pages of fiction into a southern oral tradition. His function as story-teller—as with Scheherazade's Arabian tales and Aesop's Greek fables—puts him in control of story selection, execution, and moralizing. Of the suspense generated by serialized dramatic monologues, Uncle Remus warns, "Der ain't no way fer ter make tattlers en tale-b'arers turn out good." (Harris 1982, 107) Applying his incantatory trade as griot, he gains a hold over "Miss Sally's little boy" by threatening to withhold "tales ter bad chilluns." To the child's plain-tive disclaimer, Remus poses rhetorical questions: "Who dat chunkin' dem chick-ens dis mawnin'? Who dat knockin' out fokes's eyes wid dat Yallerbammer [Alabama] sling des 'fo' dinner? Who dat sickin' dat pinter [pointer] puppy atter my pig? Who dat scatterin' my ingun [onion] sets? Who dat flingin' rocks on top er my house, w'ich a little mo' en one un em would er drap spang on my head?" (Harris 1982, 70) The ingenuous child, who lacks the expertise in lying to cover his trail, replies that he "didn't go to do it" and "won't do so any more." (Harris 1982, 71) Child-fashion, he delivers teacakes purloined from the house so the storyteller will complete the story of the fox saddled like a riding-horse.

The archetypal father figure, Remus flaunts the mask of the mischievous but harmless old darky. Like the gladsome child running back from the big house with pockets bulging with pastries, he plans a surprise party: "I'm gwineter bounce in on Marse John en Miss Sally, en holler Chris'mus gif' des like I useter endurin' de fahmin' days fo' de war, w'en old Miss wuz 'live." (Harris 1982, 74) Without the social means to broach white adults as an equal, he impishly intervenes in the child's behalf by singing about the "little Crickety Cricket" under the parlor window and by ingratiating himself with flattery and self-abnegation to get his way. (Harris 1955, 587) To the shift in the familial power base, old Remus mutters to the overmanaged grandson, "'Twa'n't yo' granma dat had you shot [shut] up in dar. No, suh, not her—never in de roun' worl." (Harris 1955, 588) The consummate pragmatist, he applies a servile pose when the mask suits the situation. Such posturing has drawn ire, but critics of Harris's storyteller are forced to admit that they have the toadying Remus to thank for the survival of Afro-American lore.

On the surface of his complex being, the gray-haired old storyteller relates in folk speech his interwoven series of preliterate animal fables. At the heart of his moralizing, he embodies the ethos of Harris, a literate white man who adapted the character to suit newspaper features and books. Through Remus's shrewd observations and witty animal fables, Harris preserved the central Georgia plantation vernacular, a richly textured, flowing dialect for which the South is famous. Remus, a patched and bespectacled composite of plantation models who coddled the fatherless Harris in boyhood, expanded the capabilities of an office-bound writer who suffered pathological timidity and a severe speech impediment. Embedded in Harris's exacting recreation of mid-nineteenth-century patois lay the folkways, political opinions, and day-to-day wisdom for surviving the caprices of history and the malice of southerners, the first Americans to fight on the losing side.

In the man-to-boy story sessions each evening after supper, Harris assumes multiple roles for his "seances." He distances himself from the mentoring of a seven-year-old white aristocrat by standing outside the fictive realm like a properly objective newsman observing events. By cloaking himself in blackface, he also plays the venerable old man's part and salts his rambling discourse with advice for southerners who had survived the Civil War only to face the virulence and random violence of Reconstruction. In loco parentis, Remus looks out for the child by meting out stories and warning the sleepy-eyed boy, "Chilluns can't speck ter know all 'bout ev'ything 'f' dey git some res'. Dem eyeleds er yone wanter be propped with straws dis minnit." (Harris 1982, 83–84) The third segment of a triad of identities is the boy himself, Miss Sally's endearing charge, who displays the wide-open curiosity and trust of the young Joe Harris, who had sat among kindly ex-slaves to enjoy their patter and adventures. By playing all the parts, Harris is able to deconstruct the complex post-war social order and reassemble its elements into an ideal relationship of giver and receiver of advice and admonition. Without lapsing too far into the mellow old gentleman, on Christmas Eve he is capable of snapping, "Now, den, I bin a-beggin' un you fer ter quit yo' 'havishness [misbehavior] de long ez I'm a-gwine ter, en I ain't gwine beg you no mo' kaze I'm des teetotally wo' out wid beggin', en de mo' I begs de wus you gits. You des go you' ways en I'll go mine." (Harris 1955, 403–404) The threat works; the child runs after the old man, who stalks toward the big house, and declares, "I was just playing."

Uncle Remus, the focus of Harris's bonhomie, was totally fiction. By way of explanation, the author claims to have "walloped together" his spokesman from three or four black griots. (Brookes 1950, 47) The result is the portrait of a venerable, self-possessed individual who demanded respect. In Harris's estimation, "He had always exercised authority over his fellow-servants. He had been the captain of the corn-pile, the stoutest at the log-rolling, the swiftest with the hoe, the neatest with the plough, and the plantation hands still looked upon him as their leader." (Brookes 1950, 48) A far cry from grinning, head-ducking fieldhands or wretched laborers who strove against servitude under threat of whipping, selling down the river, or worse, Remus is a house slave and carriage driver. A genial dictator, he seems content to the point of vanity and dozes by the fireside, reaching easily for his hat and cane or a poker to stir the fire, honing a pocket knife, swirling coffee to blend with sweetening in his cup, complaining mildly of rheumatism in his bones, resoling his shoes and waxing laces, and grasping a darning needle to sew one more calico square to his coat. For the fractious boy, Remus settles him instantly by producing a hand-plaited whip, "with a red snapper all waxed and knotted." (Harris 1982, 111) A humble, undemanding old man, he roasts yams for supper and cooks gingersnaps in his Dutch oven to sell to plantation folk.

Uncle Remus's status suggests the thorough acculturization of black slavery in a fantasy world where the greatest test of courage and endurance is a scolding from Miss Sally for keeping a child beyond his bedtime. On Christmas Eve, old Remus ascends to a madonnaesque pose:

> The old man took the child in his arms and carried him to the big house, singing softly in his ear all the way; and somehow or other the song seemed to melt and mingle in the youngster's dreams. He thought he was floating in the air, while somewhere near all the Negroes were singing, Uncle Remus's voice above all the rest; and then, after he had found a resting-place upon a soft warm bank of clouds, he thought he heard the songs renewed . . . until at last (it seemed) Uncle Remus leaned over him and sang *Good Night*. (Harris 1955, 407)

As has been obvious to black critics from the inauguration of the lovable slave figure, Remus is a figment of the moderate white's hopes for peace and forgiveness for the more than three centuries of enforced servitude. The illiterate griot fulfills Harris's desire to smooth over decades of political wrangling and years of war and reprisal with an old man's lively, nonthreatening stories enacted by animal figures, with whom all races can identify.

Yet, at the edge of the moral commentary that accompanies Uncle Remus's stories lurks a criticism of black culture implicit in the reminder that the creatures are amoral, not knowing "nothin' 'tall 'bout dat dat's good en dat dat ain't good. Dey dunno right fum wrong. Dey see what de want, en dey git it ef dey kin, by hook er by crook. Dey don't ax who it b'longs ter, ner wharbouts it come fum. Dey dunno de diffunce 'twix' what's dern [theirs] en what ain't dern." (Harris 1955, 560) Although Remus directs the accusation toward amoral animal figures, the sting of the statement shadows the harsh white mindset that ex-slaves lack the moral development to differentiate between right and wrong. As though divesting himself of subconscious antiblack sentiment, Harris retreats into the persona of Uncle Remus and exclaims self-righteously that he prefers animal stories to "tales 'bout folks" because human beings can't "play no tricks, ner git even wid der neighbors, widout hurtin' somebody's feeling's er breakin' some law er nudder, er gwine 'g'inst what de preacher say." (Harris 1955, 563)

In the 34 stories of *Uncle Remus: His Songs and His Sayings* (1880), Remus stands free and easy on home turf. The first story, "Uncle Remus Initiates the Little Boy," achieves pictorial reality by moving directly to the storyteller's lair—the cabin beyond the big house, where the boy leans his head against a strong, black arm, ignores the old man's poverty, and settles in rapt wonder for real riches—the next installment of Brer Rabbit's mischief. Without fanfare, Remus begins, "Bimeby, one day, arter Brer Fox bin doin' all dat he could fer ter ketch Brer Rabbit." (Harris 1982, 55) From the initial episode, Remus segues easily into "The Wonderful Tar-Baby Story," which gains momentum after the child insists on knowing whether the fox caught his prey. As a narrative brake, the speaker hedges on absolutes and replies, "He come mighty nigh it, honey, sho's you bawn—Brer Fox did." (Harris 1982, 57) Like the Big Muddy churning its way to the sea, the surface of Remus's stories retains a languid drift, but underneath the current threatens disaster.

The format of Uncle Remus's stories blends narration with animal characterizations, for which he supplies voice and gesture. He follows Aesopic themes and motifs that tend to humble the proud and elevate the lowly. In *Uncle Remus and His Friends*, Remus states the underlying credo of fable: "The ruse of the old speaking felicitous folk wisdom to the young maintains the innocence of Remus's underlying philosophy. If Harris substituted Miss Sally for the child, the hidden slave agenda might find opposition from a more sophisticated audience less interested in bestial lore and more attuned to the kind of discontented underdog capable of spawning bloody plantation insurrection." (Brooks 1950, 49)

The griot has a way with incongruity. His syncretism of African creation myth with the biblical story of Noah's ark demonstrates in genial story form the accommodation of two traditions, African with Hebrew. To pave over the gap between animist and orthodox versions, Remus raises the question of variance, then resorts to his usual ploy: "Dey mout er bin two deloojes, en den agin dey moutent. Ef dey wuz enny ark, in dish yer w'at de Crawfishes brung on, I ain't heern tell un it, en w'en dey ain't no arks 'roun, I ain't got no time fer ter make um en put um in dere. Hit's gittin' yo' bedtime, honey." (Harris 1955, 205) Although disarmed by southern bigotry and the constraints of old age, Remus retains the energetic thrust and parry of storytelling, an adaptable weapon to the deadly enforcement of whites over blacks, the mid-nineteenth-century's rigid social order. He softens murderous exchanges between animal enemies with humorous onomatopoeia, which resounds with a "Kerblinkity-blunk" and "Jug-er-rum-kum-dum" rather than a burst of gunfire or thudding hooves of advancing night riders. (Harris 1982, 89) Even though the world outside the plantation produced the dreaded patrollers and Ku Klux Klan, emasculations, and lynchings to uppity blacks, Harris's beloved microcosm shelters the young aristocrat beside Remus's hearth, where the boy perches on the teller's lap and feels the soft stroke on his hair as Brer Rabbit once more tries the limits of the animal kingdom. As if sublimating an urge to flee the reach of lethal white masters, Remus puts into the rabbit's mouth the taunts of a survivor wriggling free one more time, tossing over his shoulder, "Bred en bawn in a brier-patch" as he "skip out des ez lively ez a cricket in de embers."

From his vantage of 80 years, Uncle Remus bears the protective aura of the elderly. Under the aegis of age, he looks the white race in the eye and speaks plainly a well-deserved chastisement. To the boy, he insists "I ain't seed no tattler come ter no good en'." (Harris 1982, 107) When the boy catches Remus crafting new ventures for Brer Fox, who supposedly died in a former installment, the cagey teller wrinkles his brow and remarks, "Bless grashus! ef chilluns ain't gittin so dey knows mo'n ole fokes." (Harris 1982, 110) To a sudden spurt of tears from the tenderhearted boy, Remus declares, "I 'clar' to goodness . . . ef you ain't de ve'y spit en image er ole Miss w'en I brung 'er de las' news er de war. Hit's des like skeerin' up a ghos' w'at you ain't fear'd un." (Harris 1982, 111)

The text of Harris's books encompasses more than storytelling. Among the animal fables, Remus scatters his stock of idiom, witticisms, work songs, and field lore. Drawing on the natural grace of black conversation, he speaks easily of being "bleedzd ter" [obliged to] and "prop-en-tickler" [proper and particular], complains of illness that "hid de ole nigger a joe-darter," and threatens to "put my name down wid de migrashun niggers." (Harris 1982, 203, 126, 204) In a serious moment, Remus scolds his charge for playing with the Favers children, who "wa'n't no 'count 'fo' de war, en dey wa'n't no 'count endurin' er de war, en dey ain't no 'count atterwards, en w'iles my head's hot you ain't gwineter go mixin' up yo'se'f wid de riff-raff er creashun." (Harris 1982, 130) To Pegleg Charley, a ne'er-do-well, Remus observes good-naturedly, "It's 'bout time dat I wuz spectin' fer ter hear un you in de chain-gang, an', stidder dat, hit's de chu'ch." (Harris 1982, 214) On the subject of educating blacks, Harris in the guise of Remus warns, "Wid one bar'l stave I kin fa'rely lif' de vail er ignunce." (Harris 1982, 216)

The songs, too, reflect traditions and folkways, from corn shuckin' and plowin' to camp meetin' and revivals. From an era of farm labor that wrested tobacco plantations and rice fields from the wild, he recalls the rhythmic chant of workers:

Spit in yo' han's en tug it en toll it,
En git behine it, en push it, en pole it;
Spit in yo' han's en r'ar back en roll it.
(Harris 1982, 118)

From the agricultural economy, which fed on slavery like a cannibal on prime flesh, the old griot comes up with a cheery planting ditty:

Ti-yi! Tungalee!
I pick um pea, I eat um pea.
Hit grow in de groun', hit grow so free;
Ti-yi! dem goober pea.
(Harris 1982, 118)

After a spooky session in which Remus relates superstitions about witches, he must lead the boy home in the dark and remain outside to sing a reassuring spiritual, which declares "Hit's eighteen hunder'd, forty-en-eight,/Christ done made dat crooked way straight—." (Harris 1982, 146)

At times, Harris pulls the strings of his spokesman too tight with Remus's sayings. Part of the series of exchanges supposedly occurs at the newspaper office, where the old man appears when he wants to relay an opinion or offer salient moralizing on such subjects as fistfights and courtesy. In "Uncle Remus's Church Experience," he complains that "de members 'uz a blame sight too mutuel fer ter suit my doctrines." (Harris 1982, 190) To contrast the central Georgia dialect with Gullah, Harris contrives "Uncle Remus and the Savannah

Darkey," an outright parody of the high-stepping coastal manservant who attempts to impress the land-based black. Remus's trip to the dentist prompts him to a serious boast: If the pronged molar had grown upside down in the jaw, "I'd a bin a bad nigger long arter I jin'd de chu'ch. You year'd my ho'n!" [You heard my horn]. (Harris 1982, 198)

See also Brer Rabbit; Harris, Joel Chandler.

Sources Bradbury 1963; Brookes 1950; Brunvand 1996; Davis 1970; Dorson 1959; Ehrlich and Carruth 1982; Harris 1955, 1982; Harlow 1941; Lester 1988, 1994; O'Shea 1996; Smith 1967; Snodgrass, *Encyclopedia of Satirical Literature* 1997, *Encyclopedia of Southern Literature* 1997.

WILDE, OSCAR

One of England's facile dramatists and fabulists of the nineteenth century, Dubliner and noted aesthete Oscar Wilde excelled in a range of genres, including verse, critical essay, autobiography, satire, and wry, entertaining aphorism. A flagrant homosexual in a grimly moralistic age that abhorred fops, dandies, and sybarites, Wilde adopted bizarre ruses to conceal his lifestyle. Early in the twentieth century, his legendary libertinism swamped his literary and humanitarian reputation, but incisive epigrams—such as "To love oneself is the beginning of a life-long romance" and "A man cannot be too careful in the choice of his enemies"—echoed in print and public declamation, often by speakers who misunderstood the source and Wildean nature of their origin. Because of his perceptive observations of social behaviors, Wilde wrote wisely and well about superficiality and moral compromise. He achieved stardom with two masterworks: *Lady Windermere's Fan* (1892), a complex comedy about parental sacrifice and the vehicle for some of his cleverest one-liners, and *The Importance of Being Earnest* (1895), a witty farce replete with well-paced dialogue and satiric jabs at England's stuffiness and shallow, conventional morals. In a more tolerant era, his work thrives throughout Europe and America and on the kabuki stage. To believers in art for art's sake, he is regarded as a champion of individualism and artistic freedom.

Oscar Fingal O'Flahertie Wills Wilde, son of poet Jane Francisca "Speranza" Elgee and Sir William Robert Wills Wilde, a distinguished ear and eye surgeon and oculist to Queen Victoria, was born October 15, 1856, and came of age during the height of smug middle-class hypocrisy. He set himself apart from the accepted youthful rough and tumble by collecting peacock feathers and blue china, carrying lilies, and wearing a sunflower as a boutonniere. Marked by brilliance as well, he achieved a scholarly reputation at the Portora Royal School, Enniskillen, earned awards in classical literature at Dublin's Trinity College and Magdalen College, Oxford, and won the Newdigate Prize for his poem "Ravenna" (1878). He attuned himself to art and extolled the works of the Pre-Raphaelites, John Ruskin, Matthew Arnold, and Walter Pater.

A public figure for his dramatic appearance, exhibitionist acts, and effete mannerisms, Wilde openly courted attention. At age 23, he settled in London and issued minor essays and poems in the popular press. His wit and eccentric

Photograph of Oscar Wilde in his signature dapper dress

charm adorn contributions to the *Pall Mall Gazette, Irish Monthly, Kottobos, Pan,* the *Catholic Mirror*, *Month*, and the *Woman's World*, which he edited from 1887–1889. In the early 1880s, he toured and lectured in America, where his play *Vera* (1882) introduced his parodies of stage convention. His gothic melodrama, *The Picture of Dorian Gray* (1891), brought fame after it was serialized in *Lippincott's Magazine*. Lesser works—*A Woman of No Importance* (1893) and *An Ideal Husband* (1895)—reprised the light social comedy of the Restoration era. London's Lord Chamberlain rejected his last melodrama, *Salomé* (1893); it opened in Paris to a worldly, shockproof audience.

Despite literary success, however, Wilde's career as London's chief wit began to upend and slide to the depths of shame and recrimination. His enemies declared that his 1884 marriage to Constance Lloyd, a wealthy heiress, was a cover for blatant homosexuality. For a brief time, he carried off the sham relationship and, while living in Chelsea, published a fable collection, *The Happy Prince and Other Tales* (1888), for his sons, Cyril and Vyvyan. Like Ambrose Bierce, his American contemporary, Wilde reveled in smartly derisive fables on human failings. For "The Artist," he creates a dramatic scenario of the worker in bronze reclaiming a sculpture of "The Sorrow That Endureth for Ever" and casting it into the furnace to provide molten material for a new statue. From the raw material he fashions "The Pleasure that Abideth for a Moment." A skillful rendering is Wilde's restatement of the Greek myth of Narcissus. Entitled "The Disciple," the fable captures the paradox of reflected beauty. The Oreads comfort the pool for losing the beautiful male figure who had once lain on the banks and gazed at his beauty reflected on the surface. The pool answers, "But I loved Narcissus because, as he lay on my banks and looked down at me, in the mirror of his eyes I saw my own beauty mirrored." (Komroff 1935, 486) Other examples from the collection include "The Nightingale and the Rose," a sweetly poignant fable that concludes with the bird's wasted martyrdom on a rose thorn, "The Remarkable Rocket," a far-fetched story of aspiration and sacrifice, "The Devoted Friend," a story-within-the-story that a linnet tells a crass water rat," and "The Selfish Giant," a fable about a giant who learns to value children and who is rewarded by a visit from the Christ Child.

Although Wilde's fable collection is spotty and spoiled by heavy-handed moralizing, it redeems itself on the strength of the title story. "The Happy Prince," set in a nameless monarchy in an unidentified city, tells of the unlikely friendship between a gilded statue and a love-sick swallow. A fanciful dialogue unfolds with a storyteller's simplicity to tell of the prince, who once "lived in the Palace of Sans-Souci [without care], where sorrow is not allowed to enter." (Wilde 1983, 237) In his years as a monument to happiness, he gazes on "all the ugliness and all the misery of my city, and though my heart is made of lead, yet I cannot choose but weep." The crux of "The Happy Prince" lies in one of fable's standard ploys—the alliance of unlike beings. The statue begs the swallow to serve as emissary to the suffering. Though the swallow yearns for Egypt and his love, his heart gradually alters from self-centered longing to caring for the people whom the prince rewards with anonymous acts of kindness and charity. Wilde builds his theme of altruism on subtle digs at callous city officials who pull down the worn statue and push aside the dead swallow at its feet. Unable to melt the broken leaden heart, they toss it away on a dust-heap, where God's angels gather it along with the bird's corpse. The fabulist confers immortality on good deeds in the final line, in which God chooses the bird for an eternal songster and the prince as a resident of the heavenly city of gold. Unusually pious for Wilde's canon, the story reflects a time when his fatherhood demanded a conservative mindset.

Succeeded by *The House of Pomegranates* (1891), the new addition of fables to Wilde's literary accomplishments balanced the arch, gossipy stage works with a grace and felicity uncommon to his canon. Among the "The Young King," "The Star-Child," and "The Fisherman and His Soul," a parallel of Hans Christian Andersen's "The Little Mermaid," is "The Birthday of the Infanta," a romance set in the Spanish Renaissance. Better developed than the rest, the story expresses the grief of a widower king, who worships before the embalmed figure of the queen on a tapestried beir like the prince in Hans Christian Andersen's "Snow White." In the dizzying rapture common to fairy tale, the king immures himself in sorrow and yearning: "He had hardly ever permitted her to be out of his sight; for her, he had forgotten, or seemed to have forgotten, all grave affairs of State. . . . When she died he was, for a time, like one bereft of reason." (Wilde 1983, 247)

Wilde breaks the story into two segments. The first is dominated by the sadness of the king and his daughter, the infanta, who grows up in the vagaries of court life, which the king has abdicated in honor of his wife's memory. In the second, a focus on the little princess pairs her with a delightful dwarf who knows nothing of his ugliness. In search of the infanta, he steals into the palace and confronts a mirror, which shatters his innocence and ends his life. The infanta, a spoiled darling who demands obedience, stamps her food and cries, "My funny little dwarf is sulking . . . you must wake him up and tell him to dance for me." (Wilde 1983, 262) Declaring herself Infanta of Spain and the Indies, she bids him amuse her until the chamberlain explains that the dwarf has died of a broken heart. The royal child curls her lip and declares, "For the future let those who come to play with me have no hearts." (Wilde 1983, 263) The story foretells the future of the realm, which is likely to be shadowed by yet another cynical, demanding royal.

The childlike delicacy of Wilde's fable collections belies the misery of his declining years. His creation of the altruistic prince and unsuspecting infanta suggests a father who composes illustrative fables for the instruction of children whom Wilde would protect from the forces that bring him low. A public scandal arose after the marquis of Queensberry publicly reviled the poet for his relationship with his son, Lord Alfred Douglas. A sensational trial created a stir over Wilde's suggestive imagery, which barristers read aloud to the jury. The failed lawsuit for libel against Queensberry collapsed. Sentenced to two years at hard labor in Wandsworth Prison, Wilde never again saw his sons. Transferred to the infamous Reading Gaol, he continued writing and submitted letters to the *Daily Chronicle* protesting floggings of the insane, indecent sanitation, repulsive rations of gruel and suet, persistent diarrhea, punishment on the tread-mill, and imprisonment of children.

Overcome with self-abasement, Wilde dramatized himself as an unwelcome ghost. His last years in self-imposed exile in Italy, Sicily, and France cost him friends, copyrights of his works, and a fortune in art and rare books. He immortalized his imprisonment the following year in *The Ballad of Reading Gaol* (1898), a plea for justice that he signed with his prison number, C.3.3. Obsessed with the sufferings of those still incarcerated, he continued to petition for prison reform and published fiction under the pseudonym Sebastian Melmoth. In his final desperate weeks, Wilde underwent an operation to ease the pain of cerebral meningitis, then died on November 30, 1900, in the Hotel d'Alcace in Paris. A cult figure and curiosity, he was buried nearby, then relocated in 1909 to Pére Lachaise cemetery to an ornate art deco vault that lured streams of mourners.

Sources Bartlett 1992; Bermel 1982; Brockett 1968; Gassner and Quinn 1969; Grigson 1963; Hart-Davis 1962; Hornstein et al. 1973; Komroff 1935; Magill 1958; McArthur 1992; Miller 1989; Wilde, "The Happy Prince," http://sunsite.unc.edu, "The House of Pomegranates," http://sunsite.unc.edu.

A TIME LINE OF FABLE

2300–2200 B.C.E.	"The Tamarisk and the Palm," anonymous Babylonian
2000 B.C.E.	*The Book of Achiqar*, anonymous Arabic "Nisaba and Wheat," anonymous Babylonian
1700–1600 B.C.E.	"The Fable of the Fox," anonymous Babylonian
1500 B.C.E.	"The Ox and the Horse," anonymous Babylonian
1500–1200 B.C.E.	"The Snake and the Eagle," anonymous Babylonian
960 B.C.E.	I Kings 3:16–28
925 B.C.E.	Judges 9:8–15
8th century B.C.E.	*Works and Days*, Hesiod
790 B.C.E.	II Kings 14:9
650 B.C.E.	"The Fox Avenging His Wrongs on the Eagle," Archilochus
6th century B.C.E.	II Samuel 12:1–6
530 B.C.E.	*Fables*, Aesop
5th century B.C.E.	*Panchatantra*, Bidpai
462 B.C.E.	*Agamemnon*, Aeschylus
460 B.C.E.	*Myrmidones*, Aeschylus
451 B.C.E.	*Ajax*, Sophocles
425 B.C.E.	*The Histories*, Herodotus
422 B.C.E.	*The Wasps*, Aristophanes
414 B.C.E.	*The Birds*, Aristophanes
4th century B.C.E.	*Alcibiades*, Plato *Historia Animalium*, Aristotle *Memoirs of Socrates*, Xenophon *Meteorologica*, Aristotle *Phaedo*, Plato *Phaedrus*, Plato *Rhetorica*, Aristotle *Symposium*, Plato
350 B.C.E.	*Aesop*, Alexis of Thurii
3rd century B.C.E.	*Aesopia*, Phaedrus
290 B.C.E.	*Aesop's Fables*, Demetrius of Phalerum

270 B.C.E.   *Epigrammata*, Callimachus

30 B.C.E.   "The City Mouse and the Country Mouse," Horace

14 C.E.   *Ab Urbe Condita*, Livy

100   *Vita Aesopi*, Plutarch

2nd century   *Aetia Graeca*, Plutarch
Conjugalia Praecepta, Plutarch
De Capienda ex Inimicis Utilitate, Plutarch
The Life of Aratus, Plutarch
The Life of Themistocles, Plutarch
Praecepta, Plutarch
Progymnasmata, Theon
Questiones Convivales, Plutarch
Vitae Decem Oratorium, Plutarch

170   "The Sorcerer's Apprentice," Lucian
Cynicus, Lucian

175   *Hermotimus*, Lucian

180   *Noctes Atticae*, Aulus Gellius

3rd century   *Historia Animalium*, Aelian
Popular Proverbs, Diogenes Laertius
Vitae Philosophorum, Diogenes Laertius

200   *Jatakamala*, Aryasura

207   *Hermeneumata*, Pseudo-Dositheus

215   *Novus Aesopus*, Alexander Neckham
Novus Avianus, Alexander Neckham

4th century   *Avionnets*, anonymous French

6th century   *The Miracles of St. Martin*, Gregory of Tours

7th century   *Hümayun-name*, anonymous Turkish

613   "Al-kahf," Koran

750   *Kalilah wa Dimnah*, Ibn al-Muquaffa

9th century   *Hazar Afsanah*, anonymous Persian

10th century   *Androcles and the Lion*, Romulus
Kalilah wa Dimnah, Rudaki

940   *Ecbasis Captivi*, anonymous Latin

11th century   *Stephanites kai Ichnelates*, anonymous Greek

1070   *The Tales from the Kathasaritsagara*, Somadeva

1075   *Konjaku Monogatari*, Minamoto Takakuni

12th century   *Carmina Burana*, anonymous central European
Historia Septem Sapientum, Johannes of Alta Silva
Hitopadesha, anonymous
Novus Aesopus, Baldo
Panchatantra, Rabbi Joel
Speculum Stultorum, Nigel of Longchamps

1100   *Novus Avianus*, anonymous

1148	*Ysengrimus,* Nivard of Ghent
1154	*Consolation Philtres for the Man of Authority,* Ibn Zafar
1175	*Isopet,* Galterus Anglicus
	Progymnasmata, Nikephoros Basilakis
1180	*Isopet I,* Galterus Anglicus
	Reinhart Fuchs, Heinrich der Glîchezaere
1189	*Fables,* Marie de France
1190	*The Owl and the Nightingale,* anonymous English
13th century	*Chartres Isopet,* anonymous French
	De Nugis Curialium, Walter Map
	Directorium humanae vitae, John of Capua
	El libro de los gatos, anonymous Spanish
	Isopet II, anonymous French
	Meshal ha-Kadmoni, Isaac Sahula
	Mishlei Shu'alim, Berechiah ha-Nakdan
	Speculum Majus, Vincent de Beauvais
1200	*Rainardo e Lesengrino,* anonymous French-Italian
1215	*Novus Aesopus,* Alexander Neckham
	Novus Avianus, Alexander Neckham
1220	*Fabulae,* Odo of Cheriton
1230	*Sermones Vulgares,* Jacques de Vitry
1250	*Reinaert de Vos,* Willem
	Roman de Renart, anonymous French
	Van den Vos Reinaerde, anonymous Flemish-Dutch
	Of the Vox and of the Wolf, anonymous English
1251	*Calila e Digna,* anonymous Spanish
1261	*Renard le Bestourné,* Rutebeuf of Champaign
1270	*La Couronnement de Renart,* anonymous Flemish
	Masnavi-ye Ma'navi, Jalal ad-Din ar Rumi
1288	*Renart le Nouvel,* Jacquemart Gielée
14th century	*The Byzantine History of 1204–1359,* Nikephoras Gregoras
	Conde Lucanor, Don Juan Manuel
	El Libro do buen amor, Juan Ruiz
1300	*Tuti Nameh,* anonymous Persian
1324	*Gesta Romanorum,* anonymous
1330	*Der Edelstein,* Ulrich Boner
1340	*Renart le Contrefait,* anonymous French
1353	*The Decameron,* Giovanni Boccaccio
1370	*Reinaerts Histoire,* anonymous Flemish
1377	*The Parliament of Fowls,* Geoffrey Chaucer
1387	*The Canterbury Tales,* Geoffrey Chaucer
1390	*The Churl and the Bird,* John Lydgate
	Confessio Amantis, John Gower

1398	*Isopes Fabules*, John Lydgate
	The Horse, Goose, and Sheep, John Lydgate
15th century	*El Libro de los exenplos por a. b. c.*, Clemente Sénchez
	Liber Facetiarum, Bracciolini Poggio
1476	*Äsop*, Joachim Liebhard
1477	*Aesop's Life and Fables*, Ernst Voulliéme
	Aesop's Life and Fables, Heinrich Steinhöwel
1479	*Aesop's Fables*, Liberale da Verona
	Die Hystorie van Reynaert die Vos, Gheraert Leeu
1481	*The Historye of Reynart the Foxe*, William Caxton
1483	*Das Buch der Beyspiele*, anonymous German
1485	*Aesop's Life and Fables*, anonymous Italian
	The Boke of Subtyl Historyes and Fables of Esope, William Caxton
1489	*La vida del Ysopet con sus fabulas hystoriadas*, Johan Hurus
1497	*Aesopo Historiado*, anonymous Italian
1498	*Rienaerts Histoire*, anonymous Dutch
	Reinke de Vos, anonymous Dutch
1500–1505	*Anwar-e Suhayli*, Hoseyn Wa'ez-e Kashefi
1513	*Phaedrus*, Martin Dorp
1515	*Ein kurtzweilig Lesen von Dyl Vlenspiegel*, anonymous German
1522	*Schimpf und Ernst*, Johannes Pauli
1534	*Fabeln*, Erasmus Alberus
1548	*Esopus*, Burkhard Waldis
1552	*La Moral Philosophia*, Antonio Francesco Doni
1553	*Le Piacevoli Notti*, Giovanni Straparola
1555	*Kuh Buch*, Abraham ben Mattathias
1556	*Aesop's Leyned og Fabler*, Christien Pedersen
1560	*Churchyard Chippes*, Thomas Churchyard
	Here beginneth a merye Jest of a man that was called Howleglas, anonymous English
1562	*Gargantua and Pantagruel*, François Rabelais
1563	*The Legend of Shore's Wife*, Thomas Churchyard
1565	*Fabulae Centum*, anonymous Italian
1567	*De Warachtighe Fabulen der Dieren*, Marcus Geeraerts
1570	*The Morall Fabillis of Esope the Phrygian, compylit in eloquent & ornate Scottis meter*, Robert Henryson
	The Morall Philosophie of Doni, Thomas North
1577	*Cento Favole Morali*, anonymous Italian
1585	*Aesopz Fablz in Tru Ortography with Grammar-notz*, William Bullokar
1591	*Mother Hubberds Tale*, Edmund Spenser
17th century	*Aesop's Fables with His Life*, Francis Barlow
1605	*Coriolanus*, William Shakespeare

1606   *Volpone, the Fox*, Ben Jonson

1610   *Mythologia Aesopica*, Isaac Nicholas Nevelet

1625   *Of Vainglory*, Francis Bacon

1631   *Les Fables d'Esope phrygien*, Jean Baudoin

1637   *Il Pentamerone*, Giambattista Basile

1644   *La Livre des Lumières*, David Sahid

1654   *The Most Delectable History of Reynard the Fox, Newly Corrected & Purged from all grossness in Phrase & Matter*, John Shirley

1665   *Fables of Aesop Paraphras'd in Verse*, John Ogilby

1668   *Aesopics, or a Second Collection of Fables*, Wenceslaus Hollar
        Fables choisies, Jean de La Fontaine

1673   *La Malade imaginaire*, Molière

1676   *The Most Delectable History of Reynard the Fox*, anonymous Dutch

1678   *Fables choisies*, Vol. II, Jean de La Fontaine

1687   *Aesop's Fables in English and Latin*, Charles Hoole
        Aesop's Fables with His Life, Aphra Behn
        The Hind and the Panther, John Dryden

1692   *Fables of Aesop and Other Eminent Mythologists: with Morals and Reflexions*, Sir Roger L'Estrange

1697   *Sefer Meshalim*, Rabbi Moses Wallich

1700   *Fables Ancient and Modern*, John Dryden

1703   *Aesop's Fables*, John Locke
        Fables, Moral and Political, anonymous English
        Some Fables after the Easie and Familiar Method of Monsieur de la Fontaine, Bernard de Mandeville

1704   *Aesop Dress'd or A Collection of Fables Writ in Familiar Verse*, Bernard de Mandeville

1706   *The Crafty Courtier: or the Fable of Reynard the Fox*, anonymous English

1708   *Les Mille et Une Nuits, contes arabes traduits en français*, Antoine Galland

1711   *Spectator* essay, Joseph Addison

1713   *The Atheist and the Acorn*, Anne Kingsmill Finch

1714   *The Fable of the Bees or Private Vices, Publick Benefits*, Bernard de Mandeville

1717   *Les Mille et une nuits*, Antoine Galland

1720   *Divine Songs*, Isaac Watts

1722   *The Fables of Aesop and Others Newly Done into English*, Samuel Croxall

1723   *Remarks on Mandeville's Fables of the Bees*, William Law

1724   *Les contes et fables indiennes de Bidpai et de Lokmam*, Antoine Galland

1727   *Fifty-one Fables in Verse*, John Gay

1729	*The Fable of the Bees, Part II*, Bernard de Mandeville
1739	*Aesop's Fables*, Samuel Richardson
1747	*Fabeln und Erzählungen in Reimen*, Gotthold Lessing
1748	*Fabeln und Erzählungen*, Christian Gellert
1755–1759	*Fables choisies,* Jean de La Fontaine
1757	*Fables in Verse for the Improvement of the Young and the Old by Abraham Aesop Esq*, Christopher Smart
1759	*Candide*, Voltaire *Fabeln: Drei Bücher*, Gotthold Lessing *The History of Rasselas, Prince of Abyssinia*, Samuel Johnson
1760	*A Poetical Translation of the Fables of Phaedrus*, Christopher Smart
1761	*Fables for Grown Gentlemen*, John Hall Stevens
1764	*Select Fables of Esop and Other Fabulists*, Robert Dodsley
1771	*The Fables of Flora*, John Langhorne
1772	*Fables Moral and Sentimental*, William Russell
1778	"Ephemera: An Emblem of Human Life," Benjamin Franklin
1779	*Fabliaux ou contes du XIIe et du XIIIe siècles*, Pierre d'Aussy
1780	*An Easy Introduction to the Knowledge of Nature*, Sarah Kirby Trimmer
1781	*Fábulas morales*, Félix Samaniego
1782	*El asno erudito*, Juan Pablo Forner *Fábulas literarias*, Tomás de Iriarte *Favole e Novelle*, Lorenzo Pignotti
1783	*Cobwebs to Catch Flies; or Dialogues in Short Sentences,* Lady Eleanor Fenn *Fables by Mrs. Teachwell*, Lady Eleanor Fenn *Para casos tales suele tenor los maestros oficiales*, Tomás de Iriarte
1784	*Bewick's Select Fables*, Oliver Goldsmith *Select Fables of Aesop and Others*, Thomas Bewick
1787	*The Oeconomy of Charity*, Sarah Kirby Trimmer
1788	*La Mélange tirés d'une grande bibliothèque*, Marc d'Argenson
1788–1789	*Family Magazine*, Sarah Kirby Trimmer
1789	*The Ladder to Learning*, Sarah Kirby Trimmer
1792	"Der Zauberlehrling," Johann Goethe *Fables*, Jean de Florian
1794	*Reinecke Fuchs*, Johann Goethe
19th century	*Hazar Dastan*, Totaram Sháyán
1801	*How Gertrude Educates Her Children*, Johann Heinrich Pestalozzi
1805	*Fables Ancient and Modern*, William Godwin
1806–1808	*Der Knaben Wunderhorn,* Clemens Brentano and Achim von Arnim
1807	*Friends in a New Dress*, Richard Scrafton Sharpe

1809   *Basni*, Ivan Krylov

1811   *A New Work of Animals Principally Designed from the Fables of Aesop, Gay and Phaedras*, Samuel Howitt

1812–1822   *Kinder und Hausmärchen*, Jacob and Wilhelm Grimm

1815   *Lieder der alten Edda*, Jacob and Wilhelm Grimm

1818   *Aesop's Fables,* Thomas Bewick and Robert Elliott Bewick

1820   *Fables*, Andreas Fay

1821   *Aesop in Rhyme, with Some Originals*, Jeffreys Taylor
     Oeuvres Complètes de La Fontaine, Jean de La Fontaine

1824   "The Devil and Tom Walker," Washington Irving

1826   *Irische Elfenmärchen*, Jacob and Wilhelm Grimm

1833–1834   *Fables de La Fontaine*, Georges Gouget

1834   *Reinhart Fuchs*, Jacob and Wilhelm Grimm

1835   *Eventyr, fortalte for børn*, Hans Christian Andersen

1837   *Eventyr,* Hans Christian Andersen
     Noch fünfzig Fabeln für Kinder, Wilhelm Hey

1838   *Fables de La Fontaine*, J. J. Grandville

1840   *Billedbog uden Billeder*, Hans Christian Andersen
     The Fairy Tale of My Life, Hans Christian Andersen

1843   *A Christmas Carol*, Charles Dickens

1844   *Reynard the Fox, a renowned Apologue of the Middle Age, reproduced in Rhyme*, Samuel Naylor

1852   *The Christmas Books,* Charles Dickens
     The Fairy Godmothers and Other Tales, Margaret Scott Gatty
     Reynard the Fox, a Poem in Twelve Cantos, E. W. Holloway

1853   *The Chimes*, Charles Dickens

1855   *The Parables from Nature*, Margaret Scott Gatty

1857   *The Fables of Aesop and Others Translated from Human Nature*, Charles Bennett

1859   *Aunt Judy's Tales*, Margaret Scott Gatty

1861   *Ka Hae Hawai'i,* G. W. Kahiolo

1865   *Alice in Wonderland*, Lewis Carroll
     Max und Moritz, Wilhelm Busch

1866   *La Légende de les aventures héroiques, joyeues, et glorieuses d'Ulenspiegel et de Lamme Goedzak au pays de Flandres et ailleurs*, Charles de Coster (1866)

1866–1873   *Aunt Judy's Magazine*, Margaret Scott Gatty

1867   "The Celebrated Jumping Frog of Calaveras County," Mark Twain

1868   *Fables de La Fontaine*, Gustave Doré

1871   *Through the Looking Glass and What Alice Found There*, Lewis Carroll

1872   *Fairy Tales and Stories*, Hans Christian Andersen

1873–1885   *Aunt Judy's Magazine*, Juliana Horatia Gatty Ewing

1875   *Fiabe, novelle e racconti popolari Siciliani,* Giuseppe Pitré
        Popular Italian Tales, Domenico Comparetti

1877   "Folklore of Southern Negroes," William Owens

1880   *The Book of the Thousand Nights and a Night: A Plain and Literal*
           Translation of the Arabian Nights Entertainment, Richard Burton
        Uncle Remus: His Songs and His Sayings, Joel Chandler Harris
        Sessanta novelle popolari Montanesi, Gherardo Nerucci
        "The Wonderful Tar-Baby Story," Joel Chandler Harris

1883   *Nights with Uncle Remus: Myths and Legends of the Old Plantation,*
           Joel Chandler Harris

1884   *The Book of the Thousand Nights and One Night,* John Payne
        Mingo and Other Sketches in Black and White, Joel Chandler Harris
        The Poetical Works of Alice and Phoebe Cary

1886   *The Baby's Own Aesop,* Walter Crane
        The Strange Case of Dr. Jekyll and Mr. Hyde, Robert Louis Stevenson

1887   *Free Joe and Other Georgian Sketches,* Joel Chandler Harris

1888   *The Book of the Thousand Nights and One Night,* John Payne
        The Happy Prince and Other Tales, Oscar Wilde
        Histoire d' Alá al-Din ou La Lampe Merveilleuse, Texte Arabe, Hermann
           Zotenberg

1889   *Daddy Jake the Runaway and Short Stories Told after Dark,* Joel
           Chandler Harris
        Fables of Aesop, Joseph Jacobs

1891   *The House of Pomegranates,* Oscar Wilde

1892   *Uncle Remus and His Friends,* Joel Chandler Harris

1893   *The Tale of Peter Rabbit,* Beatrix Potter

1894   *The Jungle Book,* Rudyard Kipling

1895   *The Second Jungle Book,* Rudyard Kipling

1896   *The Bad Child's Book of Beasts,* Hilaire Belloc
        Fables, Robert Louis Stevenson
        The Story of the Other Wise Man, Henry Van Dyke

1897   *The First Christmas Tree,* Henry Van Dyke

1898   *De l'Angélus de l'aube à l'Angélus du soir,* Francis Jammes

1899   *Chantecler,* Edmond Rostand
        Fantastic Fables, Ambrose Bierce
        The Moral Alphabet, Hilaire Belloc

1900   *Fables in Slang,* George Ade
        Myths of the Cherokee, James Mooney
        The Southern Mountaineer, Caleb A. Ridley

1902   *Just-So Stories for Little Children,* Rudyard Kipling

1903   *The Souls of Black Folks,* W. E. B. Du Bois
        The Tale of Squirrel Nutkin, Beatrix Potter
        Told by Uncle Remus, Joel Chandler Harris

1904   *The Tar-Baby and Other Rhymes of Uncle Remus,* Joel Chandler Harris

1905	"The Gift of the Magi," O. Henry
1906	*Uncle Remus and Brer Rabbit,* Joel Chandler Harris
1907	*Cautionary Tales*, Hilaire Belloc *Hawaiian Folk Tales: A Collection of Native Legends*, Thomas G. Thrum
1908	*Penguin Island*, Anatole France *The Tale of Samuel Whiskers*, Beatrix Potter *The Wind in the Willows*, Kenneth Grahame
1909	"A Fable," Mark Twain
1910	"The Ransom of Red Chief," O. Henry *Uncle Remus and the Little Boy*, Joel Chandler Harris
1911-1915	*The Golden Bough: The Roots of Religion and Folklore*, James Frazer
1912	*Androcles and the Lion*, George Bernard Shaw
1914	*Panchatantra*, Johannes Hertel
1915	*Treemonisha*, Scott Joplin
1916	*Aesop's Fables*, Arthur Rackham
1918	*Folklore in the Old Testament*, James Frazer *Johnny Town-Mouse*, Beatrix Potter
1918	*Uncle Remus Returns,* Joel Chandler Harris
1919	*A Collection of Hawaiian Antiquities and Folklore*, Abraham Fornander
1921	*Journal of American Folklore,* Elsie Clews Parsons *The Witch Wolf: An Uncle Remus Story,* Joel Chandler Harris
1923	*Jungle Beasts and Men*, Dan Gopal Mukerji *More Hawaiian Folk,* Thomas G. Thrum
1927	*Gay-Neck: The Story of a Pigeon*, Dan Gopal Mukerji
1928	*Till Eulenspiegel*, Gerhart Hauptmann
1929	*The Green Pastures*, Marc Connelly
1931	*Fables of Aesop According to Sir Roger L'Estrange*, Alexander Calder
1935	*The Great Fables of All Nations*, Manuel Komroff *Mules and Men*, Zora Neale Hurston
1938	*Tell My Horse*, Zora Neale Hurston
1939	*Il Tempo d'allora, figure, storie e proverbi*, Eugenio Cirese *Old Possum's Book of Practical Cats*, T. S. Eliot
1940	*Fables for Our Time and Famous Poems Illustrated*, James Thurber
1943	*Le Petit Prince*, Antoine de Saint-Exupéry
1944	*Sumerian Mythology*, Samuel Noah Kramer *A Treasury of American Folklore*, B. A. Botkin
1945	*Animal Farm*, George Orwell
1946	*Jonathan Draws the Long Bow*, Richard M. Dorson
1948	*Seven Tales of Uncle Remus*, Joel Chandler Harris
1949	"Babette's Feast," Isak Dinesen
1952	*Who Blowed Up the Church House and Other Ozark Folk Tales*, Vance Randolph

1953   *9 Aesop's Fables*, Antonio Frasconi
         A Woman as Great as the World and Other Fables, Jacquetta Hawkes
         A Word on the Brazos: Negro Preacher Tales from the Brazos Bottoms of Texas, J. Mason Brewer

1954   *Twelve Fables of Aesop*, Antonio Frasconi

1956   *The Blue Dog and Other Fables for the French*, Anne Bodart
         Further Fables for Our Time, James Thurber

1957   *The Best of Simple*, Langston Hughes

1958   *The Book of Negro Folklore*, Langston Hughes and Arna Bontemps

1960   *99 Fables by William March*

1962   *Burmese Law Tales: The Legal Element in Burmese Folklore*, Maun Htin Aung
         La Ville de la chance, Elie Wiesel
         Silent Spring, Rachel Carson

1963   *Aesop: A Portfolio of Color Prints*, Joseph Low

1964   *Les Portes de la forêt*, Elie Wiesel

1965   *Hot Springs and Hell and Other Folk Jests and Anecdotes from the Ozarks*, Vance Randolph

1966   *La Chant des morts*, Elie Wiesel

1967   *American Negro Folktales*, Richard M. Dorson
         Vendredi, Michael Tournier

1968   *Zalmen; ou, La Folie de Dieu*, Elie Wiesel

1970   *I Know Why the Caged Bird Sings*, Maya Angelou
         Jonathan Livingston Seagull, Richard Bach
         One Hundred Years of Solitude, Gabriel García Marquez

1971   *A Dictionary of British Folk-Tales*, Katherine Briggs

1972   *Bless Me, Ultima*, Rudolfo Anaya
         Fables of Man, Mark Twain
         Watership Down, Richard Adams

1975   *Georgia Place-Names*, Kenneth K. Krakow

1976   *The Night with the Hants and Other Alabama Folk Experiences*, Ray B. Browne

1978   *Shuckin' and Jivin': Folklore from Contemporary Black Americans*, Daryl Cumber Dance

1979   *I Love Myself: When I Am Laughing . . . and Then Again When I Am Looking Mean and Impressive: A Zora Neale Hurston Reader*

1980   *The Unbroken Web: Stories and Fables*, Richard Adams

1981   *The Sanctified Church: The Folklore Writings of Zora Neale Hurston*
         Sources and Analogues of the Uncle Remus Tales, Florence Baer

1982   *Coyote &*, Joe Hayes
         The Day It Snowed Tortillas, Joe Hayes
         La casa de los espíritus, Isabel Allende

1984   *Mouth Open Story Jump Out*, Grace Hallworth

1985   *Afro-American Folktales: Stories from Black Traditions in the New World*, Roger D. Abrahams
          Anansi's Secret, Grace Hallworth
          Spunk: The Selected Short Stories of Zora Neale Hurston
          The People Could Fly: American Black Folktales, Virginia Hamilton

1986   "The Enchanted Raisin," Jacqueline Balcells
          Neveryona, Samuel R. Delaney
          No Way, Jose!/De Ninguna Manera, José!, Joe Hayes

1987   *The Jewish Stories One Generation Tells Another*, Peninnah Schram
          Tall Betsy and Dunce Baby: South Georgia Folktales, Marielle Glenn Hartsfield
          Why Mosquitoes Buzz in People's Ears, Bobby Norfolk

1988   *The Alchemist*, Paulo Coelho
          Norfolk Tales, Bobby Norfolk

1989   *The Frog Who Wanted to Be a Singer*, Linda McNear Goss

1990   *Animal Tales*, Jim Weiss
          Animal Tales, Dan Yashinsky
          Arabian Nights, Dan Yashinsky
          Cric Crac, Grace Hallworth
          Eight Tales for Eight Nights: Stories for Chanukah, Peninnah Schram and Steven M. Rosman
          Keepers of the Animals, Joseph Bruchac and Michael Caduto
          Mule Bone: A Comedy of Negro Life, Zora Neale Hurston
          Tales for an Unknown City, Dan Yashinsky

1991   *Native American Stories*, Joseph Bruchac

1992   *Animal's Ball Game*, Lloyd Arneach
          Cajun Folktales, J. J. Reneaux
          Everyone Knows Gato Pinto: More Tales from Spanish New Mexico, Joe Hayes
          Uncle Remus con Chile, Américo Paredes

1993   *The Butterflies Trick Coyote*, Joe Hayes
          Native American Animal Stories, Joseph Bruchac
          Soft Child: How Rattlesnake Got Its Fangs, Joe Hayes
          "Tales of Aesop from Jamal Koram," Mary Carter Smith

1994   *Anansi at the Pool*, Grace Hallworth
          The Girl Who Married the Moon, Joseph Bruchac and Gayle Ross
          How Rabbit Tricked Otter and Other Cherokee Trickster Stories, Gayle Ross
          Nanaue the Shark Man and Other Hawaiian Shark Stories, Emma M. Nakuina et al.

1995   *The Boy Who Lived with the Bears and Other Iroquois Stories*, Joseph Bruchac
          The Dog People: Native Dog Stories, Joseph Bruchac
          The Gift of Music, Dayton Edmonds
          Her Stories: African American Folktales, Fairy Tales, and True Tales, Virginia Hamilton

1995   *(continued)*
       How Turtle's Back Was Cracked: A Traditional Cherokee Tale, Gayle Ross
       The Jungle Book, Dan Yashinsky
       Native Wisdom, Joseph Bruchac
       Why Alligator Hates Dog, J. J. Reneaux

1996   *Children of the Longhouse*, Joseph Bruchac
       A Christmas Carol and Other Favorites, Dan Yashinsky
       The Gift of Rabbit, Dayton Edmonds

1997   "Bouki Dances the Kokioko," Diane Wolkstein
       The Farmer's Three Sons, Dayton Edmonds
       The Gift of Fire, Dayton Edmonds
       Tales from Watership Down, Richard Adams

MAJOR AUTHORS OF FABLE
AND FABLE-BASED LITERATURE

Abrahams, Roger D., *Afro-American Folktales: Stories from Black Traditions in the New World* (1985)

Abu-Bakr, Caliph (630)

Adams, Richard, *Tales from Watership Down* (1997)
   The Unbroken Web: Stories and Fables (1980)
   Watership Down (1972)

Addison, Joseph, *Spectator* essay (1711)

Ade, George, *Fables in Slang* (1900)

Aelian, *Historia Animalium* (third century)

Aeschylus, *Agamemnon* (462 B.C.E.)
   Myrmidones (ca. 460 B.C.E.)

Aesop, *Fables* (ca. 530 B.C.E.)

Alexis of Thurii, *Aesop* (ca. 350 B.C.E.)

Allende, Isabel, *La casa de los espíritus* (1982)

Anaya, Rudolfo, *Bless Me, Ultima* (1972)

Andersen, Hans Christian, *Billedbog uden Billeder* (1840)
   Eventyr (1837)
   Eventyr, fortalte for børn (1835)
   The Fairy Tale of My Life (1840)
   Fairy Tales and Stories (1872)

Angelou, Maya, *I Know Why the Caged Bird Sings* (1970)

Anglicus, Galterus, *Isopet* (1175)
   Isopet I (ca. 1180)

anonymous Arabic, *The Book of Achiqar* (ca. 2000 B.C.E.)
   Hitopadesha (twelfth century)

anonymous Babylonian, "The Fable of the Fox" (1700–1600 B.C.E.)
   "Nisaba and Wheat" (2000 B.C.E.)
   "The Ox and the Horse" (ca. 1500 B.C.E.)
   "The Snake and the Eagle" (1500–1200 B.C.E.)
   "The Tamarisk and the Palm" (2300–2200 B.C.E.)

anonymous central European, *Carmina Burana* (twelfth century)

anonymous Dutch, *The Most Delectable History of Reynard the Fox* (1676)
    Reinke de Vos (1498)
    Rienaerts Histoire (1498)

anonymous English, *The Crafty Courtier: or the Fable of Reynard the Fox* (1706)
    Fables, Moral and Political (1703)
    Here beginneth a merye Jest of a man that was called Howleglas (ca. 1560)
    The Owl and the Nightingale (ca. 1190)
    Of the Vox and of the Wolf (ca. 1250)

anonymous Flemish, *La Couronnement de Renart* (1270)
    Reinaerts Histoire (ca. 1370)

anonymous Flemish-Dutch, *Van den Vos Reinaerde* (ca. 1250)

anonymous French, *Avionnets* (fourth century)
    Chartres Isopet (thirteenth century)
    Isopet II (thirteenth century)
    Renart le Contrefait (ca. 1340)
    Roman de Renart (ca. 1250)

anonymous French-Italian, *Rainardo e Lesengrino* (ca. 1200)

anonymous German, *Das Buch der Beyspiele* (1483)
    Ein kurtzweilig Lesen von Dyl Vlenspiegel (1515)

anonymous Greek, *Stephanites kai Ichnelates* (eleventh century)

anonymous Italian, *Aesopo Historiado* (1497)
    Aesop's Life and Fables (1485)
    Cento Favole Morali (1577)
    Fabulae Centum (1565)

anonymous Latin, *Ecbasis Captivi*, (ca. 940)
    Gesta Romanorum (1324)
    Novus Avianus (ca. 1100)

anonymous Persian, *Hazar Afsanah* (ninth century)
    Tuti Nameh (ca. 1300)

anonymous Spanish, *Calila e Digna* (1251)
    El libro de los gatos (thirteenth century)

anonymous Turkish, *Hümayun-name* (seventh century)

Aphthonius (315)

Archilochus, "The Fox Avenging His Wrongs on the Eagle" (ca. 650 B.C.E.)

Aristides (second century)

Aristophanes, *The Birds* (414 B.C.E.)
    The Wasps (422 B.C.E.)

Aristotle, *Historia Animalium* (fourth century B.C.E.)
    Meteorologica (fourth century B.C.E.)
    Rhetorica (fourth century B.C.E.)

Arneach, Lloyd, *Animal's Ball Game* (1992)

Aryasura, *Jatakamala* (200)

Aulus Gellius, *Noctes Atticae* (ca. 180 C.E.)

Aung, Maun Htin, *Burmese Law Tales: The Legal Element in Burmese Folklore* (1962)

Ausonius (fourth century)

Avianus, fables (fifth century)

Axum (third century)

Babrius, Valerius (second century)

Bach, Richard, *Jonathan Livingston Seagull* (1970)

Bacon, Francis, *Of Vainglory* (1625)

Baer, Florence, *Sources and Analogues of the Uncle Remus Tales* (1981)

Balcells, Jacqueline, "The Enchanted Raisin" (1986)

Baldo, *Novus Aesopus* (twelfth century)

Barlow, Francis, *Aesop's Fables with His Life* (seventeenth century)

Basilakis, Nikephoros, *Progymnasmata* (ca. 1175)

Basile, Giambattista, *Il Pentamerone* (1637)

Baudoin, Jean, *Les Fables d'Esope phrygien* (1631)

Beauvais, Vincent de, *Speculum Majus* (thirteenth century)

Behn, Aphra, *Aesop's Fables with His Life* (1687)

Belloc, Hilaire, *The Bad Child's Book of Beasts* (1896)
    Cautionary Tales (1907)
    The Moral Alphabet (1899)

ben Hananiah, Joshua (117)

ben Mattathias, Abraham, *Kuh Buch* (1555)

ben Zakkai, Johannan (second century)

Bennett, Charles, *The Fables of Aesop and Others Translated from Human Nature* (1857)

Bewick, Thomas, *Select Fables of Aesop and Others* (1784)

Bewick, Thomas, and Robert Elliott Bewick, *Aesop's Fables* (1818)

Bidpai, *Panchatantra* (fifth century B.C.E.)

Bierce, Ambrose, *Fantastic Fables* (1899)

Boccaccio, Giovanni, *The Decameron* (1353)

Bodart, Anne, *The Blue Dog and Other Fables for the French* (1956)

Boner, Ulrich, *Der Edelstein* (1330)

Botkin, B. A., *A Treasury of American Folklore* (1944)

Brentano, Clemens, and Achim von Arnim, *Der Knaben Wunderhorn* (1806–1808)

Brewer, J. Mason, *The Word on the Brazos: Negro Preacher Tales from the Brazos Bottoms of Texas* (1953)

Briggs, Katherine, *A Dictionary of British Folk-Tales* (1971)

Browne, Ray B., *A Night with the Hants and Other Alabama Folk Experiences* (1976)

Bruchac, Joseph, *The Boy Who Lived with the Bears and Other Iroquois Stories* (1995)
    Children of the Longhouse (1996)
    The Dog People: Native Dog Stories (1995)
    Native American Animal Stories (1993)
    Native American Stories (1991)
    Native Wisdom (1995)

Bruchac, Joseph, and Gayle Ross, *The Girl Who Married the Moon* (1994)

Bruchac, Joseph, and Michael Caduto, *Keepers of the Animals* (1990)

Bullokar, William, *Aesopz Fablz in Tru Ortography with Grammar-notz* (1585)

Burton, Richard, *The Book of the Thousand Nights and a Night: A Plain and Literal Translation of the Arabian Nights Entertainment* (1880)

Burzoe (570)

Busch, Wilhelm, *Max und Moritz* (1865)

Calder, Alexander, *The Fables of Aesop According to Sir Roger L'Estrange* (1931)

Callimachus, *Epigrammata*, (ca. 270 B.C.E.)

Carroll, Lewis, *Alice in Wonderland* (1865)
   Through the Looking Glass and What Alice Found There (1871)

Carson, Rachel, *Silent Spring* (1962)

Cary, Alice, and Phoebe Cary, *The Poetical Works of Alice and Phoebe Cary* (1884)

Caxton, William, *The Boke of Subtyl Historyes and Fables of Esope* (1485)
   The Historye of Reynart the Foxe (1481)

Cent, Siô (1430)

Chaucer, Geoffrey, *The Canterbury Tales* (1387)
   The Parliament of Fowls (ca. 1377)

Churchyard, Thomas, *Churchyard Chippes* (ca. 1560)
   The Legend of Shore's Wife (1563)

Cirese, Eugenio, *Il Tempo d'allora, figure, storie e proverbi* (1939)

Comparetti, Domenico, *Popular Italian Tales* (1875)

Connelly, Marc, *The Green Pastures* (1929)

Crane, Walter, *The Baby's Own Aesop* (1886)

Croxall, Samuel, *The Fables of Aesop and Others Newly Done into English* (1722)

d'Argenson, Marc, *La Mélange tirés d'une grande bibliothèque* (1788)

d'Aussy, Pierre, *Fabliaux ou contes du XIIe et du XIIIe siècles* (1779)

da Vinci, Leonardo (sixteenth century)

Dance, Daryl Cumber, *Shuckin' and Jivin': Folklore from Contemporary Black Americans* (1978)

de Coster, Charles, *La Légende de les aventures héroiques, joyeues, et glorieuses d'Ulenspiegel et de Lamme Goedzak au pays de Flandres et ailleurs* (1866)

Delaney, Samuel R., *Neveryona* (1986)

Demetrius of Phalerum, *Aesop's Fables* (ca. 290 B.C.E.)

Demosthenes of Athens (fourth century B.C.E.)

Dickens, Charles, *The Chimes* (1853)
   The Christmas Books (1852)
   A Christmas Carol (1843)

Dinesen, Isak, "Babette's Feast" (1949)

Dio Chrysostom (first century)

Diogenes Laertius, *Popular Proverbs* (third century)
   Vitae Philosophorum (third century)

Dodsley, Robert, *Select Fables of Esop and Other Fabulists* (1764)

Doni, Antonio Francesco, *La Moral Philosophia* (1552)

Doré, Gustave, *Fables de La Fontaine* (1868)

Dorp, Martin, *Phaedrus* (1513)

Dorson, Richard M., *American Negro Folktales* (1967)
    Jonathan Draws the Long Bow (1946)

Dryden, John, *Fables Ancient and Modern* (1700)
    The Hind and the Panther (1687)

Du Bois, W. E. B., *The Souls of Black Folks* (1903)

Edmonds, Dayton, *The Farmer's Three Sons* (1997)
    The Gift of Fire (1997)
    The Gift of Music (1995)
    The Gift of Rabbit (1996)

Eliot, T. S., *Old Possum's Book of Practical Cats* (1939)

Ennius (second century B.C.E.)

Erasmus Alberus, *Fabeln* (1534)

Ewing, Juliana Horatia Gatty, *Aunt Judy's Magazine* (1873–1885)

Fay, Andreas, *Fables* (1820)

Fenn, Lady Eleanor, *Cobwebs to Catch Flies; or Dialogues in Short Sentences* (ca. 1783)
    Fables by Mrs. Teachwell (1783)

Finch, Anne Kingsmill, *The Atheist and the Acorn* (1713)

Florian, Jean de, *Fables* (1792)

Fornander, Abraham, *A Collection of Hawaiian Antiquities and Folklore* (1919)

Forner, Juan Pablo, *El asno erudito* (1782)

France, Anatole, *Penguin Island* (1908)

Franklin, Benjamin, "The Ephemera: An Emblem of Human Life" (1778)

Frasconi, Antonio, *9 Aesop's Fables* (1953)
    Twelve Fables of Aesop (1954)

Frazer, James, *Folklore in the Old Testament* (1918)
    The Golden Bough: The Roots of Religion and Folklore (1911–1915)

Galland, Antoine, *Les contes et fables indiennes de Bidpai et de Lokmam* (1724)
    Les Mille et une nuits (1717)
    Les Mille et une nuits, contes arabes traduits en français (1708)

Gatty, Margaret Scott, *Aunt Judy's Magazine* (1866–1873)
    Aunt Judy's Tales (1859)
    The Fairy Godmothers and Other Tales (1852)
    The Parables from Nature (1855)

Gay, John, *Fifty-one Fables in Verse* (1727)

Geeraerts, Marcus, *De Warachtighe Fabulen der Dieren* (1567)

Gellert, Christian, *Fabeln und Erzählungen* (1748)

Gielée, Jacquemart, *Renart le Nouvel* (1288)

Glîchezaere, Heinrich der, *Reinhart Fuchs* (ca. 1180)

Godwin, William, *Fables Ancient and Modern* (1805)

Goethe, Johann Friedrich von, "Der Zauberlehrling" (1792)
　　Reinecke Fuchs (1794)

Goldsmith, Oliver, *Bewick's Select Fables* (1784)

Goss, Linda McNear, *The Frog Who Wanted To Be a Singer* (1989)

Gouget, Georges, *Fables de La Fontaine* (1833–1834)

Gower, John, *Confessio Amantis* (1390)

Grahame, Kenneth, *The Wind in the Willows* (1908)

Grandville, J. J., *Fables de La Fontaine* (1838)

Gregoras, Nikephoras, *The Byzantine History of 1204–1359* (fourteenth century)

Gregory of Nazianzus (fourth century)

Gregory of Tours, *The Miracles of St. Martin* (sixth century)

Grimm, Jacob, and Wilhelm Grimm, *Irische Elfenmärchen* (1826)
　　Kinder und Hausmärchen (1812, 1815, 1822)
　　Lieder der alten Edda (1815)
　　Reinhart Fuchs (1834)

ha-Nakdan, Berechiah, *Mishlei Shu'alim* (thirteenth century)

Hallworth, Grace, *Anansi at the Pool* (1994)
　　Anansi's Secret (1985)
　　Cric Crac (1990)
　　Mouth Open Story Jump Out (1984)

Hamilton, Virginia, *Her Stories: African American Folktales, Fairy Tales, and True Tales* (1995)
　　The People Could Fly: American Black Folktales (1985)

Harris, Joel Chandler, *Daddy Jake the Runaway and Short Stories Told after Dark* (1889)
　　Free Joe and Other Georgian Sketches (1887)
　　Mingo and Other Sketches in Black and White (1884)
　　Nights with Uncle Remus: Myths and Legends of the Old Plantation (1883)
　　Seven Tales of Uncle Remus (1948)
　　The Tar-Baby and Other Rhymes of Uncle Remus (1904)
　　Told by Uncle Remus (1903)
　　Uncle Remus: His Songs and His Sayings (1880)
　　Uncle Remus and Brer Rabbit (1906)
　　Uncle Remus and His Friends (1892)
　　Uncle Remus and the Little Boy (1910)
　　Uncle Remus Returns (1918)
　　The Witch Wolf: An Uncle Remus Story (1921)
　　"The Wonderful Tar-Baby Story" (1880)

Hartsfield, Marielle Glenn, *Tall Betsy and Dunce Baby: South Georgia Folktales* (1987)

Hauptmann, Gerhart, *Till Eulenspiegel* (1928)

Hawkes, Jacquetta, *A Woman as Great as the World and Other Fables* (1953)

Hayes, Joe, *The Butterflies Trick Coyote* (1993)
　　Coyote & (1982)
　　The Day It Snowed Tortillas (1982)
　　Everyone Knows Gato Pinto: More Tales from Spanish New Mexico (1992)

No Way, Jose!/De Ninguna Manera, José! (1986)
Soft Child: How Rattlesnake Got Its Fangs (1993)

Hebel, Johann Peter (nineteenth century)

Henry, O., "The Gift of the Magi" (1905)
"The Ransom of Red Chief" (1910)

Henryson, Robert, *The Morall Fabillis of Esope the Phrygian, compylit in eloquent & ornate Scottis meter* (1570)

Herder, Johann (eighteenth century)

Herodotus, *The Histories* (ca. 425 B.C.E.)

Hertel, Johannes, *Panchatantra* (1914)

Hesiod, *Works and Days* (eighth century B.C.E.)

Hey, Wilhelm, *Noch fünfzig Fabeln für Kinder* (1837)

Himerius (fourth century)

Hollar, Wenceslaus, *Aesopics, or a Second Collection of Fables* (1668)

Holloway, E. W., *Reynard the Fox, a Poem in Twelve Cantos* (1852)

Hoole, Charles, *Aesop's Fables in English and Latin* (1687)

Horace, "The City Mouse and the Country Mouse" (30 B.C.E.)

Howitt, Samuel, *A New Work of Animals Principally Designed from the Fables of Aesop, Gay and Phaedras* (1811)

Hughes, Langston, *The Best of Simple* (1957)

Hughes, Langston, and Arna Bontemps, *The Book of Negro Folklore* (1958)

Hurston, Zora Neale, *I Love Myself: When I Am Laughing . . . and Then Again When I Am Looking Mean and Impressive: A Zora Neale Hurston Reader* (1979)
Mule Bone: A Comedy of Negro Life (1990)
Mules and Men (1935)
Tell My Horse (1938)
The Sanctified Church: The Folklore Writings of Zora Neale Hurston (1981)
Spunk: The Selected Short Stories of Zora Neale Hurston (1985)

Hurus, Johan, *Las vida del Ysopet con sus fabulas hystoriadas* (1489)

Ibn al-Muquaffa, *Kalilah wa Dimnah* (750)

Ibn Zafar, *Consolation Philtres for the Man of Authority* (1154)

Iriarte, Thómas de, *Fábulas literarias* (1782)
Para casos tales suele tenor los maestros oficiales (1783)

Irving, Washington, "The Devil and Tom Walker" (1824)

Jacobs, Joseph, *The Fables of Aesop* (1889)

Jammes, Francis, *De l'Angélus de l'aube à l'Angélus du soir* (1898)

Joel, Rabbi, *Panchatantra* (twelfth century)

Johannes of Alta Silva, *Historia Septem Sapientum* (twelfth century)

John of Capua, *Directorium humanae vitae* (thirteenth century)

Johnson, Samuel, *The History of Rasselas, Prince of Abyssinia* (1759)

Jonson, Ben, *Volpone, the Fox* (1606)

Joplin, Scott, *Treemonisha* (1915)

Judges 9:8–15 (925 B.C.E.)

Kahiolo, G. W., *Ka Hae Hawai'i* (1861)

Kanem-Bornu fables (ninth–seventeenth centuries)

Kashefi, Hoseyn Wa'ez-e, *Anwar-e Suhayli* (ca. 1500–1505)

I Kings 3:16–28 (960 B.C.E.)

II Kings 14:9 (790 B.C.E.)

Kipling, Rudyard, *The Jungle Book* (1894)
 Just-So Stories for Little Children (1902)
 The Second Jungle Book (1895)

Komroff, Manuel, *The Great Fables of All Nations* (1935)

Koran, "Al-kahf" (613)

Krakow, Kenneth K., *Georgia Place-names* (1975)

Kramer, Samuel Noah, *Sumerian Mythology* (1944)

Krylov, Ivan, *Basni* (1809)

Kush (fourth century B.C.E.–second century C.E.)

La Fontaine, Jean de, *Fables choisies* (1668)
 Fables Choisies, Vol. II (1678)
 Fables Choisies (1755–1759)
 Oeuvres Complètes de La Fontaine (1821)

Landi, Giulio (1575)

Langhorne, John, *The Fables of Flora* (1771)

Law, William, *Remarks on Mandeville's Fables of the Bees* (1723)

Leeu, Gheraert, *Die Hystorie van Reynaert die Vos* (1479)

Lessing, Gotthold, *Fabeln: Drei Bücher* (1759)
 Fabeln und Erzählungen in Reimen (1747)

L'Estrange, Sir Roger, *Fables of Aesop and Other Eminent Mythologists: with Morals and Reflexions* (1692)

Liebhard, Joachim, *Äsop* (1476)

Livy, *Ab Urbe Condita* (ca. 14 C.E.)

Loango (fifteenth–eighteenth centuries)

Locke, John, *Aesop's Fables* (1703)

Lokman (ca. 1100 B.C.E.)

Low, Joseph, *Aesop: A Portfolio of Color Prints* (1963)

Lucan (first century)

Lucian, *Cynicus* (ca. 170)
 Hermotimus (ca. 175)
 "The Sorcerer's Apprentice" (ca. 170)

Lucilius (second century B.C.E.)

Luther, Martin (sixteenth century)

Lydgate, John, *The Churl and the Bird* (ca. 1390)
 The Horse, Goose, and Sheep (ca. 1398)
 Isopes Fabules (ca. 1398)

Mandeville, Bernard de, *Aesop Dress'd or A Collection of Fables Writ in Familiar Verse* (1704)
    The Fable of the Bees or Private Vices, Publick Benefits (1714)
    The Fable of the Bees, Part II (1729)
    Some Fables after the Easie and Familiar Method of Monsieur de la Fontaine (1703)

Mandingo (thirteenth–sixteenth century)

Manuel, Don Juan, *Conde Lucanor* (fourteenth century)

Map, Walter, *De Nugis Curialium* (thirteenth century)

March, William, *99 Fables by William March* (1960)

Marie de France, *Fables* (ca. 1189)

Marquez, Gabriel García, *One Hundred Years of Solitude* (1970)

Maximus of Tyre (second century)

Meissner, August (eighteenth century)

Molière, *Le Malade imaginaire* (1673)

Mooney, James, *Myths of the Cherokee* (1900)

Mukerji, Dan Gopal, *Gay-Neck: The Story of a Pigeon* (1927)
    Jungle Beasts and Men (1923)

Nakuina, Emma M. et al., *Nanaue the Shark Man and Other Hawaiian Shark Stories* (1994)

Naylor, Samuel, *Reynard the Fox, a renowned Apologue of the Middle Age, reproduced in Rhyme* (1844)

Neckham, Alexander, *Novus Aesopus* (ca. 1215)
    Novus Avianus (ca. 1215)

Nerucci, Gherardo, *Sessanta novelle popolari Montanesi* (1880)

Nèvelet, Isaac Nicholas, *Mythologia Aesopica* (1610)
    Romulus Niveleti

Nigel of Longchamps, *Speculum Stultorum* (twelfth century)

Nivard of Ghent, *Ysengrimus* (1148)

Norfolk, Bobby, *Norfolk Tales* (1988)
    Why Mosquitoes Buzz in People's Ears (1987)

North, Thomas, *The Morall Philosophie of Doni* (1570)

Odo of Cheriton, *Fabulae* (ca. 1220)

Ogilby, John, *Fables of Aesop Paraphras'd in Verse* (1665)

Orwell, George, *Animal Farm* (1945)

Owens, William, "Folklore of Southern Negroes" (1877)

Paredes, Américo, *Uncle Remus con Chile* (1992)

Parsons, Elsie Clews, *Journal of American Folklore* (1921)

Pauli, Johannes, *Schimpf und Ernst* (1522)

Paulus Diaconus (eighth century)

Payne, John, *The Book of the Thousand Nights and One Night* (1884)

Pedersen, Christien, *Aesop's Leyned og Fabler* (1556)

Pestalozzi, Johann Heinrich, *How Gertrude Educates Her Children* (1801)

Petrus Alphonsus (thirteenth century)

Phaedrus, *Aesopia* (third century B.C.E.)

Philo Judaeus (first century)

Pignotti, Lorenzo, *Favole e Novelle* (1782)

Pitré, Giuseppe, *Fiabe, novelle e racconti popolari Siciliani* (1875)

Planudes, Maximus (ca. 1330)

Plato, *Alcibiades* (fourth century B.C.E.)
    Phaedo (fourth century B.C.E.)
    Phaedrus (fourth century B.C.E.)
    Symposium (fourth century B.C.E.)

Plutarch, *Aetia Graeca* (second century)
    Conjugalia Praecepta (second century)
    De Capienda ex Inimicis Utilitate (second century)
    The Life of Aratus (second century)
    The Life of Themistocles (second century)
    Praecepta (second century)
    Questiones Convivales (second century)
    Vita Aesopi (ca. 100 C.E.)
    Vitae Decem Oratorium (second century)

Poggio, Bracciolini, *Liber Facetiarum* (fifteenth century)

Potter, Beatrix, *Johnny Town-Mouse* (1918)
    The Tale of Peter Rabbit (1893)
    The Tale of Samuel Whiskers (1908)
    The Tale of Squirrel Nutkin (1903)

Pseudo-Dositheus, *Hermeneumata* (207 C.E.)

Rabelais, François, *Gargantua and Pantagruel* (1562)

Rackham, Arthur, *Aesop's Fables* (1916)

Randolph, Vance, *Hot Springs and Hell and Other Folk Jests and Anecdotes from the Ozarks* (1965)
    Who Blowed Up the Church House and Other Ozark Folk Tales (1952)

Reneaux, J. J., *Cajun Folktales* (1992)
    Why Alligator Hates Dog (1995)

Richardson, Samuel, *Aesop's Fables* (1739)

Ridley, Caleb A., *The Southern Mountaineer* (ca. 1900)

Romulus, *Androcles and the Lion* (tenth century)

Ross, Gayle, *How Rabbit Tricked Otter and Other Cherokee Trickster Stories* (1994)
    How Turtle's Back Was Cracked: A Traditional Cherokee Tale (1995)

Rostand, Edmond, *Chantecler* (1899)

Rudaki, *Kalilah wa Dimnah* (tenth century)

Ruiz, Juan, *El Libro do buen amor* (fourteenth century)

Rumi, Jalal ad-Din ar, *Masnavi-ye Ma'navi* (ca. 1270)

Russell, William, *Fables Moral and Sentimental* (1772)

Rutebeuf of Champaign, *Renard le Bestourné* (1261)

Sahid, David, *La Livre des Lumières* (1644)

Sahula, Isaac, *Meshal ha-Kadmoni* (thirteenth century)

Saint-Exupéry, Antoine de, *Le Petit Prince* (1943)

Samaniego, Félix, *Fábulas morales* (1781)

II Samuel 12:1–6 (sixth century B.C.E.)

Schram, Peninnah, *The Jewish Stories One Generation Tells Another* (1987)

Schram, Peninnah, and Steven M. Rosman, *Eight Tales for Eight Nights: Stories for Chanukah* (1990)

Sénchez, Clemente, *El Libro de los exenplos por a. b. c.* (fifteenth century)

Shakespeare, William, *Coriolanus* (ca. 1605)

Sharpe, Richard Scrafton, *Friends in a New Dress* (1807)

Shaw, George Bernard, *Androcles and the Lion* (1912)

Sháyán, Totaram, *Hazar Dastan* (nineteenth century)

Shirley, John, *The Most Delectable History of Reynard the Fox, Newly Corrected & Purged from all grossness in Phrase & Matter* (1654)

Simonides (fifth century B.C.E.)

Smart, Christopher, *Fables in Verse for the Improvement of the Young and the Old by Abraham Aesop Esq.* (1757)
A Poetical Translation of the Fables of Phaedrus (1760)

Smith, Mary Carter, "Tales of Aesop from Jamal Koram" (1993)

Somadeva, *The Tales from the Kathasaritsagara* (1070)

Songhay (thirteenth–sixteenth century)

Soninke fables (fourth–thirteenth century)

Sophocles, *Ajax* (ca. 451 B.C.E.)

Spenser, Edmund, *Mother Hubberds Tale* (1591)

Steinhöwel, Heinrich, *Aesop's Life and Fables* (ca. 1477)

Stephens, Robert (1546)

Stevens, John Hall, *Fables for Grown Gentlemen* (1761)

Stevenson, Robert Louis, *Fables* (1896)
The Strange Case of Dr. Jekyll and Mr. Hyde (1886)

Straparola, Giovanni, *Le Piacevoli Notti* (1553)

Sylvester II (1000)

Takakuni, Minamoto, *Konjaku Monogatari* (1075)

Taylor, Jeffreys, *Aesop in Rhyme, with Some Originals* (1821)

Tehmistius (third century)

Theon, *Progymnasmata* (second century)

Thrum, Thomas G, *Hawaiian Folk Tales: A Collection of Native Legends* (1907)
More Hawaiian Folk Tales (1923)

Thurber, James, *Fables for Our Time and Famous Poems Illustrated* (1940)
Further Fables for Our Time (1956)

Timocreon (fifth century B.C.E.)

Tournier, Michael, *Vendredi* (1967)

Trimmer, Sarah Kirby, *An Easy Introduction to the Knowledge of Nature* (1780)
    Family Magazine (1788–1789)
    The Ladder to Learning (1789)
    The Oeconomy of Charity (1787)

Twain, Mark, "The Celebrated Jumping Frog of Calaveras County" (1867)
    "A Fable" (1909)
    Fables of Man (1972)

Vallo, Lorenzo (fifteenth century)

Van Dyke, Henry, *The First Christmas Tree* (1897)
    The Story of the Other Wise Man (1896)

Verona, Liberale da, *Aesop's Fables* (1479)

Vitry, Jacques de, *Sermones Vulgares* (ca. 1230)

Voltaire, *Candide* (1759)

von Minden, Gerhard (thirteenth century)

Voulliéme, Ernst, *Aesop's Life and Fables* (ca. 1477)

Waldis, Burkhard, *Esopus* (1548)

Wallich, Rabbi Moses, *Sefer Meshalim* (1697)

Watts, Isaac, *Divine Songs* (1720)

Weiss, Jim, *Animal Tales* (1990)

Wiesel, Elie, *La Ville de la chance* (1962)
    Le Chant des morts (1966)
    Les Portes de la forêt (1964)
    Zalmen; ou, La Folie de Dieu (1968)

Wilde, Oscar, *The Happy Prince and Other Tales* (1888)
    The House of Pomegranates (1891)

Willem, *Reinaert de Vos* (ca. 1250)

Wolkstein, Diane, "Bouki Dances the Kokioko" (1997)

Xenophon, *Memoirs of Socrates* (fourth century B.C.E.)

Yashinsky, Dan, *Animal Tales* (1990)
    Arabian Nights (1990)
    A Christmas Carol and Other Favorites (1996)
    The Jungle Book (1995)
    Tales for an Unknown City (1990)

Zotenberg, Hermann, *Histoire d' Alá al-Din ou La Lampe Merveilleuse, Texte Arabe* (1888)

FILMS OF FABLE

MAJOR SOURCES OF FABLE

A

Ab Urbe Condita, Livy (ca. 14 C.E.)

Aesop, Alexis of Thurii (ca. 350 C.E.)

Aesop: A Portfolio of Color Prints, Joseph Low (1963)

Aesop Dress'd or A Collection of Fables Writ in Familiar Verse, Bernard de Manville (1704)

Aesop in Rhyme, with Some Originals, Jeffreys Taylor (1821)

Aesopia, Phaedrus (third century C.E.)

Aesopics, or a Second Collection of Fables, Wenceslaus Hollar (1668)

Aesopo Historiado, anonymous Italian (1497)

Aesop's Fables, Thomas Bewick and Robert Elliott Bewick (1818)

Aesop's Fables, Demetrius of Phalerum (ca. 290 C.E.)

Aesop's Fables, John Locke (1703)

Aesop's Fables, Arthur Rackham (1916)

Aesop's Fables, Samuel Richardson (1739)

Aesop's Fables, Liberale da Verona (1479)

Aesop's Fables in English and Latin, Charles Hoole (1687)

Aesop's Fables with His Life, Francis Barlow (seventeenth century)

Aesop's Fables with His Life, Aphra Behn (1687)

Aesop's Leyned og Fabler, Christien Pedersen (1556)

Aesop's Life and Fables, anonymous Italian (1485)

Aesop's Life and Fables, Heinrich Steinhöwel (ca. 1477)

Aesop's Life and Fables, Ernst Voulliéme (ca. 1477)

Aesopz Fablz in Tru Ortography with Grammar-notz, William Bullokar (1585)

Aetia Graeca, Plutarch (second century)

Afro-American Folktales: Stories from Black Traditions in the New World, Roger D. Abrahams, (1985)

Agamemnon, Aeschylus (462 C.E.)

Ajax , Sophocles (ca. 451 C.E.)

Alcibiades, Plato (fourth century C.E.)

Alice in Wonderland, Lewis Carroll (1865)

"Al-kahf," Koran (613)

American Negro Folktales, Richard M. Dorson (1967)

Anansi at the Pool, Grace Hallworth (1994)

Anansi's Secret, Grace Hallworth (1985)

Androcles and the Lion, Romulus (tenth century)

Androcles and the Lion, George Bernard Shaw (1912)

Animal Farm, George Orwell (1945)
Animal Tales, Jim Weiss (1990)
Animal Tales, Dan Yashinsky (1990)
Animal's Ball Game, Lloyd Arneach (1992)
Anwar-e Suhayli, Hoseyn Wa'ez-e Kashefi (ca. 1500–1505)
Arabian Nights, Dan Yashinsky (1990)
Äsop, Joachim Liebhard (1476)
The Atheist and the Acorn, Anne Kingsmill Finch (1713)
Aunt Judy's Magazine, Juliana Horatia Gatty Ewing (1873–1885)
Aunt Judy's Magazine, Margaret Scott Gatty (1866–1873)
Aunt Judy's Tales, Margaret Scott Gatty (1859)
Avionnets, anonymous French (fourth century)

B
"Babette's Feast," Isak Dinesen (1949)
The Baby's Own Aesop, Walter Crane (1886)
The Bad Child's Book of Beasts, Hilaire Belloc (1896)
Basni, Ivan Krylov (1809)
The Best of Simple, Langston Hughes (1957)
Billedbog uden Billeder, Hans Christian Andersen (1840)
The Birds, Aristophanes (414. B.C.E.)
Bless Me, Ultima, Rudolfo Anaya (1972)
The Blue Dog and Other Fables for the French, Anne Bodart (1956)
The Boke of Subtyl Historyes and Fables of Esope, William Caxton (1485)
The Book of Achiqar, anonymous Arabic (ca. 2000 B.C.E.)
The Book of Negro Folklore, Langston Hughes and Arna Bontemps (1958)
The Book of the Thousand Nights and a Night: A Plain and Literal Translation of the Arabian Nights Entertainment, Richard Burton (1880)
The Book of the Thousand Nights and One Night, John Payne (1884)
"Bouki Dances the Kokioko," Diane Wolkstein (1997)
The Boy Who Lived with the Bears and Other Iroquois Stories, Joseph Bruchac (1995)
Burmese Law Tales: The Legal Element in Burmese Folklore, Maun Htin Aung (1962)
The Butterflies Trick Coyote, Joe Hayes (1993)
The Byzantine History of 1204–1359, Nikephoras Gregoras (fourth century)

C
Cajun Folktales, J. J. Reneaux (1992)
Calila e Digna, anonymous Spanish (1251)
Candide, Voltaire (1759)
The Canterbury Tales, Geoffrey Chaucer (1387)
Carmina Burana, anonymous central European (twelfth century)
Cautionary Tales, Hilaire Belloc (1907)
"The Celebrated Jumping Frog of Calaveras County," Mark Twain (1867)
Cento Favole Morali, anonymous Italian (1577)
Chantecler, Edmond Rostand (1899)
Chartres Isopet, anonymous French (thirteenth century)
Children of the Longhouse, Joseph Bruchac (1996)
The Chimes, Charles Dickens (1853)
The Christmas Books, Charles Dickens (1852)
A Christmas Carol and Other Favorites, Dan Yashinsky (1996)

A Christmas Carol, Charles Dickens (1843)
Churchyard Chippes, Thomas Churchyard (ca. 1560)
The Churl and the Bird, John Lydgate (ca. 1390)
"The City Mouse and the Country Mouse," Horace (30 C.E.)
Cobwebs to Catch Flies; or Dialogues in Short Sentences, Lady Eleanor Fenn (ca. 1783)
A Collection of Hawaiian Antiquities and Folklore, Abraham Fornander (1919)
Conde Lucanor, Don Juan Manuel (fourth century)
Confessio Amantis, John Gower (1390)
Conjugalia Praecepta, Plutarch (second century)
Consolation Philtres for the Man of Authority, Ibn Zafar (1154)
Coriolanus, William Shakespeare (ca. 1605)
Coyote &, Joe Hayes (1982)
The Crafty Courtier: or the Fable of Reynard the Fox , anonymous English (1706)
Cric Crac, Grace Hallworth (1990)
Cynicus, Lucian (ca. 170)

D
Daddy Jake the Runaway and Short Stories Told after Dark, Joel Chandler Harris (1889)
Das Buch der Beyspiele, anonymous German (1483)
The Day It Snowed Tortillas, Joe Hayes (1982)
The Decameron, Giovanni Boccaccio (1353)
De Capienda ex Inimicis Utilitate, Plutarch (second century)
De l'Angélus de l'aube à l'Angélus du soir, Francis Jammes (1898)
De Nugis Curialium, Walter Map (thirteenth century)
De Warachtighe Fabulen der Dieren, Marcus Geeraerts (1567)
Der Edelstein, Ulrich Boner (1330)
Der Knaben Wunderhorn, Clemens Brentano and Achim von Arnim (1806–1808)
"Der Zauberlehrling," Johann Goethe (1792)
"The Devil and Tom Walker," Washington Irving (1824)
A Dictionary of British Folk-Tales, Katherine Briggs (1971)
Die Hystorie van Reynaert die Vos, Gheraert Leeu (1479)
Directorium humanae vitae, John of Capua (thirteenth century)
Divine Songs, Isaac Watts (1720)
The Dog People: Native Dog Stories, Joseph Bruchac (1995)

E
An Easy Introduction to the Knowledge of Nature, Sarah Kirby Trimmer (1780)
Ecbasis Captivi, (ca. 940)
Eight Tales for Eight Nights: Stories for Chanukah, Peninnah Schram and Steven M. Rosman, (1990)
Ein kurtzweilig Lesen von Dyl Vlenspiegel, anonymous German (1515)
El asno erudito, Juan Pablo Forner (1782)
El Libro de los exenplos por a. b. c., Clemente Sénchez (fifteenth century)
El libro de los gatos, anonymous Spanish (thirteenth century)
El Libro do buen amor, Juan Ruiz (fourth century)
"The Enchanted Raisin," Jacqueline Balcells (1986)
"Ephemera: An Emblem of Human Life," Benjamin Franklin (1778)
Epigrammata, Callimachus (ca. 270 C.E.)
Esopus, Burkhard Waldis (1548)
Eventyr, Hans Christian Andersen (1837)

Eventyr, fortalte for børn, Hans Christian Andersen (1835)
Everyone Knows Gato Pinto: More Tales from Spanish New Mexico , Joe Hayes (1992)

F
Fabeln, Erasmus Alberus (1534)
Fabeln: Drei Bücher, Gotthold Lessing (1759)
Fabeln und Erzählungen, Christian Gellert (1748)
Fabeln und Erzählungen in Reimen, Gotthold Lessing (1747)
"A Fable," Mark Twain (1909)
The Fable of the Bees or Private Vices, Publick Benefits, Bernard de Mandeville (1714)
The Fable of the Bees, Part II, Bernard de Manville (1729)
"The Fable of the Fox," anonymous Babylonian (1700–1600 B.C.E.)
Fables, Aesop (ca. 530 B.C.E.)
Fables, Andreas Fay (1820)
Fables, Jean de Florian (1792)
Fables, Marie de France (ca. 1189)
Fables, Robert Louis Stevenson (1896)
Fables, Moral and Political, anonymous English (1703)
Fables Ancient and Modern, John Dryden (1700)
Fables Ancient and Modern, William Godwin (1805)
Fables by Mrs. Teachwell, Lady Eleanor Fenn (1783)
Fables choisies, Jean de La Fontaine (1668)
Fables choisies, Jean de La Fontaine (1755–1759)
Fables choisies, Vol. II, Jean de La Fontaine (1678)
Fables de La Fontaine, Gustave Doré (1868)
Fables de La Fontaine, J. J. Grandville (1838)
Fables d'Esope phrygien, Jean Baudoin (1631)
Fables for Grown Gentlemen, John Hall Stevens (1761)
Fables for Our Time and Famous Poems Illustrated, James Thurber (1940)
Fables in Slang, George Ade (1900)
Fables in Verse for the Improvement of the Young and the Old by Abraham Aesop Esq, Christopher Smart (1757)
Fables Moral and Sentimental, William Russell (1772)
Fables of Aesop, Joseph Jacobs (1889)
Fables of Aesop According to Sir Roger L'Estrange, Alexander Calder (1931)
Fables of Aesop and Other Eminent Mythologists: with Morals and Reflexions, Sir Roger L'Estrange (1692)
The Fables of Aesop and Others Newly Done into English , Samuel Croxall (1722)
The Fables of Aesop and Others Translated from Human Nature, Charles Bennett (1857)
Fables of Aesop Paraphras'd in Verse, John Ogilby (1665)
The Fables of Flora, John Langhorne (1771)
Fables of Man, Mark Twain (1972)
Fabliaux ou contes du XIIe et du XIIIe siècles, Pierre d'Aussy (1779)
Fabulae, Odo of Cheriton (ca. 1220)
Fabulae Centum, anonymous Italian (1565)
Fábulas literarias, Tomás de Iriarte (1782)
Fábulas morales, Félix Samaniego (1781)
The Fairy Godmothers and Other Tales, Margaret Scott Gatty (1852)
The Fairy Tale of My Life, Hans Christian Andersen (1840)
Fairy Tales and Stories, Hans Christian Andersen (1872)

Family Magazine, Sarah Kirby Trimmer (1788–1789)
Fantastic Fables, Ambrose Bierce (1899)
The Farmer's Three Sons, Dayton Edmonds (1997)
Favole e Novelle, Lorenzo Pignotti (1782)
Fiabe, novelle e racconti popolari Siciliani, Giuseppe Pitré (1875)
Fifty-One Fables in Verse, John Gay (1727)
The First Christmas Tree, Henry Van Dyke (1897)
Folklore in the Old Testament, James Frazer (1918)
"Folklore of Southern Negroes," William Owens (1877)
"The Fox Avenging His Wrongs on the Eagle," Archilochus (ca. 650 B.C.E.).
Free Joe and Other Georgian Sketches, Joel Chandler Harris (1887)
Friends in a New Dress, Richard Scrafton Sharpe (1807)
The Frog Who Wanted To Be a Singer, Linda McNear Goss (1989)
Further Fables for Our Time, James Thurber (1956)

G

Gargantua and Pantagruel, François Rabelais (1562)
Gay-Neck: The Story of a Pigeon, Dan Gopal Mukerji (1927)
Georgia Place-Names, Kenneth K. Krakow (1975)
Gesta Romanorum, anonymous (1324)
The Gift of Fire, Dayton Edmonds (1997)
The Gift of Music, Dayton Edmonds (1995)
The Gift of Rabbit, Dayton Edmonds (1996)
"The Gift of the Magi," O. Henry (1905)
The Girl Who Married the Moon, Joseph Bruchac and Gayle Ross (1994)
The Golden Bough: The Roots of Religion and Folklore, James Frazer (1911–1915)
The Great Fables of All Nations, Manuel Komroff (1935)
The Green Pastures, Marc Connelly (1929)

H

The Happy Prince and Other Tales, Oscar Wilde (1888)
Hawaiian Folk Tales: A Collection of Native Legends, Thomas G. Thrum (1907)
Hazar Afsanah, anonymous Persian (ninth century)
Hazar Dastan, Totaram Sháyán (ninth century)
Her Stories: African American Folktales, Fairy Tales, and True Tales, Virginia Hamilton (1995)
Here beginneth a merye Jest of a man that was called Howleglas, anonymous English (ca. 1560)
Hermeneumata, Pseudo-Dositheus (207 C.E.)
Hermotimus, Lucian (ca. 175)
The Hind and the Panther, John Dryden (1687)
Histoire d' Alá al-Din ou La Lampe Merveilleuse, Texte Arabe, Hermann Zotenberg (1888)
Historia Animalium, Aelian (third century)
Historia Animalium, Aristotle (fourth century B.C.E.)
Historia Septem Sapientum, Johannes of Alta Silva (twelfth century)
The Histories, Herodotus (ca. 425 B.C.E.)
The Historye of Reynart the Foxe, William Caxton (1481)
The History of Rasselas, Prince of Abyssinia, Samuel Johnson (1759)
Hitopadesha, anonymous (twelfth century)
The Horse, Goose, and Sheep, John Lydgate (ca. 1398)
Hot Springs and Hell and Other Folk Jests and Anecdotes from the Ozarks, Vance Randolph (1965)

The House of Pomegranates, Oscar Wilde (1891)
How Gertrude Educates Her Children, Johann Heinrich Pestalozzi (1801)
How Rabbit Tricked Otter and Other Cherokee Trickster Stories, Gayle Ross (1994)
How Turtle's Back Was Cracked: A Traditional Cherokee Tale, Gayle Ross (1995)
Hümayun-name, anonymous Turkish (seventh century)

I

I Kings 3:16–28 (960 B.C.E.)
II Kings 14:9 (790 B.C.E.)
II Samuel 12:1–6 (sixth century B.C.E.)
I Know Why the Caged Bird Sings, Maya Angelou (1970)
I Love Myself: When I Am Laughing . . . and Then Again When I Am Looking Mean and Impressive: A Zora Neale Hurston Reader (1979)
Il Pentamerone, Giambattista Basile (1637)
Il Tempo d'allora, figure, storie e proverbi, Eugenio Cirese (1939)
Irische Elfenmärchen, Jacob and Wilhelm Grimm (1826)
Isopes Fabules, John Lydgate (ca. 1398)
Isopet, Galterus Anglicus (1175)
Isopet I , Galterus Anglicus (ca. 1180)
Isopet II, anonymous French (thirteenth century)

J

Jatakamala, Aryasura (200 C.E.)
The Jewish Stories One Generation Tells Another, Peninnah Schram (1987)
Johnny Town-Mouse, Beatrix Potter (1918)
Jonathan Draws the Long Bow, Richard M. Dorson (1946)
Jonathan Livingston Seagull, Richard Bach (1970)
Journal of American Folklore, Elsie Clews Parsons (1921)
Judges 9:8–15 (925 B.C.E.)
Jungle Beasts and Men, Dan Gopal Mukerji (1923)
The Jungle Book, Rudyard Kipling (1894)
The Jungle Book, Dan Yashinsky (1995)
Just-So Stories for Little Children, Rudyard Kipling (1902)

K

Ka Hae Hawai'i, G. W. Kahiolo (1861)
Kalilah wa Dimnah, Ibn al-Muquaffa (750)
Kalilah wa Dimnah, Rudaki (tenth century)
Keepers of the Animals, Joseph Bruchac and Michael Caduto (1990)
Kinder und Hausmärchen, Jacob and Wilhelm Grimm (1812, 1815, 1822)
Konjaku Monogatari, Minamoto Takakuni (1075)
Kuh Buch, Abraham ben Mattathias (1555)

L

La casa de los espíritus, Isabel Allende (1982)
La Chant des morts, Elie Wiesel (1966)
La Couronnement de Renart, anonymous Flemish (1270)
The Ladder to Learning, Sarah Kirby Trimmer (1789)
La Légende de les aventures héroiques, joyeues, et glorieuses d'Ulenspiegel et de Lamme Goedzak au pays de Flandres et ailleurs, Charles de Coster (1866)

La Livre des Lumières, David Sahid (1644)

La Malade imaginaire, Molière (1673)

La Mélange tirés d'une grande bibliothèque, Marc d'Argenson (1788)

La Moral Philosophia, Antonio Francesco Doni (1552)

La vida del Ysopet con sus fabulas hystoriades, Johan Hurus (1489)

La Ville de la chance, Elie Wiesel (1962)

The Legend of Shore's Wife, Thomas Churchyard (1563)

Le Petit Prince, Antoine de Saint-Exupéry (1943)

Le Piacevoli Notti, Giovanni Straparola (1553)

Les Contes et fables indiennes de Bidpai et de Lokmam, Antoine Galland (1724)

Les Fables de La Fontaine, Georges Gouget (1833–1834)

Les Mille et une nuits, Antoine Galland (1717)

Les Mille et une nuits, contes arabes traduits en français, Antoine Galland (1708)

Les Portes de la forêt, Elie Wiesel (1964)

Liber Facetiarum, Bracciolini Poggio (fifteenth century)

Lieder der alten Edda, Jacob and Wilhelm Grimm (1815)

The Life of Aratus, Plutarch (second century)

The Life of Themistocles, Plutarch (second century)

M

Masnavi-ye Ma'navi, Jalal ad-Din ar Rumi (ca. 1270)

Max und Moritz, Wilhelm Busch (1865)

Memoirs of Socrates, Xenophon (fourth century B.C.E.)

Meshal ha-Kadmoni, Isaac Sahula (thirteenth century)

Meteorologica, Aristotle, (fourth century B.C.E.)

Mingo and Other Sketches in Black and White, Joel Chandler Harris (1884)

The Miracles of St. Martin, Gregory of Tours (sixth century)

Mishlei Shu'alim, Berechiah ha-Nakdan (thirteenth century)

The Moral Alphabet, Hilaire Belloc (1899)

The Morall Fabillis of Esope the Phrygian, compylit in eloquent & ornate Scottis meter, Robert Henryson (1570)

The Morall Philosophie of Doni, Thomas North (1570)

More Hawaiian Folk Tales, Thomas G. Thrum (1923)

The Most Delectable History of Reynard the Fox, anonymous Dutch (1676)

The Most Delectable History of Reynard the Fox, Newly Corrected & Purged from all Grossness in Phrase & Matter, John Shirley (1654)

Mother Hubberds Tale, Edmund Spenser (1591)

Mouth Open Story Jump Out, Grace Hallworth (1984)

Mule Bone: A Comedy of Negro Life, Zora Neale Hurston (1990)

Mules and Men, Zora Neale Hurston (1935)

Myrmidones, Aeschylus (ca. 460 B.C.E.)

Mythologia Aesopica, Isaac Nicholas Nevelet (1610)

Myths of the Cherokee, James Mooney (1900)

N

Nanaue the Shark Man and Other Hawaiian Shark Stories, Emma M. Nakuina et al. (1994)

Native American Animal Stories, Joseph Bruchac (1993)

Native American Stories, Joseph Bruchac (1991)

Native Wisdom, Joseph Bruchac (1995)

Neveryona, Samuel R. Delaney (1986)

A New Work of Animals Principally Designed from the Fables of Aesop, Gay and Phaedras,
   Samuel Howitt (1811)
The Night with the Hants and Other Alabama Folk Experiences, Ray B. Browne (1976)
Nights with Uncle Remus: Myths and Legends of the Old Plantation, Joel Chandler
   Harris (1883)
9 Aesop's Fables, Antonio Frasconi (1953)
99 Fables by William March (1960)
"Nisaba and Wheat," anonymous Babylonian (2000 B.C.E.)
No Way, Jose!/De Ninguna Manera, José!, Joe Hayes (1986)
Noch fünfzig Fabeln für Kinder, Wilhelm Hey (1837)
Noctes Atticae, Aulus Gellius (ca. 180 C.E.)
Norfolk Tales, Bobby Norfolk (1988)
Novus Aesopus, Alexander Neckham (ca. 1215)
Novus Aesopus, Baldo (twelfth century)
Novus Avianus, Alexander Neckham (ca. 1215)
Novus Avianus, anonymous (ca. 1100)

O

The Oeconomy of Charity, Sarah Kirby Trimmer (1787)
Oeuvres Complètes de La Fontaine, Jean de la Fontaine (1821)
Of the Vox and of the Wolf, anonymous English (ca. 1250)
Of Vainglory, Francis Bacon (1625)
Old Possum's Book of Practical Cats, T. S. Eliot (1939)
One Hundred Years of Solitude, Gabriel García Marquez (1970)
The Owl and the Nightingale, anonymous English (ca. 1190)
"The Ox and the Horse," anonymous Babylonian (ca. 1500 C.E.)

P

Panchatantra, Bidpai (fifth century B.C.E.)
Panchatantra, Johannes Hertel (1914)
Panchatantra, Rabbi Joel (twelfth century)
Para casos tales suele tenor los maestros oficiales, Tomás de Iriarte (1783)
The Parables from Nature, Margaret Scott Gatty (1855)
The Parliament of Fowls, Geoffrey Chaucer (ca. 1377)
Penguin Island, Anatole France (1908)
The People Could Fly: American Black Folktales, Virginia Hamilton (1985)
Phaedo, Plato (fourth century C.E.)
Phaedrus, Martin Dorp (1513)
Phaedrus, Plato (fourth century C.E.)
A Poetical Translation of the Fables of Phaedrus, Christopher Smart (1760)
The Poetical Works of Alice and Phoebe Cary (1884)
Popular Italian Tales, Domenico Comparetti (1875)
Popular Proverbs, Diogenes Laertius (third century)
Praecepta, Plutarch (second century)
Progymnasmata, Nikephoros Basilakis (ca. 1175)
Progymnasmata, Theon (second century)

Q

Questiones Convivales, Plutarch (second century)

R

Rainardo e Lesengrino, anonymous French-Italian (ca. 1200)
"The Ransom of Red Chief," O. Henry (1910)
Reinaert de Vos, Willem (ca. 1250)
Reinaerts Histoire, anonymous Flemish (ca. 1370)
Reinecke Fuchs, Johann Friedrich von Goethe (1794)
Reinhart Fuchs, Heinrich der Glîchezaere (ca. 1180)
Reinhart Fuchs, Jacob and Wilhelm Grimm (1834)
Reinke de Vos, anonymous Dutch (1498)
Remarks on Mandeville's Fables of the Bees, William Law (1723)
Renard le Bestourné, Rutebeuf of Champaign (1261)
Renart le Contrefait, anonymous French (ca. 1340)
Renart le Nouvel, Jacquemart Gielée (1288)
Reynard the Fox, a Poem in Twelve Cantos, E. W. Holloway (1852)
Reynard the Fox, a renowned Apologue of the Middle Age, reproduced in Rhyme, Samuel Naylor (1844)
Rhetorica, Aristotle, (fourth century B.C.E.)
Rienaerts Histoire, anonymous Dutch (1498)
Roman de Renart, anonymous French (ca. 1250)
Romulus Niveleti, Isaac Nicholas Nèvelet (1610)

S

The Sanctified Church: The Folklore Writings of Zora Neale Hurston (1981)
Schimpf und Ernst, Johannes Pauli (1522)
The Second Jungle Book, Rudyard Kipling (1895)
Sefer Meshalim, Rabbi Moses Wallich (1697)
Select Fables of Aesop and Others, Thomas Bewick (1784)
Select Fables of Esop and Other Fabulists, Robert Dodsley (1764)
Sermones Vulgares, Jacques de Vitry (ca. 1230)
Sessanta novelle popolari Montanesi, Gherardo Nerucci (1880)
Seven Tales of Uncle Remus, Joel Chandler Harris (1948)
Shuckin' and Jivin': Folklore from Contemporary Black Americans, Daryl Cumber Dance (1978)
Silent Spring, Rachel Carson (1962)
"The Snake and the Eagle," anonymous Babylonian(1500–1200 B.C.E.)
Soft Child: How Rattlesnake Got Its Fangs, Joe Hayes (1993)
Some Fables after the Easie and Familiar Method of Monsieur de la Fontaine, Bernard de Manville (1703)
"The Sorcerer's Apprentice," Lucian (ca. 170)
The Souls of Black Folks, W. E. B. Du Bois (1903)
Sources and Analogues of the Uncle Remus Tales, Florence Baer (1981)
The Southern Mountaineer, Caleb A. Ridley (ca. 1900)
Spectator essay, Joseph Addison (1711)
Speculum Majus, Vincent de Beauvais (thirteenth century)
Speculum Stultorum, Nigel of Longchamps (twelfth century)
Spunk: The Selected Short Stories of Zora Neale Hurston (1985)
Stephanites kai Ichnelates, anonymous Greek (eleventh century)
The Story of the Other Wise Man, Henry Van Dyke (1896)
The Strange Case of Dr. Jekyll and Mr. Hyde, Robert Louis Stevenson (1886)

Sumerian Mythology, Samuel Noah Kramer (1944)
Symposium, Plato (fourth century B.C.E.)

T
The Tale of Peter Rabbit, Beatrix Potter (1893)
The Tale of Samuel Whiskers, Beatrix Potter (1908)
The Tale of Squirrel Nutkin, Beatrix Potter (1903)
Tales for an Unknown City, Dan Yashinsky (1990)
The Tales from the Kathasaritsagara, Somadeva (1070)
Tales from Watership Down, Richard Adams (1997)
"Tales of Aesop from Jamal Koram," Mary Carter Smith (1993)
Tall Betsy and Dunce Baby: South Georgia Folktales, Marielle Glenn Hartsfield (1987)
"The Tamarisk and the Palm," anonymous Babylonian (2300–2200 B.C.E.)
The Tar-Baby and Other Rhymes of Uncle Remus, Joel Chandler Harris (1904)
Tell My Horse, Zora Neale Hurston (1938)
Through the Looking Glass and What Alice Found There, Lewis Carroll (1871)
Till Eulenspiegel, Gerhart Hauptmann (1928)
Told by Uncle Remus, Joel Chandler Harris (1903)
A Treasury of American Folklore, B. A. Botkin (1944)
Treemonisha, Scott Joplin (1915)
Tuti Nameh, anonymous Persian (ca. 1300)
Twelve Fables of Aesop, Antonio Frasconi (1954)

U
The Unbroken Web: Stories and Fables, Richard Adams (1980)
Uncle Remus: His Songs and His Sayings, Joel Chandler Harris (1880)
Uncle Remus and Brer Rabbit, Joel Chandler Harris (1906)
Uncle Remus and His Friends, Joel Chandler Harris (1892)
Uncle Remus and the Little Boy, Joel Chandler Harris (1910)
Uncle Remus con Chile, Américo Paredes (1992)
Uncle Remus Returns, Joel Chandler Harris (1918)

V
Van den Vos Reinaerde, anonymous Flemish-Dutch (ca. 1250)
Vendredi, Michael Tournier (1967)
Vita Aesopi, Plutarch (ca. 100 C.E.)
Vitae Decem Oratorium, Plutarch (second century)
Vitae Philosophorum, Diogenes Laertius (third century)
Volpone, the Fox, Ben Jonson (1606)

W
The Wasps, Aristophanes (422 B.C.E.)
Watership Down, Richard Adams (1972)
Who Blowed Up the Church House and Other Ozark Folk Tales, Vance Randolph (1952)
Why Alligator Hates Dog, J. J. Reneaux (1995)
Why Mosquitoes Buzz in People's Ears, Bobby Norfolk (1987)
The Wind in the Willows, Kenneth Grahame (1908)
The Witch Wolf: An Uncle Remus Story, Joel Chandler Harris (1921)
A Woman as Great as the World and Other Fables, Jacquetta Hawkes (1953)

"The Wonderful Tar-Baby Story," Joel Chandler Harris (1880)
A Word on the Brazos: Negro Preacher Tales from the Brazos Bottoms of Texas, J. Mason
    Brewer (1953)
Works and Days, Hesiod (eighth century B.C.E.)

Y
Ysengrimus, anonymous Belgian (1148)
Ysengrimus, Nivard of Ghent (1148)

Z
Zalmen; ou, La Folie de Dieu, Elie Wiesel (1968)

PRIMARY SOURCES

Adams, Richard. *Tales from Watership Down*. New York: Alfred A. Knopf, 1997.

———. *The Unbroken Web: Stories and Fables*. New York: Crown Publishers, 1980.

———. *Watership Down*. New York: Avon Books, 1972.

Adventures in World Literature. New York: Harcourt, Brace and World, 1970.

Aeschylus. Herbert Weir Smyth, trans. Cambridge, Mass.: Harvard University Press, 1936.

Aesop: Five Centuries of Illustrated Fables. John J. McKendry, ed. New York: Metropolitan Museum of Art, 1964.

Aesop's Fables. George Fyler Townsend, trans. New York: Doubleday, 1968.

Aesop's Fables. John E. Keller and L. Clark Keating, trans. Lexington: University Press of Kentucky, 1993.

Aesop's Fables. V. S. Vernon Jones, trans. New York: Ravenel Books, n. d.

Allende, Isabel. *The House of the Spirits*. New York: Bantam Books, 1982.

Ancient O'ahu: Stories from Fornander & Thrum. Honolulu, Hawaii: Kalamaku Press, 1996.

Angelou, Maya. *I Know Why the Caged Bird Sings*. New York: Bantam Books, 1970.

Aristophanes. Vols. 1 and 2. Benjamin Bickley Rogers, trans. London: William Heinemann, 1930.

Aristotle. *Meteorologica*. W. E. Webster, trans. Oxford: Clarendon Press, 1931.

———. *Politica*. Benjamin Jowett, trans. Oxford: Clarendon Press, 1921.

———. *Rhetorica*. W. Rhys Roberts, trans. Oxford: Clarendon Press, 1946.

Arneach, Lloyd. *Animal's Ball Game*. San Francisco, Calif.: Children's Press, 1992.

Arnott, Kathleen. *African Myths and Legends*. New York: Henry Z. Walck, 1963.

Aulus Gellius. *The Attic Nights*. Vols. 1–3. Cambridge, Mass.: Harvard University Press, 1946.

Babbitt, Ellen C. *Jataka Tales: Animal Stories*. New York: Appleton-Century-Crofts, 1940.

Bach, Richard. *Jonathan Livingston Seagull: A Story*. New York: Avon Books, 1970.

Balcells, Jacqueline, "The Enchanted Raisin," in *Literature and the Language Arts*. St. Paul, Minn.: EMC/Paradigm Publishing, 1996.

Bancroft, Bronwyn. *Dirrangun*. Sydney, Australia: Angus & Robertson, 1994.

———. *Minah.* Sydney, Australia: Angus & Robertson, 1995.

———. *The Whalers.* Sydney, Australia: Angus & Robertson, 1996.

Basile, Giambattista. *The Pentameron.* London: Spring Books, n. d.

Belloc, Hilaire. *The Bad Child's Book of Beasts*. New York: Alfred A. Knopf, 1965.

———. *Cautionary Verses.* New York: Alfred A. Knopf, 1959.

———. *More Beasts for Worse Children.* New York: Alfred A. Knopf, 1966.

Bennett, J. A. W., and G. V. Smithers. *Early Middle English Verse and Prose*. Oxford: Clarendon Press, 1968.

Bierce, Ambrose. *Civil War Songs*. New York: Dover, 1994.

———. *The Complete Short Stories of Ambrose Bierce*. Lincoln: University of Nebraska Press, 1984.

———. *The Devil's Dictionary.* New York: Laurel, 1991.

———. *Ghost and Horror Stories of Ambrose Bierce*. New York: 1964.

———. *The Sardonic Humor of Ambrose Bierce*. New York: Dover, 1963.

———. *The Stories and Fables of Ambrose Bierce*. Owings Mills, Md.: Stemmer House, 1977.

Bierhorst, John, ed. *The White Deer and Other Stories Told by the Lenape*. New York: William Morrow, 1995.

Bodart, Anne. *The Blue Dog and Other Fables for the French*. Boston, Mass.: Houghton Mifflin, 1956.

Botkin, B. A., ed. *A Treasury of American Folklore: Stories, Ballads, and Traditions of the People*. New York: Crown, 1944.

Bruchac, Joseph. *The Boy Who Lived with the Bears and Other Iroquois Stories*. New York: HarperCollins, 1995.

———. *Children of the Longhouse.* New York: Dial, 1996.

———. *Dog People: Native Dog Stories.* New York: Fulcrum, 1995.

———. *The Girl Who Married the Moon* (coauthor Gayle Ross). Greenville, S.C.: Bridgewater, 1994.

———. *Native American Animal Stories.* New York: Fulcrum, 1993.

———. *Native Wisdom.* San Francisco, Calif.: Harper, 1995.

Bruchac, Joseph, and Michael Caduto. *Keepers of the Animals*. New York: Fulcrum, 1990.

———. *Native American Stories*. New York: Fulcrum, 1991.

Cabral, Len. *Anansi's Narrow Waist* (easy reader in English and Spanish). Addison-Wesley 1994.

———. *Len Cabral's Storytelling Book*, Neal-Schuman 1997.

Callimachus. *Hymns and Epigrams*. A. W. Mair, trans. Cambridge, Mass.: Harvard University Press, 1955.

Calvino, Italo. *Italian Folktales*. New York: Pantheon Books, 1980.

Carmina Burana: Die Gedichte des Codex Buranus Lateinisch und Deutsch. Zurich: Artemis Verlag, 1974.

"The Carol of the Birds." Kurt Schindler and Deems Taylor, trans., Philadelphia: G. Schirmer, 1953.

Carson, Rachel, "A Fable for Tomorrow," in *Reading Literature*. Evanston, Ill.: McDougal, Littell, 1986.

Cary, Alice, and Phoebe Cary. *The Poetical Works of Alice and Phoebe Cary*. Boston, Mass.: Houghton, Mifflin, 1884.

Chaucer, Geoffrey. *The Canterbury Tales*. Boston, Mass.: Houghton Mifflin, 1961.

———. *The Canterbury Tales*. London: Cresset Press, 1992.

———. *Chaucer's Canterbury Tales: The Prologue*. Lincoln, Neb.: Cliffs Notes, 1966.

———. *Chaucer's Canterbury Tales: The Wife of Bath*. Lincoln, Neb.: Cliffs Notes, 1966.

———. *Selected Canterbury Tales*. New York: Holt, Rinehart & Winston, 1969.

Chekhov, Anton, "A Slander," in *Adventures in Appreciation*. New York: Harcourt Brace Jovanovich, 1958.

Connelly, Marc. *The Green Pastures, A Fable*. New York: Farrar & Rinehart, 1929.

Cooper, Frederic Taber, ed. *An Argosy of Fables: A Representative Selection from the Fable Literature of Every Age and Land*. New York: Frederick A. Stokes, 1921.

Cowen, Jill Sanchia. *Kalila wa Dimna: An Animal Allegory of the Mongol Court*. New York: Oxford University Press, 1989.

Crafts, George, "Coyote Drives Away the Winter," *Storytelling*, November 1996, 38–39.

Crane, Ronald S., ed. *A Collection of English Poems, 1660–1800*. New York: Harper & Row, 1932.

Creeden, Sharon. *Fair Is Fair: World Folktales of Justice*. Little Rock, Ark.: August House, 1994.

Dargin, Peter. *Aboriginal Fisheries of the Darling-Barwon Rivers*, 3rd ed. Dubbo, New South Wales: DAP, 1991.

———. *Swagman's Stone Soup*. Dubbo, New South Wales: DAP, 1997.

De Spain, Pleasant. *The Dancing Turtle*. Little Rock, Ark.: August House, 1998.

———. *Eleven Nature Tales: A Multicultural Journey*. Little Rock, Ark.: August House, 1996.

———. *Eleven Turtle Tales: Adventure Tales from around the World*, Little Rock, Ark.: August House, 1994.

Dickens, Charles. *A Christmas Carol*. New York: Airmont, 1963.

———. *A Christmas Carol* in *The Annotated Dickens*. New York: Clarkson N. Potter, 1986.

Dinesen, Isak. *Babette's Feast and Other Anecdotes of Destiny.* New York: Vintage Books, 1953.

Dorson, Richard M. *American Folklore.* Chicago, Ill.: University of Chicago Press, 1959.

———. *American Negro Folktales.* Greenwich, Conn.: Fawcett, 1967.

Duff, J. Wight, and Arnold M. Duff, trans. *Minor Latin Poets.* Vol. 2. Cambridge, Mass.: Harvard University Press, 1982.

Edmonds, Dayton. *The Farmer's Three Sons.* Devo'Zine 1997.

———. *The Gift of Fire.* United Methodist Church Board of Higher Education and Ministry, 1997.

———. *The Gift of Music.* United Methodist Church Board of Higher Education and Ministry, 1995.

———. *The Gift of Rabbit.* United Methodist Church Board of Higher Education and Ministry, 1996.

Emerson, Nathaniel B. *Unwritten Literature of Hawaii: The Sacred Songs of the Hula.* Honolulu, Hawaii: Pohaku Press, 1997.

Evans-Wentz, W. Y. *The Fairy-Faith in Celtic Countries.* New York: Carol Publishing, 1994.

Faison, Edward, Jr. *African-American Folk Tales.* New York: Vantage Press, 1989.

Forest, Heather. *Songspinner: Folktales and Fables Sung and Told* (audiocassette). New York: Weston Woods, 1982.

———. *Tales around the Hearth* (audiocassette). New York: Gentle Wind, 1989.

Gatty, Mrs. Alfred. *Parables from Nature.* Vols. 1–4. London: Bell and Daldy, 1869.

Ghose, Sudhin, N. *Folk Tales and Fairy Stories from India.* Mineola, N.Y.: Dover Publications, 1996.

Gillman, Jackson. *Just So Stories* (videocassette). Mt. Desert, Maine: Chip Taylor Communications, 1996.

Goethe, Johann Friedrich von. *Poems and Ballads of Goethe.* New York: Holt and Williams, 1871.

———. *The Story of Reynard the Fox.* New York: Heritage Press, 1954.

"Goliardic Verse," in *The Medieval Reader.* New York: HarperCollins, 1994.

Goss, Clay, and Linda Goss. *Jump Up and Say; Anthology of African-American Storytelling.* New York: Simon & Schuster, 1995.

Goss, Linda. *The Frog Who Wanted To Be a Singer.* New York: Orchard Books, 1996.

Green, Margaret, ed. *The Big Book of Animal Fables*. New York: Franklin Watts, 1965.

Grimm, the Brothers. *The Complete Grimms' Fairy Tales*. New York: Random House, 1972.

———. *Grimms' Fairy Tales*. New York: Grosset & Dunlap, n. d.

Hale, Thomas A., ed. and trans. *The Epic of Askia Mohammed*. Bloomington: Indiana University Press, 1996.

Hallworth, Grace. *Anansi at the Pool*. London: Longman, 1994.

———. *Cric Crac*. Portsmouth, N.H.: Heinemann, 1990.

———. *Mouth Open Story Jump Out*. London: Methuen, 1984.

Hamilton, Virginia. *Her Stories: African American Folktales, Fairy Tales, and True Tales*. New York: Blue Sky Press, 1995.

———. *The People Could Fly*. New York: Alfred P. Knopf, 1985.

Haney, Marie. *Over Nine Waves: A Book of Irish Legends*. London: Faber & Faber, 1995.

Harrington, Karl Pomeroy, ed. *Mediaeval Latin*. Boston, Mass.: Allyn & Bacon, 1925.

Harris, Joel Chandler. *The Complete Tales of Uncle Remus*. Boston, Mass.: Houghton Mifflin, 1955.

———. *Uncle Remus: His Songs and His Sayings*, intro. by Robert Hemenway. New York: Penguin Books, 1982.

———. Uncle Remus Stories in *The Literature of the South*. Chicago, Ill.: Scott, Foresman, 1952.

Hawkes, Jacquetta. *A Woman as Great as the World and Other Fables*. New York: Random House, 1953.

Hayes, Joe. *Soft Child: How Rattlesnake Got Its Fangs*. Tucson, Ariz.: Harbinger House, 1993.

Henry, O. "The Gift of the Magi" in *Reading Literature*. Evanston, Ill.: McDougal, Littell, 1986.

Herodotus. *The Histories*. Aubrey de Sélincourt, trans. London: Penguin, 1961.

Hesiod, trans. Richmond Lattimore. Ann Arbor: University of Michigan Press, 1973.

Hesiod and Theognis, trans. Dorothea Wender. London: Penguin Books, 1973.

Holy Bible. King James Version. Iowa Falls, Iowa: World Bible Publishers, 1986.

Homer. *The Odyssey*. E. V. Rieu, trans. London: Penguin Books, 1946.

Horace. *The Odes, Epodes, and Carmen Saeculare*. New York: American Book, 1902.

———. *The Satires*. New York: American Book, 1909.

———. *The Satires and Epistles*. Boston, Mass.: Ginn, 1888.

———. *Satires and Epistles*. Chicago, Ill.: Phoenix Books, 1959.

———. *Selections from Horace*. Philadelphia, Pa.: Eldredge & Brother, 1899.

———. *The Works of Horace*. New York: Harper & Brothers, 1891.

———. *The Works of Horace*. New York: Hinds, Noble & Eldredge, 1892.

Hurston, Zora Neale. *The Complete Stories*. New York: HarperCollins, 1995.

———. *Dust Tracks on a Road*. New York: Harper Perennial, 1991.

———. *Mule Bone: A Comedy of Negro Life*. New York: Harper Perennial, 1991.

———. *Mules and Men*. New York: Harper Perennial, 1990.

———. *The Sanctified Church*. Berkeley, Calif.: Turtle Island Foundation, 1981.

———. *Their Eyes Were Watching God*. New York: Harper & Row, 1990.

———. *Zora Neale Hurston: Folklore, Memoirs, and Other Writings*. New York: Library of America, 1995.

Ingpen, Robert, and Barbara Hayes. *Folk Tales and Fables of the Americas and the Pacific*. New York: Chelsea House, 1994.

———. *Folk Tales and Fables of Asia and Australia*. New York: Chelsea House, 1994.

Johnson, Samuel, "The Fable of the Vultures," *Ideas and Patterns*. New York: Harcourt, Brace & World, 1970.

Jones, Charles C. *Negro Myths from the Georgia Coast*. Detroit, Mich.: Singing Tree Press, 1969.

Jones, Matt, et al. *Native America in the Twentieth Century: An Encyclopedia*. New York: Garland Publishing, 1994.

Kame'eleihiwa, Lilikala K. *A Legendary Tradition of Kamapua'a, the Hawaiian Pig-God*. Honolulu, Hawaii.: Bishop Museum Press, 1996.

Kipling, Rudyard. *A Diversity of Creatures*. Garden City, N.Y.: Doubleday, Page, 1917.

———. *The Humorous Tales of Rudyard Kipling*. Garden City, N.Y.: Doubleday, Doran, 1931.

———. *The Jungle Book*. Garden City, N.Y.: Doubleday, Doran, 1893.

———. *Just-So Stories*. New York: Signet, 1974.

Komroff, Manuel, comp. *The Great Fables of All Nations*. New York: Tudor Publishing, 1935.

The Koran Interpreted. A. J. Arberry, trans. New York: Touchstone Books, 1955.

Krylov, Ivan. *Krylov's Fables*. New York: Harcourt Brace, 1927.

La Fontaine, Jean de, "Le Loup et l'Agneau," in *A Survey of French Literature*. New York: Harcourt Brace Jovanovich, 1965.

———. *The Fables of La Fontaine*. Marianne Moore, trans. New York: Viking Press, 1954.

———. *Selected Fables*. Oxford, England: Oxford University Press, 1995.

Lamson, Roy, and Hallett Smith. *Renaissance England*. New York: W.W. Norton, 1942.

Leach, Maria. *How the People Sang the Mountains Up: How and Why Stories*. New York: Viking Press, 1967.

Lem, Stanislaw, "The First Sally (A) OR Trurl's Electronic Bard" in *World Masterpieces*. Englewood Cliffs, N.J.: Prentice Hall, 1991.

Lester, Julius. *The Last Tales of Uncle Remus*. New York: Dial Books, 1994.

———. *More Tales of Uncle Remus*. New York: Dial Books, 1988.

Livo, Norma, and Dia Cha. *Folk Stories of the Hmong*. Englewood, Colo.: Libraries Unlimited, 1991.

Livy. *The Early History of Rome*. London: Penguin Books, 1971.

Loya, Olga. *Momentos Mágicos/Magic Moments*. Little Rock, Ark.: August House 1997.

Mandeville, Bernard de. *The Fable of the Bees*. New York: Penguin, 1989.

Mann, Jill. *Ysengrimus*. Leiden, The Netherlands: E. J. Brill, 1987.

March, William. *99 Fables by William March*. Mobile: University of Alabama Press, 1960.

"Marie de France" in *The Medieval Reader*. New York: HarperCollins, 1994.

Marie de France. *Fables*. Toronto, Ontario: University of Toronto Press, 1994.

———. *The Lais of Marie de France*. London: Penguin Books, 1986.

Mayer, Mariana. *The Sorcerer's Apprentice: A Greek Fable*. New York: Bantam Skylark, 1989.

Mbitu, Ngangar, and Ranchor Prime. *Essential African Mythology*. Glasgow: Thorson's, 1997.

McDermott, Tom, "The Caged Bird," *Storytelling*, May 1997, 28–29.

Nakuina, Emma M., et al. *Nanaue the Shark Man and Other Hawaiian Shark Stories*. Honolulu, Hawaii: Kalamaku Press, 1994.

"Numskull and the Rabbit" from the *Panchatantra* in *Literature: World Masterpieces*. Englewood Cliffs, N.J.: Prentice Hall, 1991.

"Old Man Coyote and Buffalo Power" in *Plains Indian Mythology*. New York: Meridian Books, 1975.

Orwell, George. *Animal Farm*. New York: Signet, 1946.

O'Sullivan, Sean, ed. *Folktales of Ireland*. London: Routledge & Kegan Paul, 1966.

Palmer, Martin, and Zhao Xiaomin. *Essential Chinese Mythology*. London: Thorsons, 1997.

Parlett, David. *Selections from the Carmina Burana*. London: Penguin Books, 1986.

Perry, Ben Edwin. *Aesopica*. Urbana: University of Illinois Press, 1952.

———. *Babrius and Phaedrus*. Cambridge, Mass.: Harvard University Press, 1965.

———. "Fable," in *Studium Generale*, Cambridge, Mass.: Harvard University Press 1959, 17–37.

Plato. *Alcibiades*. W. R. M. Lamb, trans. Cambridge, Mass.: Harvard University Press, 1960.

———. *Phaedo*. Harold North Fowler, trans. Cambridge, Mass.: Harvard University Press, 1947.

Potter, Beatrix. *The Complete Tales of Beatrix Potter*. London: F. Warne, 1989.

———. *Letters to Children*. New York: Harvard College Library, 1966.

Radice, Betty, ed. *The Greek Anthology*. London: Penguin, 1981.

Ranke, Kurt, ed. *Folktales of Germany*. London: Routledge and Kegan Paul, 1966.

"Renard the Fox: Bourgeois Contempt for the Nobility" in *The Medieval Reader*. New York: HarperCollins, 1994.

Reneaux, J. J. *Cajun Folktales*. Little Rock, Ark.: August House, 1992.

———. *Why Alligator Hates Dog*. Little Rock, Ark.: August House, 1995.

The Romance of Reynard the Fox. D. D. R. Owen, trans. New York: Oxford University Press, 1994.

Ross, Gayle. *How Rabbit Tricked Otter and Other Cherokee Trickster Stories*. New York: HarperCollins 1994.

———. *How Turtle's Back Was Cracked: A Traditional Cherokee Tale*. New York: Dial 1995.

Rostand, Edmond. *Chantecler*, serialized in *Hampton's Magazine*, June–September 1910.

Saint-Exupéry, Antoine de. *The Little Prince*. New York: Harcourt, Brace & World, 1943.

Sanfield, Steve, "John's Memory," *Storytelling*, May 1996, 22–23.

Sarma, Visnu. *The Pancantantra*. London: Penguin Books, 1993.

Schram, Peninnah, and Steven M. Rosman. *Eight Tales for Eight Nights: Stories for Chanukah*. New York: Jason Aronson, 1990.

———. *Jewish Stories One Generation Tells Another*. New York: Jason Aronson, 1987.

Shah, Idries. *Tales of the Dervishes*. London: Octagon Press, 1982.

Shakespeare, William. *The Riverside Shakespeare*. Boston, Mass.: Houghton Mifflin, 1974.

Shaw, G. B. *Androcles and the Lion*. Baltimore, Md.: Penguin, 1951.

Simonov, Pyotr. *Essential Russian Mythology*. London: Thorsons, 1997.

Somadeva. *Tales from the Kathasaritsagara*. London: Penguin Books, 1994.

Sophocles. *The Tragedies of Sophocles*. Richard C. Jebb, trans. Cambridge, Mass.: Harvard University Press, 1936.

Squire, Charles. *Celtic Myths and Legends*. New York: Gramercy Books, 1994.

Stevenson, Robert Louis. *Dr. Jekyll and Mr. Hyde*. New York: Bantam Books, 1981.

———. *Fables*. New York: Charles Scribner's Sons, 1905.

Swearingen, Roger G. *The Prose Writings of Robert Louis Stevenson: A Guide*. New Haven, Conn.: Shoe String Press, 1980.

Thompson, Vivian L. *Hawaiian Legends of Tricksters and Riddlers*. New York: Holiday House, 1969.

Thurber, James. *Fables for Our Time and Famous Poems Illustrated*. New York: Harper & Row, 1940.

———. *Further Fables for Our Time*. New York: Simon & Schuster, 1956.

———. "The Last Flower" in *The United States in Literature*. Glenview, Ill.: Scott Foresman, 1987, 320–329.

Tong, Diane. *Gypsy Folktales*. San Diego: Harvest Books, 1989.

Twain, Mark. *The Complete Short Stories of Mark Twain*. New York: Bantam Books, 1958.

Van Dyke, Henry. *The Story of the Other Wise Man*. New York: Harper & Brothers, 1923.

Walker, Alice, "A South without Myths," *Sojourner's Magazine*, December 1994/January 1995, n. p.

Walker, Warren S., and Ahmet E. Uysal. *Tales Alive in Turkey*. Cambridge, Mass.: Harvard University Press, 1966.

Warmington, E. H., ed. and trans. *Remains of Old Latin*. Cambridge, Mass.: Harvard University Press, 1938.

Werner, Edward T. C. *Ancient Tales and Folklore of China*. London: Senate, 1995.

Widdows, P. F., ed. and trans. *The Fables of Phaedrus*. Austin: University of Texas Press, 1992.

Wiesel, Elie. *All Rivers Run to the Sea*. New York: Alred A. Knopf, 1995.

Wilde, Oscar. *The Complete Oscar Wilde*. New York: Crescent Books, 1995.

———. *The Complete Works of Oscar Wilde*. Volume 11. Garden City, N.Y.: Doubleday, 1923.

———. *De Profundis*. New York: Philosophical Library, 1965.

———. *The Picture of Dorian Gray and Selected Stories*. New York: Signet, 1983.

Wolkstein, Diane. *The Banza: A Haitian Folk Tale*. New York: Dial, 1995.

———. *Bouki Dances the Kokioko: A Haitian Story*. New York: Harcourt, 1997.

Wolkstein, Diane, and Samuel Noah Kramer. *Inanna: Queen of Heaven and Earth, Her Stories and Hymns from Sumer*. New York: HarperCollins, 1983.

Xenophon. *Memorabilia and Oeconomicus*. E. C. Marchant, trans. Cambridge, Mass.: Harvard University Press, 1959.

Yolen, Jane, ed. *Favorite Folktales from around the World*. New York: Pantheon Books, 1986.

Yriarte, Thomas de. *Literary Fables of Yriarte*. Boston, Mass.: Ticknow and Fields, 1855.

Ysengrimus. Ernst Voigt, ed. Halle: Verlag der Buchhandlung des Waisenhauses, 1884.

Zipes, Jack. *Arabian Nights: The Marvels and Wonders of the Thousand and One Nights*. New York: Signet, 1991.

Audiovisual

Cabral, Len, *Ananzi Stories and Others* (audiocassette), Story Sound Productions, 1988.

———. *Nho Lobo and Other Stories* (audiocassette), Story Sound Productions, 1984.

Chaucer, Geoffrey. *The Wife of Bath's Tale* (audiocassette), Prince Frederick, Md.: Recorded Books, 1993.

Edmonds, Dayton, *A Storyteller's Story* (audiocassette), self-published, 1994.

Goss, Linda, *Afro-American Tales and Games* (LP). Washington, D.C.: Folkways Records, 1981.

Hallworth, Grace. *Anansi's Secret* (audiocassette), Granada TV, 1985.

Moses, Johnny. *Johnny Moses, Storyteller* (video), American Indian Voices, 1992.

Nilsson, Harry. *The Point* (video), Van Nuys, Calif.: Family Home Entertainment, 1985.

Norfolk, Bobby. *Norfolk Tales* (audiocassette), Earwig Music, 1988.

———. *Why Mosquitoes Buzz in People's Ears* (audiocassette), Earwig Music, 1987.

Patrix, Abbi. *The War of the Crows and the Owls* (audiocassette), Paris: Audivis/ Jeunesse, 1995.

Reneaux, J. J. *Wake, Snake!* (audiocassette), self-published, 1997.

Saint-Exupéry, Antoine. *The Little Prince* (video), Paramount, 1975.

Smith, Mary Carter. "Tales of Aesop from Jamal Koram," *Mary Carter Smith—Nearing Seventy-Five* (audiocassette), self-published, 1993.

Twain, Mark. "The Celebrated Jumping Frog of Calaveras County" (audiocassette and guide), Prince Frederick, Md.: Recorded Books, 1995.

Weiss, Jim. *Animal Tales* (audiocassette), Benicia, Calif.: Greathall Productions, 1990.

———. *Arabian Nights* (audiocassette), Benicia, Calif.: Greathall Productions, 1990.

———. *The Jungle Book* (audiocassette and CD), Benicia, Calif.: Greathall Productions, 1995.

Wilde, Oscar, "The Canterville Ghost" (audiocassette), New York: Recorded Books, 1995.

Internet

"Aesop's Fables," http://www.ai.mit.edu/people/torrance/literature.html.

Andersen, Hans Christian, "Fairy Tales," http://www.math.technion.ac.il/~rl/ Andersen/vt/.

"Anthology of Spanish Poetry," http://www.ipfw.indiana.edu/cm/jehle/web/ poetry.htm.

"Beatrix Potter," http://www.cyberramp.net/~startrek/.

Bierce, Ambrose. *Can Such Things Be*. http://www-cgi.cs.cmu.edu/cgi-bin/book/ makeauthorpage, June 25, 1996.

———. *The Devil's Dictionary*. http://www-cgi.cs.cmu.edu/cgi-bin/book/ makeauthorpage, June 25, 1996.

———. *Fantastic Fables*. http://www-cgi.cs.cmu.edu/cgi-bin/book/ makeauthorpage, June 25, 1996.

"Bierce Papers," http://sunsite.berkeley.edu:8008/findaids/Berkeley/bierce/1.toc, June 24, 1996.

Dryden, John, "The Hind and the Panther," http://www.library.utoronto.ca/www/ utel/rp/poems/dryden6b.htm.

Eliot, T. S., "Old Possum's Book of Practical Cats," http://www.kirtland.cc.mi.us/ honors/possums.htm.

Gullette, Alan, "Ambrose Bierce, Master of the Macabre." www.creative. net/~alang/ lit/horror/bierce.sht, June 24, 1996.

"Hans Christian Andersen's Fables," http://www.math.technion.ac.il/~rl/ Andersen/vt.

"Martial *Epigrammiton*," http://www.gmu.edu/departments/fld/CLASSICS/ mart5.html.

Moses, Johnny, "The Boy Who Wished for a Bicycle," http://www. hometownet.com/moses.html, May 23, 1997.

Wilde, Oscar, "The Happy Prince," http://sunsite.unc.edu/pub/docs/books/ gutenberg/etext97/hpaot10.txt.

———. "The House of Pomegranates," http://sunsite.unc.edu/pub/docs/books/ gutenberg/etext97/hpomg10.txt.

BIBLIOGRAPHY

Abbott, Walter M., et al. *The Bible Reader: An Interfaith Interpretation*. New York: Bruce Publishing, 1969.

Abrahams, Roger D., comp. and ed. *African Folktales*. New York: Pantheon Books, 1993.

———. *Afro-American Folktales: Stories from Black Traditions in the New World*. New York: Pantheon Books, 1985.

Abrams, M. H. *A Glossary of Literary Terms*. New York: Holt, Rinehart & Winston, 1971.

Addison, Joseph, Richard Steele, et al. *The Spectator.* Vol. 2. London: J. M. Dent & Sons, 1907.

Ade, George. *Fables in Slang*. Chicago, Ill.: Herbert S. Stone, 1900.

Afanasyev, Alexander Nikolaievitch. *Russian Folk Tales*. Boulder, Colo.: Shambhala, 1980.

Alok, Roi. *Orwell and the Politics of Despair: A Critical Study of the Writings of George Orwell*. New York: Cambridge University Press, 1989.

Asante, Molefi K., and Mark T. Mattson. *Historical and Cultural Atlas of African Americans*. New York: Macmillan, 1992.

Auden, W. H., and Louis Kronenberger, comps. *The Viking Book of Aphorisms*. New York: Dorset Press, 1966.

Baldick, Chris. *The Concise Oxford Dictionary of Literary Terms*. New York: Oxford University Press, 1990.

Banerji, Sures Chanra, and Chhanda Chakraborty. *Folklore in Ancient and Medieval India*. Calcutta, India: Punthi Pustak, 1991.

Barker, Keith, "Animal Stories," in *The International Companion Encyclopedia of Children's Literature*. London: Routledge, 1996.

Barnet, Sylvan, Morton Berman, and William Burto. *A Dictionary of Literary Terms.* Boston, Mass.: Little, Brown, 1960.

Bartlett, John. *Familiar Quotations*. Boston, Mass.: Little, Brown, 1992.

Bauer, Helen. *Rudyard Kipling: A Study of the Short Fiction*. New York: Twayne, 1994.

Baugh, Albert C., ed. *A Literary History of England*. New York: Appleton-Century-Crofts, 1948.

Beatty, Richmond Croom, et al., eds. *The Literature of the South.* Chicago, Ill.: Scott, Foresman, 1952.

Beckson, Karl, and Arthur Ganz. *Literary Terms: A Dictionary*. New York: Noonday Press, 1989.

Bemister, Margaret. *Thirty Indian Legends of Canada.* Vancouver, B.C.: Douglas & McIntyre, 1973.

Bennett, J. A. W., and G. V. Smithers. *Early Middle English Verse and Prose*, Oxford, England: Clarendon Press, 1968.

Bentley, Gerald E. *Shakespeare: A Biographical Handbook*. New Haven, Conn.: Yale University Press, 1961.

Bermel, Albert. *Farce: A History from Aristophanes to Woody Allen.* New York: Simon and Schuster, 1982.

Bernstein, Burton. *Thurber*. New York: Dodd, Mead, 1975.

Biblia Sacra: Vulgatae Editionis. Rome: Editiones Paulinae, 1957.

Bishop, Morris. *A Survey of French Literature: Volume One: The Middle Ages to 1800.* New York: Harcourt Brace, 1965.

Blackham, H. J. *Fable As Literature*. London: Athlone Press, 1985.

Blain, Virginia, et al. *The Feminist Companion to Literature in English*. New Haven, Conn.: Yale University Press, 1990.

Blair, Walter. *Tall Tale America*. New York: Coward-McCann, 1944.

Blankenship, Russell. *American Literature As an Expression of the National Mind*. New York: Henry Holt, 1931.

Bloom, Harold, intro. *Mark Twain*. New York: Chelsea House, 1986.

———. *Zora Neale Hurston*. New York: Chelsea House, 1986.

Boas, Franz. Preface. *Mules and Men*. Bloomington: Indiana University, 1990.

Boorstin, Daniel J. *The Creators: A History of Heroes of the Imagination*. New York: Vintage Books, 1992.

Booss, Claire, ed. *Scandinavian Folk & Fairy Tales*. New York: Avenel Books, 1984.

Bowder, Diana, ed. *Who's Who in the Roman World*. New York: Washington Square Press, 1980.

———. *Who's Who in the Greek World*. New York: Washington Square Press, 1982.

Boyce, Charles. *Shakespeare A to Z*. New York: Facts on File, 1990.

Bradbury, John. *Renaissance in the South.* Chapel Hill: North Carolina Press, 1963.

Bradbury, Malcolm. *The Atlas of Literature*. London: De Agostini, 1996.

Breeze, Andrew. *Medieval Welsh Literature*. Dublin: Four Courts Press, 1997.

Briggs, Katharine. *British Folktales*. New York: Pantheon Books, 1977.

———. *A Dictionary of British Folk-Tales in the English Language*. London: Routledge, 1991.

Brockett, Oscar G. *History of the Theatre*. Boston, Mass.: Allyn & Bacon, 1968.

Brookes, Stella Brewer. *Joel Chandler Harris, Folklorist*. Athens: University of Georgia Press, 1950.

Brunvand, Jan Harold. *American Folklore: An Encyclopedia*. New York: Garland, 1996.

Buck, Claire, ed. *The Bloomsbury Guide to Women's Literature*. New York: Prentice Hall, 1992.

Budd, Louis J. *Critical Essays on Mark Twain*. Boston, Mass.: G.K. Hall, 1983.

Buitehuis, Peter, and Ira B. Nadel, eds. *George Orwell: A Reassessment*. New York: St. Martin's Press, 1988.

Bulfinch, Thomas. *Bulfinch's Mythology: The Age of Fable*. Philadelphia, Pa.: Courage Books, 1990.

Burdick, Jacques. *Theater*. New York: Newsweek Books, 1974.

Burrison, John A., ed. *Storytellers: Folktales & Legends from the South*. Athens: University of Georgia Press, 1989.

Calder, Jenni. *Animal Farm and Nineteen Eighty-Four*. New York: Taylor and Francis, 1987.

———. *Robert Louis Stevenson: A Critical Celebration*. New York: Barnes & Noble Imports, 1980.

———. *Stevenson & Victorian England*. New York: Columbia University Press, 1981.

Campbell, Oscar James. *Shakespeare's Satire.* New York: Oxford University Press, 1943.

Cantor, Norman F., ed. *The Medieval Reader*. New York: HarperCollins, 1994.

Carey, Gary, and Mary Ellen Snodgrass. *A Multicultural Handbook to Literature*. Jefferson, N.C.: McFarland, 1998.

Cavendish, Marshall. *Man, Myth and Magic*. New York: Marshall Cavendish, 1970.

Christiansen, Reider Thorwald. *Folktales of Norway*. Chicago, Ill.: University of Chicago Press, 1964.

Chute, Marchette. *Geoffrey Chaucer of England*. New York: E. P. Dutton, 1946.

———. *An Introduction to Shakespeare*. New York: E. P. Dutton, 1951.

———. *Shakespeare of London*. New York: E. P. Dutton, 1949.

Cizevskij, Dmitrij. *Comparative History of Slavic Literature*. Nashville, Tenn.: Vanderbilt University Press, 1971.

Classical and Medieval Literature Criticism. Detroit, Mich.: Gale Research, 1991.

Commire, Anne, ed. *Yesterday's Authors of Books for Children*. Detroit, Mich.: Gale Research, 1978.

Connelly, Mark. *The Diminished Self: Orwell and the Loss of Freedom*. Pittsburgh, Pa.: Duquesne, 1986.

Contemporary Authors. (CD-ROM) Detroit, Mich.: Gale Research, 1994.

Cooper, Frederic Taber, ed. *An Argosy of Fables*. New York: Frederick A. Stokes, 1921.

Courlander, Harold. *A Treasury of African Folklore*. New York: Marlowe, 1996.

———. *The Fourth World of the Hopis*. New York: Crown Publishers, 1971.

Crick, Bernard. *George Orwell: A Life*. Boston, Mass.: Little, Brown, 1980.

Cross, Tom Peete, and Clark Harris Slover, eds. *Ancient Irish Tales*. New York: Barnes & Noble, 1996.

Cuddon, J. A. *A Dictionary of Literary Terms*. New York: Penguin, 1984.

Cuevas, Lou. *Apache Legends*. Happy Camp, Calif.: Naturegraph, 1991.

Curtin, Jeremiah. *Myths and Folklore of Ireland*. Avenel, N.J.: Wings Books, 1996.

Curtius, Ernst Robert. *European Literature and the Latin Middle Ages*. Princeton, N.J.: Princeton University Press, 1953.

Dailey, Sheila. *Putting the World in a Nutshell: The Art of the Formula Tale*. New York: H. W. Wilson, 1994.

Dames, Michael. *Mythic Ireland*. London: Thames & Hudson, 1992.

Danaher, Kevin. *The Year in Ireland: Irish Calendar Customs*. Dublin: Mercier Press, 1972.

Davey, Gwenda Beed, and Graham Seal. *The Oxford Companion to Australian Folklore*. Melbourne, Australia: Oxford University Press, 1993.

Davidson, Cathy N., and Linda Wagner-Martin. *The Oxford Companion to Women's Writing*. New York: Oxford University Press, 1995.

Davis, Richard Beale, et al. *Southern Writing: 1585–1920*. New York: Odyssey Press, 1970.

Dillon, Myles, ed. *Irish Sagas*. Dublin: Mercier Press, 1968.

Dobreé, Bonamy. *Rudyard Kipling, Realist and Fabulist*. London: Oxford University Press, 1967.

Dorson, Richard M., ed. *Folklore and Folklife*. Chicago, Ill.: University of Chicago Press, 1972.

Douglas, George William. *The American Book of Days*. New York: H.W. Wilson, 1948.

Drabble, Margaret, ed. *The Oxford Companion to English Literature*. New York: Oxford University Press, 1985.

Draper, James P., ed. *World Literature Criticism, 1500 to the Present*. Detroit, Mich.: Gale Research, 1992.

Durant, Will. *The Life of Greece*. New York: Simon & Schuster, 1939.

Eagle, Dorothy, and Meic Stephens, eds. *The Oxford Illustrated Literary Guide to Great Britain and Ireland*. New York: Oxford University Press, 1992.

Edmonds, J. M., ed. and trans. *Greek Elegy and Iambus.* Vol. 2. London: Loeb Classical Library, 1931.

Ehrlich, Eugene, and Gorton Carruth. *The Oxford Illustrated Literary Guide to the United States.* New York: Oxford University Press, 1982.

Ekstrom, Reynolds R. *The New Concise Catholic Dictionary.* Mystic, Conn.: Twenty-Third Publications, 1995.

Emerson, Everett. *The Authentic Mark Twain: A Literary Biography of Samuel L. Clemens.* Philadelphia: University of Pennsylvania Press, 1985.

The Encyclopedia of World Biography. New York: McGraw-Hill, 1973.

Enroth, C. A., gen. ed. *Selected Canterbury Tales.* New York: Holt, Rinehart & Winston, 1969.

Feder, Lillian. *The Meridian Handbook of Classical Literature.* New York: New American Library, 1986.

Feinberg, Leonard. *Introduction to Satire.* Ames: Iowa State University Press, 1967.

Feldmann, Susan, ed. *The Storytelling Stone: Traditional Native American Myths and Tales.* New York: Laurel Books, 1965.

Ferrell, Keith. *George Orwell: The Political Pen.* New York: M. Evans, 1988.

Fife, Austin, and Alta Fife. *Saints of Sage and Saddle.* Bloomington: Indiana University Press, 1956.

Flaceliere, Robert. *A Literary History of Greece.* New York: Mentor, 1962.

Fowler, Alastair. *A History of English Literature.* Cambridge, Mass.: Harvard University Press, 1989.

Foxx, Redd, and Norma Miller. *The Redd Foxx Encyclopedia of Black Humor.* Pasadena, Calif.: W. Ritchie Press, 1977.

Fraser, Frances. *The Bear Who Stole the Chinook.* Vancouver, British Columbia: Douglas & McIntyre, 1968.

Frazer, Sir James G. *Folklore in the Old Testament.* New York: Avenel Books, 1988.

Gág, Wanda. *Tales from Grimm.* Eau Claire, Wis.: E. M. Hale, 1936.

Gardner, Averil. *George Orwell.* Boston, Mass.: G. K. Hall, 1987.

Gardner, John. *The Life and Times of Chaucer.* New York: Alfred A. Knopf, 1977.

Garland, Henry, and Mary Garland, ed. *The Oxford Companion to German Literature.* Oxford, England: Clarendon Press, 1976.

Garraty, John A., ed. *Dictionary of American Biography.* New York: Charles Scribner's Sons, 1955.

Gassner, John, and Edward Quinn, eds. *The Reader's Encyclopedia of World Drama.* New York: Thomas Y. Crowell, 1969.

Gentz, William H., gen. ed. *The Dictionary of Bible and Religion.* Nashville, Tenn.: Abingdon, 1973.

Ghazali. *The Alchemy of Happiness*. New York: Orientalia, 1964.

Gibb, H. A. R. *Arabic Literature*. New York: Oxford University Press, 1963.

Giuliano, Edward, and Philip Collins, eds. *The Annotated Dickens*. 2 vols. New York: Clarkson N. Potter, 1986.

Godolphin, Francis R. B., ed. *The Latin Poets*. New York: Modern Library, 1949.

Goring, Rosemary, ed. *Larousse Dictionary of Writers*. Edinburgh, Scotland: Larousse, 1994.

Goss, Linda, and Marian E. Barnes, eds. *Talk That Talk: An Anthology of African-American Storytelling*. New York: Touchstone Books, 1989.

Graham, Ilse. *Goethe and Lessing: The Wellsprings of Creation*. New York: Harper & Row, 1973.

Grauer, Neil A. *Remember Laughter: A Life of James Thurber*. Lincoln: University of Nebraska, 1995.

Gray, Martin. *A Dictionary of Literary Terms*. Essex, England: Longman, 1992.

Green, Roger Lancelyn, ed. *Kipling: A Critical Heritage*. New York: Barnes & Noble, 1971.

Grenander, M. E. *Ambrose Bierce*. New York: Twayne, 1971.

Grigson, Geoffrey. *The Concise Encyclopedia of Modern World Literature*. New York: Hawthorn Books, 1963.

Gross, John, ed. *The Age of Kipling*. New York: Simon & Schuster, 1972.

Hadas, Moses. *Ancilla to Classical Reading*. New York: Columbia University Press, 1954.

———. *A History of Latin Literature*. New York: Columbia University Press, 1952.

Hammond, N. G. L., and H. H. Scullard, eds. *The Oxford Classical Dictionary*. Oxford, England: Clarendon Press, 1992.

Harlow, Alvin F. *Joel Chandler Harris (Uncle Remus): Plantation Storyteller*. New York: Julian Messner, 1941.

Hart, James D. *The Oxford Companion to American Literature*. New York: Oxford University Press, 1983.

Hart-Davis, Rupert, ed. *The Collected Letters of Oscar Wilde*. New York: Harcourt-Brace, 1962.

Harvey, Sir Paul, and J. E. Heseltine. *The Oxford Companion to French Literature*. Oxford, England: Clarendon Press, 1959.

Haskins, Jim. *The Harlem Renaissance*. Brookfield, Conn.: Millbrook Press, 1996.

Hemenway, Robert. *Zora Neale Hurston: A Literary Biography*. Champaign: University of Illinois Press, 1977.

Henry, Laurie. *The Fiction Dictionary*. Cincinnati, Ohio: Story Press, 1995.

Highet, Gilbert. *The Anatomy of Satire*. Princeton, N.J.: Princeton University Press, 1962.

Hill, Eldon C. *George Bernard Shaw*. Boston, Mass.: G. K. Hall, 1978.

Hine, Darlene Clark, et al., eds. *Black Women in America: An Historical Encyclopedia*. Bloomington: Indiana University Press, 1993.

Hobbs, Anne Stevenson. *Beatrix Potter's Art*. London: Frederick Warne, 1989.

———, ed. *Fables*. London: Victoria and Albert Museum, 1986.

Hoffman, A. J. *Twain's Heroes, Twain's Worlds*. Philadelphia: University of Pennsylvania Press, 1988.

Holloway, Karla F. *The Character of the Word*. Westport, Conn.: Greenwood, 1987.

Holman, C. Hugh, and William Harmon. *A Handbook to Literature*. New York: Macmillan, 1992.

Holroyd, Michael. *Bernard Shaw*. New York: Random House, 1989.

Hopper, Vincent, and Bernard D. N. Grebanier. *Essentials of European Literature*. Great Neck, N.Y.: Barron's Educational Series, 1952.

Hornstein, Lillian Herlands, et al., eds. *The Reader's Companion to World Literature*. New York: New American Library, 1973.

Howard, Lillie P. *Zora Neale Hurston*. Boston, Mass: Twayne, 1980.

Howatson, M. C., ed. *The Oxford Companion to Classical Literature*. New York: Oxford University Press, 1989.

Indries Shah, Sayyid. *The Sufis*. New York: Doubleday, 1964.

The International Who's Who, 1987–1988. London: Europa Publications, 1987.

The Interpreter's Dictionary of the Bible. New York: Abingdon Press, 1962.

Ish-Kishor, Judith. *Tales from the Wise Men of Israel*. Philadelphia: J. B. Lippincott, 1962.

Islam, Shamsul. *Kipling's Law*. New York: St. Martin Press, 1975.

Jeffrey, David Lyle. *A Dictionary of Biblical Tradition in English Literature*. Grand Rapids, Mich.: William B. Eerdman's, 1992.

Jobes, Gertrude. *Dictionary of Mythology, Folklore and Symbols*. New York: Scarecrow Press, 1962.

Johnson, J. W., ed. *Utopian Literature: A Selection*. New York: Modern Library, 1968.

Jones, Alison. *Dictionary of World Folklore*. New York: Larousse, 1995.

Kaplan, Justin, gen. ed. *Mister Clemens and Mark Twain: A Biography*. New York: Simon and Schuster, 1966.

Kato, Shuichi. *A History of Japanese Literature: The Years of Isolation*. New York: Kodansha International, 1979.

Keates, Jonathan, and Angelo Hornak. *Canterbury Cathedral*. London: Scala Books, 1994.

Kemp, Sandra, *Kipling's Hiddern Narratives*. Oxford, England: Basil Blackwell, 1988.

Kernan, Alvin. *The Cankered Muse: Satire of the English Renaissance*. New Haven, Conn.: Yale University Press, 1959.

Kesterson, David B., ed. *Critics on Mark Twain.* Baltimore, Md.: University of Miami, 1979.

Kilpatrick, R. C. Corneille. *Horace.* Wolfeboro, N.H.: Longwood, 1981.

Kirkpatrick, D. L., ed. *Twentieth Century Children's Writers.* New York: St. Martin's, 1978.

Kitto, H. D. F. *The Greeks.* London: Penguin, 1951.

Knight, R. C. Corneille. *Horace.* Wolfeboro, N.H.: Longwood, 1981.

Kohlschmidt, Werner. *A History of German Literature, 1760–1805.* New York: Holmes & Meier, 1975.

Krappe, Alexander H. *The Science of Folklore.* New York: W. W. Norton, 1964.

Kunitz, Stanley. *Twentieth Century Authors.* New York: H. W. Wilson, 1942.

———. *Twentieth Century Authors: First Supplement.* New York: H. W. Wilson, 1955.

Kunitz, Stanley J., and Howard Haycraft, eds. *British Authors before 1800: A Biographical Dictionary.* New York: H. W. Wilson, 1952.

Lagarde, André, and Laurent Michard, eds. *XXe Siecle: Les Grandes Auteurs Français.* Paris: Bordas, 1973.

Lamar, Howard R., ed. *The Reader's Encyclopedia of the American West.* New York: Harper & Row, 1977.

Lamb, Sidney, ed. *Chaucer's Canterbury Tales: The Prologue.* Lincoln, Neb.: Cliffs Notes: 1966.

———. *Chaucer's Canterbury Tales: The Wife of Bath.* Lincoln, Neb.: Cliffs Notes: 1966.

Lambert, W. G. *Babylonian Wisdom Literature.* London: Oxford University Press, 1960.

Landman, Isaac, ed. *The Universal Jewish Encyclopedia.* New York: Universal Jewish Encyclopedia Co., 1948.

Lang, D. M., and D. R. Dudley, eds. *The Penguin Companion to Classical, Oriental and African Literature.* New York: McGraw-Hill, 1969.

Lanier, Emilia. *The Poems of Shakespeare's Dark Lady.* New York: Clarkson N. Potter, 1978.

Leeming, David Adams. *The World of Myth.* New York: Oxford University Press, 1990.

Lesky, Albin. *A History of Greek Literature.* London: Methuen, 1966.

Letters of a Sufi Master. Titus Burckhardt, trans. Middlesex, England: Perennial Books, 1969.

Lewis, David Levering. *When Harlem Was in Vogue.* New York: Alfred A. Knopf, 1981.

Lewis, Jayne Elizabeth. *The English Fable: Aesop and Literary Culture, 1651–1740.* Cambridge, England: Cambridge University Press, 1996.

Linder, Leslie. *The History of the Writings of Beatrix Potter.* London: Frederick Warne, 1971.

Low, W. Augustus, and Virgil A. Clift, eds. *Encyclopedia of Black America.* New York: Da Capo, 1981.

Lummis, Charles F. *Pueblo Indian Folk-Stories.* Lincoln: University of Nebraska Press, 1992.

Lüth, Max. *European Folktale: Form and Nature*. Bloomington: Indiana University Press, 1982.

Lyons, Mary E. *Sorrow's Kitchen: The Life and Folklore of Zora Neale Hurston.* New York: Macmillan, 1990.

MacDonald, Ruth K. *Beatrix Potter*. New York: Twayne, 1986.

Mackay, Agnes Ethel. *La Fontaine and His Friends.* New York: George Braziller, 1973.

Maggio, Rosalie. *Quotations by Women.* Boston, Mass.: Beacon Press, 1992.

Magill, Frank N., ed. *Cyclopedia of World Authors.* New York: Harper & Brothers, 1958.

Magnusson, Magnus, gen. ed. *Cambridge Biographical Dictionary.* New York: Cambridge University Press, 1990.

Maixner, Paul. *Robert Louis Stevenson: The Critical Heritage.* London: Routledge Chapman & Hall, 1981.

Major Twentieth-Century Writers. Detroit, Mich: Gale Research, 1990.

Manguel, Alberto, and Gianni Guadalupi. *The Dictionary of Imaginary Places.* New York: Harcourt Brace Jovanovich, 1987.

Mantinband, James H. *Dictionary of Latin Literature.* New York: Philosophical Library, 1956.

Marriott, Alice, and Carol K. Rachlin. *Plains Indian Mythology.* New York: Meridian Books, 1975.

Massignon, Genevieve, ed. *Folktales of France.* Chicago, Ill.: University of Chicago Press, 1968.

Mays, James L., gen. ed. *Harper's Bible Commentary*. San Francisco, Calif: Harper & Row, 1988.

McArthur, Tom, ed. *The Oxford Companion to the English Language*. New York: Oxford University Press, 1992.

McGlathey, James M., ed. *The Brothers Grimm and Folktales.* Urbana: University of Illinois Press, 1988.

McGreal, Ian P., ed. *Great Literature of the Eastern World*. New York: HarperCollins, 1996.

Meckler, Laura, "Zora Neale Hurston's Unknown Work Found," *Charlotte Observer*, December 17, 1996, 6A.

Meigs, Cornelia, et al. *A Critical History of Children's Literature.* New York: Macmillan, 1953.

Merriam Webster's Reader's Handbook. Springfield, Mass.: Merriam-Webster, 1997.

Miller, Corki, and Mary Ellen Snodgrass. *Storytellers.* Jefferson, N.C.: McFarland, 1998.

Miller, Luree. *Literary Villages of London.* Washington, D.C.: Starrhill Press, 1989.

Monagan, John S. *Horace: Priest of the Poor.* Washington, D.C.: Georgetown University Press, 1985.

Morris, Roy, Jr. *Ambrose Bierce: Alone in Bad Company.* New York: Crown, 1995.

Morsberger, Robert. *James Thurber.* New York: Twayne, 1964.

Moses, Daniel David, and Terry Goldie, eds. *An Anthology of Canadian Native Literature in English.* Toronto, Ontario: Oxford University Press, 1992.

Moskovit, Leonard, trans. *Horace: Twelve Odes.* Boston, Mass.: Rowan Tree, 1983.

Moss, Robert F. *Rudyard Kipling and the Fiction of Adolescence.* New York: St. Martin's Press, 1982.

Muir, Kenneth, and Samuel Schoenbaum. *A New Companion to Shakespearean Studies.* Cambridge, Mass.: Harvard University Press, 1971.

Muir, Percy. *English Children's Books: 1600 to 1900.* London: Batsford, 1954.

Naito, Hirshi, ed. *Legends of Japan.* Rutland, Vt.: Charles E. Tuttle, 1972.

Nathiri, N. Y., ed. *Zora! A Woman and Her Community.* Crystal River, Fla.: Sentinel, 1991.

Negley, Glenn, and J. Max Patrick. *The Quest for Utopia.* New York: Henry Schumann, 1952.

Newbigging, Thomas. *Fables and Fabulists: Ancient and Modern.* London: Elliot Stock, 1895.

Nicholson, R. A. *Rumi, Poet and Mystic.* London: George Allen & Unwin, 1950.

Nickerson, Roy. *Robert Louis Stevenson in California: A Remarkable Courtship.* San Francisco, Calif.: Chronicle Books, 1982.

Nitze, William A., and E. Preston Dargan. *A History of French Literature: From the Earliest Times to the Present.* New York: Holt, Rinehart & Winston, 1950.

Noel, Thomas. *Theories of the Fable in the Eighteenth Century.* New York: Columbia University Press, 1975.

Oldsey, Bernard, and Joseph Browne, eds. *Critical Essays on George Orwell.* Boston, Mass: G. K. Hall, 1986.

Orel, Harold. *Critical Essays on Rudyard Kipling.* New York: G. K. Hall, 1989.

Paffard, Mark. *Kipling's Indian Fiction.* New York: St. Martin's Press, 1989.

Paredes, Américo, ed. *Folktales of Mexico.* Chicago, Ill.: University of Chicago Press, 1970.

Patterson, Lotsee, and Mary Ellen Snodgrass. *Indian Terms of the Americas.* Englewood, Colo.: Libraries Unlimited, 1994.

Peppard, Murray B. *Paths through the Forest: A Biography of the Brothers Grimm.* New York: Holt, Rinehart & Winston, 1971.

Person, James E., Jr., ed. *Literature Criticism from 1400 to 1800.* Detroit, Mich.: Gale Research, 1988.

Philip, Alex J., and W. Laurence Gadd. *A Dickens Dictionary.* Leipzig, Germany: G. Hedeler, 1928.

Pierpont, Claudie Roth, "A Society of One: Zora Neale Hurston, American Contrarian," *New Yorker*, February 17, 1997, 80–91.

Pino-Saavedra, Yolando, ed. *Folktales of Chile*. Chicago, Ill.: University of Chicago Press, 1967.

Ploski, Harry A., and James Williams, eds. *The Negro Almanac*. Detroit, Mich.: Gale Research, 1989.

Pollard, Arthur. *Satire*. London: Methuen, 1970.

Polley, Jane, ed. *American Folklore and Legend*. Pleasantville, N.Y.: Reader's Digest, 1978.

Porter, A. P. *Jump at de Sun: The Story of Zora Neale Hurston*. Minneapolis, Minn.: Carolrhoda, 1992.

Raby, F. J. E. *A History of Christian-Latin Poetry from the Beginnings to the Close of the Middle Ages*. Oxford, England: Clarendon Press, 1997.

Radice, Betty, ed. *Who's Who in the Ancient World*. New York: Penguin Books, 1973.

Radin, Paul. *The Trickster: A Study in American Indian Mythology*. New York: Schocken Books, 1972.

Rampersad, Arnold. *The Life of Langston Hughes*. New York: Oxford University Press, 1986.

Rankin, Nicholas. *Dead Man's Chest: Travels after Robert Louis Stevenson*. Winchester, Mass.: Faber & Faber, 1987.

Rao, K. Bhaskara. *Rudyard Kipling's India*. Norman: University of Oklahoma Press, 1967.

Rasmussen, R. Kent. *Mark Twain A to Z: The Essential Reference to His Life and Writings*. New York: Facts on File, 1995.

Reilly, Patrick. *George Orwell: The Age's Adversary*. New York: St. Martin's Press, 1989.

Renoir, Alain. *The Poetry of John Lydgate*. London: Routledge & Kegan Paul, 1967.

Roberts, Vera Mowry. *On Stage: A History of Theatre*. New York: Harper & Row, 1962.

Robinson, F. N., ed. *The Works of Geoffrey Chaucer*. Boston, Mass.: Houghton Mifflin, 1957.

Roby, Kinley E., ed. *Rudyard Kipling*. Boston, Mass.: Twayne, 1982.

Rollins, Hyder E., and Herschel Baker, eds. *The Renaissance in England; Non-dramatic Prose and Verse of the Sixteenth Century*. Boston, Mass.: D. C. Heath, 1954.

Rosen, Michael J., ed. *People Have More Fun Than Anybody: A Centennial Celebration of the Drawings and Writings of James Thurber*. San Diego, Calif.: Harvest Books, 1995.

Rosenberg, Donna. *Folklore, Myths, and Legends*. Lincolnwood, Ill.: NTC Publishing, 1997.

Ross, Norman P., ed. *American Folklore*. New York: Time, 1961.

Rubin, Louis D., Jr. *Gallery of Southerners*. Baton Rouge: Louisiana State Press, 1982.

Rudd, Niall. *The Satires of Horace and Persius*. Berkeley: University of California Press, 1982.

Sandler, Robert, ed. *Northrop Frye on Shakespeare*. New Haven, Conn.: Yale University Press, 1986.

Saposnik, Irving S. *Robert Louis Stevenson*. New York: G. K. Hall, 1974.

Schimmel, Annemarie. *Mystical Dimensions of Islam*. Chapel Hill: University of North Carolina Press, 1975.

———. *As through a Veil: Mystical Poetry in Islam*. New York: Columbia University Press, 1982.

Scott, A. F. *Who's Who in Chaucer*. New York: Hawthorn Books, 1974.

Seymour-Smith, Martin. *Rudyard Kipling*. New York: St. Martin's Press, 1989.

Shackleton, Bailey. *A Profile of Horace*. Cambridge, Mass.: Harvard University Press, 1982.

Shah, Amina. *Folk Tales of Central Asia*. London: Octagon Press, 1975.

Shattock, Joanne. *The Oxford Guide to British Women Writers*. Oxford, England: Oxford University Press, 1993.

Sheffey, Ruthe T., ed. *Zora Neale Hurston Forum*. Milwaukee, Wis.: Morgan, 1992.

Sherr, Lynn, and Jurate Kazickas. *Susan B. Anthony Slept Here: A Guide to American Women's Landmarks*. New York: Random House, 1994.

Smith, C. Alphonso. *Southern Literary Studies: A Collection of Literary, Biographical, and Other Sketches*. Port Washington, N.Y.: Kennikat Press, 1967.

Smith, Eric. *A Dictionary of Classical Reference in English Poetry*. Cambridge, Eng.: D.S. Brewer, 1984.

Smith, Gregory. *The Transition Period*. London: William Blackwood & Sons, 1900.

Snodgrass, Mary Ellen. *Encyclopedia of Frontier Literature*. Santa Barbara, Calif.: ABC-Clio, 1997.

———. *Encyclopedia of Satirical Literature*. Santa Barbara, Calif.: ABC-CLIO, 1997.

———. *Encyclopedia of Southern Literature*. Santa Barbara, Calif.: ABC-CLIO, 1997.

———. *Encyclopedia of Utopian Literature*. Santa Barbara, Calif.: ABC-CLIO, 1995.

———. *Greek Classics*. Lincoln, Nebr.: Cliffs Notes, 1988.

———. *Roman Classics*. Lincoln, Nebr.: Cliffs Notes, 1988.

Something about the Author. Vol. 53. Detroit, Mich.: Gale Research, 1988.

Steinberg, S. H., ed. *Cassell's Encyclopaedia of World Literature*. New York: Funk & Wagnalls, 1954.

Stephen, Sir Leslie, and Sir Sidney Lee. *The Dictionary of National Biography*. London: Oxford University Press, 1922.

Stewart, J. I. M. *Rudyard Kipling*. Indianapolis, Ind.: Dodd, Mead, 1966.

Strayer, Joseph R., ed. in chief. *Dictionary of the Middle Ages*. New York: Charles Scribner's Sons, 1989.

Swearingen, Roger G. *The Prose Writings of Robert Louis Stevenson: A Guide.* New Haven, Conn.: Shoe String Press, 1980.

Tatar, Maria. *The Hard Facts of the Grimms' Fairy Tales.* Princeton, N.J.: Princeton University Press, 1987.

Taylor, Judy, comp. *Beatrix Potter's Letters.* London: Frederick Warne, 1989.

Ten Brink, Bernhard. *History of English Literature.* Vol. 2. London: George Bell & Sons, 1895.

Thompson, Stith. *The Folktale.* Berkeley: University of California Press, 1977.

Thurman, Judith. *Isak Dinesen: The Life of a Storyteller.* New York: St. Martin's Press, 1981.

Trent, William Peterfield, et al., eds. *The Cambridge History of American Literature.* New York: Macmillan, 1946.

Tripp, Edward. *The Meridian Handbook of Classical Mythology.* New York: New American Library, 1970.

Turner, Frederick, ed. *The Portable North American Indian Reader.* New York: Penguin, 1974.

Twain, Mark. *Life on the Mississippi.* New York: Oxford University Press, 1990.

Twentieth Century Literary Criticism. Vols. 2, 56. Detroit, Mich.: Gale Research, 1979, 1995.

Van Doren, Mark, ed. *An Anthology of World Poetry.* New York: Harcourt, Brace, 1936.

Waley, M. I. *Sufism: The Alchemy of the Heart.* San Francisco, Calif.: Chronicle Books, 1993.

Wall, Cheryl A. *Women of the Harlem Renaissance.* Bloomington: Indiana University Press, 1995.

Wallich, Reb Moshe. *Book of Fables.* Detroit, Mich.: Wayne State University Press, 1994.

Walker, Alice, ed. *I Love Myself When I Am Laughing: A Zora Neale Hurston Reader.* New York: Feminist Press, 1979.

———. *In Search of Our Mothers' Gardens.* New York: Feminist Press, 1983.

Ward, Philip, ed. *The Oxford Companion to Spanish Literature.* Oxford, England: Oxford University Press, 1978.

Warner, Rex. *The Greek Philosophers.* New York: New American Library, 1958.

Washington, Mary Helen. *Invented Lives: Narratives of Black Women, 1860–1960.* New York: Anchor, 1987.

Watt, William Montgomery. *Companion to the Qur'an.* Oxford: Oneworld, 1994.

Weinreich, Beatrice Silverman, ed. *Yiddish Folktales.* New York: Pantheon Books, 1988.

Weygandt, Ann M. *Kipling's Reading.* Philadelphia: University of Pennsylvania Press, 1939.

Who's Who in American Art. New York: Bowker, 1976.

Wiggins, Robert A. *Ambrose Bierce.* Minneapolis: University of MInnesota Press, 1964.

Willard, Frances E., and Mary A. Livermore. *A Woman of the Century.* Detroit, Mich.: Gale, 1967.

Williams, Jay. *The Wicked Tricks of Tyl Uilenspiegel.* New York: Four Winds Press, 1978.

Wilson, Charles Reagan, and William Ferris, eds. *Encyclopedia of Southern Culture.* Chapel Hill: University of North Carolina Press, 1989.

Wilson, John Harold. *A Preface to Restoration Drama.* Boston, Mass.: Houghton Mifflin, 1965.

Witcover, Paul. *Zora Neale Hurston.* New York: Chelsea House, 1991.

Woods, George B., et al., eds. *The Literature of England.* Chicago: Scott, Foresman, 1947.

Yates, Janelle. *Zora Neale Hurston: A Storyteller's Life.* Staten Island, N.Y.: Ward Hill, 1991.

Articles and Monographs

Alston, Charlotte Blake, "Introducing African Storytelling," *Tales as Tools: The Power of Story in the Classroom.* Nashville, Tenn.: National Storytelling Press, 1994, 174–175.

Butcher, Fanny, "Review," *Chicago Sunday Tribune*, August 2, 1953, 5.

Dailey, Sheila, "Rediscovering the Formula Tale," *Storytelling*, May 1994, 16–19.

Dobrée, Bonamy, "Review," *Spectator*, June 12, 1953, 763.

Einstadt, Margaret, and Donna Tamaki, "Kamishibai," New York: Kamishibai for Kids, n.d.

Freedman, Samuel G., "Bearing Witness: The Life and Work of Elie Wiesel," *New York Times Magazine*, October 23, 1983.

Fremantle, Anne, "Review," *Commonweal*, August 7, 1953, 448.

Gilman, Richard, "Review," *New York Times Book Review*, March 24, 1974, 3–4.

Keding, Dan, "The Endless Tale: Heather Forest," *Sing Out*, May/June/July 1995, n. p.

Kreuzer, Terese Loeb, "Elie Wiesel's Jewish Tales," *The Reporter*, 1995, 12–14.

Lerman, Leo, "Written by Candlelight, in Black Coal," *New York Times Book Review*, September 16, 1956, 41.

Maddock, Melvin, "The Light That Triumphed," *Time*, September 8, 1975, 66.

———. "Rabbit Redux," *Time*, March 18, 1974, 92–93.

Mano, D. Keith, "Banal Bunnies," *National Review*, April 26, 1974, 484–485.

Matthews, Nancie, "Review," *New York Times*, August 2, 1953, 4.

McGregor, Lurline Wailana, "Holo Mai Pele: The Performance Documentary," *Storyboard*, January 1998, 4–5.

Perry, B. E., "Demetrius of Phalerum and the Aesopic Fables," *Transactions and Proceedings of the American Philological Association*, 1962, 287–346.

———. "Fable," *Studium Generale*, 1959, 17–37.

Prescott, Peter S., "Rabbit, Read," *Newsweek*, March 18, 1974, 114.

"Rabbit's Tale Continues," *Hickory Daily Record*, February 2, 1997, 8A.

Rexroth, Kenneth, "Goethe," *Saturday Review*, April 19, 1969, 21.

Rubin, Merle, "The Muse Who Midwifed 'Treasure Island,'" *Wall Street Journal*, June 5, 1995, 5A.

Ryan, Alan, "Saint-Exupéry in Full Flight," *USA Today*, January 12, 1995, 5D.

Samuels, Charles Thomas, "Call of the Wild," *New Republic*, March 23, 1974, 28–29.

Sax, Boria, "The Allure of Animal Anecdotes," *Storytelling*, Spring 1992, 10–13.

Sheppard, R. Z., "The Demon and the Muse," *Time,* March 13, 1978, 92–95.

Sherwin, Elisabeth, "Something About Thurber Makes Him Perfect for China," *Printed Matter*, August 25, 1996.

Skow, John, "The Fabulous Invalid," *Time*, February 27, 1995, n. p.

Smith, Janet Adam, "Exodus," *New York Review of Books*, April 18, 1974, 8–9.

Stinton, T. C. W., "Phaedrus and Folklore: An Old Problem Restated," *Classical Quarterly*, 1979, 432–435.

Wolkstein, Diane, "Bouki Dances the Kokioko," *Storytelling*, May 1997, 11–13.

Internet

"Alice Walker Web Page," http://www.utexas.edu/~mmaynard/Walker/walker.htm, May 3, 1996.

Beck, Sanderson, "Literature of India," http://www.west.net/~beck/EC12.literature.html, 1996.

"Bierce Papers," http://sunsite.berkeley.edu:8008/findaids/Berkeley/bierce/1.toc, June 24, 1996.

"Brewer: Dictionary of Phrase and Fable," http://www.bibliomania.com/Reference/PhraseAndFable/data/437.html#fables

Brick, Scott, "Dickens's 'A Christmas Carol,'" http://www.willandcompany.com/tattler/nov97/dickens.html.

Chapman, Heather, "Pathfinder: James Grover Thurber," http://ils.unc.edu/~chaph/thurber.html.

"Charles Dickens," http://cp-tel.net/miller/BilLee/quotes/dickens.html.

"Charles Dickens," http://www.mala.bc.ca/~mcneil/dickens.htm.

"A Christmas Carol," http://www.neurop2.ruhr-uni-bochum.de/~porr/ChristmasCarol/index.html.

"A Christmas Carol," http://www.susqu.edu/ac_depts/arts_sci/english/lharris/class/dickens/cult.htm.

Corbett, William, "Review: Remember Laughter," http://www.bookwire.com/bbr/life/James-Thurber.html.

"Dickens Page," http://ernie.lang.nagoya-u.ac.jp/~matsuoka/Dickens.htm.

"Dickens Project: University of California," http://hum.ucsc.edu/dickens/Dickens.Project.Home.html.

DISCovering Multicultural America, http://www.galenet.gale.com.

"The Grimm Brothers," http://nova.med.nyu.edu/lit-med/lit-med-db/webdocs/webauthors.

"The Grimm Brothers Home Page," http://www.pitt.edu/~dash/grimm.html.

Gullette, Alan, "Ambrose Bierce, Master of the Macabre." www.creative.net/~alang/lit/horror/bierce.sht, June 24, 1996.

"Hans Christian Andersen Museum," http://www.odkomm.dk/int/hcamuk.htm.

Hooks, Rita, "Conjured into Being: Zora Neal's Hurston's Their Eyes Were Watching God," http://splavc.spjc.cc.fl.us/hooks/zoraint.html, February 12, 1997.

"James Thurber," http://us.imdb.com/M/person-exact?James%20Thurber.

"Jean de La Fontaine," http://www.callisto.si.usherb.ca/~gisweb/gis/fables/renrai06.htm.

"Jean de La Fontaine," http://www.metdanse.com/poesie/lafon2.htm.

"La Fontaine," http://www.argyro.net/gem/LFONTAIN.htm.

"La Poesía de los Siglos de Oro," http://www.geocities.com/Hollywood/Hills/7985/literature 3.htm.

Long, John R., "Aesop's Fables," http://www.pacificnet.net/~johnr/aesop.

"Marie de France," *Catholic Encyclopedia*, http://www.knight.org/advent/cathen/09667a.htm.

"Musée Jean de la Fontaine," http://perso.wanadoo.fr/museelafontaine/.

O'Shea, Brian. *Joel Chandler Harris Home Page*. http://www.ajc.com/staff/oshea/preswalk.thm, December 8, 1996.

"The Other Wise Man," http://www.spirituality.org/issue05/page 13.html.

"The Real *Watership Down* Homepage," http://members.aol.com/thlayli959/index.htm.

"Robert Louis Stevenson," http://www.halcyon.com/jeanluc/RLS.html.

"St. Exupery," http://www.westegg.com/exupery.

"Sanskrit Literature," http://www.connect.net/ron/sanskritliterature.html.

"Thurber's World (and Welcome to It)!" http://home.earthlink.net/~ritter/thurber/index.html.

"The Widow of Ephesus in Petronius, Phaedrus, and Romulus," http://www.und.ac.za/und/classics/bxdw/html.

"Zora Neale Hurston," http://www.ceth.rutgers.edu/projects/hercproj/hurston/front.htm., February 12, 1997.

"Zora Neale Hurston," http://www.detroit.freenet.org/gdfn/sigs/l-corner-world/hurston/html, February 12, 1997.

ILLUSTRATION CREDITS

ILLUSTRATION CREDITS

135   Archive Photos

143   Archive Photos

148   North Wind Picture Archives

157   Archive Photos

162   Photofest

170   Archive Photos

175   Library of Congress/Corbis

182   Bibliotheque Nationale, Paris. Giraudon/Art Resource, NY

188   Bibliotheque Nationale, Paris. Giraudon/Art Resource, NY

192   Bibliotheque Nationale, Paris. Giraudon/Art Resource, NY

203   North Wind Picture Archive

214   Library of Congress

225   North Wind Picture Archives

229   Archive Photos

259   Giraudon/Art Resource, NY

262   Giraudon/Art Resource, NY

271   Archive Photos

295   Archive Photos

305   Giraudon/Art Resource, NY

314   Archive Photos

319   Archive Photos

321   Archive Photos

324   North Wind Picture Archives

327   Archive Photos

331   North Wind Picture Archives

332   Courtesy of Gayle Ross

336   North Wind Picture Archives

339   North Wind Picture Archives

364   Popperfoto/Archive Photos

INDEX

[Note: Page numbers in **boldface** denote major entry headings. Numbers in brackets indicate illustrations.]

INDEX